Values and Faith

Activities for Family and Church Groups

Roland S. Larson and Doris E. Larson

Winston Press
430 Oak Grove
Minneapolis, Minnesota 55403

Library of Congress Catalog Card Number: 76-9549
ISBN 0-86683-673-X (previously ISBN 0-03-018046-5)
Printed in the United States of America

Winston Press, Inc.
Minneapolis, MN 55403

9 8 7 6 5 4

Acknowledgments

Many, many persons have been a part of this book in one way or another. The cliché is true — there are too many to mention. But a number of people have been especially influential or helpful in this venture.

Our work with Howie and Barb Glaser-Kirschenbaum, Merrill Harmin, Sid Simon, Thomas Gordon, and Ralph Jones helped shape our understanding and use of methodologies in the area of values education.

Wayne Paulson, Jack Cole, Jerry Glashagel, Mick Johnson, Bob Phipps, and John Ziegler sharpened our facilitating and training skills in values education.

Ron Rising, Dorothy Williams, and Miriam Frost gave us appreciated editorial help in writing.

Thanks go to these dear friends who provided feedback on portions of the book's content: Douglas and LaVonne Anderson, Glen and Shirley Espelien, and Clint and Violet Sprain.

Special thanks to Merton Strommen for his constant encouragement and support during the seven years we worked together at Youth Research Center. His openness to new approaches gave impetus to developing much that is in this book.

We are also grateful to three of our children — Tom, Mary Lee, and Jane Larson-Wipf, for contributing their ideas and reactions throughout the book's period of development.

Lastly, we acknowledge valuable input from workshop participants throughout the country. In our interaction with them, we tested and modified our ideas and methods. These many persons contributed to our own understanding and personal growth.

To representatives of two generations,
our parents,
Elvina and Elmer Linell and Judith and Petrus Larson,
who provided a caring, loving atmosphere to nurture our values growth
and our children,
Dan, Tom, Jane, and Mary Lee,
who helped us translate our values for the 1970's and 80's

Table of Contents

Foreword

An Historical Perspective

Oscar Wilde once said, "A cynic is one who knows the price of everything and the value of nothing." The promulgators of the value-free style of education which was popular after World War II should hardly be surprised that it bred a fair number of cynics, young people strong on facts but weak on how to attach a value to them.

What was the cause of value-neutral education? It resulted from a reaction against a doctrinaire imposition of values, leaving little room for free choice. Processes of decision making were barely considered. Anger over such intimidating value forcing caused educators to divorce values from facts: Forget about values. Be neutral and objective. Concentrate on the fact of the matter. Think of the classroom as though it were the lab of a white-smocked scientist. Peel away the impact of biases, prejudgments, presumptions, and values. Let sanitized information hold sway. Use a process method to teach, but exorcise values in that procedure.

The teachers who adopted this studied forgetfulness of values were well-intentioned, but they gave students the impression that values in life were not important. And once they had convinced the students that values had no place in the learning environment, they set the stage for cynicism and the consequent loss of trust in authority and institutions. In fact, students stopped trusting the teacher, since this "value" was just as absent as all the others.

Teachers floundered as they hammered away at the objective view of persons and institutions. Whereas teachers used to point up the values surrounding the heroes of history—courage, loyalty, maturity, love, fidelity, perseverance, imagination, and the capacity to withstand failure—now, by refusing to advert to these values, teachers drew attention to the faults and sins of the heroes. Ironically, objective, value-free teaching became equated with debunking the once heart-stirring figures of the past and present. Governments, churches, businesses and other institutions, viewed from a vantage point of veneration (admittedly, too much at times), met a similar fate. They were now portrayed too much in their worst light.

The old values education did indeed often hold up unreal heroes and paint institutions with too sentimental a brush. But the reactionary, value-free education faltered by morosely featuring only the clay feet in people and institutions. Many teachers became hucksters of anti-values. No wonder the young began to champion the anti-hero and the anarchic communities of recent years.

The value-free educators became just as imperialistic as their presumed adversaries. Their non-directive rhetoric made cold objectivity appear to reign in the classroom. That was a magician's illusion. Once the ritual of disallowance ("banish those values") had been pronounced, the teacher was perversely free to become a propagandist for anti-values.

A Return To Values

We are now at Act III in this continuing saga of value education. Values are back in the picture, due largely to the influence of humanistic psychology advanced by Maslow, May, Perls, Erikson, Rogers, and others.

The translation of their work into practical educational methods was first spurred by Dr. Sidney Simon and then widely adapted and developed by other insightful educators, among them, Roland and Doris Larson, the authors of this excellent book.

How does this new approach to values differ from the two earlier ones mentioned?

1) It differs from value-free education in that it frankly acknowledges that values continually brood in, over, and around the facts of life.

2) It differs from the doctrinaire approach to values education in that it concentrates on inductive valuing processes that evoke free and candid expression of personal values in a nonthreatening and receptive atmosphere.

This new approach is an intriguing adaptation of Carl Rogers' one-to-one, nondirective counseling techniques to a group situation. From Rogers, it borrows the capacity to create a nonthreatening situation. To make the process more useful for group work, it adds the techniques of "gaming" to facilitate interaction.

Faith As a Central Value

In this book, Roland and Doris Larson move the discussion of value education to the level of faith. Rightfully, they view faith itself as a central value. They have provided numerous ways to help learners express and clarify their religious values, which flow from the value of faith itself. Moreover, they establish a smooth linkage between human and religious values so that these two dimensions come through as interrelated, complementary, and supportive of each other.

In so doing, the authors have taken the imperious sting out of considerations of religious values. Their ecumenical sense has also softened the wrong kind of sectarian bias that often hovers around the discussions about religious values. They clearly have a peaceable perspective that should have a healing effect upon the lucky users of this book.

It is also evident that the authors speak from a compassion well-tempered by long experience in practicing the wealth of suggestions which they offer in this book. Here they are preaching what they have already practiced. The educational field is fortunate that the authors have taken the time to share the immensely varied number of exercises which have worked so well for them in countless seminars, classes, and institutes.

Prepare, then, both to read a stimulating book and to be encouraged by a multitude of useful exercises, enabling participants to become both deeply human and profoundly religious in the best sense of these expectations.

Reverend Alfred McBride, Director
National Forum of Religious Educators

Values and Faith

Introduction

This book contains many practical exercises which can be used in a variety of ways — particularly with large and small groups in church-related settings or within the family. Its purpose is to help create a positive, caring, supportive environment in which individuals of all ages have an opportunity to:

— share with each other and learn from one another;
— look at what is important in their own lives;
— examine their own opinions, attitudes, beliefs, and values in a Christian context;
— discover congruencies or discrepancies between what they do and what they say they believe and value;
— take actions to make their behaviors more consistent with their beliefs and values;
— learn and practice a way to continually examine their beliefs and values;
— feel better about themselves through constructive, positive human interaction.

Too Many Choices

Recently a friend expressed thankfulness at not being a teenager in today's world. "The choices would do me in," she confided. "When I think about how many things kids have to decide nowadays, I wish I knew some way to help." Then she sighed and smiled ruefully, "But telling them doesn't do the job anymore, does it?"

Indeed it doesn't. But "telling them" didn't do the job for us either. Like the youth of today, we face many choices, too. Many of us are confused and groping for help in clarifying our priorities and values. We, too, need the opportunity to explore, to share, and to say out loud our opinions, thoughts, and ideas on important matters. We need to be listened to and to listen to others as we clarify our beliefs and values in these changing and challenging times.

We need to think about the ways we were helped in the past and decide how we will help others today.

Advice used to be one of the chief ways we tried to help other people make choices. But for the most part, the time is gone when a person can hope to achieve change in another's behavior or belief simply by outlining what ought to be done.

It's a pity, too. *Moralizing* — telling "the way it ought to be" — is such a nice, easy method for the person who assumes the role of teacher or helper or counselor. It's relatively simple for one who has lived through a given experience or time of life to tell someone younger or less experienced how to handle a new situation. Imparting the wisdom of age and experience also gives us an ego boost; it makes us feel helpful and good. But the chief drawback to moralizing is that it just doesn't work.

Moralizing is, of course, only one of the time-tested and much-venerated methods we have used to help people make choices. Another method, usually adopted by people who have tried the first one and failed, is the *laissez-faire* technique — throwing up the hands and saying, "I can't do a thing about it. Since you won't listen to me, you'll have to figure it out on your own." Even when accompanied by fervent hopes that everything will turn out right, the use of laissez-faire simply seems to make recipients suspect that people don't really care what happens to them.

Modeling — teaching by example — is a third, widely-respected method for influencing and guiding the behavior and choices of another person. In some situations, modeling seems to work. We do find people — influenced not by conscious teaching but by modeling — who imitate an admired person. Modeling has drawbacks, however. We seldom know how many people our own example affects. Moreover, few of us have the patience or the opportunity to bide our time and observe how well the modeling works. But most importantly, too many models, as well as the inconsistent behavior some of these models display, can confuse those who are trying to make decisions on the basis of what their "heroes" do.

Suggestions, guidelines, and pressures impinge on people from a host of varied sources — Mom and Dad, playmates, fellow students, teachers, church leaders, TV commercials, movie stars, popular magazines. Confusion often results from trying to determine which source is right.

Although we are concerned with passing on certain values that are important to us, down deep we know it's futile to impose them on others. But we can create an open, accepting, loving environment which encourages persons to examine various choices and find answers that make sense for their own lives.

Background For This Book

Values and Faith grew out of our experiences over the past six years in conducting many value-clarifying classes, seminars, workshops, and study programs for people of all ages in a wide variety of settings.

We have discovered that well-thought-out exercises, presented in an encouraging and accepting atmosphere, cause learning that leads to informed choices and changed lives. Typically, we discover enthusiasm, eagerness, and seriousness of purpose breaking out in these sessions. In one group, a 92-year-old told us, with a twinkle in her eye, "Learning in the church should always be fun like this." Likewise, kindergarteners have enthusiastically entered into similar exercises, conducted at their level of understanding.

One concern has frequently surfaced in these groups: Where can a person obtain a collection of value-clarifying exercises specifically designed for use in a Christian context? *Values and Faith* is our attempt to provide an answer to that question.

Viewpoint

We, the authors, assume throughout this book that God is the absolute, the beginning point of ourselves and of our world.He loves us and acts to make himself known to us through the Bible, the Church, the life of Christ, and the activity of the Holy Spirit among us — revealing himself and his will to us through what we read, what we learn from other people, and what we experience every day.

We hope the values exercises described in *Values and Faith* will help raise people's awareness of God's presence in their lives and thus help them become more conscious of the wealth of resources available for making decisions about life. This is a book to help stretch our minds and to keep us growing. We are aware, not only of the resources outside ourselves, but of the resources within. As Jesus said, "The Kingdom of God is within you."

Jesus used ways similar to some of these values exercises to help people clarify choices. He frequently laid out important questions — in what must have been, at times, a disturbing and challenging way — to make people think through the implications of what they were doing. "For what does it profit a man, to gain the whole world, and forfeit his life? For what can a man give in return for his life?" (Luke 9:25)

Jesus also told stories and asked people what they learned from them. After telling the parable of the two sons whose father sent them to a vineyard, Jesus asked, "Which of the two did the will of his father?" (Matthew 21:31) This question must have caused some thought in His day, as it does in ours. Or, following the parable of the Good Samaritan, "Which of these three, do you think, proved neighbor to the man who fell among the robbers?" (Luke 10:36)

Effective education does not give people answers; rather, it draws their own answers from them. Answers given are easily forgotten; answers discovered from within are remembered. *Values and Faith* raises questions, compelling individuals to discover answers from within themselves.

Some of what we do in this book will be recognized by those who know the values-clarification work done by Raths, Harmin, Kirschenbaum and Simon, as they developed it during the past decade or more. They have greatly influenced our methodology. We have used, adapted, and modified parts of their approach and have found the resulting values exercises to be excellent tools for Christian education in a variety of settings: young adult programs, church schools, youth groups, Bible study groups, parent groups, retreats, camps, boards and councils, special-interest small groups, family discussions.

Use in the Family

We have found practical use for these exercises with families. In our own home, we used some exercises at the mealtime table, around a fireplace or campfire, in the car, on a family vacation. Many parents who have used values exercises in their homes have been pleased to find new kinds of discussions, more openness in communications, and shared decision making within the family.

Enhancing the Learning Process

Our own excitement about using values exercises with the family and with church groups comes from seeing the following things happen in the learning process:

1. *The learner participates actively.* Discussion, we have always thought, is an improvement on most lectures. If we are free to talk, we are more interested. We have sometimes gone to sleep when other people are talking but never while outlining our beliefs to someone else! Many of the exercises in this book invite participants to talk out their beliefs with one another, with partners, or with small groups. To counteract passivity, participants are often active physically. Sometimes the action involves walking around, crossing the room, finding a particular location within the room. This process gets people involved — even those who may have privately decided beforehand to sit on the sidelines. People don't fall asleep when they're involved; they're too busy doing things, and when they do things they remember them.

2. *The resources of the total group are used.* As long as there's only one teacher, the resources of a group are limited to what comes out of the thinking of that one person. All of us together can contribute more than any one of us. Getting everyone involved gives all of us a greater fund of information and feelings to draw on. It has been our experience that — far from causing everyone to think and act alike — the group experience causes people to become more individual, more of what they want to be.

3. *The leader or parent participates as a learner.* As a group leader or parent you have certain responsibilities that other participants do not have. But you are also free to participate along with the others in the activity of valuing. No matter how often we have used them, we always learn from these exercises. Something has changed about us since the last time we did them, or someone new in the group changes it for us — something happens that helps us learn.

4. *The learner changes.* People seldom leave a session quite the same as they began it. Something happens to them. They change their beliefs slightly, or they widen their concept of a particular issue, or they stumble onto new questions that they had never before asked of themselves.

5. *People learn to minister to one another.* In the process of clarifying values, participants have an opportunity to make their witness to one another and to be heard. Both are a way of giving and receiving ministry. We do not have to talk about the ministry of the laity and hope that somewhere people will minister to one another; we can help it happen right here, within the session.

6. *People learn to listen to one another.* Through sharing with others and respecting one another, people learn to appreciate each other's viewpoints. People get to know each other better as persons and begin to discover and understand one another in new ways. Sometimes they even find themselves enlightened, appreciative, instructed.

Although you may begin with the values exercises given here, you might soon begin constructing some of your own. You may find your whole teaching and learning pattern altered, opened up, freed to help more new things happen in your work, in your own family, in your life.

This book, then, comes filtered through our own thinking and experience with many different kinds of groups, all seeking answers for their lives. We hope that you and the people with whom you interact will find it helpful.

Leadership

Resources within People

As a leader using *Values and Faith,* you do not have to have all the answers, for you will not be teaching, in the usual sense of the word. Rather, you will be facilitating a process in which people grow and minister to each other through sharing their beliefs, attitudes, and experiences. We've learned that people have great resources within themselves to help one another think about life's important matters.

Resources of the Christian Faith

These values exercises, however, do not propose "the blind leading the blind." Christians share a rich background of biblical history, a body of writings of religious thinkers. They believe that God acts in human history, especially through the life of Jesus and the ever-present activity of the Holy Spirit. In addition to making use of the person-resources in the group, we also assume that you will draw on the great resources of the Christian faith in presenting a framework within which people can test assumptions and make decisions.

How and when should these resources be brought into the discussion? Feel free to trust your own sense of what will be most appropriate for your situation and for your group.

Our main caution is to avoid imposing your own ideas on the group; rather, involve group members in a discovery process — using all available resources as guides.

Ideally, you will have received some group leadership training. (We realize, however, this is not always possible.) Familiarity with values theories, rationale, and methodology are recommended, as well, and we have provided a bibliography for this purpose.

Caring, Accepting Leadership

More important, however, we hope you will be a caring, warm, genuine, and accepting person. A good leader is a person first and an expert second. Techniques and methods are helpful, but your sensitivity, acceptance of others, and support for them are essential. Using these exercises, you will be most effective as a leader if you have these characteristics —

— You are open and willing to learn along with others.
— You want to be more accepting.
— You want to grow.
— You wish to increase your listening skills because you are really interested in what other people think and feel, even though you might disagree with them.
— You realize you might not have all the "right" answers for complex problems and issues, especially the problems and issues that others face.

Creating an Atmosphere

Creating an atmosphere is a highly important function of the leader. Without it, the exercises may become mere games. They are far too potentially meaningful to be used only as time-fillers or only for "fun." Their purpose is serious, and though fun often occurs for people who use them, the fun is merely a fortunate by-product.

To create the necessary atmosphere, clearly indicate the guidelines which all will follow during the exercises. If you post them as well, participants may remember them better.

The following are guidelines for participants:

1. *Everyone has the right to pass.* Every person is permitted *not* to give his or her answer to a question. The signal for passing is to fold the arms or to say "I pass." An answer of "pass" is just as acceptable as any other answer. If the atmosphere is properly established, very few people pass after the first few minutes. Remind people occasionally that they have this right and may exercise it.

2. *Accept each other.* Encourage the group to accept the answer a person gives as the right one for him or her at that time. Remind people of this guideline if arguments or challenges of statements occur. We have grown up so used to arguing and challenging one another that accepting other views is foreign to us. But acceptance contributes greatly to an atmosphere of trust and openness. Children are great correctors of one another, often denying the feeling behind a statement as well as its accuracy: "Oh, you did not. You're just making that up; you don't either like strawberries better than cherries." But children enjoy the freedom of the accepting atmosphere when they find they can trust it. So do adults.

3. *Speak for yourself.* Encourage participants to say what they think and what they feel. (A nonjudgmental climate facilitates the use of this guideline.) But ask them to relate their comments to themselves rather than to speak for others. For example: say "I think . . ." rather than "Most of us . . ." or "We . . . ."

4. *Expect unfinished business.* Unfinished business occurs when you have more to say on a values issue or when you're curious about something someone else said and would like to explore the thought further. Having to stop a discussion or having to move on to another subject before everything has been said by everyone is a fact of the process. Remind the group at the beginning of every session that they will have unfinished business with other members of the group. Encourage them to complete it between exercises, at break time (if you have one), or after the session.

In the next section, there are some other important ideas which can increase the effectiveness of your leadership. You should have them firmly in your mind.

Further Suggestions for the Leader

In using this process most effectively, you *put aside the function of judge* which is often an accepted part of the teacher's role. Do not feel compelled to decide, as a judge would, whether an answer is good or bad, right or wrong. In your verbal acknowledgments try to avoid comments that imply either a negative or a positive reaction. When participants generate conflicting ideas and responses, leader acknowledgments such as "good," "you don't mean that do you?", "fine," "great," "that's right," "that's not right, is it?" indicate particular approval of one response over another. Acceptable acknowledgments that are not judgmental would be "thank you," and "O.K."

To be a group facilitator who is nonjudgmental, we think it is important for you to —

present a stimulus (the exercise);

elicit responses to the stimulus;

accept those responses;

help each person clarify what he or she means by that response;

accept again.

At some point, *join the group* in giving your own answer or response to the exercise. It is a good idea, as in voting for instance, to delay your response a bit so that the group doesn't mirror your viewpoint. But do join them. You are a participant as well as a presenter, leader, facilitator. And your participation is valuable in several ways. First, your participation will encourage other individuals in the group to see themselves as participants with you in a shared venture. Second, what you value, how you vote, what you choose, will be observed and listened to. If you want to be influential — to have your preferences, values, choices known — this is an opportunity to present them, without foisting them on anyone. Finally, it is also important for the group to know that you, the leader, are not asking them to do something you're not willing to do yourself.

The Basic Exercises

Each of the next chapters in this book present several basic exercises as a means to explore chapter topics in depth. On pages 19 through 34, the basic exercises you will be using are thoroughly described. An explanation of how to present and share each of these simple exercises is also given. These exercises are —

Voting
Ranking
Continuum
Either/Or
Listening
Dilemma
Interviewing
Goal Setting

Each of the remaining chapters explores specific topics using examples of the exercises.

You may choose to present a seminar or workshop around a particular theme from a chapter; for example, you might develop a seminar for couples based on the exercises presented in "Valuing My Family." We have noted the specific exercises which deal with marriage, divorce, roles of husbands and wives, etc., and you can choose a combination of them for your seminar.

Using Values Exercises in the Family

At a leisurely evening meal a news item triggered a thought: "How awful to be blind!" Using the values exercise of Ranking, we asked our children to rank in 1, 2, 3-order this question:

Which condition would you least prefer?

____ blindness
____ deafness
____ paralysis

We all voiced our rankings without discussion or judgment. Then each of us talked about our ranking, explaining the reason for that particular order of choice. In the process, we learned something new about one of our daughters. She least preferred deafness. For her, deafness would be most difficult to live with because she would miss hearing beautiful music. We could tell from the way she responded that her love of music was deep — deeper than we realized. Through this simple values exercise we gained new insight into her feelings, and she was able to verbalize those feelings to us.

Sometimes these values exercises can be helpful in complex decision making within the family. Recently, tragedy struck the family of one of our friends. The youngest of three children, a seven-year-old, was hit by a car and killed on her way home from school. That evening the parents and the two children began making plans for the funeral. In this time of sudden grief, a question arose which the family needed to deal with immediately: How shall we take care of the body? Their spontaneous inclination for this family decision was to explore the options through a values Ranking:

____ We prefer a conventional burial.

____ We prefer to donate her body for organ transplants.

____ We prefer to cremate her body.

After individual ranking and discussion, a family decision was reached — to offer the child's body for organ transplants. The wisdom of their decision was confirmed when letters arrived, thanking them for eyesight restored to others. After transplants, the body was donated to medical science for training of pediatric physicians.

Careful Family Use

You might find Ranking, Voting, and the Either/Or exercises (see pages 19-24) the easiest to use within the family. It is important to remember that these exercises are not games. They should be used responsibly with openness, acceptance, sharing, listening, and facilitating. This is not easy. We have seen meaningful discussions suddenly become threatening to the parent's or authority figure's own personal beliefs and values. Then the temptation to impose one's own beliefs is strong, and the sharing session can become simply an advice-giving lecture. At that moment of disagreement, the challenge is to listen to the other people and try to feel accepting toward them. Acceptance does not mean that you will always agree with them. As parents, you will express your own ideas along with everyone else. Your children will want and need to know where you stand. Acceptance means rather that family members are willing to help each other express themselves; that together families can build a climate in which each person's ideas, thoughts, and feelings are respected; that they can learn to share in a spirit of mutual trust and understanding. Within this kind of climate, family members can clarify their own personal values and help each other to build strong family relationships.

Eight Basic Exercises

Eight basic exercises are used in *Values and Faith.* Nearly all of the following types will be found in each of the book's sections.

The insignia shown below will be used to help you quickly locate and identify each of the eight basic exercises throughout the book.

A description of the purpose and procedural steps for each of these eight exercises is provided in this chapter. Be familiar with these steps before using the exercises. Have them at your fingertips and refer to them frequently.

Each section of the book also includes a variety of additional exercises, often one of a kind. Instructions are included with each of these miscellaneous exercises.

Voting

Definition and Purpose:

The *Voting* exercise consists of a series of statements or questions to which participants respond by agreeing or disagreeing with each statement or question.

Voting gives each participant a chance, without talking, to take a stand and to note the responses of the rest of the group. Although values Voting is useful in a wide variety of situations, it is probably most frequently used as an opening exercise — a quick way to start people thinking about the various dimensions of one issue or about a variety of different issues. Examples of Voting questions are "How many of you think the size of families should be limited to two children?" or "How many of you agree with this statement: Our liturgy is no longer very meaningful?"

Voting gives you an opportunity to see where the group generally agrees or disagrees and helps you determine where to "zero in" for more in-depth discussion. Participate in the voting yourself, but delay your response until others have committed themselves. Otherwise, some will tend to follow your lead.

Voting can take as little time as 2 or 3 minutes. Or it may require an hour or more, depending on the number of voting items you choose and the time you allow for discussion.

Procedure:

1. Before you begin the exercise, give these instructions: "I will be asking questions or reading statements to which I'd like your response. If you agree, raise your hand high. Wave it if you agree strongly. If you disagree, make a fist and put your thumb down. Shake it if you disagree strongly. If you wish, you may pass by folding your arms across your chest. Do this if you have no opinion on the question, or if you don't want to answer the question."

2. Give participants a chance to try out the hand positions by asking one or two questions. Each time start with "How many of you. . .?" or "How many of you agree with the following statement?" Repeat each question or statement so that everyone has a chance to hear it.

3. Judge how much, if any, discussion you will allow. Voting moves quickly, but certain issues need to be discussed in depth. You may want to set aside time for discussion or allow brief discussion on the spot.

At any time during or after the exercise you may wish to draw from our Christian heritage resources that pertain to the topic. Be sure to elicit contributions from group members as well.

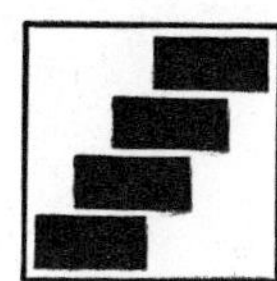

Ranking

Definition and Purpose:

The *Ranking* exercise presents three or more possible choices for participants to rearrange in their order of preference or priority (for example, from best to worst, or from most important to least important).

Ranking helps participants consider different options and make their own personal choices. Through the process of ranking or prioritizing, persons examine their thoughts, attitudes, feelings, beliefs, and behaviors. Ranking gives participants practice in choosing among alternatives and provides opportunities to explain and defend their choices, while being exposed to the thinking and choices of others.

Several Rankings can be done in 10-15 minutes. More time must be allotted if small- or large-group discussions are planned following the exercise.

Here is an example of a Ranking exercise:

What time of the year do you enjoy most with your family?

_____ Easter
_____ Thanksgiving
_____ Christmas

Procedure:

1. Read a question or statement with three or more different response items, writing them on newsprint or on a chalkboard if possible.

2. Sometimes all items are appealing and meaningful. Sometimes none of them is. In either case, ask people to rank all the items in order of importance or preference to them (1 = most important; 2 = next most important, etc.).
3. Invite volunteers to share their rankings and their reasons. After accepting seven or eight responses, you may wish to give your own ranking, with reasons why.

Sharing might also take place in small groups, with each group including persons who made different rank orders. Allow time for discussion.

Again, bring resources from our Christian heritage to the discussion.

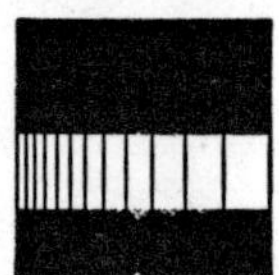

Continuum

Definition and Purpose:

The *Continuum* exercise presents two opposite choices or viewpoints. Respondents select that place on the continuum — between the choices — which most closely represents their personal views.

A wide array of response is possible on many value issues. The Continuum exercise opens the possibility for many gradations of choice between two extremes. Participants examine their own opinions and beliefs and take stands where they feel most comfortable between the extremes. In addition, they become aware of the range of views that exist in the thinking of a seemingly homogeneous group of people. Discussing one's point of view with another person often brings the issue into clearer focus and helps participants improve their ability to hear and understand one another.

A Continuum exercise can sometimes be done quickly in 5 or 10 minutes. However, more time is often needed, depending upon the amount and intensity of discussion which follows.

Here is an example of a Continuum exercise:

What should be the main emphasis in church life?

|———————————————————————————————|

Worship Services　　　　　　　　　　　　　　　　Social Action

Procedure:

1. Ask a question which raises an issue. Then describe two disparate responses to that issue.

2. Designate an imaginary line across the room, asking participants to respond to the issue by placing themselves at a point on the line representing their own personal view. (Afterward, you may wish to take your own position on the continuum.)

3. Encourage participants to share reasons for their choices with one or two people nearby.

4. After a few minutes, elicit from several people (particularly those at the extremes) their reasons for standing where they are. Focus on respondents, listening and accepting their statements.

5. General discussion may then follow. Or discussion might be continued in small groups.

If you decide on small-group discussion, number off the total group (1, 2, 3, 4; 1, 2, 3, 4, etc.) from one end of the continuum to the other. Have all one's meet together, two's together, etc.

Later, come together and share discoveries, learnings, and observations. Questions to consider: 1) As a result of the sharing, did anyone get an insight that encouraged you to change your position? 2) What did you learn from this experience?

If Continuum exercises are used in sequence, have people come to the middle of the room each time before announcing the next issue and describing the two extreme positions.

At some point, you may introduce data and material from Christian resources, asking, for example, "What does God's Word say about this issue? Let's search it out together."

Either/Or

Definition and Purpose:

The *Either/Or* exercise is a forced choice between two

options. Respondents select the option with which they most closely identify.

Often a choice boils down to one of two alternatives. Sometimes both choices are appealing; sometimes neither one is. Nevertheless, people are often forced to choose one of two options. In this exercise, participants are asked to examine choices and are exposed to the choices and thoughts of others.

Here is an example of an Either/Or choice:

Which are you most like?
leader / follower

Either/Or is sometimes set up as a metaphorical exercise. For example, you might ask participants, "Which are you more like, a hardwood floor or wall-to-wall carpeting?" Participants exercise their imaginations and intuitions to relate themselves to these items, considering the implications of each choice: Am I plain or fancy? Do I prefer things simple or luxurious? Am I old-fashioned or modern?

Time required for the Either/Or exercise is variable. Plan for a minimum of 10 minutes. If multiple Either/Or exercises are used, you may wish to shift to another type of exercise after 20-25 minutes.

Procedure:

1. Clear the room so that people can move about easily.
2. Ask a question with two alternatives. Repeat it.
3. Point to the opposite sides of the room and ask those identifying with the first alternative to go to one side and those identifying with the second alternative to the other.
4. Have each participant find a partner on the same side and share reasons for their choices with each other. (Or, people can find partners at the opposite side and share.) In general, limit discussion on an item to about 2 or 3 minutes.
5. Before the next Either/Or choice, call the group to the middle of the room, so that an active choice has to be made each time.

Listening

Definition and Purpose:

The *Listening* exercise consists of a stimulus statement or paragraph to which each person in a group of three responds individually while the others listen to him or her. The individual responder is called the *focus person*.

Small groups typically carry on discussions which are dominated by a few people, while other members seldom are encouraged or have a chance to express their ideas. The Listening exercise gives all group members equal time to express their personal views and reactions to an issue. When closely followed, this exercise provides an opportunity for each person to be listened to and to be a listener. Each Listening exercise requires 20 minutes or more to complete.

Controversial statements provide the content to which participants respond. For example, a statement might be read which suggests a controversial way in which a worship service should be conducted.

Procedure:

Prior to beginning the exercise:

1. Select a content area for discussion and choose an appropriate Listening statement.
2. Divide the total group into smaller groups of three.
3. Have groups sit together while you give the instructions.
4. Announce that a provocative statement will soon be made and that each person will have an opportunity to respond to the statement, receiving the full attention of the other two group members.
5. Give the following guidelines for the Listening exercise (post these guidelines, stressing their importance to successful completion of the exercise):

Focusing Give these instructions:

Taking turns, each person will be on focus for 5 minutes. During this period the focus person will respond to the Listening statement — commenting on it, agreeing or disagreeing with portions of it, adding new thoughts. Other group members should not let the attention shift from the focus person. While focusing on another's comments, hold your own thoughts or reactions until it is your turn to be on focus.

Drawing Out Give these instructions:

Listen as intently as you can. You may not agree with what the focus person says, but try not to indicate this in any way, for the time being. Instead, try to understand his or her attitudes, beliefs, and feelings. Ask questions to help clarify the focus person's comments and feelings, but do not allow attention to shift from the focus person to yourself.

Acceptance Give these instructions:

Try to feel accepting, even when you don't agree with what the focus person is saying. You can demonstrate your acceptance by listening, smiling, and nodding. Keep eye contact; be warm and supportive. And then listen some more!

Begin the exercise:

1. Ask each group to designate the first focus person.

2. Read the selected Listening statement and ask the focus person in each group to begin talking.

3. When 5 minutes are up, ask groups to stop wherever they are and move clockwise to the next focus person. (Repeat until each has had a turn.)

4. By this point, many individual reactions typically have been generated within the small groups. They may want to simply talk and share for a few minutes. Allow for normal small-group conversation so that some feeling of closure on the subject matter is reached.

5. Reassemble the total group and share learnings, observations. Ask, "Does the Word of God speak to this issue? What does it say?" Then talk about it: in the total group, or in small groups again.

Dilemma

Definition and Purpose:

A values *Dilemma* is a story that presents a dilemma but stops short of the solution. Participants try to solve the dilemma.

Values Dilemmas give participants practice in generating alternative solutions and considering the possible consequences of each. Based on the data generated, they choose a "best" solution to the problem.

The time required for a dilemma is usually 20-30 minutes, sometimes more.

Here is an example of a Dilemma: You are a high school junior. A person representing a social agency in your neighborhood speaks at your church. His message is interesting, but you feel he unjustly criticizes the young people in your community's churches for their "lack of concern for other youth." You think he is not in touch with what the youth in the churches are attempting to do. By the time he finishes, you are furious. As you leave the church, you notice that the speaker is greeting people at the door. You will have to pass by him on your way out. STOP

What could you do right now? What might happen?

Procedure:

1. Have participants form small discussion groups of 3-4 and sit together. Pass out paper to each group; then read the Dilemma story.

2. Give the following steps, asking that they be followed carefully:

Step one: Brainstorm. Give these instructions to the group: Each small group brainstorm together all possible alternative responses to the dilemma-situation and list them on your paper. List the possibilities quickly *without discussing or judging,* at this point, whether or not they will work. See how many you can list in 4 minutes.

Step two: Consider consequences of each alternative. After 5 minutes, continue with these instructions:

Go over your list, one item at a time. As you look at each alternative, discuss what possible consequences it might have. Jot them down.

(Move from group to group to monitor the progress. Many groups are ready to move from Step two after 6-8 minutes.)

Step three: Make a decision. Give these instructions:

Each person make an individual decision. Consider also the Christian perspective. What would you personally do? Choose one response.

Prior to beginning Step four, challenge people to really try to hear one another. Allow ample time for listening and understanding.

Step four: Share individual responses. Give these instructions:

In your small groups, take turns explaining why you made your particular decision.

Step five: Reflect on choices. Give these instructions:

In your groups, reflect on these questions: Did Christianity have anything to do with the choice you made? What? Do the Scriptures provide any guidelines for this situation?

3. Reassemble the entire group.

4. Ask for volunteers to tell the total group what their decision was. Then ask for any other key ideas that emerged in the small groups.

Some small groups may wish to role play their "best" solution and possibly reenact their situation for the entire group. Why not give an invitation to do so?

Interviewing

Definition and Purpose:

The values Interview consists of questions asked by the leader of a volunteer from the group.

Interviewing gives that volunteer an opportunity to share some information with the total group about self, personal thoughts, feelings, attitudes, and values. The

Interview allows the group to learn from the life of another in a short time. It is an excellent way to help people in ongoing groups and classes to get acquainted and understand one another.

Time required for a public Interview is often 15-20 minutes. An additional 20 minutes must be allotted for a paired Interview.

An Interview might be used, for example, with a Confirmation class. A class member is interviewed in order for the group to learn about that person's life, experiences, beliefs, and values. (You can also interview someone from outside the group. In this case, perhaps, a pastor, youth worker, or someone recently confirmed.)

Procedure:

Interviewing before a group:

1. Explain that you would like to conduct an interview with someone from the group.

2. Select the interviewee or ask for a volunteer. While people are thinking (and perhaps hesitating), announce these simple ground rules for the interview:

— The person to be interviewed answers honestly and openly.

— The interviewee has the right to pass on any question.

— The interviewee controls the interview. At any point he or she can terminate the interview by stating, "Thanks for the interview." The interviewer (you) can bring it to a close in the same manner.

— When the interview is completed, the person interviewed will have the privilege of asking the interviewer any question he or she was asked.

3. In selecting a volunteer, you can interview the first person who responds, or you can wait until three or four have volunteered and then choose one. Quickly review the ground rules, or ask the interviewee to restate them in his or her own words.

4. Proceed with the interview, allowing about 10-15 minutes for completion. It is important to keep track of time and not carry the interview on too long, especially with children.

5. Begin with questions which elicit basic information. For example:

— What is your full name?
— Where did you grow up as a child?
— Do you have brothers and sisters?
— Where did you attend school?
— What hobbies do you have now?

6. Use your own style to listen, to reflect thoughts and feelings, to paraphrase, and to ask more questions, but add no input of your own. (Focus on the person being interviewed; do not discuss the person's responses.) As you begin to hear attitudes, beliefs, values, you may go into some depth as seems appropriate — sometimes following the interviewee's train of thought, sometimes changing to a desired topic with a direct question again.

7. If the group has been dealing with a certain topic, the interviewee can be asked some questions or opinions about it. Here is also a chance to find out about the person's background, experience, and thoughts about the church. You might want to ask questions like these:

— Did you attend church as a child? Where?
— Did you attend church school or Sunday school?
— Was there a particular class or teacher you liked best?
— Have you been involved in any church activities or groups during the last five years?
— What is your most meaningful church involvement now?
— Was there any one person in your life who had an influence on what you believe now? Do you care to share anything about it?

8. At the end, give the interviewee the option to question the interviewer.

Interviewing in pairs:

A follow-up to the exercise described above is to involve everyone in an interview, at the same time, in pairs.

1. Instruct the participants to find a partner — someone in the group they don't know very well.

2. Explain that in each pair, one person is the interviewer, the other the interviewee.
3. After 6-8 minutes, call time. Have pairs switch roles, and begin a final interview.
4. Before the pairs come back to the total group, provide time for them to talk for a minute or two about their experience together, how it felt to interview and to be interviewed.

Interviews are most effective when the interviewer does not use a predetermined list of questions. If you have some general issues in mind, yet are flexible and a good listener, your interview will be comfortable and informative.

Goal Setting

Definition and Purpose:

Value learning is incomplete unless values are linked to one's commitments and behavior. Throughout this book, therefore, Goal Setting is used intermittently, often at the end of a miscellaneous exercise.

Goal Setting helps translate discussed ideas into planned action. It helps individuals to act on a decision. The individual tells others in the group of his or her goal and makes a commitment to accomplish it. Thus, Goal Setting is a way of getting things done, changing something, helping a person become more the person he or she wants to be.

Sometimes Goal Setting is done as a one-time-only activity. But in groups that meet weekly (or on some other regular basis) it may be a part of each session. Setting goals is most often a closing activity and usually can be done in small groups in about 10 minutes.

Here are examples of goals which persons might set:

— To complete a specific project for school.
— To write a long overdue letter to a friend.
— To confront a person about a difficult matter.

Procedure:

1. Give this goal-setting sequence:

— Select a goal you want to attain.
— Carry out your plan.
— From achieving your goal, you will feel satisfaction.
— Set another goal, carry it out, and continue to experience more feelings of satisfaction and achievement.

2. Post these eight guidelines for goal setting and review them with the group. A goal should be —

conceivable: can be put into words;
believable: is appropriate to your own set of values;
achievable: can be accomplished;
controllable: does not depend on another person for its attainment;
measurable: is countable, observable;
desirable: is something you really want to achieve;
definite: there are no alternatives — you *will* reach it — not just try to;
beneficial: has a positive effect on a person and/or society.

Stress the importance of following the guidelines, encouraging participants to make sure that their goals fit each. This will greatly improve the chance for successful attainment of goals. You can demonstrate how this works by setting a personal goal, stating it to the group, and showing how it fits each of the guidelines.

3. Sometimes participants can set goals quietly and alone. At other times they may want to work in small groups where they can use each other as resources — discussing their ideas, formulating their goals, and finally stating the goals (word for word) to one another.

4. It is important for individuals to report the actual attainment of a goal. With ongoing groups, individuals can report to the group at the opening of the next session. If no additional session is planned, encourage participants to arrange a time by which they will check in with a specific person in their group — perhaps by telephone, or however they wish.

5. If you hold another session for the same group, provide time at the beginning for reporting on goals. You might start by saying, "My goal was . . . and here's what happened. . . ." Encourage others to summarize their goals and tell what happened.

Miscellaneous Exercises

At the end of each chapter, exercises appear which are one-of-a-kind. These Miscellaneous Exercises are designed to help participants further examine what they believe and value. Directions and procedures accompany each.

Three Levels of Learning

In learning we typically deal with three levels:
— Facts
— Concepts
— Values

Learning begins at the facts level. We need factual information in order to understand concepts and formulate our own values. Biblical passages contain rich material at each level. Obviously, a great amount of value-laden content is provided.

Each section of this book includes an exercise which focuses on each of the three levels. All or part of this insignia is used in those exercises.

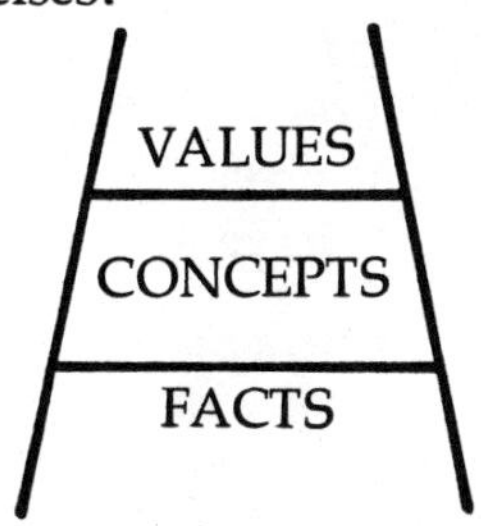

The insignia is a reminder of the three levels. In teaching-learning activities, we think it is important to spend considerable time at the values level.

Write Your Own Exercises

You may want to write your own exercises when dealing with content areas not covered in this book. The following forms provide an outline for creating new exercises to fit specific issues or subject matter content. Winston Press, Inc. gives permission to reproduce the forms for group and family use.

Consider and complete the following items on each form:

— the setting for your group
— the group or activity you will be working with
— the age, sex, and other relevant characteristics of participants
— the value issue, goal, or objective to be considered
— methods for sharing
— helpful resources you can draw from

The outline helps develop a specific exercise to be used with a specific group of people dealing with a specific value issue in a specific way.

Prior to the group session, take time to carefully define the value issue, goal, or objective to be considered. The questions and exercises you develop should be ones that capture a group's interest and stimulate participants to think. Try out the question or exercise on one or two others in advance.

Sharing is an important part of learning; it gives participants a chance to express what they think and feel and to hear others express themselves. Using different sharing modes (pairs, small groups, large group) helps maintain interest.

Voting

Setting:
Group/activity:
Participant characteristics:
Value issue, goal, or objective:

"How many of you ______________________________?"

"How many of you ______________________________?"

"How many of you ______________________________?"

"How many of you ______________________________?"

"How many of you ______________________________?"

"How many of you ______________________________?"

"How many of you ______________________________?"

"How many of you ______________________________?"

"How many of you ______________________________?"

Sharing methods:

_____ total group

_____ small groups

_____ pairs

_____ other ______________________________

Resources:

Ranking

Setting:
Group/activity:
Participant characteristics:
Value issue, goal, or objective:

Question "____?"

(choices to be ranked)

Question "____?"

(choices to be ranked)

Question "____?"

(choices to be ranked)

Sharing:

_____ total group

_____ small groups who disagree

_____ small groups who agree

_____ pairs

_____ other ____

Resources:

Continuum

Setting:

Group/activity:

Participant characteristics:

Value issue, goal, or objective:

Question "______________________________________ ?"
(describe one extreme) (describe other extreme)

Question "______________________________________ ?"
(describe one extreme) (describe other extreme)

Question "______________________________________ ?"
(describe one extreme) (describe other extreme)

Sharing:

____ turn to person near you and share

____ total group

____ number off to form small groups of persons representing different positions

____ other ______________________________

Resources:

Either/Or

Setting:

Group/activity:

Participant characteristics:

Value issue, goal, or objective:

Which do you identify more with?

____________________ or ____________________

____________________ or ____________________

____________________ or ____________________

____________________ or ____________________

____________________ or ____________________

____________________ or ____________________

Sharing:

____ total group

____ pairs who made same choice

____ pairs who made opposite choice

____ other ____________________________________

Resources:

Listening

Setting:

Group/activity:

Participant characteristics:

Value issue, goal, or objective:

Listening Statement:

Sharing:

____ groups of 3

____ groups of 4

____ other ______________________________

Resources:

Interviewing

Setting:

Group/activity:

Participant characteristics:

Value issue, goal, or objective:

Factual or informational questions:

Deeper questions:

Sharing:

_____ interviewing in total groups

_____ interviewing in pairs

Resources:

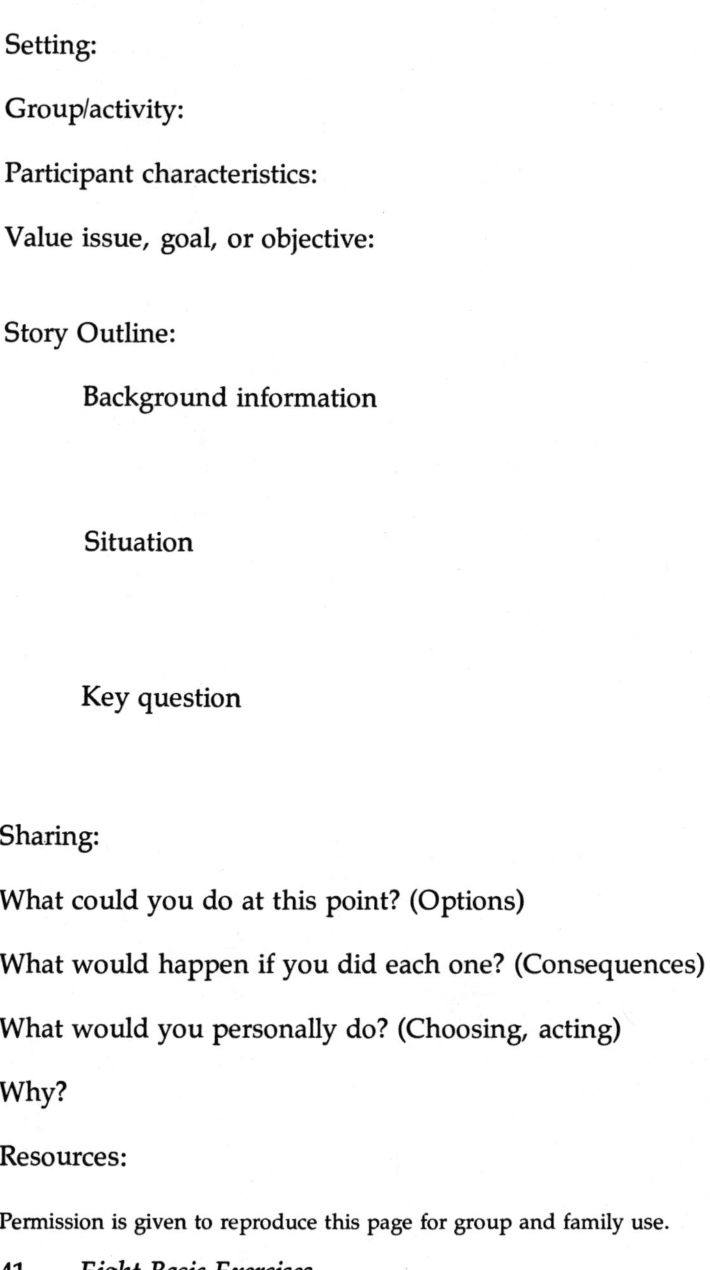

Dilemma

Setting:

Group/activity:

Participant characteristics:

Value issue, goal, or objective:

Story Outline:

Background information

Situation

Key question

Sharing:

What could you do at this point? (Options)

What would happen if you did each one? (Consequences)

What would you personally do? (Choosing, acting)

Why?

Resources:

Valuing My Faith

Values and Faith centers around the Christian faith. Faith provides the context in which persons examine their opinions, attitudes, and beliefs.

The exercises in this section are designed to help participants clarify their own personal faith and its importance in their lives. Further, the intent of these exercises is to give persons an opportunity to:

— Develop a deeper appreciation of their faith.
— Think about faith as a source of their personal values.
— Think about how their faith is related to their actions.
— Think about how their faith provides a framework for living out their lives.
— Seek to discover who Christ is to them.
— Explore areas of uncertainty and struggle in their faith life.
— Become aware of ways to share their faith and to set personal goals to accomplish this.

Before using this chapter, please review the chapter on leadership.

Voting

Instructions: Pages 20-21 give purpose and procedure for the Voting exercise.

Participants vote in the following manner:

Agree?	(Raise hand.)
Strongly agree?	(Wave hand.)
Disagree?	(Thumb down.)
Strongly disagree?	(Shake thumb.)
Pass?	(Fold arms across chest.)

General Voting Questions on Faith

How many of you:

- — think that faith in God "just happens"?
- — find that your ideas about God have changed a lot since grade school?
- — are at a loss for words when someone challenges your beliefs?
- — sometimes have doubts about your faith?
- — believe that God makes himself best known through Jesus?
- — think that a Christian needs other people in order to live fully?
- — think that every Christian should be able to identify a conversion experience in his or her life?
- — think most people find it difficult to share their faith?
- — think that Jesus continues to live in people through the presence of the Holy Spirit?
- — think the Bible is relevant to every person's life?
- — think it's important to participate in Communion at least once a month?
- — think it's important to participate in Communion more than once a month?
- — believe that prayers are always heard?
- — think we can learn from other religious faiths?
- — think that people have trouble accepting salvation as a free gift?
- — view death as a beginning rather than an ending?

Faith and God

How many of you agree with this statement?

- — God is always pursuing us.
- — It is really difficult to know if there is a God.
- — God supplies our needs.
- — God gives us choices in our everyday life.
- — Faith in God is based on a personal relationship with God.
- — A person may believe in God and yet not have faith.
- — A person may believe that God is good and yet not have faith.
- — No one has ever seen God.

— We all need redemption.
— God gives a person direction in deciding what is right or wrong.
— God controls our every thought and act.
— A person can believe God is good, even when there is evil and suffering in the world.
— All evil and suffering in the world is a result of sin.
— Satan is real.
— Satan is the source of all evil.
— God intends only good for us.
— God suffers with us in times of tragedy.
— God daily rescues people from evil.
— God uses our sin to teach us of his love.
— God makes himself known through others.

Faith and Jesus

How many of you:
— think that Jesus is truly divine and truly human?
— think that Christ is the Son of God?
— wonder about Jesus' childhood?
— think that deep down, many Christians wish Jesus weren't Jewish?
— really rejoice that Jesus, as the Bible says, was a human being like us in all ways, but without sin?
— believe that Jesus is the only way to God?
— think that because Jesus was tempted he is better able to understand and help others who are tempted?
— believe that Jesus actually rose from the dead?
— feel that Christians must take the resurrection story literally?
— feel that it is important to prove things about Jesus, such as that he was an historical person, that he rose from the dead?
— think it is harder for us to believe in Jesus than it was for first-century Christians?

Faith and the Holy Spirit

How many of you:

— think of God in three ways — as Father, Son, and Holy Spirit?

— think belief in the Holy Spirit is less essential than belief in the Father and Jesus?

— believe that the Holy Spirit can give power to your life?

— are uncertain about the nature and working of the Holy Spirit?

— believe that God's Spirit is active in us?

— think that Jesus continues to live in people through the presence of the Holy Spirit?

— really don't understand the way the Holy Spirit works?

— ever wish for an empowering by the Holy Spirit like the early disciples received on the day of Pentecost?

— think the Holy Spirit comes to chosen people in the Church?

— believe you cannot understand or believe in Jesus except with the help of the Holy Spirit?

— think of the Holy Spirit as a counselor?

— believe that the gifts you have are the work of the Holy Spirit?

— believe that the Holy Spirit gives different gifts to people?

— believe that one needs to experience a definite "baptism by the Spirit" in order to know the Spirit?

— think the Holy Spirit is the one who makes God's Word clear to you?

— think the Holy Spirit gives people power to live for God and others?

— believe the Church is held together by the power of the Holy Spirit?

— believe that the Spirit can work in people's lives even when they are not open to it or aware of it?

Faith and the Bible

How many of you agree with this statement?

— The Bible is the Word of God.

— What a person gets out of the Bible depends on what that person brings to the Bible.

— Each person is free to interpret the Bible in his or her own way.
— Some people twist Scripture to say what they want it to say.
— The Bible is relevant to every person's life.
— The Bible provides as much insight into our problems and needs today as it provided people throughout the ages.
— Sometimes it's hard to know what the Bible originally said because of translation changes.
— The Bible contains no errors.
— The Bible is a revelation of God.
— The Bible teaches much about human nature.
— The Bible is not a science book.
— The Bible is a personal revelation, something between God and an individual.
— An important way to learn what the Bible has to say is through studying and discussing it with others.
— The Bible reveals new truths and meanings for us as we change and grow.

Baptism and Communion

How many of you:
— usually listen to a sermon as if God himself were speaking to you?
— think most people overlook the joy of the Lord's Supper?
— think that participating in the Lord's Supper makes a person more certain of God's love and forgiveness?
— feel that the Lord's Supper is a very personal experience?
— find that the promise of forgiveness in both Baptism and the Lord's Supper is a reason for rejoicing?
— view Baptism as a command of Christ?
— think a person must be baptized to be saved?
— believe God adopts a person into his family through Baptism?
— find Baptism a helpful reminder of who you are?
— think prayer is an important preparation for Communion?
— think it's important to participate in Communion as often as possible?

Life and Death

How many of you:

- — think that the way you view death is related to the way you view life?
- — think that death is a result of evil in the world?
- — think that eternal life as Jesus promised it begins here and now?
- — think it is possible to fear life more than death?
- — believe in life after death?
- — find God's Word a source of strength in thinking about death?
- — think of your own death more as an enemy than as a friend?
- — view death as a beginning rather than an ending?
- — sometimes wonder just what the Creed means by "the resurrection of the body"?
- — think there is a difference in the way Christians and non-Christians face death?
- — think that some Christians fear death because they fear eternal punishment?

Grace

How many of you:

- — think grace might mean God loving us with no strings attached?
- — think that personal salvation depends solely on God?
- — think most people strive to worship "properly" and live "correctly" in order to earn God's favor?
- — have experienced a special instance of grace in your own life?
- — find it difficult to believe God loves you even when you are at your worst?
- — think that God's love for us depends on the good things we do?
- — think that God's love for us depends on our belief in him?
- — think that God's love for us depends on our feelings toward him?
- — think that God's love for us depends on whether we refuse

or accept that love?
— find the concept of grace difficult to understand?

How many of you agree with this statement?
— God sees us as sinners whom he loves.
— God's acceptance of us depends on how much we know about the Bible.
— God is less accepting of people who use drugs or alcohol than those who don't.
— God's acceptance of us depends on how we treat our neighbor.
— All people are given God's grace; they only need to accept it.

Faith and Doubt

How many of you:
— think that faith is a gift from God?
— think that you can prove your faith by attending church regularly?
— think that we can't trust God unless we fully understand him?
— think that faith is a greater risk than downhill skiing?
— think that having a religious faith is important?
— see your faith as your highest value?
— are bothered when other people express doubts about God?
— are bothered when you have doubts about God?
— think we should be ashamed to have doubts about our religious beliefs?
— think that faith needs to be tested to be real?
— think that doubts often lead to real certainty about our faith?
— think that to be of help to a person who doubts, you must have experienced doubt yourself?
— think that faith is something you have to work at constantly?
— think that religion has become too academic and complicated?

— think that God never intended that religion be complicated?
— think that churches would be better off if people did not choose their religion until they were capable of making a mature choice?
— think that most people need proof of something before they will believe it?

Change through Conversion

How many of you agree with this statement?
— Conversion happens at a certain time and place.
— Conversion happens every day.
— Human nature changes at the time of conversion.
— Anger disappears at the time of conversion.
— A person can be completely changed after conversion.
— A person should be able to state definitely whether he or she is saved.
— After conversion, a person never reverts to the old self.
— Conversion is a private matter between a person and God.
— Other people are often instrumental in the conversion experience of individuals.
— If a family member or a friend is struggling with his or her life and faith, you should help them toward a conversion experience.
— Conversion happens when God breaks into a person's life.
— A person's own efforts and attitudes are important in bringing about a conversion experience.

Personal Beliefs

How many of you:
— think that belief in God is necessary for a meaningful life?
— have difficulty putting into words what you believe about God?
— are not sure what you really believe?
— don't think much about why you believe as you do?
— have the same basic religious beliefs as your parents?
— have beliefs that are quite different from those of your parents?

— try to pass on your beliefs to your friends or family members?
— think that one's personal faith should lead to more relationships that are supportive and caring?
— think that Christian life is meaningful only if one holds certain beliefs?
— think that any relationship to God based only on feeling is very flimsy?

Sharing Beliefs

How many of you:
— think it is impossible to persuade someone to become a Christian?
— think that faith is more corporate than private?
— think that if we really know what we believe, we will share that belief?
— think most Christians do not share their faith easily because they are embarrassed to talk about it with others?
— think most Christians do not share their faith easily because it is a private matter?
— think that Christians often set poor examples for non-Christians?
— have ever told another person what your faith means to you?
— think that Christians ought to respect what other people believe, without trying to alter those beliefs?
— would like to tell a friend about your faith, but don't know where to begin?
— had an opportunity to share your personal faith with someone but did not make use of it?
— shared your personal faith with someone, and it made a real difference in his or her life?
— think that preaching the Gospel is almost useless to people struggling for physical survival?
— think the best way to transmit your faith to others is to tell what it means to you?
— think the best way to transmit your faith to others is simply to live it?

Prayer

How many of you:

— often pray silently in public places?
— believe that public prayer is hypocritical?
— pray silently at work or in school?
— pray with your family?
— wish your family had prayed more when you were younger?
— would rather pray alone than in a group?
— have a set time and place for prayer each day?
— feel that praying is not necessary?
— wish you knew more about praying?
— like to pray in unison at church worship?
— feel closer to God when you pray?
— are not sure God hears when you pray?
— know that God hears your prayers?
— have experienced answers to prayer?
— think that prayer is like magic?
— prefer to pray the written prayers of others?
— usually create you own prayers?
— often use hymns as prayers?
— pray for others who are ill?
— pray mostly for your own needs?
— pray every day?
— believe that God hears prayerful requests but does not always grant them?
— think that it isn't possible for God to hear all people's prayers at the same time?
— think God often answers prayer in more than one way?
— pray even when you feel doubt and disbelief?
— wonder why we need to pray at all when God is all-knowing and all-wise?
— think that answers to prayer are possible but improbable?
— think God answers prayer in proportion to your faith?
— are comfortable praying?
— find prayer difficult?
— find it difficult to pray in public?
— are embarrassed to bow your head in public before you eat?

Christian Life

How many of you agree with this statement?

— If God is in your life, you are never a "nobody."
— The Christian faith helps you decide what's important in life.
— Personal ambition can keep you from finding faith in God.
— Personal ambition can keep you from living out faith in God.
— Christians should be able to bear more sorrows and burdens than non-Christians.
— God can use our personal tragedies to build better disciples.
— All Christians have a cross to bear.
— The Apostles' Creed should begin with the words "we believe" rather than "I believe."
— An important mission of the Church is to help liberate poor and oppressed people and to heal human misery.

How many of you:

— wonder what being a Christian really means?
— think that a Christian should not get angry?
— think Christians should always "turn the other cheek"?
— think that people should be free to dress as they wish for church?
— think that you can't be a Christian without other people?
— think that a person does not have to be an active church member to be a Christian?
— think that the local church is the main source of fellowship, support, and strength for a Christian?
— have questions about your relationship to God?
— wish you had a closer relationship to Christ?
— feel a closer relationship to God because of Christ?
— feel a closer relationship to God through other people?
— think that change is part of God's order, and nothing is absolute except God's love for us?
— think that to love God you must also love your fellow human beings?

Other Religions

How many of you agree with this statement?

— We do not learn from other faiths because we generally ignore them or actively reject them.
— Good people of non-Christian faiths are often more virtuous than Christians.
— Persons of the Christian faith generally listen carefully to the ideas of persons of other faiths.
— We can learn much from other groups and other cultures, but people in our church seldom take the opportunity to do so.
— Most Christians would feel uncomfortable having a Buddhist in their home.
— Doctrine divides, and that is why different denominations have trouble working closely together.
— The ecumenical movement can be destructive if it is carried too far.
— Non-Christians will not have eternal life with God.
— It doesn't matter so much what you believe as long as you believe in some kind of God.
— Different faiths are just different means to the same end.
— Christians should not try to convert those who believe differently.
— If all religions are seen as equally valid, the real meaning of the Christian faith is diminished.
— First-century traditions are not important to Christians today.
— Christians need to continually examine and reexamine their faith in the light of other world views.
— Both ancient and modern ideas are needed to fully understand and strengthen one's Christian faith.
— Modern science conflicts with the Christian world view.
— Evolution and the biblical account of Creation are compatible.
— The Christian faith is an extension of the Jewish faith.
— Most Christians have not closely examined the relationship of the Jewish Passover to the Lord's Supper.

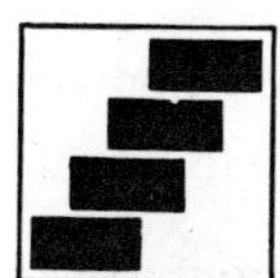

Ranking

Instructions: Pages 21-22 give purpose and procedure for the Ranking exercise.

Participants rank all items in order of preference or priority (1 = most important; 2 = next most important, etc.)

General Faith Rankings

Which of the following would help you most in learning the meaning of faith?
____ exploring the way the Bible defines faith
____ listening to a theologian talk on faith
____ putting yourself in Jesus' hands in a risky situation
____ listening to experiences of others who have lived in faith

Faith in Jesus is most like which of these?
____ venturing into a love relationship with someone
____ knowing your parents will help you if you ask
____ trusting the airplane to get you from Minneapolis to Los Angeles
____ knowing water will come out of the tap when you turn the spigot

Which statement is most important in relating to God?
____ Doubts are okay; God understands them.
____ Faith becomes even stronger when it is tested through doubt.
____ We should never doubt.

Our salvation depends upon:
____ God's action.
____ our own works.
____ making a decision for Christ.
____ fate — it's already decided who will be saved.

Which is most important to you?
_____ faith in the ability of education to develop human potential
_____ faith in God's work in people's lives
_____ faith that science will assure continual progress
_____ faith in the goodness of people

What is the greatest hindrance to your faith in God?
_____ your own weaknesses
_____ personal tragedy
_____ faith's conflict with science
_____ difficulty in knowing God

What steps are most important after a person has put God in command of his or her life?
_____ reading the Bible and other Christian books
_____ sharing one's faith and doubts with other Christians
_____ praying and attending church
_____ caring for others

How is the Christian faith most often passed on to others?
_____ through words
_____ through personal witness
_____ through the Holy Spirit
_____ through loving actions

Faith and God

What is the most important belief you hold about God and Creation?
_____ God created the world in six days.
_____ God created man and woman.
_____ God is continually creating.

Where do you see the most evident signs of God's presence?
_____ in the faith of others
_____ in the life of Jesus
_____ in the Bible
_____ in the world around us

What quality comes to your mind first when you think of God?
_____ loving
_____ stern
_____ holy
_____ just
_____ all-knowing
_____ all-powerful
_____ merciful

Faith and Jesus

Which of these wonders surrounding the birth of Jesus have most meaning to you?
_____ God became human in Christ Jesus.
_____ Jesus was born of a virgin.
_____ Mary's faith was so great, she believed this would happen to her.

Which answer best describes who Jesus is for you?
_____ I don't know.
_____ a great teacher
_____ God who became fully human
_____ a savior who came to redeem broken people
_____ a worker of miracles

When you think of Jesus, what quality comes first to your mind?
_____ impartial
_____ loving
_____ compassionate
_____ kind
_____ firm
_____ forgiving
_____ forceful

Faith and Prayer

What changes occur when you pray?
_____ I change.
_____ Little or nothing changes.
_____ Circumstances change.
_____ My outlook changes.

Why is prayer important in your life?
_____ It serves as a powerful resource.
_____ It enables me to cope.
_____ It gives me what I need.
_____ It helps me communicate with God.
_____ It helps me see things in perspective.

When are you most likely to pray?
_____ When I am frightened.
_____ When someone is ill.
_____ When I want something very much.
_____ When I am thankful for something.
_____ When I am confused.

How often do you pray?
_____ every day
_____ several times a day
_____ about once a week
_____ hardly ever

For whom do you pray most?
_____ myself
_____ my family
_____ my friends
_____ people in need whom I don't know

The Bible

To understand the Bible it is best to approach it:
_____ as a scientist.
_____ as a poet.
_____ as an historian.
_____ as a believer.
_____ as a skeptic.

The Devil

Evil's greatest victory in human lives is in convincing people:
_____ they don't need God.
_____ there is no God.
_____ it doesn't matter what faith you have.
_____ all religions have some good in them.
_____ God was invented by weak people as a crutch.

Grace

Which is grace most like?
_____ God's acceptance of the past, allowing us to move into the future without guilt
_____ God loving us with no strings attached
_____ a reward from God

Christian Life

Which is most important to know about the membership of a church you are interested in joining?
_____ its denomination
_____ if it is liberal, conservative, fundamental, radical
_____ if it is Christian
_____ other

What season in the church year has the most meaning to your faith?
_____ Pentecost
_____ Advent
_____ Christmas
_____ Lent
_____ Easter

Which is most important in your life?
_____ happiness
_____ security
_____ success

Which is most important to you?
_____ God
_____ other people
_____ a sense of fulfillment

Which do you think is the most difficult commandment for most people to keep? (Rank four of them only.)
_____ Thou shalt have no other gods before Me.
_____ Thou shalt not take the Name of the Lord thy God in vain; for the Lord will not hold him guiltless that taketh His Name in vain.
_____ Remember the Sabbath day, to keep it holy.
_____ Honor thy father and thy mother.
_____ Thou shalt not kill.
_____ Thou shalt not commit adultery.
_____ Thou shalt not steal.
_____ Thou shalt not bear false witness against thy neighbor.
_____ Thou shalt not covet thy neighbor's house.
_____ Thou shalt not covet thy neighbor's wife, nor his manservant, nor his maidservant, nor his cattle, nor anything that is thy neighbor's.

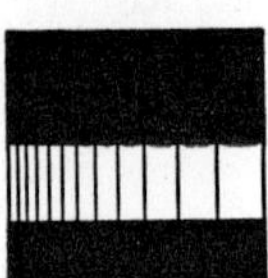

Continuum

Instructions: Pages 22-23 give purpose and procedure for the Continuum exercise.

Participants choose that place on the continuum, between two opposite extremes, which most closely represents their personal viewpoint.

General Faith Continuums

What is sin to you?

|—————————————————————|

Sin is separation from God and need not be a part of our life.	Sin is part of human nature — we are born with sin, and everything we do is tainted with it.

How do you feel about the Christian faith as a way of life?

I am skeptical of anything that tries to tell me the right way to live. — I am glad for a faith that gives my life direction.

What place does doubt have in religious faith?

You must accept all religious beliefs without question. — Demand proof before you accept any religious belief.

How do you view the Bible?

as a literal interpretation of God's Word — as a guide, to be individually interpreted

How do you feel about the existence of Satan?

The Devil is within us. — The Devil is dead.

How free are you to affect the course of your life?

Most of life is decided for us, rather than by us. — We are responsible for what happens with our lives.

When do you find faith most meaningful?

When I experience it on a personal, private level. — When I share it with others.

Which is most important to you?

Thou shalt! — Thou shalt not!

Either/Or

Instructions: Pages 23-24 give the purpose and procedure for the Either/Or exercise.

Participants select, between two choices, the option with which they most closely identify.

General Faith Either/Or Exercises

Faith is more like:
- believing / hoping
- action / surrender
- a miracle / a gift

The Lord's Supper is more like:
- a feast / a snack
- sorrow / joy
- one / many
- law / gospel
- command / promise
- earth / heaven

Repentance is more like:
- I can do better. / I can't do it by myself.

The Holy Spirit is more like:
- new / old
- past / present
- open / closed
- structure / no structure
- inside / outside

The main purpose of the Bible is to give people guidelines for:
doing / knowing
performing good acts / avoiding evil acts

Praying is more like:
stumbling in the dark / walking in the light
God within us / God around us
seeing / hearing
noise / quiet
thanking / asking
crying / laughing
looking up / looking down
outward / inward

God

Which is God more like?
out looking for us / looking out for us

How do you understand the term "God"?
humans projecting highest ideals / supernatural being

Love for God is more like:
visible / invisible
outer acts of love for people / inner devotion to God

Which do you think is most important to God?
the beliefs we hold / the life we live

How do you see our relationship to God?
God needs us. / We need God.

Jesus

What do you think of when you think of Jesus?

charisma / humility
the calm / the storm
acceptance / rejection
dove / hawk
lion / lamb
stop / go
liberal / conservative
intense / mild
poor / rich
talker / listener
doctor / teacher
loner / many friends
human / divine
lives / lived
the king / the commoner
superstar / cheerleader

Faith

Which is your faith more like?

rain / sunshine
skiing / mountain climbing
a balloon / a bowling ball
hammer / nail
a butterfly / a cocoon
a closed window / an open door
a pillow / a rock
a question / an answer
knowing / searching
mining for gold / planting a garden
trusting an old friend / making a new friend

Christian Life

Life with Christ is more like:
autumn / spring
summer / winter
a walk through woods / a walk through meadows
a pool / a river

Which best describes persons professing the Christian faith?
They are Christians. / They are Christian.

The Christian life is more:
inner-directed / outer-directed

A Christian is more like:
a candle / a mirror
asking / telling
a child / an adult

Following Christ is more like:
costly / free
riding / walking
falling / climbing

Life and Death

Death is more like:
beginning / end
a dark closet / a sun-filled doorway
day / night
joy / sorrow
a period / an exclamation mark
closing a door / opening a door
a friend / an enemy
prison / lighthouse

Life is more like:
a beating heart / an active mind
work / play
fire / water
coming / going
a journey / a home

What do you believe about life after death?

Life goes on after death. / Death is the end.

I have eternal life. / I'm not sure I have eternal life.

Listening

Instructions: Pages 25-26 give the purpose and procedure for the Listening exercise. Study the procedures carefully.

Participants respond to a stimulus statement in groups of three. Each person is "on focus" for five minutes.

Faith and Doubt

In class one day, Joan announced, "The Apostle Paul says that nothing — not even death — can separate us from God. This should be comforting, but it just doesn't work out that way for most of us. Harsh realities like sickness and hunger and poverty and death often *do* separate us from God."

In a conversation with a friend, George said, "Bill told me people should *know* that they have eternal life. How can one be that presumptuous? A person just can't know for sure."

Cathy included this statement in a letter she wrote: "It's easy to talk about God when things are going great. But I'm not really so sure any more about a God who really looks after each of us and answers our prayers. Maybe that kind of God is just a projection of our needs and hopes. Looking to God for help is just a way of kidding yourself. You really have to make it on your own."

Personal Beliefs

Chris told Andrea: "I don't remember one big moment in my life like Paul had on the road to Damascus — when

God's spirit came upon him and changed his life. Some call that conversion. I know my parents baptized me and that the pastor then called me 'a child of God.' But maybe my Baptism, like Paul's conversion, was just the beginning of my growth as a Christian — like a seed that takes a long, long time to become a grain of wheat."

❖❖❖

Mary said to Alice: "I've always believed what the Book of Proverbs says: 'Train up a child in the way he should go, and when he is old he will not depart from it.' I've always counted on that for my children. But sometimes I wonder. I can give them Christian training and set good examples, but I can't really pass my faith on. My kids must work out their own faith themselves."

❖❖❖

Ted said: "You can never know for sure what other people think or feel about their religious faith. One person can be a faithful church member and lack assurance of eternal life. Another person can work on many church committees and have no personal relationship with Jesus Christ. On the other hand, a person who isn't active at all may have a really firm faith. You just can't tell a book by its cover."

Sharing Beliefs

Jane said to Mike: "I can't *give* faith to another person, because faith is a gift from *God.* In my own case, I didn't reach faith by studying church dogmas or by inheriting it from my parents. I helped deepen my faith by experiencing life and reflecting on my life-experience. And I can help others who are struggling with faith by listening to them, telling them what my faith means to me, and above all, living out my faith."

❖❖❖

Mr. Johns said: "There's much Gospel in many of us. It doesn't come from the pulpit only. By sharing with one another we examine our own faith and discover we can minister to one another and help one another. The Church should find more ways to help its members do this."

Church Influence

This is what Marge had to say: "The Church is just another exclusive club. The Church requires our attendance, our money. It requires that we believe doctrines and uphold traditions. But it does not ask that we measure up to the standard of our leader Jesus Christ, who said, 'If any man would come after me, let him deny himself and take up his cross and follow me.' If the Church is serious about what it stands for, it should set stricter, higher standards."

Jim said to Tom: "The Church today really confuses me. It needs to take a stand. We must stop changing basic Christian beliefs so that they will conveniently fit today's life-style and world. Cultures may come and go, but basic Christianity must continue as Christ proclaimed it in the Gospel."

Harry responded to a neighbor's question by saying: "No, I still don't belong to any church — nor do I have a faith of any kind. I've always been puzzled by those who claim to be Christians. The ones I know seem to be joyless, and yet Christianity is supposed to be a faith with joy. Christians don't seem to be any better at handling life than anyone else, and yet the Christian faith claims a kind of power. Many Christians I know seem overly anxious about life, which doesn't jibe with the Christian faith's claim of peace. And I frankly don't understand bickering and strife within a Church that proclaims love and forgiveness."

Christian Life

Rachel confided to Bruce, "Tension and anxiety really help a person be a better Christian. When I have everything I need and things are comfortable, I find it difficult to think about spiritual realities. But when the rug is pulled from under me and I encounter many problems and anxieties, then I really examine my life and question its meaning. That's when faith begins to grow! So — we should rejoice and be thankful for discomfort and pain."

❖❖❖

Al said to his brother: "Today a girl in my class said, 'It's my life, and I can live it as I want.' But I think a real Christian always asks first of all, 'How will this action of mine affect others?' A true Christian always thinks of others before self."

❖❖❖

After receiving a letter from his friend, Ben was puzzled; he asked: "How can this be? Art just wrote me from his work with the poor in this remote, deprived area. He says he never thinks about money and trusts God for it completely. And a check seems to arrive whenever money is needed. Now, he thinks he can depend solely on faith and live by what Jesus said: 'Don't be anxious about tomorrow.' But I don't see how a responsible person can live like that. He has to get his money some place. That means other people have to be continually supporting him."

Interviewing

Instructions: Pages 28-31 give purpose and procedure for the Interviewing exercise.

A volunteer from among the participants is interviewed before the group.

In addition to members of your group, you might consider a faith interview with a layperson, your pastor, a youth worker, a parent, a person in one of the trades, a doctor, a teacher, a person in any occupation.

Select appropriate questions from page 30. In addition, you might want to consider these questions:

— Do you think a religious faith is an important part of life?
— Would you like to share how religion is important in your life?
— What part has your church life played in your religious faith?
— Have any church activities given you an outlet for living or practicing your religious beliefs?
— Have you experienced times when your faith was stronger than at other times?
— Do you think most people have periods of doubt?
— How do you think a person can deal with doubt?
— How would you respond to a person who asked, "Are you saved?"
— Have you had any real crises of faith?
— Are you more like a person who has found the answers, or like a person who is still searching?
— Is there anything that I have not asked that you'd like to comment on, or to add?

Miscellaneous Exercises

The remaining exercises in this section are one of a kind. The purpose of each is to help participants further examine what they believe and value about their faith.

Procedures are given for each.

Interviewing Historical Figures

(Time required: 10-15 minutes)

1. Ask group members to review the life and thought of an historical figure such as Saint Paul, Saint Thomas Aquinas, Martin Luther, Mary Baker Eddy, Saint Theresa.

2. Either you or another group member can conduct an interview with the figure chosen; for example, with Saint Paul. Have one person answer as Paul might have answered. Interview Paul to find out about turning points in his life, his faith and particular beliefs, why he did certain things.

Who Is Jesus?

(Time required: 20-30 minutes)

Jesus said: I am . . .

the Good Shepherd	John 10:14
the Bread of Life	John 6:35, 48, 51
the Way	John 14:6
the Truth	John 14:6
the Life	John 14:6
the Door	John 10:9
the Resurrection	John 11:25-26
the True Vine	John 15:5
Teacher	John 13:13
Lord	John 13:13

Give the following instructions:

1. Share your answers to the following questions in groups of four:

— Does one of these "I am's" mean more to you than the others? If so, explain.

— How does it help you know who Jesus is?

— Do you learn anything about yourself as you think about who Jesus is? If so, what?

2. Think for a few minutes about who you are. Complete the statement "I am . . ." with six different responses.

3. Share your "I am . . ." completions with a partner. What does your own religious experience have to do with these answers?

4. Pretend your partner does not know Jesus, and you do. Introduce Jesus to your partner. Tell him or her who Jesus is to you personally.

Definition of Faith

(Time required: 15-20 minutes)

1. Give the following instructions: "In groups of 4, think of the word *faith*. Brainstorm definitions of faith — as many as you can think of — whatever occurs to you. Write them down quickly. Don't evaluate them yet."

2. Ask each group to reach a consensus on one definition.

3. Now reassemble the total group. Compile one list from all groups.
4. Ask the total group to consider these questions: Is there a common theme that runs through these definitions? Did you discover any new insights into the definition of faith? What are they? Do they clarify your definition? How?

Faith Shield

This exercise gives individuals an opportunity to think about the characteristics of their own personal faith and to depict their faith experiences on a personal Faith Shield. (Time required: 20-30 minutes)

1. Reproduce the Faith Shield shown on page 73, or ask each participant to make a facsimile of the shield.
2. Have participants fill in each section of the Faith Shield by drawing a picture, symbol, or design in the designated area to represent their responses. (Written words are acceptable if response is difficult to translate pictorially.) Give the following instructions:

- — In section A, depict the key ingredient of your faith.
- — In section B, depict an action you once took because of your religious faith.
- — In section C, depict a person who was important in the development of your faith.
- — In section D, depict one thing that sometimes interferes with your living your faith.
- — In section E, depict one belief about which you are very certain.
- — In section F, write or depict three words that describe your faith.

3. Have participants share, in groups of 4, the drawings on their shields, explaining to each other the meanings behind the symbols. (A sharing option is to post all shields, having them available for everyone to see.)

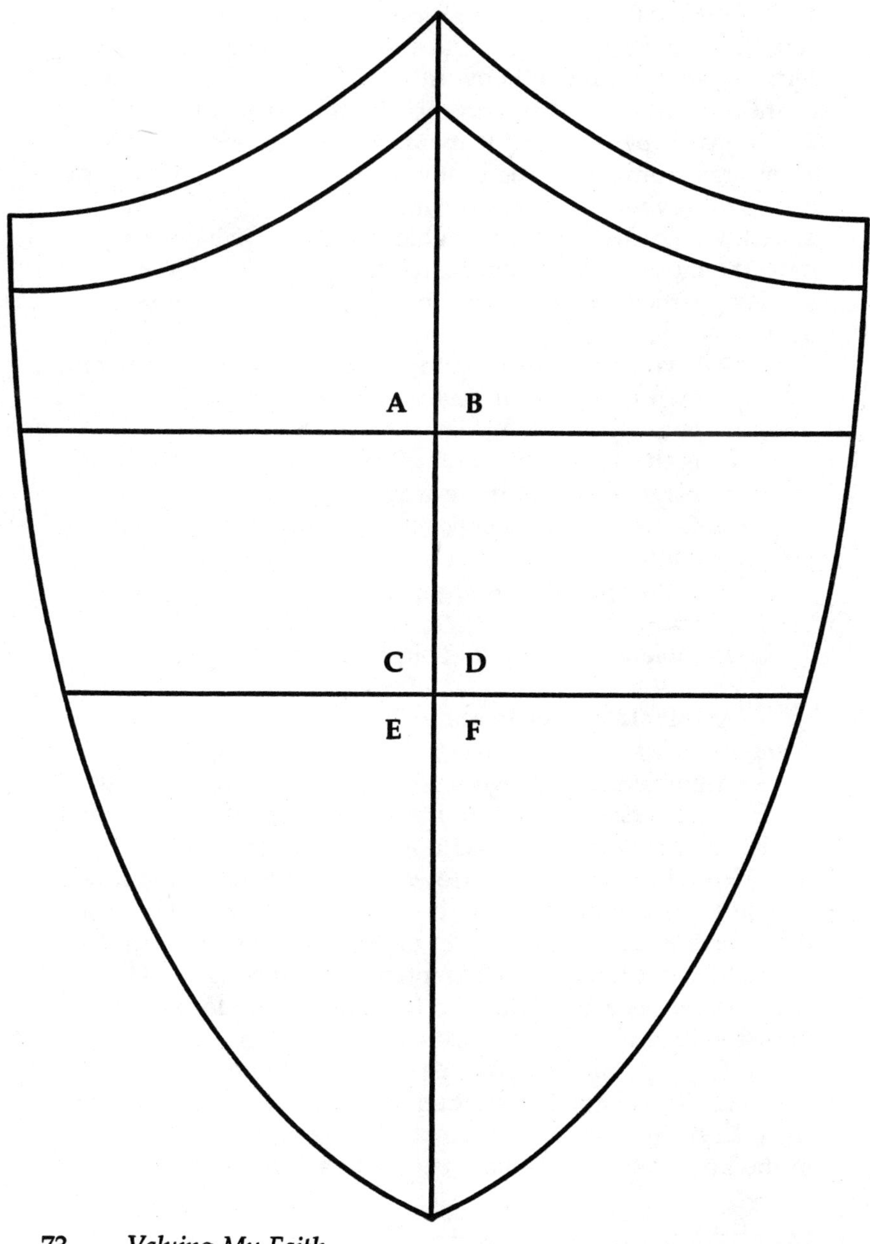
A
B
C
D
E
F

Sharing Faith

(Time required: 15-20 minutes)

1. Read the following to the group: "Terry, a high school senior, said, 'I know Christ and value my relationship with him so I want others to know him too.' His method was to confront another person with the question, 'Are you saved?' "

2. Ask participants to think about how they share their faith. Then brainstorm, with the group, as many possibilities as you can, writing them on a chalkboard.

3. Ask the group to consider which of the ways listed might have the most influence on them.

4. Have participants consider, in groups of 4, the following questions:

- — If you wished to communicate something about your own faith, which way would be most comfortable for you?
- — Is there a "best" way? (Groups might try role playing each of these ways.)
- — Can you reach a consensus of two or three effective ways?
- — Is it impossible to argue anyone into the Christian faith? Explain.

5. Reassemble total group and share learnings.

Archibald's Experiment

(Time required: 30-40 minutes)

Archibald is a college student who is confused about his faith. He was brought up in a Christian home but rejected Christianity as a teenager. He now takes great pride in telling others that he is an atheist. However, he is curious about how people express faith and is writing a term paper — due in three days — on the subject. In order to get people to open up, he decides to *pretend* he is interested in changing. He goes to see the college chaplain who has been trying for two years to talk with Archibald about conversion.

The chaplain is glad to see Archibald and listens to his false tale. The chaplain tells Archibald that he will be able to solve all his future problems by believing and putting his trust in the Lord. When Archibald begins to ask some questions, the chaplain explains that he can't spend any more time with him that day, because he has promised to meet a friend at the golf course. Archibald tells him that it's very important and that he needs a couple of hours right away. The chaplain promises to meet with him after the weekend, spending as much time as necessary then.

After leaving the chaplain, Archibald calls Candy and asks if he can come over because there's something important on his mind. Candy was raised as a Christian, but she is not too sure of her beliefs. Recently, she began a meditation course and has found meditation to be a positive force in her life. She assures Archibald that meditation is just what he needs, ignoring Archibald's apparent desire to return to the Church. She adds, "A lot of that stuff they teach you at church just isn't worth anything."

The next morning, Archibald goes to see his friend Dr. Leroy, who is taking a day's vacation from his dental practice. Dr. Leroy gladly agrees to spend any time needed with Archibald. After hearing what Archibald has to say, Dr. Leroy points out that it's really not important what you believe, just so you believe something. He adds: "All religions are the same as far as I am concerned. I go to church myself every Sunday. Actually, it's been good for my practice. Most of the people in our church have their dental work done at my office. Join us next Sunday if you'd like to try it out."

Continuing to pretend, Archibald calls a former Sunday school teacher, Mrs. Davis. He takes Mrs. Davis to dinner that night so that he will have enough time to collect plenty of information for his paper. She is thrilled at his possible change of heart and can hardly contain her enthusiasm. Archibald barely has a chance to tell her of his interest in returning to the fold, when she begins telling him how she has disapproved of his actions in the past and what he should do to change his life. Archibald has lots of questions, but doesn't have a chance to ask them because Mrs. Davis is so busy admonishing him to read the Bible, pray every day, and change his behavior.

1. Read the story aloud; then have the total group split into groups of 5 or 6.
2. Ask the groups to rank the characters from best to worst and then to share their rankings with each other.
3. Ask the groups to make a consensus ranking.
4. After about 15 minutes, have each group report their consensus if they reached one.
5. You might wish to tabulate on the chalkboard the "best" person and the "worst" person choices of all participants using the following format:

	Best Person	Worst Person
Archibald		
Chaplain		
Candy		
Dr. Leroy		
Mrs. Davis		

6. Invite any brief statements by participants.
7. Have small groups discuss how people can be most helpful to another person who is searching for meaning in life and using them as a resource.

Faith Questions

(Time required: 25-30 minutes)
1. Ask each person to write down two questions he or she has about the Christian faith.
2. Divide the group into pairs. Have pairs designate person A and person B in each.
3. Explain that in each pair, person A will ask person B one question, and person B will answer to the best of his or her ability. Then person B will ask one question, and person A will answer. This procedure is repeated. (Set a time limit of 10 minutes.)
4. When each pair has completed their questions and answers, ask all A's to remain seated while B's select a new partner. Repeat the asking and answering process described above. (This can be repeated with yet another partner.)

5. Reassemble the group and ask them to share one thing they learned.

Optional: Have the large group place all their questions in a box. Immediately (or at a later time in the session), ask your priest, minister, or some knowledgeable layperson for an interview. Use the questions from the group as the basis for the interview.

Faith Celebration

Easter — New Life!

(Time required: approximately 35-40 minutes)

1. Have everyone in your family or group list the feeling words they associate with Good Friday and the feeling words they associate with Easter.

2. Ask participants the following questions:

— At what time in your life have you had Good Friday feelings?

— Have you had a time when you moved from Good Friday feelings to Easter feelings?

3. Have participants share their responses with another person or in a group of 4.

4. Now ask participants to spend a few minutes thinking about Jesus Christ, his death and Resurrection. Ask:

— What does Jesus' Resurrection mean to you?

— How might your life be different if Jesus had not risen?

5. Ask the group to reflect in silence.

6. After this time of silence, ask the group to find some way to express their thoughts about Jesus. Give these suggestions: "Look around the room for an object, take a walk outdoors, create something, write a poem or a song. Let your imagination go. After 10-15 minutes, return to the group and share your creativity and findings."

7. After sharing, have the group think of a special way to celebrate Easter.

Three Levels of Learning

Give Me the Facts! (See Hebrews 11)

Questions to answer:

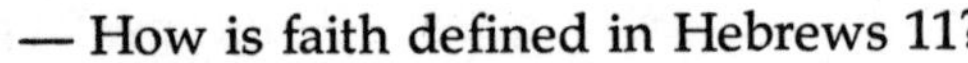

— How is faith defined in Hebrews 11?

— List the examples of faith noted in this chapter.

— What people were involved?

— What did they do that illustrated the kind of faith they had?

— What was their goal? (Hebrews 11:14-16)

— Why, according to the writer of Hebrews, did they not receive all that was promised to them?

FACTS

What's the Idea?

Concepts to explore:

— What were the results of their faith?

— What characteristics within them enabled them to go out in faith?

— What kind of a relationship did they have with God?

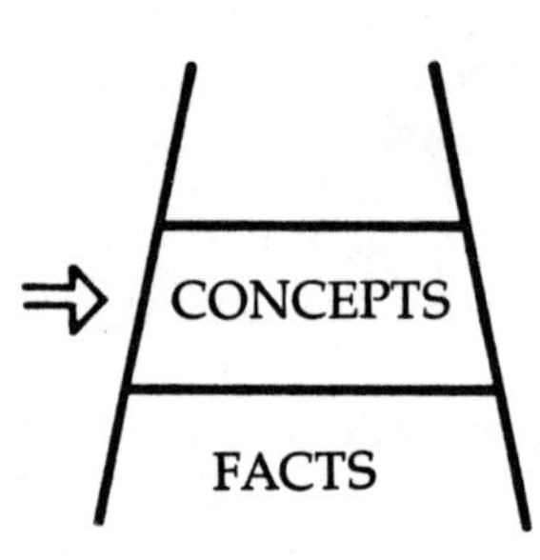

— List some contemporary people who exemplify faith. What did they do that made them outstanding examples of faith?

— Can their deeds be matched with some of the words used of the people in Hebrews 11?

— What might the writer have meant by "God had foreseen something better for us"?

What's In It for Me?

Valuing suggestions:

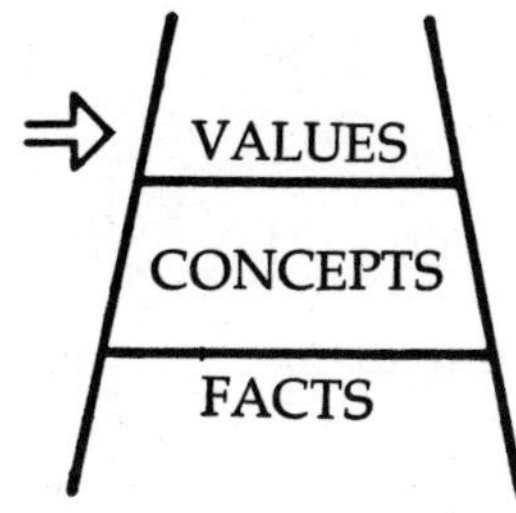

— Give your definition of faith.
Do the words "obey," "trust," "believe," "vision," "courage" say anything to you about your faith?

— Compare your relationship to God with those of the Old Testament people of faith.
Are some of their characteristics of faith also in your relationship with God? Which ones? Are some missing? Which ones? Is God calling you to some special task today?

— How can you strengthen your faith?
Think of something specific you can do about it. Set a goal that will lead you in that direction.

— Share some of the feelings about your faith with another person.

Resources from the Bible (for optional use)

God

Genesis 1	"In the beginning God. . . ."
Job 38:1-7	"Where were you. . . ?"
1 Kings 19:9-12	The hidden God.
Psalm 104	God the Creator
Isaiah 40:12-31	No words can describe God.

Romans 11:33	A great God.
Psalm 139:1-10	God searches for his people.
Romans 1:19-20	God makes himself known to people.
John 12:44	Jesus declares God as the authority.
Ephesians 4:6	One Lord — one God.

Faith — What Is It?

Hebrews 11:1	Faith defined.
Hebrews 11	Faith of Old Testament figures.
Genesis 12:1-8	Abraham obeyed.
Genesis 22:1-10	Abraham is tested.
Exodus 14:21-31	Crossing the Red Sea.
Psalm 14:1	To the fool there is no God.
Mark 4:35-41	Why have you no faith?
Matthew 17:14-21	Faith to move mountains.
John 20:24-29	Honest doubt.
Luke 1:26-38	Mary believes she is to bear the Savior.
2 Corinthians 5:6-10	By faith, not by sight.
James 2:14-18	Faith and works.
Romans 3:20-26 and Galatians 3:23-26	Justified by faith.
Ephesians 2:8	Faith, a gift from God.
Mark 9:24	"I believe; help my unbelief!"
Romans 10:17	Faith by hearing the preaching of Christ.

Life and Teachings of Jesus

Matthew
Mark
Luke
John

Who Is Jesus?

Isaiah 9:6	"Wonderful, Counselor, Mighty God, Everlasting Father, Prince of Peace."
Isaiah 53	"A man of sorrows."
Matthew 7:24-29	Jesus speaks with authority.
Matthew 1:21	"Jesus."
Matthew 1:23	"Emmanuel."
Luke 31-36	"Jesus." "Son of the Most High." "Son of God."
John 1:1-5	"The Word."
John 1:14	"Word made flesh."
John 1:29	"Lamb of God."
John 4:42	"Savior of the World."
John 6:35	"Bread of Life."
John 7:12	"Light of the World."
John 10	"The Good Shepherd."
John 11	"The Resurrection and the Life."
John 14:6-7	"The Way, the Truth, the Life."
John 15:5	"The Vine."
Matthew 16:16	"Christ, Son of the Living God."

Christian Life

Galatians 2:15-21	Life lived in faith.
Romans 5	Faith in Christ makes us friends with God.
Romans 8	A healthy spiritual life.
Ephesians	New life in Christ.
Philippians	Joy.
1 Corinthians 12	Spiritual gifts.
1 Corinthians 13	Faith, Hope, Love.
2 Timothy 1:2	"I know whom I have believed."
Matthew 10:39	Cost of following Christ.

Sharing Faith

Matthew 28:16-20	Tell others — to all the world.
Romans 1:16-17	Sharing the Good News.
Romans 10:9-10	Tell others that Jesus is Lord.

Prayer

Matthew 14:23	Jesus prayed.
Psalm 50:15	God hears prayer.
Luke 11:1-13	"Teach us to pray."
Matthew 6:5-15	"When you pray. . . ."
Matthew 5:44	Pray for enemies.
Matthew 7:7-8	Ask, seek, knock.
Matthew 18:19-20	Promise to answer prayer requests.
Matthew 21:22	Ask in faith.
Luke 18:10-14	Two men praying in the Temple.
Romans 8:26-27	The Holy Spirit helps us pray.
Ephesians 6:18	"Pray at all times in the Spirit."
James 5:13-16	Results of prayer.

Life — Death

John 5:24	Eternal life begins now.
Job 19:25	"I know that my Redeemer lives."
Matthew 28:20	"I am with you always."
Psalm 23	"The Lord is my Shepherd."
1 Thessalonians 4:13	Christians have hope.
Romans 8:38-39	Nothing separates us from God.
Romans 12:15	Empathy with others.
Philippians 1:19-26	Paul's dilemma — death, or life?
John 14:1-7	"Let not your hearts be troubled. . . ."
John 14:18-19	"Because I live, you will live."
Romans 14:7	In life or death we belong to God.

Death Is Conquered — Christ Lives

John 11

Romans 5

1 Corinthians 15

2 Corinthians 4

Revelations 5 and 7

Holy Spirit

John 14:25-31	Promise of the Holy Spirit.
John 16:13-14	Spirit of Truth.
John 3:5-8	Born of the Spirit.
Luke 11:13	Asking for the Holy Spirit.
Acts 1:8	Power promised.
Acts 2:1-13	Tongues of fire.
Book of Acts	Work of the Holy Spirit in the early Church.

2 Corinthians 1:21-22	God's guarantee.
Galatians 5:22-23	Fruit of the Spirit.

The Trinity

Matthew 28:19
Romans 5:1-8
2 Corinthians 13:14

Word of God

Romans 10:17	Faith comes from hearing the Word.
Hebrews 4:12	Word of God is "living and active."
Psalm 119:11	God's Word in the human heart.
Psalm 119:105	"A lamp unto my feet."
John 8:31	"Truth will make you free."
1 Corinthians 1:18	The Word — folly, or power?

Baptism

Matthew 28:19-20
John 1:33
Ephesians 4:5
Colossians 2:12
1 Peter 3:21-22
Romans 6:1-11

The Lord's Supper

Matthew 26:20-29
Mark 14:17-25
Luke 22:14-23
John 13:21-30
1 Corinthians 11:17-34

Prayer

Lord, I have said "Yes" to you. I love you! I believe in you and am sure of your love — a love that followed me every time I tried to run away. I no longer want to run away, but every once in awhile I still cry out, "I believe, Lord; help my unbelief!"

Thank you for the people who touch my life and encourage me in my faith. Thank you for forgiving and loving me so much you were willing to die on the cross for me. May your own constant trust and obedience, even in the most trying times, be a model and an inspiration for me.

Valuing My Family

We are optimistic about the family's potential, for we firmly believe that family life can provide a unique climate for individual and group growth and support.

But family life is not easy these days. Each family member must make many value-laden choices — choices which frequently involve the entire family. Communication is often difficult and conflicts become a part of every family's experience. The crucial question is: How do we handle these difficulties?

We think that people can profit from greater in-depth discussions with their own family members as well as with persons from other families. They need to practice listening to one another, developing sensitivity to diverse viewpoints.

These exercises provide a chance for family members to examine their own ideas, to listen to one another, to understand each other, and to grow in mutual respect. The result is often greater peace, joy, and harmony.

The exercises can be used:

— at group meetings in which parents and children collect in family units to complete the exercises.

— at group meetings in which only individuals (not families) are present.

— at home, with one's own family.

In general, the directions for exercises are written for group meetings at which a number of families are present. For other uses, modification in procedures might be necessary.

Before using this chapter, please review the chapter on leadership.

Voting

Instructions: Pages 20-21 give purpose and procedure for the Voting exercises.

Participants vote in the following manner:

Agree?	(Raise hand.)
Strongly agree?	(Wave hand.)
Disagree?	(Thumb down.)
Strongly disagree?	(Shake thumb.)
Pass?	(Fold arms across chest.)

General Voting Questions on Family

How many of you:

— would like to develop more family unity but don't know how?
— think family size should be limited?
— see the Church as a family?
— think children should interact with grandparents as much as possible?
— think family members should share in decision making?
— think the family, as a unit, will survive?
— think many couples are unprepared for marriage?
— think the Church should help more to prepare people for marriage?
— think the Church should do more to help family members listen to one another?
— think Christian faith stabilizes families?
— think devotions should be a part of everyday family life?
— wish you could share your faith more easily with your family?

Marriage

How many of you:

— think there are alternate kinds of marriage permissible for Christians?
— would approve of contract marriages in which the contract would come up for renewal every few years?

— wish you know (or had known) more about what to look for in a mate?
— would like to know more about marriage?
— have read a book on marriage within the last year?
— think a marriage built on long-term friendship is the strongest?
— think the rate of marriage breakdowns in the over-forty age bracket is alarming?
— think that living together before marriage can be a good way to test a relationship?
— think that sexuality today is viewed in a more positive way than ever before?
— think that how people live and develop their sexuality is their own business?
— think the Church should do more to help persons deal with themselves as sexual beings?
— think that one person can meet all or most of another person's human needs?
— would marry someone from a different race?
— would marry someone from a different ethnic group?
— would marry someone from a different religion?
— are concerned about the divorce rate?
— know of a separation or divorce that worked out best for everyone?
— know of a separation or divorce that caused more harm than good?
— think that both partners are always responsible for a broken marriage?
— think young people are not trying hard enough to make their marriages work?
— think teenage marriages usually end in divorce?
— think most couples marry too young?
— think divorce is sinful according to traditional Christian teaching?
— think a Christian should not marry a non-Christian?
— think people who do not marry in their early twenties usually do not marry at all?

Role of Husband and Wife

How many of you agree with this statement?

— The woman's traditional role of wife and mother should be given priority over any position outside the home.
— A father should have as much responsibility for raising the children as the mother.
— The feminist movement frequently contributes to breakdown in marriages.
— The feminist movement has strengthened marriage.
— "As the Church is subject to Christ, so let wives be subject in everything to their husbands." (Ephesians 5:24)
— No-fault divorce laws contribute to the breakdown of marriages.
— The husband should have the final say in the home.
— Husband and wife should share authority equally.
— A woman's obedience to her husband can weaken her own authority.
— The family needs one person as the recognized final authority.
— Most women are proud of a husband who will assume the role of leadership and authority in the home.

How many of you:

— think a woman's place is in the home?
— work outside your home?
— are happy in your work?
— are housewives but feel you should also be working outside your home?
— are spending a lot of time working outside your home but would like more time at home?
— think your home life is enhanced by a job outside the home?
— think women make better single parents than men?
— think freedom for women means freedom for men?

Parenting

How many of you:

— think most young people take their problems to their parents?

— think communication is more open in families today than in the past?

— think the moral character of youth is declining?

— think the moral character of adults is declining?

— think that the family's view of a child greatly influences the child's view of himself or herself?

— think children should share their joys, fears, and problems with their parents?

— think parents should share their joys, fears, and problems with their children?

— would like to air more problems in the family?

— think that all of your family members feel they actually share in making decisions?

— look (or looked) to your parents for help in making decisions?

— think parents tend to underestimate the abilities of their children?

— think children should have some say in the way family money is spent?

— think many parents hesitate to guide their children in religious matters because their own beliefs are not clear?

— think most young people have trouble talking about their beliefs?

— think most parents have trouble talking about their beliefs?

— have been strongly influenced by your parents?

— confide in a member of your family?

— feel comfortable telling your parents your personal problems?

— wish you could be a happier person in your home?

— think your parents have helped you understand yourself?

— think children should have to work for an allowance?

— would (or do) raise your own children more strictly than you were raised?

— think parents should be totally consistent in handling family matters?

— think a fifteen-year-old should obey his or her parents even if the parents' best reason seems to be "because I said so"?
— think young people today are spoiled?
— think a breakdown in family relationships contributes to teenage drug abuse?
— think parents should always try to understand the child's point of view, no matter how different from their own?
— think that being close friends with their parents is good for children?
— wish there were more children in your family?
— will never spank your children?
— were sometimes spanked when you were young?
— agree that if one member of a family hurts, then all hurt?
— think a good family life once shielded many teens from trouble?

Church Influence

How many of you:
— see the Church as a family?
— think that exclusive concern for your own church family can stunt your church's growth?
— think the total congregation should do more things together?
— think your church is a community of people who really care about one another?
— wish more people would talk to one another at church?
— wish there were more opportunities to work together as a family within the church family?
— think that at worship it's important to mention the names of people in need?
— think the sexual freedom and sexual attitudes of our society can be clearly labeled as Christian or un-Christian?
— think a church should not allow discussion of matters such as homosexuality, masturbation, and premarital sex?
— think Christian churches should avoid sex education?
— think that the Church should speak out on issues that affect family life, such as abortion and divorce?

— think the Church should do more to educate families and parents about sex, marriage, and family life?
— think the Church should initiate programs and activities to strengthen family life?
— think that, in the long run, family life is often fragmented by the Church?
— would want your own children to have the same kind of church life you had as a youngster?
— think the Church ignores single adults?
— think the Church is a lonely place if you're not married?

How many of you agree with the following statement?
— The Church could easily and satisfactorily substitute as a family for those who either have no families or who live alone.
— The Christian faith is the best foundation on which to build a satisfying family life.

Family Traditions

How many of you:
— love to celebrate special family occasions?
— think it's important to keep up traditional celebrations like Christmas and birthdays?
— think traditional family celebrations are unimportant?
— like to be remembered on your birthday with a celebration?
— think celebrating is a bother?
— have recently begun a family tradition?
— exchange gifts at Christmas?
— received gifts on your last birthday?
— think traditional celebrations have become too commercialized?
— think giving gifts is a pleasure?
— think giving gifts is overdone?
— think sending Christmas cards is a tradition that has lost its meaning?
— like to create your own cards as a family?
— think Christmas is a lonely time of year?
— celebrated last Christmas in much the same way you did when you were a small child?

— have ever shared your Christmas Eve supper with someone who was lonely?
— rarely give to needy people except at Christmas?
— think the Christmas spirit has diminished?

Family and Social Issues

How many of you:
— have worked together as a family on a social issue?
— think your parents are well informed on social issues?
— know what others in your family think about current issues?
— wish your family were more interested in social issues?
— are aware of your parents helping others in need?
— agree with your family on most political issues?
— think it's difficult getting your family to work together?

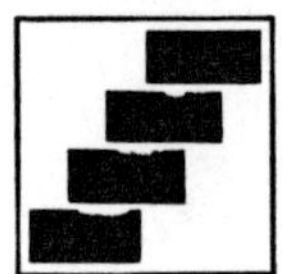

Ranking

Instructions: Pages 21-22 give purpose and procedure for the Ranking exercise.

Participants rank all items in order of preference or priority (1 = most important; 2 = next most important, etc.).

General Family Rankings

Which is most important in family life?
_____ sharing
_____ loyalty
_____ respect

Which is the most important in family life?
_____ fidelity
_____ love
_____ discipline

Which is the most important factor in a successful family?
_____ husband or wife with a good job
_____ mother who remains in the home
_____ regular church attendance
_____ love among family members

Which has had the greatest influence on your religious beliefs?
_____ parents and family
_____ friends
_____ teachers, clergy
_____ personal experiences

Which should the Christian family be most concerned about?
_____ service
_____ love
_____ personal growth

What best characterizes a Christian family?
_____ caring for one another
_____ forgiving one another
_____ spiritual commitment
_____ acceptance of one another

What is the best way to share your religious faith with your family?
_____ sharing Christian books
_____ living the faith
_____ encouraging the family to attend church
_____ leading family devotions

Marriage

What do you see as the greatest obstacle to a successful marriage?
_____ unfaithfulness
_____ careless use of money
_____ career ambition
_____ lack of common interests

Which is the most important characteristic in a mate?
_____ thoughtfulness
_____ strength
_____ gentleness

What communication skill do you most value in your mate?
_____ ability to articulate ideas
_____ ability to listen
_____ ability to understand your feelings

Which kind of marriage do you think holds the greatest promise for satisfaction and happiness?
_____ marriage with a renewable contract
_____ traditional marriage
_____ open marriage

Which would you rather do?
_____ Review our present marriage contract to see what each of us expected to give and receive when we got married.
_____ Renegotiate the marriage contract to meet our present needs.
_____ Leave things as they are.

Which of these men do you disagree with most?
_____ John said, "A woman's place is in the home. Working women deprive their husbands and children of certain family relationships. They are too tired at the end of the day."
_____ Joe said, "Behind every successful man there's a woman."
_____ Archie said, "When a wife greets her husband at the door after he's put in a hard day at work, she should be freshly scrubbed and have a cheery, positive attitude."

Parenting

Which is the greatest influence on a child's life today?
_____ church
_____ home
_____ school
_____ friends
_____ television

What do parents most need to effectively raise their children?
_____ common sense
_____ special training in parenting
_____ adequate help from school and church

What is the most important parental characteristic?
_____ consistency
_____ fairness
_____ acceptance

What is the main goal of parenting?
_____ to raise obedient children
_____ to "provide" for the children
_____ to help the children become independent
_____ to foster mutual respect between parent and child

You are a parent. Which problem would be hardest for you to work out with your child?
_____ dropping out of high school
_____ sexual promiscuity
_____ shoplifting
_____ running away from home
_____ drug or alcohol abuse

You are a high school sophomore. Which would be the most difficult problem to talk over with your parents?
_____ You want to quit school.
_____ Your steady is pressuring you to become sexually involved.
_____ Your use of alcohol/drugs has gotten out of control.

As a parent, which quality in a teenager most disturbs you?
_____ disobedience
_____ irresponsibility
_____ preoccupation with self
_____ conformity to peers

As a teenager, which quality in a parent bugs you the most?
_____ nagging
_____ pressuring
_____ lack of interest
_____ inability to see your point of view

When are parents most apt to interfere?
_____ in the selection of a mate
_____ in child-rearing decisions
_____ in educational choices
_____ in the choice of life-style

What do you do when your child is being bullied?
_____ tell the child to fight back
_____ talk with the bully's parents
_____ allow child to handle it
_____ ignore it

What do youth want most from adults?
_____ They want respect.
_____ They want to be heard.
_____ They want to participate in decision-making.
_____ They want honesty.

In getting children to take responsibility, which parent would you agree with most?
_____ Parent A rewards children for obedience; punishes children for disobedience.
_____ Parent B allows children to make mistakes; says that's how children learn.
_____ Parent C avoids conflict; ignores or tolerates behavior problems.

Church Influence

Whom does the Church influence most?
____ young children
____ teenage youth
____ adults
____ elderly

The Church could be more helpful to families by:
____ offering sex education.
____ sponsoring social service projects.
____ helping family members communicate.
____ offering preparation for marriage.

What aspect of the Church has had the most influence on your family?
____ worship
____ Bible study
____ music
____ recreational activities

Family Traditions

What time of the year do you enjoy most with your family?
____ Easter
____ Christmas
____ Thanksgiving

Which Christmas project might your family enjoy most?
____ making Christmas cards together
____ finding and decorating the Christmas tree together
____ baking Christmas cookies together
____ caroling together

Which do you remember with the most fondness?
____ a family trip
____ a family celebration
____ a family reunion

Which would be the best vacation for your family?
_____ a camping trip
_____ a sight-seeing trip
_____ visiting special places of interest near home

Which do you enjoy most with your family?
_____ picnics
_____ attending shows
_____ participating in sports
_____ music

Which do you wish your family had more of?
_____ sense of togetherness
_____ greater support for one another in crises
_____ humor
_____ common interests

What do you like least at mealtime?
_____ everyone eating at different times
_____ fighting
_____ hurrying
_____ silence

How often do you attend church as a family?
_____ almost always
_____ never
_____ occasionally

Family and Social Issues

A forty-five-year-old woman, with a grown family, becomes pregnant. What do you think is her best course of action?
_____ to have the child and keep it
_____ to have the child and give it up
_____ to have an abortion

Whom would you prefer as next-door neighbors?
_____ an elderly couple
_____ a young couple with a mentally-retarded child
_____ a family of a different race from yours
_____ a group of young singles

Which might your family prefer to do?
_____ support an orphan
_____ visit sick persons
_____ raise money for the needy

Dinner Table Rankings

What bothers you most?
_____ shoplifting
_____ pushing drugs
_____ careless driving

What do you think is most harmful to the human body?
_____ cigarettes
_____ marijuana
_____ alcohol
_____ sleeping pills
_____ tranquilizers

Which chore would you prefer to do?
_____ housecleaning
_____ repair work
_____ cooking
_____ laundry

If you found a wallet, which would you do?
_____ keep the money and put the wallet in a postal box
_____ return the wallet to its owner
_____ keep the money and throw away the wallet

Which would be the greatest loss to you?
_____ eyesight
_____ hearing
_____ speech

Which of these subjects makes the most interesting reading?
_____ world events
_____ famous people
_____ sports

Which would you most like to be?
_____ an astronaut
_____ a deep-sea diver
_____ a balloonist

Which person do you think has the most challenging job?
_____ an athletic coach
_____ an engineer
_____ a business executive
_____ a nurse
_____ a machinist

How would you choose to spend your spare time?
_____ alone
_____ with one or two friends
_____ with a group

Which do you think is worst?
_____ to be punished by a teacher
_____ to have friends make fun of you
_____ to get poor grades on a report card

Which is the most enjoyable?
_____ reading a good book
_____ playing a game
_____ working a puzzle

Which would you rather use?
_____ hands
_____ mind
_____ body

Which do you prefer?
_____ movies
_____ radio
_____ TV

Which are you most likely to use as an escape at times?
_____ television
_____ drugs or alcohol
_____ work
_____ religion
_____ recreation
_____ solitude

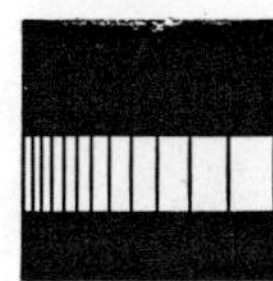

Continuum

Instructions: Pages 22-23 give the purpose and procedure for the Continuum exercise.

Participants choose that place on the continuum, between two opposite extremes, which most closely represents their personal viewpoint.

General Family Continuums

How long should a marriage contract last?

forever; can never be broken under any circumstances. — three-year marriage contract; reassess every three years.

How willing are you to forgive in your family?

always — seldom

How dependent are you on your family?

totally dependent — totally independent

How important are traditions in your family?

very important — not important

To what extent should the Church be involved in sex education?

not at all | much more

Role of Husband and Wife

Who should have the final authority in the home?

husband | wife

What do you think about working wives?

A woman's place is in the home, and women should be proud to be homemakers. Their families suffer if they aren't there every day.

A woman should have a job outside the home. She can probably do more for her family and herself by working.

Parenting

To what extent should a parent influence a child's values?

Parents should influence children's values as much as possible or they'll never learn to live decent lives. Telling children what to value is the best policy.

Parents should leave children alone to develop their own values. In fact, they should try to disguise their own values so as not to influence their children.

Who should select a child's friends?

Parents should choose the friends.

Children should choose their own friends.

How do you think children should be raised?

strictly | permissively

Either/Or

Instructions: Pages 23-24 give the purpose and procedure for Either/Or exercises.

Participants select, between two choices, the option with which they most closely identify.

General Family Either/Or Exercises

Which seems more important in family life?

happy relationships / knowledge of the Christian faith
tradition / change
spirit of the Gospel / spirit of the law

In your family, which are you more like?

giver / taker
strict / permissive
listener / talker
leader / follower
arguing / agreeing
thinking / doing
coach / team member
yes / no
jeans / dress slacks
today / tomorrow

Which is your family more like?

birds in a nest / bees in a hive
live and learn / look before you leap
purse strings / boot straps
sweet and sour / moonlight and roses
meat and potatoes / yogurt and granola
a camper / a motel
chess / spin the bottle
rock groups / string ensemble

Parenting

Rules are most effective when they are set by:
parents alone / parents and children together

Children need love most when they:
get a poor report card / break a neighbor's window

Would you rather face parenthood in the middle:
1970s / 1980s

In communicating your love to family members, which is more important?
tell them / show them

Church Influence

It is more important to spend time in:
church activities / family activities

The influence of the Church tends to make husband and wife:
more equal / less equal

Which best describes the influence of church activities on the family?
pulling together / pulling apart

Marriage

Which married couples tend to be happier?
those with children / those without children

Which are young people more concerned about?
career / marriage

In marriage, which is more important between mates?
friendship / romance

Family and Social Issues

If a new family moved into your neighborhood, what would you most likely do?

call on them / wait for them to drop in

Married couples should have:

more children / fewer children

Listening

Instructions: Pages 25-26 give purpose and procedure for the Listening exercise. Study the procedures carefully.

Participants respond to a stimulus statement in groups of three. Each person is "on focus" for five minutes.

Church Influence

Orville said, "The Church has been too timid about discussing male-female relationships. The Church should listen to human needs and help interpret them in the light of Christ's message. The Church is the place to introduce sex education courses and premarital counseling. The Church community needs to have a warm, loving, healing atmosphere where its people can experience healthy interaction and develop close bonds without endangering marriage ties."

Frank said, "Churches today are just too liberal regarding male-female relationships. The Church's traditional approach has withstood the test of time; God's authority and history make it clear what marriage should be. The tendency to accept diverse life-styles and moods of the moment will ultimately harm family life and interfere with the effective rearing of children. The Church knows what is right and should put people on the right track. We can't be wishy-washy on this matter."

Parenting

Mrs. Evans said, "A father's word should be absolute law in a family. Whatever the father says must be obeyed without question. Children have to be trained early so they really understand this and can follow the Bible's teaching: 'Children, obey your parents in the Lord, for this is right.' "

❖❖❖

Tim, a young adult, said, "Families usually feel powerless when they try to combat drug abuse in their own children. But families could do a lot more than they think. They can listen to their children. Most parents really don't listen. They want to listen and think they actually do. But the main thing that comes across to the kid is judgment and advice plus more judgment and advice!"

❖❖❖

At lunchtime, Harley said to the fellows at work, "Things are too easy for kids these days. Nothing is demanded of them anymore. Young people need and want direction and guidance. We adults are making a big mistake by not giving it to them. Parents and other adults should set higher standards. We need to discipline kids — let them know who's boss."

❖❖❖

A parent said, "I hate to hear my kids quarreling. I know it's part of growing up, but it's one of the most irritating parts of being a parent. I know I sometimes confuse and puzzle them by yelling at them and condemning them for their actions. But there doesn't seem to be any alternative."

❖❖❖

Kathy said, "A lot of us subtly try to mold our children in our own image and likeness. We pretend to be liberal, pretend we want them to become themselves, but we keep downgrading their hair-styles, the music they like, the heroes they admire, the life's work they want. What's behind it is that we want them to be just like us, but we're afraid to admit we're that tyrannical."

A frustrated, middle-aged father said, "Most parents just don't have the know-how for raising children in our complex world. Nobody has taught them how, in school or elsewhere. We should have training courses which provide the knowledge and skills for being a good parent. Completion of such training courses should be an absolute requirement for expectant parents."

❖❖❖

A teenager had this to say: "Let's say parents model concern for human beings. The child learns this, but he or she does it in a different style, maybe in a commune. The parent gets kind of sidetracked by the style, and can't see that in the commune the same kinds of values are present — real respect for the other people who live there. It'd be great if a kid could say, 'But I really do respect the things you've taught me. I'm just doing it a different way.' "

❖❖❖

Mrs. Allen firmly stated to her neighbor, "It's wrong to keep a child tied to the apron strings. We mustn't do things *for* them; we should help them do things for themselves. If we refrain from making a child's decisions for him or her, we're helping the child learn how to make decisions wisely and boldly."

❖❖❖

Nancy, a college junior, said to a group of adults, "Something that goes on between parents and kids my age really bothers me. The kid will just be following the parents' values but the parent can't recognize it. For example, the parents have always modeled moderation in drinking. These parents don't use drink as an escape. They use it as sort of a sharing thing — have wine for dinner and that sort of thing. The kid will pick up those values and use marijuana in the same way, but the parents can't see this because the issue of marijuana is so emotion-laden."

Dilemma

Instructions: Pages 27-28 give purpose and procedure for the Dilemma exercise.

Participants respond to a dilemma situation, exploring alternatives and consequences and finally choosing their own best solution.

Marriage

Twenty-year-old Ruth has been going steady with Herb for a year or so. She really likes him, has thought a lot about marriage, but isn't sure if he's the one. After a pleasant and fun-filled evening, Herb is silent for awhile. Then he says, "Ruth, I've been offered a job on the Coast. I'd like you to come with me. Will you marry me?" What might Ruth do?

Parenting

Your daughter started confirmation class recently. The class has been studying Genesis. Today your daughter came home upset and said, "I sure don't believe all that creation stuff." What do you say to her?

Your seven-year-old son has been playing a lot with eight-year-old Timmy, whose family recently moved into the house next door. On occasion you have heard a good deal of loud shouting and abusive language coming from their house. You have good reason to believe that the parents drink quite heavily at times. After dinner tonight your son comes to you in great excitement and says, "Hey, Mom, where are my pajamas? Timmy wants me to stay over at his house tonight and it's O.K. with his parents." What do you do?

Your eighth grader had a lot of trouble in English class last year. Today he comes home with his report card, and you comment on his improvement in English. He says, "You have to cheat to get by in that class. All the kids do it." What do you say?

Part I: Your fifteen-year-old daughter Tracy promised to be home shortly after the youth meeting, which was to be finished at 10:00 P.M. You know she had planned to study for a biology test tomorrow. By 11:00 P.M. you are getting panicky. There is no word from Tracy. What might you do?

Part II: You are sitting in the kitchen, waiting. At 12:10 the door opens and you hear Tracy tip-toeing up the stairs to her bedroom. What do you do?

Six-year-old Michelle returns from school after a month in first grade. She is unusually quiet. The next morning after breakfast she cries and says, "I'm not going to school today." What do you do?

Nine-year-old Bill frequently fights with his older brother and sister. You pull him away as he is hitting and scrapping with them again. Bill says, "You're always blaming me when they really started it. Why don't you punish them, too? You just like them better than you like me!" What do you do?

Your son, a bright, active, and motivated high school senior, has been considering a number of colleges. He comes to you one evening to talk. You are disappointed to hear him say, "I've decided against college." What do you say to him?

Your fifteen-year-old son Joe has been attending Sunday school regularly since age four. Lately he has been very unhappy about Sunday school, and two weeks ago he asked if he could quit because he was "not learning anything."

You said, "No. I expect all of our family to attend."

Sunday morning your entire family is getting ready to go to Sunday school classes. You are almost ready to leave when you discover Joe sitting in his room in his pajamas. He says, "I'm not going to Sunday school today or ever again." What can you do?

Interviewing

Instructions: Pages 28-31 give purpose and procedure for the Interviewing exercise.

A volunteer from among the participants is interviewed before the group.

In addition to members of your group, you might consider an interview with a middle-aged couple, a senior citizen, an engaged couple, your pastor, a youth worker, a divorced person, a marriage counselor, a social worker.

Select appropriate questions from page 30. In addition, you might want to consider these questions:

— What do you think is the difference between a Christian family and a non-Christian family?
— How long have you been married?
— When did you first meet each other?
— How long did you go together before being married?
— What do you think has been responsible for the higher rate of marriage breakups?
— How do you view divorce?
— Do you think it is important for husband and wife to have the same religious faith?
— Has your religious faith made a difference in your married life together? How?

— In marriages you have seen break up, what is often the cause?
— Could some of these breakups have been prevented? How?
— Do you have advice for youth today? In your experience, what is important in a happy marriage?
— Do you have children?
— Have children enriched your marriage?
— Has your relationship with your spouse changed during your married life?
— Is there anything that I have not asked that you'd like to comment on or to add?

Goal Setting

Instructions: Pages 31-33 give purpose and procedure for the Goal Setting exercise.

Participants, individually, select a goal they wish to achieve, make a commitment to achieving that goal, and report their successful accomplishment of it.

You may have seen a change or two you would like to make in your family life — a change you could help bring about. Why not construct and sign a contract that will help you set a goal in the direction you want to go.

To strengthen my family life, I will . . .

____

(signature)

You may have seen a change you would like to make to strengthen your marriage — a change you could help bring about. Why not construct and sign a contract that will help you set a goal in the direction you want to go.

To make our marriage stronger, I will . . .

____

(signature)

Miscellaneous Exercises

The remaining exercises in this section are one of a kind. The purpose of each is to help participants further examine what they believe and value about the family. Procedures are given for each.

Heart Attack

This exercise gives family members an opportunity to examine their life-styles and priorities when illness strikes a member of the family. (Time required: 15-20 minutes)

1. Have the total assembly split into family groups, or small groups of 4-5 if families are not present.

2. Ask participants to think of the family in which they are now living. Present this situation: "Your family life has been quite busy. Three weeks ago the parent providing the main source of income had a heart attack. The doctor's report has just come in: complete rest and no more work for a year; thereafter, work may be possible but only on a part-time basis."

3. Have the groups talk about these questions:

- Would some things change immediately for you personally? For the other family members? What immediate decisions would you need to make?
- How would people outside your family unit be involved?
- Would a typical day be different for you?
- Are there things you would have to give up? What?
- Would some things possibly change for the better? Why?
- As you think about this situation, do you find any new insights or implications for your present family life?

Family Communications Questionnaire

This exercise is for use with family groups who are willing to risk by going into considerable depth about how their own family members talk with and relate to one another.

The questionnaire is designed to help youth and their parents better understand how they communicate. Sharing perceptions and insights about family communications helps clear the air and can lead to deeper understanding and constructive action in family relationships. (Time required: 5 minutes to complete questionnaire and 15-20 minutes or more to share perceptions)

1. Duplicate the questionnaire and provide participants with a copy.

2. Have each family member complete the form in the appropriate columns, checking one of the three options (yes, no, pass). There are no right or wrong answers.

3. Have youth relate each item to their own personal experience in their family and have parents think of a specific child in their family, preferably one who will also fill out the questionnaire.

4. After participants have completed the form, invite parents and children to discuss the questionnaire content in any way they feel comfortable. Some family members may choose to compare their answers. Others may just want to discuss some issues raised. Participants who have no family members present can be combined into small groups for discussion. Some challenges to the small groups might be:

- — Share your perceptions in any way you feel comfortable.
- — Do you find one or two items your family can work on to improve communications? Decide who will do what to improve those communications.
- — Set a goal. (Pages 31-33 give purpose and procedure for Goal Setting.)

Family Communications Questionnaire

Permission is given to reproduce this form for group and family use.

Our family communicates well together.
Our family does things together as a group.
Parent shows an interest in child's interests.
Child shows an interest in parent's interests.
Family members talk things over with each other.
Parent gives too much advice and lectures a lot.
Child respects parent's ideas and opinions.
Parent respects child's ideas and opinions.
Parent trusts child.
Child can discuss personal problems with parent.
Parent finds it hard to share feelings with family.
Child finds it hard to share feelings with parent.
Matters of sex are discussed.
Parent really listens to child.
Child really listens to parent.
Child hesitates to disagree with parent.
Parent explains reason for not letting child do something.
Parent tries to see child's side of things.
Child tries to see parent's side of things.
Parent shows confidence in child's abilities.

This column answered by PARENT			This column answered by YOUTH					
			My Mother			My Father		
Yes	No	Pass	Yes	No	Pass	Yes	No	Pass

Generations Dialogue

This exercise works best if there are approximately equal numbers of youth and adults present. Its purpose is to create a setting for an intergenerational discussion, allowing youth and adults to share and learn from one another about important issues in family life. (Time required: at least 35-40 minutes)

1. Ask all youth to go to one side of the room, all adults to the other side.

2. Further divide the group into smaller units of 4 people, again keeping youth and adults separate. Note: Have the same number of subgroups on each side of the room (even if the number of persons in each subgroup is not the same).

3. Pass out a blank sheet of paper to each group and give the following instructions to everyone: "Shortly, I will be asking each of your groups to make a list of five things. You might think of more, but decide among yourselves on the top five. Appoint a recorder to write down the five things you decide on. Each group will need this list, because you will soon be breaking into new groups and sharing your list with some people on the other side of the room."

4. Give these instructions to the youth groups: "When you young people think about family life, what are some really important things (anything!) that you think adults should know about? Discuss these and put the five most important ones on your list."

Give these instructions to the adult groups: "When you adults think about family life, what are some really important things (anything!) that you think young people should know about? Discuss these and put the five most important ones on your list.

5. Allow 15 minutes for groups to generate the list of items. Because groups work at different paces, slower ones may need to be pushed a bit. After 10 minutes, give a 5-minute warning. Call time and check to see that each group has a completed list.

6. Now pair each youth group with an adult group. Each group now has two lists.

7. Begin a sharing process. Have groups take the top item from one list, read it, and discuss it. They will then take the top item from the second list and repeat the process, taking alternate items until both lists have been shared and discussed. (Allow at least 15-20 minutes for this.) Check to see how the various groups are doing. Even though some groups will want more time, you may decide to call time while interest is still high. Or, if this is an ending exercise, groups can be allowed to finish at their own pace.
8. An optional way of concluding the exercise is to call everyone back together again to share their experiences and learnings with the total assembly.

Runaway

This exercise helps participants examine their thoughts, feelings, behaviors, and ways of communicating in a parent-child confrontation. (Time required: 15-20 minutes)
1. Read the following situation to the group:
"Fourteen-year-old Connie and her parents have had quite a few disagreements recently about Connie's attitudes and behavior. She runs away from home and is gone three days and nights. The parents are desperate when they receive no word about her or from her. Late on the third day, Connie suddenly appears at the door."
2. Ask the group how they would probably react to this situation if they were Connie's parents.
3. On a chalkboard set up the columns and possible reactions as shown below.
4. Have the group rank their reactions in Column 1, from "most likely" to "least likely" (1 = most likely).

Column 1	Column 2	
____	____	persuade her to see a counselor
____	____	talk with her about what she has done
____	____	accept and love her, no strings attached
____	____	tell her she can't stay unless she promises to change
____	____	ground her for a certain length of time
____	____	other:

5. Ask participants if they wish their ranking were different. If so, have them do a ranking in Column 2 from their "most preferred" action to their "least preferred."

6. Ask the total group to break into smaller groups of 3 or 4 and share:

- — their rankings; what they would most likely do and why.
- — the changed rankings they would like to make.
- — how their feelings and ranking would change if Connie were a boy; if Connie were seventeen years old instead of fourteen.
- — whether Scripture gives any guidelines here.

7. Reassemble the total group and share comments and learnings.

Family Strengths

This exercise may be completed together or individually. It helps family members become aware of their own strengths and one another's strengths. (Time required: 10-15 minutes)

1. Have participants make columns on a piece of paper. Number of columns should equal the number of people in their family. At the top of the columns, have people write the names of family members, including themselves.

2. Have participants look at one name at a time and think about that person.

- — What do you like about that person?
- — What strengths or good qualities does that person have? Have people write, in the columns, five strengths they see in each person listed. Caution participants to think only of strong points — nothing negative.

3. Ask participants to share their lists with their family. Offer these questions to think about:

- — What did you learn about your family while completing the exercise? About yourself?
- — What were your feelings about yourself and your family?

Marriage Poll

Polling gives participants an opportunity to state an important belief or idea and learn how others respond to it. Each person is also challenged to evaluate many other statements — a process which helps participants examine or reexamine their own attitudes, beliefs, and values regarding the marriage relationship. (Time required: 20 minutes plus discussion time)

1. Pass out one 4″ x 6″ card to each person.

2. Ask participants to think about the marriage relationship.

— What makes it rich and rewarding?

— Or, what makes it difficult?

3. Ask each person to write, at the top of the card, a short statement, summing up an important idea that he or she personally holds about marriage. The statement should be one that the individual believes strongly, can express in a sentence, and is willing to share.

4. Allow about 3 minutes for composing and writing the statements.

5. Ask participants to write the words *Agree, Strongly Agree, Disagree, Strongly Disagree,* and *Pass* in a column on the back of their cards.

6. Have participants spend about 10 minutes milling around the room, sharing their statement with each other and asking each person whether he or she agrees with the statement. Participants should get as many responses to their statements as they can, moving quickly from person to person and tabulating the responses on the back of the card. Caution participants not to discuss the issues. If need be, they should quickly clarify the statement to someone who doesn't understand it.

7. When time is up, reassemble the total group. Ask participants to determine what percent of the people agreed with their statements (number who agreed divided by total number of people who voted). Assure them that no value judgment is placed on the number who agree or disagree with their statement.

8. Ask for volunteers to read their statement and report on the number of persons who agreed with them.

9. Then ask the group to quickly call out words that describe underlying values about marriage which seem important to this group, identify areas of disagreement or conflict of values within the group, and call out any quotations from Scripture which they are reminded of.
10. Depending on time available, discussion may follow, either in the total group or in small groups.

Family Celebration

Christmas Gift-Giving

This exercise helps participants focus on giving and on the wide array of gifts associated with Christmas. It emphasizes the context in which gift-giving should take place for Christians. (Time required: 10-15 minutes)
1. Reproduce the following page for each participant beforehand. Pass these out and allow 5-8 minutes of quiet time. Instruct persons to work alone, writing in responses to questions for each item.
2. After time is called, ask participants to think about these questions:

— What kinds of feelings emerged as you completed this gift-giving exercise?

— Which gifts were most difficult for you to identify?

3. Ask participants to share their thoughts and feelings with one other person.

What two talents would you like to share with others?
What Christmas message about the Christian faith would you give to all?
What gift would you like to give to your family?
What gift that you gave another was especially liked?
What would you give to Jesus Christ?
What gift could you give to the Church?
What is the best gift you ever got?
What Christmas gift you received has special memories?
What is a gift you created?

Celebration

1. Have each family member list ten things they love to do at Christmas.

2. After participants have completed their lists, give these instructions:

- — Star your top four.
- — Put a dollar sign by those that cost money.
- — Put an **F** by those you do as a family.
- — Put an **A** by those you prefer to do alone.
- — Put an **O** by those that involve doing something for other people.
- — Put a **T** by those that involve a tradition in your family.
- — Put a **C** by those that involve church.
- — Put a **W** by those you wish you would do with your family.

3. Have participants study their coded lists for a few minutes. Ask if they see any patterns regarding the things they love? Allow time to share any discoveries.

4. For family discussion:

- — Compare your top four with others in your family.
- — Can you come to a consensus on what is your favorite thing to do at Christmas as a family?
- — How many preferences do you share with the other members of your family?
- — What is one thing you would like to see become a part of your family's celebration at Christmas? Why is it important to you?
- — Are there some things you would like to change in your Christmas celebration? Which?
- — Action: If there are some new things you would like to introduce, or some changes you would like to make, why not try them?

Three Levels of Learning

This exercise provides an opportunity for parents and/or youth to examine parent-child relationships, focusing on the importance of keeping the relationship intact despite differences.

Give Me the Facts! (See Luke 24:41-52)

Questions to answer:

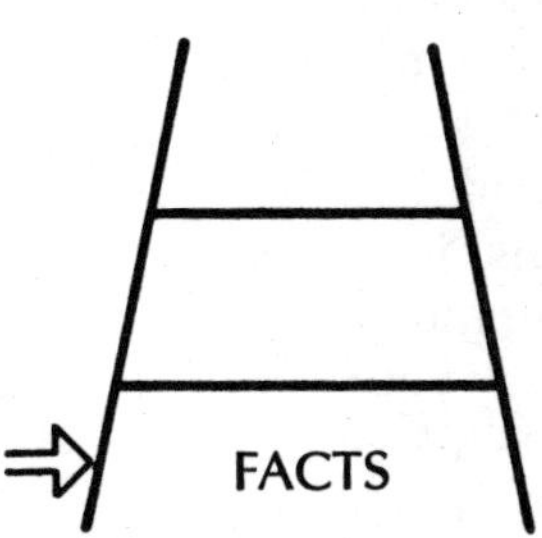

— When did Jesus and his family go to Jerusalem?
— What concern did Mary and Joseph have as they started back home?
— Where did they find Jesus? How many days had he been gone?
— What was he doing?
— What did Mary say to him?
— How did Jesus answer?

What's the Idea?

Concepts to explore:

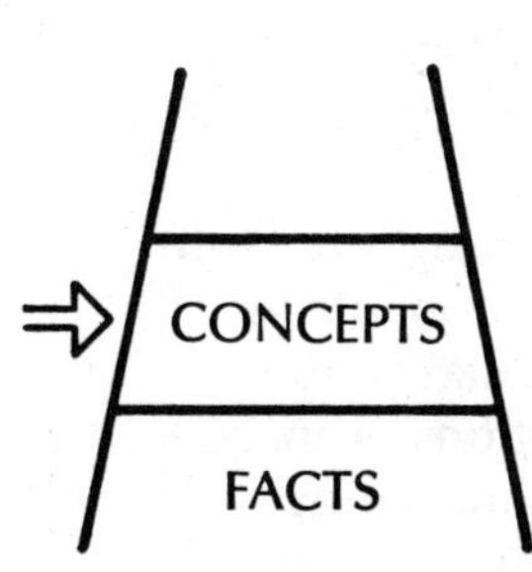

— Why was the Feast of the Passover celebrated every year? Find out all you can about it.
— What time in the life of a Christian youth parallels this time when Jesus went to the Temple?
— What kind of feelings did Jesus probably have for the Temple?
— What kind of understanding do you think Mary had for Jesus' deep interest in the Temple?

What's in It for Me?

Valuing suggestions: (Time required: at least 20-30 minutes)

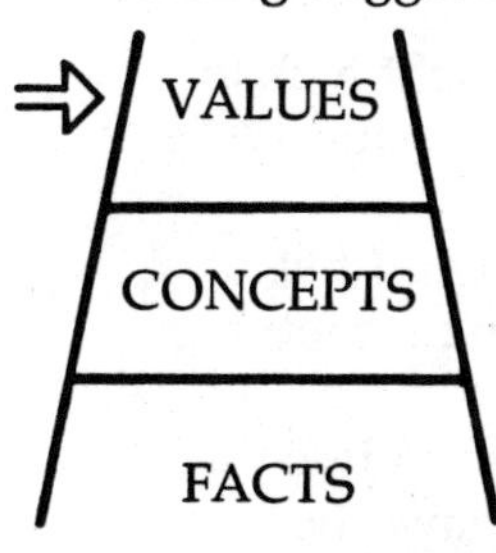

1. Have participants try to get into the role of Jesus' mother and father in this situation. Ask them to close their eyes and imagine they are Jesus' mother. Say: "Your son hasn't come home, and it's getting late. What are you feeling? With your eyes closed, think about it silently for a couple of minutes."

2. Now ask them to imagine they are Jesus' father, wondering where their son is. Say: "What are you feeling? What are you saying to your spouse at this frantic moment? Think about it for a minute or so."

3. Have participants open their eyes and pair up with a person alongside them. Have the pairs spend 2-3 minutes sharing the thoughts and feelings they had as Jesus' parent.

4. Have each pair quickly designate a parent and a son in their pair and close their eyes again. Say: "Sons, imagine you have spent three busy days learning from others in the Temple. Parents, imagine you go on a search for your son. After three days you find him in the Temple. What is the first thing you do when you catch sight of each other? (Pause.) What do you say to each other?"

5. Now have participants open their eyes and try a brief dialogue between parent and son. Say: "Parents, express your thoughts and feelings to your son in any manner you feel appropriate at this moment. Say the words — along with any gestures and feelings. Sons, how do you view the situation? What are your thoughts and feelings? Try expressing them to your parent. You may begin."

6. After a 2-3 minute dialogue, stop the pairs and have them take a couple of minutes to talk with each other about the dialogue they shared. Ask: "What are your thoughts and feelings about it?" Have them share their reactions or insights.

7. Have each pair combine with another pair into groups of 4 to talk about the experience. They may want to consider one or more of these questions:

- — Do you think Jesus' parents saw him as rebelling?
- — Does this situation relate to your own family experience? How?
- — Adults, are there times when you thought a child was rebelling, and he or she was only doing something in a different way?
- — Young people, was there a time when you felt misunderstood because you were doing something different from what was expected?

8. After terminating the small group exercise, form two larger groups — an adult group and a youth group. Have the two groups meet separately to do some quick brainstorming. Instruct the groups to brainstorm some differences of opinion which tend to separate the generations. (Caution the groups not to discuss or judge the items — just list as many as they can think of.)

9. Have the groups compare their lists.

— Were there any similar discoveries? What were they?

10. Have groups agree on a topic that needs particular clarification or better communication.

11. Plan another session on that topic, using a Listening exercise, Interview, etc.

Resources from the Bible (for optional use)

Marriage

Ephesians 5:21	Be subject to one another out of reverence for Christ.
Galatians 3:28	Neither male nor female; all one in Jesus Christ.
Genesis 2:18	Companionship.
Genesis 2:24	One flesh.
Matthew 19:3-9	Christ confirms the Old Testament creation pattern of marriage.
Malachi 2:14-16	Faithfulness.
Ephesians 5:33	Love and respect.
Proverbs 31:10-31	A good wife — who can find?
1 John 4:7	Loving one another.
Matthew 19:3-12 and Mark 10:2-12	Jesus appealed to Genesis 1:27 and 2:24 for his basic argument.
Ruth 1:16	Wherever you go.

Women

John 4:1-42	Jesus talked with women frequently, announced his messiahship to a Samaritan woman.
Luke 10:38-42	Jesus talked with women about religion.
Gospel of Luke	Much about women.
John 20:11 Matthew 28:9 Mark 16:9	Women bear witness of the risen Jesus.

Women and the Church

1 Corinthians 11:7-16
1 Corinthians 14:26-35
1 Timothy 2:9-14

Children and Parents

Ephesians 6:1-4	Do not provoke your children to anger.
Colossians 3:20	Obedience to parents.
Colossians 3:21	Do not provoke your children, lest they become discouraged.
Deuteronomy 6:4-7	Teaching in family.
1 Timothy 5:3-4	Children's duty to family.
Ephesians 4:12-16; Colossians 3:12-25; Romans 12; 1 Corinthians 13	Building each other up in love for a Gospel-oriented family.
Proverbs 22:6	Child-raising.

New Life in Christ

Colossians 1:9-14; 2:1-23; 3:1-25 through 4:1
2 Corinthians 5:17

New Commandment

Matthew 22:37-39

A New Way of Love

1 Corinthians 13:8-13
Ephesians 4:13-16
1 John 3:1-14

Prayer

Lord, thank you for the family. What a beautiful creation! We have sometimes distorted and lost sight of what you meant it to be. Forgive us!

I want to be a loving family member — a listener, an encourager, and a support to those around me. I know that the kind of love a family desperately needs is the love that you introduced — a patient, giving kind of love.

Give each one of us a rich measure of that love so that we will grow into a healthy, whole, and caring family.

Valuing Myself and My Gifts

We believe that each person is a special gift of God and that each person has God given talents that can be shared with others. But many personal strengths and gifts go undiscovered throughout a person's life. Or they often get lost in a climate which tends to emphasize the negative rather than the positive.

We believe that people need to take time to identify their talents and strengths; but being aware of them is not enough. We need to ask ourselves: Are we using these gifts in our day-to-day living not only to please ourselves but also to please others and God?

When we know who we are and to whom we belong, we are more free to use our talents and to celebrate them. Through greater awareness, caring, and sharing, we become whole persons who feel better about ourselves as creatures of God.

Before using this chapter, please review the chapter on leadership.

Voting

Instructions: Pages 20-21 give purpose and procedure for the Voting exercise.

Participants vote in the following manner:

Agree?	(Raise hand.)
Strongly agree?	(Wave hand.)
Disagree?	(Thumb down.)
Strongly disagree?	(Shake thumb.)
Pass?	(Fold arms across chest.)

General Voting Questions

How many of you:

— think that the real meaning of life can be found mainly through service to others?
— think that, should you die today, your life has been worthwhile?
— think that your faith makes a difference in your outlook on life?
— feel O.K. about not going along with the crowd?
— are sometimes concerned about what others think?
— like to try new things?
— measure success by your own standards, rather than by others' standards?
— would like to offer your talents to the Church but don't know how to go about it?
— are satisfied with how you spend your time?
— think that giving always means sacrifice?
— think that most people feel guilty when they are not doing something "productive"?
— find it hard to discipline your use of time?
— often find that what you actually do contradicts what you say you believe?
— think sacrificial giving should be a condition of church membership?
— stop and think occasionally about the worth of what you're doing?
— take time to think about what you value in life?
— have nearly the same values you had five years ago?
— are often torn between what you want to do and what you believe is right?
— feel that your values form a real basis for your decisions and actions?
— think that values come naturally to a person, with no need to "work" at them?
— think certain things we value actually become false gods?

My Outlook on Life

How many of you:
- — think that life is brimming over with exciting, good things?
- — think that most people spend more time thinking about themselves than about others?
- — think that to admire ourselves as we are makes us too complacent?
- — think that most people have trouble dealing with their real feelings?
- — think that most people have negative feelings about themselves?
- — think that people who expect the worst in life usually find it?
- — think that some are lucky in life and some are not?
- — think that most people value good looks more than inner beauty?
- — think that a person's ideas and beliefs are greatly influenced by how much money he or she has?
- — think that people are basically good and have great potential to love and care?
- — think that people have a natural desire to grow and learn?

My View of Myself

How many of you:
- — understand yourself pretty well?
- — are often a puzzle to yourself?
- — would like to understand yourself better?
- — think that God has something to do with who you are right now?
- — depend on God for direction?
- — think that you have to step on someone to get ahead?
- — did something this week that you are proud of?
- — are bored by routine?
- — feel on top of the world when you reach a goal you set?
- — think you learn more when you go through the struggles of making your own choices?
- — think that talking over the consequences of your choice helps clarify your thoughts?
- — gave up a hobby because you weren't good at it?
- — are perfectionists?

My View of Myself and Others

How many of you:
— are happy with your life-style?
— have experienced feelings of loneliness?
— believe that good can come from your struggles?
— are greatly influenced by your family?
— are easily swayed by your friends?
— wish people really knew you as you are?
— feel that people appreciate you for who you are?
— worry a lot?
— usually want to please others?
— usually work too hard at pleasing yourself?
— did not share a new idea with someone because you were afraid the person might laugh at you?
— would be willing to take a cut in salary as part of a long-range effort to improve living conditions for others?
— love others as much as you love yourself?

Things I Like

How many of you:
— like to be around people?
— like to daydream?
— would like to fly an airplane?
— enjoy skiing?
— like to meditate?
— would like to meet a well-known leader?
— would like to be a famous leader?
— like to sleep late in the morning?
— like to be around older people?
— would like to be rich?
— like birthday parties?
— enjoy making things?
— like to play with young children?
— make music an important part of your life?

Loving My Neighbor and Myself

How many of you agree with this statement?
— Showing love is hard to do.
— Loving oneself is difficult.

— Loving oneself is healthy.
— "Keeping up with the Joneses" is a way for some people to feel O.K.
— Being "successful" doesn't prove we're good persons.
— Being self-critical is necessary for growth.
— We are all worthwhile human beings.
— We begin to love ourselves when we stop condemning and accusing ourselves.
— How a person acts is determined more by other people than by oneself.
— It is easy to be yourself.
— God accepts you as you are.
— God wants you to be different than you are now.
— God has a special mission for you.
— People usually act first and then find reasons to explain their behavior.

Success

How many of you:
— feel successful?
— think that success takes hard work?
— think that a successful person is usually wealthy?
— think that success is the feeling that you are doing your best?
— have changed your ideas of what success means during the last five years?
— think that for many people, success refers only to material things?
— have ever felt successful, yet found that no one recognized your success?
— think that Jesus was successful?
— think that success is liking yourself?
— think that success is knowing and standing up for what you believe?
— think that success is a goal to be reached by age 50 or 60?
— think that success is the capacity to change?
— think that success is allowing yourself to become the person God intends?

— think that success is living responsibly in society?
— think that ambition makes people do inhuman things?
— think that the amount of money a person makes depends on how hard that person works?
— think jobs with power and prestige mean increased satisfaction and happiness?
— get most of your satisfaction in life from your job?
— would like to retire early?
— think that people who work only for their own glory seldom find real joy in their work?

My Gifts

How many of you agree with this statement?
— Musical ability is a gift.
— Leadership ability is a gift.
— A warm smile is a gift.
— You are a capable person.
— You have many strengths.
— You have a unique contribution to make to the world.
— Talking about personal strengths is embarrassing.
— Talking about personal strengths is boastful.
— A person can have a Christian vocation outside the Church.
— It is difficult to be open and honest with other church members about one's personal concerns.
— People need the Church as a support when they have problems.
— The Church is accepting of people as they are.
— Some people participate in a church activity because they feel it is their duty.
— Using our gifts to serve others is one way of thanking God.

Management of Time

How many of you:
— can usually account for your time?
— think you usually manage your time wisely?
— clutter your days with trivia?
— often set daily goals?

— try to set aside time for meditation and devotions each day?
— often put off doing distasteful tasks?
— wish you could organize your time better?
— consider time as a gift from God?
— think it's better to take each day as it comes rather than planning far ahead?
— feel O.K. about taking time to "goof off"?
— think you waste a lot of time watching TV?
— think mostly about the past?
— think more about the future than the past?
— think that one can spend too much time with community or church activities at the expense of one's personal life?

Gifts of Money

How many of you agree with this statement?
— People should give first and think about it later.
— People *think* about giving more than they actually give.
— The things people spend money on tell a lot about the quality of their faith.
— Those who give generously to the Church are usually blessed materially in return.
— The tithe (10% of income) is a good standard to use in giving to the Church.
— Church members should be allowed to designate the use of their tithe.
— To be both rich and Christian is not possible.
— If we are Christians, we are not free to spend our money as we wish.
— People should use any extra money to help others.
— The more you have, the more you should give to others.
— Money is the root of all evil.
— Money is a gift from God.
— The Lord will provide, so we don't need to.
— There is nothing wrong with money if it's used for a good cause.

Leisure

How many of you:
— set aside a special time each week for leisure activities you enjoy?
— think everyone needs free time?
— think that Christians should observe the Sabbath by resting from work?
— think that Americans are too driven by the "work ethic"?
— would like a four-day work week?
— would take a salary cut for a shorter work week?
— feel that leisure time is a luxury for the rich?
— think that one needs to discipline the use of free time?
— would rather spend most of your leisure time by yourself than with others?
— feel that having a hobby or a special interest would encourage you to use more leisure time?
— feel that leisure time implies neglect in other areas?

Work

How many of you:
— like your job?
— work long hours?
— are hooked on work?
— get more enjoyment from your leisure hours than you get on the job?
— find your work interfering with your personal life?
— are sometimes frustrated with too much free time?

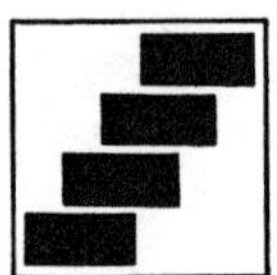

Ranking

Instructions: Pages 21-22 give purpose and procedure for the Ranking exercise.

Participants rank all items in order of preference or priority (1 = most important; 2 = next most important, etc.).

Outlook on Life

Which is most important to you?
_____ living responsibly
_____ being insightful
_____ being well liked
_____ being physically attractive

Which gives you the most satisfaction?
_____ high marks
_____ learning something new
_____ solving a problem

Which is most important to you?
_____ new adventures
_____ service to others
_____ good personal relationships

What is most important to you in life?
_____ to be a good spouse
_____ to be a good parent
_____ to be a whole person
_____ to be a good friend
_____ to be a good daughter or son

What is most important to you?
_____ to do well in a chosen job
_____ to have a good social life
_____ to feel good about yourself

Which is most important to you?
_____ status
_____ money
_____ comfort

View of Self

How do you see yourself?
____ as a decision maker
____ as a peacemaker
____ as an innovator

Which most nearly describes you?
____ critical
____ easygoing
____ demanding of others

From which do your talents stem?
____ hands
____ head
____ heart

How do you feel you are using your talents?
____ very well
____ pretty well
____ not so well

How do you see yourself?
____ I am attractive to others.
____ I'm not too popular.
____ I get along with others.

Compared to most others, which describes you?
____ more intelligent
____ less intelligent
____ just as intelligent

Which is most important in your life?
____ feeling good about yourself
____ a family that loves you
____ good friends to relate to
____ financial security

Which would you rather risk?
_____ the effects of permanent unemployment
_____ the effects of lung cancer
_____ the effects of an earthquake

Which quality do you most prefer in others?
_____ friendliness
_____ honesty
_____ unselfishness

Which would you rather be?
_____ a well-liked boss
_____ a respected politician
_____ a famous artist

Which would you rather be?
_____ a farmer
_____ a business person
_____ a youth corrections worker

What trait would you prefer in a friend of the opposite sex?
_____ creativity
_____ humor
_____ attractiveness

With which church group would you rather work?
_____ youth group
_____ council/board
_____ church-school children

How would you rather spend a free afternoon?
_____ alone outdoors
_____ puttering around the house
_____ socializing with friends

How do you rank the following statements?
_____ Playing and relaxing is as important as hard work.
_____ Free time should be used to help others.
_____ Hard work is a virtue; time not spent on work is time wasted.

Gifts to the Church

Which church activities would enable you to become more aware of your personal strengths or your personal gifts? (Rank each group of three separately.)

_____ attending church worship
_____ attending confirmation class
_____ attending church summer camp

_____ visiting a nursing home
_____ helping on a church-sponsored car wash
_____ being an usher

_____ helping serve Communion
_____ teaching church school
_____ singing in the choir

_____ serving on the church council
_____ working on a stewardship drive
_____ becoming a priest or minister

What keeps you from sharing more of your money?
_____ material needs and desires
_____ saving for the future
_____ supporting family members

How much money should people give to the Church?
_____ all they can spare
_____ a tenth of their gross income
_____ no set amount

Success

Which is success most like?
_____ winning
_____ feeling you've done your best
_____ accomplishing something

What is most important to you in choosing a career?
_____ prestige
_____ money
_____ service
_____ personal fulfillment

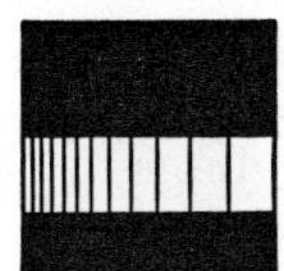

Continuum

Instructions: Pages 22-23 give purpose and procedure for the Continuum exercise.

Participants choose that place on the continuum, between two opposite extremes, which most closely represents their personal viewpoint.

Work and Leisure Time

How do you prefer to spend your time?

alone ———————————————— with people

How much do you use your talents?

never ———————————————— always

Given the opportunity would you work more, or less?

much more ———————————————— much less

How do you spend your leisure time?

pleasing myself ———————————————— serving others

How much time do you spend watching television?

never turn it on ———————————————— never turn it off

What does Sunday mean to you?

|—————————————————————————|

It's a special day to be observed by worship and rest. — It's the same as any other day.

View of Self

To what extent should a person express feelings to others?

|—————————————————————————|

Be open; express all feelings. — Keep feelings to oneself.

Which describes you most of the time?

|—————————————————————————|

pessimistic — optimistic

How should a person deal with anger?

|—————————————————————————|

Express it freely. — Hold it in.

Which best describes you?

|—————————————————————————|

I always lead. — I always follow.

How do you deal with conflict?

|—————————————————————————|

Avoid conflict at all costs. — Confront — bring conflict into open.

Which are you more like?

|—————————————————————————|

private — social

Success

How do you feel about competition?

|—————————————————————————|

Win at all costs. — Winning is unimportant.

When you accomplish something what do you do?

Tell everyone about it. — Tell no one about it.

Giving

Do you feel that you have talents to share?

none at all — many

Do you enjoy sharing the talents you have?

not much — very much

Are you a spender or a saver?

spender — saver

Either/Or

Instructions: Pages 23-24 give purpose and procedure for the Either/Or exercise.

Participants select between two choices that option with which they most closely identify.

View of Self

Which are you more like:
giving / taking
arguing / agreeing
helping / watching
active / passive
willow / oak
cello / trumpet
competitive / cooperative
taking off / digging in
problem solver / worrier

Which is more important to you?
personal freedom / following the rules
a lucrative job / a meaningful job
adventure / recognition

In the biblical story of Mary and Martha (Luke 10:38-42) which are you more like?
Mary / Martha

Success

Which are you most apt to admire?
leader / poet
entertainer / teacher
scientist / artist
athlete / doctor
courage / generosity
wisdom / honor
ability / good will

Giving

Which is more important to the Church?
how much I give / how much I do

Which do you spend more on?
wants / needs
self / others

To which would you most likely give?
medical research / recreation facilities
save our schools / save our parks
chemical dependency program / day-care center
political candidate / guest-lecture program
congregational needs / world relief

Listening

Instructions: Pages 25-26 give purpose and procedure for the Listening exercise.

Participants respond to a stimulus statement in groups of three. Each person is "on focus" for five minutes.

General Listening Statements

Jack complained: "There's just too much disagreement among Christians about what's right and what's wrong. The reason, I think, is that sometimes the Bible itself isn't very clear. Like, is killing or stealing always wrong? Most Christians don't seem to know for sure, so they end up doing whatever they want."

Spence said, "A friend of mine is the most thankful person I've ever met. I don't know how he does it, but he's able to thank God for everything, good or bad. He can actually offer thanks to God when something destructive or negative happens to him. Personally, I can't thank God for the suffering that happens to another person. I can't thank God for hunger and oppression in the world. I think that's going a bit too far — thanking God for those kinds of things."

Work and Leisure

Jan said, "Time is a gift from God. We should make the best use of every moment, every day. A person should decide what's important to do today and let nothing interfere. God is going to ask us to account for every minute we waste."

Ron wanted the fellows to know how he felt so he said, "A Christian is a person who knows how to work, how to give 110 percent in everything he or she does. God intended people to work and work hard. This is how we can fulfill our lives and further the Kingdom of God."

Giving

Norma said, "Every Christian should be a servant. It's more important to put the needs of other persons before your own, even if you have to suffer. We need to forget about ourselves and serve God by helping others. This is what Jesus meant when he said, 'Anyone who wants to become great among you must be slave to all.' "

Mark listened intently as Richard said, "You might think I'm un-Christian, but frankly I think money is one of the most important things in life. It's true that Jesus warned against the dangers of riches, but he also praised the unjust steward for being prudent. When I was young our family was really poor, and I can tell you that poverty didn't bring us closer to God. God expects us to use common sense — to take care of our families now and to provide for a decent old age."

Kate said, "The early Christians owned everything in common. A life-style like that would be good for our society. We could ease poverty if we shared more of our wealth. And think what we could do for ecology by sharing cars, land, and appliances. We would also discover how important we are to each other. Most Americans don't realize that."

Dilemma

Instructions: Pages 27-28 give purpose and procedure for the Dilemma exercise.

Participants respond to a dilemma situation, exploring alternatives and consequences and finally choosing their own best solution.

Sharing Gifts

Your spouse confides to you: "I don't know why, but our neighbor has offered to teach Sunday school. She doesn't seem to like kids much and yells at them when they come into her yard. She knows we're short of teachers and wants to help, but our son will be in her class and he's frightened of her. What can we do?" What do you say?

You are the church choir director. One day a member of the congregation stops you and says: "I'd like to sing in the choir, but I don't have much of a voice, and I can't read music. I suppose I ought to confine my singing to the shower." What do you say?

Your church is sponsoring a drive for a cause you do not believe in. One of your neighbors is heading the drive and has asked you to contribute.

What do you do?

Interviewing

Instructions: Pages 28-31 give purpose and procedure for the Interviewing exercise.

A volunteer from among the participants is interviewed before the group.

Select appropriate questions from page 30. In addition you might want to consider these questions:

— What do you like to do when you are alone?
— How important are people in your life?
— What special skills do you have?
— What major influences have made you the person you are today?
— What does the word *success* mean to you?
— Have your ideas about success changed over the years?
— Was there a time you felt particularly successful?
— In what area do you feel most successful now?
— What news items most disturb you these days?
— Is there one thing you would like to do or accomplish before you die?
— What will you probably be doing five or ten years from now? What would you like to be doing then?

Miscellaneous Exercises

The remaining exercises in this section are one of a kind. The purpose of each is to help participants further examine what they believe and value about themselves and their gifts. Procedures are given for each.

Modern Exodus

This exercise helps participants think about their most meaningful possessions and prioritize them. (Time required: 10-15 minutes)

1. Give these instructions: "A catastrophe is upon your city, and you must leave your home without ever returning to claim your possessions. You are allowed to take a maximum of eight items with you. You must be able to carry them to an evacuation station about four blocks away. Quickly list the eight items. Do not include other people. They are taken care of." (Allow about 3 minutes.)

2. After participants have completed their lists, have them gather in groups of 4 and share:

— the three or four most important items you saved.
— why they are important to you.
— what you thought of as you made your choices.
— what you learned about yourself from the choices you made.

Self-Evaluation I

1. Reproduce the Self-Evaluation form which follows and pass out a copy to each participant.

2. Have participants read the instructions and complete the form independently.

3. When the forms have been completed, ask participants if they would prefer to be at different places on any of the continuums. If so, suggest that they might wish to set a goal to accomplish that. (Pages 31-33 give purpose and procedure for Goal Setting.)

Self-Evaluation Form

Instructions: On each continuum below, underline the number that best represents where you are now and circle the number that best represents where you'd like to be.

Living up to my beliefs:

1 2 3 4 5 6 7 8 9 10

Never Always

Attending church:

1 2 3 4 5 6 7 8 9 10

Never Always

Giving according to my ability:

1 2 3 4 5 6 7 8 9 10

Never Always

Sharing myself with others:

1 2 3 4 5 6 7 8 9 10

Never Always

Listening to members of my family:

1 2 3 4 5 6 7 8 9 10

Never Always

Spending time with people I love:

1 2 3 4 5 6 7 8 9 10

Never Always

Spending time alone with God:

1 2 3 4 5 6 7 8 9 10

Never Always

Using my talents:

1 2 3 4 5 6 7 8 9 10

Never Always

Self-Evaluation II

1. Have participants compile the following lists:

— three things you like to do on a rainy day
— three books you have read and enjoyed
— three things you like best about yourself
— three new and good things in your life
— three things you can do well
— three concerns you have

2. Ask volunteers to share one thing they learned about themselves from completing their lists.

Motivations for Attending Church

This exercise helps participants examine and discuss some reasons why people attend church and also gives them insights into their own motivations. (Time required: about 30 minutes, depending on group size)

1. Have the group form two circles, one inside the other, facing each other. Have each participant in the outer circle pair with a participant in the inner circle. Explain that the group will be exploring some possible motivations for attending church.

2. From the list given below, read the first possible motivation for attending church. You might say: "People attend church for various reasons. One reason may be social: to meet people and be with friends."

3. Ask each pair to react to the social motivation by discussing these questions:

— What do you think of this as a reason for attending church?
— Do you, personally, ever attend church for this reason?

(Allow 2-3 minutes for pairs to discuss these two questions.)

4. After the pairs have completed their discussion, give these instructions: "We are now ready to consider the next motivation, but first we will change partners. People in the inside circle stay seated. Persons in the outside circle move one seat to the left."

5. Give the new partners another motivation from the list below, and have them follow the same procedure.

6. Repeat, until participants have considered 6-8 reasons, or until everyone has talked with every possible partner.

Motivations for attending church:

— To meet people and be with friends.
— To grow in faith.
— Out of a sense of duty.
— To make business contacts.
— To appear respectable.
— To get out of the house.
— To hear a good sermon.
— To satisfy conscience.
— Because friends belong.
— To set an example.
— To be intellectually challenged.
— To find a mate, a girlfriend or boyfriend.
— As an excuse to dress up for a change.
— To help fulfill a commitment to Jesus Christ.
— (Any others participants wish to add.)

7. Reassemble the group. Invite volunteers to share insights, reactions.

Work Motivations

This exercise gives an opportunity to examine some motivations for pursuing a career. (Time required: 20-30 minutes or more, depending on group size)

Pages 154-155 (Motivations for Attending Church) give the procedure for this exercise.

Possible motivations for working:

— To further personal and family interests; to support a family.
— To develop and use personal talents.
— To help other people; to make the world a better place to live.
— To be challenged and stimulated.
— To further the work of God on earth.
— To have money for a few luxuries.

— To keep from being bored or feeling useless.
— (Any others participants wish to add.)

Success Motivations

This exercise helps participants examine some of their thoughts, feelings, and drives related to success. (Time required: 20-30 minutes, depending on group size)

Pages 154-155 (Motivations for Attending Church) give the procedure for this exercise.

Possible motivations for wanting to be "successful":

— To have more material things.
— To gain the respect of others.
— To keep up with others.
— To demonstrate self-achievement.
— To please parents or other people.
— For personal security.
— For influence and power.
— (Any others participants wish to add.)

My Gifts

This exercise helps people recognize and value the gifts God has given them. (Time required: 25-30 minutes or more)

1. Hand out blank sheets of paper, and have each participant number down the page from one to ten.
2. Ask them to list the gifts they have — the things they do well.
3. Have participants look over their lists and place a star beside the gifts they really enjoy using.
4. Have participants gather in groups of 4 to share their lists. Ask that they focus on one person at a time, helping that person identify the gifts and abilities he or she might have missed.
5. Ask the group to spend a moment or two considering their abilities and how they might use them to help others.
6. Have each group of 4 divide into pairs. Ask that each person choose one or two of their gifts and help one another

think of ways these gifts can be of value to others. Questions to discuss:

— How can these gifts be used to help another person or a community of people?

— Can they be used in your church?

7. Invite participants to set a goal. (Pages 31-33 give the procedure for Goal Setting.)

8. Reassemble the total group, and give these suggestions:

— Think about the list you made. Was it difficult to identify your gifts? Were you surprised to discover you could list so many? Or so few?

— Can a few of you tell what you learned or share an insight you gained? Try completing this sentence, "I learned that. . . ."

Windfall

(Time required: 15-20 minutes)

1. Present this situation to the total group:

"Your wealthy uncle, who was a great philanthropist, just died and left you a large sum of money. After taxes and other costs, you have $160,000.

"The will stipulates that you must give away at least half of your inheritance within the next two years. The money must be given 'to further the growth of Christianity in individual lives, in any manner that seems effective to you.'

"The terms are open. Apparently your uncle knew you well enough to trust your judgment.

"Without worrying about legal procedures or other details, and working alone, consider where and how you will allocate the $80,000."

2. After about 5 minutes, have participants gather in groups of 4 to share choices and discuss the values that underlie those choices.

Relationships

This exercise gives people an opportunity to examine the influence of relationships on their lives. (Time required: about 15 minutes)

1. Ask each participant to draw a line down the middle of a piece of paper. In one column, have them list people who have been important in their lives. In the other column, have them list why the person has been important.
2. When participants have completed their lists, have the group pair off. In pairs, participants take turns talking about their lists with one another. Have them see if they find any common elements that tell something about their meaningful relationships with others.
3. Invite volunteers from the total group to complete this statement: "My most meaningful relationships seem to be. . . ."

The Gift of Leadership

Throughout history we find a wide variety of leadership styles. Effective leadership takes many forms — often reflecting the personality, background, and past experiences of the leader. This exercise provides participants with the opportunity to reflect on styles of leadership, including their own. (Time required: 15-20 minutes)
1. Have each participant think about committees on which they have served in the community, church, or school. Have them try to recall various styles of leadership from their experiences. Then ask participants to rank, from most effective (1) to least effective (4), the examples given below. You may wish to write these descriptions on the chalkboard:

Person A: Keeps things moving; influences group decisions subtly and tactfully.

Person B: Participates as member of group; seeks others' contributions; guides group to its own decisions.

Person C: Asserts self in strong and direct manner; efficient; gets results.

Person D: Keeps peace at all costs; avoids conflict; often assumes major responsibility to get the job done.

2. When the group has completed their rankings, have them gather in groups of 4 to share their rankings. (Allow 2-3 minutes.)

3. Ask each group if it can agree on some important principles for effective leadership. (Allow 2-3 minutes.)

4. Ask participants to think about the following individually:

- — Which of the four styles most nearly reflects your own personal way of leading?
- — Are you satisfied with that?
- — Are there changes you would like to try which might increase your effectiveness in leadership?

5. Have participants find a partner and share some thoughts about their own style of leadership. Ask that they try to be helpful to one another — listening and giving feedback. (Allow 5-10 minutes.)

Portrait

This exercise gives people an opportunity to become more visually aware of others and more aware of themselves by using feedback from others' impressions of them. (Time required: 10-15 minutes)

1. Ask participants to find a partner. Give these instructions:

"Sit facing your partner. In each pair designate Person A and Person B.

"Imagine that each of you is a portrait painter; you will have a chance to paint a mental portrait of your partner.

"Without talking, look at your partner and observe his or her features — eyes, hair, coloring, expression — for about 30-40 seconds. (Pause.)

"Now close your eyes. Person A, describe to Person B the portrait you are mentally painting of him or her."

2. After a few minutes, have partners reverse roles. Person B describes Person A.

3. Ask pairs to share:

- — what you learned about yourself.
- — what you learned about each other.
- — what you see as important in your own physical appearance.
- — what you see as important in the other's appearance.

Memories

(Time required: 10-15 minutes)

Jesus said: ". . . unless you change and become like little children you will never enter the kingdom of heaven. And so, the one who makes himself as little as this little child is the greatest in the kingdom of heaven." (Matthew 18:3-4)

1. Have each participant think of himself or herself as a small child; or have them think of a small child they have recently observed. Ask: "What qualities or characteristics attract you? Make a list of these characteristics." (Allow 5 minutes.)

2. Have participants share the following in pairs:

- Which of the qualities you listed do you have now?
- Have some that you had as a small child been lost along the way? Which?
- Are there one or two you would really like to have again? If so, discuss ways you can recapture these. (Allow 5 minutes.)

3. Invite participants to set a personal goal. (Pages 31-33 give procedure for Goal Setting.)

Birthday Celebration

Celebrating My Strengths

This exercise invites participants to identify and celebrate their successes, strengths, and values.

1. Duplicate the form "Celebrating My Strengths" and provide a copy for each participant.

2. Have participants think about their most recent birthday. Suggest that they probably accomplished many things over the years and that some of these may have gone unrecognized. Explain to participants that they will be doing a birthday inventory to give their accomplishments and strengths recognition.

3. Have participants list as many of their accomplishments as they can think of in the "success" candle, using words or short phrases to describe them. (Allow about 5 minutes.)

4. Have each participant find a partner, preferably someone he or she knows quite well. Have partners share their accomplishments with each other. Give these instructions: "As you look over your list, what strengths do you find in yourself? With your partner, identify your personal strengths and list them in the "strengths" candle. (Allow about 10 minutes.)

5. Now have participants work alone for a few minutes, adding other strengths — ones that were not identified with their partners. Encourage them to list as many positive qualities as they can think of. (Allow another 2-3 minutes.)

6. Give these instructions: "As you think about your accomplishments and your strengths, what do they suggest to you about the values you hold? List the five values that seem most important to you. Write them in the "values" candle. (Allow 5 minutes.)

7. Continue: "Look at your list of strengths and your list of important values. If you apply your strengths to the things that are important to you, what is one new success you could make happen? With your partner, set a goal to make this success happen. Tell your partner what you will do, how you will do it, and when." (Pages 31-33 give procedure for Goal Setting. Allow 10-15 minutes.)

8. Have partners combine with another pair to share some of their discoveries.

9. Invite the group to think of a special way to celebrate their personal successes and strengths.

Celebrating My Strengths

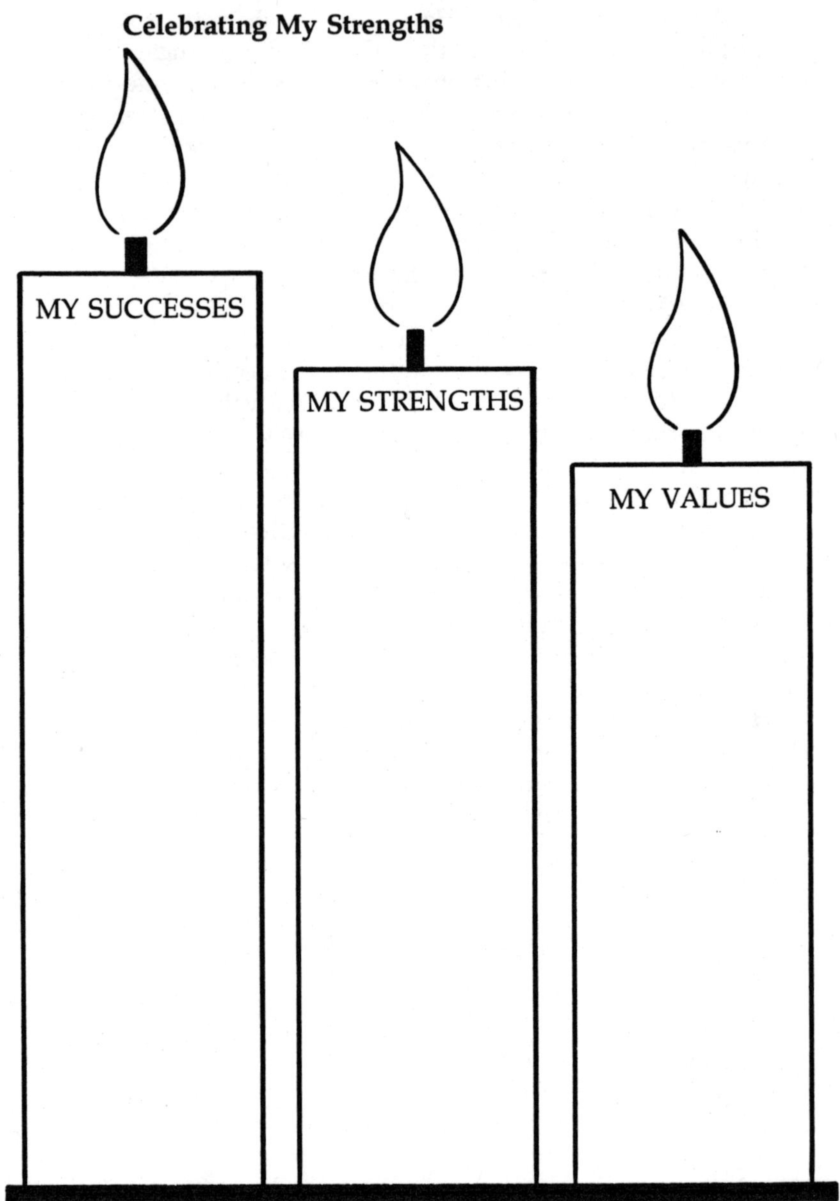

Three Levels of Learning

Give Me the Facts! (See Matthew 25:14-30, the Parable of the Talents)

Questions to answer:

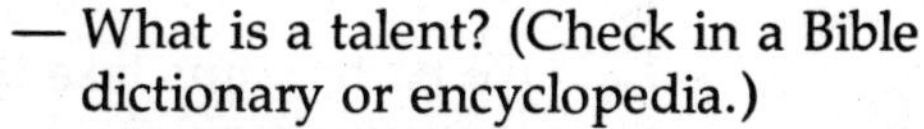

— What is a talent? (Check in a Bible dictionary or encyclopedia.)
— How did the man divide his property?
— Why were different amounts given to each servant?
— How did the first two servants account for their stewardship when the master returned?
— What did the master say to these two servants when he learned how each had used the talents?
— How did the servant with the one talent use his? What reason did he give?
— How did the master respond to him?
— What did Jesus say that summed up the meaning of this parable?

What's the Idea?
Concepts to explore:

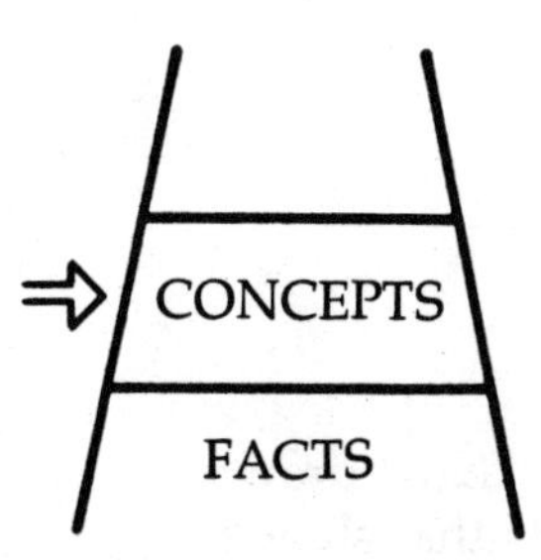

— What does this parable tell us about the way God views our gifts?
— How might the master have responded if the servant with one talent had risked in a business venture and lost some or all of it?
— How might this statement be explained: "Every Christian is a steward of the gospel."
— What are some obstacles to Christian stewardship?
— What excuses might be offered to avoid stewardship responsibilities?

— To what extent are people in the Church today guilty of hoarding their gifts?
— What modern-day title could be given to this parable?

What's in It for Me?

Valuing suggestions:

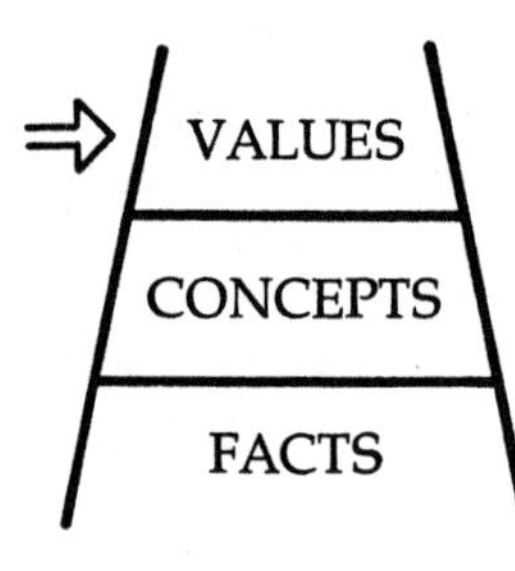

1. Have participants take time to reflect on their lives and then list their talents.
2. Ask participants to imagine themselves in a parable similar to the Parable of the Talents in which they must account for their use of talents. Ask if anything keeps them from using their talents?
3. Have participants consider their use of time as well as talents. Ask:
— How long have you lived?
— Can you describe how you have used that time?
— How do you hope to use your time in the future?
4. When participants have had a chance to consider the preceding questions, give these instructions: "Think about your typical day. Draw a circle and divide it into segments that show how you use your day." (You might wish to draw this example on the chalkboard.)

Allow about 5 minutes, then continue: "Now draw another circle and divide it into time-segments that show how you *wish* you would spend your day."

5. Have participants share their drawings in pairs.

Resources from the Bible (for optional use)

Self-Awareness

Romans 7:14-25	I do the very things I don't want to do.
Galatians 5:22-23	Fruit of the Spirit: love, joy, peace, patience, etc.

Self-Worth

Psalm 8	"What is man . . .?"
Psalm 23	The Lord is my Shepherd.
Psalm 100	God made us: we are his people.
Isaiah 49:16	God does not forget us.
Matthew 10:28-31	God's love and the sparrows.
Luke 15:3-10	The worth of each individual.
John 3:16	God's love for the world.
John 14:1-4	A place for us.
1 Corinthians 3:16-17	Our body is God's temple.
1 John 3:1-3	We are God's children.

Success; Happiness

Joshua 1:8	Guidelines for "good success."
Ecclesiastes 5:19	Enjoyment in work.
Matthew 5:1-11	Beatitudes — a blessed life.
John 13:3-17	Happiness is serving.
1 Timothy 6:6-10	Secret of contentment.

Talents, Time, and Money

Romans 12:1-8	Different gifts.
Matthew 6:25-33	Concern for material things.
Mark 10:17-22; Luke 12:13-21	Wealth and abundance can create obstacles.
Matthew 6:19-24	The heart is where the treasure is.
Luke 12:48	High expectations for some people.
Matthew 25:14-30	Parable of the Talents.

Ephesians 5:15-17	Responsible living and use of time.
Luke 6:38	Generosity.
Mark 12:41-44	The Widow's Mite — gave all she had.
2 Corinthians 8 and 9	Generous and cheerful giving.
Acts 20:35	Joy in giving.
1 Timothy 6:7; Matthew 19:23-24	It isn't easy to be rich.
Genesis 28:22	A tenth to God.

Serving

Matthew 5:16	Giving God the glory.
Luke 10:25-28	Great commandment: Love God, love your neighbor as yourself.
Matthew 20:20-28	Key to true greatness.
2 Corinthians 3:2-3	People's lives are like letters.
Galatians 6:9	Service can be tiring.
1 Peter 5:2	Serve gladly — not grudgingly.

Life-style

Acts 2:44-47	Life-style of the early Church.
Acts 4:32-35	Everything in common.

Work, Leisure

Ecclesiastes 3	A time and a season for everything.
Ecclesiastes 3:10-22	Enjoyment in work is one of God's gifts.
2 Thessalonians 3:6-10	No work, no eat.

Prayer

Lord, I truly believe you created me — a marvelous, unique creation. I belong to you. Sometimes, this gift of life troubles me at the same time that it amazes me. Sometimes I become confused trying to live up to the expectations of others and yet wanting to be myself.

But your constant reminder is that I am yours, that you care about me just the way I am. Thank you for making me whole. I can be myself again — appreciating the worth, the beauty of your creation. Help me to be all that I might be, as a special part of that creation, so that I may add to your glory.

Valuing Others

How do we see other persons, especially those who are in need and who are hurting? What is our responsibility to them, to ourselves, and to our God? And how do we handle things when we are hurting and need others?

Christian teachings challenge people to live a life which reflects their love for God, their neighbor, and themselves. Jesus taught that these relationships are intertwined. He said that we should love our neighbor as ourselves. This love becomes a very part of our being. It is expressed in our everyday life and thought and in our interaction with other persons.

This section is intended to help people examine human relationships in the light of God's love and forgiveness. How much do we really care about others? How do we think, feel, and behave as human beings in relation to other human beings and as a part of God's total creation?

Before using this chapter, please review the chapter on leadership.

Voting

Instructions: Pages 20-21 give purpose and procedure for the Voting exercise.

Participants vote in the following manner:

Agree?	(Raise hand.)
Strongly Agree?	(Wave hand.)
Disagree?	(Thumb down.)
Strongly Disagree?	(Shake thumb.)
Pass?	(Fold arms across chest.)

General Voting Questions on Valuing Others

How many of you:
— are disturbed because you don't know how to help people?
— find that recognizing one's own limitations makes a person more accepting of another's shortcomings?
— think listening to another person is one way of accepting him or her?
— think that modern conveniences have cut people off from one another?
— think too many people are indifferent to the world around them?
— think most people practice what they preach?
— think that sin is an unavoidable part of human nature?
— find it difficult to say you're sorry?
— think that people have unlimited rights over their bodies?
— think that self-concern causes ecological crises?
— think that poor people have a right to protest their circumstances?
— think men need liberating as well as women?

Helping Others

How many of you:
— willingly help others?
— think that people need each other's help in order to mature?
— ever received an unexpected kindness from someone?
— ever received help from a whole group of people?
— were ever refused when you requested help?
— feel obligated to someone who helps you?
— expect your favors to be returned?
— quickly defend someone who is being ridiculed?
— ever stood up for a person who was not present to defend himself or herself?
— think others suspect your motives when you try to help?
— would stop to help someone fix a flat tire?
— help people who are unable to repay you?
— think that gratitude for God's gift of life requires that we devote our life to serving others?

— think that new ideas in technology usually help relieve human needs?
— think that some oppressed people are worthy of help, but some are not?
— think we can't really help poor people unless we understand their oppression?
— think that by helping minority groups and the poor, we help ourselves?
— find it difficult to understand and really help people of the Third World?
— are bothered when the Church sends food and clothing to communist countries or to protesting minorities?
— think the poor should receive free medical care?
— think better housing should be available to those who need it but can't afford it?

Sharing

How many of you:
— think there is a limit to how much a person can bear of another's burdens?
— think the Church community does not share enough with one another?
— think our relationships in groups would be richer if we would rely more on God's Spirit?
— feel that sharing deeply with another person is often too risky?
— think some people are afraid to be free and open with you?
— have ever betrayed a confidence?
— know one or two persons who can really confide in you?
— have tried to share and be open but were turned away?
— have a close friendship with someone because you shared a troubled period of time together?
— think that if you take the Gospel seriously, you really need to share the suffering and joy of others?
— think that greed underlies all the world's problems?
— think that if we use our resources wisely, there's plenty for everyone.

Loving

How many of you:

— think all people are lovable in some way?
— know someone you really don't like?
— think we will know how to love others if we know God?
— think it's impossible to love everybody?
— think loving means, specifically, taking care of the needy?
— think we grow as persons when we love others as ourselves?
— think that the more deeply we love, the more deeply we feel pain?
— think that the more deeply we love, the more deeply we are alive?

Listening and Accepting

How many of you:

— sometimes wonder if you listen carefully enough to what others say?
— think listening to another person is one way of accepting him or her?
— are often concerned only with what *you* want to say in a conversation?
— think everyone has an idea worth listening to?
— ever felt that nobody was listening to you?
— sometimes feel angry with another person who monopolizes a conversation?
— accept people whose lifestyles differ greatly from yours?
— accept people whose lifestyles you consider "unproductive"?
— think that yours is the only true religion?
— ever dropped a friend because his or her ideas were incompatible with yours?
— think that if we do not fear and hate, we do not arouse fear and hatred in others?
— sometimes make snap judgments about people?
— became friends with someone you didn't think you would like?
— think that most people are influenced too much by the opinions of others?

— believe people of all races are similar but shouldn't mingle?
— would vote for the best-qualified presidential candidate regardless of his or her race?
— would feel O.K. about living next door to a person of another race?
— think that people of all races have basically the same needs?
— have had a person of another race in your home during the past year?
— would date a person of another race?
— think manual labor is inferior to intellectual pursuits?
— would not object to a "half-way house" for chemically dependent persons in your neighborhood?
— think we should be careful about allowing persons of certain religions into our country?
— are interested in learning about others with different religious beliefs from yours?

Reaching Out to Our Neighbors and Others

How many of you:
— have a good relationship with most of your neighbors?
— have neighbors who are friendly but are not your friends?
— have a neighbor you could depend on in an emergency?
— are usually one of the first in your area to meet a new neighbor?
— would probably be one of the last in your area to meet a new neighbor?
— wish your neighborhood had a "sense of community"?
— have ever wondered what your neighborhood would be like if all of you depended on one another?
— feel that sometimes neighbors intrude on each other?
— have ever been annoyed by an overly helpful neighbor?
— have tried to reach out to a lonely person in the last month?
— tried to reach out to another person and were rejected?
— think people in your generation don't seem to need one another as much as they did in your parents' generation?
— think that modern conveniences have cut people off from one another?

— wish people weren't so private?
— prefer privacy?
— find that it is difficult today to get to know people deeply?
— would like to reach out more to people?
— would rather have one or two close friends than many friends?
— spend time with older people and enjoy it?
— find it depressing to be with people who have many problems?
— avoid people who have problems?
— avoid contacts with the handicapped?
— enjoy contacts with the handicapped?

Taking a Stand and Being Responsible

How many of you:
— think your vote counts?
— think your ideas about most things count?
— would like to take a stand on an issue but don't have enough facts?
— would like to know more about what your pastor thinks about social issues such as war, abortion, drugs, etc.?
— find it difficult to defend an unpopular view before a group?
— have nevertheless defended such a view before a group?
— think it's a waste of time to worry about political issues?
— think you should be involved in political and social issues?
— have ever carried a picket sign?
— have ever publicly taken a stand on an issue?
— think that participation in a demonstration is sometimes a Christian duty?
— think that as long as you are law-abiding, you needn't show any other interest in government?
— think other people should be completely responsible for themselves?
— think each nation should determine its own socio-economic and political systems?
— concentrate more on the needs of others than on your own needs?
— think it is possible to care so much for others that we neglect ourselves?

— think the oppressed have a right to resort to violence to obtain their rights?
— worry about violence in cities?
— worry about starving people in the world?
— think that a person should mostly worry about himself or herself and let others fend for themselves?
— think most Christians are concerned about oppressed people?
— think a Christian has the responsibility to prevent an acquaintance from committing suicide?
— think social reformers, in emphasizing the reform, sometimes forget the people?
— think people often neglect their families in order to be involved in community and church life?
— think a Christian can expect to suffer some inconvenience or persecution?
— would be willing to take a cut in salary as a part of a long-range effort to feed the hungry?

How many of you agree with this statement?
— What you do is your own business as long as you don't harm others.
— Conversion to Christianity implies having a sense of responsibility for others.
— We are accountable for the choices we make.
— We are accountable for what our choices do to others.
— The Church has an obligation to speak up on social and political issues.
— The Church should spend more time, energy, and money serving people in prisons, nursing homes, and hospitals.

How many of you agree with this statement on population?
— Population growth in the United States is harmful to our economy.
— Fewer people means less pollution.
— The population problem is manageable and can be dealt with gradually over the years.
— The population explosion will lead to the end of the human race.
— Legislation should restrict the number of children per family.

How many of you agree with this statement on war?
— Nuclear warfare can never be justified, even if some other forms of war can.
— War is always wrong.
— Citizens should have more choice in whether they have to fight in a war.
— Christians should serve their country willingly in any war.
— Both sides lose in any war.
— Many Christians have changed their attitudes toward war in recent years.
— Traditional "conditions for a just war" cannot be defended today.

How many of you agree with this statement on women?
— Women should be allowed and encouraged to serve and hold office in all areas of the Church's life.
— The Church has made second-class citizens of women.
— Men need liberating as well as women.
— Jesus treated women as persons more than men do today.
— The Church should encourage women to enter all fields of human endeavor.
— Men are naturally superior to women in administrative positions.
— Women's insights are needed in such fields as theology and politics.
— Women are harming themselves by wanting equality with men.
— Marriage and family life can be as good or better if women enter more into fields where men now predominate.
— The government should help support day-care centers for the children of working mothers.

How many of you agree with this statement on unwanted pregnancy?
— Women have unlimited rights over their bodies.
— The unborn child should have the same rights as a child at birth.
— The Scriptures are clear on the morality of abortion.

— Abortion should be a medical decision between the pregnant woman and her doctor.
— There are psychological, social, or economic circumstances that justify abortion in some cases.
— Abortion is allowable as long as it is not used as a means of birth control.
— From the moment of conception, life is to be protected by all reasonable means.
— More understanding and help should be given to unwed mothers.
— In some situations, families should be encouraged to put a child out for adoption.
— More men should take responsibility for birth control by vasectomy.
— There would be fewer abortions if more help were given parents of unwanted children.
— The Church provides little help when a woman is faced with the dilemma of an unwanted pregnancy.

How many of you agree with this statement on the treatment of the terminally ill?
— A patient has the right to know of his or her terminal illness.
— Terminally-ill patients should have the right to determine how long their life will be prolonged.
— Life is a gift from God, and a person has no option to terminate it.
— It is possible to decide at what point being alive becomes meaningless.
— A terminally-ill person should be kept alive as long as possible by whatever means, regardless of whether there is hope of recovery.
— There is no moral obligation to use extraordinary means to preserve the life of a terminally-ill person who does not wish his or her life prolonged.

Sin and Forgiveness

How many of you agree with this statement?

— Defining the word "sin" is difficult.
— Sin is too strong a word.
— Sin and crime are the same.
— Stealing food for a starving child is wrong.
— Sin is basically separation from God.
— Sin is an unavoidable part of human nature.
— We are born sinful.
— Sin is basically selfishness.
— An act is either right or wrong; there is nothing in between.
— Telling a lie is always wrong.
— Sin always hurts someone.
— You sin against God when you wrong another person.
— Society often excuses sin by calling it "mental illness."
— Guilt feelings are a healthy deterrent to wrongdoing.
— Sex crimes should be dealt with more severely.

How many of you:

— have wondered what it would be like if there were no forgiveness?
— think human beings cannot completely forgive and forget?
— have been forgiven and felt a sense of relief?
— have ever forgiven someone who never found out about it?
— ever asked someone to forgive you?
— find it difficult to say you're sorry?
— have been deeply hurt by another person and then forgave that person?
— think forgiveness sometimes involves a promise in return?
— think most people have trouble practicing forgiveness?
— think there is something for which you could never forgive a person?
— know someone you cannot forgive?

Ecology and the Environment

How many of you agree with this statement?

— Increasing the gross national product increases the junk piles around us.

— Most Americans believe that the consumption of "things" makes people happy.
— We consume too much.
— We need to re-evaluate our lifestyles.
— Economic progress and protection of the environment are not compatible.
— The wealthy cause more pollution than the poor.
— Our country is the major polluter of the world.
— The world needs more technology.
— We need to humanize the technology that already exists.

How many of you:
— think we don't really appreciate and use the natural resources God created for us?
— think we must learn to live with nature rather than to control nature?
— think that concern for profit is the main cause of ecological crises?
— think that most industrialists are as concerned about pollution as environmentalists are?
— spend much time in the out-of-doors?
— would like to spend more time in nature but are too busy?
— are concerned about the use of land in America?
— have ever written a letter to a government official regarding the use and care of natural resources?
— feel we have ignored the wisdom of American Indians in matters of conservation?

How many of you:
— overspend?
— own two cars?
— save your glass bottles and cans for recycling?
— often walk instead of drive?
— feel you have more clothes than you need?
— think it's a good idea to increase auto registration fees with increased engine size?
— would be willing to ride in a car pool or take the bus regularly?
— could get along without a car? could get by with one car?

— would be willing to share major appliances such as freezers or lawn mowers with other neighbors?
— would feel lost if you had no TV?
— own an air conditioner?
— would consider communal living to reduce the use of land and appliances?

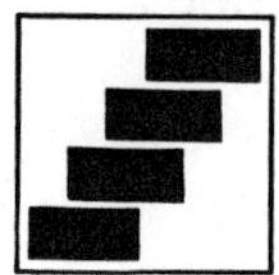

Ranking

Instructions: Pages 21-22 give purpose and procedure for the Ranking exercise.

Participants rank all items in order of preference or priority (1 = most important; 2 = next most important, etc.)

General Ranking

For me, the joy of being a Christian is:
_____ knowing my sins are forgiven.
_____ sharing in Christ's work by serving others.
_____ sharing in fellowship with other Christians.

For me, the "Good News" of the Gospel is that there is:
_____ a God who loves us.
_____ freedom for the poor and oppressed.
_____ new life for us as sinners.
_____ life after death.

My faith helps me to see people:
_____ as brothers and sisters in Christ.
_____ as sinners.
_____ as people who need my love and service.

For life together in my congregation it is most important:
_____ to know each other as individuals.
_____ to know God and his Word.
_____ to know and respond to the needs of society.

Your teenage daughter is pregnant; what do you think would be best for her?

_____ Place the child for adoption.
_____ Have an abortion.
_____ Keep the child.
_____ Marry immediately.

What is the best way to be involved in life?

_____ Spend free time helping others.
_____ Develop one's self to the fullest potential.
_____ Be friendly to everyone.
_____ Join a group that helps others.

Which do you think Jesus would choose as most important for his followers to be concerned about? (Rank five.)

_____ knowledge of the Bible
_____ being active in one's church
_____ feeding the hungry
_____ housing for those without shelter
_____ companionship for the lonely
_____ developing one's own potential
_____ working with others for the common good
_____ converting the world to Christianity

Helping

Your friend has a problem and you want to help. In which situation do you think you would be most effective?

_____ unwed daughter becomes pregnant
_____ spouse is an alcoholic
_____ parent is dying of cancer
_____ parent is in a nursing home
_____ child is taking drugs

Which is the most helpful to people in need?

_____ church
_____ family
_____ welfare agency
_____ psychiatry

In the parable of the Good Samaritan, the Samaritan took several risks in befriending another person. Which risk would concern you most in helping another person?
_____ getting too involved
_____ becoming a victim
_____ interference with other plans
_____ losing money

What do you think persons in trouble need most?
_____ advice
_____ understanding
_____ God's Word

Accepting

What do you usually do when confronted with a person whose values are different from yours?
_____ accept the person
_____ accept his or her values
_____ try to change the person

Homosexuals:
_____ are immoral.
_____ need understanding.
_____ are sick.
_____ are normal people.

What quality is most important to you in a friend (or substitute one of these: boyfriend, girlfriend, child, mate, parent, pastor, etc.)? Rank each group of three.
_____ dependability
_____ honesty
_____ generosity

_____ self-confidence
_____ fairness
_____ sense of purpose

_____ similar interests
_____ same race
_____ similar religious faith

_____ intelligence
_____ sense of humor
_____ outgoing nature
_____ charm
_____ respect for opinions of others
_____ responsibility

My faith helps me to accept others because:
_____ Jesus says I should.
_____ we are all sinners who have fallen short of the glory of God.
_____ I believe that we are all equally children of God.

Reaching Out

How can we best enrich the lives of the aging?
_____ Keep them in touch with persons of all ages.
_____ Help them share their wealth of experience.
_____ Allow them to be themselves.
_____ Visit them often.

Which is most likely to cut people off from one another?
_____ mobility
_____ conveniences
_____ privacy

Loving

Love is . . .
_____ helping
_____ risking
_____ forgiving
_____ accepting others
_____ sharing
_____ listening

Which definition of love is probably closest to what Jesus talked about?

_____ Creating the best possible conditions for developing the potential of other persons.
_____ Loving the Lord your God with all your heart, mind, soul, and your neighbor as yourself.
_____ Giving to another when you see him or her in need.

Sin and Forgiveness

When you think of the word *sin,* which is it most like? Rank each group of three.

_____ eating too much
_____ wasting money
_____ working on Sunday

_____ ruthlessly cutting down forests
_____ strip mining
_____ being cruel to animals

_____ premarital sex
_____ drug abuse
_____ alcohol abuse

_____ not keeping your word
_____ not keeping society's rules
_____ ignoring people's needs

_____ separation from God
_____ disobeying God's commands
_____ following the flesh instead of the spirit

_____ hating your brother or sister
_____ making money your number one priority
_____ stealing a TV set

_____ divorce
_____ deceit
_____ abortion

_____ a temper tantrum
_____ a sulk
_____ a putdown

Which of the following is the most meaningful title for the story of the Prodigal Son? (Luke 15:11-24)
_____ "A Son Comes Home"
_____ "Three Prodigals"
_____ "A Loving, Forgiving Parent"
_____ "The Prodigal Son"
_____ other:

For your past mistakes, which is most difficult for you to accept?
_____ forgiveness of God
_____ forgiveness of others
_____ forgiveness of yourself

Which is forgiving most like?
_____ totally forgetting
_____ restoring a relationship
_____ taking a load off another's back
_____ not judging another's behavior

Which do you think best expresses reconciliation?
_____ "Let's get together and figure out what went wrong."
_____ "I told you so. But let's forget it."
_____ "I'll be here if you need me."
_____ "What you did doesn't matter to me."

Taking a Stand and Being Responsible

What do you consider the most important concerns facing our society today? (Rank five.)
_____ racism
_____ war
_____ drugs
_____ violence
_____ poverty
_____ dishonesty in government
_____ juvenile delinquency
_____ aging
_____ sexual promiscuity
_____ vandalism
_____ abortion
_____ death and dying
_____ women's rights
_____ hunger
_____ population control
_____ ecology
_____ other:

What would best bring about international peace?
_____ Examine why people fight.
_____ Examine what Jesus says about love and peace.
_____ Become acquainted with people from other countries.
_____ Study the history and effects of war on nations.
_____ Share our knowledge and wealth with other nations.

A woman in her late 40s raised several children and wants no more. What do you think she should do if she becomes pregnant?
_____ raise the child
_____ place the child for adoption
_____ have an abortion

What would be the best reason for permitting mercy killing if an eighty-seven-year-old person were dying from cancer?
_____ to save the family money
_____ to spare the person needless suffering
_____ to save society expense

Which is worst?
_____ killing in war
_____ mercy killing
_____ capital punishment
_____ fatality resulting from careless or drunk driving

In what order does a Christian rank these responsibilities?
_____ self
_____ family
_____ others

Ecology and Environment

What do you see as the biggest underlying cause of environmental problems?

_____ population growth
_____ high consumption
_____ profit-motivated systems
_____ political leaders who fear to act on their beliefs
_____ indifferent Church leaders
_____ apathetic citizens

What modern convenience could you do without most easily?

_____ paper towels
_____ plastic bags
_____ nonreturnable containers

What could the American people do that would best relieve the ecological crisis?

_____ get along with less
_____ curb population growth
_____ do more recycling

Continuum

Instructions: Pages 22-23 give purpose and procedure for the Continuum exercise.

Participants choose that place on the continuum, between two opposite extremes, which most closely represents their personal viewpoint.

General Continuums

How do you view your relationship with people in positions of influence and power?

|—————————————————————————————|

dependent upon ... independent of

What do you usually do when you meet a person whose values are different from yours?

accept them — reject them

To what extent should poor people in your community be helped?

Give the shirt off your back. Share everything you possess. — Give them nothing. Let them work and earn for themselves.

How do you share thoughts with friends?

tell them everything — tell them nothing

Reaching Out

Whom do you trust?

everyone — no one

Which are you more like with potential friends?

I choose. — I am chosen.

Taking a Stand and Being Responsible

How responsible do you think people are for their behavior?

An individual is totally responsible. — An individual is not personally responsible.

Do you think abortion is morally permissible?

any time — never

How necessary are wars?

Our greed and fighting instincts guarantee wars. — People have the freedom and intelligence to resolve all differences.

How do you feel about preserving wilderness areas?

leave them untouched — open them up

Either/Or

Instructions: Pages 23-24 give purpose and procedure for the Either/Or exercise.

Participants select, between two choices, the option with which they most closely identify.

General Either/Or Exercises

Which are you more like?

ask / tell
think / act
repair the old one / buy a new one
feed the world / care for yourself
pragmatist / idealist
forgiving and forgetting / forgiving but not forgetting

Which is more important in a friend?

openness / loyalty
willingness to help / willingness to listen
generosity / intelligence

dependability / humor
an outgoing nature / a private nature
independence / stability
tolerance / honesty

Which are your relationships with others more like?
winter / spring
basket of eggs / building blocks
agony / ecstasy
sand castle / fortress
welcome mat / no trespassing
cozy / rocky

Which should Christians be more concerned about?
listening / telling
opposing / supporting
giving money / giving time
teaching / learning
spiritual growth / social change

Which better illustrates sin?
gossiping / telling a lie
cheating on income tax / cheating in an exam
harmful thoughts / harmful deeds
harming oneself / harming another
abortion / child abuse
indifference / acts of revolt
misuse of power / misuse of knowledge

Which is more dehumanizing to people?
caste system / racial discrimination
cruel punishment / total neglect
active dislike / silence
prison system / lack of education
poverty / welfare
pornography / stereotyping

Listening

Instructions: Pages 25 -26 give purpose and procedure for the Listening exercise.

Participants respond to a stimulus statement in groups of three. Each person is "on focus" for five minutes.

Sin and Forgiveness

Tim and Bob had these reactions to the story of the adulterous woman and Jesus' response to her in John 7:53-8:11.

Tim: "Jesus must have recognized the woman's strong sexual drive and felt bad about the trouble she was in. The way he handled the situation — with compassion and strength — probably kept her from committing adultery again."

Bob: "I don't agree with you. Jesus was understanding, all right, but I think he was too permissive. He hardly mentioned her sinfulness. I think she'd have been better off if He'd forced her to admit her guilt openly."

❖❖❖

When asked about her views on homosexuality, Harriet said, "I consider homosexuality a sin, but God forgives all persons regardless of their sexual sins, so we should forgive them too."

Myra responded: "I get upset when people say that homosexuals are sinful or sick. It seems to me that one's unselfish commitment to another person is the important thing, not what society thinks. Why can't we consider homosexuals to be as unselfish and loving as other people? Why call homosexuality a sin at all?"

Taking a Stand and Being Responsible

Mary Ellen said, "I know what to do when there's a sick neighbor down the street or when there's a family in our church needing food. But when I hear about the millions who are starving, or some huge area of the world suffering from a natural disaster, then I'm stumped. Those people are my neighbors too, but I don't know how to respond. My contribution of money or clothes seems so meaningless. I think that the Church must become more socially active, that it must help shape the social conscience of society by giving its members an understanding of the problems and issues. Then Church members would be able to respond intelligently to make this a more humane world."

❖❖❖

Louise told her husband, "I'm really bothered by the way the Church and the gospels keep telling us to take care of others, to love our neighbors as ourselves. It's hard enough just raising a family these days without worrying about others as well."

❖❖❖

Colleen attended a congregational meeting of her church. One agenda item was world hunger, and the response of most people seemed less than enthusiastic for supporting this cause. In irritation Colleen rose to her feet and said, "Can you imagine half of the world being hungry and many starving — right this very minute? Here we are, you and I, with more than we need while millions of people are in desperate need of food just to survive. It seems to me," Colleen continued, "that Jesus said, 'I was hungry and you gave me food; I was thirsty and you gave me drink.' If our congregation doesn't respond, we are downright disobedient, immoral!"

Karen responded, "You're an idealist, Colleen. We can't change the world. Besides, how do you know our help would ever reach those people? It would simply line the pockets of the few who control the power. Let's concentrate on helping the people in our own parish."

❖❖❖

Bert said, "In my travels around the world I've noticed that material wealth isn't the goal many poor people reach for. They want dignity and identity — and they wouldn't trade that for a piece of property or for a lot of expensive possessions. When we judge the motives and life-styles of poor people, we ought to be sure it's not just from our own middle-class perspective."

Dilemma

Instructions: Pages 27-28 give purpose and procedure for the Dilemma exercise.

Participants respond to a dilemma situation, exploring alternatives and consequences and finally choosing their own best solution.

Reaching Out

In your church, you've noticed a family that is often alone and appears uninterested in everyone else. You've never met them and feel a bit shy and uncomfortable about approaching them because they seem so distant. Today, you notice the mother and her three young children attending the morning service alone. The woman looks like she is holding back tears.

What can you do? What might happen?

Ann has made friends with a new girl in her class. The new girl is shy and has a speech impediment, and some of the other students have made fun of her. But Ann likes her and wants her to get to know Sue, who is Ann's best friend. Ann calls Sue to see if the three of them can do something together on Saturday. Before she has a chance to ask, Sue says, "Hey, I'm glad it's just you and me getting together next Saturday. Your new friend, Linda, is kind of a drag."

What could Ann do? What might happen?

Helping

You are an avid golfer and play every Saturday. This Saturday you long to be out on the course, but your regular playing companions had other plans. Your neighbor comes to your door in real despair, asking if you have time to discuss a personal problem that has been brewing all month. You say, "Sure!" Just then, the phone rings. It's your new boss who enthusiastically says, "Guess what! We've got reservations at the Club. I'll pick you up in ten minutes. O.K.?"

What can you do? What might happen?

A disheveled-looking person stops you on the street and asks you for a quarter to buy some coffee.

What could you do? What might happen?

An 18-year-old girl whose parents live next door to you has written to you in confidence from another city. Last month she had a big hassle with her parents and left home. She is expecting a child, and there is no possibility of marriage. She expresses feelings of loneliness, confusion, and fear. She pleads with you to tell nobody, but wants your advice on what to do.

What can you do? What might happen?

Andy's peers look down on him because he comes from a poor family, isn't very well educated, wears shabby clothes, and generally lacks social graces.

Today, in despair, Andy confides in you: "There really ain't any hope for me to be any different kind of person than I am. I'm stuck with me. I can't help it . . . I'm made that way."

What can you do? What might happen?

Accepting

Your best friend just arrived, very pleased with a new outfit. You think the outfit looks baggy and drab. Your friend says, "I blew my whole paycheck on this outfit. How do you like it?"

What can you say or do right now? What might happen?

Your 16-year-old daughter, Lisa, is quite popular with the kids at school. She has told you about a boy she likes named Gene. (You have not met Gene, but have heard that he is very nice. However, you were a little uptight when you found out that Gene is of a different race and religious faith than your family.) Lisa says, "Gene asked me to go to the big school party next Saturday. I said I'd let him know tomorrow. Is it O.K. with you?"

What can you do? What might happen?

Taking a Stand and Being Responsible

You are 15 years old and live in an all-white suburban community. Your folks have always encouraged you to love and accept everyone. Last week an interracial couple moved into the house down the block. Tonight the husband called and asked if you could sit with their three children. You were happy to get the call, but when you told your mother, she said, "Honey, Dad and I don't want you to baby-sit over there."

What could you do? What might happen?

Jan told her friends that she just met Vivian Davis, a woman running for Congress, and was impressed with how articulate and knowledgeable she seemed. One of her friends commented, "Maybe so, but no woman will get my vote."

What could Jan say? What might happen?

You feel your political views are your own business, so although you are registered with a party, others are not aware of which one. A friend in your church is running for office, backed by the opposing political party. The friend calls you on the phone and says, "May I use your name in my campaign?"

What could you do? What might happen?

You are 13 years old and your friends mean more to you than almost anything. Five of you are at a friend's house, and the parents are gone. One of the girls suddenly appears with an opened bottle of whiskey and quickly pours five small glasses. You really don't want any, but all of a sudden one friend holds out a glass to you and says, "You're not a baby, are you?"

What can you do? What might happen?

A married couple in their middle forties have almost finished raising a family of four children. Their youngest is in junior high school. The marital relationship has been strained throughout the years, partly because of the demands of child rearing, and the couple plan to be divorced. Today the wife learns that she is pregnant and is completely distraught.

What can she do? What might happen?

You are a passenger in another person's car. He stops to buy gas and pays for it with a ten-dollar bill. You notice that the attendant gives him change of almost eleven dollars. The driver sticks the money into his pocket and mumbles something about "a lousy mathematician."

What can you do? What might happen?

A doctor tells a colleague about an elderly patient in Room 210: "That woman is terminally ill and suffering a lot. Her husband is dead and she has very little money. Her only son, some 500 miles away, hasn't much either. I can keep her alive with modern medicine for several months at enormous expense to her son's family, but again today she pleaded that I let her die now."

What can the doctor do? What might happen?

Miscellaneous Exercises

The remaining exercises in this section are one of a kind. The purpose of each is to help participants further examine what they believe about others. Procedures are given for each.

Name Tag

The purpose of this exercise is to help people get acquainted and begin sharing with one another. (Time required: 10-15 minutes)

1. Pass out a 4 x 6 card and a small piece of masking tape to each person. Then give these directions:

- In the center of the card, print your first name.
- In the upper left-hand corner, write or draw a place you would like to visit.

— In the upper right-hand corner, write or draw something you can do well.
— In the lower left-hand corner, write or draw a belief or value you hold strongly.
— In the lower right-hand corner, put the name or initials of a person who has had a strong, positive influence in your life.

2. Have participants attach masking tape to their card and wear it. (Remind them of their right to pass. They can omit everything but their name if they wish.)

3. Have participants spend a few minutes milling about the room, meeting as many people as they can and talking about one or two of the items on their name tags if they wish.

Note: Hundreds of suggestions can be used for the Name Tag exercise. Certain ones might be especially appropriate for a particular group, and you may wish to write your own items. Here are additional suggestions to get you started:

— Write one thing you'd like to see happen in this community (or church).
— Write the name of a living person you greatly admire.
— Write the name of an historical figure you admire.
— Complete this sentence: "Church is a place in which I. . . ."
— Write the name of a favorite teacher, coach, or youth worker.
— Complete this sentence: "Our community is a place where. . . ."

How Do I Forgive?

This exercise is designed to help participants examine their attitudes about forgiveness in relation to the behavior of others. (Time required: 10-15 minutes)

1. Write the situations described below on a chalkboard.

2. Have participants read the situations. Have them choose the three persons they are *most willing* to forgive; then have them choose the three they are *least willing* to forgive.

3. Ask each participant to find a partner and talk about the following:

— why they made the choices they did;
— the person that bothers them most of all;
— how God might see some of these situations.

Here are the people and the situations:

— *Mrs. Jones* steals food for her hungry family.
— *Billy* steals fifty cents from his father's wallet.
— Fifteen-year-old *Rita* shoplifts with a group of friends for kicks.
— Bartender *Louie* goes looting during a riot in the inner city.
— *Judy* requisitions small articles from the place where she works and takes them home for her personal use.
— *Jimmy* snatches a purse from an old lady who has just cashed her welfare check.
— *Mary* steals money from a wealthy home where she is baby-sitting.
— *Nancy* pads her expense account.
— *Mike* steals drugs to support his habit.
— Once again *Perry* steals your time — promises to meet you for lunch and doesn't show up.

What Is Sin?

1. Duplicate the following page and provide each participant with a copy.
2. Allow participants 3-4 minutes to read and rank the responses.
3. Have participants gather in groups of 3 and share their rankings. Option: You may wish to use this as a Listening exercise. (See pages 25-26 for purpose and procedure.)

Margaret and Joan are in a church-school class which has been discussing the meaning of sin. They were assigned to talk with several members of their congregation to find out what some of the adults think about sin.

Here is what the owner of a small business said: "Sin is real and people sin by choice. We are free to commit good or evil. This God-given freedom makes us personally responsible for how our choices affect others. We hurt others when we sin."

A homemaker described sin in this way: "Sin, as I see it, is putting other things before God. Sin is separation from God. In other words, when we don't keep God's commandments or when worldly things take priority in our lives, that is sin."

An engineer had a different viewpoint: "I don't think there's anything such as sin. Wrong-doing can be traced to people's environment or upbringing. Some people live in such poverty that they're sometimes forced to steal, even kill, just to stay alive. Some children grow up never knowing what's right or wrong. I know a young boy who was recently caught stealing. His father is an alcoholic and his mother really doesn't love him. You can't tell me that boy is responsible for his stealing. Maybe he did wrong, but I don't call that sin."

Which response came closest to your understanding of sin? Rank them.
_____ business owner
_____ homemaker
_____ engineer

Values Statements

1. Choose a content area: ecology, hunger, equal rights, war, etc., and select voting items from the Voting section of this chapter (or create your own voting items).
2. Write the word *agree* on a piece of paper. Write the words *strongly agree* on another, *disagree* on a third, and *strongly disagree* on a fourth.
3. Post the sheets of paper, one in each corner of the room.
4. Call people to the middle of the room before you read a voting item. Then read the item and ask participants to select the corner of the room which best reflects their reaction (agree, disagree, etc.).
5. As it seems appropriate, give time to talk in pairs.
6. Call all to the center of the room again and repeat the procedure.
7. Keep a record of people's responses to each item you use.
8. For a closing activity, ask volunteers to quickly complete the statement, "I learned. . . ."

Report Card

This exercise gives participants an opportunity to reflect on their attitudes and behaviors toward others, particularly on acceptance and forgiveness in their personal relationships. (Time required: 10-15 minutes)

1. Pass out paper and then give these instructions: "Working alone, consider what forgiveness means to you. Using your own definition of forgiveness, describe and grade yourself in the following areas:

— forgiving others in your family
— forgiving others outside of your family
— specific acts of forgiveness you have performed
— forgiving others and forgetting."

Allow 5-8 minutes.
2. Have each participant find a partner and share "report cards" with each other, along with some of their thoughts and feelings. Ask: "Is there an area you want to improve on? Why not describe it and set a goal?" (See pages 31-33 for Goal Setting.)

Butterfly

This exercise uses the biblical story of the Prodigal Son to help participants focus on the topic of reconciliation, examining their own thoughts, feelings, and experiences in the light of human forgiveness and God's forgiveness. (Suggested time: 20 minutes)

1. Participants will be working in groups of 4. Beforehand, prepare one set of Butterfly Cards for each small group. Cards can be made by duplicating the following page, cutting, and assembling into sets of four cards each.
2. Read Luke 15:11-32 to the entire group.
3. Have participants gather in groups of 4. Give each group one set of cards.
4. Give these instructions: "Silently look at the cards. Think about how you would arrange them to tell the story of the Prodigal Son as you understand it. Use your imagination; there are no right or wrong answers. Just visualize a story-telling sequence for the four cards." (Allow 1 or 2 minutes.) "Now, taking turns, each person arrange the cards and share why you chose your arrangement. When the last person has finished, consider these questions:

- — How do you think the older son who stayed home would have arranged the cards? Try it, put them in a sequence. Tell why.
- — How do you think the father would have arranged the cards? Share why.
- — Have you had a similar experience when you felt forgiven? Can you arrange the cards to describe it? If you wish, share something about that experience.
- — What does all of this say to you about God's forgiveness?"

5. Have participants reassemble into one large group and share their learnings and their insights into God's forgiveness.

Butterfly Cards

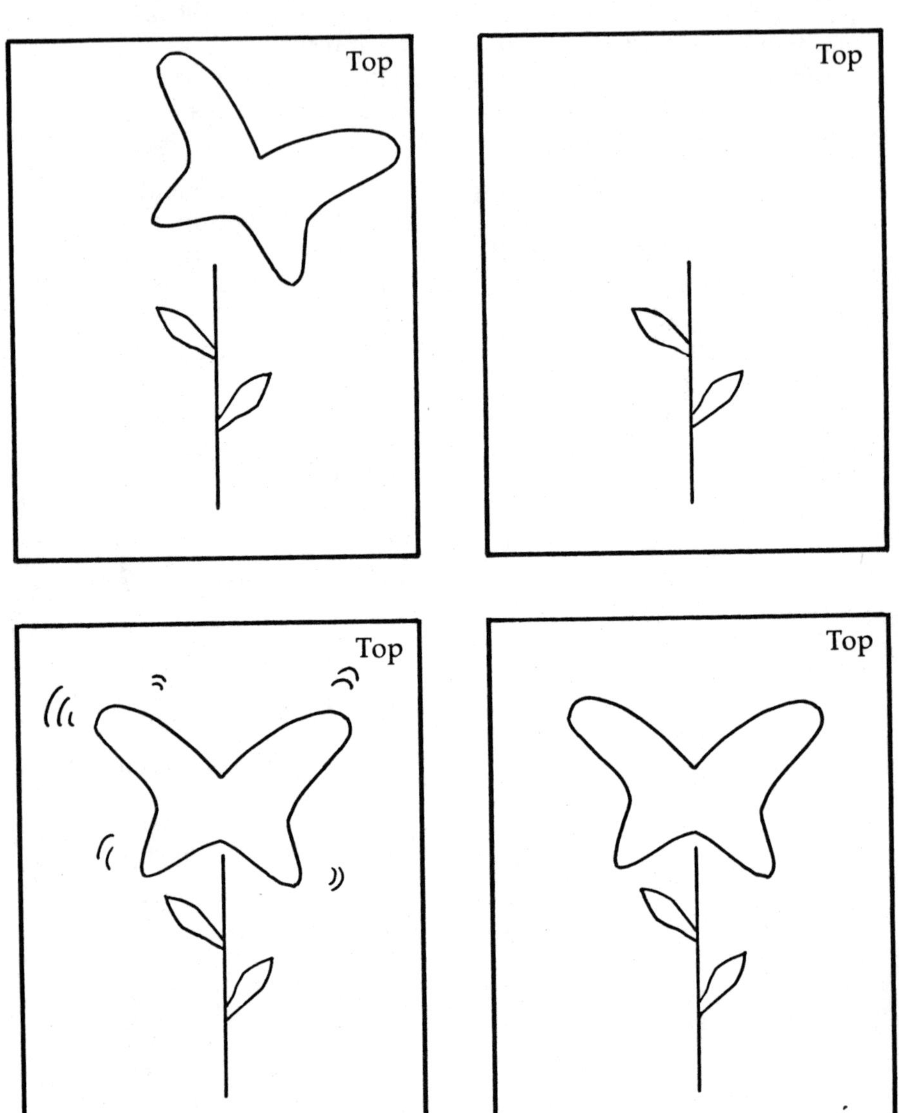

Permission is given to reproduce this page for family and group use.

Forgiveness Discussion

(Suggested time: 20-25 minutes)

1. You may wish to write the questions below on a chalkboard. Then give these instructions: "Consider these questions one at a time. Jot down some notes on your responses. You will have a chance to share your reactions with others later on."

— What is the first word you think of when you hear the word *forgiveness?* What does forgiveness mean to you?

— If you were the Prodigal Son, would you have returned home? Why or why not?

— If you were the father, how might you have responded to your son's return?

— As you look at your life, are you more like the son who *left* home or the son who *stayed* home?

— Think of times when you felt forgiven. What feelings did you experience? Jot them down.

— Have you ever found it difficult to forgive another person? How do you deal with hurt and anger so that you are able to forgive another?

— Have you known a situation where human forgiveness seemed almost as complete as God's?

2. Have participants share their responses in groups of 4.

Food Crisis

This exercise helps participants examine their feelings, attitudes, and values on the problem of hunger. (Time required: 30-40 minutes)

1. Have participants gather in small groups of 5 or 6 prior to giving instructions. Write the list of Food Users on the chalkboard. Then set up the situation: "World population is up; there was poor weather for growing crops again this year; the supply of food is down, and the back-up supply is down to approximately seven to ten days."

2. Give these instructions to the groups:

"You are members of the United States Commission on Food Use and Hunger. The immediate situation dictates that your group must plan to reduce food consumption in the

United States by 25-30 percent. Your decisions will be implemented within sixty days.

"Your plan will probably be in effect for several years, as the situation is not expected to improve.

"During the past year your commission has worked on voluntary food saving plans. These have failed.

"Your task for today (you will have about 15 minutes) is to negotiate and decide which *four* of the food users must have their supply of available food cut drastically. If you have time, also designate four which you would be most reluctant to cut."

Food Users:

- — restaurants, eating places
- — American families
- — friendly countries who need food, and are willing to pay two times the going rate for it
- — hostile countries who need food, and are willing to pay three times the going rate for it
- — producers of alcoholic beverages who require grain for their products
- — hospitals, nursing homes, etc.
- — people in the world who are starving
- — needy persons in the United States (includes free school breakfasts in poverty areas, meals on wheels, etc.)
- — schools, colleges, and agencies whose subsidized programs provide meals at reduced rates
- — livestock, for meat production
- — household pets

3. When most groups have finished, bring everyone together again. Ask groups to report:

- — whether or not they were able to reach a consensus
- — which areas they chose to be cut drastically
- — what values were behind their decisions

4. Ask participants if there is one thing they could do about hunger individually. Invite them to set a goal. (See pages 31-33 for Goal Setting.)

Thanksgiving Celebration

Thank List

(Time required: approximately 20-30 minutes)

1. Give these instructions to the group: "Think about positive things that have happened to you or are a part of your life today. Then list ten things you are thankful for." (Allow 5-10 minutes.)

2. Have participants look at their lists and ask that they do the following:

- — Star the three you are most thankful for.
- — Put an F by those things that involved your family.
- — Put a G by those things that involved your relationship with God in some direct way.
- — Put an O by the things that involved people outside your family.
- — Put an M by the things that largely involved money.

3. Ask participants to look over their completed Thank Lists and consider what they learned about the things they are thankful for.

4. Divide the total group into smaller groups of 4 people. Have them talk about their three starred items, those for which they are most thankful. Ask:

- — What feelings do you have as you look over your list? Share them.
- — Together can you think of a way to celebrate your thankfulness?

Three Levels of Learning

Give Me the Facts

Bible passages to read:

Two young persons named David and Jonathan had a close friendship. Read about them in 1 Samuel 20 and 1 Samuel 23:15-18, ". . . he loved him as he loved his own soul. And Jonathan went to David . . . and strengthened his hand in God."

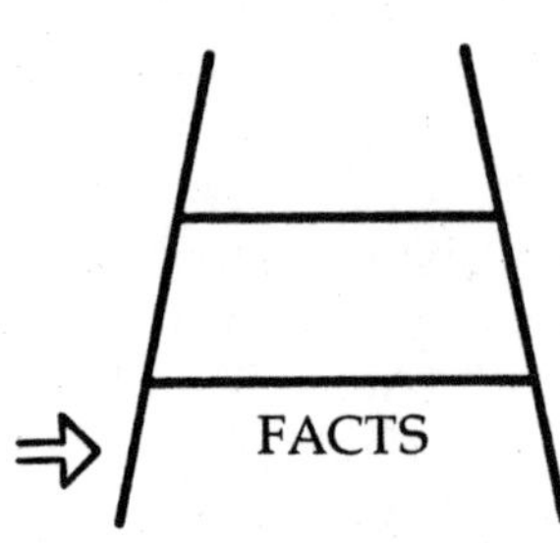

Naomi and Ruth, Naomi's daughter-in-law, had a beautiful relationship. See Ruth 1:16-17, ". . . entreat me not to leave you . . . where you go I will go. . . ."

Jesus was comfortable with Mary, Martha, and Lazarus at their home in Bethany. He often stayed with them. One gets the feeling that each of them would be at home with the other(s). See Luke 10:38-42; John 11:1-44; and John 12:1-8.

What's the Idea?

Concepts to explore:

— What are the key aspects behind each of these friendships?
— Why are friendships important?
— What is meant by "Friendship is a gift"?

What's In It for Me?

Valuing suggestions:

— Think of a person whose friendship has meant a lot to you. List that person's three or four most important characteristics which have enriched your relationship.
— In the total group, make a composite list on the chalkboard of all the personal qualities mentioned.
— To think about individually:

Which qualities do you possess?
Which would you like to strengthen, or add?
Which characteristics would you value in a mate? Do you have those same qualities?
Is there a specific goal you might set for your own growth in one or more of the desirable qualities?

Resources from the Bible (for optional use)

Relationships

Matthew 5, 6, 7	Sermon on the Mount
Matthew 5:1-12	The Beatitudes
Matthew 7:12	The Golden Rule
Matthew 22:34-40	The Great Commandments
Luke 10:29-37	Parable of the Good Samaritan
John 15:12	Love one another.
Proverbs 17:17	A friend loves at all times.
Romans 12:9-21	Love everyone, including enemies.
Romans 14	On judging others. Supporting one another.
1 Corinthians 13	". . . and the greatest of these is love."
Hebrews 13	Discipline in the Christian life.
1 Corinthians 12	Working together as one body.
1 John 3, 4	The love of God.
1 Thessalonians 5:11	"So give encouragement to each other. . .
Ephesians 6:5-9	Employer-worker relationships.
Malachi 3:5	
Ephesians 2:14	Christ brings people of different values together.
Philippians 4:8	". . . fill your minds with. . . ."
Galatians 6:1-5	Bearing one another's burdens.

Taking a Stand and Being Responsible

Genesis 4:1-9	Brother's keeper?
Jeremiah 26	A faithful prophet risks death.
1 Corinthians 10:24	Seek your neighbor's good.
1 John 3:17-24	Responding to a brother in need.
Daniel 1-6	Daniel took a stand.
Acts 6:8-15; 7:1-60	Stephen the martyr.
Acts, especially 4:1-22; 5:27-33; 12:1-19; 16:16-40 18:1-11; 22:1-27:44	Peter and Paul, courageous apostles.

Behavior and Forgiveness

1 Corinthians 6	The body is God's temple.
Romans 13:8-14	Love one another.
Galatians 5	Christian freedom.
1 John 2:9-10	Hate and love.
Psalm 51	David's cry for forgiveness.
1 John 1:9	Confession and forgiveness.
Luke 15:11-24	A forgiving father.
Matthew 5:21-26	Reconciliation comes first.
Matthew 6:14-15	If you forgive others. . . .
Matthew 18:23-35	Parable of the unforgiving servant.
Jeremiah 31:34	God forgives and forgets.

Social Issues

Genesis 1	"And God saw that it was good. . . ."
Genesis 1:26-28; 2:15	Care for the earth.
Job 38:4-7	"The morning stars sang together. . . ."
Psalm 33:6-9	The word of the Lord and Creation.
Psalm 19	"The heavens are telling. . . ."
Romans 8:19-21	Creation will be set free.
Revelation 21:1	". . . a new heaven and a new earth."
Revelation 22:1-2	". . . for the healing of the nations."
1 Peter 2:13-17; Romans 13:1-7; Luke 12:11-12; 20:24-25	Attitudes toward civil authority.
Acts 5:27-29	"Obey God rather than men."
Isaiah 10:1-3	Injustice condemned.
Isaiah 58:6-7	A true fast: free the oppressed, share with the hungry and homeless.
Amos 5:21-24	". . . but let justice roll down like waters."
Micah 6:8	". . . justice . . . kindness . . . and walk humbly."
Galatians 3:26-28	". . . neither Jew nor Greek, neither slave nor free, neither male nor female . . . all one in Christ Jesus."

Prayer:

Lord, I hear you say, "Love your neighbor as yourself." I find it easy to love my friends and am grateful for each one of them. I need them; they are important to me. But I'm beginning to find out who my neighbor really is — the hungry, the lonely, the oppressed. There are so many in need. I want to love them — not just in word, but by doing something for them.

I need your courage and encouragement. Lord, teach me to accept your forgiveness in my own life. And help me to love myself so that I can reach out to others, loving them more fully and experiencing the joy of giving.

Valuing the Old and the New

People today are constantly challenged to examine tradition and change as these affect their own lives, their family life, and the life of the Church.

Christianity offers many resources which apply to our examination of the new and the old. And we think that the Christian faith is always a present reality, oriented to the past, the present, and the future.

Tradition and change can work side by side in harmony, or they can produce discord and divisiveness. Deep feelings are often involved as we examine our opinions, attitudes, beliefs, and values. Thus, it is most helpful if these exercises can be used in a climate of mutual respect, acceptance, understanding and love.

Before using this chapter, please review the chapter on leadership.

Voting

Instructions: Pages 20-21 give purpose and procedure for the Voting exercise.

Participants vote in the following manner:

Agree? (Raise hand.)
Strongly agree? (Wave hand.)
Disagree? (Thumb down.)
Strongly disagree? (Shake thumb.)
Pass? (Fold arms across chest.)

General Voting Questions on Old and New

How many of you agree with this statement?
— Change is O.K. if it doesn't happen too fast.
— The present is influenced by the past.

— Change just happens, and you have little or no control over it.
— Change is a fact of life—but a regrettable fact.
— Most people nowadays want too much change.
— The "good old days" were the best.
— Tradition is important, but change is important too.
— Change provides a chance for growth or renewal.
— It is practically impossible for a person to grow and change without having some feelings of discomfort.

How many of you:
— feel there's too much change in your life right now?
— have experienced growth through change in the last two years?
— have found by experience that old ways of doing things are usually better than new ways?
— have changed at least one traditional way of doing something in the past year?
— have changed jobs within the last year?
— think changing jobs is a risk?
— were nervous about moving from the lower grades to junior high or senior high?
— have changed an important belief within the last five years?
— have found it upsetting to move to a new place?
— have found it upsetting to try something new?
— have found change to be challenging?
— think God is active in change?

The Church and Change

How many of you:
— think people will support only that which they are a part of?
— think the Church should concern itself with all the current issues of society?
— think the Church has a great chance today to lead people into life-styles which are exciting and meaningful?
— think your own church is moving closer to the characteristics of the early Church?
— think there are many possible forms of church life in modern society?

— think most churches need to spend some time in squabbling and in argument?

How many of you agree with this statement?
— A good church-school teacher helps children think for themselves.
— Good church-school teachers should not try to make the pupil think and believe as they do.
— There is little hope for the Church's future unless pastors and congregations begin to communicate more.
— In thirty years your church body will unhesitatingly accept women as members of the clergy.
— A woman should be seriously considered as a senior pastor the next time your church has an opening.
— The bureaucracy of the Church often keeps people from the true Gospel and its meaning.
— If Jesus were a member of your church today, he would fit into your church life.
— The Christian church should encourage and support its traditions.
— Although many other things change, the Church should be the same yesterday, today, and forever.
— There is a sense of urgency to proclaim the Gospel in the Church today.
— Business organizations operate more efficiently than the Church.
— The Church doesn't set high enough standards for Christians today.
— The Church is a community of both saints and sinners.
— Most Christians do not really study the Bible and think through their faith.
— Most church members have lost the thrill of learning about their religion.
— The world sets the agenda for the Church.
— The Church sometimes establishes certain doctrines and practices which God never intended.
— A salesclerk can be carrying on a ministry as important as that of a pastor of a church.

Personal Reactions To Church

How many of you:
— feel protected in church?
— like stained-glass windows?
— like to pray in unison in church?
— sometimes fall asleep in church?
— wish your parents had accompanied you to church as a child?
— would want your own children to have the same kind of church life you had as a youngster?
— think most churches operate in a spirit of peace, love, and light?
— think that the local parish is an impersonal place?
— would be upset if organized religion did not exist?

Worship

How many of you agree with this statement?
— Worship can happen while you study.
— Worship can happen while you work.
— The Sunday morning service is really the only place of worship.
— Most people prefer simple hymns to chorales.
— The liturgy as we usually practice it is not meaningful.
— Group feedback after sermons would be helpful.
— Some of our worship meetings should be held in private homes.

How many of you:
— think your church listens when young people want to try something new?
— would like to be more involved in Sunday worship?
— would like new forms of worship?
— think the prayers in worship services are too long?
— wish the prayers in your church worship service were more personal?
— think your church's way of praying helps to create a worshipful atmosphere?
— can't relate to the prayers at Sunday worship?

— usually experience a feeling of joy in your worship services?
— think there needs to be a stronger relationship between church worship service and real life?
— habitually think of "other things" during the Sunday morning sermon?
— think that the effectiveness of a sermon depends primarily on the listener?
— cannot easily accept new forms in church worship such as contemporary music, dance, drama?
— feel uncomfortable with your present liturgy?
— would like to see contemporary worship used as an alternative form of worship?
— would like more hymn singing?
— prefer the old hymns?
— wish there were a wider variety of hymns sung during services?
— wish you knew more about the meaning behind Church symbols?

Holy Communion

How many of you agree with this statement?
— Before receiving Communion, a person should be certain of his or her worthiness.
— Everyone should be invited to receive Holy Communion.
— Children who have not completed confirmation should not be allowed to participate in Holy Communion.
— Only members of a congregation should be allowed to receive Communion with the congregation.
— Children should be encouraged to accompany their families to Communion and receive a blessing even if they do not receive the bread and wine.
— Lay people should share in distributing the bread and wine.
— The Communion liturgy should be very formal.
— The common cup should not be used.
— Communion is a joy-filled experience.

Ranking

Instructions: Pages 21-22 give purpose and procedure for the Ranking exercise.

Participants rank all items in order of preference or priority (1 = most important; 2 = next most important, etc.).

General Rankings on Old and New

If you were stranded alone on a deserted island, which would you rather have along?
_____ the New Testament
_____ the Old Testament
_____ an anthology of great literature
_____ an encyclopedia

Which is most effective in imparting values?
_____ school
_____ family
_____ religious institutions
_____ world leaders

Which most often happens when you experience change?
_____ I'm stimulated to risk new things.
_____ I feel more hopeful.
_____ I ask more questions.

For life together in our congregation, it is most important:
_____ to know each other as individuals.
_____ to know God and his Word.
_____ to know and be responsive to the needs of society.

How involved should your church be in the life of the outside community? Rank each group separately.
_____ somewhat involved
_____ heavily involved
_____ slightly or not at all involved

_____ The Church should keep a balance between evangelism and community building.
_____ The Church's first emphasis should be on evangelism.
_____ The Church's first emphasis should be on community building.
_____ The Church's first duty is to be a servant to others.

Which would most likely happen in your church?
_____ A black family would be welcomed as visitors.
_____ A black family would be invited to join.
_____ A black family would be ignored.

What changes are most needed in your church?
_____ changes in facilities
_____ changes in worship service
_____ changes in education programs
_____ changes in methods of community outreach

If Jesus looked at your church program, which do you think he would find most nearly fulfilling his goals for the church? (Rank each group of three.)
_____ church school
_____ youth groups
_____ music

_____ money-raising efforts for your own parish
_____ giving to missions
_____ membership pledges

_____ council meetings
_____ women's groups
_____ Sunday worship

Holy Communion

For whom should Communion be available?
_____ all those baptized
_____ only those baptized and confirmed
_____ anyone above ten years of age who is a believer

How often should your congregation receive Holy Communion?

_____ weekly
_____ monthly
_____ every three months
_____ oftener than weekly

How long should confirmation preparation last?

_____ one year
_____ two years
_____ three years

Church Worship

Which is of most importance to you in a worship service?

_____ experiencing a positive feeling
_____ being alone with God
_____ reaffirming faith in God
_____ feeling kinship with others

Which is the most important part of a worship experience for you?

_____ sermon
_____ music
_____ people

Which type of sermon is most effective at a morning worship?

_____ One that challenges the intellect.
_____ One that preaches the Gospel.
_____ One that challenges me to reach out to others.

In sermons, which should be emphasized most?

_____ repentance
_____ Church teachings
_____ forgiveness

Which is closest to your meaning of worship?
_____ sharing
_____ thanking
_____ praising
_____ listening

Which hymn do you prefer? (Rank each group of three.)
_____ "One in the Spirit" ("They'll Know We Are Christians By Our Love")
_____ "A Mighty Fortress"
_____ "What a Friend We Have in Jesus"

_____ "Mine Eyes Have Seen the Glory" ("Battle Hymn of the Republic")
_____ "Beautiful Savior"
_____ "Jesus Loves Me, This I Know"

_____ "Kumbaya"
_____ "Joy to the World"
_____ "In the Garden"

Which season of the Church year do you relate to most?
_____ Advent
_____ Christmas
_____ Lent
_____ Easter
_____ Pentecost

Which do you think is the most appropriate musical instrument for worship?
_____ guitar
_____ organ
_____ violin
_____ piano

Which kind of setting do you prefer for worship?
_____ church
_____ nature
_____ home

Continuum

Instructions: Pages 22-23 give purpose and procedure for the Continuum exercise.

Participants choose that place on the continuum, between two opposite extremes, which most closely represents their personal viewpoint.

General Continuum Exercises

Who should be members of a church council?

Youngsters — the majority of the council should be young people, including teenagers. Older adults inhibit change. The Church needs the idealism and energy of youth.	Oldsters — only older members should be allowed on the council. The Church needs their experience and maturity. Young people are too impulsive — they want to change everything.

Which best enhances one's own spiritual quest?

Go it alone — a person today needs more time alone, in quiet meditation, to reflect on his or her spirituality.	Be with others — people today need more corporate life, freed *for* each other and freed *from* self-isolation, for mutual love and caring.

How important are church facilities to the Christian life?

Our church should be large and beautiful to attract people. People want to feel reverence and awe. And our learning facilities should accommodate many children and young adults.	We don't need a building at all. There's no need to be enclosed to worship. We should seek out people and minister to them wherever they are.

How do you feel about sharing leadership in a church?

Enlarge the church staff and give them complete responsibility for all decisions. We want our church to run smoothly and efficiently.	Every lay person should be involved in all aspects of church life. Then we won't need a staff. We can handle everything ourselves, including the sermons.

How can people nurture their own Christian lives?

Only through worship, Bible study, and church-related activities.	Only through involvement with the many people "out there" who haven't yet been reached.

Should the national Church body take a stand on social issues?

Absolutely, on each and every issue! We should be united, for an individual's stand is meaningless.	Absolutely not! Never! Stands on social issues are personal. The Church can't possibly represent all its members.

How do you relate to others at worship service?

I stay apart. Worship is a private experience and involves just God and me.

I get together with others. An important part of worship is mingling with others and making people feel welcome.

Either / Or

Instructions: Pages 23-24 give purpose and procedure for the Either / Or exercise.

Participants select between two choices that option with which they most closely identify.

General Either/Or Exercises

With which do you more closely identify?

It is safe. / It is right.
individual spiritual growth / social change
social action / evangelism
Life is a journey. / Life is a destination.
Change is challenging. / Change is threatening.
hearing or reading theology / experiencing theology
future / present
satisfaction with the present / hope for the future

Which change is more difficult to adjust to?

moving to a new city / taking a new job
getting married / having children
separation from family / losing a job
a new school / a new house
a new church / new neighbors
a new pastor / new liturgy
a new form of worship / a new biblical interpretation
breaking a tradition / breaking a habit

Which do you prefer?
contemporary worship / traditional worship
chorales / Gospel hymns
group prayer / individual prayer
worship in church / worship in nature
worship in church / worship at home
singing in the choir / teaching Sunday school
sermons / group Bible study
piano music / organ music
working with youth / working with the elderly
church wedding / home wedding
baptism during church / baptism after church
common cup for Communion / individual cups
children at services / separate worship for children
colorful banners/stained glass windows
formal liturgy / folk liturgy

Which is happening to the Church today?
It is breaking down. / It is breaking open.

Which is Holy Communion more like?
a fellowship dinner / lunch with a friend
celebrating / meditating
joyful / solemn

Regarding church attendance for confirmands, which is best?
required attendance / voluntary attendance

Which is worship more like?
ministering to others / our inward response to God

Listening

Instructions: Pages 25-26 give purpose and procedure for the Listening exercise.

Participants respond to a stimulus statement in groups of three. Each person is "on focus" for five minutes.

The Church and Change

Adele said: "We should appreciate the old in the Christian Church — there's so much good in it. Many traditions have taken centuries to develop and have stood the test of time. Many people find their roots in such traditions. Traditions give meaning to their Christian experience. Too many people today want change just for change's sake. Let's hold on to our good, old ways."

Mary Jane wrote to a friend, "Fear seems to dominate most of a young person's church life. The Ten Commandments always come first, with all of the 'Thou shalt not's.' That's why the Church is turning kids off. That's why you don't see kids around after the ninth or tenth grade."

When Larry read Mark 2:21-22 (new wineskins), he interpreted it to mean: "Staying young in mind is of utmost importance. You've got to be able to change and adapt. Creating something new is really necessary, because the old can always be improved. You shouldn't patch a sinking ship — let it sink and build a new one."

Congregational Life

Eric, a high school sophomore, said: "In most of the churches in our community, people don't really care about one another. They don't even get acquainted — only a lot of surface stuff. Our worship would draw us closer together if it provided feeling-level experiences, not just an intellectual trip. And we should have more group participation in deciding what kinds of church services to have and how to carry them out."

Tillie gave this pitch to the Membership Committee of her church: "The church is not requiring enough of its members. Members should have to tithe; to attend church regularly; to serve in some capacity; to devote more of their time to the church. After all, Jesus said, 'If any man would come after me, let him deny himself and take up his cross and follow me.' If people can't measure up to those standards, they shouldn't be allowed to keep their church membership."

The Church and the Community at Large

Abraham Lincoln once said, "The only assurance of our nation's safety is to lay our foundations in morality and religion." More recently a businesswoman said to her friend, "Religious institutions are no longer as influential as they once were, and their lack of influence has contributed to a decline in our moral standards. We need to recover the kind of religion our predecessors practiced. Apparently the separation of Church and state was a mistake. Church and government should unite to raise our moral standards. We've got to reverse the present trend before it's too late."

Church council members Elmer and Dan were talking about new directions for the Church's mission program. Elmer said, "The essential work of the Church of Jesus Christ is the propagation of the Gospel truth. The fundamental job of Christians is to reach as many people as possible. We've already spent much money and time on unbelievers in this community, but few have been responsive. Now we should broaden our mission effort — like that verse says — 'go into all the world.' Churches should greatly increase their budgets to support mission work in countries where people haven't even had a chance to hear the Word of God."

Worship

Greg said, "True worship needs to include the great prayers of the Church, written or spoken, in language that is dignified. The Sunday service music should be worshipful and bring the congregation closer to God. I like guitar music and informal prayers at home, but they have no place in a Sunday service, because they don't create an atmosphere for religious worship."

Sherrie said, "A friend of mine thinks that people are the most important part of attending church. She loves to be with others, singing and praying and enjoying their fellowship. But you can be with other people at home, at work, in the neighborhood — every place. At church you should concentrate on God and on your response to him. It's a time of getting closer to God in order to know him better. I attend church because God is there — not because people are there."

Interviewing

Instructions: Pages 28-31 give purpose and procedure for the Interviewing exercise.

A volunteer from among the participants is interviewed before the group.

Identify from your group a person who is either more traditional (likes things as they are; prefers things not to change), or a person who is more contemporary (likes new ways of doing things; finds change exciting).

Select appropriate questions from page 30. In addition, you might want to consider these questions:

— How long have you attended church here?
— What are some activities you have enjoyed or been involved in?
— Do you think this church has changed since you have been here? How would you describe the changes?
— What is one good thing about tradition?
— What is one good thing about change?
— Can you describe the kind of worship service you enjoy most?
— What does worship mean to you?
— Some people say that the old is better than the new; others say the new is better than the old. What do you think?
— Weddings take various forms these days. Do you prefer any particular type or format?
— Do you have any other thoughts about change that I haven't asked you?

In addition to members of your group, you may wish to interview one or more of the following:

— a person who has recently made a decision to enter a new occupation.
— a youth who has recently been confirmed.
— your pastor, asking some questions about the new and the old.
— a college student.
— an elderly person who is active in the congregation.
— a youth from a family whose work requires that they move frequently.
— a person who works in an area of specialty that is constantly changing.
— a career counselor who helps other people deal with change.

— a person who has made a major change in some area of life.
— a new convert to the Christian faith.
— your parents, using the form on page 230.

Miscellaneous Exercises

The remaining exercises in this section are one of a kind. The purpose of each is to help participants further examine what they believe and value about the new and old in the Christian church. Procedures are given for each.

Reaching Out

1. Write this list on a chalkboard or large sheet of paper.

education	ethnic minorities
health	celebrations
food	economics
energy	family
work	community
prisons	housing
women	other

2. Have participants copy the list and check any items that they think your church should be more concerned about.
3. Ask participants to rank in order of importance those three items your church should be most concerned about.
4. Have participants share their responses in groups of four.

When You Were My Age Interview

"When I was your age . . ." always seems to be followed by a lecture. This exercise invites youth to question adults, beginning with "When you were my age . . .," to get in touch with the past and to find out what was important to adults when they were younger.

1. Duplicate the form on the next page and provide a copy for each participant.

2. Have participants interview one or both parents, grandparents, or another adult, jotting responses on the form.

3. Ask participants to bring their completed form to the next session.

4. At the next session have participants review the responses made to their questions. Give these instructions: "From what you've learned in your interviews, write a short paragraph about each person you interviewed, summarizing what seemed to be most important to them when they were your age.

Option: Have participants share their learnings in small groups or in the total group.

When You Were My Age

What was your favorite thing to do after school?
What kind of house did you live in?
What kind of games did you play?
Did you have a pet? What?
What did you like to eat?
What scary experience did you have?
What was the most important thing you owned?
What did you like to daydream about?
What worried you most?
Did you have a favorite book? Which one?
Where did you go when you wanted to be alone?
What fun things did you do with your family?
Did you fight with your sister or brother?
Who was your best friend?
What did you do together?
What person influenced you most?
When you were in trouble, who helped you?

1st Person	2nd Person

Church Future

1. Write the following Ranking exercise on the board.

For the future of the Christian Church, it is most important that its members:

_____ accept responsibility for justice and peace.
_____ seek healing and creative encounter.
_____ explore new ways of witness to Christ.
_____ release the full potential in every person.
_____ grow in personal faith and discipline in commitment to the faith.

2. Have participants gather in groups of 4 and consider their local church — its location, facilities, staff, and members — in terms of the items listed. Ask which items are already important, active ingredients in the life of their church.
3. Have each group member rank the items in terms of the needs of their local church. Then have each group reach a consensus on the two most important needs.
4. When the groups have reached a consensus, have them examine the two items and brainstorm ways to fill those needs. (Page 27 gives the procedure for brainstorming.)
5. Have each group decide which are the best three solutions and rank those three. Ask: "Do you see one first step toward a goal you might set? A step that is realistic, believable, and achievable? What is it and how might you accomplish it? How about setting an action goal?" (Page 32 gives procedure for Goal Setting.)

Examining Beliefs

1. Duplicate the following page and pass out copies to each participant.
2. Have individuals rank the items given.
3. When participants have completed their rankings, have them find partners and share their rankings and reasons for their rankings.

Optional sharing: Participants could react to these three items in groups of 3, following the procedures for the Listening exercise. (See pages 25-26)

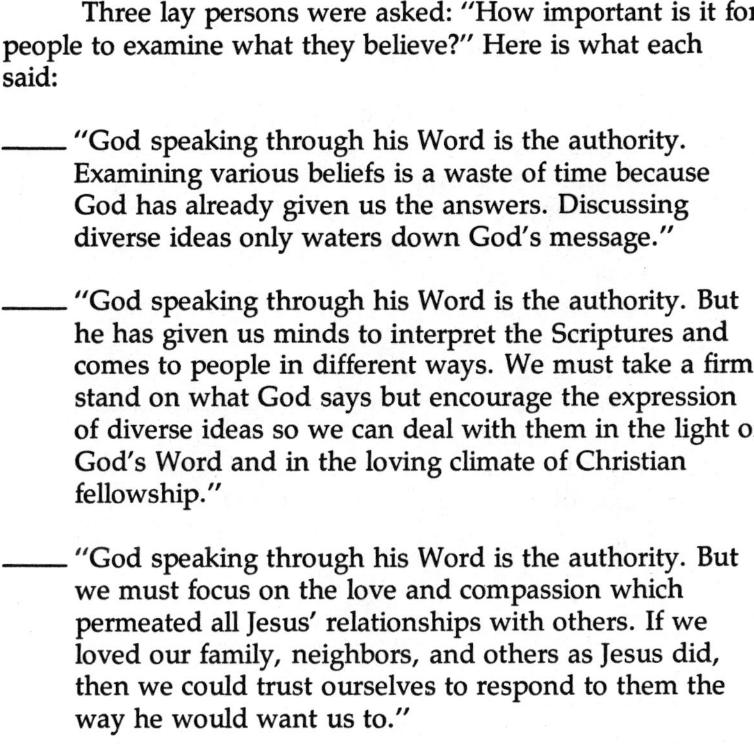

Three lay persons were asked: "How important is it for people to examine what they believe?" Here is what each said:

____ "God speaking through his Word is the authority. Examining various beliefs is a waste of time because God has already given us the answers. Discussing diverse ideas only waters down God's message."

____ "God speaking through his Word is the authority. But he has given us minds to interpret the Scriptures and comes to people in different ways. We must take a firm stand on what God says but encourage the expression of diverse ideas so we can deal with them in the light of God's Word and in the loving climate of Christian fellowship."

____ "God speaking through his Word is the authority. But we must focus on the love and compassion which permeated all Jesus' relationships with others. If we loved our family, neighbors, and others as Jesus did, then we could trust ourselves to respond to them the way he would want us to."

Church Search

1. Duplicate the following page and pass out copies to each participant.
2. Have individuals rank the items from most to least attractive to them as prospective church members.
3. When rankings are completed, have participants gather in groups of three and give these instructions:

- — Each person share your ranking, without giving reasons at this point.
- — Now talk about some of the reasons behind your choices.
- — What feelings did you experience?
- — What are important attitudes, opinions, beliefs, and values behind your rankings?
- — Would you have preferred a fourth type of church? Can you describe it to your group?

You have just moved into a new city with your family. You've boiled your choice of churches down to three which are quite similar in membership and size. They appear to be equally committed to the Gospel, and each sees a strong congregational life as part of its mission. The respective pastors make these statements to you:

____ Pastor A: "We want to grow quickly and respond to the needs of youth and young adults. Thus our worship services are contemporary, and changes often occur. You wouldn't recognize this place two years ago."

____ Pastor B: "We've tried different kinds of services, but considerable strife occurred when we tried to change things too much. Consequently, our church is very much like it was twenty years ago. We plan to keep it that way, for we've learned that what we have now is the most effective."

____ Pastor C: "Our church is becoming a house church. We don't have many meetings in our church. In fact, we're thinking of selling it. Our council and congregation would like to use most of the money for missions — both abroad and in our city. I plan to coordinate this program so that most of our fellowship and worship will be done in our members' homes."

Dimensions of the Christian Church

1. Write the word *proclamation* on a large piece of paper. Write *faith* on another, *fellowship* on a third, and *service* on a fourth.
2. Post the sheets of paper, one in each corner of the room.
3. Have participants gather in the middle of the room and give these instructions: "In a moment you will be choosing, from four interwoven dimensions of the Christian church, the one you think the Church should be most concerned about. You will see that a key word is posted in each corner of the room. When you have made your choice, please move to that corner. Here are the four interwoven dimensions:

— to proclaim God's message to people.
— to encourage a personal faith centered in Christ.
— to encourage fellowship in the life of the Holy Spirit.
— to be of service to the Christian community and to the larger human community.

"This might be a difficult choice since all of these may be important to you. But if you were to choose one, which would it be?" (Repeat the four items if necessary.)
4. Allow time for discussion.

Church Goals

One church council used this four-corner Voting exercise to begin thinking about its own goals. (See procedures 1-8 on page 200. They were asked if they agreed with the following statements:

— It's hard to make your true feelings known in most church groups and church activities.
— Concern for family programs in a church means that "singles" are ignored.
— Ours is a warm, friendly church.
— Church provides something for everyone if people search it out.
— Sunday morning coffee is a positive factor in promoting fellowship at our church.
— Our church needs more small groups within it, to meet individual needs.
— New members at our church are integrated quite readily into the mainstream of church life.
— There are lots of cliques at our church.
— Most people at our church go out of their way to make a new member feel welcome.

— On Sundays we should have one traditional service and one contemporary service.
— Youth should be encouraged to participate regularly in activities such as ushering and adult Bible study groups.
— Our church provides ample intellectual challenge for its members.
— Our church needs more fellowship suppers.

The Auction Barn

1. Duplicate the Auction Barn Form on the next pages. Pass out a copy to each participant.
2. Give these instructions: "Each of you represents a different church. You will have $4,000 with which to bid on the items you feel are most important for you and your fellow church members. You will be bidding competitively with each other. You will now have about five minutes to study the items and decide which ones you value most. Allot portions of the $4,000 and record the amounts in Column 1."
3. After 5 minutes, begin the auction. Go through the items one by one and award each to the highest bidder. Ask each person to keep track of the items he or she bid on, which ones he or she won, and the amount of money remaining after he or she won a bid. Nobody can spend more than $4,000. Persons failing to bid successfully on an item can reallocate their funds in Column 2 for bids on other items.
4. After the auction is completed, have participants gather in groups of 4-6 and share:
 — the items on which you made your two highest original bids and your reasons.
 — the values that lie behind these choices.
5. Give these instructions to the entire group:
 — Individuals, share your learnings by completing one of these sentence beginnings:
  I learned . . . I wonder . . .
  I think . . . I was surprised . . .
 — Small groups, what values predominated in each of your groups? What issues were raised that you would like the total group to know about?
 — Assembly, is there an appropriate follow-up? Any next steps? (Invite suggestions.)

Auction Barn Form

1 Unlimited church budget for 3 years.
2 Ability of your church council to make only wise decisions for the next 5 years.
3 Assurance that the Christian faith is active in the lives of people in your community.
4 An opportunity to donate $100,000 to foreign mission programs.
5 A magic formula which would make everyone responsive to God's Word.
6 Complete trust within your congregation.
7 Double your church staff.
8 A beautiful, functional church complete with the finest pipe organ, debt free.
9 Absolute wisdom for your decision-makers.
10 A perfect personal relationship for yourself with God.
11 Assurance that you will fully know the meaning of life.
12 A membership which is committed to giving ten percent of all gross income.
13 An openness and honesty formula with a lifetime effect for everyone.
14 Assurance that you will be personally involved in the church in ways that give you complete satisfaction in service.
15 The opportunity to spend a full month with the religious figure of your choice — anyone throughout history.
16 Listen-ears which enable all to hear each other's thoughts and feelings.
17 The ability to be the most effective Christian in your personal outreach.
18 Absolute assurance that you will have eternal life with God.

Amount You Originally Budgeted	Your Revised Bid	Items You Won

Tornado

This exercise gives participants an opportunity to examine the entire life of their church, in the event that it were to be rebuilt. (Time required: at least an hour is recommended, and some groups may need considerably more time)

1. Have participants gather in groups of 6-8 prior to instructions.

2. Present this situation:

"Your church congregation has recently received two shocks. First, you are without a pastor, because he resigned to accept a call at another church. Then last month a tornado completely destroyed the church building, the only structure owned by the congregation. Insurance coverage paid off the mortgage. Five hundred people remain on the membership rolls.

"Your national church body has decided to fund your congregation as a three-year pilot project to begin a program from scratch. They have made it clear that all decisions are to be made by a laypersons' committee; they insist that this be a grass-roots effort, with all responsibility and authority kept at the local level. Their only mandate is that whatever you develop must promote, for you and your fellow parishioners, growth in the Christian life. Their gift is $600,000 over a three-year period ($200,000 each year). Thus you are able to commit $200,000 for the current year.

"You are assembled today to begin your work. Your group is the committee. You have the opportunity for a completely fresh start, scrapping part or all of the past if you wish. All facets of church life need to be considered — goals, staffing, physical structures, program, etc. Your committee's task is to begin developing plans for this new venture, in your own way. Designate one person to keep careful notes on all specific decisions made by your group."

3. Allow 30-40 minutes for small-group discussion and decision making. Challenge individuals to practice really listening to one another, hearing everyone's ideas and feelings.

4. Ask the total assembly to share their decisions, one group at a time. Then have them consider:

— Are there any common threads that run through the various group decisions?
— What dominant values underlie the decisions?
— What did your discussions tell you about where your own church is right now?
— What are some of the strengths in your present program? (Do you wish to reaffirm and celebrate these in any ways?)
— Are there some areas which need modifying, changing, adding to?
— Do the words of Christ give you any ideas, any directions?

5. Have small groups reassemble and consider the following:

— What might be the priority area for possible change?
— What available resources can help bring about that change? (Have groups list the available resources.)
— Are there any specific actions to take — as individuals, small group, total assembly, or congregation? (Have groups list them.)
— Who will take responsibility for the first step?

6. Give the total assembly these instructions: "Without lengthy discussion, quickly share personal thoughts, feelings, observations, decisions, or actions to be taken."

7. *Optional:* Pass out copies of the Telegram Form on the next page and ask each participant to write a telegram urging an individual or group to take a specific action. Have volunteers read their telegrams to the group.

8. Give the group these questions to ponder on the way home:

— Think about your personal involvement during this entire exercise. What did you learn about yourself? What did you learn about how you interact with others? Did you listen? Were you listened to? How can the Church best encourage input from people like you?

T E L E G R A M

To:

Message:

____

(signed)

Mining for Gold

This exercise builds on the positive aspects of one's church-life experience and can lead to action that will strengthen and enhance it. (Time required: 25-35 minutes)

1. Have participants list five things in church life that bring them satisfaction or happiness and circle the two main ones.
2. Now have them list three things in church life that cause them some concern and circle the main one.
3. Ask participants to gather in groups of 4 and share their lists, considering the following from the first list:
- — the important things your church has given your group members.
- — ways you can acknowledge, give thanks, or celebrate these.

4. Then give the group these instructions: "Using your second list, identify any common concerns within your group. Decide which main concern people like yourselves could conceivably do something about. Brainstorm possible solutions." (Page 27 gives the procedure for brainstorming.)
5. Have groups reach a consensus on the best possible solution. Invite them to set a goal within their group and draw up a contract to achieve that goal. (Pages 31-33 give the procedure for Goal Setting.)

Church Cup

This exercise helps participants think about their own church — what it is now and how it might be changed. You will need a Styrofoam cup and a pencil for each group of 5 or 6 people. (Time required: 15 minutes)

1. Ask participants to gather in small groups of 5 or 6 people.
2. Give each group one cup and one sharp pencil. Explain: "Let this cup represent your church. Without talking, do anything you wish with the cup to express your feelings on what your church should be. What values do you envision as most important for your church? Represent these nonverbally in your own way — drawing on the cup, filling it, writing on

it, puncturing it. The beginning person takes a minute or two to respond, then passes the cup to the next person. Repeat until each has had a turn."

3. Have participants take turns within their groups, explaining how they changed the cup and what that change represents. Then allow time for small-group discussion.

4. Reassemble the entire group and invite participants to share meaningful happenings, insights, observations. Encourage free expression regarding unmet needs of your church and possible new directions.

Thank-You Telegram

1. Reproduce the form on page 242, and provide each participant with a copy.

2. Give these instructions: "Think about your church. (Pause.) Then think about positive experiences in your church life. Think of a person who has helped you deal with the meaning of your life or who has enriched your church experience. Send that person a Thank-You Telegram, using fifteen words or less. If you like, send more than one telegram."

3. Allow 4-5 minutes. Encourage volunteers to read their telegrams to the entire group.

Celebrating the Old and the New

Remembering the Old Year and Anticipating the New

The Church values celebration; just note the many seasons of the year it celebrates — Advent, Christmas, Easter, Pentecost, among others. The New Year is important too, and celebrating it suggests looking to the future and reflecting on the past. This exercise provides participants with a chance to examine the important things about the old year. (Time required: 20-25 minutes)

1. List the following items on newsprint or chalkboard. Allow time for individuals to work quietly and alone, completing each item.

— things I like most to remember about last year
— a positive change in me during the old year

— one new thing I'd like to change for the new year
— a hope for the new year
— my goal during the next year

2. When participants have completed their lists, ask them to consider the following questions: "Do any of the things you listed relate to your religious faith? If so, in what way? How has your faith changed over the past year?"
3. Introduce Goal Setting. (Pages 31-33 give procedures.) Challenge individuals to set a goal for themselves, write it down, and sign it.
4. Ask each participant to find a partner and take ten minutes to share their thoughts and goals.

Three Levels of Learning

Give Me the Facts!

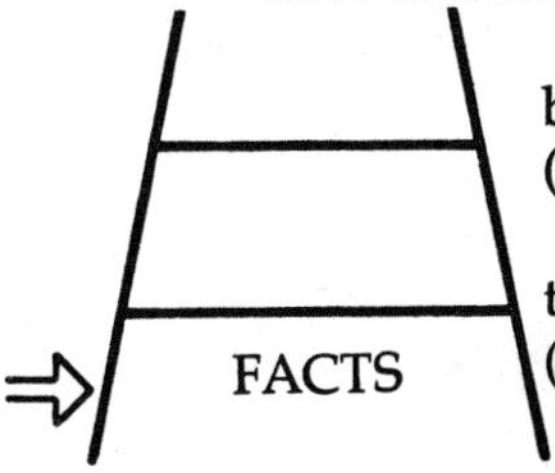

FACTS

God called *Abraham* to pack his belongings and go to another country. (Genesis 11:31-32 and 12:1-9)

Christ called *Matthew* to leave his job as tax collector and said, "Follow me!" (Matthew 9:9-13 and Luke 5:27-32)

Christ confronted *Paul* in a vision and called him to change his ways. (Acts 9:1-22)

Questions to answer:
— Where did Abraham's family come from?
— What was his response to God's command and promise?
— What effect did Abraham's obedience to God's call have on him and on others? (Hebrews 11:8-19)
— By what name was Matthew also called?
— What was Matthew's response to Jesus' call?
— What special thing did Matthew do for Jesus?
— How had Paul been treating the disciples and Christians?
— What happened on the road to Damascus?
— How did Paul respond?
— Describe the events that followed. Who were the people involved?
— What was the result of the change in Paul's life?

What's the Idea?

Concepts to explore:

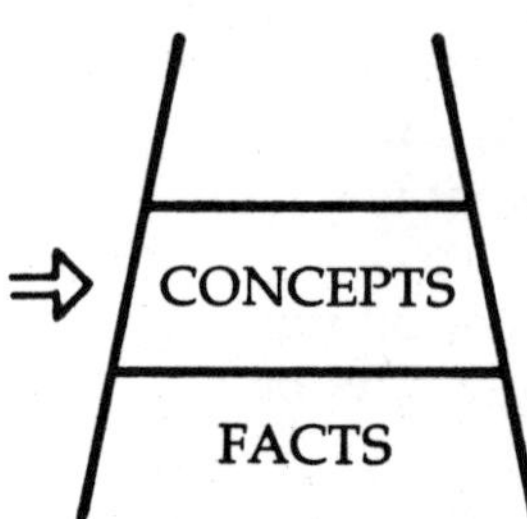

— What adjustments do you think Abraham and his family had to make in the new land?
— What problems confront a family moving to a new location within their country? To a foreign land?
— What changes do you think Matthew encountered when he left his position as a tax collector to follow Jesus?
— Was a sacrifice involved? Explain.
— What is meant by the term "sacrifice"?
— What is a conversion? Does it last?
— Paul knew the time and place of his conversion. Is it always possible to know this? Explain.
— How can one explain the unquestioning, obedient response of each of these three men — Abraham, Matthew, and Paul — to a change in their life?

What's in It for Me?

Valuing suggestions:

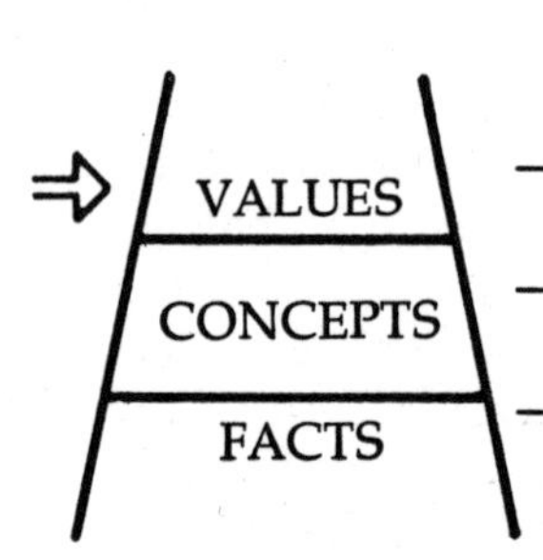

1. Have participants take time to reflect on the following questions:
— What do the lives of Abraham, Matthew, and Paul say to you about responding to change? About coping with change?
— What feelings do you associate with change?
— Have you ever moved? What feelings and adjustments did you encounter?
— Have you known anyone who has sacrificed a good salary to take a new job that was more fulfilling than his or her present position?

Paul writes in 2 Corinthians 5:17 about the new and the old. "If anyone is in Christ, he is a new creation; the old has passed away, behold the new has come."

— What implications does this verse have for your life?
— Have you known a person who made a major change in life-style like Paul did? If so, what sort of change?

2. Have participants share the following in pairs:
— Talk about any of the above that relates to your own life.
— Think about one change you have wanted to make to enrich your life — a change in a personal relationship, a job, a life-style, etc. What might you do to make the change? Discuss it with your partner.
— Consider setting a goal. Tell your partner specifically what you are going to change and how you will go about it.

3. Invite all participants to keep a list of the new and different experiences they have had recently, considering how those experiences have been meaningful.

Resources from the Bible (for optional use)

Personal Change

Ezekiel 36:26	A new heart and a new spirit.
2 Corinthians 5:17	People can become a new creation.
John 3:3-4	"How can a grown man be born?"
Mark 1:18	Change of career.
Acts 9:1-22	A changed life.

Church

Proverbs 29:18	With no vision, the people perish.
Ephesians 3:14-21	Christ is at the center of the Church
Ephesians 4:13-16	Importance of unity — one body, one Spirit.
Romans 15:1-7	Encourage and help one another.
Philemon 1-7	Early house church.
1 John 3:19-24	God is truth.
1 John 4:7-12	Love one another.

Lay Involvement

Colossians 3:12-17	Life together in the Church.
Romans 12:1-2	God changes people.
John 8:31-32	Truth means freedom.
Galatians 3:28	All people are one in Christ Jesus.
Ephesians 1:3-15	A common faith, a common commitment.
1 Corinthians 12:4-6	Varieties of gifts, but same Spirit.
2 Timothy 2:15	Teaching — passing the Word along.
1 Peter 5:1-3	The importance of a good example.

Worship

John 4:19-24	True worship defined.
Psalm 95:5	A call to worship.
Hosea 6:6	The attitude in worship is important.
Matthew 4:10, Revelation 22:8	Worship focuses on God.
Luke 4:16	Jesus worshiped "as was his custom."

Jesus and Change

Matthew 5	Jesus suggests changed attitudes.
Mark 2:15-17	Ate with tax collectors.
Mark 2:23-28	Worked on the Sabbath.
Mark 3:1-5	Healed on the Sabbath.
Mark 2:18-22	New wine in old wineskins.

Prayer

You loved tradition, Lord, and yet you were always open to new things; you didn't let rules and old ways of doing things interfere with your love for people. Help me to be open to the beauty of the old and the challenge of the new so that I might be an effective person in your kingdom.

Bibliography

In addition to the Bible, you may find these books useful.

Augenstein, Leroy G. *Come, Let Us Play God.* New York: Harper & Row, Publishers, 1969.

Bach, Marcus. *Had You Been Born in Another Faith.* Engelwood Cliffs, N.J.: Prentice-Hall, Inc., 1973.

Becker, Ernest. *Denial of Death.* New York: The Free Press, 1973.

Bonhoeffer, Dietrich. *Cost of Discipleship.* 2d ed. New York: The Macmillan Company, 1967.

———. *Life Together.* Translated by J. W. Doberstein. New York: Harper & Row, Publishers, 1954.

Bovet, Theodor. *Handbook of Marriage.* rev. ed. Garden City, N.Y.: Doubleday & Company, Inc., 1969.

———. *Have Time and Be Free.* Atlanta: John Knox Press, 1964.

Brand, Eugene. *Rite Thing.* Minneapolis: Augsburg Publishing House, 1970.

Clinebell, Charlotte H., and Clinebell, Howard J., Jr. *Intimate Marriage.* New York: Harper & Row, Publishers, 1970.

Feucht, Oscar. *Family Relationships and the Church.* St. Louis: Concordia Publishing House, 1971.

Fowler, James. "Religious Socialization: The Faith Development Perspective." Paper presented at annual meeting of Religious Research Association, October 1975.

Frankl, Viktor E. *Man's Search for Meaning.* rev. ed. Boston: Beacon Press, 1963.

Freire, Paulo. *Pedagogy of the Oppressed.* Translated by Myra B. Ramos. New York: Herder/The Seabury Press, 1971.

Gelatt, H. B.; Varenhorst, B.; and Carey, R. *Deciding: A Decision-Making Program For Students.* New York: College Entrance Examination Board, 1972.

Ginott, Haim G. *Between Parent and Child.* New York: Avon Books, 1969.

———. *Between Parent and Teenager.* New York: Avon Books, 1971.

Glashagel, Jerry. *Valuing Families.* Youth Values Project. New York: National YMCA Board, 1975.

Gordon, Thomas. *Parent Effectiveness Training: The No-Lose Program for Raising Responsible Children.* New York: Peter H. Wyden, Inc., 1970.

Harmin, Merrill; Kirschenbaum, Howard; and Simon, Sidney B. *Clarifying Values Through Subject Matter.* Minneapolis: Winston Press, Inc., 1973.

Howe, Reuel L. *Miracle of Dialogue.* New York: The Seabury Press, Inc., 1963.

Hudnut, Robert K. *Sleeping Giant: Arousing Church Power in America.* New York: Harper & Row, Publishers, 1971.

Jourard, Sidney M. *Transparent Self.* 2d ed. New York: Van Nostrand Reinhold Company, 1971.

Kirschenbaum, Howard, and Simon, Sidney B., eds. *Readings in Values Clarification.* Minneapolis: Winston Press, Inc., 1973.

Kohlberg, Lawrence. "The Child as a Moral Philosopher." *Psychology Today,* September 1968.

Lewis, C. S. *Chronicles of Narnia.* 7 paperback volumes for children and adults. New York: The Macmillan Company, n.d.

———. *A Grief Observed.* New York: The Seabury Press, Inc., 1963.

———. *Mere Christianity.* New York: The Macmillan Company, 1953.

Menninger, Karl, M.D. *Whatever Became of Sin?* New York: Hawthorn Books, Inc., 1973.

Miller, Keith. *Second Touch.* 2d ed. Waco, Tex.: Word Books, Inc., 1972.

———. *Taste of New Wine.* Waco, Tex.: Word Books, Inc., 1965.

Mooneyham, W. Stanley. *What Do You Say To a Hungry World?* Waco, Tex.: Word Books, Inc., 1975.

O'Connor, Elizabeth. *Eighth Day of Creation: Gifts and Creativity.* Waco, Tex.: Word Books, Inc., 1971.

———. *Our Many Selves.* New York: Harper & Row, Publishers, 1971.

Olsson, Karl. *Finding Your Self in the Bible.* Minneapolis: Augsburg Publishing House, 1974.

Paulson, Wayne. *Deciding for Myself: A Values-Clarification Series.* Minneapolis: Winston Press, Inc., 1974.

Phillips, John B. *Your God Is Too Small.* New York: The Macmillan Company, 1961.

Raths, L. E.; Harmin, Merrill; and Simon, Sidney B. *Values and Teaching.* Columbus, Oh.: Charles E. Merrill Publishing Company, 1967.

Satir, Virginia. *Peoplemaking.* Palo Alto, Calif.: Science and Behavior Books, Inc., 1972.

Simon, Arthur. *Faces of Poverty.* New York: The Macmillan Company, 1968.

Simon, Sidney B.; Howe, Leland; and Kirschenbaum, Howard. *Values Clarification: A Handbook of Practical Strategies for Teachers and Students.* New York: Hart Publishing Company, 1972.

Smith, JoAnn Kelley. *Free Fall.* Valley Forge, Penn.: Judson Press, 1975.

Strommen, Merton P. *Five Cries of Youth.* New York: Harper & Row, Publishers, 1974.

Tournier, Paul. *Meaning of Persons.* New York: Harper & Row, Publishers, 1957.

Trexler, Edgar R., ed. *Creative Congregations.* Nashville: Abingdon Press, 1972.

Trueblood, Elton. *A Place to Stand.* New York: Harper & Row, Publishers, 1969.

Westerhoff, John G., 3rd. *Values for Tomorrow's Children.* Philadelphia: United Church Press, 1970.

Winter, Gibson. *Love and Conflict: New Patterns in Family Life.* Garden City, N.Y.: Doubleday & Company, Inc., 1958.

———. *The New Creation as Metropolis.* New York: The Macmillan Company, 1963.

Wold, Margaret. *The Shalom Woman.* Minneapolis: Augsburg Publishing House, 1974.

Zdenek, Marilee, and Champion, Marge. *Catch the New Wind.* Waco, Tex.: Word Books, Inc., 1972.

Additional Titles

Clarke, Jean Illsley. *Self-Esteem: A Family Affair.* Minneapolis: Winston Press, Inc., 1978.

Larson, Roland S. and Doris E. *I Need to Have You Know Me, A Guide to a Better Marriage.* Minneapolis: Winston Press, Inc., 1979.

Feedback Telegram

We, the authors, would appreciate hearing about your experiences in using this book. If you have modified or adapted an exercise that worked well for you, we would like to hear about it. Or, maybe you've invented a new one that you'd like to tell us about. While we cannot promise to answer every "telegram," we would value knowing what was or was not helpful, interesting, effective, or facilitating for you. Your reactions will help us grow and become more aware of new ways for using these exercises. Thanks!

T E L E G R A M

To: Doris and Rollie Larson
2442 Gettysburg Avenue, South
Minneapolis, MN 55426

From:

Message:

____

(signature)

About the Authors

Dr. Roland Larson is an educational consultant/trainer who also counsels individuals in private practice. He is a licensed consulting psychologist who earned his doctorate at Michigan State University and the B.S. and M.A. at the University of Minnesota. As a training consultant since 1967, Dr. Larson has conducted some 600 workshops for a wide variety of organizations and groups. For several years he directed a training center for Search Institute in Minneapolis, Minnesota.

Doris Larson is Administrative Assistant in the firm of Roland S. Larson and Associates, Minneapolis. While her professional background and experiences are in social work, she has devoted most of her time and energies to homemaking and sharing in the raising of the family's four children. Together, the Larsons have led workshops and seminars in the United States, Canada, Europe, Central America, and the Pacific Islands.

A year after *Values and Faith* was published in the United States, it was translated into Swedish and published by Skeab of Sweden under the title *Värderingar och tro.* Since then, this book has become widely used in Sweden, and the Larsons have conducted many workshops there.

Doris and Rollie have also co-authored *I Need to Have You Know Me: A Guide to a Better Marriage* (Winston Press, 1979) and are involved with marriage enrichment training programs. Through the years they have participated greatly in community and church activities, and they have a special interest in wellness, preventive mental health, and holistic health — integrating body, mind, and spirit.

संघ
की
अनसुनी कहानियाँ

संघ की अनसुनी कहानियाँ

डॉ. हरीश चंद्र बर्णवाल

प्रकाशक

प्रभात प्रकाशन प्रा. लि.

4/19 आसफ अली रोड, नई दिल्ली–110002

फोन : 011–23289777 • हेल्पलाइन नं. : 7827007777

इ–मेल : prabhatbooks@gmail.com ❖ वेब ठिकाना : www.prabhatbooks.com

संस्करण

द्वितीय, 2026

चित्र सौजन्य

अभिलेखागार, राष्ट्रीय स्वयंसेवक संघ

पेपरबैक मूल्य

सात सौ पचास रुपए

मुद्रक

आर–टेक ऑफसेट प्रिंटर्स, दिल्ली

———————— ★ ————————

SANGH KI ANSUNI KAHANIYAN

by Dr. Harish Chandra Burnwal

Published by **PRABHAT PRAKASHAN PVT. LTD.**

4/19 Asaf Ali Road, New Delhi-110002

ISBN 978-93-5521-723-3

₹ 750.00 (PB)

माँ–पापा
को समर्पित।

साथ ही,
उन लाखों स्वयंसेवकों को नमन
जो संघ की शतवर्षीय यात्रा में
समाज को रोशन करते हुए
माँ भारती की सेवा में विलीन हो गए।

शुभाकांक्षा

राष्ट्रीय स्वयंसेवक संघ पर केंद्रित डॉ. हरीश चंद्र बर्णवाल की यह एक विलक्षण पुस्तक है। उन्होंने संघ से जुड़ी कम जानी और ज्यादातर अनजानी कहानियों को खोजकर अपने अध्यवसाय तथा अध्ययन से इसे लिखा है। यह पुस्तक है 'संघ की अनसुनी कहानियाँ'। इसकी पांडुलिपि मुझे मिली। मैंने इसे देखा और पढ़ा। यह प्रयास बहुत सराहनीय है। यह पुस्तक संघ के योगदान को ऐतिहासिक साक्ष्यों के साथ प्रस्तुत करती है। हर कहानी थोड़े शब्दों में है। इस शैली का अपना आकर्षण है।

पिछली सदी के तीसरे दशक में सांस्कृतिक राष्ट्रीयता की विलुप्त धारा को पुनः जाग्रत् करने के उद्देश्य से संघ की यात्रा प्रारंभ हुई। समाज में चरित्र निर्माण और हिंदू समाज के संगठन के उस प्रयास ने धीरे-धीरे राष्ट्रव्यापी रूप लिया। संघ की भूमिका और बलिदान को अकसर राजनीतिक कारणों से उपेक्षित किया गया। यह पुस्तक संघ और स्वयंसेवकों की साधना को चित्रित करती है।

इतिहास की विविध घटनाओं को समेटते हुए लेखक ने संघ की बहुआयामी भूमिका को गहराई से सामने रखने का प्रयास किया है। स्वतंत्रता संग्राम में भारत छोड़ो आंदोलन, भारत विभाजन, गुजरात और बिहार आंदोलन, आपातकाल में लोकतंत्र की बहाली का राष्ट्रीय प्रयास और प्राकृतिक आपदा एवं दुर्घटनाओं के समय संघ के निस्स्वार्थ सेवाकार्यों को बहुत सारगर्भित ढंग से पुस्तक में समाहित किया गया है। यह पुस्तक हर प्रसंग को एक 'अनसुनी कहानी' के रूप में प्रस्तुत करती है, जो पाठक को संघ के स्वयंसेवकों के त्याग, बलिदान और अथक परिश्रम से परिचित कराती है।

पुस्तक कई ऐतिहासिक महत्त्वपूर्ण प्रसंगों को भी सामने लाती है। मोतीलाल नेहरू, विट्ठल भाई पटेल, वीर सावरकर, बाबासाहेब आंबेडकर, जयप्रकाश नारायण और प्रणब मुखर्जी जैसे अनेक नेताओं ने समय-समय पर संघकार्य की प्रशंसा की और उसके कार्यक्रमों में भी शामिल हुए। ये तथ्य प्रामाणिक हैं। समाज में संघ की स्वीकार्यता के प्रतीकात्मक उदाहरण हैं।

यह पुस्तक उन अनगिनत स्वयंसेवकों की गाथा भी है, जो इतिहास की पुस्तकों

में नहीं मिलते, लेकिन जिनकी निष्ठा और समर्पण के कारण आज का भारत जीवंतता के साथ खड़ा है। डॉ. हरीश चंद्र बर्णवाल की यह पुस्तक स्वयंसेवकों को सामाजिक, सांस्कृतिक, नैतिक और ऐतिहासिक नजरिए से देखने का एक विनम्र प्रयास है। इस शोधपरक प्रयास ने तथ्य, संवेदना और राष्ट्रभाव से परिपूर्ण एक अनुपम साहित्यिक कृति समाज को प्रदान की है। मुझे पूरा विश्वास है कि यह पुस्तक सामान्य पाठक और शोधार्थियों के लिए संदर्भकोश सिद्ध होगी। इस अनूठी पुस्तक के लिए वरिष्ठ पत्रकार और लेखक डॉ. हरीश चंद्र बर्णवाल को मेरी हार्दिक शुभाकांक्षा।

—दत्तात्रेय होसबाले

सरकार्यवाह, राष्ट्रीय स्वयंसेवक संघ

आश्विन शुक्ल एकम्

विक्रमी संवत् 2082

प्रथम नवरात्र, तदनुसार 22 सितंबर, 2025

पुरोकथन

भारत के सुदीर्घ इतिहास में राष्ट्रीय स्वयंसेवक संघ एक बड़ा और अनुकरणीय उदाहरण हो गया है। वह क्या है ? हर उत्सुक व्यक्ति इसे जानना चाहेगा। जो विरोधी हैं, वे भी इसे इस समय समझना चाहते हैं। जो स्वयंसेवक हैं, वे इसे अपने जीवन का अनुभव बनाना चाहेंगे। जो अनुकरणीय उदाहरण है, वह शब्दों में सरल है। लेकिन आचरण में अत्यंत चुनौतीपूर्ण होता है। वह यह कि जो चलना शुरू कर देते हैं, वे रास्ता खोज लेते हैं। महापुरुषों ने भी यही कहा है कि चलते रहो, उठो और चलो। निरंतर चलने वाले को पहाड़ भी रास्ता दे देता है। राष्ट्रीय स्वयंसेवक संघ के 100 साल का यशोगान आज हो रहा है तो इसका एक प्रमुख कारण यही है कि जबसे यह संस्था शुरू हुई तो रुकी नहीं, बाधाएँ आईं, लेकिन अपने पाँव पर भरोसे से संघ ने अपने कदम रोके नहीं, हर कदम जो उठाया, वह यात्रा का विश्वास था। कदम उठते गए। उनकी संख्या बढ़ती गई। उसी अनुरूप साधन, समर्थन, अवसर और यश की कहानियाँ बनती चली गईं। उन कहानियों को स्वयंसेवकों ने अपने पुरुषार्थ से सार्थक किया। यह सिद्ध किया कि सफल संस्था वह होती है, जो कठिनाइयों से हार नहीं मानती। जीतने के अपने भरोसे को सकर्म में रूपांतरित करती है।

राष्ट्रीय स्वयंसेवक संघ ने एक सामाजिक शक्ति अर्जित की है। वह कठिनाइयों से पार पाने का परिणाम है। संघ की कहानियों में उस पर प्रतिबंध की घटनाएँ भी हैं। इस समय इन घटनाओं को अलग दृष्टिकोण से देखा जा रहा है। वह यह कि कितनी बार प्रतिबंध लगाए गए, इसका प्रश्न नहीं है, बल्कि यह है कि प्रतिबंध के बावजूद संघ की यात्रा में निरंतरता बनी रही और उसका विस्तार होता रहा। संघ को रोकने, घायल करने और मार डालने के प्रयास बार-बार होते रहे। उन प्रयासों या षड्यंत्रों को विफल कर संघ अपनी राख से उठ खड़ा हुआ और कुछ अधिक ही ऊर्जा उसमें दिखी, क्योंकि संघ में निश्चय प्रबल था। प्रतिबंधों ने संघ को डराया नहीं। उसमें अधिक विश्वास पैदा किया। इससे यह सिद्ध होता है कि राष्ट्रीय स्वयंसेवक संघ कोई सांयोगिक संस्था के रूप में यों ही नहीं जनमी, बल्कि एक सुविचारित सांस्कृतिक

क्रांति की उससे शुरुआत हुई, जिसने अपने आरोहण के 100 सोपान पूरे कर लिये हैं। यात्रा अनवरत चल रही है। उसका संदेश गूँज रहा है। जो संदेश है, उसमें 'पंच परिवर्तन' की मंदाकिनी के मधुर स्वर हैं।

सरसंघचालक मोहन भागवत ने 26-28 अगस्त, 2025 को नई दिल्ली के विज्ञान भवन की अपनी व्याख्यानमाला में बताया कि स्वाधीनता संग्राम में चार धाराएँ थीं—क्रांतिकारी, राजनीतिक, समाज सुधार और धार्मिक। संघ के संस्थापक डॉ. केशवराव बलिराम हेडगेवार को इन चारों धाराओं में कार्य करने का अनुभव था। उस आधार पर उन्होंने 'एक नया प्रयोग करने की ठानी'। वह नया प्रयोग राष्ट्रीय स्वयंसेवक संघ है। जिस समय राष्ट्रीय स्वयंसेवक संघ का संस्था के रूप में बीजारोपण हुआ, उस दौर में अनेक वैचारिक धाराएँ संस्था के रूप में पैदा हुईं। समाजवादी धारा करीब 90 साल पुरानी है। कम्युनिस्ट 100 पूरे कर रहे हैं। इनके कितने टुकड़े हुए? यह शोध का विषय है। समय साक्षी है कि राष्ट्रीय स्वयंसेवक संघ बीज से वृक्ष बना और संस्था के रूप में एक वटवृक्ष बन गया है, जिसके तने और शाखाओं का उपवन मनोरम होता जा रहा है। ऐसे जीवंत राष्ट्रीय स्वयंसेवक संघ की 'अनसुनी कहानियाँ' इस पुस्तक में हैं। ये संख्या में 225 हैं।

यह पुस्तक कई साल के निरंतर अध्ययन और खोज का परिणाम है। ठीक-ठीक तारीख और साल मुझे याद नहीं है। यह याद है कि एक दिन डॉ. हरीश चंद्र बर्णवाल ने यों ही बातचीत में बताया कि वे संघ पर अपनी एक शोध टोली से अध्ययन करा रहे हैं। वे स्वयं भी संघ पर छपी पुस्तकें पढ़ने के लिए रतजगा कर रहे हैं। यह सुनकर मेरी उत्सुकता बढ़ी। इसके दो कारण हैं, क्योंकि हरीश बर्णवाल संघ में इतनी गहरी रुचि लेंगे, इससे मैं अनजान था। जिस हरीश बर्णवाल को मैं जितना जानता था, वह परिचय अधूरा था। दूसरा कि उसी समय संघ में देवरस बंधु के योगदान का मैं स्वयं भी अध्ययन कर रहा था। मैंने सोचा कि इस कार्य में हरीश बर्णवाल से भी कुछ मदद मिलेगी। उस दिन मैंने यह समझा कि वे संघ के इतिहास को खोज रहे हैं और खोजवा रहे हैं। इसका अर्थ यह हुआ कि वे स्वयं उस टीम का नेतृत्व कर रहे हैं, जो उपलब्ध साहित्य में से संघ के इतिहास को ढूँढ़ रही है। इसमें दो-तीन साल का समय लगा है। हर कहानी थोड़े शब्दों में है, लेकिन अपने आप में पूरी है। इसलिए यह ज्यादा पढ़ी जाएगी, क्योंकि उसे पढ़ने में कुछ मिनट ही लगेंगे। इस तरह यह पुस्तक अब तक की संघ पर छपी पुस्तकों से भिन्न है। मेरा अनुमान है कि नई पीढ़ी की नजर में यह

पुस्तक बेहतर समझी जाएगी। इस पुस्तक की कहानियों में समय और संघ के दर्द भी हैं। इसे जो पढ़ेगा, वह हर शब्द में उस अनुभव से गुजरेगा। अनेक कहानियों में संघ के संघर्ष का इतिहास है। उसे जानना, संघ को जानना है। यह भी जानना संभव है कि जिसे संघ ने अपने लिए चुनौती माना और यात्रा जारी रखी, तभी तो कहानियाँ आगे बढ़ीं। इस प्रकार संघ की वह विचार-यात्रा थी। वही है भी और उसके बने रहने की हर संभावना है। यहीं यह समझने की भी जरूरत है कि संघ के विचार में अपने अस्तित्व के प्रति सगजता बनी रही। दुष्प्रचार और आक्षेप से संघ निर्लिप्त रहा। हो सकता है कि इस पर कुछ लोगों को यकीन न हो। लेकिन जिन्हें यकीन नहीं होगा, वे भी यह तो मानने ही लगे हैं कि यात्रा अविराम बनी रही। भला! बिना निर्लिप्त रहे, ऐसी यात्रा संभव है ?

इस पुस्तक में वे कहानियाँ भी हैं, जो इतिहास के पन्नों में तो हैं पर उपेक्षित हैं। उन पर इतिहासकारों, राजनीतिक नेताओं और अंधविरोधियों ने अपने-अपने हिस्से की रंग-बिरंगी मिट्टी भी डाली है। इस पुस्तक की कहानियों को पढ़ने से पाठक की संवेदना जगेगी। हर कहानी से वह अपने को जोड़ सकेगा। तब वह पाएगा कि इन कहानियों से संघ का वर्तमान अस्तित्व अपने गौरवपूर्ण इतिहास से प्रकट होता है। इसका यह अर्थ नहीं है कि इस पुस्तक से संघ के बारे में संपूर्ण कथा निकलती है। इतना ही अर्थ है कि संघ के अस्तित्व की इन कहानियों में एक झलक है। संघ अपनी परिभाषा स्वयं है। उसे शब्द-चित्र में दिखाएँ तो जो भाव इस पुस्तक से प्रगट होता है वह है, हालात जिसे हिला नहीं सके, वह राष्ट्रीय स्वयंसेवक संघ है। 100 साल के संघ की कहानियों को एक सीमा में बाँधना बड़ा कठिन कार्य है, जिसे हरीश बर्णवाल ने इस पुस्तक में प्रस्तुत करने का प्रयास किया है।

उन्होंने अपनी भूमिका में बताया है कि पुस्तक की प्रेरणा क्या है। पत्रकारिता के कार्य में उन्हें जो संगी-साथी मिले, वे अपने चश्मे से संघ को देखते और दिखाते थे। उनका चश्मा उन्हें मुबारक हो, हरीश बर्णवाल अपनी इस भावना पर अडिग रहे। यह आमतौर पर होता नहीं है। संगी-साथी कुछ प्रभाव तो डालते ही हैं। वे ही बच पाते हैं, जो अपने में बने रहते हैं और अपनी आंतरिक समृद्धि को विचार की अपनी संपदा बनाते हैं। इसके विपरीत एक खतरा बना रहता है। वह होता खतरनाक है। हरीश बर्णवाल उस खतरे को पार कर पहचान सके कि उनका मार्ग क्या है। इसलिए उन्होंने स्वयं से प्रश्न पूछे और इतिहास में गोते लगाकर संघ के मोती चुनने

का अध्यवसाय किया। अध्ययन और अध्यवसाय से जो उन्हें मिला, वह इस पुस्तक में अपने ढंग के शिल्प से प्रस्तुत हो सका है।

यह शिल्प पाठकों को लुभाएगा, उन्हें फुसलाएगा भी। फुसलाना आसान नहीं होता, धैर्य की माँग करता है। शिल्प से पाठकों में रुचि पैदा होगी। वह पढ़ते समय जब मन से अनुकूलन की रासायनिक प्रक्रिया से गुजरेगा तो उसमें जो भाव पैदा होगा, वही उसे बिना कहे फुसलाएगा। यहाँ एक स्पष्टीकरण आवश्यक है। अंग्रेजी का जो शब्द परसुएशन है, वह यहाँ फुसलाने के अर्थ में इस्तेमाल किया गया है। क्या यह पुस्तक संघ के आलोचकों को उत्तर देने के लिए लिखी गई है? ऐसा दिखता नहीं है। क्योंकि इन कहानियों में तथ्य हैं और उनको एक कहानी बनाने के लिए आवश्यक संदर्भ हैं। अगर उत्तर देने के लिए यह पुस्तक होती तो उसका कथानक बदल जाता। भाषा भी बदल जाती। कहानी कहानी न होकर एक तलवार होती और जिस पर चलती, उसे ढाल का सहारा लेने का अवसर भी नहीं देती। आम धारणा है कि संघ की कहानी उसकी स्थापना से शुरू होती है। यह एक मायने में सही भी है और इतिहास की दृष्टि से गलत भी है। सही इसलिए है, क्योंकि 1925 में डॉ. केशवराव बलिराम हेडगेवार ने एक घोषणा की। वह वास्तव में नए प्रयोग की घोषणा थी। उसका पहला प्रमाण कुछ साल बाद मिला, जब राष्ट्रीय स्वयंसेवक संघ का नाम निर्धारित हुआ। आमतौर पर संस्था का नाम पहले तय होता है और उसकी गतिविधियाँ बाद में शुरू होती हैं।

इस पुस्तक से प्रमाण सहित यह जानना संभव है कि संघ के संस्थापक स्वाधीनता आंदोलन के उत्कृष्ट योद्धा थे। स्वाधीनता सेनानी थे। वीरव्रती थे। लकीर के फकीर नहीं थे। उनसे संबंधित कई कहानियाँ इसमें हैं। एक कहानी 'हेडगेवार ने जंगल कानून तोड़कर किया सत्याग्रह' है। इसे पढ़ें तो दो बातें स्पष्ट होती हैं। पहली कि नमक सत्याग्रह के दौरान वह जंगल सत्याग्रह था। दूसरी कि वे स्वयं सत्याग्रह में शामिल होने के लिए गए क्योंकि स्वाधीनता आंदोलन की वह माँग थी। लेकिन सरसंघचालक पद पर रहते हुए वे सत्याग्रह में सम्मिलित नहीं हुए। वह पद एक योग्य सहयोगी को दिया और तब तक सँभालने के लिए कहा, जब तक वे लौटकर आते नहीं। उन्हें उस सत्याग्रह में नौ महीने के कठोर कारावास की सजा मिली। उस सत्याग्रह ने संघ को स्वाधीनता संग्राम में सम्मिलित होने के लिए एक खिड़की भी खोली। आँगन में संघ था और खिड़की से बाहर युद्ध के मैदान में स्वयंसेवक थे। इसे

ही अहिंसक छापामार युद्ध कहते हैं।

बिना जाने-समझे कुछ पूर्वाग्रही लोग कहते-सुने जाते हैं कि 1942 में संघ कहाँ था। यह उनकी जिज्ञासा नहीं होती है, उनका फरमान होता है। ऐसे लोग इस पुस्तक की पहली कहानी पढ़कर चाहें तो अपना विचार बदल सकते हैं। इसके लिए वैचारिक ईमानदारी की जरूरत पड़ेगी। इस कहानी को पढ़ते वक्त मुझे याद आया कि हिंदी दैनिक 'जनसत्ता' में अगस्त क्रांति के तीन पहलुओं पर मैंने तीन लेख लिखे थे। उसमें एक लेख 'आंदोलन की तीन धाराओं का प्रवाह' था। वह 26 सितंबर, 1992 को छपा था।

उसका प्रासंगिक अंश पढ़िए—'उस दौर में स्वाधीनता आंदोलन के तीन रूप थे। वे अपने-अपने दृष्टिकोण से चलाए जा रहे थे। पहला कांग्रेस, यानी महात्मा गांधी के नेतृत्व में स्वाधीनता का अहिंसात्मक आंदोलन था। दूसरा क्रांतिकारी धारा थी, जिसका प्रतिनिधित्व नेताजी और वीर सावरकर अपने-अपने ढंग से कर रहे थे। तीसरी धारा राष्ट्रीय स्वयंसेवक संघ की थी। कांग्रेस मुख्यधारा थी। महात्मा गांधी ने अंग्रेजों को भारत छोड़ने के लिए आदेश देकर एक नैतिक संदेश अपने देशवासियों को दिया कि वे 9 अगस्त, 1942 से खुद को आजाद मानें। वे आजादी के लिए जिएँ और जरूरत पड़े तो मौत को गले लगाएँ। इसके जरिए उन्होंने दुनिया को बताया कि अंग्रेजी साम्राज्य का आधार खत्म हो गया है। कोई साम्राज्य तभी तक शासन कर सकता है, जब तक लोग उसकी सत्ता को कबूल करते हैं।'

इन तीन प्रवाहों में संघ कैसे भिन्न था? उसी लेख का यह अंश बताता है—'राष्ट्रीय स्वयंसेवक संघ इससे भिन्न धरातल पर खड़ा था। 1940 में उसके संस्थापक केशवराव बलिराम हेडगेवार का निधन हो गया था। राष्ट्रीय स्वयंसेवक संघ उस दौर में 15 साल का था। विश्व युद्ध छिड़ गया था। संघ के सरसंघचालक का आह्वान था कि भारत माता की वेदी पर बलिदान में ही जीवन की सार्थकता है। संघ के सरकार्यवाह रहे एच.वी. शेषाद्रि की पुस्तक 'आर.एस.एस. : अ विजन इन ऐक्शन' में 1942 का प्रसंग है। उसमें लिखा है कि भारत छोड़ो आंदोलन के आह्वान से पहले कांग्रेस ने अन्य संगठनों और देशभक्त समूहों से बात नहीं की। उसने संघ से भी संपर्क नहीं किया, फिर भी संघ के स्वयंसेवकों ने आंदोलन में भरपूर हिस्सा लिया। विदर्भ के मशहूर अष्टी-चिमूर विद्रोह में संघ के स्वयंसेवक ही थे। दिल्ली-मुजफ्फरनगर रेल लाइन को दिल्ली के स्वयंसेवकों ने उखाड़ा था। सतारा में समानांतर सरकार (जिसे

पत्री सरकार भी कहा जाता है, क्योंकि सरकार के प्रतीक नाना पाटिल पेड़ पर टीन की पत्री ठोंक देते थे। अंग्रेज हुकूमत पत्री हटाने में परेशान रहती थी) कायम करने वाले नाना पाटील को उनके भूमिगत जीवन में औंध के संघचालक श्रीपाद दामोदर सातवलेकर के घर में शरण मिली। साने गुरुजी पुणे के संघचालक यादव साहब देशमुख के घर में रहकर सरकार से बच सके। दिल्ली में लाला हंसराज के यहाँ जे.पी. और अरुणा आसफ अली ठहरे। संघ संगठन के तौर पर तटस्थ रहा।'

डॉ. हरीश चंद्र बर्णवाल की यह पुस्तक पाठक को समझा सकने में समर्थ है कि शाखा, प्रार्थना, अनुशासन, समरसता, सेवा और शौर्य जैसे मूल तत्त्वों पर खड़ा राष्ट्रीय स्वयंसेवक संघ एक देशव्यापी सामाजिक क्रांति का पर्याय है। भारत का स्वतंत्रता संग्राम केवल बंदूक और जेल की सलाखों के इर्द-गिर्द रचा गया इतिहास नहीं है। यह एक ऐसा महासंग्राम था, जिसमें असंख्य व्यक्तियों, समूहों और संगठनों ने अपने-अपने स्तर पर देश की स्वतंत्रता और पुनर्निर्माण के लिए बलिदान, त्याग और तपस्या की। किंतु दुर्भाग्यवश, स्वतंत्रता के बाद इतिहास लेखन की धारा ने अनेक महत्त्वपूर्ण संगठनों और उनके योगदान को या तो हाशिए पर डाल दिया या पूरी तरह से भुला दिया। राष्ट्रीय स्वयंसेवक संघ उन्हीं संगठनों में से एक है, जिसकी ऐतिहासिक भूमिका का उचित मूल्यांकन नहीं हो पाया।

संघ के हजारों स्वयंसेवकों ने व्यक्तिगत और सामूहिक स्तर पर सविनय अवज्ञा आंदोलन, जंगल सत्याग्रह और भारत छोड़ो आंदोलन में हिस्सा लिया। डॉ. हेडगेवार स्वयं दो बार जेल गए। उनका संघर्ष केवल प्रतीकात्मक नहीं था—उन्होंने अंग्रेजों की आँखों में आँखें डालकर न्यायालय में कहा था, "मैं आदेशों का पालन नहीं करूँगा, क्योंकि वह मेरे राष्ट्रधर्म के विरुद्ध है।" राष्ट्रीय स्वयंसेवक संघ की शुरुआत से पहले डॉ. हेडगेवार ने 'राष्ट्रीय उत्सव मंडल' की स्थापना कर समाज में राष्ट्रवादी भावना जगाई, जबकि 'कागजी आंदोलन' के माध्यम से उन्होंने ब्रिटिश नीति के विरुद्ध सटीक वैचारिक संघर्ष छेड़ा। डॉ. हरीश चंद्र बर्णवाल की इस पुस्तक में वह पहलू भी शामिल किया गया है, जहाँ संघ के स्वयंसेवकों ने 'आजाद हिंद फौज' के साथ कंधे-से-कंधा मिलाकर ब्रिटिश शासन को चुनौती दी। ऐसे सैकड़ों स्वयंसेवक थे, जो नेताजी सुभाषचंद्र बोस के नेतृत्व में अंग्रेजों के विरुद्ध संग्राम में शामिल हुए। नेताजी ने स्वयं डॉ. हेडगेवार से संवाद किया और अपने प्रतिनिधि उनके पास भेजे थे। यह केवल एक संगठनात्मक मेल नहीं था, बल्कि एक राष्ट्रवादी विचारधारा की गूँज थी।

कई ऐतिहासिक तथ्यों को डॉ. बर्णवाल ने इस पुस्तक में पहली बार संगठित रूप में प्रस्तुत किया है, जैसे महात्मा गांधी का संघ के शिविर में जाना और उनका उस अनुशासन और आत्मबल से प्रभावित होना। गांधीजी ने स्पष्ट शब्दों में कहा था कि "अगर ऐसा संगठन पूरे भारत में हो जाए तो देश का भविष्य उज्ज्वल है।" विट्ठलभाई पटेल, बाबासाहेब आंबेडकर, जयप्रकाश नारायण, मदन मोहन मालवीय जैसे कई स्वतंत्रता सेनानियों ने न केवल संघ की सराहना की, बल्कि इसे भारत के सर्वसमावेशी भाव को विकसित करने का सशक्त माध्यम बताया। कई ने संघ की शाखाओं में जाकर संवाद और सहयोग को भी बढ़ावा दिया। आंबेडकर ने स्वयंसेवकों के साथ भोजन किया—वह भी एक ऐसे समय में जब जातीय भेदभाव चरम पर था।

देश का विभाजन भारतीय इतिहास की सबसे बड़ी मानवीय त्रासदी थी। इस संदर्भ में यह पुस्तक एक दस्तावेज की तरह काम करेगा कि किस प्रकार इस संकट की घड़ी में जब प्रशासन, पुलिस और सेना भी असहाय हो गई थी, तब संघ के स्वयंसेवक ही थे जो सीमा पर, शिविरों में, रेल स्टेशनों पर, मोहल्लों में डटे रहे। सैकड़ों स्थानों पर उन्होंने हिंसा को रोका, हजारों राहत शिविर चलाए और हजारों जीवन बचाए। लाहौर से लेकर अमृतसर तक, कोटली से लेकर पुंछ तक, संघ के स्वयंसेवक अपने प्राणों की परवाह किए बिना हिंदू, सिख और यहाँ तक कि मुसलिम बहनों-बेटियों को भी सुरक्षित स्थानों पर पहुँचाने में लगे रहे। यह भी उल्लेखनीय है कि सरदार वल्लभभाई पटेल और लाल बहादुर शास्त्री ने संघ से सहायता ली और संघ की भूमिका की प्रशंसा की। विभाजन के दौरान कई कांग्रेस नेताओं ने भी अपने परिवारों की रक्षा के लिए संघ की शरण ली। आदरणीय गुरुजी गोलवलकर के कूटनीतिक प्रयासों से कश्मीर का भारत में विलय संभव हो पाया।

भारत के स्वतंत्र हो जाने के बाद संघ की भूमिका और अधिक व्यापक हो गई। जब-जब देश संकट में आया—बाढ़, भूकंप, रेल दुर्घटनाएँ, आतंकी हमले, महामारी या युद्ध—संघ के स्वयंसेवक सबसे पहले सेवा में उपस्थित रहे। 1962 के चीन युद्ध और 1965 के पाकिस्तान युद्ध में, संघ ने न केवल सेना को सहायता दी, बल्कि 'गणतंत्र दिवस की परेड' में शामिल होकर राष्ट्रीय गौरव में अपना महत्त्वपूर्ण स्थान बनाया। भूदान आंदोलन, तिब्बती शरणार्थियों की सहायता, आपातकाल में लोकतंत्र की रक्षा, कारगिल युद्ध में कोष का गठन और कोविड काल में भोजन

बैंक, दवा वितरण जैसे अनेक सेवा कार्यों में संघ का योगदान अब किसी प्रमाण का मोहताज नहीं रहा। यह पुस्तक उन प्रसंगों को भी उजागर करती है, जहाँ राजनीतिक भिन्नताओं के बावजूद, कांग्रेस के अनेक नेताओं ने संघ की सराहना की। मोतीलाल नेहरू ने जेल से बाहर आने पर डॉ. हेडगेवार का स्वागत किया तो नेहरू ने संघ को 'राष्ट्रवादी' कहा, जाकिर हुसैन ने कहा कि "देश को संघ से बहुत कुछ सीखना चाहिए", इंदिरा गांधी ने संघ के प्रमुख प्रचारक एकनाथ रानाडे को आई.सी.सी.आर. का सदस्य नियुक्त किया था।

इस पुस्तक में एक कहानी का शीर्षक है, 'देवरस से कई बार मिले राजीव गांधी, सोनिया को रखा बेखबर'। यह कहानी सच है, लेकिन अज्ञात सी है। जो जानते हैं, वे भी इसका उल्लेख नहीं करते। आज यह कहानी सनसनी पैदा कर सकती है। एक समय में जब इंदिरा गांधी दोबारा सत्ता में आ गई थी, तब उन्होंने राजीव गांधी को संघ के एक शिखर पुरुष भाऊराव देवरस के पास भेजा। वहाँ से शुरुआत हुई। जो संवाद उस समय हुआ वह चलता रहा। इसे जानना भी कठिन सा है। ऐसी अनेक बातें और अनेक प्रसंग इस पुस्तक में हैं। जिससे यह जानना संभव है कि राजनीति के मंच पर जो संघ को कोसते रहते हैं, वे भी अपने सुरक्षित भविष्य के लिए संघ से संवाद बनाने के लिए तत्पर रहते हैं।

इस अर्थ में राष्ट्रीय स्वयंसेवक संघ एक जनआंदोलन है। जनआंदोलन की प्रचलित परिभाषा की परिधि का संघ निरंतर विस्तार कर रहा है। विचार, कर्म और निष्ठा की त्रिवेणी ने उसे एक आत्मानुशासन उपलब्ध कराया है। इसीलिए हिमालय की चोटियों से लेकर रण कच्छ के बियाबान तक संघ का आकाश फैला हुआ है। केदारनाथ आपदा, नेपाल भूकंप, चेन्नई बाढ़, केरल रेल दुर्घटना, ओडिशा रेल हादसा या वैश्विक महामारी—हर संकट में संघ निस्स्वार्थ भाव से सेवा में जुटा रहा। 'अहसास यात्रा' जैसे कार्यक्रमों ने कश्मीरी युवाओं के सोचने का नजरिया बदल दिया तो विद्या भारती और एकल विद्यालयों ने ग्रामीण भारत को शिक्षित और संस्कारित करने का बीड़ा उठाया। सहयोग, समर्पण और संस्कार के त्रिवेणी संगम पर खड़ा यह संगठन अब 1 करोड़ से अधिक स्वयंसेवकों का विश्व का सबसे बड़ा नागरिक संगठन बन चुका है। इन सभी तथ्यों को डॉ. हरीश चंद्र बर्णवाल की इस पुस्तक में खूबसूरती के साथ समाहित किया गया है।

इतिहास तब अधूरा होता है, जब वह केवल विजेताओं या सत्ता में रहे लोगों की

कहानी कहे। यह पुस्तक उस ऐतिहासिक संतुलन को स्थापित करने की एक कोशिश है, जो दिखाती है कि कैसे एक विचार, एक संगठन ने राष्ट्र को उसकी जड़ों से जोड़े रखा, समाज को जोड़ा, सेवा को धर्म माना और समर्पण को साधना। डॉ. बर्णवाल की यह पुस्तक आपको बताएगी कि गणवेश में खड़ा वह स्वयंसेवक केवल झंडा नहीं फहराता, वह संस्कार भी प्रदर्शित करता है, वह केवल शाखा में समय नहीं बिताता, वह समाज को समर्पित करता है। यह एक यात्रा है—डॉ. हेडगेवार की आखिरी चिट्ठी से लेकर महाकुंभ में 54 हजार लोगों को उनके परिजनों से मिलाने तक। यह एक गाथा है—जेल में भूख हड़ताल करने वाले स्वयंसेवकों से लेकर चक्रवात और कोविड जैसी आपदाओं में मोरचा सँभालने तक। इस पुस्तक के माध्यम से उस 'अनकही गाथा' को सामने लाया गया है, जो भारत की मिट्टी से उपजी, भारत के मन में गूँजी और भारत के भविष्य को गढ़ने में सतत सक्रिय रही।

इस पुस्तक में 'स्वतंत्रता संघर्ष और संघ', 'संघ और स्वतंत्रता सेनानी', 'स्वतंत्रता संघर्ष और डॉ. हेडगेवार', 'विभाजन की त्रासदी और आजादी', 'स्वतंत्र भारत के पाँच दशक', 'इक्कीसवीं सदी और संघ' और 'संगठन' शीर्षक से अलग-अलग खंड हैं। इससे इस पुस्तक की पठनीयता बढ़ेगी और पाठक को जिसमें रुचि होगी, वह खोजने में सुविधा होगी। यह पुस्तक इसलिए अत्यंत महत्त्वपूर्ण है। इसके रचनाकार डॉ. हरीश चंद्र बर्णवाल को हार्दिक साधुवाद! उन्होंने अथक परिश्रम कर इसे संभव बनाया है। इसमें जहाँ श्रमसाध्य शोध है, वहीं निष्पक्ष दृष्टिकोण भी है। इसमें तथ्य, कथ्य, विश्लेषण और निष्कर्ष का ऐसा समन्वय है, जो हर दृष्टि से सम्यक् और संतुलित है। यह एक सराहनीय सृजनात्मक प्रयास है।

—रामबहादुर राय

अध्यक्ष, इंदिरा गांधी राष्ट्रीय कला केंद्र

विजयादशमी

2 अक्तूबर, 2025

भूमिका

वर्ष 2019 तक 8 पुस्तकें लिखने के बाद मैंने यह निर्णय लिया था कि अब पुस्तक लेखन से विराम लूँगा, परंतु कुछ घटनाओं ने एक ऐसी परिस्थिति पैदा की, जिसने मुझे संघ को और करीब से जानने के लिए विवश कर दिया। जाहिर है लगातार पढ़ने, सुनने और संघ को नजदीक से समझने का आग्रह इतना प्रबल रहा कि मुझे पुनः लेखन के लिए प्रेरित होना पड़ा। पुस्तक लिखने का संकल्प दरअसल, केवल बौद्धिक अभ्यास नहीं है, बल्कि जीवन के उन अनुभवों का पुनरावलोकन भी है, जिन्होंने मुझे संघ को देखने का न केवल एक नया नजरिया दिया, बल्कि उसे समग्रता से पेश करने का अवसर भी प्रदान किया। आज जब राष्ट्रीय स्वयंसेवक संघ पर यह पुस्तक आप सुधी पाठकों को समर्पित कर रहा हूँ तो कुछ स्मृतियाँ मन के किसी कोने में दस्तक दे रही हैं। संघ से मेरा पहला वास्ता अस्सी के दशक में पश्चिम बंगाल के आसनसोल की छोटी गलियों वाले मुहल्ले में पड़ा, जहाँ बाल्यकाल में मैं पहली बार शाखा में गया था। हालाँकि उस समय मुझे ये पता नहीं था कि शाखा या संघ क्या चीज है, परंतु वहाँ बड़ों के साथ बच्चों को अनुशासन में खेलते हुए देखना एक ऐसा अनुभव था, जो आज भी मेरी स्मृति में जीवंत है।

दिल्ली विश्वविद्यालय में ग्रेजुएशन के दौरान संघ से एक बार फिर वास्ता पड़ा, जब मुझे कुछ महीनों के लिए 'संकल्प' छात्रावास में रहने का अवसर मिला। यहाँ उत्साही स्वयंसेवकों के साथ बिताए गए पल आज भी ताजा हैं। उस दौरान वे मुझे संघ गीत गाने के लिए विशेष रूप से प्रेरित करते थे और सामूहिक तरीके से राष्ट्रभक्ति के उन गीतों को गाकर मुझे एक अद्‍भुत संतोष और प्रेरणा मिलती थी, लेकिन संघ को लेकर हुई एक घटना ने उस समय मुझे झकझोरकर रख दिया, जब मैं एक प्रतिष्ठित मीडिया संस्थान 'न्यूज 18' में कार्यरत था।

दरअसल, मैंने हरिद्वार में गायत्री परिवार के एक यज्ञ में हिस्सा लिया था और भगवा धोती-कुरते में अपनी तसवीर फेसबुक पर पोस्ट कर दी थी। इसी तसवीर

को देखकर मेरे एक एंकर सहकर्मी ने भरे न्यूजरूम में हिकारत भरी नजरों से मुझसे सवाल किया, 'क्या तुम भी संघी हो?' उसका यह सवाल मेरे लिए किसी निजी आघात या तिरस्कार से कम नहीं था। यह क्षण मेरे लिए एक महत्त्वपूर्ण मोड़ साबित हुआ। अब तक मेरा जब भी संघ या स्वयंसेवकों से पाला पड़ा तो ऐसा कुछ भी नहीं दिखा, जो आपत्तिजनक हो। उस समय से मैंने संघ पर नियमित रूप से पढ़ना शुरू कर दिया। परंतु पुस्तक लेखन का विचार तब और प्रगाढ़ हो गया, जब नरेंद्र मोदी की सरकार आने के बाद संघ पर विपक्ष का हमला और तीखा होता चला गया।

जाहिर है संघ के प्रति मेरी दिलचस्पी उन शक्तियों की वजह से पैदा हुई, जो लगातार संघ को कठघरे में खड़ा करने का प्रयास करती रहती हैं। एक पत्रकार होने के नाते मेरे सामने भी निरंतर कई प्रश्न खड़े होते रहे। इनमें एक सवाल जो सबसे महत्त्वपूर्ण था, वह था कि आखिर इतनी सारी आलोचनाओं के बावजूद संघ 100 वर्षों से क्यों और कैसे टिका हुआ है? एक जागरूक नागरिक होने के नाते मेरी जिज्ञासा निरंतर बढ़ती रही। यही जिज्ञासा मुझे गहराई तक ले गई और मैंने संघ के बारे में अधिक जानने के लिए व्यवस्थित शोध आरंभ किया। संघ से जुड़ी न जाने कितनी पुस्तकें खरीदीं और पढ़ीं। यह भी बताना मुश्किल है कि मैंने कितने घंटे के ऑडियो-वीडियो सुने-देखे हैं। इसके अलावा संघ से जुड़े कई संगठनों के बीच जाने का प्रयास किया, जमीनी स्तर पर अनगिनत स्वयंसेवकों से संवाद किया। इस परिश्रम से जो निचोड़ निकला, उसी का परिणाम यह पुस्तक है।

यह भी सुखद संयोग है कि बरसों की मेहनत के बाद इस पुस्तक की रचना उस समय पूरी हुई है, जब संघ की स्थापना के 100 साल पूरे हुए हैं। किसी संस्था के जीवन में 100 वर्ष का विस्तार एक महत्त्वपूर्ण उपलब्धि है। यह उसकी प्रासंगिकता, सहजता, संवेदनशीलता और प्रभावशीलता का भी प्रमाण है, जो यह दरशाता है कि संस्था अपने तय लक्ष्यों को प्राप्त करने और समाज पर सकारात्मक प्रभाव डालने में कितना सक्षम रही है। संघ के बारे में बहुत सी बातें ज्ञात हैं तो कई ऐसी बातें भी हैं, जो अल्पज्ञात हैं। इस पुस्तक के माध्यम से संघ के द्वारा किए गए देशहित और समाज सेवा के कार्यों को एक स्थान पर लाने की कोशिश की गई है, जो कि भूली-बिसरी या कि कम ज्ञात हैं।

संघ का फलक इतना व्यापक है कि उसके कार्यों को 225 छोटी कहानियों

में समेट पाना मुश्किल ही नहीं, असंभव कार्य है। तथापि इस पुस्तक के माध्यम से यथासाध्य उन कहानियों को सामने लाने का प्रयास किया गया है, जो कभी हेडलाइन नहीं बन पाईं या चर्चा में नहीं आ पाईं। मीडिया में कई दशकों तक काम करने के बाद ये अनुभव हुआ कि अधिकतर लोगों की यह सोच होती है कि सिर्फ काम करना ही नहीं चाहिए, बल्कि करते हुए दिखना भी चाहिए। मगर संघ का सिद्धांत एकदम अलग है। यहाँ काम करते तो हैं, मगर करते हुए दिखने और प्रकाशित होने से उन्हें परहेज है, इसलिए जब कई कहानियों की पुष्टि के लिए हमने जतन किया तो भी मुश्किलों का सामना करना पड़ा। इस पुस्तक की कहानियों को कम-से-कम शब्दों में लिखने का प्रयास किया गया है। ऐसा इसलिए, क्योंकि किसी घटनाक्रम के बारे में अगर छोटी कहानी के माध्यम से बताया जाए तो वे ज्यादा सरल, सहज और सुग्राह्य होता है। इस पुस्तक के माध्यम से जहाँ एक तरफ संघ की दुर्लभ और अनसुनी कहानियों को सामने लाने की कोशिश की गई है, वहीं ये कहानियाँ संघ के खिलाफ फैलाई गई कई भ्रांतियों को भी दूर करती हैं।

इस पुस्तक की रचना के समय यह कोशिश थी कि आजादी के आंदोलन के दौरान और विभाजन के समय तक की कहानियों को पुस्तक में समेटा जाए, लेकिन प्रबुद्धजनों की राय के बाद इसमें संघ से जुड़ी अद्यतन कहानियों पर भी मैंने काम किया और उन्हें भी जोड़ने का प्रयास किया है। इसमें स्वाधीनता आंदोलन, विभाजन, आपातकाल से लेकर कोरोनाकाल और इसके बाद की भी अद्यतन कहानियों को शामिल किया गया है, लेकिन इस बात को स्वीकार करने में मुझे तनिक भी संकोच नहीं है कि रिसर्च के दौरान मुझे यह आभास हुआ कि ये कहानियाँ संघ के प्रयासों को सामने लाने की एक झलक भर हैं। जितना मैंने लिखा है, वह ऊँट के मुँह में जीरा के समान है। ऐसी अनगिनत कहानियाँ हैं, जिनमें संघ के कार्यकर्ताओं ने 'नेकी कर दरिया में डाल' की भावना के साथ काम किया और अब वे कहीं भी उपलब्ध नहीं हैं। मैंने इस पुस्तक में उन्हीं कहानियों को सम्मिलित किया है, जिनका उल्लेख किसी-न-किसी स्रोत ग्रंथ में हुआ है। इस पुस्तक की रचना हेतु जिस प्रकार लोगों का प्रत्यक्ष या अप्रत्यक्ष रूप से सहयोग मिला, मैं उन सभी का हृदय से आभार प्रकट करता हूँ।

'संघ की अनसुनी कहानियाँ' अब आपके हाथों में है। उम्मीद है कि संघ

को जानने–समझने में यह मददगार बनेगी और शोधार्थियों के लिए सहायक एवं महत्त्वपूर्ण साबित होगी। आपकी सकारात्मक समीक्षा, तार्किक आलोचना एवं महत्त्वपूर्ण सुझाव मेरा उत्साहवर्धन करेंगे। पुस्तक आपको कैसी लगी, अपने मंतव्य से जरूर अवगत कराइएगा।

—डॉ. हरीश चंद्र बर्णवाल

hcburnwal@gmail.com

महाअष्टमी
30 सितंबर, 2025

अनुक्रम

स्वतंत्रता संघर्ष और डॉ. हेडगेवार

विभाजन की त्रासदी और आजादी

स्वतंत्र भारत के 5 दशक

इक्कीसवीं सदी और संघ

संगठन

कहानियों का संदर्भ देखने के लिए
क्यूआर कोड स्कैन करें।

स्वतंत्रता संघर्ष और संघ

प्रारंभिक प्रचारक

श्री प्रभाकरराव फैजपूरकर

श्री के. बापूराव मोघे

श्री बापूसाहेब महाशब्दे

श्री के.डी. जोशी

श्री दिनकरराव बुचे

श्री मुकुंदराव मुंजे

श्री वासुदेवराव विश्वेकर

श्री अण्णाजी चट्टे

श्री भौय्याजी जुगादे

श्री मनोहर डोंगरे

श्री दिगंबर शंकरराव तिजारे

अखिल भारतीय बैठक की एक तसवीर

(पुणे की तसवीर)
बाएँ से—
(1) गणपतराव नलावडे,
(2) डॉ. हेडगेवार,
(3) छात्र जगद्‌गुरु,
(4) अण्णासाहब भोपटकर,
(5) तात्यासाहब करंदीकर।

(शुद्धि समारोह)

बैठे हुए (बाएँ से)—(2) दाजीसाहब बुटी, (4) डॉ. हेडगेवार, (7) डॉ. कुर्तकोटी, (8) राजा लक्ष्मणराव भोंसले, (10) डॉ. मुंजे।

* श्री न.गो. देशपांडे के घर, आर्वी में दत्तविधान समारोह में बैठे हुए (बाएँ से)—
सीतारामपंत हेडगेवार, (मध्य में) श्री न.गो. देशपांडे, पत्नी तथा दत्तक पुत्र,
कोट, टोपी पहने हुए डॉ. हेडगेवारजी।

बैठे हुए (बाएँ से)
(1) डॉ. इंगले,
(2) डॉ. बी.आर कानिटकर,
(3) डॉ. लूले।

कुरसी पर बैठे हुए
(बाएँ से)—
(1) डॉ. शंकरराव
नाईक, मुर्तिजापुर,
(2) श्री अण्णासाहब
खापर्डे, अमरावती।

डॉ. हेडगेवार के दुर्लभ चित्र

ब्रिटिश सरकार के खिलाफ संस्थाओं में संघ सबसे ऊपर

स्वतंत्रता आंदोलन में राष्ट्रीय स्वयंसेवक संघ की भूमिका कितनी महत्त्वपूर्ण है, इसे इसी बात से समझा जा सकता है कि ब्रिटिश सरकार ने वर्ष 1940 में स्वयंसेवी संस्थाओं की जो सूची बनाई थी, उसमें संघ को सबसे मजबूत स्वयंसेवी संस्था के रूप में दिखाया गया था। दरअसल संघ ने उस समय जो रणनीति अपनाई, उसकी वजह से अंग्रेज अफसरों को संघ की गतिविधियों पर नजर रखने में काफी कठिनाई हो रही थी। स्वयंसेवक उस समय सक्रिय अनुशीलन समिति, हिंदुस्तान समाजवादी प्रजातांत्रिक सेना, बब्बर खालसा, गदर पार्टी, कांग्रेस पार्टी व अभिनव भारत जैसे 20 से अधिक संगठनों में सीधे सक्रिय होकर स्वाधीनता के लक्ष्य को परिणति तक पहुँचा रहे थे। वर्ष 1938-39 आते-आते संघ की गतिविधियों में तेजी आ गई थी। इससे ब्रिटिश हुकूमत दहशत में आ गई और संघ को कमजोर करने के लिए अगस्त 1940 में स्वयंसेवी संस्थाओं के शारीरिक प्रशिक्षण कार्यक्रमों पर प्रतिबंध लगा दिया गया। सरकारी महकमे में संघ की उपस्थिति पर ब्रिटिश खुफिया विभाग ने टिप्पणी की थी, 'संघ के स्वयंसेवकों को चिह्नित करना कठिन कार्य है, क्योंकि प्रत्येक को छद्म नाम दिया जाता है। खुफिया रिपोर्ट में उदाहरण देते हुए बताया गया कि पंजाब के दिलबाग राय सेठ, जो सरकारी कर्मचारी हैं और ओम प्रकाश वैद्य जो सेना में हैं, वे क्रमशः प्रसन्नचित्त और विष्णु सहाय के नाम से संघ में जाने जाते हैं।' ब्रिटिश राज के लिए परेशानी का सबब यह था कि चाहे कांग्रेस पार्टी हो, आजाद हिंद फौज हो या फिर स्थानीय स्तर पर हो रहे आंदोलन हों, वे संघ के स्वयंसेवकों को हर जगह पाते थे।

□

स्वतंत्रता प्राप्ति के लिए संघ ने बनाई थी योजना

राष्ट्रीय स्वयंसेवक संघ ने स्वतंत्रता प्राप्ति के लिए एक बड़ी योजना तैयार की थी। इस बात से डरकर अंग्रेजी हुकूमत ने संघ पर निगरानी रखने के लिए अपने खुफिया विभाग को लगा दिया था। इस संबंध में ब्रिटिश शासन के गुप्तचर विभाग ने वर्ष 1943 में जो रिपोर्ट प्रस्तुत की, वह राष्ट्रीय अभिलेखागार की फाइलों में सुरक्षित है। इसमें कहा गया है कि संघ योजनाबद्ध तरीके से स्वतंत्रता प्राप्ति की ओर बढ़ रहा है। रिपोर्ट में गुप्तचर विभाग ने संघ के अधिकारियों के प्रवास, कार्यक्रमों एवं शस्त्र प्रशिक्षण पर चिंता प्रकट की थी। गुप्तचर विभाग की रिपोर्ट में संघ के क्रांतिकारियों से संबंधों का भी उल्लेख किया गया था। मई-जून 1943 तक संघ का कार्य तेजी से फैल रहा था। संघ ने 11 शहरों में अधिकारी शिक्षण शिविर लगाए। इन शिविरों में युद्ध कौशल और लड़ाई के तरीकों पर चर्चा की गई और बताया गया कि संगठन के शक्तिशाली होने पर भारत की स्वाधीनता के लिए अंग्रेजों से संघर्ष को तेज किया जाएगा। ब्रिटिश सत्ता को इसकी भनक न लगे, इसलिए इन शिविरों तथा कार्यक्रमों में पूर्ण गोपनीयता बरती जाती थी।

□

संघ के असर से डरकर अंग्रेजों ने 'गणवेश' पर लगाई पाबंदी

अंग्रेजी हुकूमत संघ की बढ़ती ताकत से इतना घबरा गई थी कि उसने संघ की यूनिफॉर्म 'गणवेश' पर पूरी तरह से पाबंदी लगा दी। देश भर में संघ के प्रभाव से वो किस कदर खौफ में थी, इसका अंदाजा उसके गुप्तचर विभाग की रिपोर्ट से ही लगाया जा सकता है। इस रिपोर्ट के आधार पर ही ब्रिटिश शासन ने 5 अगस्त, 1940 को एक अध्यादेश जारी किया। इसमें भारत सुरक्षा कानून 56 व 58 के अंतर्गत किसी भी गैर-सरकारी संगठन द्वारा सैनिक वरदी पहनने और परेड (पथ संचलन) करने पर कानूनी प्रतिबंध लगा दिया गया। ये आदेश सीधे-सीधे संघ को कुचलने का प्रयास था। ब्रिटिश शासन के गुप्तचर विभाग की रिपोर्टों में साफ तौर पर ये लिखा था, 'संघ का वास्तविक उद्देश्य तो अंग्रेजों को भारत से खदेड़कर देश को स्वतंत्र करवाना है।' गुप्तचर विभाग ने संघ अधिकारियों के भाषणों को भी इकट्ठा करना शुरू कर दिया था। रिपोर्ट में यह भी कहा गया, 'संघ का बड़ी तेजी से विस्तार हो रहा है। उसकी शाखाएँ अब देसी रियासतों सहित पूरे भारत में लग रही हैं। सरकारी सेवाओं में भी संघ की घुसपैठ हो चुकी है और यहाँ तक कि सेना भी इससे अछूती नहीं है।'

□

सविनय अवज्ञा आंदोलन में संघ ने निभाई सक्रिय भूमिका

महात्मा गांधी ने वर्ष 1930 में सविनय अवज्ञा आंदोलन की शुरुआत नमक सत्याग्रह और दांडी मार्च के साथ की थी। उन्होंने नमक पर टैक्स लगाने के अंग्रेजों के फैसले के खिलाफ अहमदाबाद में साबरमती आश्रम से नमक सत्याग्रह की शुरुआत की थी। स्वतंत्रता का आंदोलन हो और स्वयंसेवक भाग न लें, ऐसा कैसे हो सकता है! युवा स्वयंसेवकों की टोलियाँ निश्चित स्थानों पर पहुँचकर सत्याग्रह करने लगीं। स्वयंसेवकों का मनोबल देखकर संघचालकों की बैठक में यह निश्चित किया गया कि सत्याग्रह में संघ समर्पित भाव से भाग लेगा। कुछ स्वयंसेवकों ने गणवेश पहनकर भगवा ध्वज के साथ सत्याग्रह में जाने की इच्छा प्रकट की। हालाँकि डॉ. हेडगेवार ने उनकी निष्ठा का सम्मान करते हुए समझाया, "आंदोलन में पूरी तरह समरस होने का प्रयास करना चाहिए। सभी स्वयंसेवक व्यक्तिगत तौर पर आंदोलन में संघचालक की अनुमति से भाग लें।" डॉ. हेडगेवार ने स्वयंसेवकों से कहा, "इस भ्रम में नहीं रहना चाहिए कि वर्तमान आंदोलन स्वतंत्रता प्राप्ति की अंतिम लड़ाई होगी। हमें सर्वस्व त्याग कर उसमें कूदने के लिए तैयार रहना चाहिए।" उन्होंने स्वयंसेवकों को अति उत्साह से बचने और अपने पाँव धरती पर टिकाए रखते हुए स्वाधीनता आंदोलन में भाग लेने का निर्देश दिया। यहाँ तक कि संघ ने सत्याग्रहियों की सुरक्षा के लिए 100 स्वयंसेवकों की टोली भी बनाई थी।

□

हेडगेवार ने जंगल कानून तोड़कर किया सत्याग्रह

एक तरफ देश में अंग्रेजों के खिलाफ नमक टैक्स को लेकर नमक सत्याग्रह चल रहा था, उसी दौरान राष्ट्रीय स्वयंसेवक संघ के संस्थापक डॉ. हेडगेवार ने अंग्रेजों द्वारा थोपे गए जंगल कानून को तोड़कर जंगल सत्याग्रह किया। दरअसल, उन दिनों मध्य प्रांत की सरकार ने प्रदेश के 1618 वर्ग मील जंगल को प्रतिबंधित घोषित कर दिया। कानून के तहत कोई भी व्यक्ति चारे के लिए एवं निर्माण कार्य के लिए लकड़ी नहीं काट सकता था। इससे अनेक लोगों के कारोबार प्रभावित हो रहे थे। इस मुश्किल को समझते हुए डॉ. हेडगेवार ने एक जत्था तैयार किया और 21 जुलाई, 1930 को जंगल कानून को तोड़ने का निश्चय किया। सत्याग्रह के पूर्व उन्होंने सरसंघचालक का दायित्व डॉ. परांजपे को सौंप दिया। इस अवसर पर उन्होंने स्पष्ट किया कि जो लोग इस आंदोलन में भाग ले रहे हैं, वे व्यक्तिगत स्तर पर ऐसा कर रहे हैं। सत्याग्रह स्थल यवतमाल से 10 किलोमीटर दूर लोहारा के जंगल में था। स्वयंसेवकों ने भगवा ध्वज को प्रणाम करके पूजा की और फिर घास एवं लकड़ी काटने के औजार लेकर सत्याग्रह के लिए निकल पड़े। इस सत्याग्रह को देखने के लिए 10 हजार से ज्यादा लोग इकट्ठे हो गए थे। जैसे ही स्वयंसेवकों ने घास काटना शुरू किया, कानून टूट गया। पुलिस ने उन्हें गिरफ्तार कर लिया। इस सत्याग्रह के लिए डॉ. हेडगेवार को नौ महीने के कठोर कारावास की सजा सुनाई गई। □

स्वतंत्रता संग्राम के दौरान डॉ. हेडगेवार दो बार जेल गए

स्वतंत्रता संग्राम में हिस्सा लेने की वजह से डॉ. हेडगेवार एक नहीं, बल्कि दो बार जेल गए। यहाँ तक कि आजादी की लड़ाई में हिस्सा लेने के लिए उन्होंने अपना सरसंघचालक का दायित्व भी छोड़ दिया था। दायित्व छोड़ने का सीधा मतलब था कि स्वयंसेवक संगठन के तौर पर नहीं, एक प्रेरणा के तौर पर व्यक्तिगत हैसियत से आजादी के आंदोलन में हिस्सा लें। इस तरह से हजारों की संख्या में स्वयंसेवकों ने इसमें भाग लिया और कइयों ने अपना जीवन बलिदान कर दिया। डॉ. हेडगेवार पहली बार असहयोग आंदोलन में अपने उग्र भाषण के कारण वर्ष 1921 में जेल गए थे और एक साल कठोर कारावास की सजा पूरी करने के बाद 12 जुलाई, 1922 को जेल से छूटे थे। वहीं दूसरी बार वर्ष 1930 में जंगल सत्याग्रह में हिस्सा लेने की वजह से 22 जुलाई, 1930 को यवतमाल में अंग्रेजों ने उन्हें गिरफ्तार कर लिया। उन्हें नौ महीने जेल की सजा सुनाई गई। वर्ष 1930 तक डॉ. हेडगेवार काफी लोकप्रिय हो गए थे। डॉ. हेडगेवार और सत्याग्रहियों को जब यवतमाल से अकोला ले जाया जा रहा था, तब भीड़ इकट्ठा हो जाने के कारण पुलिस ने सभी सत्याग्रहियों को हथकड़ी लगाने का आदेश दिया। इसका विरोध करते हुए, डॉ. हेडगेवार ने चेतावनी दी कि अगर हथकड़ी लगाने का प्रयास किया गया तो वे पुलिसवालों को ही खदेड़ देंगे। इसके बाद हथकड़ी नहीं लगाई गई।

□

1200 गणवेशधारी स्वयंसेवक देख अंग्रेज हुए भयभीत

वर्ष 1932 के विजयादशमी में करीब 1200 गणवेशधारी स्वयंसेवक शामिल हुए। इतनी बड़ी संख्या में स्वयंसेवकों को देख अंग्रेज भयभीत हो गए। संघ को खतरा मानते हुए वे उस पर प्रतिबंध लगाने की जुगत में जुट गए। 15 दिसंबर, 1932 को मध्य प्रांत के गवर्नर-इन-काउंसिल ने सरकारी कर्मचारियों के संघ की शाखाओं में जाने पर रोक लगाने का आदेश जारी कर दिया। यही नहीं, कुछ समय बाद यह आदेश नगर पालिका और जिला स्थानीय बोर्ड के कर्मचारियों पर भी लागू कर दिया गया। बोर्ड और नगर पालिका समितियों ने इसका विरोध किया। समाज के अन्य वर्गों द्वारा भी इसका विरोध हुआ। 7 मार्च, 1934 को विधायक वी.डी. कोलते ने इस प्रतिबंध के विरोध में विधानसभा में प्रस्ताव पेश किया। एक के बाद एक वक्ताओं ने इन आदेशों की निंदा की। नागपुर विश्वविद्यालय के डॉ. डी.टी. मंगल मूर्ति ने गृहमंत्री ई. राघवेंद्र राव को याद दिलाया कि 1929 में उन्होंने खुद बिलासपुर में एक अखाड़े की आधारशिला रखी थी, जो कि संघ का केंद्र था। अमृताबाई डागा कॉलेज की प्रिंसिपल रमाबाई ताँबे ने कहा, "राष्ट्रीय स्वयंसेवक संघ एक सार्थक आंदोलन है। इसे मध्य प्रांतों में शुरू किया गया है और मैं कह सकती हूँ कि यह पूरे भारत में फैलेगा और सभी समुदायों को एक साथ संगठित करेगा। मुझे संघ में प्रशिक्षित लड़कों का व्यवहार देखना अच्छा लगता है। मैं नहीं मानती कि संघ उन्हें अराजकतावादी बनाता है। किसी ने कुछ शरारत की है।" दो दिन की बहस के बाद प्रस्ताव पारित हो गया और सरकार को हार का मुँह देखना पड़ा। इस तरह सरकार का प्रतिबंध का आदेश निष्प्रभावी हो गया।

□

भारत छोड़ो आंदोलन में कई स्वयंसेवकों ने जेल की सजा काटी

वर्ष 1942 में भारत छोड़ो आंदोलन शुरू होने से पहले डॉ. हेडगेवार का निधन हो चुका था। इसके बाद संघ के दूसरे सरसंघचालक माधवराव सदाशिवराव गोलवलकर उपाख्य 'श्रीगुरुजी' को यह फैसला करना था कि आंदोलन में संघ किस प्रकार से हिस्सा लेगा। आंदोलन की दशा और दिशा का आकलन करने के लिए श्रीगुरुजी ने प्रांत स्तर के कार्यकर्ताओं की एक बैठक बुलाई। इसके बाद यह निर्णय लिया गया, "संघ संगठन के रूप में इस आंदोलन में भाग नहीं लेगा, लेकिन चूँकि यह आंदोलन देश की स्वतंत्रता के लिए किया जा रहा है, इसलिए नागरिक के रूप में स्वयंसेवक इस आंदोलन में देश के किसी भी हिस्से में भाग ले सकते हैं।" इसके बाद स्वयंसेवक अपनी-अपनी सामर्थ्य के अनुसार आम जनता के साथ सहयोग करने के लिए इस लड़ाई में कूद गए। इस बात की पुष्टि राष्ट्रीय अभिलेखागार में रखी गुप्तचर विभाग की एक रिपोर्ट से भी होती है। यह रिपोर्ट एक फाइल में सुरक्षित तरीके से रखी गई है। इस फाइल में संघ के उन कार्यकर्ताओं के नाम लिखे हैं, जिन्होंने 1942 के आंदोलन में भागीदारी की और हिरासत में लिये गए।

□

आजाद हिंद फौज में स्वयंसेवकों ने दिया योगदान

द्वितीय विश्वयुद्ध के दौरान वर्ष 1942 में भारत को अंग्रेजों के कब्जे से स्वतंत्र कराने के लिए महान् स्वतंत्रता सेनानी सुभाष चंद्र बोस ने आजाद हिंद फौज यानी इंडियन नेशनल आर्मी (INA) नामक सशस्त्र सेना का गठन किया। आजाद हिंद फौज के गठन और उसके संचालन में राष्ट्रीय स्वयंसेवक संघ की भी महत्त्वपूर्ण भूमिका थी। संघ के तीन प्रचारक व सैकड़ों स्वयंसेवक आजाद हिंद फौज में भेजे गए थे। संघ किस तरह आजाद हिंद फौज से जुड़ा हुआ था, इसका पता 20 सितंबर, 1943 को नागपुर में संघ की एक गुप्त बैठक से भी चलता है। इसमें जापान की सहायता से आजाद हिंद फौज के भारत की ओर रवाना होने के समय संघ की संभावित योजना पर विचार हुआ। आजाद हिंद फौज और संघ के बीच किस प्रकार का संबंध था, इसे बोस और डॉ. हेडगेवार के बीच मुलाकातों से भी समझा जा सकता है। बोस और डॉ. हेडगेवार पहली बार 1928 में कांग्रेस पार्टी के कलकत्ता सेशन में मिले थे। वहाँ दोनों के बीच स्वयंसेवकों को तैयार करने पर चर्चा हुई। इसके बाद वर्ष 1938 में बोस जब कांग्रेस पार्टी के अध्यक्ष के नाते नागपुर पहुँचे थे तो वे डॉ. हेडगेवार से मिलना चाहते थे, लेकिन प्रोविंशियल कांग्रेस कमेटी ने इसकी अनुमति नहीं दी। वर्ष 1939 में बोस ने डॉ. हेडगेवार के पास संदेश भिजवाया कि वे सशस्त्र विद्रोह की योजना बना रहे हैं। इसके बाद बोस का संदेश लेकर त्रिलोकीनाथ चक्रवर्ती डॉ. हेडगेवार से मिले थे। 20 जून, 1940 को बोस खुद डॉ. हेडगेवार से मिलने पहुँचे थे, लेकिन उनके नींद में होने की वजह से मुलाकात नहीं हो पाई। इसके एक दिन बाद ही 21 जून, 1940 को डॉ. हेडगेवार ने अंतिम साँस ली।

□

स्वतंत्रता आंदोलन के दौरान संघ ने बनाई थी स्वतंत्र सरकार

राष्ट्रीय स्वयंसेवक संघ ने वर्ष 1942 में भारत छोड़ो आंदोलन के दौरान स्वतंत्र सरकार की स्थापना की थी। इसकी भनक ब्रिटिश सत्ता को लग गई थी, जिसकी पुष्टि उसकी खुफिया रिपोर्ट से होती है। संघ के बढ़ते प्रभाव की वजह से ब्रिटिश अधिकारी स्वयंसेवकों की गतिविधियों की जासूसी करवाने लगे थे। नरेंद्र सहगल ने अपनी पुस्तक 'भारतवर्ष की सर्वांग स्वतंत्रता' में लिखा है—"राष्ट्रीय अभिलेखागार में गुप्तचर विभाग की यह रिपोर्ट बड़े साइज की मोटी फाइल में सुरक्षित रखी हुई है। इसी फाइल में संघ के अनेक कार्यकर्ताओं के नाम भी मिलते हैं, जो वर्ष 1942 के भारत छोड़ो आंदोलन में भागीदारी करने के कारण विभिन्न स्थानों पर हिरासत में लिये गए और जेलों में सजा भुगतते रहे। इन रिपोर्टों से यह भी पता चलता है कि विदर्भ के अष्टी-चिमूर नामक स्थान पर तो संघ के कार्यकर्ताओं ने स्वतंत्र सरकार की स्थापना भी कर ली थी। संघ के स्वयंसेवकों ने अंग्रेजों की पुलिस द्वारा किए गए कई प्रकार के अमानुषिक अत्याचारों का सामना किया। गुप्तचर विभाग की रिपोर्टों से पता चलता है कि अपनी सरकार स्थापित करने के बाद सरकारी आदेशों से हुए लाठीचार्ज और गोलीबारी में एक दर्जन से अधिक स्वयंसेवक बलिदान हुए थे।"

□

स्वतंत्रता आंदोलन में संघ का दूसरा केंद्र बना वर्धा

स्वतंत्रता आंदोलन के समय नागपुर एक महत्त्वपूर्ण केंद्र था और इसमें राष्ट्रीय स्वयंसेवक संघ के संस्थापक डॉ. हेडगेवार का अहम योगदान रहा। यों तो नागपुर में संघ की स्थापना वर्ष 1925 में हुई, लेकिन संघ के गठन के पूर्व से ही वे अलग-अलग माध्यमों से युवाओं में देशप्रेम और स्वाधीनता की अलख जगा रहे थे। इसका परिणाम यह हुआ कि वर्ष 1920 में असहयोग आंदोलन और वर्ष 1923 में झंडा सत्याग्रह का मुख्य केंद्र यह शहर रहा। नागपुर के बाद संघ की दूसरी शाखा 18 फरवरी, 1926 को वर्धा में स्थापित हुई तो यह शहर स्वतंत्रता आंदोलन का दूसरा केंद्र बन गया। वर्धा में संघ द्वारा किए गए कार्य से ऐसा अनुकूल वातावरण बना कि महात्मा गांधी साबरमती आश्रम छोड़कर वर्ष 1936 में वर्धा आ गए और सेवाग्राम आश्रम में रहने लगे। भारत छोड़ो आंदोलन की रूपरेखा भी इसी शहर में तैयार हुई। संघ की दूसरी शाखा वर्धा में स्थापित होने की रोचक कहानी है। एक बार संघ के संस्थापक डॉ. हेडगेवार ने कार्यकर्ता-बैठक में कहा कि क्या केवल संघकार्य किसी के जीवन का ध्येय नहीं बन सकता? यह सुनकर हरिकृष्ण जोशी ने उन 56 संस्थाओं से त्याग-पत्र दे दिया, जिनसे वे संबद्ध थे और 18 फरवरी, 1926 को वर्धा में शाखा प्रारंभ कर दी। हरिकृष्ण जोशी बाद में 'अप्पाजी जोशी' के नाम से प्रसिद्ध हुए। यह नागपुर के बाहर राष्ट्रीय स्वयंसेवक संघ की पहली शाखा थी। डॉ. हेडगेवार ने उन्हें वर्धा जिला संघचालक का दायित्व दिया था। वर्ष 1946 में वे कुछ समय के लिए सरकार्यवाह बने।

□

संघ और स्वतंत्रता सेनानी

(जंगल सत्याग्रह) कुरसी पर बैठे (बाएँ से)—(1) विट्ठलराव देव, (2) दादाराव परमार्थ, (3) डॉ. हेडगेवार, (4) भैयाजी कुंबलवार, (5) आप्पाजी जोशी।

(दि आइडियल डेमोक्रेटिक इंश्योरेंस कंपनी लि., नागपुर) बैठे हुए (बाएँ से)—(1) दत्तोपंत परांजपे, (2) दामुपंत देशमुख, (3) शेषराव पाँढरीपांडे, (4) दादासाहब खापर्डे, (5) नाना साहब तेलंग, (6) डॉ. हेडगेवार, (7) डी. डी. देशपांडे।

डॉ. हेडगेवार के दुर्लभ चित्र

स्वतंत्रता आंदोलन के समय स्वयंसेवक।

सेवा भारती के शिविर में कार्यकर्ता।

स्वयंसेवकों से प्रभावित होकर गांधीजी पहुँच गए संघ के शिविर

महात्मा गांधी जमनालाल बजाज के आमंत्रण पर वर्धा पहुँचे थे। बापू जिस दोमंजिला घर में रुके, उसके सामने विशाल मैदान में संघ के स्वयंसेवकों का जिलास्तरीय शीतकालीन शिविर 23 से 25 दिसंबर, 1934 के बीच आयोजित किया गया था। इसमें करीब डेढ़ हजार कार्यकर्ताओं ने भाग लिया था। महात्मा गांधी सेवाग्राम आश्रम में ठहरे हुए थे, जो कि संघ के शिविर से काफी नजदीक था। उन्होंने अपने कमरे से संघ के शिविर को काफी करीब से देखा। उन्होंने देखा कि किस प्रकार कार्यकर्ताओं ने खुद पूरे मैदान को साफ किया, इसके बाद अथक परिश्रम करते हुए तंबू लगाए और उसे एक व्यवस्थित शिविर का रूप दिया। गांधीजी इस पूरे प्रकरण को देखकर बहुत प्रभावित हुए। उन्होंने महादेव देसाई से इसे पास जाकर देखने की इच्छा जताई। इस बारे में जमनालाल बजाज के बेटे कमलनयन बजाज ने अप्पाजी जोशी से बात की। अप्पाजी जोशी ने तुरंत ही महात्मा गांधी को शिविर में आने का न्योता दिया। गांधीजी ने भी संघ के शिविर को देखने में देर नहीं लगाई। अगले दिन ही सुबह 6 बजे शिविर में पहुँच गए। यह घटना 24 दिसंबर, 1934 की है।

□

संघ के शिविर में जाकर भाव-विभोर हुए गांधीजी

महात्मा गांधी राष्ट्रीय स्वयंसेवक संघ के वर्धा शिविर में मीरा बेन, महादेव देसाई और अन्य लोगों के साथ पहुँचे। शाखा में स्वयंसेवकों को योग अभ्यास करते देखकर गांधीजी ने अप्पाजी के कंधे पर हाथ रखा और कहा, "मैं बहुत प्रसन्न हूँ। देश में मैंने ऐसा नजारा कहीं नहीं देखा।" जब भगवा ध्वज फहराया गया तो गांधीजी अन्य लोगों की तरह सावधान की मुद्रा में खड़े हो गए और ध्वज को सलामी दी। उसके बाद गांधीजी ने शिविर घूमने की इच्छा व्यक्त की। शिविर में लोगों से मिलते समय उन्होंने एक जगह कुछ स्वयंसेवकों की जाति पूछी। वे यह जानकर आश्चर्य से भर गए कि उनमें से एक महार था, दूसरा तेली, तीसरा मराठा और चौथा ब्राह्मण था। गांधीजी चकित थे कि संघ ने किस प्रकार विभिन्न जातियों को एक साथ रहने, खेलने और खाने के दौरान जोड़कर रखा। संघ शिविर से जब गांधीजी की विदाई का समय आया तो अप्पाजी जोशी ने उनसे पूछा कि आपको कोई कमी नजर आई हो तो बताइए। इस पर गांधीजी ने कहा, "कोई कमी नहीं। हर तरह से आप बेहतरीन कार्य कर रहे हैं।"

□

गांधीजी ने डॉ. हेडगेवार को बताया देश का दूसरा ऑर्गेनाइजर

महात्मा गांधी 25 दिसंबर को वर्धा में डॉ. हेडगेवार से मिले। डॉ. हेडगेवार के साथ अप्पाजी जोशी और पुणे के एल.बी. भोपटकर भी मौजूद थे। गांधी संघ शिविर का दौरा कर चुके थे और इससे काफी प्रभावित थे। शुरुआती अभिवादन के बाद गांधीजी ने कहा, "डॉ. हेडगेवार, मुझे लगा कि मैं भारत में एकमात्र ऑर्गेनाइजर हूँ, लेकिन एक और भी है, और वह डॉ. हेडगेवार हैं।" उन्होंने आगे कहा, "आपके पास बहुत बढ़िया बैंड है। मुझे संगीत सुनने का शौक है। आपका बैंड रात नौ बजे के बाद बजता है और नौ बजे मेरा सोने का समय होता है। फिर भी मैं छत पर जाकर इसे सुनता हूँ।" गांधीजी को यह जानकर आश्चर्य हुआ कि संघ के स्वयंसेवक अपने भोजन, वरदी और यात्रा का खर्च स्वयं उठाते हैं और पूर्ण अनुशासन बनाए रखते हैं, जबकि अन्य स्वयंसेवी संगठनों में उन्हें ये सभी चीजें मुफ्त दी जाती हैं और फिर भी कोई अनुशासन नहीं होता। डॉ. हेडगेवार ने बताया, "संघ के व्याख्यानों में हम राष्ट्रीय एकता, चरित्र और धर्म, समाज, संस्कृति और राष्ट्र के प्रति प्रेम को बढ़ावा देने वाले विचार रखते हैं। हम उन्हें 'रामायण' और 'महाभारत' की ऐतिहासिक कहानियाँ और घटनाएँ सुनाते हैं। इससे स्वयंसेवकों में नेक भावनाएँ और आदर्शवाद पैदा होता है।" उन्होंने कहा, "जहाँ अन्य संगठन अपने स्वयंसेवकों को 'मुफ्त का मजदूर' मानते हैं, वहीं संघ अपने स्वयंसेवकों को प्रथम श्रेणी का देशभक्त मानता है, जो देश के लिए कुछ भी कर सकते हैं।"

□

गांधीजी के सामने डॉ. हेडगेवार ने बताईं कांग्रेस की कमियाँ

महात्मा गांधी वर्धा के संघ शिविर का दौरा कर इस कदर प्रभावित हुए कि जब वे डॉ. हेडगेवार से मिले तो सवालों की झड़ी लगा दी। इस दौरान गांधीजी ने कांग्रेस पार्टी से संबंधित सवाल भी पूछे। गांधीजी ने पूछा—"आपका संगठन सराहनीय है। मैं जानता हूँ कि आप कई वर्षों तक कांग्रेस के कार्यकर्ता रहे हैं। आपने कांग्रेस जैसे लोकप्रिय संगठन में ऐसा स्वयंसेवक कैडर क्यों नहीं बनाया? आपने अलग संगठन क्यों बनाया?" डॉ. हेडगेवार ने कहा, "यह सच है कि मैंने कांग्रेस में काम किया है। मैं कांग्रेस के वर्ष 1920 के अधिवेशन के समय स्वयंसेवक दल का सचिव भी था। उस समय मेरे मित्र डॉ. परांजपे दल के अध्यक्ष थे। इसके बाद हम दोनों ने कांग्रेस के अंदर एक ऐसा स्वयंसेवक कैडर बनाने की कोशिश की, लेकिन हमारे प्रयास सफल नहीं हुए।" गांधीजी ने पूछा—"आपका प्रयास क्यों विफल हुआ? क्या यह वित्तीय सहायता की कमी के कारण था?" डॉ. हेडगेवार ने कहा, "नहीं। नहीं! धन की कोई कमी नहीं थी। हमारे सामने जो समस्या थी, वह धन की नहीं, बल्कि दृष्टिकोण की थी।" गांधीजी ने पूछा, "क्या आपका यह मानना है कि कांग्रेस में नेकदिल लोग नहीं थे या अब नहीं हैं?" हेडगेवार ने कहा, "कांग्रेस में कई नेक इरादे वाले लोग हैं। मुद्दा कुछ बुनियादी दृष्टिकोणों का है।" हेडगेवार ने आगे कहा, "कांग्रेस के नेता स्वयंसेवकों को अवैतनिक सेवकों के रूप में देखने के आदी हैं। कांग्रेस यह नहीं मानती कि राष्ट्र की समस्याओं का प्रभावी समाधान तभी हो सकता है, जब समर्पित स्वयंसेवकों का एक बड़ा और अनुशासित समूह अपनी इच्छा से, और कहीं और से प्रेरणा की प्रतीक्षा किए बिना देश की सेवा करने के लिए उत्सुक हों।"

□

गांधीजी ने डॉ. हेडगेवार को दी सफल होने की शुभकामना

वर्धा में जब महात्मा गांधी और डॉ. हेडगेवार की मुलाकात हुई तो इस दौरान उन्होंने डॉ. हेडगेवार को अपने मिशन में सफल होने की शुभकामनाएँ भी दीं। गांधी और हेडगेवार के बीच हुई यह बातचीत एक ऐतिहासिक दस्तावेज की तरह है। गांधीजी ने पूछा, "स्वयंसेवक के बारे में आपकी क्या धारणा है?" डॉ. हेडगेवार ने कहा, "स्वयंसेवक वह है, जो राष्ट्र के सर्वांगीण उत्थान के लिए प्रेमपूर्वक अपना जीवन समर्पित कर दे। ऐसे स्वयंसेवकों का निर्माण करना ही संघ का उद्‌देश्य है।" गांधीजी ने कहा, "मैं वास्तव में बहुत खुश हूँ। आपके प्रयासों की सफलता से देश को निश्चित रूप से लाभ होगा। मैंने सुना है कि वर्धा जिले में संघ ने बहुत बड़ी संख्या में कार्यकर्ता तैयार कर लिये हैं। आप इतने बड़े संगठन का खर्च कैसे उठाते हैं?" डॉ. हेडगेवार ने कहा, "स्वयंसेवक स्वयं खर्च उठाते हैं; सब अपना-अपना योगदान गुरु-दक्षिणा के रूप में देते हैं।" गांधीजी ने फिर पूछा, "ऐसा लगता है कि आपका पूरा समय इसी काम में बीतता है। आप अपना चिकित्सा पेशा कैसे चलाते हैं?" इस पर डॉ. हेडगेवार ने जवाब दिया कि उन्होंने चिकित्सा को पेशे के तौर पर नहीं अपनाया है। गांधीजी ने फिर कौतूहल से पूछा, "तो फिर आप अपने परिवार का भरण-पोषण कैसे करते हैं?" गांधीजी यह जानकर और भी चकित रह गए कि डॉ. हेडगेवार ने राष्ट्र सेवा के लिए अविवाहित रहने का प्रण लिया है। गांधीजी को अब संघ की सफलता का रहस्य पता चल गया था। उन्होंने डॉ. हेडगेवार को शुभकामना देते हुए कहा, "आपका समर्पण इस बात का सबूत है कि आपने इतने कम समय में कितनी शानदार सफलता हासिल की है। डॉक्टरजी, आपके चरित्र और ईमानदारी के साथ, इसमें कोई संदेह नहीं है कि आप सफल होंगे।"

□

स्वाधीनता के बाद फिर संघ की शाखा पहुँचे गांधीजी

देश की स्वाधीनता के साथ विभाजन के दौर में सांप्रदायिक दंगे शुरू हो चुके थे। हर तरफ मारकाट मची हुई थी। पाकिस्तान से आए शरणार्थियों का भी बहुत बुरा हाल था। महात्मा गांधी दिल्ली की एक दलित बस्ती में ठहरे हुए थे। उधर संघ शरणार्थियों की सेवा में जुटा हुआ था। उसी दौरान संयोग से संघ का कार्यक्रम दिल्ली की उसी बस्ती में आयोजित हुआ, जहाँ महात्मा गांधी ठहरे हुए थे। गांधीजी को जैसे ही पता चला, उन्होंने फिर से संघ की शाखा में जाने का फैसला किया। 16 सितंबर, 1947 को वे न केवल संघ की शाखा में पहुँचे, बल्कि स्वयंसेवकों की सभा को भी संबोधित किया। गांधीजी ने संघ के स्वयंसेवकों का अनुशासन और जात-पाँत की भावना से ऊपर उठकर एक साथ काम करते देखकर काफी प्रसन्नता व्यक्त की। महात्मा गांधी ने यहाँ अपने पुराने अनुभव के बारे में बताया, "बरसों पहले मैं वर्धा में राष्ट्रीय स्वयंसेवक संघ के एक शिविर में गया था। वहाँ मैं उन लोगों का कड़ा अनुशासन, सादगी और छुआछूत की पूर्ण समाप्ति देखकर अत्यंत प्रभावित हुआ था।"

□

मोतीलाल नेहरू ने वर्ष 1922 में किया था डॉ. हेडगेवार का स्वागत

महात्मा गांधी की अगुवाई में वर्ष 1921 में चले असहयोग आंदोलन में डॉ. हेडगवार ने महत्त्वपूर्ण भूमिका निभाई थी। इसके कारण उन पर राजद्रोह का मुकदमा चला और वे 19 अगस्त, 1921 से 11 जुलाई, 1922 तक कारावास में रहे। वे तब तक इतने लोकप्रिय हो चुके थे कि 12 जुलाई को जब उन्हें जेल से रिहा किया गया तो जगह-जगह पर उनके स्वागत में लोगों की भीड़ जमा हो गई थी। डॉ. हेडगेवार के लिए उसी दिन शाम को चिटणीस पार्क में 'स्वागत सभा' आयोजित की गई थी। इसी समय मोतीलाल नेहरू, विट्ठल भाई पटेल, हकीम अजमल खाँ, राजगोपालाचारी, कस्तूरी आयंगर आदि नेता कांग्रेस कार्य समिति की बैठक के लिए नागपुर आए हुए थे। स्वागत सभा में हेडगेवार के स्वागत का प्रस्ताव रखा गया, जो तालियों की गड़गड़ाहट के बीच स्वीकृत हुआ। इसके बाद मोतीलाल नेहरू तथा हकीम अजमल खाँ के स्वागत भाषण हुए। नागपुर के बाद यवतमाल, वणी, आर्वी, वाढोणा, मोहोपा आदि अनेक स्थानों पर डॉ. हेडगेवार को आमंत्रित किया गया तथा उनकी शोभायात्रा निकालकर सत्कार समारोहों का आयोजन किया गया।

□

विट्ठल भाई पटेल
जब स्वयं पहुँच गए मोहिते बाड़ा शाखा

सरदार पटेल के बड़े भाई और महान् स्वतंत्रता सेनानी विट्ठल भाई पटेल ने जब संघ की स्थापना के तीन वर्ष बाद ही कई लोगों से इसकी प्रशंसा सुनी तो उन्हें स्वयं शाखा जाकर इसे देखने की इच्छा हुई। वर्ष 1928 में विट्ठल भाई पटेल नागपुर के मोहिते बाड़ा शाखा पहुँचे। वे जब पहुँचे तो उस समय शाखा में 100 से ज्यादा स्वयंसेवकों ने हिस्सा लिया था। विट्ठल भाई स्वयंसेवकों के कड़े अनुशासन और देशभक्ति को देखकर काफी प्रभावित हुए और शाखा से लौटने के बाद अपने छोटे भाई सरदार पटेल से संघ की काफी प्रशंसा की। शाखा देखने के बाद उन्होंने कहा, "आजतक मैंने धन और दूसरे साधनों को जुटाने में लगे बहुत से संगठनों को देखा है, लेकिन संघ शाखा में काम करने का बिल्कुल नया तरीका देखने को मिला है। मैंने देखा कि कैसे राष्ट्रीय चरित्र को गढ़ा जा रहा है। इसने वास्तव में मेरे दिल को छू लिया है।"

□

एक स्वयंसेवक के साहस के प्रशंसक हुए नेहरू

बात वर्ष 1936 की है। महाराष्ट्र के जलगाँव स्थित फैजपुर में कांग्रेस का अधिवेशन हुआ था। इस अधिवेशन की अध्यक्षता जवाहरलाल नेहरू ने की थी। कार्यक्रम के दौरान जब नेहरू झंडा फहराने लगे तो झंडा रस्सी के साथ ऊपर अटक गया और इससे उनकी किरकिरी हो गई। करीब 80 फीट ऊँचे खंभे पर चढ़कर उसे सुलझाने का साहस कोई नहीं कर पा रहा था। इसी बीच किशन सिंह राजपूत नाम का तरुण स्वयंसेवक भीड़ में से दौड़ा और तेजी से खंभे पर चढ़ गया। उसने रस्सियों की गुत्थी सुलझाई, ध्वज को ऊपर ले जाकर फहरा दिया और नीचे आ गया। हजारों लोगों ने ताली बजाकर उसकी प्रशंसा की। नेहरू ने भी शाबाशी देते हुए उसकी पीठ थपथपाई। अधिवेशन में उसे सम्मानित किए जाने की बात कही गई, लेकिन यह पता चलते ही कि किशन सिंह संघ से जुड़ा हुआ है और वह शाखा में जाता है, उसे सम्मानित नहीं किया गया। बाद में जब संघ के संस्थापक डॉ. हेडगेवार को पता चला तो उन्होंने किशन सिंह का अभिनंदन किया। यह एक घटनाक्रम बताता है कि तिरंगे के प्रति संघ और स्वयंसेवकों के मन में सदैव कितना सम्मान भाव था।

□

बाबासाहेब आंबेडकर ने स्वयंसेवकों के साथ भोजन किया

बाबासाहेब डॉ. भीमराव आंबेडकर 2 जनवरी, 1940 को महाराष्ट्र के सतारा जिले के कराड में संघ की एक शाखा में पहुँचे थे। इस दौरान उन्होंने संघ के स्वयंसेवकों से मुलाकात की और उन्हें संबोधित भी किया। वहाँ उन्होंने संघ के सभी कार्यक्रमों को देखा और इससे काफी प्रभावित हुए। उन्होंने कहा, "मुझे यह देखकर आश्चर्य होता है कि यहाँ पर स्वयंसेवक किसी भी प्रकार के भेदभाव के बिना, एक-दूसरे की जाति जाने बगैर परस्पर भाईचारे से रह रहे हैं।" उन्होंने दोपहर में डॉ. हेडगेवार और अन्य स्वयंसेवकों के साथ भोजन किया। इसके बाद डॉ. हेडगेवार के अनुरोध पर बाबासाहेब ने एक घंटे तक वंचितों के उत्थान की चर्चा करते हुए स्वयंसेवकों को संबोधित किया। उन्होंने कहा, "यह पहली बार है जब मैं संघ के स्वयंसेवकों के शिविर का दौरा कर रहा हूँ। मैं सवर्णियों और वंचितों के बीच पूर्ण समानता देखकर खुश हूँ।" डॉ. आंबेडकर के इस दौरे के बारे में एक खबर 9 जनवरी, 1940 को पुणे के प्रसिद्ध मराठी दैनिक 'केसरी' में प्रकाशित हुई थी।

□

डॉ. हेडगेवार से मिलने पहुँचे सुभाष चंद्र बोस के प्रतिनिधि

जून 1939 में डॉ. हेडगेवार की तबीयत खराब थी और उस समय नागपुर में काफी गरमी पड़ रही थी। नागपुर के संघचालक बाबासाहब घटाटे ने नासिक से आठ-नौ मील दूर देवलाली में एक बँगला किराए पर लिया। स्वास्थ्य की दृष्टि से यहाँ की जलवायु अनुकूल थी। पुणे से लौटते वक्त घटाटे ने डॉ. हेडगेवार से आग्रह किया कि वे कुछ दिनों तक देवलाली में रुकें। डॉ. हेडगेवार के साथ श्रीगुरुजी और तात्या तैलंग भी देवलाली आए। इसी दौरान सुभाष चंद्र बोस और डॉ. हेडगेवार के बीच बैठक की तिथि निश्चित करने के लिए 8-9 जुलाई को स्वयंसेवक बालाजी हुद्दार देवलाली पहुँचे। उनके साथ बोस ने बंबई के डॉ. वसंतराव रामराव संझगिरी को भी भेजा था। सुभाष चंद्र बोस उस दौरान कांग्रेस छोड़ने के बाद फॉरवर्ड ब्लॉक का गठन कर अंग्रेजों से लड़ाई की तैयारी कर रहे थे। डॉ. हेडगेवार की तबीयत खराब थी, लेकिन फिर भी उन्होंने उनकी बातें ध्यान से सुनीं। उनका कहने का यही आशय था कि बोस युद्ध की परिस्थिति का लाभ उठाकर अंग्रेजों के विरुद्ध विद्रोह करना चाहते हैं। उनको सुनने के बाद डॉ. हेडगेवार ने पूछा, "यह तो सही है कि समय अनुकूल होता जा रहा है। लेकिन क्रांति के लिए आपकी तैयारी कितनी है? प्रारंभ में कम-से-कम 50 प्रतिशत तो सिद्धता चाहिए। इस दृष्टि से सुभाष बाबू के पास अभी कितने व्यक्ति हैं? अपनी तैयारी के बिना स्वतंत्रता के लिए केवल परायों पर भरोसा करके काम नहीं होगा।" चूँकि उस समय डॉ. हेडगेवार की तबीयत ठीक नहीं थी तो उन्होंने कहा, "फिर कभी शांति के साथ विचार करने के लिए आप नागपुर आइए।"

□

डॉ. हेडगेवार से मिलने पहुँचे नेताजी सुभाष चंद्र बोस

डॉ. हेडगेवार और नेताजी सुभाष चंद्र बोस के बीच एक गहरा नाता था। इसकी झलक इसी बात से मिलती है कि डॉ. हेडगेवार जब गंभीर रूप से बीमार थे तब 20 जून, 1940 को उनसे मिलने नेताजी नागपुर आए थे। बोस जब पहुँचे तब डॉ. हेडगेवार की तबीयत काफी खराब थी और उन्हें नींद आ गई थी। सुभाष बाबू ने उन्हें उठाना ठीक नहीं समझा। वे इतना कहकर चले गए, "अभी इनके आराम में खलल डालना ठीक नहीं होगा। इन्हें सोने दीजिए, मैं जल्दी ही फिर लौटकर किसी दिन मिलूँगा।" उन्होंने हाथ जोड़कर प्रणाम किया और चले गए। हालाँकि बाद में जब डॉ. हेडगेवार को इसका पता चला तो उन्होंने नाराजगी जताई कि उन्हें क्यों नहीं जगाया गया। वे स्नेहवश मन-ही-मन बुदबुदाए 'सुभाष' और उन्हें प्रणाम निवेदित किया। उस दिन वे 106 डिग्री बुखार से तप रहे थे। इसके अगले ही दिन 21 जून, 1940 को डॉ. हेडगेवार का निधन हो गया। उल्लेखनीय है कि सुभाष चंद्र बोस इससे पहले वर्ष 1928 में कांग्रेस के कलकत्ता अधिवेशन में डॉ. हेडगेवार से मिल चुके थे। डॉ. हेडगेवार कांग्रेस नेता के रूप में अधिवेशन में भाग लेने पहुँचे थे।

□

संघ ने सिंध में नेहरू की जनसभा को सुरक्षा प्रदान की

बात वर्ष 1946 की है। उस वक्त तक कांग्रेस पार्टी ने देश का विभाजन स्वीकार नहीं किया था। इससे मुसलिम लीग बौखलाई हुई थी। जवाहरलाल नेहरू 1946 में सिंध के एक प्रमुख शहर हैदराबाद में (अब पाकिस्तान में) एक जनसभा को संबोधित करने वाले थे। कांग्रेस कार्यकर्ता सार्वजनिक सभा की तैयारी में जुटे थे, लेकिन उन्हें इस बात की आशंका थी कि अन्य स्थानों की तरह मुसलिम लीग उनकी इस सभा में भी रंग में भंग डाल सकती है। इस आशंका को देखते हुए कांग्रेस पार्टी ने राष्ट्रीय स्वयंसेवक संघ से मदद माँगी। इसके बाद संघ ने बड़ी संख्या में नौजवान स्वयंसेवकों को तैयार किया और वे सभी सभा स्थल पर पहुँच गए। बड़ी संख्या में स्वयंसेवकों को देखकर मुसलिम लीग के गुंडे उपद्रव करने की हिम्मत नहीं जुटा सके और नेहरू की सभा बिना किसी बाधा के सुचारू रूप से संपन्न हुई। इससे यह पता चलता है कि संघ ने विभाजन के समय बड़े पैमाने पर हुई सांप्रदायिक हिंसा से पहले भी शांति और स्थिरता लाने में महत्त्वपूर्ण भूमिका निभाई थी। सिंध एक समृद्ध हिंदू सांस्कृतिक विरासत वाला क्षेत्र था। हालाँकि विभाजन के समय इसकी हिंदू आबादी को व्यापक हिंसा, जबरन धर्मांतरण और बड़े पैमाने पर विस्थापन का सामना करना पड़ा।

□

राजगुरु पढ़ाई के दौरान ही बन गए थे स्वयंसेवक

महान् स्वतंत्रता सेनानी भगत सिंह और सुखदेव के साथ खुशी-खुशी फाँसी के फंदे पर चढ़ जाने वाले क्रांतिकारी राजगुरु वर्ष 1926-27 में नागपुर पहुँचे और उसी दौरान नागपुर की भोंसले वेदशाला में पढ़ते समय स्वयंसेवक बन गए। राजगुरु संघ की मोहिते बाड़ा शाखा के स्वयंसेवक थे और संघ संस्थापक डॉ. हेडगेवार के बेहद करीबी रहे। लाला लाजपत राय की हत्या का बदला लेकर राजगुरु दिसंबर 1928 में लाहौर से सुरक्षित आ गए थे। डॉ. हेडगेवार ने उमरेड में भैयाजी दाणी (जो बाद में संघ के सरकार्यवाह बने) के फार्महाउस पर उनके टिकने की व्यवस्था की थी। डॉ. हेडगेवार ने राजगुरु को अपने गाँव पुणे नहीं जाने की सलाह दी थी, क्योंकि वहाँ पर उनके गिरफ्तार होने का खतरा था, लेकिन राजगुरु किसी कारणवश पुणे चले गए और वहाँ से उन्हें गिरफ्तार कर लिया गया। राजगुरु ने 19 दिसंबर, 1928 को भगत सिंह के साथ मिलकर लाहौर में सहायक पुलिस अधीक्षक पद पर नियुक्त अंग्रेज अधिकारी जेपी सांडर्स को गोलियों से भून दिया था। बाद में ब्रिटिश सरकार ने 23 मार्च, 1931 को भगत सिंह, राजगुरु और सुखदेव को लाहौर सेंट्रल जेल में फाँसी दे दी।

□

जयप्रकाश नारायण और अरुणा आसफ अली को शरण

अंग्रेजी हुकूमत के खिलाफ महात्मा गांधी ने 8 अगस्त, 1942 को 'भारत छोड़ो आंदोलन' की शुरुआत की थी। संघ ने इस आंदोलन को परिणति तक पहुँचाने के लिए एड़ी-चोटी का जोर लगा दिया था। देश के कोने-कोने में फैले स्वयंसेवक भारत की स्वतंत्रता के लिए इस आंदोलन को सफल बनाने में जी-जान से जुटे थे। इस आंदोलन के दौरान जयप्रकाश नारायण और अरुणा आसफ अली जब अंडरग्राउंड होकर ब्रिटिश सरकार के खिलाफ आंदोलन कर रहे थे, तब दिल्ली के संघचालक लाला हंसराज गुप्त ने इनके लिए अपने घर पर ठहरने का प्रबंध किया था। अगस्त 1967 में हिंदी दैनिक 'हिंदुस्तान' में प्रकाशित एक साक्षात्कार में अरुणा आसफ अली ने बताया, "मैं वर्ष 1942 के आंदोलन में भूमिगत थी, दिल्ली के संघचालक लाला हंसराजजी ने मुझे 10-15 दिनों के लिए अपने घर में शरण दी और मेरी पूरी सुरक्षा का प्रबंध किया। उन्होंने इस बात का ध्यान रखा कि किसी को भी उनके घर पर मेरे रहने की खबर न मिले।" वहीं प्रख्यात समाजवादी नेता अच्युत पटवर्धन और साने गुरुजी पुणे के संघचालक भाऊसाहब देशमुख के घर पर टिके थे। इसी तरह 'पतरी सरकार' गठित करने वाले क्रांतिकारी नाना पाटिल को औंध (जिला सतारा) में संघचालक पंडित सातवलेकरजी ने आश्रय दिया था। उस समय संघ के विभिन्न कार्यकर्ताओं के घर ही क्रांतिकारियों के लिए गुप्त ठिकाने बन गए थे। यह आंदोलन वर्ष 1942 के अंत तक चला, जिसमें स्वयंसेवकों सहित सैकड़ों लोगों ने भारत माता की मुक्ति के लिए अपना जीवन बलिदान कर दिया।

□

मदन मोहन मालवीय ने दो भवन किए संघ के नाम

काशी हिंदू विश्वविद्यालय के संस्थापक महामना मदन मोहन मालवीय संघ से काफी प्रभावित थे। एक बार मालवीयजी ने डॉ. हेडगेवार से कहा था, "लोग मुझे 'Royal Beggar' कहकर बुलाते हैं। अगर आप चाहें तो मैं संघ के लिए धन जुटाऊँगा।" इस पर संघ की तरफ से उत्तर मिला था, "हमें धन नहीं, आप जैसे महानुभावों का आशीर्वाद चाहिए। वही हमारे लिए पर्याप्त है।" मदन मोहन मालवीय संघ के प्रति किस प्रकार का भाव रखते थे, इसका अंदाजा 8 अप्रैल, 1938 के कार्यक्रम से लगा सकते हैं। रामनवमी के दिन बनारस हिंदू विश्वविद्यालय में संघ का एक कार्यक्रम आयोजित था। इस कार्यक्रम में महामना के साथ संघ के संस्थापक डॉ. हेडगेवार और श्रीगुरुजी भी एक ही मंच पर उपस्थित थे। इस अवसर पर मदन मोहन मालवीय ने कहा था—"संघ राष्ट्र के लिए काम कर रहा है।" यहाँ इस बात की जानकारी बहुत महत्त्वपूर्ण है कि वर्ष 1929 से ही डॉक्टर हेडगेवार का बी.एच.यू. में आना-जाना था। महामना हेडगेवार के व्यक्तित्व और संघ के कार्यों से इतने प्रभावित हुए कि लॉ कॉलेज के दो भवन उन्होंने संघ को अलॉट कर दिए। इन्हें संघभवन कहा जाने लगा और ये संघ का कार्यालय हो गया।

□

जो काम सैकड़ों लेख नहीं कर सकते वह संघ की शाखा कर रही

नागपुर में वर्ष 1933 में 'अखिल भारतीय मराठी साहित्य सम्मेलन' हुआ। सम्मेलन में बड़ी संख्या में प्रख्यात साहित्यकार शामिल हुए। इस सम्मेलन के अध्यक्ष प्रसिद्ध पत्रकार और साहित्यकार कृष्णाजी प्रभाकर खाडिलकर थे, जो कि काकासाहब खाडिलकर के नाम से प्रसिद्ध थे। उस समय राष्ट्रीय स्वयंसेवक संघ का विस्तार तेजी से हो रहा था। साहित्य सम्मेलन के उपरांत डॉ. हेडगेवार ने काकासाहब खाडिलकर को संघ के शिविर में आने का न्योता दिया। काकासाहब ने उनका न्योता स्वीकार कर लिया और करीब 10 से ज्यादा साहित्यकार संघ का काम देखने के लिए उनके साथ शिविर आए। शाखा में आकर वे सभी काफी प्रभावित हुए। संघ की अवधारणा को जानने, कार्यशैली को समझने और शाखा के स्वरूप को देखकर काकासाहब ने कहा, "हम साहित्यिक लोग तो वाग्वीर हैं। परंतु यहाँ तो शक्ति की प्रत्यक्ष उपासना हो रही है। यही शक्ति का दृश्य स्वरूप है। सहस्त्रों व्याख्यान तथा लेख लिखकर हम जो काम सिद्ध नहीं कर सकते, जो भाव लोगों के मन पर अंकित नहीं कर सकते, वह संघ के इस दृश्य मात्र से ही संभव है। प्रत्यक्ष दृश्य मात्र से ही महान् तत्त्वों का बोध हो सकता है, संघ इसका अत्यंत प्रभावी उदाहरण है।"

उल्लेखनीय है कि महाराष्ट्र में आधुनिक पत्रकारिता की नींव काकासाहब ने ही रखी थी। उनके योगदान को रेखांकित करते हुए साहित्य अकादेमी ने 'भारतीय साहित्य के निर्माता' सीरीज के अंतर्गत उन पर पुस्तक भी प्रकाशित की है।

□

स्वतंत्रता संघर्ष और डॉ. हेडगेवार

डॉ. हेडगेवार के जंगल सत्याग्रह और अदालत में पेशी के साथ ही स्वतंत्रता आंदोलन एवं सत्याग्रह के विभिन्न अवसरों की चित्रांकन के माध्यम से झलकियाँ

स्वतंत्रता आंदोलन के समय डॉ. हेडगेवार के दुर्लभ चित्र

(सरस्वती सिनेटोन, पूना में स्वागत) कुरसी पर बैठे हुए (बाएँ से)—(1) भाऊराव अभ्यंकर, (2) दादा साहब तोरणे, (3) डॉ. हेडगेवार, (4) माधव गोलवलकर, (5) नाना साहब तेलंग।

डॉ. हेडगेवार ने स्वतंत्रता संग्राम के लिए छोड़ दी डॉक्टरी

डॉ. हेडगेवार वर्ष 1915 में डॉक्टरी की पढ़ाई पूरी कर कलकत्ता से नागपुर वापस आए। वे चाहते तो कहीं नौकरी करके अथवा डॉक्टरी की प्रैक्टिस करके आराम से बेहतर जीवनयापन कर सकते थे, लेकिन भारत को ब्रिटिश राज से पूर्ण स्वतंत्रता दिलाने और देश सेवा के लिए उन्होंने ऐशो-आराम की जिंदगी को ठोकर मार दी। ब्रिटिश भारत में आज के मध्य प्रदेश, छत्तीसगढ़, महाराष्ट्र को मिलाकर मध्य प्रांत हुआ करता था और इसकी राजधानी नागपुर थी। वर्ष 1911 की जनगणना में मध्य प्रांत की जनसंख्या 1,60,33,310 आँकी गई थी। उस समय पूरे मध्य प्रांत में केवल 75 चिकित्सक थे। यह आबादी के लिहाज से काफी कम था। ऐसे में एक डॉक्टर के लिए प्रैक्टिस करना काफी फायदेमंद रहता। यही नहीं, डॉ. हेडगेवार के पास बर्मा (म्याँमार) में नौकरी का प्रस्ताव भी था, लेकिन माँ भारती के लिए उन्होंने डॉक्टरी को पेशा के रूप में नहीं अपनाया। डॉ. हेडगेवार डॉक्टर तो थे, लेकिन उन्होंने लोगों की बीमारी के बजाय उस बीमारी का इलाज करना जरूरी समझा, जिससे देश पीड़ित था। इतिहास से सबक लेते हुए उन्होंने पाया कि देशभक्ति की भावना की कमी, राष्ट्रीय चेतना का अभाव और हिंदुओं में व्याप्त सामाजिक कुरीतियाँ जैसे—छुआछूत, जाति प्रथा और आपसी वैमनस्य के कारण भारत को विदेशी आक्रमणकारियों के हाथों हार मिली और विदेशी शासन के अधीन गुलामी का दंश झेलना पड़ा। उन्होंने इन मुद्दों को हल करने के लिए एक सशक्त संगठन स्थापित करने का फैसला किया।

□

देश सेवा के लिए डॉ. हेडगेवार ने लिया बड़ा प्रण

संघ संस्थापक डॉ. हेडगेवार ने जब वर्ष 1915 में डॉक्टरी की पढ़ाई पूरी कर ली तो उनके लिए विवाह के भी अनेक प्रस्ताव आने लगे। मगर डॉ. हेडगेवार के मन में तो देशभक्ति का ज्वार हिलोरे मार रहा था। अंग्रेजों की गुलामी से वे इतने व्यथित थे कि एक झटके में उन्होंने अपना पूरा जीवन देश को समर्पित करने का फैसला कर लिया। हेडगेवार जब महज 13 वर्ष के थे, तभी उनके माता-पिता का निधन हो चुका था। ऐसे में उन्होंने अपने चाचा को पत्र लिखा और कहा, "मैंने आजीवन ब्रह्मचर्य का पालन करते हुए देश के लिए जीवन जीने की प्रतिज्ञा की है।" उन्होंने साफ कहा, "मुझे इस जीवन में विवाह नहीं करना है।" डॉ. हेडगेवार की इस प्रतिज्ञा की जानकारी जैसे ही लोगों को मिली, उसके बाद उनके लिए विवाह के प्रस्ताव आने बंद हो गए। उस समय स्वतंत्रता आंदोलन के सभी प्रमुख नेता विवाहित और गृहस्थ थे। हरेक का अपनी गृहस्थी के लिए आवश्यक धनोपार्जन का कोई-न-कोई साधन था। इसके साथ-साथ वे स्वतंत्रता आंदोलन में अपना योगदान दे रहे थे। डॉ. हेडगेवार भी ऐसा ही सोच सकते थे। परंतु उन्होंने अपने व्यक्तिगत जीवन का कोई विचार न करते हुए अपनी सारी शक्ति, समय और क्षमता राष्ट्र को अर्पित कर दी और डॉक्टरी पेशे को त्यागने के साथ-साथ अविवाहित रहने की भी प्रतिज्ञा कर ली।

□

क्रांतिकारियों ने डॉ. हेडगेवार को दिया कोड नेम

डॉ. हेडगेवार वर्ष 1910 में जब मेडिकल की पढ़ाई के लिए कलकत्ता गए तो वहाँ क्रांतिकारी समूह 'अनुशीलन समिति' से जुड़ गए। यहाँ उनका प्रमुख कार्य स्वाधीनता के दीवानों के लिए न केवल भूमिगत साहित्य और हथियारों को जुटाना था, बल्कि उन तक सही-सलामत पहुँचाना भी था। इस काम को करने में उनके मित्र संदेशवाहक की भूमिका निभाते थे। वे जब भी नागपुर जाते थे तो वहाँ क्रांतिकारियों के लिए रिवॉल्वर लेकर जाते थे। क्रांतिकारियों ने उनके लिए एक कोड वर्ड रखा था और उन्हें 'कोकेन' के नाम से बुलाते थे। डॉ. हेडगेवार वर्ष 1911 से 1913 तक कलकत्ता में क्रांतिकारी कार्यों में काफी सक्रिय रहे। उन दिनों अनुशीलन समिति से जुड़े प्रसिद्ध क्रांतिकारी त्रिलोक नाथ चक्रवर्ती के मार्गदर्शन में वे शस्त्र संग्रह का काम करते थे। इस बात की पुष्टि त्रिलोक नाथ चक्रवर्ती ने भी अपनी पुस्तक 'जेले त्रिश बछर' (जेल में 30 वर्ष) में की है। उल्लेखनीय है कि अनुशीलन समिति के प्रमुख पुलिन बिहारी दास और त्रिलोक नाथ चक्रवर्ती को अंडमान में काले पानी की सजा हुई थी।

□

डॉ. हेडगेवार ने अंग्रेजों के विरुद्ध चलाया था 'कागजी आंदोलन'

डॉ. हेडगेवार ने कलकत्ता में मेडिकल की पढ़ाई के दौरान अंग्रेजों के विरुद्ध एक 'कागजी आंदोलन' चलाया था। दरअसल अंग्रेज सरकार एक कानून लाने वाली थी, जिसके कारण विद्यालय और कॉलेज में पढ़ने वाले आंदोलनकारी छात्रों को मिलने वाले प्रमाण-पत्र अवैध घोषित किए जाने थे। उस समय समाज में इस विषय को लेकर बड़ा आंदोलन करना संभव नहीं था। ऐसे में डॉ. हेडगेवार को एक नई तरकीब सूझी। उन्होंने कलकत्ता के हर मोहल्ले में घूम-घूमकर प्रमुख लोगों से बात की और कहा कि कोई अधिकारी आकर आपसे पूछे कि सरकार के इस प्रस्ताव के विरोध में आपके यहाँ कोई सभा हुई तो आप कहिए "हाँ, सभा हुई थी।" यही नहीं वो बाकायदा प्रेस नोट बनाकर अखबारों में जनसभाओं की खबर भेजते थे। डॉ. हेडगेवार की यह रणनीति काम कर गई, क्योंकि समाचार-पत्रों में जनसभा की जानकारी प्रकाशित होने लगी। इसमें हजारों लोगों के जमा होने की रिपोर्ट भी सामने आई। उधर सरकार के पास यह रिपोर्ट गई कि इस विषय को लेकर बड़ा जन असंतोष है। यदि यह कानून लाया गया तो परिणाम घातक हो सकते हैं। इसके बाद ब्रिटिश सरकार को झुकना पड़ा और वो कानून को नहीं ला सकी।

□

डॉ. हेडगेवार 'यूनियन जैक' की जगह फहराना चाहते थे 'भगवा ध्वज'

डॉ. हेडगेवार में राष्ट्रीय भावना किस कदर कूट-कूटकर भरी थी, इसे उनके बालजीवन की एक घटना से समझा जा सकता है। उस समय देश पर अंग्रेजों का शासन था और नागपुर में सीताबर्डी किले पर अंग्रेजों का झंडा 'यूनियन जैक' लहराता था। केशव को यह पसंद नहीं था। वे चाहते थे कि इसके स्थान पर हिंदवी स्वराज का प्रतीक 'भगवा ध्वज' फहराए। सीताबर्डी किले पर यूनियन जैक की जगह भगवा ध्वज फहराने की योजना बनाने के लिए केशव ने अपने साथियों के साथ बात की। योजना यह बनी कि सुरंग खोदकर किले तक पहुँचा जाए और वहाँ पहुँचकर किले से विदेशी 'यूनियन जैक' को उतारकर उसके स्थान पर अपना 'भगवा ध्वज' फहरा दिया जाए। योजना के अनुरूप निश्चित तिथि पर केशव और उनके साथी सीताबर्डी किले के पास पहुँच गए। वहाँ पहुँचकर सुरंग खोदने का काम शुरू कर दिया। लेकिन इसी बीच इस बात की जानकारी केशव के गुरु को हुई तो उन्होंने ऐसा नहीं करने की नसीहत दी और केशव और उनके साथियों को पढ़ाई पर ध्यान देने और इस काम को करने से रोक दिया।

□

डॉ. हेडगेवार की प्रेरणा से हटा 'हिंदू कॉलोनी' का बोर्ड

डॉ. हेडगेवार 21 और 22 फरवरी, 1937 को डॉ. मुंजे द्वारा स्थापित 'द सेंट्रल मिलिट्री एजुकेशन सोसाइटी' की प्रबंध समिति की बैठक में भाग लेने के लिए नासिक पहुँचे। उस समय उन्होंने संघ शाखा का भी निरीक्षण किया। इस अवसर का एक महत्त्वपूर्ण प्रसंग सामने आया। एक दिन शाखा का कार्यक्रम समाप्त करके जब डॉ. हेडगेवार वकील राजाभाऊ साठे के घर की ओर जा रहे थे तो उनकी दृष्टि 'हिंदू कॉलोनी' नाम के एक बोर्ड पर पड़ी। नासिक में यह एक नई बस्ती बन रही थी तथा वहाँ के कुछ उत्साही लोगों ने इस कॉलोनी को यह नाम दिया था। लेकिन डॉ. हेडगेवार को यह बात रास नहीं आई। उन्होंने राजाभाऊ से इस विषय पर चर्चा करते हुए कहा, "अपने देश में किसी भी बस्ती को 'हिंदू कॉलोनी' नाम देना उचित नहीं है। मैं पिछली बार जब बंबई गया था तो वहाँ भी दादर में 'हिंदू कॉलोनी' नाम देखा था। उस संबंध में मैंने श्री बाबाराव सावरकर से कहा कि 'पारसी कॉलोनी' होना तो ठीक है, लेकिन अपने ही देश में 'हिंदू कॉलोनी' नाम रखकर तो हम यही सिद्ध करेंगे कि मानो हम परदेसी हैं। यदि हम इंग्लैंड या किसी अन्य देश में जाएँ और वहाँ अपनी बस्ती बसाएँ तो उसे 'हिंदू कॉलोनी' नाम देना युक्तिसंगत होगा।" डॉ. हेडगेवार की बात पर सभी लोगों ने गौर किया और इसकी गंभीरता समझ में आने के बाद हिंदू कॉलोनी का बोर्ड हटा दिया गया। आज नासिक की यह बस्ती 'गोले कॉलोनी' के नाम से जाना जाती है।

□

सत्याग्रह के लिए डॉ. हेडगेवार पर लगा 25 रुपए जुर्माना

पुणे में प्रसिद्ध सोन्या मारुति मंदिर में शाम को होने वाली आरती में घंटा बजाया जाता था। इस मंदिर के पास में ही एक मसजिद थी, जिसमें मुसलमान नमाज अदा करते थे। वे चाहते थे कि मंदिर में घंटा बजना बंद हो जाए। उन्होंने इस बारे में स्थानीय कांग्रेस नेताओं से बात की। तुष्टीकरण की नीति पर चलने वाले स्थानीय कांग्रेसी नेताओं ने प्रशासन को घंटा बजाने पर प्रतिबंध लगाने की सलाह दे डाली। उनकी सलाह पर प्रशासन ने मंदिर में वाद्य वादन, भजन-कीर्तन पर 24 अप्रैल, 1937 से 14 मई, 1937 तक प्रतिबंध लगा दिया। इस रोक की वजह से भजन-कीर्तन में व्यवधान उत्पन्न हो गया, जिससे हिंदू समाज आक्रोशित हो उठा। इस अन्यायपूर्ण फैसले के खिलाफ हिंदुओं ने 'सोन्या मारुति सत्याग्रह' शुरू कर दिया। संघ के स्वयंसेवक अपनी पहचान को पीछे रखकर एक आम नागरिक की तरह इस सत्याग्रह में शामिल हुए। 13 मई को डॉ. हेडगेवार भी इस सत्याग्रह में शामिल हुए और सांकेतिक गिरफ्तारी दी। इसके बाद मुकदमा चला और 17 मई को डॉ. हेडगेवार पर 25 रुपए का जुर्माना लगाया गया। इससे पहले पुणे पहुँचने पर डॉ. हेडगेवार से कुछ लोगों ने प्रश्न किया था, "सत्याग्रह में संघ क्या करेगा?" इस पर जवाब देते हुए, डॉ. हेडगेवार ने कहा था, "यह सत्याग्रह सभी नागरिकों का है। सैकड़ों स्वयंसेवक इसमें एक नागरिक के रूप में सहभागी हो रहे हैं।"

□

डॉ. हेडगेवार ने संघ को इस तरह बनाया छुआछूत मुक्त

डॉ. हेडगेवार मानते थे कि स्वतंत्रता आंदोलन में एक बड़ी बाधा सामाजिक कुरीतियाँ भी हैं। इन कुरीतियों में जाति प्रथा बड़ी कुरीति के रूप में नजर आती थी, इसलिए उन्होंने इसे दूर करने का फैसला किया। वे समाज को जाति की कुरीतियों से तो मुक्त करना ही चाहते थे, साथ ही संघ में भी जाति प्रथा, ऊँच-नीच और अस्पृश्यता को पनपने नहीं देना चाहते थे। बात वर्ष 1932 की है। नागपुर में संघ के शीत शिविर में कुछ ऐसे लोग आए, जिनको समाज में अस्पृश्य माना जाता था। वे शाखा में शामिल हुए। लेकिन जब भोजन की बारी आई तो उसी मोहल्ले से आए अन्य जाति के कुछ स्वयंसेवकों ने एक अजीब शर्त रख दी कि हम इनके साथ एक पंक्ति में बैठकर भोजन नहीं करेंगे। अब डॉ. हेडगेवार के सामने बड़ी दुविधा उत्पन्न हो गई। कुछ सोच-विचार के बाद उन्होंने कहा, "ठीक है, आप लोग अलग पंक्ति बनाकर भोजन कीजिए। मैं तो उनके साथ ही भोजन करूँगा।" इसके बाद 10-12 स्वयंसेवक तो अलग पंक्ति में बैठे, जबकि हेडगेवार ने 300 स्वयंसेवकों के साथ पंक्तियों में बैठकर भोजन किया। इस घटना ने विशिष्ट जाति के स्वयंसेवकों के मन पर इतना प्रभाव छोड़ा कि शीत शिविर के दूसरे दिन उन 10-12 स्वयंसेवकों ने भी सबके साथ पंक्ति में बैठकर भोजन किया।

□

रानी विक्टोरिया के समारोह की मिठाई कूड़े में फेंक दी

डॉ. हेडगेवार बचपन से ही क्रांतिकारी स्वभाव के थे। उन्होंने छोटी आयु में ही यह प्रमाण दे दिया था कि राष्ट्रप्रेम उनके अंदर कूट-कूटकर भरा हुआ है। इसकी गवाही देता है उनका स्कूल का जीवन। 22 जून, 1897 को हुई एक घटना से उनके व्यक्तित्व का भी पता चलता है। देश पर ब्रिटिश हुकूमत थी और रानी विक्टोरिया के राज्यारोहण की साठवीं वर्षगाँठ के उपलक्ष्य में हेडगेवार के स्कूल में मिठाई बाँटी गई थी। हेडगेवार को जब यह मिठाई दी गई तो उन्होंने इसका तिरस्कार करते हुए, उसे कूड़े में फेंक दिया। हेडगेवार ने यह कहते हुए मिठाई कूड़ेदान में फेंक दी, "हिंदुओं के राज्य को जीतने वाले विक्टोरिया के समारोह का आनंद हम क्यों मनाएँ?" हो.वे. शेषाद्रि ने अपनी पुस्तक 'डॉ. हेडगेवार : द एपोक मेकर' में लिखा है, "घरवालों ने पूछा केशव क्या तुझे मिठाई नहीं मिली? केशव ने जवाब दिया, "मिली थी, लेकिन इन अंग्रेजों ने हमारे भोंसले खानदान को खत्म कर दिया, फिर हम इनके समारोह में कैसे हिस्सा ले सकते हैं?"

□

अंग्रेज इंस्पेक्टर के सामने 'वंदे मातरम्' का गगनभेदी नारा

डॉ. हेडगेवार जब नागपुर के नीलसिटी स्कूल में नौवीं कक्षा के छात्र थे, तब उन्होंने अंग्रेज इंस्पेक्टर के आगमन पर अपने साथियों के साथ मिलकर निर्भय होकर वंदे मातरम् का गगनभेदी नारा लगाया था। बालक हेडगेवार को भली-भाँति मालूम था कि अपनी इस राष्ट्रभक्ति के लिए उन्हें स्कूल से निष्कासित भी किया जा सकता है, परंतु मातृभूमि के प्रति अपने अटूट प्रेम के कारण उन्हें किसी दंड की परवाह नहीं थी। उन्हें स्कूल से निष्कासित कर दिया गया, लेकिन इसका उन्हें जरा सा भी अफसोस नहीं था। अगर डॉ. हेडगेवार चाहते तो क्षमायाचना कर सकते थे और इससे उनका निष्कासन भी रद्द हो सकता था, लेकिन उन्होंने ऐसा नहीं किया। वे देश के लिए किसी भी हद तक जा सकते थे। बाकी छात्र तो क्षमायाचना करके फिर से स्कूल लौट गए, लेकिन डॉ. हेडगेवार ने माफी नहीं माँगी। इसके बाद उन्होंने आगे की पढ़ाई पुणे से की और वहीं से मैट्रिक की परीक्षा पास की। इसके बाद वे मेडिकल की पढ़ाई के लिए कलकत्ता चले गए। उल्लेखनीय है कि अंग्रेजों ने वर्ष 1906 में 'वंदे मातरम्' गाने पर प्रतिबंध लगा दिया था।

□

डॉ. हेडगेवार ने ब्रिटिश जज से कहा : मैं आदेशों का पालन नहीं करूँगा

महाराष्ट्र के नागपुर जिले के कटोट और भरतवाड़ा में मई 1921 में डॉ. हेडगेवार ने आक्रामक भाषण दिया था। ब्रिटिश सरकार इससे खासा नाराज थी और राजद्रोह का आरोप लगाकर उन्हें गिरफ्तार कर लिया। इस मुकदमे की सुनवाई 14 जून, 1921 को शुरू हुई। कुछ दिनों की सुनवाई के बाद डॉ. हेडगेवार जन-जन तक अपना संदेश देने के लिए स्वयं पैरवी करने लगे। अदालत में पैरवी के दौरान वे और अधिक आक्रामक हो गए। डॉ. हेडगेवार का बयान सुनने के बाद ब्रिटिश न्यायाधीश ने कहा, "उनका अपना बचाव बयान उनके मूल बयान से अधिक राष्ट्रविरोधी है।" अदालत ने उन्हें एक साल तक देशद्रोही भाषण नहीं देने और 3000 रुपए की जमानत राशि पर छोड़ने की बात कही। इस पर डॉ. हेडगेवार ने कहा, "मेरी आत्मा कहती है कि मैं पूरी तरह से निर्दोष हूँ। मुझे और मेरे साथी भारतीयों को दबाना सरकार की कुनीतियों के कारण पहले से ही जल रही आग में पेट्रोल डालने के समान है। मैं स्पष्ट रूप से कहता हूँ कि मैं आदेशों का पालन नहीं करूँगा।" जैसे ही उन्होंने अपना उत्तर समाप्त किया, न्यायाधीश ने उन्हें एक वर्ष कठोर कारावास की सजा सुना दी। □

हेडगेवार के दिंडी सत्याग्रह के बाद निकल पाई गणेश यात्रा

यह बात वर्ष 1923 की है। महाराष्ट्र के नागपुर में शुक्रवार तालाब के पास पूजा स्थान 'गणेश पेठ' था। इसी के बगल में एक खुले स्थान पर कुछ मुसलिम नेताओं ने एक झोपड़ी बना दी और बाद में उसे मसजिद का रूप दे दिया। स्थानीय हिंदुओं ने इसका कोई विरोध नहीं किया। वहीं कट्टरपंथी मुसलिमों ने जिला प्रशासन पर दबाव डालकर यह आदेश जारी करवा दिया कि मसजिद के पास हिंदुओं की कोई भी धार्मिक यात्रा गाजे-बाजे के साथ नहीं निकल सकती। इसके कारण वर्ष 1923 में होने वाला गणेश विसर्जन कार्यक्रम नहीं हो सका। इस आदेश का विरोध करते हुए राजा लक्ष्मणराव भोंसले, डॉ. हेडगेवार, डॉ. मुंजे और परांजपेजी ने सत्याग्रह करने का फैसला किया। इसके बाद डॉ. हेडगेवार के मार्गदर्शन में 11 नवंबर, 1923 को दिंडी सत्याग्रह का आयोजन किया गया। इसमें 40 हजार से अधिक लोग सम्मिलित हुए। सत्याग्रह के बावजूद 19 नवंबर को निकाली जा रही गणेश यात्रा पर कट्टरपंथी मुसलिमों ने हमला कर दिया। इसके बाद हर मोहल्ले में युवकों को लाठी-भालों से लैस किया गया, जिससे यात्रा के समय कोई अप्रिय घटना न हो सके। हिंदुओं को संगठित देख फिर कोई हमला नहीं हुआ। इसके बाद 25 नवंबर को कार्तिक पूर्णिमा के दिन 'गणेश पेठ' में काकड़ आरती के साथ यात्रा भी निकली और गणेश विसर्जन शांति एवं उत्साह से संपन्न हुआ।

□

स्वाधीनता की अलख जगाने डॉ. हेडगेवार ने निकाला था अखबार

डॉ. हेडगेवार ने पूर्ण स्वतंत्रता के लक्ष्य को जन-जन तक पहुँचाने, लोगों में स्वतंत्रता की अलख जगाने और दैनिक अखबार निकालने के लिए एक 'स्वातंत्र्य प्रकाशन मंडल' की स्थापना की थी। नागपुर के देनीगिरी महाराज के बाड़े में 'स्वातंत्र्य दैनिक' का कार्यालय खोला गया। वर्ष 1924 से इसके तहत एक दैनिक समाचार-पत्र 'स्वातंत्र्य' का प्रकाशन शुरू हो गया। विश्वनाथ राव केलकर को इस अखबार के संपादन का दायित्व सौंपा गया। डॉ. हेडगेवार एक प्रकार से समाचार-पत्र के संचालक की भूमिका का निर्वाह कर रहे थे। धन से लेकर लेख-सामग्री तक जिसकी भी कमी होती, वे इसे पूरा करते थे। इस अखबार में उन्होंने कई लेख लिखे, जिनसे उनकी सशक्त एवं प्रभावशाली लेखनी की भी जानकारी मिलती है। पैसे के अभाव के कारण यह पत्र एक वर्ष से अधिक नहीं चल पाया, लेकिन इस एक वर्ष के बहुत छोटे से कालखंड में भी डॉ. हेडगेवार ने कई लेखकों, साहित्यकारों एवं पत्रकारों को अपनी भविष्य की योजना में भागीदार बनने के लिए तैयार कर लिया।

□

डॉ. हेडगेवार ने संघ से पहले किया था, 'राष्ट्रीय उत्सव मंडल' का गठन

डॉ. हेडगेवार ने राष्ट्रीय स्वयंसेवक संघ का गठन वर्ष 1925 में किया, लेकिन इससे पहले वर्ष 1919 में उन्होंने 'राष्ट्रीय उत्सव मंडल' का गठन किया था। डॉक्टरी की पढ़ाई पूरी कर कलकत्ता से लौटने के बाद नागपुर में डॉ. हेडगेवार विद्यार्थियों की सभा आयोजित करने लगे थे और उनमें देशभक्तिपूर्ण भाषण देने शुरू कर दिए थे। वे मेलजोल बढ़ाने के लिए छात्रों के घर भी जाते रहते थे। वे युवाओं को राष्ट्रीय जागरण के अभियान में भाग लेने के लिए प्रेरित करते थे। जब डॉ. हेडगेवार को लगा कि सक्षम युवाओं की टोली तैयार हो गई है और वे देश के लिए कुछ करने के लिए तैयार हो गए हैं, तब उन्होंने एक संस्था 'राष्ट्रीय उत्सव मंडल' का गठन किया, जिससे वे संगठित होकर स्वतंत्रता आंदोलन में अपना योगदान दे सकें। वे स्वयं कई वर्षों तक इस संस्था के महामंत्री की जिम्मेदारी निभाते रहे। इस संस्था के अनेक कार्यक्रमों में छात्रों को राष्ट्रीय संस्कृति, स्वतंत्रता का महत्त्व तथा ब्रिटिश सरकार के द्वारा हिंदुओं के अस्तित्व को मिटा देने के षड्यंत्र की जानकारी दी जाती थी।

□

संघ की एक पहचान—काम एक, नाम अनेक

डॉ. हेडगेवार संघ की गतिविधियों के विस्तार के लिए अकसर यात्रा पर रहते थे। उनका प्रचार का तरीका निराला था। उनका मानना था, "हमें तब तक गुमनाम रहना चाहिए, जब तक हम कुछ महत्त्वपूर्ण हासिल नहीं कर लेते; हमें पृष्ठभूमि में रहकर काम करना चाहिए।" यही वजह रही कि डॉ. हेडगेवार ने विविध रियासतों में अपने संगठन का काम 'राष्ट्रीय स्वयंसेवक संघ' के नाम से न करते हुए अन्य किसी और नाम से शुरू करने की नीति अपनाई। इस नीति के अनुसार महाराष्ट्र के कोल्हापुर रियासत में 'राजाराम स्वयंसेवक संघ' और ग्वालियर रियासत में 'राणोजी स्वयंसेवक संघ' और हैदराबाद में 'हिंदू स्वयंसेवक संघ' के नाम से संघ का काम शुरू हुआ। हैदराबाद में इससे पहले वर्ष 1930 में हिंदू हित को बढ़ावा देने के लिए 'कर्मयोगी सेवा दल' और 'हिंदू नागरिक स्वातंत्र्य संघ' के नाम से अभियान शुरू किया गया था। इन संस्थाओं के माध्यम से कई तरह के उपक्रम चलाए जाते थे, जिनमें प्रमुख रूप से वाचनालय, नमस्कार और प्रार्थना मंडल, दंगा पीड़ित सहायता निधि आदि प्रमुख थे।

□

हर समस्या का समाधान बन गए डॉ. हेडगेवार

डॉ. हेडगेवार का समूचा जीवन समाज को संगठित करने के लिए समर्पित रहा। समाज और देश की सेवा के लिए उन्होंने एक तरफ जहाँ डॉक्टरी जैसे सम्मानित पेशे को छोड़ दिया, वहीं दूसरी तरफ जीवन भर अविवाहित रहने का निर्णय लिया। वे समाज से इस तरह जुड़े हुए थे कि हर तबके के लोग अपनी मुश्किलें लेकर उनके पास पहुँचते थे। जो नहीं पहुँच पाते थे और अगर उनको पता चल जाता था तो वे स्वयं उनकी मदद करने पहुँच जाते थे। नागपुर के बाहर आर्वी नामक स्थान में वर्ष 1925 में दंगा हुआ। इस मामले में 14 हिंदू नेताओं को गिरफ्तार कर लिया गया। उनके जेल में रहने के दौरान उनके परिवार के जीवनयापन की व्यवस्था डॉ. हेडगेवार ने की। वर्ष 1924 में 12 व 13 जुलाई को ईद और आषाढ़ी एकादशी एक ही समय हुई। ऐसे में दंगे की आशंका को देखते हुए उन्होंने युवकों की टोली बनाई, जिससे सामाजिक सद्भाव बना रहे। यहाँ तक कि विभाजन के मामले निपटाने, वर संशोधन और विषम विवाह की समस्या को सुलझाने के लिए भी लोग डॉ. हेडगेवार के पास पहुँचते थे और वे खुशी-खुशी लोगों की परेशानी हल करते थे। समाज के हर तबके से न जाने कितने छोटे-बड़े कामों के लिए पीड़ित डॉ. हेडगेवार के पास पहुँचते थे। वे विवाह, उपनयन, सत्यनारायण व्रत कथा, नामकरण आदि आयोजनों में भी जाने से कतराते नहीं थे। इस तरह उनका संपर्क का दायरा तो बढ़ता ही था, समाज को एकजुट करने के उनके मिशन के कार्य को विस्तार भी मिल जाता था।

□

विभाजन की त्रासदी और आजादी

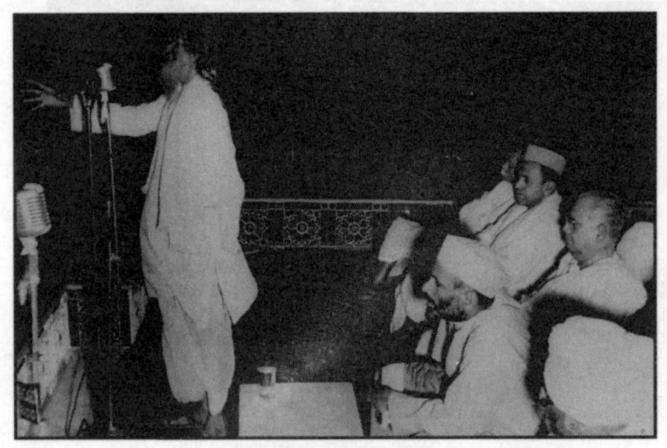

पूर्वी बंगाल के हिंदुओं तथा अन्य अल्पसंख्यक संबंधित अखिल भारतीय सम्मेलन (18 अप्रैल, 1964)

श्रीगुरुजी व ग.ना. का. खरे, बापूजी अणे, वि.घ. देशपांडे इत्यादि। (27.10.57)

मंगल कामना समारोह पर उपस्थित संघचालकगण, इसमें माधवराव मूले भी बैठे हैं (चंडीगढ़)

51वीं वर्षगाँठ—दिल्ली समारोह (1956)

लाला हंसराज गुप्ता का केन्या (अफ्रीका) दौरा।

श्रीगुरुजी कला भवन, दिल्ली (1949)

श्रीगुरुजी, सिंहगडावर, मोरोपंत पिंगले (1952)

आनंद पार्क, दिल्ली में श्रीगुरुजी (1950)

संघ द्वारा लगाया गया बाढ़ पीड़ित सहायता केंद्र।

दिल्ली में बाढ़ पीड़ितों को भोजन कराते स्वयंसेवक।

कांग्रेस के अनुरोध पर संघ ने मुसलिम लीग के गुंडों को खदेड़ा

02 सितंबर, 1946 को देश में जवाहरलाल नेहरू के नेतृत्व में अंतरिम सरकार बनी। यह कांग्रेस और मुसलिम लीग की मिली-जुली सरकार थी, लेकिन मुसलिम लीग अंतरिम सरकार के लिए मुसीबत का सबब बन गई। हर कामकाज में उसने अड़ंगा डालना शुरू कर दिया। केंद्रीय असेंबली में जब इसका अधिवेशन शुरू हुआ, तब मुसलिम लीग के गुंडों ने विरोध-प्रदर्शन और पथराव कर कांग्रेसी नेताओं को अपमानित किया। अगले दिन और बड़ी संख्या में एकत्र होकर उन्होंने कांग्रेस नेताओं को परेशान करना जारी रखा। मुसलिम लीग की हरकतों से तंग आकर कांग्रेस नेता देशबंधु गुप्त ने दिल्ली में संघ के कार्यालय जाकर इस चुनौती से निपटने के लिए मदद माँगी। संघ ने उन्हें मदद का भरोसा दिया और तुरंत अपने स्वयंसेवकों को कार्यालय आने की सूचना दी। आनन-फानन में सैकड़ों स्वयंसेवकों को तैयार कर लिया गया। इसके बाद स्वयंसेवक असेंबली पहुँच गए। संघ के नौजवान स्वयंसेवकों की टोलियों को देखकर मुसलिम लीग के गुंडे डरकर भाग खड़े हुए। उसके बाद दोबारा उन्होंने ऐसी हरकत करने की हिम्मत नहीं की।

□

संघ से मदद के लिए रक्षा मंत्री ने पटेल को लिखी चिट्ठी

भारत का विभाजन विश्व के रक्तरंजित इतिहास की सबसे बड़ी घटनाओं में से एक है। इस त्रासदी में कई लोगों के घर छूटे, कई लोगों के घर लूट लिये गए, कई लोग जिंदगी भर के लिए लापता हो गए। वर्ष 1947 में विभाजन के समय पाकिस्तान में हिंदू बच्चियों और महिलाओं के साथ सामूहिक बलात्कार हो रहे थे। उस समय तत्कालीन रक्षा मंत्री सरदार बलदेव सिंह ने 6 अक्तूबर, 1947 को तत्कालीन गृहमंत्री सरदार पटेल को चिट्ठी लिखकर संघ से मदद लेने की बात कही। इस पत्र की एक कॉपी उन्होंने डॉ. श्यामा प्रसाद मुकर्जी को भी भेजी। इस पत्र में बलदेव सिंह ने लिखा, "पश्चिम पंजाब में एक भी ऐसा गाँव या शहर नहीं है, जहाँ महिलाएँ पीड़ित न हों और लड़कियों का अपहरण न हो रहा हो। ऐसे में मदद लेने से झिझकना नहीं चाहिए और संघ प्रमुख गोलवलकरजी से परामर्श लिया जा सकता है।" जिस समय पत्र लिखा गया, उस समय तक पश्चिम पंजाब से 20 हजार महिलाओं और लड़कियों का अपहरण हो चुका था। उस समय संघ के स्वयंसेवकों ने पाकिस्तान जाकर अनगिनत हिंदू महिलाओं को बचाया। संघर्ष के उस दौर में कई स्वयंसेवकों ने अपने प्राणों की आहुति दी।

□

स्वयंसेवकों ने श्रीनगर में पाकिस्तानी झंडा उतरवाया

भारत के विभाजन के समय 14 अगस्त, 1947 को जम्मू-कश्मीर के श्रीनगर शहर के मुख्य पोस्ट ऑफिस (जी.पी.ओ.) के अधिकारी पाकिस्तान का झंडा कार्यालय पर लगा रहे थे। संघ के दो स्वयंसेवकों ने जब यह देखा तो आपत्ति जताई और तत्काल पोस्ट मास्टर से पूछा, "आप पाकिस्तान का झंडा यहाँ कैसे लगा सकते हैं? अभी महाराजा हरि सिंह ने कश्मीर का विलय पाकिस्तान में नहीं किया है।" इस पर उस मुसलिम पोस्ट मास्टर ने जवाब दिया, "अभी श्रीनगर पोस्ट ऑफिस, सियालकोट सर्कल के अंतर्गत आता है और सियालकोट पाकिस्तान का हिस्सा बन चुका है।" इसके बाद स्वयंसेवक जम्मू-कश्मीर के प्रांत संघचालक प्रेमनाथ डोगरा के पास पहुँचे। प्रांत संघचालक ने तुरंत इस बात की सूचना महाराजा हरि सिंह के कार्यालय में पहुँचाई। इसके साथ ही उन्होंने दस-पंद्रह स्वयंसेवकों को मुख्य पोस्ट ऑफिस भेज दिया। इन स्वयंसेवकों ने उस पोस्ट मास्टर को समझाया और अगले आधे घंटे में पाकिस्तान का झंडा उतार लिया गया।

□

500 स्वयंसेवकों ने दुश्मनों से बचाया था श्रीनगर

अक्तूबर 1947 में पाकिस्तान ने जम्मू-कश्मीर पर आक्रमण कर दिया। उस दौरान श्रीनगर में सेना की कमी थी, इसलिए राज्य के बाहर से सेना को लाया जाना था। लेकिन इसमें सबसे बड़ी मुसीबत यह थी कि श्रीनगर हवाई अड्डे पर भारी बर्फ जमा हो गई थी और भारतीय वायुसेना के लड़ाकू विमान नहीं उतर पा रहे थे। पाकिस्तानी सेना तेजी से आगे बढ़ रही थी, वहीं श्रीनगर में बर्फ हटाने के लिए मजदूर मिल नहीं रहे थे। ऐसे में सेना के अधिकारियों को संघ की याद आई। रात के 11 बजे एक सैन्य जीप संघ कार्यालय पहुँची। प्रेमनाथ डोगरा व अर्जुनजी कार्यालय में मौजूद थे। सेनाधिकारी ने पूछा—"आप हवाई अड्डे से बर्फ हटाने का कार्य कर सकेंगे क्या?" अर्जुनजी ने कहा—"कितने व्यक्तियों की सहायता चाहिए?" सेना के अधिकारी ने बताया, "कम-से-कम 150, जिससे 3-4 घंटों में सारी बर्फ हट जाए।" इस पर अर्जुनजी ने कहा, "हम 500 स्वयंसेवक 45 मिनट में तैयार हैं। आप हमें ले जाने के लिए वाहनों की व्यवस्था कीजिए।" फिर क्या था, स्वयंसेवकों ने रात भर में ही हवाई पट्टी से बर्फ साफ कर दी और इसके बाद 27 अक्तूबर की सुबह प्रथम सिख रेजिमेंट के 329 सैनिक हवाई जहाज से श्रीनगर उतरे और उन्होंने बड़े प्रेम से स्वयंसेवकों को गले लगाया। इस प्रकार संघ की मदद से भारतीय सेना ने समय पर पहुँचकर पाकिस्तान की साजिश को नाकाम कर दिया।

□

सेना के साथ अधिकांश मोरचे पर डटे थे स्वयंसेवक

पाकिस्तानी सेना ने कबायली घुसपैठ की आड़ में 22 अक्तूबर, 1947 को जम्मू और कश्मीर की तत्कालीन रियासत पर आक्रमण कर दिया। और जैसी आशंका थी, महाराजा हरि सिंह की सेना के अधिकतर मुसलमान सैनिक और अधिकारी पाकिस्तानी कबायलियों से जा मिले। पाकिस्तानी सेना और कबायली हिंदुओं की हत्या और महिलाओं का शील भंग करते हुए आगे बढ़ते जा रहे थे। हालत इतनी खराब थी कि जम्मू और कश्मीर के महाराजा हरि सिंह पुंछ में अपने मुसलिम सैनिकों द्वारा विद्रोह का सामना कर रहे थे और पश्चिमी जिलों पर अपना नियंत्रण खो दिया था। अविभाजित जम्मू-कश्मीर में कोटली मीरपुर जिले में मीरपुर नाम की तहसील का मुख्यालय था। यह पुंछ से 60 किलोमीटर दूर है। अब यह पाकिस्तान अधिकृत कश्मीर में है। यहाँ करीब चार हजार की आबादी में आधे हिंदू और आधे मुसलमान थे। कोटली में वर्ष 1941 से ही संघ की शाखाएँ लगने लगी थीं। पाकिस्तान के हमले के बाद संघ के स्वयंसेवक एक तरफ जहाँ लोगों को सुरक्षित जगह पर पहुँचाने और उनके लिए भोजन आदि का प्रबंध करने में जुट गए थे, वहीं दूसरी तरफ वे सेना का भी साथ दे रहे थे। स्वयंसेवकों व सेना के बीच पूरा तालमेल बना हुआ था। सुरक्षा की दृष्टि से कुल 26 मोरचे बनाए गए थे। इनमें से 8 पर सेना के जवान थे तो शेष 18 मोरचे स्वयंसेवक सँभाल रहे थे। हर मोरचे पर 70-75 स्वयंसेवक तैनात किए गए थे। लेकिन कोटली नगर को पाकिस्तानी सेना ने चारों तरफ से घेर रखा था और लगातार गोलियाँ बरसाई जा रही थीं। कश्मीर को बचाने के प्रयास में अनगिनत स्वयंसेवकों ने अपना जीवन बलिदान कर दिया।

□

मीरपुर नरसंहार पर स्वयंसेवकों के शौर्य की आँखों देखी कहानी

पाकिस्तान बनने के बाद जब मीरपुर पर खतरा मँडराया तो वहाँ लोगों को मदद पहुँचाने की सारी व्यवस्था संघ के स्वयंसेवकों ने सँभाल ली थी। चारों तरफ मारकाट मची थी। ऐसे में डोगरा फौज के साथ संघ के स्वयंसेवक हिंदुओं की रक्षा के लिए मोरचे पर डटे थे। मीरपुर नरसंहार के भुक्तभोगी और किसी तरह से जान बचाकर लौटे पुरुषोत्तम लाल गुप्ता ने स्वयंसेवकों के शौर्य के बारे में लिखा, "सब ओर मृत्यु-ही-मृत्यु नाच रही थी। फौज भाग खड़ी हुई थी। मीरपुर का वजीरे बजारत (जिलाधीश) राव रतन सिंह भी जनता को पाकिस्तानी भेड़ियों के सामने उनका ग्रास बनने के लिए छोड़कर भाग खड़ा हुआ था। परंतु संघ के स्वयंसेवक अपने-अपने मोरचों पर डटे थे। वह पाकिस्तानी सेना को ईंट का जवाब पत्थर से दे रहे थे। उनके सीने छलनी होते रहे और वे धरती पर सोते गए पर मोरचा नहीं छोड़ा। वे तो वीर बलिदानी अमर सेनानी थे।" मीरपुर अविभाजित जम्मू-कश्मीर का जिला केंद्र था। इसमें मीरपुर, भिंबर और कोटली तीन तहसीलें थीं। मीरपुर श्रीनगर से करीब 150 किलोमीटर दूर है। विभाजन के समय इसकी जनसंख्या करीब 10 हजार थी। यह इलाका मुसलिम बहुल था। हिंदुओं में अधिकतर महाजन थे, जो काफी संपन्न थे।

□

गुरु गोलवलकर की मदद से कश्मीर का भारत में विलय

आजादी के समय देश में 565 छोटी-बड़ी रियासतें मौजूद थीं। इन सभी रियासतों के भारत में विलय की जिम्मेदारी सरदार पटेल की थी, जबकि जम्मू-कश्मीर का मामला नेहरू के पास था। पटेल जहाँ बाकी रियासतों को भारत में विलय के लिए मनाने में सफल हो गए थे, वहीं कश्मीर मामला सुलझ नहीं रहा था। इसे सुलझाया राष्ट्रीय स्वयंसेवक संघ के तत्कालीन सरसंघचालक माधवराव सदाशिव गोलवलकर 'श्रीगुरुजी' ने। उनके हस्तक्षेप के बिना कश्मीर का भारत में विलय कठिन था। पटेल जानते थे कि कश्मीर के महाराजा हरि सिंह श्रीगुरुजी का बहुत सम्मान करते हैं, इसलिए उन्होंने इस मामले में उनसे निवेदन किया कि वे महाराजा से बात करें। पटेल के आग्रह पर श्रीगुरुजी 17 अक्तूबर, 1947 को सरकारी विमान से श्रीनगर पहुँचे। अगले ही दिन 18 अक्तूबर, 1947 को उन्होंने महाराजा हरि सिंह से भेंट की। इस मुलाकात के बाद श्रीगुरुजी वापस दिल्ली लौट आए और सरदार पटेल को पूरी जानकारी दी। कुछ ही दिन बाद 26 अक्तूबर को महाराजा हरि सिंह ने विलय पर हस्ताक्षर कर दिए और इस प्रकार जम्मू-कश्मीर का भारत में विलय हो गया।

□

विभाजन के समय शरणार्थियों के लिए बनाए 3000 शिविर

विभाजन के समय पाकिस्तान में बेघर होकर दर-बदर भटक रहे लोगों और पाकिस्तान से भारत आने की चाह रखनेवालों के लिए राष्ट्रीय स्वयंसेवक संघ बड़ा संबल बना था। संघ ने अपना सबकुछ लुटा चुके लोगों की सेवा के लिए 3000 शरणार्थी शिविर बनाए थे। इस तरह संघ ने न केवल उनकी जान की रक्षा की थी, बल्कि उनके रहने-खाने का भी प्रबंध किया। मोहम्मद अली जिन्ना ने लोगों को आश्वासन दिया था कि नए बन रहे पाकिस्तान में हर धर्म और पंथ के लोग रह सकते हैं। लेकिन विभाजन होते ही हिंदुओं समेत दूसरे धर्म के लोगों के साथ मारकाट होने लगी। इस खून-खराबे में दोनों देशों में करोड़ों लोग बेघर हो गए। लाखों लोगों की मृत्यु हो गई। इस दौरान राष्ट्रीय स्वयंसेवक संघ ने मानव सेवा को सर्वोपरि मानते हुए शरणार्थियों की मदद की। संघ ने शिविरों को राहत सामग्री भेजने के लिए लाहौर में पंजाब रिलीफ कमेटी स्थापित की थी, जो कि वाह, मुल्तान, माला, गुज्जरखाँ, गुड़ियाल, चकवाल, डेरा इस्माइल खाँ आदि शिविरों में सामान पहुँचाती थी। इसी तरह अमृतसर की कमेटी के अंतर्गत तरन तारन, पट्टी, खेमकरण, अटारी, अजनाला और डेरा बाबा नानक आदि शिविर आते थे। कई शिविर ऐसे थे, जिन्हें विभाजन से पूर्व दंगों के समय संघ ने शुरू किए थे और आजादी के बाद इसकी व्यवस्था भारत सरकार ने सँभाली।

□

जान पर खेलकर स्वयंसेवकों ने सेना की मदद की

यह कहानी 27 नवंबर, 1948 को कोटली में घटित हुई, जो इस समय पाक अधिकृत कश्मीर में है। पाकिस्तानी आक्रमण के समय सेना की मदद के लिए भारतीय वायुयानों से गोला-बारूद की कुछ पेटियाँ फेंकी गईं, जो कि पाकिस्तानी कब्जे वाले कश्मीर में जा गिरीं। उन्हें वहाँ से लाने में बहुत जोखिम था। इसे देखते हुए सेना ने संघ कार्यालय में संपर्क किया। उन दिनों स्थानीय पंजाब नेशनल बैंक के प्रबंधक चंद्रप्रकाश कोटली में नगर कार्यवाह थे। कमांडर ने कहा, "आठ युवक चाहिए।" चंद्रप्रकाशजी ने कहा, "एक तो मैं हूँ, बाकी सात को लेकर आधे घंटे में आता हूँ।" चंद्रप्रकाशजी ने जब स्वयंसेवकों को खबर की तो एक-दो नहीं, 30 युवक इसके लिए तैयार हो गए। चंद्रप्रकाशजी ने बड़ी कठिनाई से सात को चुना और सेना के पास पहुँच गए। सैनिक कमांडर ने उन्हें पूरी बात समझाई। भारतीय तथा पाकिस्तानी सेना के बीच में एक नाला था, जिसके पार वे पेटियाँ पड़ी थीं। सर्दी के बावजूद स्वयंसेवकों ने तैरकर नाले को पार किया और पेटियों को अपनी पीठ पर बाँधकर अपने क्षेत्र में ले आए। लेकिन लौटते समय पानी में हलचल से पाकिस्तानी सैनिक गोलियाँ चलाने लगे। इस मिशन को अंजाम देने के दौरान चंद्रप्रकाशजी और वेदप्रकाशजी सहित चार स्वयंसेवकों ने मातृभूमि की रक्षा करते हुए अपना बलिदान दे दिया।

□

संघ ने किया मुसलिम लीग के षड्यंत्र का भंडाफोड़

भारत के स्वाधीन होने के एक महीने बाद ही मुसलिम लीग ने भारत को संकट में डालने के लिए षड्यंत्र रचा था। मुसलिम लीग ने दिल्ली में हथियार और विस्फोटक एकत्र कर लिये थे और विशाल शस्त्रागार तैयार कर लिया था। यही नहीं, हमले को अंजाम देने के लिए प्रशिक्षित लोगों की टीम भी बना ली थी। उस संकट काल में अपनी जान जोखिम में डालकर स्वयंसेवकों ने उस षड्यंत्र का भंडाफोड़ किया। तत्कालीन कांग्रेस अध्यक्ष आचार्य कृपलानी ने इसकी पुष्टि करते हुए कहा था, "मुसलमानों ने हथियार एकत्र कर लिये थे। उनके घरों की तलाशी लेने पर बम और गोला-बारूद के भंडार मिले थे। पुलिस में मुसलमानों की भरमार थी और वे दंगाइयों से जा मिले थे। सरकार को अन्य प्रांतों से पुलिस और सेना बुलानी पड़ी।" भारत रत्न डॉ. भगवान् दास ने 19 अक्तूबर, 1948 को एक वक्तव्य में कहा, "आत्मबलिदानी स्वयंसेवकों ने नेहरू और पटेल को समय रहते सूचना न दी होती तो वर्तमान सरकार का कहीं नामो-निशान भी नहीं होता। मुसलिम लीग का विश्वास जीतकर षड्यंत्र उजागर करने के लिए कई स्वयंसेवकों ने तो मुसलमानों का वेश धारण कर लिया था।"

□

संघ न होता तो आज दिल्ली पाकिस्तान में होती!

राष्ट्रीय स्वयंसेवक संघ ने गृहमंत्री सरदार पटेल को जो सूचना दी, उससे दिल्ली पाकिस्तान के कब्जे में जाने से बच गई। संघ ने यह खुफिया जानकारी दी कि मुसलिम लीग के साथ मिलकर दिल्ली के कुछ मुसलिम अधिकारी 10 सितंबर, 1947 को संसद भवन उड़ाकर सभी मंत्रियों की हत्या करना चाहते हैं। इसके बाद वे लालकिले पर पाकिस्तानी झंडा फहराने की साजिश रच रहे हैं। संघ की इस सूचना के बाद पटेल तुरंत हरकत में आए। सबसे बड़ी बात यह कि दिल्ली के ये मुसलमान अधिकारी सरकार के वरिष्ठ पदों पर तैनात थे। गौरतलब है कि इस साजिश से जुड़े सभी दस्तावेज हासिल करने के लिए संघ की एक टोली ने जान की बाजी लगा दी थी, जो खोसला नामक स्वयंसेवक के नेतृत्व में कार्य कर रहे थे। दिल्ली के जिन-जिन स्थानों के बारे में संघ ने सूचना दी थी, उन सभी स्थानों पर एक साथ छापे मारे गए और बड़ी मात्रा में हथियार बरामद हुए। सबसे बड़ा हथियारों का जखीरा शाहदरा से बरामद हुआ—600 रायफलें और बम। पहाड़गंज और करोलबाग इलाके से भी पुलिस ने भारी मात्रा में हथियार जब्त किए।

□

कांग्रेस नेताओं ने अपने परिवारों को बचाने के लिए माँगी मदद

भारत के विभाजन के समय वर्ष 1947 में संघ के स्वयंसेवक जान की बाजी लगाकर लाहौर और अन्य शहरों में हिंदुओं को बचाने में जुटे थे। कत्लेआम के उस दौर में कांग्रेस के नेताओं ने हिंदुओं को साहसपूर्वक डटे रहने का उपदेश तो दिया, लेकिन वे खुद दिल्ली जाने का मौका मिलते ही वहाँ से निकल गए। संकट की उस घड़ी में वे हिंदुओं के प्रति अपना कर्तव्य निभाने में बुरी तरह विफल रहे। यहाँ तक कि पंजाब के कई जिलों में कांग्रेस के नेताओं ने अपने परिवारों और रिश्तेदारों को बचाने के लिए संघ से मदद माँगी थी। लाहौर में अंग्रेजी के प्रोफेसर ए.एन. बाली ने वर्ष 1949 में प्रकाशित अपनी पुस्तक 'नाउ इट कैन बी टोल्ड' (पृष्ठ 136-139) में आँखों देखी कहानी बयान की है। उन्होंने लिखा है, "कैसे संघ के स्वयंसेवकों ने जान पर खेलकर हर मोहल्ले में हिंदू-सिख महिलाओं और बच्चों को खतरनाक इलाकों से निकाला और सुरक्षित केंद्रों तक पहुँचाने का काम किया। हिंदुओं और सिखों को भारत ले जाने वाली ट्रेनों तक पहुँचाने के लिए लॉरी और बसों की व्यवस्था की गई और उनकी सुरक्षा के उपाय किए गए।"

□

स्वयंसेवकों ने लाहौर में सैकड़ों हिंदू-सिखों के प्राण बचाए

11 अगस्त, 1947 की रात से लाहौर में भड़के भीषण दंगों ने 12 अगस्त, 1947 को भयावह रूप धारण कर लिया था। 11 अगस्त, 1947 को किसी ने यह अफवाह उड़ा दी थी कि रेडक्लिफ के सीमा आयोग ने लाहौर को भारत में शामिल करने का फैसला कर लिया है। यह अफवाह फैलते ही मुसलिम लीग से जुड़े 'मुसलिम नेशनल गार्ड' ने हिंदुओं और सिखों को निशाना बनाना शुरू कर दिया। लाहौर की सड़कों पर अत्यंत भयानक दृश्य था और खून की होली खेली जा रही थी। 12 अगस्त को दोपहर तक मृतकों की संख्या 50 पार कर चुकी थी। मृतकों में अधिकांश हिंदू और सिख ही थे। लाहौर के कुछ इलाकों में संघ के स्वयंसेवकों ने साहस और शौर्य का प्रदर्शन करते हुए सैकड़ों हिंदू-सिखों के प्राण बचाए। संघ के स्वयंसेवक अपने-अपने इलाकों में डटे हुए थे और जहाँ तक संभव हो सका लोगों की जान बचाने में जुटे रहे। संघ कार्यालय हिंदू मोहल्ले में था, लेकिन वहाँ भी मुसलिम नेशनल गार्ड के हमले की आशंका को देखते हुए स्वयंसेवक उसकी सुरक्षा में मुस्तैद थे।

□

बाल स्वयंसेवक ने पुलिस को दिया चकमा

स्वाधीनता आंदोलन के दौरान हिंदू-मुसलिम दंगों के बीच स्वयंसेवकों के साहस से भरे अनेक किस्से आज भी लोगों को चकित कर देते हैं। अविभाजित पंजाब के लाहौर में विभाजन के दौर में पुलिस हिंदुओं के, विशेषकर स्वयंसेवकों के घरों पर छापे मारा करती थी। इसलिए लोग सजग रहते थे। जुगल किशोर शीतला मंदिर सायं शाखा के मुख्य शिक्षक थे। जुगलजी के निवास पर एक दिन पहले छापा पड़ा था। इस कारण वे निश्चिंत थे। लेकिन दूसरे ही दिन दोपहर पुलिस फिर छापा मारने आ पहुँची। उनके घर की दूसरी मंजिल पर एक थैले में पिस्तौल रखी हुई थी। इससे सभी चिंतित हो गए कि अगर पुलिस वहाँ तक पहुँच गई तो बड़ा अनर्थ हो जाएगा। तभी जुगलजी को फुर्तीले बाल स्वयंसेवक देवीचंद चोपड़ा की याद आई; उन्होंने उसे बुलाया और थैले की बात बताई। तत्काल देवीचंद के दिमाग में पतंग लूटने की तरकीब सूझी। वह तुरंत 'मेरी गुड्डी-मेरी गुड्डी' चिल्लाता हुआ तेजी से दौड़ता पुलिस के बीच से दूसरी मंजिल पर चढ़ गया। वहाँ से थैला लेकर पड़ोस के मकान की छतें कूदते हुए गली के दूसरी ओर स्थित किनारी बाजार में पहुँच गया और थैला अपने घर सुरक्षित पहुँचा दिया। इस प्रकार बाल स्वयंसेवक ने साहस और सूझ-बूझ से एक बड़ी मुसीबत को टाल दिया।

□

स्वयंसेवक ने अमानवीय अत्याचार सहे, लेकिन कोई भेद नहीं खोला

संघ के स्वयंसेवक ओमप्रकाश खन्ना लाहौर की जनकनगर प्रभात शाखा के मुख्य शिक्षक थे। विभाजन के दौरान पुलिस ने उन्हें एक झूठे मामले में फँसा दिया। शहर में हुए बम विस्फोट में फर्जी आरोप लगाकर उन्हें गिरफ्तार कर लिया गया। दरअसल, पुलिस उनसे संघ की योजनाओं के बारे में जानकारी जुटाना चाहती थी। पुलिस ने उन्हें अमानवीय यातनाएँ देने के लिए कुख्यात लाहौर किले में भेज दिया। वहाँ दो माह तक उन पर भीषण अत्याचार किए गए। निर्दयता से उनके सिर के बाल नोंच-नोंचकर निकाले गए। उन्हें इस तरह की यातनाएँ दी गईं कि उनकी एक आँख लगभग बेकार ही कर दी गई। उन्हें तरह-तरह की धमकी दी गई। कहा गया कि जमीन में आधा शरीर गाड़कर गोली मार दी जाएगी। ओमप्रकाश सब सहते रहे, कठोर यातनाएँ झेलते रहे, लेकिन उन्होंने एक भी भेद नहीं खोला। ओमप्रकाश को संघ की गतिविधियों की जानकारी थी, लेकिन उन्होंने इसका खुलासा नहीं किया। पुलिस जब भी उनसे पूछताछ करती, उनका उत्तर होता था—"मुझे कुछ नहीं मालूम।" पुलिस चाहकर भी उनसे संघ के अधिकारियों की गतिविधियों व योजनाओं के बारे में कुछ भी उगलवा नहीं सकी।

□

संघ के स्वयंसेवकों ने मुसलिम युवतियों को भी बचाया

विभाजन की विभीषिका में राष्ट्रीय स्वयंसेवक संघ ने जो मानवीय कार्य किए, उनमें धर्म को कभी आड़े नहीं आने दिया। हिंदू-मुसलिम दंगे जब देश के कई हिस्से में भड़क चुके थे, उस दौरान स्वयंसेवकों ने मारकाट के बीच अनेक बार मुसलिम युवतियों को भी बचाया। एक मुसलिम युवती अत्यंत भयभीत थी। पंजाब के तरन तारन जिले में खालड़ा गाँव के एक खेत में अपनी जान बचाने की कोशिश कर रही थी। इस खेत से पाकिस्तान की सीमा एकदम पास थी, लेकिन उस युवती को इस बात की जानकारी नहीं थी, इसलिए वह वहीं छिपी थी। पाकिस्तान में मुसलमानों द्वारा अनगिनत हिंदू-सिख युवतियों का अपहरण और कत्लेआम की जानकारी मिलने के बाद संघ के लोग उन दिनों सीमा पर गश्त देते थे। खालड़ा शाखा के नगर कार्यवाह शामलाल शर्मा उस समय अन्य स्वयंसेवकों के साथ गश्त पर थे। उन्होंने लड़की को देखा और उसे सांत्वना दी कि घबराओ मत। युवती के हाथ में गोली लगी थी। स्वयंसेवक उसे स्थानीय अस्पताल ले गए और उसका इलाज करवाया गया। इसके बाद पुलिस के संरक्षण में उस मुसलिम युवती को पाकिस्तान भेज दिया गया।

□

संघ ने अनाथ युवतियों का घर भी बसाया

विभाजन के दौर में अनेक ऐसी युवतियाँ थीं, जिनके परिवारवालों की नृशंस हत्या कर दी गई थी। यही नहीं, पूरे परिवार की हत्या के बाद युवतियों को या तो किसी मुसलमान को बेच दिया गया था या फिर जबरदस्ती अपने घर में रख लिया गया था। इन युवतियों के साथ अमानवीय व्यवहार किया जाता था। संघ के स्वयंसेवक ऐसी युवतियों को भी सेना की मदद से सुरक्षित निकालने का काम करते थे। जिन लड़कियों को मुसलिम घरों से बचाकर लाया जाता था, उनके लिए लाहौर के शिविर में ही एक प्रकोष्ठ बनाया गया था। इस बचाव कार्य में स्वयंसेवकों को साहसिक कार्य करने के साथ ही विषम परिस्थितियों का भी सामना करना पड़ा। संघ अधिकारी चूनीलाल कपूर ने एक मुसलमान के घर से एक युवती को सुरक्षित बचाया था। उसके पूरे परिवार को मार दिया गया था। जबकि इसी शिविर में एक युवक काफी उदास रहता था, क्योंकि उसके पूरे परिवार को भी मार दिया गया था। चूनीलाल ने दोनों को आपस में शादी के लिए रजामंद किया और भारत आकर वे दोनों सुखी जीवन बिताने लगे। संघ की मदद से दोनों को एक-दूसरे का सहारा मिल गया।

□

महाराजा हरि सिंह के अपहरण की साजिश विफल

पाकिस्तान ने अक्तूबर 1947 में जम्मू-कश्मीर पर हमला कर दिया। पाकिस्तानी हमलावरों ने जम्मू और आसपास के जिलों में लूटपाट, आगजनी व कत्लेआम शुरू कर दिया। इससे उन इलाकों में भगदड़ मच गई और लोग सुरक्षित ठिकाना तलाशने के लिए इधर-उधर भागने लगे। इन परिस्थितियों में जनता का मनोबल बनाए रखने के लिए महाराजा हरि सिंह और प्रधानमंत्री मेहर चंद महाजन ने उन इलाकों का दौरा करने का कार्यक्रम बनाया। महाराजा का 18 अक्तूबर, 1947 से छह दिनों का सीमा के पास के गाँवों में जाने का कार्यक्रम बना। मीरपुर, कोटली व कठुआ को केंद्र बनाकर वे जीपों से गाँवों का दौरा करने वाले थे, लेकिन जम्मू का पुलिस अधीक्षक और चीफ ऑफ स्टाफ दोनों मुसलमान थे। उन्होंने महाराजा के साथ विश्वासघात किया और कार्यक्रम की सूचना पाकिस्तानी हमलावरों को दे दी। पाकिस्तानी हमलावरों ने महाराजा का अपहरण कर उनसे जबरन विलय पत्र पर हस्ताक्षर करवाने का षड्यंत्र रचा, लेकिन उन्हें यह नहीं पता था कि जम्मू क्षेत्र के गाँव-गाँव तक संघ के स्वयंसेवक सक्रिय थे। पाकिस्तान समर्थक भारतीय अधिकारियों पर वे पैनी नजर रखते थे। स्वयंसेवकों को इस षड्यंत्र का पता चल गया। उन्होंने महाराजा को दो दिन पहले ही सतर्क कर दिया। उसी सूचना के आधार पर महाराजा ने अपने दौरे के कार्यक्रम में बदलाव कर दिया और इसकी सूचना प्रधानमंत्री महाजन तक को नहीं दी। इस तरह संघ के स्वयंसेवकों की सजगता के कारण यह षड्यंत्र विफल हो गया।

□

जब स्वयंसेवकों ने अपनाया मुसलिम वेश, सीखा मुसलिम रीति-रिवाज

स्वाधीनता के समय वर्ष 1947 में जालंधर में मुसलिम लीग की दंगा करने की तैयारी जोरों पर थी। ऐसे में उनकी वास्तविक तैयारी का पता लगाना आवश्यक था। इसके लिए कुछ समझदार और साहसी स्वयंसेवकों को मुसलमान की वेशभूषा में लीग के अंदर पैठ बढ़ाने की योजना बनाई गई। जालंधर के स्वयंसेवकों की पहचान उजागर होने का डर था, इसलिए इस काम के लिए जम्मू के स्वयंसेवक चरणजीत और गुरदासपुर के ओमप्रकाश को चुना गया। स्थानीय स्वयंसेवक डॉ. जितेंद्र के दवाखाने में दोनों की सुन्नत कराई गई, मुसलिम रीति-रिवाज का अच्छे से अभ्यास कराया गया और इनके नाम भी बदल दिए गए। इसके बाद ये दोनों लीग की गतिविधियों में सक्रिय होने लगे। कुछ ही दिनों में दोनों ने लीग के नेताओं का विश्वास जीत लिया। उनको लीग की आंतरिक बैठकों में भी बुलाया जाने लगा। अब उनको लीग की गुप्त योजनाओं के साथ ही अंदरूनी जानकारियाँ मिलने लगीं। वहाँ से मिली सूचनाओं के आधार पर ही लीग के अनेक षड्यंत्रों को विफल कर दिया गया।

□

संघ के स्वयंसेवकों ने अमृतसर के स्वर्ण मंदिर को बचाया

अमृतसर स्थित स्वर्ण मंदिर यानी दरबार साहिब पर मुसलिम लीग और उसके सशस्त्र दस्ते नेशनल गार्ड्स ने पहले 6 मार्च, 1947 की रात को हमला किया और फिर 9 मार्च, 1947 को भी धावा बोला। उस समय कांग्रेस नेता तो भाग खड़े हुए, लेकिन संघ के स्वयंसेवक पवित्र दरबार साहिब की रक्षा के लिए दीवार बनकर खड़े हो गए। 6 मार्च, 1947 को पाकिस्तान के नेशनल गार्ड्स के नेतृत्व में मुसलिम गुंडों की भीड़ शेरावाला गेट से अमृतसर के चौक फव्वारा तक बढ़ी। उस दौरान संघ के नेतृत्व में हिंदू-सिखों ने उन पर लाठियों, चाकुओं और बमों से चौतरफा हमला कर दिया। इस अचानक हमले से उन्मादी इतने भयभीत हुए कि वे भाग खड़े हुए। इस हमले के तीन दिन बाद 9 मार्च को मुसलिम नेशनल गार्ड और मुसलिम गुंडे सुनियोजित रूप से हमला करने के उद्देश्य से दरबार साहिब की ओर बढ़ने लगे। मुसलिम गुंडे जिहादी नारा लगाते हुए शहर के तीन तरफ से स्वर्ण मंदिर की तरफ बढ़ने लगे। ऐसा तब हो रहा था, जबकि शहर में कर्फ्यू लागू था। दरअसल उन्होंने पुलिस से भी साठगाँठ कर ली थी। उस समय अमृतसर पुलिस में मुसलिमों की संख्या ज्यादा थी। दरबार साहिब से पंजाब रिलीफ कमेटी के कार्यालय में मदद के लिए फोन आया। संघ के कार्यालय प्रमुख दुर्गादास खन्ना ने उन्हें आश्वस्त किया कि वे निश्चिंत रहें, स्वयंसेवकों ने हर गली-कूचे में मोरचा सँभाल लिया है। तरुण स्वयंसेवक छतों पर पत्थरों व सोडा वाटर की बोतलों से हमला करने के लिए मुस्तैद थे तो वहीं बाल स्वयंसेवक हमलावर के दिखते ही उबलते तेल उनके ऊपर डाल देते। इस तरह हमलावर उल्टे पाँव भाग खड़े होते। संघ के स्वयंसेवकों ने अचूक रणनीति और बहादुरी से मुकाबला कर आक्रांताओं को भागने पर मजबूर कर दिया। □

स्वयंसेवकों ने जालंधर के विक्रमपुरा में हमले को विफल किया

विभाजन के समय पंजाब में मुसलिम लीग का दावा केवल रावलपिंडी और लाहौर संभाग तक ही नहीं था। वह जालंधर, फिरोजपुर, फाजिल्का, होशियारपुर, गुरदासपुर और कपूरथला जिलों के कई हिस्सों पर भी अपना दावा जता रही थी। तर्क यह था कि यहाँ मुसलिम आबादी बहुमत में है। जिन-जिन स्थानों पर लीग दावा कर रही थी, वहाँ उसने जोर-जबरदस्ती और शक्ति के बल पर हिंदुओं को खदेड़ने की पूरी तैयारी कर ली थी। उन्होंने इसकी तैयारी जालंधर में भी की थी। जालंधर के विक्रमपुरा में हिंदू परिवार काफी संपन्न थे। इसके नजदीक ही मुसलिम लीग से जुड़े मुसलमानों की बस्ती कराड़खाँ थी। कराड़खाँ को आजकल गोपाल नगर के नाम से जाना जाता है। लीग ने वर्ष 1947 में होली के दिन विक्रमपुरा को लूटने की साजिश रची और षड्यंत्र के तहत विक्रमपुरा पर हमला कर दिया। उन्हें किसी प्रकार के प्रतिरोध की आशंका नहीं थी। लेकिन विक्रमपुरा में होली खेलने के लिए सैकड़ों की संख्या में संघ के स्वयंसेवक एकत्र हुए थे। मुसलमानों ने जैसे ही अल्लाहु-अकबर के नारे लगाए, स्वयंसेवक सक्रिय हो गए। संपन्न लोगों के अधिकतर घरों में लाठियाँ तक नहीं थीं, ऐसे में स्वयंसेवकों ने सिर पर कटोरा रखकर और उसे साड़ियों से बाँधकर हेलमेट बनाया और लीगी गुंडों का सामना किया। गुंडों ने सँकरी गलियों से तीन बार हमले का प्रयास किया, लेकिन पहले से मुस्तैद स्वयंसेवकों ने उनकी हर चाल को नाकाम कर दिया और इस तरह विक्रमपुरा को बचा लिया।

□

पुंछ शहर बचा, पाकिस्तान में जाने से

अक्तूबर 1947 में जम्मू-कश्मीर पर पाकिस्तानी हमले से मुकाबला करने के लिए कुमाऊँ रेजिमेंट का दस्ता जब पुंछ पहुँचा तो जबरदस्त गोलाबारी की जा रही थी। पुंछ को चारों तरफ से पाकिस्तानी सेना ने घेर लिया था। हालत इतनी खराब थी कि बाहर से मदद आने का कोई जमीनी रास्ता नहीं बचा था। केवल हवाई जहाज से ही मदद आ सकती थी, लेकिन पुंछ में हवाई अड्डा नहीं था। ऐसे में सेना के ब्रिगेडियर प्रीतम सिंह ने संघ के अधिकारियों और पुंछ के प्रमुख लोगों के सामने हवाई पट्टी के निर्माण का प्रस्ताव रखा। पुंछ में अमृत सागर के नेतृत्व में संघ ने हवाई पट्टी के निर्माण की जिम्मेदारी अपने कंधों पर ले ली। इसमें संघ से जुड़े नौजवानों के साथ-साथ स्थानीय ग्रामीणों ने भी अपना भरपूर योगदान दिया। काम दिन-रात चला और 72 घंटे में हवाई पट्टी बनकर तैयार हो गई। उसके बाद वहाँ जहाज उतरने लगे। इस काम में स्वयंसेवकों के साथ ही जवानों और बुजुर्गों का योगदान अतुलनीय था। इससे न केवल पुंछ पाकिस्तान के हाथों में जाने से बचा, बल्कि वहाँ के 40 हजार लोगों की जिंदगी भी बचा ली गई।

□

पटियाला के किशोर स्वयंसेवक का अदम्य साहस

विभाजन के दौर में समाना (पटियाला) में एक किलेनुमा बड़ी हवेली थी। यहाँ मुसलमानों ने मोरचा जमा लिया था। सेवानिवृत्त मुसलिम सैनिक इस मोरचे का संचालन कर रहे थे। सेना के लिए यह एक बड़ी चुनौती बन गई कि मुसलिम हमलावरों को वहाँ से किस तरह खदेड़ा जाए। सेना की सहायता के लिए संघ के स्वयंसेवक भी मौजूद थे, लेकिन लाख कोशिश के बाद भी हमलावर पीछे नहीं हट रहे थे। सेना के अधिकारी इस बाबत कोई युक्ति निकालने में जुटे थे। सेना के एक अधिकारी को एक तरकीब सूझी और उसने अपने सैनिकों व स्वयंसेवकों से कहा कि इस मोरचे को तोड़ने का एक ही उपाय है कि कोई वीर आगे बढ़े और समाना की हवेली के द्वार में आग लगा दे। अधिकारी ने जैसे ही अपनी बात समाप्त की चारों ओर सन्नाटा छा गया। भारी गोलीबारी के बीच हवेली तक जाने का प्रयास करना मतलब जान की बाजी लगाने के समान ही था। तभी एक 14 वर्षीय किशोर स्वयंसेवक ओमप्रकाश आगे बढ़ा और कहा, "मैं यह काम करने के लिए तैयार हूँ।" सभी लोग हतप्रभ उस किशोर स्वयंसेवक की ओर देखने लगे और मन-ही-मन उसके साहस का लोहा मान लिया। गोलियों की बौछारों के बीच ओमप्रकाश आगे बढ़ता गया और हवेली के द्वार पर पहुँचकर उसमें आग लगा दी। जैसे ही उसने आग लगाई, तभी वहाँ एक मुसलमान सैनिक आ गया। इससे पहले कि वह गोली चला पाता, ओमप्रकाश ने झपटकर उससे बंदूक छीन ली और बिजली की रफ्तार से दौड़ते हुए वापस अपने कैंप पहुँच गया और बंदूक सेना को सौंप दी।

□

स्वयंसेवकों ने पंजाब के कांग्रेस नेता के घर पर दिया पहरा

विभाजन के दौरान भीमसेन सच्चर पंजाब में कांग्रेस के वरिष्ठ नेताओं में गिने जाते थे। दंगों के दौरान उन्हें भी मुसलिम लीग के गुंडों के धमकी भरे पत्र मिलने लगे। इन पत्रों के कारण वे परेशान रहने लगे। उन्हें अपनी जान का भय सताने लगा। उनका संघ के अधिकारियों से परिचय था, लेकिन उन्होंने इस बारे में कोई चर्चा नहीं की। जब संघ के अधिकारियों को इस बात की जानकारी हुई कि सच्चर को धमकी मिल रही है तो उन्होंने उनकी सुरक्षा की चिंता की। सच्चर की सुरक्षा के लिए उनकी कोठी पर स्वयंसेवकों की तैनाती कर दी गई। चार-चार स्वयंसेवक बारी-बारी से उनकी कोठी पर पहरा देने लगे। सच्चर को बिना बताए यह व्यवस्था की गई थी। करीब 10-15 दिन बाद जब सच्चर को यह बात मालूम हुई तो वे आभार प्रकट करने के लिए संघ अधिकारी धर्मवीर से मिले और धन्यवाद दिया। धर्मवीर ने कहा, "हम तो अपना कर्तव्य करते हैं, किसी पर अहसान नहीं करते। कर्तव्य पालन में हम यह नहीं देखते कि कौन किस पक्ष या जाति का है।"

□

दंगा पीड़ितों की सहायता के लिए संघ ने बनाई 'पंजाब रिलीफ कमेटी'

विभाजन के दौरान पंजाब के दंगा पीड़ितों की सहायता के लिए राष्ट्रीय स्वयंसेवक संघ ने 'पंजाब रिलीफ कमेटी' का गठन किया था। रिलीफ कमेटी उस माहौल में बनी थी, जब मार्च 1946 में पश्चिम व पश्चिमोत्तर प्रांतों से हिंदू अपना सबकुछ गँवाकर लाहौर पहुँच रहे थे। वे शरणार्थी शिविरों में शरण लेने के लिए मजबूर थे। चूँकि जान बचाने के लिए वे अपना घर-बार सबकुछ छोड़कर निकल पड़े थे, इसलिए उन्हें भोजन और वस्त्र से लेकर हर तरह की सहायता की जरूरत थी। दंगे में अनेक लोगों की बर्बर तरीके से हत्या कर दी गई थी। ऐसे माहौल में वे घर से बिना कुछ सामान लिये जान बचाने के लिए इधर-उधर भाग रहे थे। इन हालातों में स्वयंसेवक उनके लिए संकटमोचक की तरह उपस्थित होते थे। वे न केवल उनके ठहरने का इंतजाम करते, बल्कि उनके लिए अन्न, वस्त्र, औषधि आदि की व्यवस्था में जी-जान से जुट जाते। दंगों के दौरान स्वयंसेवक संकटग्रस्त क्षेत्रों में फँसी महिलाओं, बच्चों और बुजुर्गों को निकालकर सुरक्षित स्थानों एवं शिविरों में पहुँचाने का काम जान जोखिम में डालकर करते थे। धर्म के आधार पर विस्थापित हुए लोगों की सेवा में संघ को समाज से अभूतपूर्व सहयोग मिला।

□

संघ ने किया था 'पंजाब रिलीफ स्काउट्स' का गठन

भारत को आजादी मिलने से पहले वर्ष 1946 में अविभाजित पंजाब में हिंदुओं पर भयानक हमले शुरू हो गए थे। इन हमलों से बचाकर उन्हें सुरक्षित स्थान तक पहुँचाने के लिए राष्ट्रीय स्वयंसेवक संघ ने 'पंजाब रिलीफ स्काउट्स' का गठन किया था। उस समय संघ का प्रचार विभाग अखबारों में विस्थापित लोगों की दशा और संघ के काम के बारे में अपील प्रकाशित करवाता था, जिससे लोग खुले मन से मदद पहुँचा सकें। इसी तरह की एक अपील में कहा गया था, "पंजाब रिलीफ कमेटी के साथ ही पंजाब रिलीफ स्काउट्स का भी गठन किया गया है। स्वयंसेवक स्काउट की भूमिका निभाते हुए जान जोखिम में डालकर गाँवों में फँसे लोगों, माताओं-बहनों और बच्चों को वहाँ से निकालकर सुरक्षित स्थान पर पहुँचाने का काम कर रहे हैं। इस काम में स्वयंसेवकों ने समाज के नवयुवकों को भी जोड़ लिया है। इन स्काउटों का एक काम यह भी रहता है कि वे अपहृत महिलाओं, बच्चों और जबरन धर्मांतरण का शिकार हुए हिंदुओं को भी सेना की सहायता से वहाँ से निकालकर ले आएँ। झूठे मामलों में फँसाए गए हिंदुओं की पैरवी हेतु वकीलों का एक संगठन भी बनाया गया है, जो ऐसे मामलों में निःशुल्क पैरवी करते हैं।" अधिक-से-अधिक नवयुवक संगठन में शामिल होकर सेवा के काम में सहयोग दें और शरणार्थियों के लिए ज्यादा-से-ज्यादा राहत सामग्री जुटाई जा सके, इसके लिए समय-समय पर अखबार में अपील प्रकाशित करवाई जाती थी।

□

स्वयंसेवक ने बैंक बैलेंस देने के साथ किया जीवन भी बलिदान

विभाजन के समय मुसलिम लीग की जिहादी सोच वाले लड़ाकों ने कई बार अमृतसर पर हमला किया, लेकिन हर बार उनकी साजिशों और हमलों को संघ के स्वयंसेवकों ने विफल कर दिया। इस संघर्ष में विजय प्राप्त कर स्वयंसेवकों ने न केवल अमृतसर को बचा लिया, बल्कि दिल्ली तक आगे बढ़ने के मुसलिम लीग के मंसूबों पर पानी फेर दिया। इस संघर्ष में समाज की रक्षा के लिए स्वयंसेवकों ने तन-मन-धन के साथ ही अपना सर्वस्व समर्पित कर दिया। ऐसा ही एक उदाहरण है अमृतसर के स्वयंसेवक लालचंद्र का। अमृतसर के खजानाकरज के रहने वाले लालचंद्र ने दंगों से उपजे हालात से द्रवित होकर अपना संपूर्ण बैंक बैलेंस शरणार्थियों की सेवा के लिए संघ द्वारा स्थापित पंजाब रिलीफ कमेटी को समर्पित कर दिया। अपना सारा धन देने के बाद भी वे दिन-रात शरणार्थियों के सेवाकार्य में जुटे रहे। कई बार जोखिम भरे इलाके से भी लोगों को सुरक्षित निकालना पड़ता था। ऐसे ही एक अभियान में समाज की रक्षा करते हुए उन्होंने अपना जीवन बलिदान कर दिया। ऐसे समर्पित स्वयंसेवकों के एक नहीं, अनेक उदाहरण मिलते हैं। □

विभाजन के दंगों के बीच स्वयंसेवकों ने जुटा लिये 10 हजार बरतन

भारत विभाजन के दौरान हुए दंगों के समय जब 70-70 घंटे के कर्फ्यू लगते थे, तब लोगों की परेशानी काफी बढ़ जाती थी। वे खाने-पीने के सामान नहीं जुटा पाते थे। ऐसे में संघ के स्वयंसेवकों ने उनकी परवाह की। पश्चिम और पश्चिमोत्तर प्रांतों से हिंदू लुट-पिटकर लाहौर की तरफ आ रहे थे और शरणार्थी शिविरों में शरण लेने को मजबूर थे। इसे देखते हुए लाहौर में संघ ने कई शरणार्थी शिविर बनाए थे। संघ ने लोगों की मदद के लिए पंजाब रिलीफ कमेटी भी बनाई थी, जिसमें समर्थ लोग हर प्रकार की वस्तु दिल खोलकर दान दे रहे थे। संघ की एक अपील पर लोग घड़े, पंखे, सुराहियाँ, नाश्ता, दूध, बिस्कुट और अन्य जरूरत की चीजें देने के लिए तत्पर रहते थे। स्वयंसेवकों को इलाके की गली-गली की जानकारी रहती थी। इस कारण वे कर्फ्यू में भी बच-बचाकर लोगों की मदद करने पहुँच जाते थे। भोजन से लेकर दवाई तक का प्रबंध स्वयंसेवक करते थे। इतना ही नहीं, शिशुओं के लिए दूध की व्यवस्था भी वे भरसक करते थे। जिनके घरों में गाएँ होती थीं, वे इस बात का ध्यान रखते थे कि दूसरे घर के बच्चे दूध के बिना न रह जाएँ, इसलिए अपने घर का दूध स्वयंसेवकों को दे देते थे और वे उसे उचित स्थान तक पहुँचाते थे। जब बरतनों की आवश्यकता पड़ी तो शाखाओं पर सूचना दी गई कि अगले दिन हर स्वयंसेवक कम-से-कम एक बरतन लाएगा। दंगों के उस कठिन दौर में भी स्वयंसेवकों के प्रयासों से 10 हजार बरतन एकत्र हो गए।

□

स्वयंसेवकों ने 80 हजार शरणार्थियों को छह माह तक भोजन कराया

वर्ष 1950 में पूर्वी पाकिस्तान, जो कि वर्तमान में बांग्लादेश है, वहाँ साजिश के तहत हिंदुओं पर हमला शुरू कर दिया गया और उनका कत्लेआम किया जाने लगा। चारों तरफ मारकाट मचने से बंगाल और असम में शरणार्थियों की बाढ़-सी आ गई थी। भारत सरकार इस स्थिति से निपटने के लिए कुछ नहीं कर रही थी, इससे नाराज होकर डॉ. श्यामा प्रसाद मुकर्जी ने मंत्री पद से इस्तीफा दे दिया। शरणार्थियों की बढ़ती संख्या को देखते हुए संघ के स्वयंसेवक तत्काल मैदान में उतरकर सेवा के काम में जुट गए। संघ ने वर्ष 1950 में कलकत्ता में वास्तुहारा सहायता समिति नाम से एक सोसाइटी की स्थापना की। पश्चिम बंगाल और असम उसका कार्यक्षेत्र था। हिंदू शरणार्थियों की सेवा के लिए उन्होंने देश भर में घर-घर जाकर सहायता की अपील की। लोगों ने भी दिल खोलकर नकदी, अनाज और कपड़े दिए। इस बाबत बंगाल में 15 और असम में 11 सहायता केंद्र बनाए गए थे, जिनमें लगभग आठ महीने तक पाँच हजार से भी अधिक कार्यकर्ताओं ने दिन-रात काम किया। खास बात यह है कि इन स्थानों पर लगातार छह माह तक प्रतिदिन 80,000 से अधिक लोगों को खाना खिलाया गया। इन केंद्रों ने लगभग डेढ़ लाख लोगों को वस्त्रों का वितरण किया। सियालदह तथा अन्य रेलवे स्टेशनों पर रेलगाड़ियों में बड़ी संख्या में शरणार्थी पहुँच रहे थे, ऐसे में उनके बीच एक लाख से अधिक भोजन के पैकेट वितरित किए गए।

□

स्वयंसेवकों ने किया शवों का अंतिम संस्कार

राष्ट्रीय स्वयंसेवक संघ विभाजन के दौरान हुए दंगों के समय न केवल लाखों जान बचाने में मददगार बना, बल्कि दंगे में जान गँवाने वाले लोगों की भी परवाह की। मुसलिम लीग के गुंडों का आतंक मचा हुआ था और हर तरफ मारकाट मची हुई थी। चारों तरफ गोलीबारी का शोर और अनगिनत हत्याएँ हो रही थीं। उस माहौल में मोहल्ले वाले शव का अंतिम संस्कार करने के लिए श्मशान तक जाने में भय का अनुभव करते थे। इसे देखते हुए संघ ने एक शवदाह विभाग बनाया था। इस शवदाह टोली में कार्यकर्ताओं के पास ट्रक भी थे। जहाँ कहीं से फोन आता, ये कार्यकर्ता वहाँ पहुँच जाते थे। कुछ कार्यकर्ता रावी नदी के निकट स्थित श्मशान घाट पर लकड़ियों की व्यवस्था में जुट जाते थे। जिस जगह भी शव होने की सूचना मिलती, स्वयंसेवक 10-10 की टोली में वहाँ तुरंत पहुँच जाते थे। स्वयंसेवक विधिवत् अंतिम संस्कार के बाद परिवारवालों को सुरक्षित घर पहुँचाने का जिम्मा भी लेते थे। यह काम भी उन्होंने जान हथेली पर रखकर गोलियों की बौछारों के बीच किया।

□

लाहौर में स्वयंसेवक कुलवंत सिंह हुए शहीद

भारत जिस दिन आजाद हो रहा था, उससे एक दिन पहले यानी 14 अगस्त, 1947 की रात को लाहौर में परिस्थिति बहुत ही भयानक हो चली थी। मुसलिम लीग के गुंडे हिंदू और सिखों को जहाँ भी पाते, जानलेवा हमला कर रहे थे। हिंदुओं-सिखों के जत्थे प्राण बचाने के लिए इधर-उधर भाग रहे थे। बड़ी संख्या में लोग संघ द्वारा संचालित 'पंजाब सहायता समिति' के शरणार्थी शिविर में पहुँच रहे थे। यह शिविर लाहौर डी.ए.वी. कॉलेज के परिसर और हॉस्टल में स्थापित किया गया था। शिविर में मदद की आस लिये पहुँचे लोगों और घायलों के लिए रोजाना दोपहर स्वयंसेवक सरदार कुलवंत सिंह भोजन लेकर आते थे। शरणार्थियों के लिए भोजन लाहौर के भाटी गेट मोहल्ले में स्वयंसेवक ही तैयार करते थे। 14 अगस्त को जब कुलवंत सिंह समय पर नहीं पहुँचे तो स्वयंसेवक दीनदयाल उनकी खोज-खबर लेने के लिए लाहौर शहर में निकले। कुछ दूर जाने के बाद बीच रास्ते में उन्हें भीड़ दिखाई दी। जब उन्होंने नजदीक जाकर देखा तो वे अवाक् रह गए। बीच रास्ते में कुलवंत सिंह खून से लथपथ पड़े थे। उन्हें जिहादियों ने मार दिया था। पास में ही उनकी मोटरसाइकिल गिरी पड़ी थी और चारों तरफ भोजन बिखरा पड़ा था।

□

विभाजन के दौरान स्वयंसेवकों ने कराची में निकाला पथ-संचलन

विभाजन के समय लाहौर में करीब तीन लाख हिंदू-सिख रहते थे। लेकिन मार्च-अप्रैल से मुसलिम लीग और मुसलिम नेशनल गार्ड के हमले बढ़ने लगे। इससे करीब एक लाख हिंदू-सिख पूर्वी पंजाब यानी भारत का रुख कर चुके थे। 5 अगस्त, 1947 को दंगों, आगजनी, लूटपाट और बलात्कार जैसी जघन्य घटनाओं के बावजूद सिंध प्रांत के कराची शहर में एक हलचल थी। कराची हवाई अड्डे पर वैसे कोई खास भीड़ नहीं रहती, लेकिन 5 अगस्त को भारी संख्या में लोग मौजूद थे। दोपहर संघ के सरसंघचालक श्रीगुरुजी टाटा एयर सर्विसेस के विमान से बंबई से कराची पहुँचे। उनकी सुरक्षा की व्यवस्था की जिम्मेदारी स्वयंसेवकों के हाथों में थी। हवाई अड्डे पर कराची महानगर के कार्यवाह लालकृष्ण आडवाणी स्वयंसेवकों के साथ उपस्थित थे। 5 अगस्त, 1947 को शाम पाँच बजे संघ का पूर्ण गणवेश में एक विशाल पथ-संचलन निकला। करीब 10 हजार स्वयंसेवकों ने पथ संचलन में हिस्सा लिया। इसके बाद कराची के प्रमुख चौराहे पर श्रीगुरुजी की आम सभा हुई। एक साथ बड़ी संख्या में स्वयंसेवकों को जुटा देखकर मुसलिम लीग के गुंडे किसी अप्रिय घटना को अंजाम नहीं दे सके। पथ-संचलन और सभा व्यवस्थित ढंग से संपन्न हुई। मुसलिम लीग के गुंडों को कठोर संदेश देने और हिंदू-सिखों में आत्मविश्वास जगाने के लिए यह आयोजन किया गया था। दंगों और आगजनी के बीच इस आयोजन की रूपरेखा तैयार करना साहसिक कदम था।

□

विभाजन के दौर में 'राष्ट्र सेविका समिति' की सक्रिय भूमिका

कराची में संघ से जुड़े एक परिवार का घर था। यहाँ की दो महिलाएँ 'राष्ट्र सेविका समिति' से सक्रिय रूप से जुड़ी थीं। इस घर की छत पर 14 अगस्त, 1947 को सेविकाओं का एक कार्यक्रम रखा गया था। चारों तरफ कत्लेआम के उस दौर में किस तरह हिंदू-सिखों को मुसलमानों के अत्याचार से बचाया जाए, इसको लेकर राष्ट्र सेविका समिति सक्रिय थी। हिंदू-सिख महिलाओं में उत्साह भरने के लिए ही समिति की संस्थापक लक्ष्मीबाई केलकर यानी मौसीजी कराची आई थीं। लक्ष्मीबाई केलकर ने अपनी धीर-गंभीर आवाज में सांत्वना देते हुए कहा, "जैसे भी संभव हो, हिंदुस्तान आ जाओ। यहाँ से निकलकर हिंदुस्तान कैसे पहुँचा जाए, केवल इस बात पर विचार करें। बंबई और अन्य शहरों में संघ ने आपके लिए व्यवस्था की हुई है, चिंता न करें। हम सभी एक ही परिवार हैं। यह कठिन समय आपस में मिल-जुलकर किसी तरह निकाल ही लेंगे।" कुछ समय सवाल-जवाब के लिए रखा गया था और लक्ष्मीबाई केलकर ने वहाँ मौजूद सेविकाओं की शंकाओं और समस्याओं का समाधान किया।

□

परिवार से छिपकर बाल स्वयंसेवक का सत्याग्रह

विभाजन के बाद वर्ष 1948 में फैले सांप्रदायिक दंगे के दौरान बिलासपुर (हि.प्र.) का एक स्वयंसेवक भूपेंद्र सिंह अभी दसवीं कक्षा का छात्र था और वह सत्याग्रह में भाग लेने के लिए निकल पड़ा था। वह अपने पाँच साथियों के साथ हिमाचल प्रदेश के हमीरपुर जिले के नादौन शहर में गिरफ्तारी देने के लिए पहुँच गया। इस बात की भनक घरवालों को लग गई। उसके पिता और चाचा उसे वापस लाने के लिए आधी रात को ही नादौन पहुँच गए। जिस सराय में भूपेंद्र और साथी ठहरे थे, वहाँ कोने में कपड़ों की एक ढेरी पड़ी थी। भूपेंद्र ने अपने साथियों से कहा कि ये जो कपड़े की ढेरी है, उसे मेरे ऊपर डाल दो और कह देना कि वह हमारे साथ नहीं आया था। उसके सारे साथी पिताजी और चाचाजी के साथ वापस चले गए। उनके जाने के बाद भूपेंद्र बड़ी मुश्किल से कपड़ों की ढेरी से बाहर निकला और सुजानपुर चला गया। स्थानीय प्रचारक भी सुजानपुर पहुँच गए। सुजानपुर में गिरफ्तारी देने के लिए वहाँ नया जत्था तैयार किया गया। इसके बाद उन पर मुकदमा चला और धर्मशाला कोर्ट ने भूपेंद्र को 3 वर्ष की सजा सुनाई। हालाँकि 6 माह की सजा पूरी होने के बाद भूपेंद्र को जेल से रिहा कर दिया गया।

□

के.एम. मुंशी ने पंजाब व सिंध में स्वयंसेवकों की बहादुरी को सराहा

स्वतंत्रता सेनानी, संविधान सभा के सदस्य और कांग्रेस नेता के.एम. मुंशी स्वयंसेवकों की दिलेरी के कायल थे। संघ के स्वयंसेवकों ने विभाजन के दौर में पंजाब और सिंध में जिस प्रकार महिलाओं और बच्चों की रक्षा की, उसकी उन्होंने जी भरकर तारीफ की थी। 02 अक्तूबर, 1949 के जालंधर से प्रकाशित 'आकाशवाणी' साप्ताहिक के पृष्ठ छह-सात पर कन्हैयालाल माणिकलाल मुंशी का एक प्रेस वक्तव्य छपा। इस वक्तव्य में मुंशी ने संघ के स्वयंसेवकों की प्रशंसा करते हुए कहा, "देश विभाजन के दिनों में संघ के नवयुवकों ने पंजाब और सिंध में अतुलनीय वीरता प्रकट की। उन नवयुवकों ने आततायी मुसलमानों का सामना करके हजारों स्त्रियों और बच्चों का सम्मान और जीवन बचाया। अनेक नवयुवकों ने इस कर्तव्य पालन में अपना जीवन बलिदान कर दिया।" के.एम. मुंशी कानून विशेषज्ञ होने के साथ ही गुजराती, अंग्रेजी, हिंदी के प्रसिद्ध साहित्यकार तथा शिक्षाविद् थे। वे उत्तर प्रदेश के राज्यपाल और भारत सरकार के खाद्य मंत्री पद पर भी रहे। उन्होंने बंबई में भारतीय विद्या भवन की स्थापना की।

□

हैदराबाद रियासत के विलय में संघ का योगदान

हैदराबाद रियासत ब्रिटिश काल की सबसे बड़ी राजशाही रियासत थी। इस रियासत में वर्तमान तेलंगाना, उत्तरी कर्नाटक और महाराष्ट्र का मराठवाड़ा इलाका शामिल था। यहाँ 85 प्रतिशत हिंदू जनसंख्या पर घोर मुसलिम मानसिकता वाला निजाम शासक था। नवाब मीर उस्मान अली खान सिद्‌दकी असफ-जाह ने भारत में हैदराबाद का विलय नहीं किया। उसने 40 हजार की सेना और 2 लाख कट्‌टरपंथी रजाकारों की मदद से हिंदुओं पर अत्याचार करना शुरू कर दिया। हैदराबाद में बढ़ते हिंदू उत्पीड़न के समाधान के लिए सरदार पटेल की प्रेरणा से तत्कालीन मध्य भारत के मुख्यमंत्री पंडित रविशंकर शुक्ल और गृहमंत्री द्वारिका प्रसाद मिश्र सक्रिय हुए। उन्होंने भयग्रस्त हिंदुओं को आश्वस्त करने हेतु संघ से सहायता माँगने का निर्णय लिया और मध्य प्रांत के संघचालक बापू साहब सोहणी से बात की। फिर क्या था, सैकड़ों स्वयंसेवक हिंदुओं की रक्षा के लिए हैदराबाद पहुँच गए। वे जनता का मनोबल बढ़ाने के साथ ही सत्याग्रहियों को सुरक्षा भी प्रदान कर रहे थे। भैयाजी दाणी सहित अनगिनत स्वयंसेवकों ने विरोध प्रदर्शन में हिस्सा लिया और जेल की सजा काटी। संघ ने आर्य समाज एवं अन्य हिंदू संगठनों को एकजुट किया और हिंदुओं के खिलाफ हो रहे अत्याचार को रोकने में महत्त्वपूर्ण भूमिका निभाई। इन प्रयासों से हैदराबाद रियासत का भारत में विलय का मार्ग प्रशस्त हुआ।

□

जब नेहरू ने श्रीगुरुजी के लिए खोला कार का दरवाजा

विभाजन के दौर में और उससे पहले संघ ने जिस प्रकार का काम किया, उसकी वजह से प्रधानमंत्री नेहरू के मन में दूसरे सरसंघचालक श्रीगुरुजी के प्रति गहरा आदर का भाव था। इसकी झलक उस समय देखने को मिली, जब सरसंघचालक श्रीगुरुजी 30 अगस्त, 1949 को जवाहरलाल नेहरू से मिलने उनके आधिकारिक आवास तीन मूर्ति भवन पहुँचे। दोनों के मिलने का समय निर्धारित था। लेकिन नेहरू कैबिनेट मीटिंग की वजह से समय पर आवास नहीं पहुँच पाए। इसका भान होते ही निर्धारित समय से पाँच मिनट पहले नेहरू ने अपने सेक्रेटरी को फोन किया और बताया, "मैंने गोलवलकरजी को मिलने के लिए बुला रखा है। जैसे ही वे आएँ, उनसे मेरी ओर से क्षमायाचना करना और कहना कि कैबिनेट की बैठक में देरी हो जाने के कारण मैं दस मिनट विलंब से वहाँ पहुँच पाऊँगा।" पंडित नेहरू जब आए तो सबसे पहले उन्होंने क्षमायाचना की। इसके बाद दोनों के बीच बातचीत शुरू हुई। बैठक समाप्त होने के बाद जैसे ही श्रीगुरुजी चलने लगे तो प्रधानमंत्री नेहरू उन्हें विदा करने न सिर्फ बरामदे तक आए, बल्कि उनके लिए खुद ही कार का दरवाजा खोला। उन दोनों का आपसी व्यवहार परस्पर आदर का था।

□

जब सरदार पटेल को माननी पड़ी श्रीगुरुजी की बात

राष्ट्रीय स्वयंसेवक संघ के दूसरे सरसंघचालक श्रीगुरुजी और सरदार वल्लभभाई पटेल के बीच गहरी दोस्ती जगजाहिर थी। लेकिन समय आने पर वे आपस में स्पष्टता से अपनी बात कहने में भी संकोच नहीं करते थे। मोहम्मद अली जिन्ना ने भारत-पाकिस्तान बँटवारे के बाद पूर्व और पश्चिम पाकिस्तान को जोड़ने के लिए एक विशेष कॉरिडोर की माँग की थी। वह कॉरिडोर अन्य प्रांतों के अलावा उत्तर प्रदेश से होकर गुजरने वाला था। इस माँग के उपरांत पाश्चिम पाकिस्तान से पूर्व पाकिस्तान तक कॉरिडोर के लिए उत्तर प्रदेश का जो हिस्सा पड़ रहा था, वहाँ दंगा हो गया। दंगे के दौरान पंडित नेहरू ने अपने सारे अधिकारियों को हिदायत दी कि संघ के लोगों को परेशान करना है। दंगा होने पर यदि 10 मुसलमानों को गिरफ्तार किया गया हो तो इसके जवाब में 10 हिंदुओं की भी गिरफ्तारी होनी ही चाहिए, चाहे उनकी दंगा में संलिप्तता हो या नहीं हो। नेहरू की इस संघ-विरोधी सोच के कारण उस दंगे में कई निर्दोष स्वयंसेवकों को गिरफ्तार कर लिया गया। यह बात जब श्रीगुरुजी के संज्ञान में आई तो उन्होंने तत्कालीन गृहमंत्री सरदार पटेल से बात की और बताया कि किस प्रकार उनकी पुलिस ने निर्दोष स्वयंसेवकों को पकड़कर जेल में डाल दिया है। पटेल ने कहा कि उनके पास ऑफिशियल रिपोर्ट आई है कि जिन्हें गिरफ्तार किया गया है, वे दंगों में संलिप्त थे। इस पर श्रीगुरुजी ने कहा कि आप जाँच तो कराइए। पहले तो इस पर विचार कीजिए कि जहाँ-जहाँ दंगे हुए हैं, उनसे हिंदुओं को क्या लाभ होने वाला है और दूसरा ये कि दंगे हुए कहाँ हैं? उन्होंने बताया कि दंगे उन्हीं इलाके में हुए हैं, जो ईस्ट-वेस्ट कॉरिडोर में आने वाले हैं। उनके कहने पर सरदार पटेल ने तत्काल मैप मँगवाकर देखा तो श्रीगुरुजी की बात अक्षरश: सत्य निकली। सारे दंगे उसी क्षेत्र में हुए थे।

□

लता मंगेशकर ने संघ के चैरिटी शो में लिया हिस्सा

राष्ट्रीय स्वयंसेवक संघ को गोवा तथा दादरा और नगर हवेली को पुर्तगालियों के कब्जे से मुक्त कराने के लिए धन की जरूरत पड़ी तो इस निमित्त एक चैरिटी शो करने का निर्णय लिया। इस चैरिटी शो का हिस्सा बनने के लिए प्रख्यात गायिका लता मंगेशकर के पास प्रस्ताव रखा गया। उन्होंने सहर्ष यह प्रस्ताव स्वीकार कर लिया। पुणे में 02 मई, 1954 को आयोजित इस चैरिटी शो में उन्होंने अपनी गायकी से तो लोगों को मंत्रमुग्ध किया ही, साथ ही देश सेवा में अपना अपूर्व योगदान दिया। उन्होंने एक इंटरव्यू में कहा, "मेरे पिता गोवा से थे। इस तरह मैं भी गोवा की हुई। मुझे नहीं पता कि चैरिटी शो से कितना धन इकट्ठा हुआ, लेकिन मुझे खुशी है कि मैंने अपने देश और पिता की भूमि की स्वतंत्रता के लिए कुछ योगदान दिया।" सतत संघर्ष के बल पर संघ ने 02 अगस्त, 1954 को दादरा और नगर हवेली को पुर्तगालियों के कब्जे से मुक्त करा लिया। पुणे में अगस्त 2011 में एक सभा का आयोजन किया गया, जिसमें उन स्वयंसेवकों को सम्मानित किया गया, जिन्होंने वर्ष 1954 के आंदोलन में भाग लिया था। संघ के जिन 103 स्वयंसेवकों ने इस आंदोलन में हिस्सा लिया था, उनमें से 55 स्वयंसेवक 2011 की इस सभा के समय जीवित थे। सभा में उन्हें आमंत्रित कर सम्मानित किया गया और बलिदानियों को श्रद्धांजलि अर्पित की गई। उल्लेखनीय है कि पुर्तगालियों ने नगर हवेली में 1783 और दादरा में 1785 में शासन करना आरंभ किया था।

□

जान हथेली पर रखकर मुक्त करवाया दादरा और नगर हवेली

भारत 15 अगस्त, 1947 को स्वतंत्र हो गया, लेकिन गोवा, दादरा और नगर हवेली तथा दमन दीव अब भी स्वतंत्र नहीं हुए थे। इन पर पुर्तगाली शासकों का कब्जा बना हुआ था। भारत के इतिहास में 02 अगस्त, 1954 इस लिहाज से एक महत्त्वपूर्ण दिवस है, क्योंकि इसी दिन दादरा और नगर हवेली पुर्तगाली शासन से मुक्त हुआ और 11 अगस्त, 1961 को भारत का हिस्सा बना था। दादरा और नगर हवेली की स्वतंत्रता में संघ ने अग्रणी भूमिका निभाई थी। इसकी स्वाधीनता के लिए यों तो आवाजें स्वतंत्रता आंदोलन के समय से उठती रहीं, लेकिन इसमें तेजी 1950 के दशक के आरंभ में आई। नाना काजरेकर और सुधीर फड़के के नेतृत्व में स्वयंसेवकों ने दादरा और नगर हवेली को पुर्तगालियों से स्वतंत्र कराने का प्रण लिया था। योजना के अनुसार 02 अगस्त, 1954 को पुणे के संघचालक विनायक राव आप्टे के नेतृत्व में 100 से अधिक स्वयंसेवकों की एक टोली ने दादरा और नगर हवेली के परिक्षेत्रों पर धावा बोल दिया। उन्होंने सिलवासा पर हमला बोल दिया। स्वयंसेवक जान की बाजी लगाकर हथियारों से लैस पुर्तगाल के सैनिकों से भिड़ गए और आत्मसमर्पण करने पर मजबूर कर दिया। इसके बाद वहाँ राष्ट्रीय तिरंगा फहरा दिया गया। पुर्तगाल की सेना की फायरिंग में कई स्वयंसेवकों की जान चली गई और कई घायल हो गए। एक तरफ मातृभूमि के लिए स्वयंसेवकों का बलिदान है, वहीं दूसरी तरफ देश के प्रथम प्रधानमंत्री जवाहरलाल नेहरू ने 15 अगस्त, 1961 को स्वतंत्रता दिवस पर लालकिले से दिए भाषण में दादरा और नगर हवेली को एक छोटा सा टुकड़ा और कुछ गाँव करार दिया। यही नहीं, उन्होंने कहा—“हमारी कोई इच्छा नहीं, हमारी नीति नहीं कि हम और देशों पर हमला करें; और देशों की जमीन पर कब्जा करें या और देश के रहने वालों को अपने देश में मिलाएँ।”

□

गोवा मुक्ति आंदोलन में 30 से अधिक कार्यकर्ताओं ने प्राणों की आहुति दी

गोवा मुक्ति आंदोलन में यद्यपि पूरे देश में सभाएँ हुईं, जाग्रति के लिए जुलूस निकाले गए और जत्थे गोवा रवाना हुए। महाराष्ट्र और मध्य प्रदेश में इस आंदोलन को व्यापक समर्थन मिला। इसमें संघ के स्वयंसेवकों की भूमिका महत्त्वपूर्ण रही। मालवा में गोवा मुक्ति के लिए चेतना जगाने का काम संघ के प्रचारक राजाभाऊ महाकाल ने किया। गोवा मुक्ति के लिए मध्य प्रदेश के उज्जैन से रवाना हुए जत्थे में सुप्रसिद्ध पुरातत्वविद डॉ. विष्णु श्रीधर वाकणकर भी शामिल थे। योजनानुसार देश भर के सभी जत्थे बंबई पहुँचे और वहाँ से गोवा रवाना हुए। गोवा सरकार की सेना ने नाकाबंदी कर रखी थी। जत्थों ने तिरंगा हाथ में लेकर आगे बढ़ने का प्रयास किया। पुर्तगाली सेना ने गोली चला दी, जिसमें 30 से अधिक कार्यकर्ताओं ने अपने प्राणों की आहुति दी और 100 से अधिक घायल हुए। बलिदान होने वालों में उज्जैन के राजाभाऊ भी थे। उनके सिर में तीन गोलियाँ लगी थीं। यह 15 अगस्त, 1955 का दिन था। वहीं इसी दिन वर्ष 1955 में स्वतंत्रता दिवस पर पंडित नेहरू ने अपने भाषण में कहा था—“आज के दिन भी हम, इस गोवा के मामले में कोई फौजी काररवाई नहीं करने वाले। हम इसको शांति के तरीकों से हल करने वाले हैं और कोई इस धोखे में न रहे कि हम वहाँ फौजी काररवाई करेंगे।” लेकिन आंदोलन तीव्र होता देख भारत सरकार पर दबाव बना और अंततः भारतीय सेना सक्रिय हुई। भारतीय सेना ने 19 दिसंबर, 1961 को इसे स्वाधीन करा लिया। गोवा मुक्ति आंदोलन में संघ के प्रचारक वसंतराव ओक को भी गोली लगी थी और जनसंघ के नेता जगन्नाथराव जोशी ने कई साल तक पंजिम जेल में सजा काटी।

□

स्वतंत्र भारत के 5 दशक

आंध्र प्रदेश में 1977 में आए चक्रवाती तूफान के दौरान संघ ने 'शवसेना' का गठन कर मृतकों के अंतिम संस्कार किए।

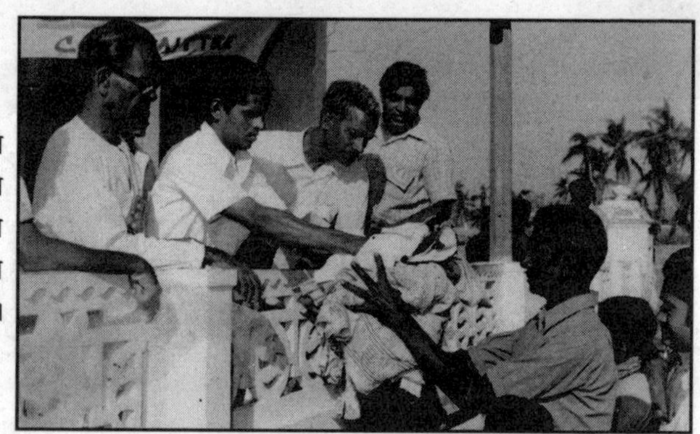

माहोलीपटनम गाँव में एक मसजिद से तूफान प्रभावितों को वस्त्र वितरण करते स्वयंसेवक।

अखिल भारतीय प्रचार प्रमुख यादवराव जोशी 11.12.1977 को चिन्नापुरम गाँव में वस्त्र वितरण करते हुए।

दीनदयाल शोध संस्थान, नई दिल्ली द्वारा तूफान प्रभावित इलाकों का हवाई सर्वेक्षण।

प्रांत प्रचारक एस. सोमैय्या, संघ के साइक्लोन रिलीफ कमेटी के वाइस प्रेसिडेंट जी.एस.के. आर्या और दीनदयाल शोध संस्थान के डॉ. जैन तूफान प्रभावित इलाके का निरीक्षण करते हुए।

तूफान प्रभावितों के लिए वामुला पल्ली,
हरिजनवाड़ा में बेघरों के लिए घरों का निर्माण करते स्वयंसेवक।

स्वयंसेवकों ने पाराचिवारा में रिकॉर्ड 20 दिनों में 61 घरों का निर्माण किया।
इस कालोनी का नामकरण संघ के दिवंगत विभाग प्रचारक भोगादी दुर्गा प्रसाद के नाम पर 'दुर्गाप्रसादपुरम' रखा गया।

1965 के भारत–पाक युद्ध के दौरान संघ की अमृतसर शाखा ने
2000 किलो मिठाई सेना के अग्रिम मोरचे पर भेजी।

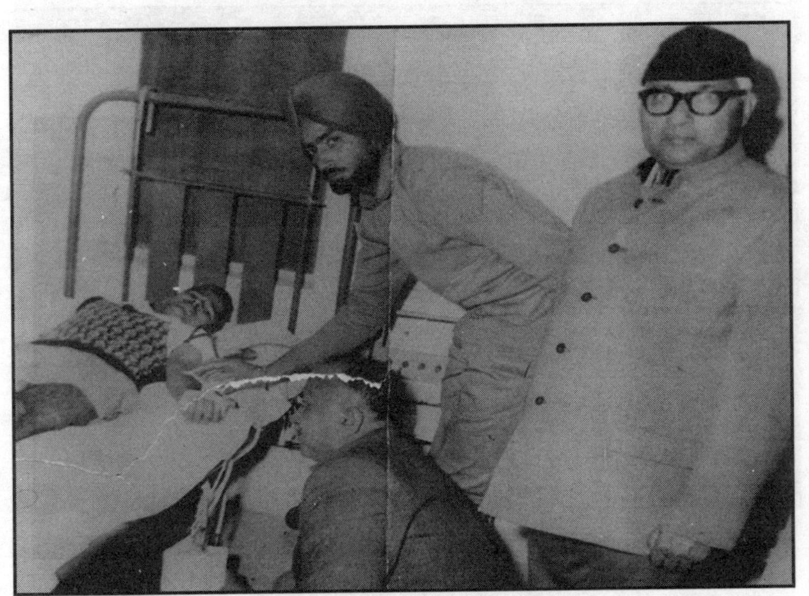

1971 के युद्ध के दौरान जालंधर के सैनिक अस्पताल में रक्तदान करते स्वयंसेवक।
साथ में हैं जिला संघचालक वतन सिंह।

1971 के भारत–पाक युद्ध के दौरान पठानकोट में
संघ के स्वयंसेवक जवानों के लिए फल और सब्जियाँ लादते हुए।

1971 के भारत–पाक युद्ध के दौरान रक्तदान के लिए तैयार संघ के स्वयंसेवकों का एक समूह। दूसरी पंक्ति (बाएँ से दाएँ) में बैठे हुए अमृतसर के एक प्रमुख कार्यकर्ता श्री देवराज, अमृतसर के रक्त बैंक प्रभारी डॉ. गुरचरण सिंह, अमृतसर के उप–जिलाधीश की पत्नी श्रीमती बेदी, अमृतसर के संघचालक श्री जी.एल. चोपड़ा, अमृतसर के रक्त बैंक अधिकारी श्री बंता सिंह।

1971 के भारत-पाक युद्ध के दौरान पठानकोट में स्वयंसेवक जवानों के लिए फल और सब्जियाँ भेजते हुए।

1971 के भारत-पाक युद्ध के दौरान संघ की अमृतसर शाखा द्वारा उपायुक्त श्री बेदी को वस्त्र आदि सौंपते हुए।

1971 भारत-पाक युद्ध के दौरान स्वयंसेवकों ने राइफल प्रशिक्षण प्राप्त किया। हमले के लिए तैयार एक स्वयंसेवक।

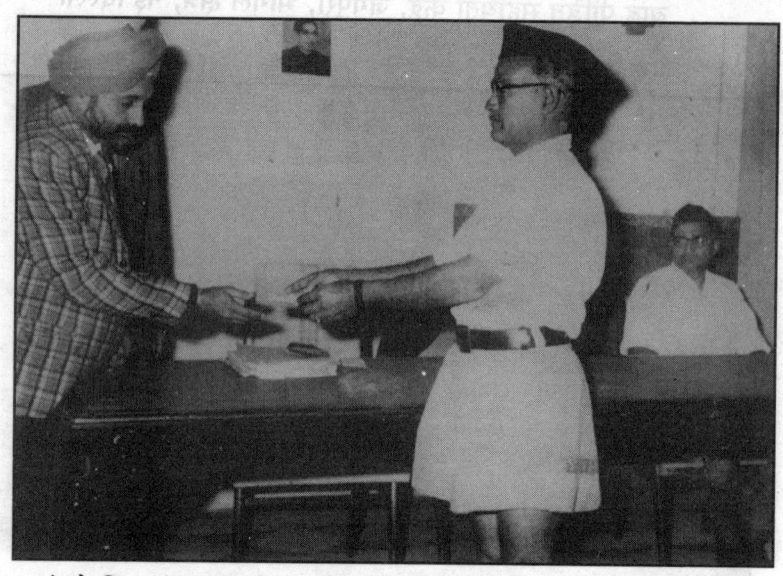

संघ के जिला संघचालक जी.एल. चोपड़ा से धनराशि प्राप्त करते हुए अमृतसर ब्लड बैंक के प्रभारी। यह राशि 1971 में भारत-पाक युद्ध के दौरान घायल सैनिकों की मदद के लिए एकत्र की गई थी।

अखिल भारतीय बौद्धिक प्रमुख एम.वी. मोघे और संघ के कुछ अन्य प्रमुख कार्यकर्ता 1971 के भारत-पाक युद्ध के दौरान पंजाब में सैन्य क्षेत्रों का दौरा करते हुए। सीमा सुरक्षा बल के कमांडर श्री भुल्लर कुछ हथियारों की कार्यप्रणाली समझा रहे हैं।

बाढ़ पीड़ित सहायता केंद्र, जंगपुरा, भोगल क्षेत्र, नई दिल्ली

श्री गीता भवन मन्दिर (पंजीकृत) तिलक नगर केन्द्र
बाढ़ पीड़ित सहायता समिति (राष्ट्रीय स्वयं सेवक संघ)
यहाँ भोजन बनता है
DHE 8436

बाढ़ पीड़ित सहायता समिति
(राष्ट्रीय स्वयंसेवक संघ)
बाढ़ पीडित भोजनालय
व्यापार मण्डल (पंजीकृत)
यूसुफ़ सराये नई दिल्ली

हरियाणा बाढ़ पीड़ितों के लिए सहायता कार्य।

दिल्ली में बाढ़ पीड़ितों के लिए स्वास्थ्य सेवा।

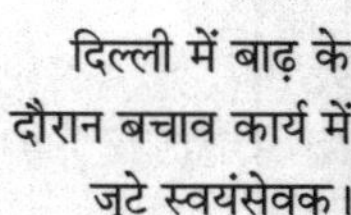

दिल्ली में बाढ़ के दौरान बचाव कार्य में जुटे स्वयंसेवक।

सेवा भारती द्वारा संचालित औद्योगिक प्रशिक्षण केंद्र।

श्रीगुरुजी के निधन पर श्रद्धांजलि कार्यक्रम में स्वयंसेवक।

कांग्रेस अध्यक्ष सीतारमैया का संघ पर बड़ा फैसला

स्वाधीनता के बाद कांग्रेस पार्टी के पहले अध्यक्ष भोगराजू पट्टाभि सीतारमैया का संघ से बहुत गहरा संबंध था। उनका संघ के नेताओं के साथ न केवल जुड़ाव था, बल्कि वे संघ की वैचारिक प्रतिबद्धता के भी कायल थे। इसलिए स्वाधीनता के बाद वर्ष 1948 में जब वे कांग्रेस के अध्यक्ष बने, तब उनकी इच्छा थी कि संघ के स्वयंसेवकों को कांग्रेस से जोड़ दिया जाए और उन्हें कांग्रेस की सदस्यता दी जाए। इसके लिए उनकी अगुवाई में कांग्रेस वर्किंग कमेटी ने स्वयंसेवकों को कांग्रेस पार्टी में शामिल होने की अनुमति भी प्रदान कर दी थी। कांग्रेस अध्यक्ष डॉ. पट्टाभि सीतारमैया ने इस अवसर पर कहा, "राष्ट्रीय स्वयंसेवक संघ कांग्रेस का दुश्मन नहीं है, बल्कि कांग्रेस के भीतर गुटबाजी सबसे बड़ा दुश्मन है।" हालाँकि नेहरू के विरोध के बाद कांग्रेस अध्यक्ष पट्टाभि सीतारमैया के इस फैसले को बदल दिया गया। संघ की कार्यप्रणाली से सीतारमैया किस हद तक प्रभावित थे, इसे इसी बात से समझा जा सकता है कि वे संघ की बैठकों और कार्यक्रमों में भी शामिल होते थे। यहाँ तक कि डॉ. हेडगेवार के साथ ही संघ के अन्य नेताओं के साथ उनके घनिष्ठ संबंध थे।

□

नेहरू ने जब श्रीगुरुजी को बताया राष्ट्रवादी

जवाहरलाल नेहरू जानते थे कि श्रीगुरुजी राष्ट्रवादी हैं और राष्ट्र के खिलाफ कुछ बरदाश्त नहीं कर सकते। इस वजह से नेहरू भी उनका काफी सम्मान करते थे। उनके मन में श्रीगुरुजी के प्रति कितनी इज्जत थी, इसे इसी बात से समझा जा सकता है कि पश्चिम बंगाल के एक लेखक हेमेंद्र पंडित ने श्रीगुरुजी की आलोचना वाली एक पुस्तक 'एंड ऑफ द ड्रीम' (End of The Dream) लिखी। एक तरह से कहें तो उस पुस्तक के माध्यम से उन्होंने गाली दी थी। उन्होंने श्रीगुरुजी के बारे में लिखा था कि वे तो ऐश और आराम में रहने वाले व्यक्ति हैं। उन्होंने अपनी यह पुस्तक डॉ. श्यामा प्रसाद मुकर्जी और जवाहरलाल नेहरू जैसी बड़ी हस्तियों को भी भेजी थी। एक दिन की बात है जवाहरलाल नेहरू से मिलने डॉ. श्यामा प्रसाद मुकर्जी उनके कार्यालय गए थे। वहाँ उनकी मेज पर मुकर्जी ने वही पुस्तक देखी तो उन्होंने नेहरू से पूछा, "क्या आप यह पुस्तक पढ़ रहे हैं।" नेहरू ने कहा, "हाँ देखी है, लेकिन अब इसे पढ़ूँगा नहीं।" मुकर्जी ने पूछा, "क्यों?" इस पर नेहरू ने कहा, "गोलवलकरजी से मेरा मतभेद जरूर है, लेकिन ये जो लिख रहा है, वो ठीक नहीं है, क्योंकि पर्सनली मैं उन्हें जानता हूँ कि वे राष्ट्रवादी हैं। उसने गलत लिखा है, शरारत के कारण लिखा है।" फिर उन्होंने वह पुस्तक नहीं पढ़ी। इससे साफ है कि वैचारिक और राजनीतिक मतभेद एक तरफ, लेकिन व्यक्तिगत तौर पर नेहरू श्रीगुरुजी का काफी सम्मान करते थे।

□

संघ पर बयान को लेकर नेहरू को हुआ गलती का एहसास

जवाहरलाल नेहरू और श्रीगुरुजी एक-दूसरे के प्रति बिना लाग-लपेट के स्पष्ट बात रखते थे। खासकर विचारों के परिप्रेक्ष्य में नेहरू से अगर कोई गलती हुई तो वे सामने स्वीकार कर लेते थे और श्रीगुरुजी को कोई बात बुरी लगती थी तो वे बेहिचक सामने कह डालते थे। एक बार लखनऊ में नेहरू का भाषण होना था। नेहरू ने अपने संबोधन के दौरान कह दिया कि संघ फासिस्ट है। संयोग की बात है कि उस कार्यक्रम के दूसरे दिन ही श्रीगुरुजी और नेहरू की दिल्ली में मुलाकात हुई। मुलाकात के दौरान श्रीगुरुजी ने नेहरू से पूछ लिया कि आपने संघ को फासिस्ट क्यों कहा और किस आधार पर कहा? श्रीगुरुजी के अचानक इस प्रकार के प्रश्न के प्रहार से नेहरू सकपका गए। उन्हें अपनी गलती का एहसास हुआ और उन्होंने तुरंत ही श्रीगुरुजी से कहा, "Don't take it seriously." (मैंने जो कहा उसे गंभीरता से न लें।) उन्होंने आगे कहा कि बोलते-बोलते आवेग में आकर ऐसा बोल गया, इसे इतनी गंभीरता से लेने की जरूरत नहीं है।

□

डॉ. जाकिर हुसैन ने संघ से सीख लेने की सलाह दी

स्वतंत्रता आंदोलन के दौरान राष्ट्रीय स्वयंसेवक संघ की संगठन-शक्ति लगातार बढ़ रही थी। इससे कांग्रेस पार्टी को यह भय सताने लगा कि संघ उसे चुनौती दे सकता है। कांग्रेस की मुसलिम लॉबी संघ के खिलाफ दुष्प्रचार में जुट गई। इसे देखते हुए स्वतंत्रता सेनानी एवं देश के प्रथम मुसलिम राष्ट्रपति डॉ. जाकिर हुसैन ने संघ के पक्ष में अपनी बात रखी और उसके कार्यों की प्रशंसा की थी। डॉ. जाकिर हुसैन ने 20 नवंबर, 1949 को बिहार के मुँगेर में आयोजित एक कार्यक्रम मिलाद महफिल में कहा, "संघ पर हिंसा फैलाने और मुसलमानों के प्रति नफरत का आरोप पूरी तरह झूठा है। मुसलमानों के प्रति घृणा फैलाने और उनके कत्लेआम करने का संघ पर लगाया जा रहा आरोप पूरी तरह निराधार और गलत है। मुसलमानों को चाहिए कि वे संघ से आपसी प्रेम, सहकार और संगठन के गुणों की शिक्षा लें।" डॉ. जाकिर हुसैन वर्ष 1967 से 1969 तक देश के राष्ट्रपति रहे।

□

स्वयंसेवकों ने जेल में किया 31 दिन का अनशन

संघ के स्वयंसेवक जात-पात और ऊँच-नीच में विश्वास नहीं रखते। वे समाज से भी इस कुरीति को दूर करने के लिए हमेशा जुटे रहते हैं। इसका एक उदाहरण वर्ष 1948 में धर्मशाला की योलकैंट जेल में देखने को मिलता है। यहाँ एक ही उद्देश्य के लिए सत्याग्रह कर रहे लोगों को भोजन के साथ ही अन्य सुविधाएँ एक जैसी नहीं थी। जेल के अधिकारी उनके साथ दोहरे मापदंड अपना रहे थे। दरअसल, उस समय कैदियों को उनकी श्रेणी के हिसाब से भोजन के लिए खर्चा मिलता था। इस तरह श्रेणी के हिसाब से किसी को भोजन का खर्च ज्यादा तो किसी को कम मिलता था। यही नहीं, अन्य सुविधाओं में भी उनके साथ भेदभाव होता था। स्वयंसेवकों ने इस नीति का विरोध करते हुए भूख हड़ताल की घोषणा कर दी। उन्होंने कहा, "सभी सत्याग्रहियों को एक समान ए श्रेणी की सुविधा मिले अन्यथा हम भोजन नहीं करेंगे।" जेल में बंद संघ प्रचारक ठाकुर राम सिंह ने उस समय बंदियों से कहा, "भूख हड़ताल वही करें, जो निर्णायक समय तक कर सकते हैं। जिनमें सामर्थ्य नहीं है, उन्हें भूखे रहने की आवश्यकता नहीं।" स्वयंसेवकों के नेतृत्व में यह हड़ताल 31 दिन चली। अनेक सत्याग्रही बीमार पड़ गए, लेकिन अंततः 31 दिन बाद जेल अधिकारियों को सत्याग्रहियों की माँगों को मानना पड़ा और सबके साथ एक समान व्यवहार किया जाने लगा।

□

भूदान आंदोलन में राष्ट्रीय स्वयंसेवक संघ की भागीदारी

विनोबा भावे द्वारा वर्ष 1951 में शुरू किया गया भूदान आंदोलन भारत में भूमि सामाजिक न्याय की एक अद्वितीय पहल थी, जिसका उद्देश्य था—जमींदारों और बड़े किसानों से स्वेच्छा से जमीन दान करवाकर भूमिहीनों में बाँटना। इस अभियान में राष्ट्रीय स्वयंसेवक संघ की भूमिका विशेष रूप से उल्लेखनीय रही। विनोबा भावे ने नवंबर 1951 में मेरठ में तत्कालीन संघ प्रमुख से भेंट की थी। श्रीगुरुजी भूमि सुधारों को प्रोत्साहित करने वाले आंदोलन से सहमत थे। इसलिए उन्होंने इस आंदोलन के लिए अपना समर्थन व्यक्त किया। इसके बाद संघ प्रचारक नानाजी देशमुख के नेतृत्व में कई स्वयंसेवकों ने आंदोलन में भाग लिया और अपनी सक्रिय भागीदारी निभाई। विभिन्न राज्यों में संघ कार्यकर्ताओं ने भूदान यात्राओं के दौरान संगठनात्मक सहयोग, स्थानीय संपर्क, रहने व भोजन की व्यवस्था तथा भाषायी अनुवाद में सहायता जैसे कार्यों में योगदान दिया। विनोबा भावे कई बार यह उल्लेख करते थे कि संघ के कार्यकर्ताओं की अनुशासन-बद्ध कार्यशैली और सेवा भावना ने भूदान आंदोलन को गाँव-गाँव तक पहुँचाने में मदद की। संघ के प्रचारकों ने ग्रामसभाओं और सामाजिक मेलों में भूदान का प्रचार किया और स्वयं भी अपनी जमीनें दान कीं और हजारों परिवारों को प्रेरित किया। विशेष रूप से उत्तर प्रदेश, महाराष्ट्र, बिहार और मध्य प्रदेश में संघ कार्यकर्ताओं ने आंदोलन को गाँवों में स्थापित करने और स्थानीय स्तर पर भूदान समितियों को सशक्त करने में मदद की। उन्होंने यह सुनिश्चित किया कि दान की गई भूमि निष्पक्ष तरीके से सुपात्र भूमिहीनों तक पहुँचे।

□

आदिवासियों के लिए कांग्रेसी मुख्यमंत्री ने संघ से माँगी मदद

ब्रिटिश शासन के दौरान भारत में ईसाई धर्म को बढ़ावा देने के लिए कई कुत्सित प्रयास किए गए। स्वाधीनता के समय सेंट्रल प्रोविंस यानी मध्य प्रांत में आदिवासियों का धर्म परिवर्तन एक बड़ा मुद्दा बन गया था। इसकी गंभीरता को देखकर तत्कालीन कांग्रेसी मुख्यमंत्री रविशंकर शुक्ल ने इस समस्या से निपटने के लिए सरसंघचालक गोलवलकर से मदद माँगी थी। श्रीगुरुजी ने संघ के स्वयंसेवक रमाकांत केशव देशपांडे यानी बालासाहब को इसकी जिम्मेदारी सौंपी। बालासाहब जनजातियों के बीच कार्य करने के लिए नागपुर से जशपुर चले आए। छत्तीसगढ़ के इस आदिवासी इलाके में सबसे बड़ी समस्या शिक्षा की थी। उन्होंने कुछ ग्रामीणों को ही ट्रेनिंग देकर शिक्षक बनाया और उन्हें बच्चों को पढ़ाने की जिम्मेदारी सौंपी। बालासाहब ने एक वर्ष के अंदर ही जशपुर के आसपास 108 विद्यालय शुरू करवा दिए। उन्होंने वनवासी बच्चों के लिए 26 दिसंबर, 1952 को छात्रावास की शुरुआत की। इसी दिन को 'वनवासी कल्याण आश्रम' के स्थापना दिवस के रूप में भी जाना जाता है। आश्रम की स्थापना का उद्देश्य आदिवासियों को शिक्षा और आर्थिक विकास से जोड़कर उन्हें मुख्यधारा में लाना है। इसके साथ ही आश्रम वनवासियों के स्वास्थ्य और सांस्कृतिक जागृति के लिए भी काम करता है।

□

संघ को रोकने के लिए तिरंगा कानून लाया गया

क्या सच में संघ ने स्वाधीनता के बाद 52 साल तक तिरंगा नहीं फहराया? समाचार माध्यमों में इस तरह की सुर्खियाँ यदा-कदा दिख जाती हैं, लेकिन सच्चाई इसके उलट है। स्वाधीनता के बाद संघ ने राष्ट्रीय पर्वों जैसे 15 अगस्त और 26 जनवरी को पूरे उत्साह के साथ मनाना शुरू किया और जनता की भागीदारी इसमें लगातार बढ़ती गई। यह सिलसिला वर्ष 1950 तक चला। संघ के कार्यक्रमों में लोगों के उमड़ने और उसकी बढ़ती लोकप्रियता से सत्ताधारी पार्टी कांग्रेस घबरा गई और इसे रोकने के उपाय ढूँढ़ने लगी। फिर राष्ट्रीय तिरंगा नियम लाया गया और National Flag Code को 1950 में लागू कर दिया गया। इसके अनुसार निजी स्थलों पर तिरंगा फहराना वर्जित हो गया। इसका मतलब कानूनन अब तिरंगा संघ की शाखाओं में नहीं फहराया जा सकता था, क्योंकि यह प्राइवेट जगह थी। इसके बाद वर्ष 2002 में सुप्रीम कोर्ट का एक ऐतिहासिक फैसला आया और उसने नेशनल फ्लैग कोड में निजी क्षेत्रों में भी तिरंगा फहराने की स्वतंत्रता को जोड़ने के लिए कहा। इसके बाद से संघ के विभिन्न कार्यालयों में पुनः तिरंगा फहराया जाने लगा।

□

भारतीय सेना के पहले कमांडर करिअप्पा 1959 में पहुँचे संघ शाखा

भारतीय सेना के पहले कमांडर इन चीफ फील्ड मार्शल के.एम. करिअप्पा संघ के प्रशंसक थे। वे वर्ष 1959 में मंगलौर की संघ शाखा में गए थे। वहाँ स्वयंसेवकों को संबोधित करते हुए उन्होंने कहा, "संघ-कार्य मुझे हृदय से प्रिय है। अगर कोई मुसलिम इसलाम की प्रशंसा कर सकता है तो संघ के हिंदुत्व का अभिमान रखने में गलत क्या है? प्रिय युवा मित्रो, आप किसी भी गलत प्रचार से हतोत्साहित न होते हुए कार्य करो। डॉ. हेडगेवार ने आपके सामने एक स्वार्थरहित कार्य का पवित्र आदर्श रखा है, उसी पर आगे बढ़ो। भारत को आज आप जैसे सेवाभावी कार्यकर्ताओं की ही आवश्यकता है।" संघ के द्वितीय सरसंघचालक श्रीगुरुजी और जनरल करिअप्पा के बीच काफी घनिष्ठता थी। 21 नवंबर, 1956 को दोनों की मुलाकात मैसूर में हुई थी। इसके बाद वर्ष 1969 में श्रीगुरुजी के निमंत्रण पर जनरल करिअप्पा उडुपी में हुए विश्व हिंदू परिषद् के सम्मेलन में शामिल हुए थे।

□

स्वयंसेवकों द्वारा तिब्बती शरणार्थियों की सहायता

वर्ष 1959 में जब चीन द्वारा तिब्बत पर कब्जा किया गया तो हजारों तिब्बती भारत में शरण लेने को मजबूर हुए। उस कठिन समय में संघ के स्वयंसेवकों ने तिब्बती शरणार्थियों की मदद के लिए आगे आकर एक ऐसी भूमिका निभाई, जो राष्ट्र की सीमाओं से ऊपर जाकर मानवीय मूल्यों को प्राथमिकता देने वाली थी। स्वयंसेवकों ने न केवल भोजन, वस्त्र और आश्रय की व्यवस्था में हाथ बँटाया, बल्कि हिमालयी क्षेत्रों में जाकर सहायता शिविर लगाने में मदद की, जहाँ तिब्बती शरणार्थी सबसे पहले पहुँचे थे। धर्मशाला, उत्तरकाशी, मसूरी और अरुणाचल जैसे क्षेत्रों में संघ के कार्यकर्ताओं ने स्थानीय जनता और प्रशासन के बीच पुल का काम किया। उन्होंने तिब्बती बच्चों की शिक्षा, चिकित्सा सेवा और सामाजिक पुनर्स्थापन में भी सहयोग किया। यह इस बात का प्रमाण है कि संघ केवल विचारधारा तक सीमित न रहकर, जरूरतमंदों की सहायता के लिए मानवीय दृष्टिकोण भी अपनाता है, चाहे वह किसी भी जाति, धर्म या राष्ट्र से संबंधित क्यों न हों। यही वजह है कि दलाई लामा ने 2014 में संघ मुख्यालय के दौरे के समय तिब्बती मुद्दे को समर्थन देने के लिए संघ की प्रशंसा की थी। संघ प्रमुख मोहन भागवत ने 20 दिसंबर, 2021 को धर्मशाला में दलाई लामा से भेंट करके करीब एक घंटे तक मंत्रणा की थी। वहाँ उन्होंने कहा था, "तिब्बत हमारा भाई देश है। इसलिए हम तिब्बत समुदाय के हर सुख-दुःख में साथ रहे हैं, और आगे भी रहेंगे।" तिब्बती शरणार्थियों के साथ संघ का संवाद और सहयोग निरंतर जारी है। इसी कड़ी में राष्ट्रीय स्वयंसेवक संघ के उत्तरी क्षेत्र के एक प्रतिनिधि मंडल ने 23 सितंबर, 2023 को निर्वासित तिब्बती संसद का दौरा किया।

□

संघ के कई गुणों ने मुझे इसकी ओर आकर्षित किया : जयप्रकाश नारायण

स्वतंत्रता सेनानी, लोकनायक और संपूर्ण क्रांति के जनक जयप्रकाश नारायण (जे.पी.) वर्ष 1960 में राष्ट्रीय स्वयंसेवक संघ की गाजीपुर शाखा में पहुँचे। वहाँ उन्होंने कहा, "हालाँकि मैं संघ के बारे में सबकुछ जानने का दावा नहीं करता, लेकिन श्रीगुरुजी के साथ हाल ही में हुई बातचीत और संघ के कई गुणों ने मुझे इसकी ओर आकर्षित किया है। संघ और सर्वोदय दोनों ही समाज में क्रांति लाने और उसे पुनर्जीवित करने के लिए राजनीति से दूर रहते हैं। समाज में क्रांति लाने का काम एक विशाल क्षेत्र है। विचारों के मतभेद किसी चीज को समझने के रास्ते में बाधा नहीं बनते। सत्य को केवल निष्पक्ष दृष्टिकोण से ही समझा जा सकता है।" जे.पी. ने बिहार में वर्ष 1966 में आए अकाल में संघ द्वारा किए गए राहत कार्यों की सराहना की थी। उन्होंने वर्ष 1975 में कहा था, "बिहार आंदोलन और संघ का काम मूल रूप से एक ही है।" मोटे तौर पर उनके वैश्विक दृष्टिकोण एक जैसे थे। जयप्रकाश नारायण और संघ दोनों ने विकेंद्रीकरण का समर्थन किया और समाजवाद व धर्मनिरपेक्षता को अस्वीकार किया।

□

□

स्वयंसेवकों की बराबरी प्रधानमंत्री भी नहीं कर सकते : जे.पी.

वर्ष 1966 में बिहार में ऐसा भयंकर अकाल पड़ा कि लोग दाने-दाने को मोहताज हो गए। संकट की उस घड़ी में हजारों स्वयंसेवक दिन-रात एक करके अकाल पीड़ितों की मदद के लिए आगे आए। पानी की किल्लत दूर करने के लिए संघ के कार्यकर्ताओं ने 971 कुएँ खोद डाले। इसी तरह भोजन की कमी से जूझ रहे लगभग 21,000 परिवारों में उन्होंने भोजन तथा वस्त्र बाँटने के साथ ही अन्य राहत सामग्री पहुँचाई। बिहार में अकाल पीड़ितों की सहायंता के लिए किए जा रहे काम की देख-रेख कर रहे जयप्रकाश नारायण स्वयंसेवकों का काम देखकर काफी प्रभावित हुए। उन्होंने देखा कि सहायता पहुँचाने के दौरान स्वयंसेवक हिंदू-मुसलिम में भेदभाव नहीं बरत रहे थे। वे सभी लोगों तक एक समान भाव से मदद पहुँचा रहे थे। स्वयंसेवक लोगों की मदद के लिए पैदल ही दूरदराज के इलाकों तक पहुँच जाते थे। 6 फरवरी, 1967 को एक अकाल पीड़ित सहायता केंद्र का उद्घाटन करते हुए जे.पी. ने कहा था, "संघ के स्वयंसेवकों की निस्स्वार्थ सेवा की बराबरी कोई नहीं कर सकता, देश का प्रधानमंत्री भी नहीं।" अकाल पीड़ितों की मदद के लिए स्वयंसेवक पैदल ही लगभग 700 गाँवों में पहुँचे और लगभग 18,000 परिवारों में 1,500 क्विंटल अनाज का वितरण किया। उस समय संघ ने 'मुष्टि धान्य' कार्यक्रम चलाया और इसके तहत हर परिवार से मुट्ठी भर अनाज एकत्र किया गया। अकाल पीड़ित पेट भर खाना खा सकें, इसके लिए कैंटीनें खोली गईं। महामारी रोकने के लिए 10 चिकित्सा केंद्र खोले गए। संघ ने मनुष्यों के साथ पशुओं की भी चिंता की और राज्य के कई हिस्सों में पशु आहार केंद्र खोले गए, जिससे सैकड़ों पशुओं की जान बच पाई।

□

नेहरू ने किया इनकार, संघ ने ली प्रवासी हिंदुओं की सुध

त्रिनिदाद एवं टोबैगो के सांसद शंभुनाथ कपिल देव वर्ष 1961 में भारत की यात्रा पर दिल्ली आए। उन्होंने त्रिनिदाद एवं टोबैगो में रह रहे हिंदुओं को लेकर यह चिंता जताई कि वे अपनी संस्कृति और जड़ों से किस प्रकार कटते जा रहे हैं। इसलिए दिल्ली आने पर भारत से उम्मीद बाँधे शंभुनाथ जवाहरलाल नेहरू से मिलने पहुँच गए। उन्होंने मुलाकात में अपनी बात रखते हुए कहा कि प्रवासी हिंदू अपनी संस्कृति और परंपराओं को जीवित रख सकें, इसके लिए भारत को कुछ करना चाहिए, लेकिन नेहरू ने यह कहते हुए इनकार कर दिया कि वर्ष 1947 से पूर्व भारत छोड़कर गए भारतीयों के लिए कुछ भी नहीं किया जा सकता। शंभुनाथ बहुत निराश हुए, लेकिन उन्होंने हार नहीं मानी और इसके बाद संघ से इस पर चर्चा करने का विचार किया। वे दिल्ली के संघचालक लाला हंसराज से मिलने पहुँचे। लाला हंसराज ने उनसे कहा कि चूँकि यह अंतरराष्ट्रीय विषय है, इसलिए इस संबंध में वे श्रीगुरुजी से मिलें। उस समय श्रीगुरुजी कर्नाटक के बेलगाम में थे। शंभुनाथ उनसे मिलने के लिए वहाँ पहुँच गए। श्रीगुरुजी ने उनकी बात ध्यान से सुनी और यही वह बैठक थी, जब वैश्विक स्तर पर हिंदुओं के एक संगठन की नींव पड़ी। इसी के फलस्वरूप वर्ष 1964 में 'विश्व हिंदू परिषद्' की स्थापना हुई। आज दुनिया के कई देशों में इसकी शाखाएँ हैं।

□

चीन से युद्ध के दौरान संघ ने निभाई महत्त्वपूर्ण भूमिका

वर्ष 1962 का चीनी आक्रमण भारत के लिए एक बदनुमा दाग की तरह है। इस युद्ध के लिए न तो भारत की सेना तैयार थी और न ही यहाँ की सरकार। दोनों ही स्तरों पर नेतृत्व की विफलता के कारण चीन ने भारतीय भूमि के एक बड़े हिस्से पर कब्जा कर लिया। युद्ध के उस दौर में जब चीनी सेना भारत की ओर बढ़ी चली आ रही थी, उन विपरीत परिस्थितियों में राष्ट्रीय स्वयंसेवक संघ ही देश की सुरक्षा और सेना का साथ देने के लिए आगे आया था। भारत-चीन युद्ध के दौरान संघ के स्वयंसेवक सेना की मदद करने के लिए देश की सीमा पर तैनात हो गए। संघ ने देश के लिए लड़ रहे जवानों की सहायता के लिए अपनी पूरी ताकत झोंक दी। सेनाओं की आवाजाही वाले मार्गों की निगरानी हो, या फिर उन्हें रसद या हथियार पहुँचाने हों, यहाँ तक कि इस युद्ध में वीरगति को प्राप्त हुए शहीदों के परिवारों की देखभाल में भी संघ ने सराहनीय भूमिका निभाई। करीब 1600 स्वयंसेवकों ने दिल्ली की सड़कों पर उतरकर ट्रैफिक के सुचारू संचालन के साथ अन्य सेवाकार्यों में दिन-रात एक कर दिया। संघ की देशभक्ति की भावना को देखते हुए जवाहरलाल नेहरू ने वर्ष 1963 में गणतंत्र दिवस की परेड में स्वयंसेवकों को शामिल होने का निमंत्रण दिया था।

□

गणतंत्र दिवस परेड में शामिल होकर संघ ने रचा इतिहास

वर्ष 1962 में चीनी हमले के दौरान संघ के कार्यकर्ताओं ने जिस प्रकार की साहसपूर्ण भूमिका निभाई, उससे तत्कालीन प्रधानमंत्री जवाहरलाल नेहरू काफी प्रभावित हुए। अगले ही साल उन्होंने संघ को गणतंत्र दिवस परेड में शामिल होने का न्योता भेजा। संघ ने प्रस्ताव को स्वीकार करते हुए एक निवेदन किया कि संघ के स्वयंसेवकों को पूरे गणवेश में सम्मिलित होने का मौका दिया जाए। उस समय दिल्ली में संघ के मंडल कार्यवाह का दायित्व सँभाल रहे विजय कुमार के मुताबिक, "प्रस्ताव देने आए सरकारी प्रतिनिधि परेड में गणवेश में शामिल होने का अनुरोध सुनकर जल्द ही सूचना देने की बात कहकर चले गए। अंत में गणतंत्र दिवस परेड के लगभग 24 घंटे पहले परेड में शामिल होने की सूचना मिली। इसके बाद संघ के करीब तीन हजार अनुशासित स्वयंसेवक परेड में शामिल हुए, वह भी पूरे गणवेश में। परेड के दौरान जब स्वयंसेवक सलामी मंच के पास से गुजर रहे थे, तब लोगों ने दर्शक दीर्घा से जोरदार तालियाँ बजाकर उनका स्वागत किया।" इस प्रकार राष्ट्रवाद का एक नया स्तंभ बन चुके संघ ने नया कीर्तिमान रच दिया।

□

नेहरू सरकार के मंत्री संघ के कार्यों के हुए कायल

कैलाश नाथ काटजू जवाहरलाल नेहरू की सरकार में मई 1952 से जनवरी 1955 तक गृह और विधि मंत्री रहे। वे केंद्र सरकार में वर्ष 1955 से 1957 तक रक्षा मंत्री भी रहे। वर्ष 1963 में उन्होंने प्रयागराज में आयोजित राष्ट्रीय स्वयंसेवक संघ की एक सभा को संबोधित किया था। उन्होंने कहा कि वे इससे पहले भी संघ की शाखाओं एवं सभाओं में हिस्सा ले चुके हैं। सभा को संबोधित करते हुए उन्होंने कहा, "चीनी आक्रमण ने राष्ट्र को अपनी महान् एकता के प्रति जागरूक किया है। लेकिन इस एकता को हमेशा के लिए बनाए रखने की आवश्यकता है। चाहे युद्ध हो या शांति काल, यह वह एकता है, जिसे राष्ट्रीय स्वयंसेवक संघ के संस्थापक ने बनाने की कोशिश की थी।" उन्होंने कहा, "कौन कहता है कि यह हिंदू राष्ट्र नहीं है ? मैं संघ में इसका लघु रूप देखकर खुश हूँ।" कैलाश नाथ काटजू स्वतंत्रता सेनानी भी थे और वर्ष 1940 में सत्याग्रह आंदोलन में हिस्सा लेने के कारण उन्हें 18 माह का कारावास मिला था। वे अगस्त 1942 से अप्रैल 1943 तक नैनी जेल में नजरबंद रहे थे। वे वर्ष 1947 से जून 1948 तक उड़ीसा के राज्यपाल और जून 1948 से 1951 तक पश्चिम बंगाल के राज्यपाल रहे।

□

जब नेपाल नरेश को संघ के कार्यक्रम में आने से रोका गया

यह घटना वर्ष 1963 की है, जब दुनिया के एकमात्र हिंदू देश नेपाल के भारत से कूटनीतिक संबंध काफी खराब हो गए थे। इसके कारण नेपाल की चीन और पाकिस्तान से निकटता बढ़ने लगी थी। उसी दौरान श्रीगुरुजी महाशिवरात्रि के समय नेपाल गए और नेपाल नरेश महाराजा महेंद्र से भेंट की। उन्होंने नेपाल नरेश के साथ हिंदू हितों और हिंदुत्व के मुद्दों पर वार्त्ता की। इस अवसर पर श्रीगुरुजी ने महाराजा को संघ के 14 जनवरी, 1965 को नागपुर में आयोजित मकर संक्रांति समारोह में संबोधित करने का निमंत्रण दिया। 25 दिसंबर, 1964 को रेडियो नेपाल ने घोषणा की कि 14 जनवरी, 1965 को नागपुर में आयोजित समारोह में शामिल होने का आमंत्रण महाराजा महेंद्र ने स्वीकार कर लिया है। वहीं स्वदेश लौटने पर श्रीगुरुजी ने प्रधानमंत्री नेहरू और गृहमंत्री लाल बहादुर शास्त्री को पत्र लिखकर नेपाल नरेश से वार्त्ता के विषय में अवगत कराया। यह एक ऐसा अवसर था, जिसे भारत सरकार नेपाल से अपने संबंध सुधारने के रूप में उपयोग कर सकती थी। लेकिन स्वागत करने की जगह भारत सरकार ने उन्हें भारत न आने का परामर्श भेज दिया। यह खुलासा उस समय हुआ, जब श्रीगुरुजी के नाम महाराजा महेंद्र का 11 जनवरी, 1965 को लिखा पत्र सार्वजनिक हुआ। उन्होंने लिखा, "आज मुझे बड़ा क्षोभ है कि एक हिंदू समारोह में मुझे हिंदू होने के नाते भाग लेने से वंचित किया जा रहा है।"

□

श्रीगुरुजी के कहने पर शास्त्रीजी ने सुधारी भूल

भारत जब स्वतंत्र हुआ तो स्वाधीनता मिलने के साथ ही पाकिस्तान के साथ युद्ध भी लड़ना पड़ गया। भारत ने वर्ष 1948 के इस युद्ध में जिस प्रकार पाकिस्तान को मजा चखाया, पाकिस्तान उसे भुला नहीं पाया था। वह कश्मीर और गुजरात के कच्छ क्षेत्र पर कब्जा कर भारत से बदला लेने की ताक में था। उसने चीन युद्ध और नेहरू के निधन के तुरंत बाद 5 अगस्त, 1965 को भारत की सीमा में घुसपैठ कर एक बार फिर आक्रमण कर दिया। पाकिस्तान घुसपैठ के जरिए जम्मू-कश्मीर में विद्रोह को बढ़ावा देना चाहता था। पाकिस्तान ने इसे 'ऑपरेशन जिब्राल्टर' नाम दिया था। भारत ने पाकिस्तान के साथ औपचारिक युद्ध की घोषणा 6 सितंबर, 1965 को की थी। वर्ष 1965 में भारत-पाक युद्ध के दौरान पाकिस्तानी सैनिकों ने पैराशूट से भारत में उतरने की कोशिश की थी। पाकिस्तान की इस करतूत को देखते हुए भारत सरकार की ओर से यह घोषणा की गई कि जो भी पाकिस्तानी सेना के जवान को पकड़ेगा, उसे इनाम दिया जाएगा। केंद्र सरकार की यह घोषणा श्रीगुरुजी को अच्छी नहीं लगी। उन्होंने शास्त्रीजी से पूछा, "देश के काम के लिए किसी को प्रलोभन या लालच देना सही है क्या?" उन्होंने कहा, "अगर पाकिस्तान के पैराशूट सैनिक हमारी धरती पर उतरते हैं तो उन्हें पकड़कर सरकार के हवाले करना हर राष्ट्रभक्त के मन में स्वत: आना ही चाहिए। राष्ट्रभक्ति और राष्ट्रीय कर्तव्य के कारण ऐसा करना हर नागरिक का नैतिक और राष्ट्रीय दायित्व होना चाहिए, जबकि प्रलोभन और लालच देकर आप उनकी राष्ट्रभक्ति को भ्रष्ट कर रहे हैं।" श्रीगुरुजी के इस विचार को सुनने के बाद लाल बहादुर शास्त्री सरकार की उस घोषणा से पीछे हट गए। यह सर्वविदित है कि राष्ट्रभक्ति का जो ज्वार देशवासियों के मन में उठा, उसकी वजह से पाकिस्तान को एक बार फिर बड़ी शिकस्त मिली।

□

शास्त्रीजी ने श्रीगुरुजी को सर्वदलीय बैठक में आमंत्रित किया

पाकिस्तान ने वर्ष 1965 में जब भारत पर आक्रमण कर दिया तो भारत की रणनीति पर विचार-विमर्श करने के लिए प्रधानमंत्री लाल बहादुर शास्त्री ने 6 सितंबर, 1965 को एक सर्वदलीय बैठक बुलाई। सभी राजनीतिक पार्टियों के नेताओं को आमंत्रित करने के साथ ही उन्होंने संघ के सरसंघचालक श्रीगुरुजी को भी इस बैठक में आमंत्रित किया। गैर-राजनीतिक संगठन होने के बाद भी संघ को इस बैठक में शामिल होने का न्योता दिया गया। बैठक में शास्त्रीजी ने श्रीगुरुजी से अनुरोध किया कि दिल्ली में कानून-व्यवस्था और ट्रैफिक संचालन स्वयंसेवक अपने हाथ में ले लें, जिससे पुलिसकर्मी इस काम से मुक्त हो जाएँ और सेना की मदद कर सकें। श्रीगुरुजी ने संघ की ओर से पूरी मदद का भरोसा दिया और स्वयंसेवकों ने दिल्ली में कानून से लेकर ट्रैफिक व्यवस्था सँभाली। युद्ध के दौरान सेना के लिए रसद आपूर्ति में भी स्वयंसेवकों ने अपना योगदान दिया। घायल जवानों के लिए रक्तदान करने वालों में भी संघ के स्वयंसेवक सबसे आगे थे। यही नहीं, सर्वदलीय बैठक के दौरान एक प्रतिनिधि प्रधानमंत्री को संबोधित करते हुए लगातार 'आपकी सेना' 'आपकी सेना' कह रहे थे। श्रीगुरुजी से जब नहीं रहा गया तो उन्होंने उस प्रतिनिधि पर चुटकी लेते कहा, "मान्यवर 'आपकी सेना' नहीं, 'हमारी सेना' कहिए।" बैठक में श्रीगुरुजी ने शास्त्रीजी से आग्रह किया कि हमारी सेना सिर्फ बचाव का ही प्रयास न करे, बल्कि हमारी सेना को समुचित समय पर आक्रामक रुख अपनाने का भी अधिकार मिले। श्रीगुरुजी की सलाह ही रही कि भारतीय सेना आक्रामक रुख अपनाते हुए लाहौर तक पहुँच गई थी।

□

□

श्रीगुरुजी ने शास्त्रीजी को स्वयं को छोटा कहने से रोका

लाल बहादुर शास्त्रीजी की सरलता सर्वविदित है। यह तो सब जानते हैं कि वे जितने सरल थे, उतने ही सज्जन थे। देश के पहले प्रधानमंत्री जवाहरलाल नेहरू के निधन के बाद लाल बहादुर शास्त्री देश के दूसरे प्रधानमंत्री बने। वह 9 जून, 1964 से 11 जनवरी, 1966 तक लगभग अठारह महीने भारत के प्रधानमंत्री रहे। प्रधानमंत्री बनने पर भी अपनी विनम्रता के चलते वे अकसर कहते थे, "जवाहरलालजी तो बड़े आदमी थे, मैं तो एक छोटा आदमी हूँ।" कुछ दिनों बाद एक दिन जब श्रीगुरुजी से उनकी भेंट हुई तो श्रीगुरुजी ने बेझिझक उन्हें ऐसा कहने से रोका। उन्होंने कहा, "व्यक्तिगत तौर पर विनम्रता में आपका स्वयं को छोटा कहना अलग बात है, लेकिन भारत के प्रधानमंत्री के रूप में ऐसा कहना बिल्कुल अलग बात है। आप भारत के प्रधानमंत्री हैं। जब आप ही कहेंगे कि मैं एक छोटा आदमी हूँ तो इसका अर्थ देश और दुनिया में गलत जाएगा। इसका तात्पर्य यह होगा कि भारत का प्रधानमंत्री छोटा आदमी है और ऐसा कहना आपके नैतिक अधिकार में नहीं आता है। क्योंकि देश के प्रधानमंत्री का अपमान करना किसी रूप में उचित नहीं होगा। इसलिए आप यह कहना छोड़ दीजिए कि 'मैं एक छोटा आदमी हूँ'।" श्रीगुरुजी के सुझाव पर लाल बहादुर शास्त्री ने न केवल स्वयं को छोटा कहना छोड़ दिया, बल्कि जवाहरलाल नेहरू को भी बड़ा बताना छोड़ दिया।

□

श्रीगुरुजी ने लाल बहादुर शास्त्री को ताशकंद जाने से मना किया था

भारत और पाकिस्तान के बीच वर्ष 1965 में युद्ध के तुरंत बाद समझौता करने के लिए प्रधानमंत्री लाल बहादुर शास्त्री को ताशकंद में आमंत्रित किया गया। परंतु राष्ट्रीय स्वयंसेवक संघ के सरसंघचालक श्रीगुरुजी गोलवलकर ने संदेश भेजकर उनसे वहाँ नहीं जाने का अनुरोध किया। इसके बाद भी जब उनका वहाँ जाना तय हो गया तो श्रीगुरुजी ने अटल बिहारी वाजपेयी के माध्यम से उनके पास एक पत्र भेजा। उसमें प्रधानमंत्री शास्त्रीजी से आग्रह किया गया था कि जनता को उन्होंने जो वचन दिया है, उस पर वे अडिग रहें, भले ही उन पर कितने भी दबाव क्यों न पड़ें। शास्त्रीजी ने अटलजी से कहा कि आगामी ताशकंद वार्त्ता के बारे में जो भ्रांतियाँ और आशंकाएँ हैं, उनके प्रति वे पूर्णतया सचेत हैं और लोगों को यह आश्वासन देना चाहेंगे कि वे ऐसा कोई काम नहीं करेंगे, जिससे देश की प्रतिष्ठा और आत्मसम्मान पर आँच आए, लेकिन ताशकंद घोषणा ने सिद्ध कर दिया कि श्रीगुरुजी की आशंकाएँ सच थीं। इस संबंध में मार्च 1966 में संघ की अखिल भारतीय प्रतिनिधि सभा ने टिप्पणी की, 'कश्मीर में हाजीपीर, टिटवाल और कारगिल जैसे सामरिक महत्त्व के क्षेत्रों से अपनी सेनाएँ हटाने के लिए सहमत होकर हमने कश्मीर के संबंध में अब तक अपनाई गई अपनी दृढ़ नीति पर गंभीर कुठाराघात किया है।' शास्त्रीजी के ताशकंद जाने को लेकर श्रीगुरुजी की घोर असहमति थी। इस यात्रा का अंत भी शोकमय हुआ और शास्त्रीजी की संदिग्ध परिस्थितियों में मृत्यु हो गई।

□

राष्ट्र सेविका समिति ने युद्ध से लेकर हर संघर्ष में दिया योगदान

राष्ट्रीय स्वयंसेवक संघ से संबद्ध राष्ट्र सेविका समिति ने युद्ध से लेकर हर संघर्ष में अपना योगदान दिया। वर्ष 1962 में जब चीन ने आक्रमण किया तो समिति की महिलाओं ने अपने स्तर पर महत्त्वपूर्ण भूमिका निभाई। समिति से जुड़ी महिलाओं ने एक स्थान से दूसरे स्थान पर जाने के दौरान रेलवे स्टेशनों पर सैनिकों के लिए भोजन की व्यवस्था की, घायल सैनिकों का प्राथमिक उपचार किया और यहाँ तक कि सैनिकों के लिए स्वेटर भी बुने। इसी तरह वर्ष 1965 में पाकिस्तान से हुए युद्ध में भी समिति की महिला कार्यकर्ताओं ने अपना भरपूर योगदान दिया। इस युद्ध के बाद एक हस्ताक्षर अभियान भी चलाया गया, जिसमें एक लाख से अधिक लोगों के हस्ताक्षर एकत्र किए गए। युद्ध जीतने के बाद प्रधानमंत्री लाल बहादुर शास्त्री समझौते के लिए ताशकंद जाने वाले थे। इससे पहले समिति से जुड़ी महिलाएँ उनसे मिलने गईं। कई और महिला संगठनों की सदस्य भी शास्त्रीजी से मिलने पहुँची थीं। अन्य संगठनों ने शास्त्रीजी को भेंट में धन एवं अन्य उपहार दिए तो राष्ट्र सेविका समिति की सदस्यों ने एक लाख से अधिक लोगों के हस्ताक्षर वाला अमूल्य उपहार भेंट किया। आपातकाल के दौरान समिति की महिलाओं ने देश भर में आंदोलन कर रहे संघ के स्वयंसेवकों एवं सत्याग्रहियों के रहने की व्यवस्था करने के साथ ही पत्रों और गुप्त संदेशों को एक स्थान से दूसरे स्थान तक पहुँचाने जैसी जिम्मेदारियाँ भी सँभालीं। समिति की महिलाओं के अथक प्रयासों से ही वर्ष 1988 में भारत सरकार द्वारा जीजा माता पर डाक टिकट जारी किया गया। उल्लेखनीय है जीजा माता मराठा सम्राट शिवाजी महाराज की माँ थीं।

□

संघ अब घर-घर का शब्द बन गया है : पूर्व मुख्य न्यायाधीश

भारत के चीफ जस्टिस रहे न्यायमूर्ति के. सुब्बाराव राष्ट्रीय स्वयंसेवक संघ की कार्यप्रणाली और सेवा भावना से बहुत प्रभावित थे और उन्होंने सार्वजनिक रूप से इसकी जमकर सराहना की थी। न्यायमूर्ति के. सुब्बाराव भारत के मुख्य न्यायाधीश के पद से 11 अप्रैल, 1967 को सेवानिवृत्त हुए। इसके बाद अगले ही वर्ष 1968 में बैंगलोर में आयोजित राष्ट्रीय स्वयंसेवक संघ के गुरु-दक्षिणा उत्सव के दौरान उन्होंने अपना संबोधन दिया था। उन्होंने कार्यकर्ताओं को संबोधित करते हुए कहा, "राष्ट्रीय एकीकरण एक नया नारा है। इसे मास मीडिया, प्रेस, मंचों और यहाँ तक कि कानूनों के माध्यम से भी आगे बढ़ाया गया है, लेकिन संघ ने वर्ष 1925 में ही इस सिद्धांत के महत्त्व को समझ लिया था।" उन्होंने कहा, "संघ को ठीक से समझा नहीं गया है। इस पर धर्मनिरपेक्ष न होने का आरोप लगाया जाता है। जबकि तथ्य यह है कि संविधान में कहीं भी 'धर्मनिरपेक्ष' शब्द नहीं पाया जाता है। हिंदू धर्म हमारी पूरी सोच और जीवन में व्याप्त है।" उन्होंने कहा, "संघ अब पूरे भारत में घर-घर में प्रचलित शब्द बन गया है और हर कोई इस देश के लिए इसके द्वारा की जा रही निस्स्वार्थ सेवा के बारे में जानता है। इसलिए मैं इसकी सफलता की कामना करता हूँ।"

□

संघ के कार्यक्रम में भाग लेने कन्याकुमारी पहुँचीं इंदिरा गांधी

संघ के प्रचारक एकनाथ रानाडे के प्रयासों से तमिलनाडु के कन्याकुमारी में स्वामी विवेकानंद की स्मृति में विवेकानंद रॉक मेमोरियल बनाया गया। मेमोरियल के उद्घाटन के लगभग एक पखवाड़े बाद 16 सितंबर, 1970 को तत्कालीन प्रधानमंत्री इंदिरा गांधी स्मारक के पूरा होने के उपलक्ष्य में आयोजित दो महीने तक चलने वाले समारोह में शामिल होने पहुँची थीं। वहाँ उन्होंने कहा, "कन्याकुमारी आना और यह देखना एक मार्मिक अनुभव है कि कैसे स्वामी विवेकानंद के संदेश में हजारों लोगों की आस्था के कारण यह स्मारक संभव हो सका। मैं कामना करती हूँ कि यह स्मारक यहाँ आने वाले सभी लोगों को प्रेरित करे और उन्हें स्वामीजी की महान् और कालजयी शिक्षाओं के अनुसार जीवन जीने का साहस प्रदान करे।" उल्लेखनीय है कि स्वामी विवेकानंद समुद्र में तैरकर 24 दिसंबर, 1892 को शिला पर पहुँचे थे और 25 से 27 दिसंबर तक लगातार इस पर ध्यानमग्न रहे। यहाँ उनके सिवा कोई और नहीं था। बताया जाता है कि इसी निर्जन स्थल पर साधना के बाद उन्हें जीवन के लक्ष्यों का पता चला।

□

नेहरू सरकार के इनकार के बाद संघ ने किया कमाल

कन्याकुमारी में जिस जगह पर आज भव्य विवेकानंद रॉक मेमोरियल बना है, 60 के दशक तक यहाँ शिला हुआ करती थी। वर्ष 1963 में जब स्वामी विवेकानंद की जन्म शताब्दी मनाई जा रही थी, तब कन्याकुमारी के कुछ लोगों के मन में विचार आया कि क्यों न यहाँ स्मारक बनाया जाए, लेकिन उन्हें सफलता नहीं मिली। इसके बाद उन्होंने संघ के तत्कालीन सरसंघचालक श्रीगुरुजी से संपर्क कर उन्हें अपने विचार से अवगत कराया। श्रीगुरुजी ने संघ के प्रचारक एकनाथ रानाडे को स्मारक निर्माण की जिम्मेदारी सौंपी। रानाडे ने जब तमिलनाडु में कांग्रेस सरकार के मुख्यमंत्री एम. भक्तवत्सलम से मेमोरियल के लिए मदद माँगी तो उन्होंने साफ मना कर दिया। नेहरू सरकार में संस्कृति मंत्री हुमायूँ कबीर ने भी कोई मदद नहीं की। रानाडे ने इसके बाद भी हार नहीं मानी। वे दिन-रात इस काम में जुट गए। उन्होंने तीन दिन के भीतर स्मारक के समर्थन में 323 सांसदों के हस्ताक्षर करवा लिये। इससे सरकार पर दबाव पड़ा और स्मारक निर्माण की मंजूरी मिल गई। स्मारक के लिए अब धन की जरूरत थी। संघ के स्वयंसेवकों ने इसके लिए संपूर्ण भारतवर्ष में 30 लाख लोगों से संपर्क किया। स्मारक के लिए जन-जन से उन्हें 1 रुपए से लेकर 5 रुपए तक का दान मिला। इस तरह स्मारक का निर्माण शुरू हो गया। 2 सितंबर, 1970 को तत्कालीन राष्ट्रपति वी.वी. गिरि ने इसका उद्घाटन किया।

□

इंदिरा गांधी ने संघ प्रचारक रानाडे को बनाया ICCR का सदस्य

पूर्व प्रधानमंत्री इंदिरा गांधी राष्ट्रीय स्वयंसेवक संघ की संगठन शक्ति को पहचान चुकी थीं और इससे भयभीत थीं। इसलिए वह संघ में कुछ लोगों से संपर्क बनाकर रखना चाहती थीं। जब श्रीगुरुजी संघ के सरसंघचालक थे, तब इंदिरा गांधी सर्वोदय के रमाकांत पाटिल के संपर्क में थीं, जिनके संघ से घनिष्ठ संबंध थे। इसी तरह जब बालासाहब देवरस संघ प्रमुख थे, तब इंदिरा गांधी संघ प्रचारक एकनाथ रानाडे और संघ प्रचारक मोरोपंत पिंगले के संपर्क में थीं। इंदिरा गांधी जब कन्याकुमारी में विवेकानंद रॉक मेमोरियल देखने गई थीं, तभी से उनका रानाडे से संपर्क हो गया था। रॉक मेमोरियल देखने के बाद वह रानाडे के काम से बहुत प्रभावित हुई थीं, लेकिन कांग्रेस को यह हजम नहीं हो रहा था कि संघ ने विवेकानंद रॉक मेमोरियल का निर्माण करवाया। कांग्रेस के नेता प्रकाश चंद्र सेठी और विद्याचरण शुक्ल ने रानाडे पर निशाना साधना शुरू कर दिया। उन्होंने आरोप लगाया कि रानाडे के नेतृत्व वाले विवेकानंद केंद्र को संघ द्वारा वित्तपोषित किया गया। तब इंदिरा गांधी ने कांग्रेस नेताओं को चुप रहने की नसीहत दी थी। वे रानाडे के खिलाफ कुछ भी सुनना नहीं चाहती थीं। यही नहीं, उन्होंने रानाडे को भारतीय सांस्कृतिक संबंध परिषद् (ICCR) का सदस्य भी बनाया।

□

संघ की लोकप्रियता से घबराकर इंदिरा गांधी ने लगाई पाबंदी

इंदिरा गांधी की सरकार ने वर्ष 1966 में सरकारी कर्मचारियों के राष्ट्रीय स्वयंसेवक संघ की गतिविधियों में शामिल होने पर प्रतिबंध लगा दिया। दरअसल 7 नवंबर, 1966 को गौ-हत्या के खिलाफ एक बड़ा विरोध प्रदर्शन हुआ था। इस विरोध प्रदर्शन के लिए संघ और जनसंघ ने लाखों लोगों का समर्थन जुटाया था। विरोध प्रदर्शन को दबाने के लिए पुलिस की गोलीबारी में कई लोग मारे गए। इसके बाद 30 नवंबर, 1966 को संघ के प्रभाव से घबराकर इंदिरा गांधी ने सरकारी कर्मचारियों के संघ में शामिल होने पर प्रतिबंध लगा दिया। जिस सिविल सेवा (आचरण) नियम वर्ष 1964 का हवाला देते हुए 58 साल पहले संघ पर प्रतिबंध लगाया गया, उस केंद्रीय सिविल सेवा (आचरण) नियम, वर्ष 1964 का नियम 5 कहता है कि कोई भी सरकारी सेवक राजनीतिक दल का सदस्य नहीं होगा। दिलचस्प बात यह है कि संघ एक सांस्कृतिक और समाजसेवी संगठन है, इसके बावजूद राजनीति वाले नियम का हवाला देते हुए प्रतिबंध लगा दिया गया। करीब 58 साल तक यह प्रतिबंध लगा रहा। इसके बाद 9 जुलाई, 2024 को प्रधानमंत्री नरेंद्र मोदी की सरकार ने इस प्रतिबंध को हटा दिया। □

□

बी.एम.एस. के श्रमिकों ने 1971 के युद्ध में दिया सेना का साथ

यह घटना वर्ष 1971 की है। पाकिस्तान की ओर से अचानक हमले के कारण भारतीय सेना को पंजाब और कश्मीर की सीमा पर मोरचा सँभालना पड़ा। ऐसे में पठानकोट से सेना को निरंतर गोला-बारूद और रसद पहुँचाना आवश्यक था। यह काम सैनिक यूनिटों के श्रमिकों का था, जो किसी जोखिम भरी चुनौती से कम नहीं था। पठानकोट सैन्य यूनिट में करीब 500 कर्मचारी कार्यरत थे। वहाँ की ऑर्डिनेंस इंप्लॉइज यूनियन भारतीय मजदूर संघ (बी.एम.एस.) से संबद्ध थी। एक यूनियन के नाते बी.एम.एस. ने संकल्प लिया कि युद्ध जारी रहने तक सभी श्रमिक कर्मचारी न सिर्फ 24 घंटे अपने सैनिक भाइयों के साथ मिलकर काम करेंगे, बल्कि कोई छुट्टी भी नहीं लेंगे। 3 से 17 दिसंबर तक चले उस युद्ध के दौरान इन कर्मचारियों ने 14 दिनों तक न केवल लगातार काम किया, बल्कि उस दौरान बने ओवरटाइम का भत्ता भी नहीं लिया। बी.एम.एस. से जुड़े सभी श्रमिकों का कहना था, "जब हमारे सैनिक साथी देश के लिए अपनी जान की बाजी लगा सकते हैं तो हमें भी देश के लिए अपना योगदान देना ही चाहिए।" युद्ध के दौरान सेना के लिए गोला-बारूद और रसद की आपूर्ति अनवरत जारी रखना राष्ट्रभक्ति के भाव के बिना असंभव है।

□

वर्ष 1975 की इमरजेंसी में लोकतंत्र का रक्षक बना संघ

संघ वैसे तो एक अराजनीतिक संगठन है, लेकिन जब देश में लोकतंत्र पर आँच आई तो संघ का हर स्वयंसेवक तानाशाही के खिलाफ उठ खड़ा हुआ। इमरजेंसी में संघ ने जिस प्रकार का योगदान दिया, आज वह भारतीय लोकतंत्र के इतिहास में स्वर्णाक्षरों में अंकित है। 25 जून, 1975 को इंदिरा गांधी ने लोकतंत्र की हत्या करके देश में आपातकाल लगा दिया। वह हर नागरिक के लिए एक गहरा सदमा था, उससे देश और समाज को संघ के उन छोटे-बड़े कार्यकर्ताओं ने निकाला, जिन्होंने लोकतंत्र के लिए भूमिगत संघर्ष के सूत्रधार की भूमिका सफलतापूर्वक निभाई। समूचे देश में काम कर रहे 1356 प्रचारकों में से 189 प्रचारकों को जेल में डाल दिया गया। शेष प्रचारकों ने भूमिगत संघर्ष की कमान सँभाली, जिनमें प्रो. राजेंद्र सिंह (रज्जू भैया), माधवराव मुले, बापूराव मोघे, लक्ष्मणराव इनामदार, दत्तोपंत ठेंगड़ी, भानुप्रताप शुक्ल और अशोक सिंहल आदि शामिल थे। आपातकाल के दौरान करीब 1 लाख 25 हजार से अधिक लोगों को बंदी बनाया गया, उनमें से 75 हजार से भी अधिक कार्यकर्ता और नेता संघ से जुड़े थे। आपातकाल के विरोध के लिए संघ ने लोक संघर्ष समिति की स्थापना की थी। आपातकाल में जेल की दीवारें भी स्वयंसेवकों के संकल्प को रोक न सकीं। वहाँ से भी उन्होंने आंदोलन का नेतृत्व करना जारी रखा। संघ ने आपातकाल के अत्याचारों को उजागर करने के लिए भूमिगत समाचार-पत्र 'सत्य समाचार' शुरू किया। तमाम सरकारी दमन के बाद भी यह पत्र निरंतर प्रकाशित होता रहा और जनता तक सच्चाई पहुँचाने का माध्यम बना रहा।

□

स्वयंसेवक ने अपनी बात पहुँचाने के लिए सिनेमा हॉल को चुना!

देश में वर्ष 1975 में लगाए गए आपातकाल के दौरान मीसा के अंतर्गत पकड़े गए राजनीतिक कैदी व सत्याग्रह कर रहे स्वयंसेवकों को सरकार अलग-अलग जेलों में डालती गई। धर्मशाला के एक स्वयंसेवक को कांगड़ा से बिलासपुर, फिर शिमला और अंत में नाहन जेल लाया गया। नाहन जेल आने के बाद वहाँ पहले से मौजूद कैदियों में उस स्वयंसेवक ने जोश भर दिया। उसने कहा, “देखो, सामने यह सिनेमा घर है। यहाँ सैकड़ों लोग प्रतिदिन सिनेमा देखने आते हैं। हमारे पास कोई अन्य साधन न भी हो तो भी हम अपनी बात को इन सिनेमा देखने वालों तक पहुँचा सकते हैं। जब भी सिनेमा के शो छूटने या इंटरवल का समय होगा, उस समय लोग सिनेमा हॉल से बाहर होते हैं। ठीक उस समय हम ‘भारत माता की जय’ के नारे लगाएँगे, अधिनायकवाद के विरोध में नारे लगाएँगे। इससे हमारी बात किसी-न-किसी तरह से शहर में फैलेगी और सरकार के विरोध में समाज का ध्यान जाएगा।” अगले दिन से ऐसा ही हुआ और नारों का असर बाहर दिखाई देने लगा। वातावरण बदलने लगा। लोग सत्याग्रहियों से जेल में मिलने आने लगे और समाज पर उसका अनुकूल असर हुआ। सरकार के लिए सत्याग्रही जेल में भी परेशानी का सबब बन गए। इसके बाद उन्हें वहाँ से अलग-अलग स्थान भेजने की योजना बनाई गई। स्वयंसेवक जहाँ भी हों, वे वहीं से अपनी आवाज उठाते हैं, ताकि समाज पर प्रभाव डाला जा सके और उन्हें एकजुट किया जा सके।

□

आपातकाल में मोदी ने बदला वेश, ट्रेनों से सूचना पहुँचाई

देश में 25 जून, 1975 को आपातकाल लगाया गया और नागरिकों के साथ क्रूरता का यह दौर 21 महीने तक चला। इस दौरान नागरिक अधिकारों का हनन किया गया, विपक्षी नेताओं को जेल भेजा गया और प्रेस की स्वतंत्रता पर 'ताला' लगा दिया गया। संघर्ष और आंदोलन के उस दौर में संघ ने काफी सक्रिय भूमिका निभाई। संघ के स्वयंसेवक अंडरग्राउंड रहकर काम कर रहे थे। उस दौरान नरेंद्र मोदी के साथ काम कर रहे वरिष्ठ संघ अधिकारी केशवराव देशमुख को गुजरात में गिरफ्तार कर लिया गया। इसे देखते हुए मोदी ने नाथा लाल जागडा को स्कूटर से सुरक्षित जगह पर पहुँचाया था। खुद की गिरफ्तारी का खतरा भाँपते हुए मोदी कभी सरदार का रूप धारण कर लेते तो कभी दाढ़ी वाले बुजुर्ग बन जाते। उन्होंने कांग्रेस सरकार की ज्यादतियों की जानकारी से जुड़े साहित्य और दस्तावेज गुजरात से अन्य राज्यों के लिए जाने वाली ट्रेनों में रखवाए। इतना ही नहीं, वह जेल में बंद वरिष्ठ कार्यकर्ताओं को भी महत्त्वपूर्ण जानकारियाँ पहुँचाते थे। मोदी ने आपातकाल के दौरान कई बार अपना वेश बदला।

□

संघ ने जब इंदिरा गांधी का प्रस्ताव ठुकराया

इंदिरा गांधी ने इमरजेंसी के बाद वर्ष 1977 में होने वाले लोकसभा चुनाव से पहले संघ के सामने सशर्त प्रतिबंध हटाने का प्रस्ताव रखा था। मार्च में लोकसभा चुनाव के लिए मतदान से ठीक 20 से 25 दिन पहले इंदिरा गांधी ने संघ पर से प्रतिबंध हटाने का प्रस्ताव दिया था और एक उच्च पदाधिकारी ने संघ के अंडरग्राउंड नेतृत्व से मुलाकात की थी। प्रतिबंध हटाने के लिए उनकी शर्त यह थी कि लाखों संघ कार्यकर्ता जो उनकी तानाशाही शासन के खिलाफ मतदाताओं को एकजुट करने के लिए जनसंपर्क कार्य में उतरे थे, उन्हें मैदान से हट जाना चाहिए, ताकि उनके लिए राह आसान हो सके। इस प्रस्ताव को संघ अधिकारियों ने खारिज कर दिया। इसका नतीजा यह हुआ कि दूसरे ही दिन से इंदिरा गांधी ने संघ के खिलाफ अनाप-शनाप बयान देना शुरू कर दिया। इसका खुलासा संघ के अखिल भारतीय बौद्धिक प्रमुख रहे बापूराव मोघे ने आपातकाल के दौरान संघ की भूमिका पर एक लेख में किया है।

□

आपातकाल में लालकिले पर सरकार की फजीहत

आपातकाल के दौरान इंदिरा गांधी ने राष्ट्रमंडल के सदस्य राष्ट्रों के सांसदों को दिल्ली में यह दिखाने के लिए बुलाया था कि भारत में सबकुछ ठीक-ठाक है। सांसदों के सार्वजनिक अभिनंदन के लिए लालकिले में कार्यक्रम रखा गया था। संघ के सत्याग्रहियों ने इंदिरा गांधी की काली करतूतों को विश्व भर में पहुँचाने के लिए इस अवसर को चुना। जनसंघ और भाजपा के वरिष्ठ नेता रहे जगन्नाथराव जोशी ने खुफिया तंत्र को धता बताते हुए अशोक होटल में ठहरे सांसदों के पास आपातकाल विरोधी साहित्य पहुँचा दिया था। बाद में जोशी का भेद खुल गया और उन्हें बंदी बना लिया गया था। 02 नवंबर, 1975 को शाम 6:30 बजे सारा कार्यक्रम शांति से हुआ। राष्ट्रगान हो चुका था। कांग्रेस नेता एच.के.एल. भगत आभार व्यक्त कर ही रहे थे कि तभी पीछे से शेम, शेम की ध्वनि उठी। सभी ने मुड़कर देखा तो संघ के कार्यकर्ता परचे बाँट रहे थे। पुलिस उधर दौड़ी तो कुछ कार्यकर्ता 'प्रजातंत्र की हत्या बंद करो', 'तानाशाही नहीं चलेगी' के नारे लगाते हुए दूसरी तरफ दौड़े। विदेशी सांसदों और पत्रकारों को परचे और साहित्य मिल गए थे। कांग्रेस की नेता अंबिका सोनी इस घटना से क्रोधित होकर पुलिसवालों को डाँट रही थी। तभी एक पत्रकार बोला, "तुम पुलिस हो, सरकार के नौकर हो, इस बहनजी के नहीं।" अंबिका बोली—"यह भी संघी है, इसे भी पकड़ो।" और अन्य सत्याग्रहियों के साथ पत्रकार को भी पकड़ लिया गया। कांग्रेसियों के चेहरे उतरे हुए थे, क्योंकि उनके झूठ का परदाफाश हो चुका था। बाद में 9 नवंबर, 1975 को अमेरिका के 'द न्यूयॉर्क टाइम्स' में इन घटनाओं के बारे में समाचार भी प्रकाशित हुआ।

□

आपातकाल के खिलाफ चाँदनी चौक से शुरू हुआ सत्याग्रह

इंदिरा गांधी ने 25 जून, 1975 को देश पर आपातकाल थोप दिया था। इसके ठीक पाँचवें दिन 29 जून, 1975 को राष्ट्रीय स्वयंसेवक संघ ने चाँदनी चौक में इसके खिलाफ सत्याग्रह का बिगुल फूँक दिया। भारतीय इतिहास के इस काले अध्याय के प्रति संघ सरकार को चेतावनी देना चाहता था। साथ ही समाज को इस तानाशाही भरे फैसले के खिलाफ साहस देना चाहता था। संघ के प्रमुख कार्यकर्ता सत्यनारायण बंसल ने इस सत्याग्रह के बारे में पत्रकारों और समाज को पहले ही सूचना दे दी थी। सत्याग्रही सामान्य वेशभूषा में 'भारत माता की जय' और 'वंदे मातरम्' के नारे लगाते हुए, चाँदनी चौक में एकत्र होने लगे। जनता का हुजूम भी उमड़ पड़ा। भीड़ जुटते ही सत्यनारायण वहाँ पहुँचे और उन्होंने आपातकाल के खिलाफ अपने विचार रखे। दो मिनट बाद ही पुलिस ने उन्हें अपने घेरे में ले लिया। जोश और उत्साह से भरे सत्याग्रही नारे लगाते रहे। सत्यनारायण जहाँ चाँदनी चौक में सत्याग्रह का नेतृत्व कर रहे थे, वहीं अजमल खाँ पार्क में मदनलाल कपूर, शिवनारायण सरसणिया और मदनमोहन अब्रोल इसका नेतृत्व कर रहे थे। कनॉट प्लेस में कंवर लाल गुप्ता के नेतृत्व में सत्याग्रह किया गया। इस कड़ी में 'इमरजेंसी हटाओ', 'तानाशाही समाप्त करो' के नारों के साथ 25 जुलाई तक देश भर में सत्याग्रह हुए।

□

स्वयंसेवकों का अनुशासन देख पुलिस अधिकारी भी रह गया दंग

14 जनवरी, 1976 को महाराष्ट्र के बुलढाणा जिले के नांदुरा में ग्रामीण क्षेत्र के संघ के 40 कार्यकर्ताओं ने सत्याग्रह किया। पुलिस ने सभी को गिरफ्तार कर लिया, लेकिन गिरफ्तारी के दौरान एक रोचक प्रसंग सामने आया। जब संबंधित पुलिस अधिकारी ने वायरलेस से अपने उच्चाधिकारियों को सूचना भेजी तो भूलवश उसने 42 सत्याग्रहियों की गिरफ्तारी की रिपोर्ट कर दी। बाद में जब उसे अपनी गलती का एहसास हुआ तो वह घबरा गया। उसे डर था कि उसके वरिष्ठ यह मान लेंगे कि दो सत्याग्रही भाग गए। घबराया अधिकारी स्वयं जत्था प्रमुख भानुदास पाटिल के पास आया और हाथ जोड़कर विनम्रता से बोला—"अब आप ही मेरी रक्षा कर सकते हैं। यदि आप दो और कार्यकर्ता गिरफ्तार करवाने के लिए भेज दें, तो मेरी नौकरी बच जाएगी।" पाटिल ने उस अधिकारी की मजबूरी को समझा और तुरंत दो और स्वयंसेवकों को संदेश भिजवाया। थोड़ी ही देर में दो कार्यकर्ता स्वयं गिरफ्तारी देने पहुँच गए। यह देख अधिकारी भावुक हो गया। उसने कहा—"सचमुच कमाल है आप संघ वालों का। ऐसा अनुशासन हो तो कोई पराजित नहीं कर सकता!" यह घटना उस दौर में संघ के कार्यकर्ताओं की संवेदनशीलता और अनुशासन की एक मिसाल बन गई।

□

□

रज्जू भैया ने जब मौलाना के वेश में दिया चकमा

आपातकाल के दौरान उत्तर प्रदेश–बिहार के तत्कालीन क्षेत्र प्रचारक प्रो. राजेंद्र सिंह (रज्जू भैया) की सक्रियता ने लोगों को खूब प्रेरित किया, जो बाद में सरसंघचालक बने। उन्होंने भूमिगत होकर देश भर में सत्याग्रह की अलख जगाने का काम किया। इस संदर्भ में एक घटना बहुत महत्त्वपूर्ण है, जब काशी में रज्जू भैया ने मौलाना का वेश धारण कर लिया था। डॉ. पी.के. बनर्जी वहाँ के एस.पी. से बातें कर रहे थे कि तभी वहाँ एक व्यक्ति ने दस्तक दी। उसने शर्ट–पायजामा पहन रखा था और उसके सिर पर मौलाना टोपी थी। आते ही वह डॉ. बनर्जी की बगल वाली कुरसी पर बैठ गया। तभी एस.पी. साहब बोले, "आप कौन हैं? कहाँ से आ रहे हैं?" अजनबी ने तत्काल सहज भाव से कहा, "डॉक्टर साहब हमारे मित्र हैं। दूर से सफर करता आ रहा हूँ। सोचा, दोस्त से मिलता चलूँ। आगे फिरोजाबाद जाना है।" डॉ. बनर्जी ने समझ लिया कि यह तो हमारे क्षेत्र प्रचारक और भूमिगत आंदोलन के सूत्रधार रज्जू भैया हैं। उन्होंने एस.पी. से कहा, "माफ कीजिए, मैं कुछ समय अपने दोस्त के साथ बिताना चाहूँगा। फिर आपको सारी जानकारी अवश्य दूँगा।" एस.पी. महोदय उठकर चले गए। डॉक्टर साहब ने राहत की साँस लेते हुए कहा, "कहिए मौलाना साहब, आपकी क्या खातिरदारी करूँ?" आपातकाल के दौरान रज्जू भैया को लगातार पुलिस ढूँढ़ रही थी और वे कई बार वेश बदलकर पुलिस वालों को चकमा देते रहे। इसी दौरान का एक और प्रसंग इलाहाबाद हाईकोर्ट का है। इस दौरान वे वकील के वेश में अपने अधिवक्ता मित्र वीरेंद्र चौधरी से मिलने सीधे कोर्ट पहुँच गए।

□

बर्फीली यातनाओं के सामने भी अडिग रहा देशभक्ति का जज्बा

जब देश पर आपातकाल की काली छाया थी, तब जम्मू में 10 जुलाई, 1975 की रात 12 वर्षीय बाल स्वयंसेवक ओंकारनाथ ने अपने कुछ मित्रों के साथ अनोखी योजना बनाई। उसने संघर्ष समिति द्वारा प्रसारित सूचनाएँ दीवारों पर चिपकाने का फैसला किया, जिससे लोगों तक संघर्ष की रूपरेखा की जानकारी पहुँच सके। जब वे पोस्टर चिपकाते हुए राजेंद्र बाजार पहुँचे तो पुलिस ने उन्हें घेर लिया और हिरासत में ले लिया। पुलिस को यकीन था कि ओंकार को संघर्ष समिति के भूमिगत केंद्र की जानकारी है। अगले तीन दिनों तक पुलिस ने ओंकार को अमानवीय यातनाएँ दीं। एक डी.एस.पी. के निर्देश पर इस नन्हे बालक को बर्फ की सिल्लियों पर लिटाकर पूछताछ की गई। यह यातना किसी भी सभ्य समाज के लिए कलंक थी, लेकिन इंदिरा गांधी की तानाशाही में पुलिस का व्यवहार बर्बर हो चुका था। अकल्पनीय पीड़ा सहते हुए भी बाल स्वयंसेवक ओंकारनाथ ने अपने साथियों और भूमिगत केंद्र के बारे में एक शब्द भी नहीं कहा। ओंकारनाथ की अडिग देशभक्ति और साहस ने पुलिस के क्रूर इरादों को ध्वस्त कर दिया। आज जब भारतीय लोकतंत्र की विकास गाथा की ओर देखते हैं तो पता चलता है कि किस प्रकार ओंकारनाथ जैसे अनगिनत सच्चे प्रहरियों ने ही भारतीय प्रजातंत्र की नींव को मजबूत बनाए रखा। □

प्रांत संघचालक ने कहा : 'जेलयात्रा पहले, पुत्र का विवाह बाद में'

1975 में जब देश पर आपातकाल का शिकंजा कस रहा था, ओडिशा के प्रांत संघचालक भूपेंद्र कुमार बसु के सामने एक कठिन फैसला था। उनके पुत्र का विवाह तय था और उन्हें विवाह या सत्याग्रह में से एक को चुनना था। उन्होंने सिद्धांतों को प्राथमिकता देते हुए कहा, "जेलयात्रा पहले, पुत्र का विवाह बाद में" और वे सत्याग्रह में शामिल हो गए। उनका यह साहसिक निर्णय आपातकाल के विरोध में एक मिसाल बन गया और अन्य लोगों के लिए प्रेरणा का स्रोत साबित हुआ। ओडिशा में उनकी प्रेरणा से कई शहरों में व्यापक प्रदर्शन हुए। राजधानी भुवनेश्वर, केंद्रपाड़ा, संबलपुर, बोलंगीर सहित कई शहरों में सैकड़ों सत्याग्रहियों ने व्यापक प्रदर्शन किया। एक जत्था गिरफ्तार होता तो दूसरा तुरंत तैयार हो जाता। इस प्रकार भूपेंद्र कुमार बसु के निस्वार्थ त्याग और नेतृत्व ने ओडिशा में आपातकाल विरोधी आंदोलन को एक नई दिशा दी और उसकी सफलता में महत्त्वपूर्ण भूमिका निभाई। इसी तरह मध्य प्रदेश के खरगौन जिले के बड़वानी में 23 नवंबर, 1975 को एक अद्भुत दृश्य देखने को मिला। बिहारीलाल जोशी के साथ 20 सत्याग्रहियों ने अपनी गिरफ्तारी दी। सत्याग्रहियों के साथ बिहारीलाल जोशी की वृद्ध माँ भी थाने पहुँच गईं और उन्होंने एक-एक कर सभी सत्याग्रहियों का तिलक किया और उन्हें आशीर्वाद दिया। यह घटना दरशाती है कि आपातकाल का विरोध सिर्फ नेताओं का नहीं, बल्कि आम जनता का आंदोलन था, जिन्होंने त्याग और देशभक्ति की मिसालें पेश कीं।

□

आपातकाल के गुमनाम नायक : त्याग और दृढ़ता की कहानी

आपातकाल की काली छाया में जब पुलिस की बर्बरता चरम पर थी, कुछ गुमनाम नायकों ने अपने असाधारण साहस और बुद्धिमत्ता से लोकतंत्र की मशाल जलाए रखी। इन्होंने त्याग, चतुराई और अटूट दृढ़ता की मिसालें पेश कीं। राजस्थान में पुलिस प्रेस मालिक दिनेश गुप्त को पकड़ने में जुटी थी, जो आपातकाल विरोधी साहित्य प्रकाशित कर रहे थे। परंतु तलाशी के दौरान पुलिस ने भूलवश एक दूसरे स्वयंसेवक दिनेश गुप्त को पकड़ा, जिनका प्रेस से कोई लेना-देना नहीं था। पुलिस की बार-बार पूछताछ के बावजूद, इस युवा स्वयंसेवक ने चुप्पी साधे रखी। वह जानता था कि अगर उसने सच बताया तो आंदोलन की रीढ़ टूट जाएगी। अपने भविष्य की परवाह किए बिना उसने गिरफ्तारी स्वीकार कर ली और अपने त्याग से आंदोलन की लौ को बुझने नहीं दिया। इसी तरह, संघ कार्यकर्ता 'पाञ्चजन्य' के संपादक भानुप्रताप शुक्ल ने अपनी चतुराई से पुलिस को चकमा दिया। वे दिल्ली में 'रविशंकर' नाम से भूमिगत होकर आंदोलन के लिए महत्त्वपूर्ण साहित्य तैयार कर रहे थे। जब एक गुप्तचर उन्हें पकड़ने आया तो शुक्लजी ने बिना घबराए खुद को 'आदित्य' बताया और इतनी सहजता से बात की कि गुप्तचर को यकीन हो गया। उनकी इस सूझ-बूझ से वे सुरक्षित रहे और आंदोलन का काम जारी रहा। उधर, केरल के कन्नानूर में सत्याग्रहियों ने अडिग दृढ़ता का परिचय दिया। पुलिस ने उन पर बेरहमी से लाठियाँ बरसाईं, लेकिन वे अपनी जगह से टस से मस नहीं हुए। लाठियाँ टूट गईं, पर उनका हौसला नहीं टूटा। ये तीनों घटनाएँ दरशाती हैं कि आपातकाल में त्याग, बुद्धिमत्ता और अटूट साहस ने लोकतंत्र बहाली की लड़ाई को जिंदा रखा।

□

आपातकाल में संघर्ष का प्रमुख भार संघ के कंधों पर था

21 मार्च, 1977 को देश में आपातकाल समाप्त होने के बाद संघ ने कर्नाटक के मंगलौर में 17 मई, 1977 को एक कार्यक्रम का आयोजन किया था। इस कार्यक्रम में आधुनिक कन्नड़ साहित्य के मूर्धन्य साहित्यकार और ज्ञानपीठ पुरस्कार विजेता डॉ. शिवराम कारंत शामिल हुए। समारोह को संबोधित करते हुए उन्होंने संघ की काफी प्रशंसा की। उन्होंने कहा था, “जब चुनाव की घोषणा हुई तो मुझे यह चिंता सताने लगी कि कौन हैं जो जनता को स्वाधीनता का संदेश देंगे और उन्हें इसकी बारीकियों से अवगत कराएँगे। संघ के हजारों कार्यकर्ता मैदान में कूद पड़े और मेरी चिंता मिट गई। चुनाव से पहले भी संघर्ष का प्रमुख भार उन्होंने अपने बलिष्ठ कंधों पर ढोया था। उन्होंने ही जनता के मनोबल को बनाए रखा था। संघर्ष करने वाला 80 प्रतिशत से भी अधिक समुदाय संघ का था। मैंने अपनी आँखों से देखा कि पूर्णत: केवल राष्ट्रप्रेम की आदर्श भावना से ओत-प्रोत हजारों युवक निष्काम भाव से संघर्ष में कूदे हैं। न उनके खाने का ठौर था और न विश्राम का। पर उनकी लगन ज्यों-की-त्यों बनी रही।” संघ ने इस तरह का संघर्ष तब किया था, जबकि आपातकाल के दौरान उस पर प्रतिबंध लगाया गया था। उल्लेखनीय है कि इंदिरा गांधी ने आपातकाल के दौरान ही 16 से 20 मार्च, 1977 के बीच लोकसभा चुनाव कराए थे। इस चुनाव में इंदिरा गांधी को भारी हार का सामना करना पड़ा। इंदिरा गांधी रायबरेली की अपनी सीट हार गईं, जबकि उनके बेटे संजय गांधी अमेठी की अपनी सीट हार गए। □

स्वयंसेवकों की सेवा भावना से इंदिरा गांधी हुईं प्रभावित

आंध्र प्रदेश में 19 नवंबर, 1977 को करीब 100 किलोमीटर प्रति घंटे की गति से आया चक्रवात काफी विनाशकारी था। समुद्र के तटवर्ती इलाकों में चक्रवात ने गाँव के गाँव लील लिये। हजारों घर तबाह हो गए और बड़े-बड़े भूखंड भी ध्वस्त हो गए। इस तबाही में 20 हजार से अधिक लोग मारे गए और लाखों लोग बेघर हो गए। चक्रवात से करीब दो हजार करोड़ रुपए की हानि का अनुमान लगाया गया। तबाही के इस मंजर में राहत और बचाव कार्य के लिए सबसे पहले स्वयंसेवक ही पहुँचे। चक्रवात के अगले ही दिन स्वयंसेवक सबसे ज्यादा तबाही वाले इलाकों में पहुँच गए और राहत कार्य शुरू कर दिया। जहाँ सरकारी तंत्र भी नहीं पहुँच सका था, वहाँ सैकड़ों स्वयंसेवक जान जोखिम में डालकर लोगों को मदद पहुँचा रहे थे। तत्काल सहायता के लिए पीड़ितों के बीच कई लाख रोटियाँ बाँटी गईं। इसके बाद जगह-जगह निःशुल्क भोजन वितरण केंद्र खोले गए। शवों का अंतिम संस्कार किया गया। हजारों कार्यकर्ताओं ने दिन-रात सहायता शिविरों में काम किया। पीड़ितों के बीच दो लाख 40 हजार कपड़े और 32 हजार बरतन बाँटे गए। बाद में घरों का भी निर्माण किया गया। स्वयंसेवकों का कार्य इस कदर प्रभावशाली था कि इंदिरा गांधी ने अपने कांग्रेस कार्यकर्ताओं को फटकार लगाते हुए कहा, "मैं जहाँ भी देख रही हूँ केवल संघ के कार्यकर्ता ही पीड़ित क्षेत्रों में कार्य करते दिखाई देते हैं।" वयोवृद्ध सर्वोदय नेता प्रभाकर राव संघ के काम से इतना प्रभावित हुए कि उन्होंने कहा, "संघ को उसके निस्स्वार्थ कार्य के कारण नया नाम दिया जाना चाहिए—रेडी फॉर सेल्फलेस सर्विस।"

□

संघ के सेवाकार्य के प्रशंसक हुए कांग्रेसी मुख्यमंत्री

आंध्र प्रदेश में 19 नवंबर, 1977 के विनाशकारी चक्रवात से आई बाढ़ में कई गाँव ऐसे थे, जो कि पूरा बह गए और उनका नामो-निशान नहीं रहा। इन्हीं में एक गाँव था 'मुलापलम'। कृष्णा जिले में स्थित इस गाँव का कोई अस्तित्व नहीं रह गया था। इस गाँव के 270 लोग बेघर हो गए थे, जिनका मुख्य पेशा मछली पकड़ना था। राष्ट्रीय स्वयंसेवक संघ के स्वयंसेवकों ने, जो कि चक्रवात से प्रभावित लोगों की मदद में जुटे हुए थे, जब बेघर हुए लोगों की दुर्दशा देखी तो इस गाँव को गोद ले लिया और नया गाँव बसाने का बीड़ा उठाया। उन्होंने 110 पक्के और कंक्रीट के मजबूत मकान बनाने का कार्य अपने हाथ में लिया। उन्होंने मजबूत मकान बनाने का फैसला इसलिए किया ताकि दोबारा चक्रवात या फिर बाढ़ आने पर उन्हें फिर बेघर न होना पड़े। सबसे महत्त्वपूर्ण बात यह है कि उन्होंने इन घरों का निर्माण रिकॉर्ड चार महीने में पूरा कर लिया, जिससे लोग अपने अस्थायी छप्पर वाले घरों से निकलकर अगले मानसून से पहले अपने नए आवास में बस सकें। इन घरों का निर्माण दिल्ली स्थित दीनदयाल शोध संस्थान के सहयोग से किया गया। यह गाँव अब दीनदयालपुरम के नाम से जाना जाता है। 22 मार्च, 1978 को हैदराबाद में सहायता कार्य से संबद्ध 250 संगठनों का सम्मेलन हुआ था। इस अवसर पर कांग्रेस पार्टी के प्रमुख नेता और तत्कालीन मुख्यमंत्री चेन्ना रेड्डी ने कहा, "संघ जो कर रहा है, कल सरकार को वही करना पड़ेगा।" तत्कालीन पुलिस महानिदेशक के. रामचंद्र रेड्डी को जब पता चला कि आंध्र पुलिस ने गाँव सोरगागुंडी के पुनर्निर्माण का जिम्मा लिया था, लेकिन उन्होंने अभी तक काम भी शुरू नहीं किया तो उन्होंने अपने जवानों को दीनदयालपुरम बुलाया और उनसे कहा, "देखो और संघ के उदाहरण का अनुसरण करो।"

□

तमिलनाडु में बाढ़ पीड़ितों के लिए नए घर बनाए

नवंबर 1977 में आए चक्रवात में आंध्र प्रदेश के साथ ही तमिलनाडु को भी काफी नुकसान झेलना पड़ा। संघ के स्वयंसेवकों ने यहाँ भी सबसे ज्यादा प्रभावित इलाकों में तत्काल पहुँचकर पीड़ितों की हरसंभव सहायता की। सबसे पहले 10 गाँवों में सहायता कार्य शुरू किया गया। इन 10 गाँवों के 5,773 परिवारों को हर प्रकार की मदद पहुँचाई गई। संघ ने तमिलनाडु में चक्रवात से प्रभावित लोगों की मदद के लिए 'चक्रवात, बाढ़-पीड़ित सहायता समिति' का गठन किया। इसके माध्यम से पीड़ितों में 3,125 क्विंटल अनाज, ढाई लाख रुपए के कपड़े के साथ ही दवाइयाँ बाँटी गईं। बाढ़ पीड़ित अपना रोजी-रोजगार फिर से चालू कर सकें, इसके लिए उनको जरूरी उपकरण उपलब्ध कराए गए। कई गाँवों में लोगों के घर बह गए थे तो कुछ घर ढह कर क्षतिग्रस्त हो गए थे। स्वयंसेवकों ने गाँवों में करीब 360 नए घर बनाए और 200 घरों की मरम्मत कर उन्हें रहने लायक बनाया। तिरुचि जिले के वायनूर गाँव में नदी की धारा बदल जाने से कई घर बह गए थे। यहाँ 30 नए घर बनाए गए, जिससे पीड़ित अस्थायी निवास से अपने स्थायी घरों में रहने के लिए जा सकें। आपदा में संघ ने बिना किसी भेदभाव के सभी वर्गों की सहायता की।

□

□

राजस्थान में गहरे पानी में उतरकर बाढ़ पीड़ितों की मदद की

राजस्थान के भरतपुर जिले में मई 1977 में आई प्रलयंकारी बाढ़ से भारी तबाही हुई। जिले के कई हिस्से पानी में डूब गए और कई गाँवों में पानी भर गया। ऐसे में नजदीकी जिलों के संघ के स्वयंसेवक तत्काल वहाँ पहुँचकर राहत कार्य में जुट गए। हालात ऐसे थे कि बाढ़ प्रभावित लोगों तक पहुँचने के लिए स्वयंसेवकों को गले तक गहरे पानी से होकर जाना पड़ा। ऐसे में सबसे चुनौतीपूर्ण यह था कि उन तक राहत सामग्री कैसे पहुँचाई जाए? लेकिन स्वयंसेवकों ने इस चुनौती का मुकाबला करते हुए पीड़ितों तक भोजन और कपड़े पहुँचाए। ठंड से बचाव के लिए गरीबों में करीब तीन हजार कंबल बाँटे गए। इस त्रासदी के करीब दो साल बाद जुलाई 1979 में एक बार फिर राजस्थान में बाढ़ की विभीषिका ने कई जिलों में कहर मचाया। उस समय भी संघ के स्वयंसेवकों ने पीड़ितों की मदद में दिन-रात एक कर दिया। करीब 10 दिन तक चले सहायता कार्य में नौ जिलों में दो हजार स्वयंसेवकों ने पीड़ितों की हरसंभव मदद की। उन्होंने बाढ़ प्रभावित इलाके से लोगों को सुरक्षित स्थानों और शिविरों में पहुँचाया। पीड़ितों तक भोजन के पैकेट पहुँचाए, उन्हें गरम कपड़े और कंबल दिए। बाढ़ के पानी को गाँवों में जाने से रोकने के लिए बाँध बनाए गए। बाढ़ का पानी कम होने के बाद स्वयंसेवकों ने पीड़ितों के पुनर्वास में भी मदद की। सरकारी अनुमान के अनुसार, बाढ़ से दो हजार लोग मारे गए और करीब पाँच लाख पशु असमय काल-कवलित हो गए।

□

एक स्वयंसेवक ने गाँव में लाया सामाजिक परिवर्तन

पुणे के स्वयंसेवक मधुकरराव देवल अपनी शिक्षा पूरी करने के बाद महाराष्ट्र के सांगली जिले में अपने गाँव महैराल लौटे। वहाँ उनकी पैतृक संपत्ति ठीक-ठाक थी। गाँव पहुँचने के बाद उन्होंने दलित समुदाय की गरीबी देखी तो उनका हृदय पिघल गया। दलित समुदाय के कई परिवार कर्ज के बोझ तले दबे थे। ऐसे में उन्होंने उनके सामाजिक उत्थान का संकल्प लिया। उन्होंने हरिजनों को 'विट्ठल कृषि सहकारी समिति' स्थापित करने की प्रेरणा दी। समिति के माध्यम से उन्हें कर्ज दिलाए, उनकी जमीन वापस दिलाई, कृषि उपज में उन्हें बचत के उपाय सिखाए और अपना घर बनाने में सहायता की। उनकी प्रेरणा से 125 दलित परिवारों ने अपने सभी कर्ज चुका दिए और ऋणमुक्त होकर राहत की साँस ली। अब प्रत्येक परिवार के पास आय के पर्याप्त साधन हो गए और रहने के लिए घर भी बन गए थे। अब धन की जरूरत होने पर उन्हें अपनी जमीन नहीं बेचनी पड़ती थी। कुछ परिवारों ने तो आय बढ़ने पर जमीन खरीदकर अपनी संपत्ति में वृद्धि भी कर ली। गाँव के विद्यालय में दलित बच्चों की संख्या बढ़ गई; बीच में पढ़ाई छोड़ने वालों की संख्या घट गई। दलित समुदाय में समृद्धि आने से सामाजिक जीवन में भेदभाव भी खत्म हुआ। महात्मा गांधी के पौत्र अरुण गांधी ने 02 दिसंबर, 1977 के 'टाइम्स ऑफ इंडिया' में एक लेख लिखकर महैराल के इस अनोखे परिवर्तन की प्रशंसा की।

□

संघ के कार्यक्रम में शामिल हुए थे पूर्व राष्ट्रपति नीलम संजीव रेड्डी

संघ से जुड़ी संस्था 'विद्या भारती' ने नवंबर 1978 में दिल्ली में एक विशाल सम्मेलन 'शिशु संगम' का आयोजन किया। इस शिविर में उत्तर भारत के अनेक प्रांतों में चल रहे सरस्वती शिशु मंदिरों के 6 से 11 साल के 15 हजार बच्चों ने हिस्सा लिया। भाग लेने वाले बच्चों में एक तिहाई बालिकाएँ थीं और 2500 शिक्षक थे। इस शिविर का उद्घाटन तत्कालीन राष्ट्रपति नीलम संजीव रेड्डी ने किया था। इस कार्यक्रम को मुख्य अतिथि के रूप में तत्कालीन केंद्रीय मंत्री बाबू जगजीवन राम ने संबोधित किया था। इस संगम में बच्चों का कार्य संचालन, अनुशासन, आचरण और अद्भुत प्रबंध क्षमता देखकर नीलम संजीव रेड्डी काफी प्रभावित हुए थे। अपने संबोधन में राष्ट्रपति ने कहा था, "प्यारे-प्यारे सुंदर बच्चों के इस विशाल सागर को देखकर मेरे हृदय में हर्ष का ज्वार उमड़ रहा है। इनके चमकते मुखमंडल और दमकती आँखें बताती हैं कि ये भविष्य की आशा और देश की अमूल्य निधि हैं। मुझे पूर्ण विश्वास है कि ये सुकुमार कलियाँ रंग-बिरंगे सुगंधित पुष्पों के रूप में पल्लवित होंगी और हमारे सपनों के भारत के गले का हार बनेंगी।" उल्लेखनीय है कि संघ प्रेरणा से कुछ लोगों ने शिक्षा-क्षेत्र को जीवन साधना समझकर वर्ष 1952 में सरस्वती शिशु मंदिर की शुरुआत की थी। समय के साथ शिशु मंदिरों की संख्या बढ़ती गई और ये प्रांतीय समिति के अंतर्गत काम करने लगीं। वर्ष 1977 में इसने अखिल भारतीय स्वरूप लिया और विद्या भारती की स्थापना की गई। □

दिल्ली में मदद के दौरान 7 कार्यकर्ताओं की हुई मृत्यु

दिल्ली में वर्ष 1978 में यमुना का जलस्तर 207.49 मीटर तक पहुँच गया था, जिससे बाढ़ आ गई और इससे काफी नुकसान हुआ। लेकिन संघ के स्वयंसेवक पहले से ही सजग थे और उन्होंने दिल्ली के निचले इलाकों के गली-मोहल्ले में जाकर बाढ़ के खतरों से लोगों को सचेत करते हुए उनसे सुरक्षित स्थानों पर जाने की अपील की। स्वयंसेवकों ने लोगों को कीमती वस्तुएँ एवं पशुओं को सुरक्षित स्थान तक ले जाने में भी मदद की। स्वयंसेवकों की चेतावनी के कारण बाढ़ से नुकसान कम हुआ, क्योंकि लोग सतर्क हो चुके थे। जब बाढ़ आई तो उसने लगभग आधी दिल्ली में तबाही मचा दी। पूर्वी दिल्ली में बाढ़ का पानी हर मोहल्ले में भर गया। लालकिला भी पानी से लबालब भर गया था। स्वयंसेवकों ने जलमग्न क्षेत्रों में लोगों के लिए भोजन के पैकेट के साथ ही आवश्यक वस्तुएँ एवं दवाइयाँ आदि पहुँचाईं। विद्यालयों एवं अन्य स्थानों में सहायता शिविर खोले गए। कई इलाकों में संघ के कार्यकर्ताओं ने कमर तक गहरे पानी में जाकर लोगों तक सहायता पहुँचाई। इसी तरह के एक अन्य प्रयास में नाव से राहत सामग्री ले जाने के दौरान दुर्घटना हो गई, जिससे सात कार्यकर्ताओं की मृत्यु हो गई। बाढ़ पीड़ितों की मदद के लिए संघ ने कुल 51 राहत शिविर खोले। इसके जरिए सैकड़ों लोगों तक मदद पहुँचाई गई। शिविरों में करीब पाँच लाख भोजन के पैकेट बाँटे गए। इस मिशन में करीब पाँच हजार स्वयंसेवकों ने लगभग एक सप्ताह तक दिन-रात एक कर लोगों की सहायता की।

□

मोरबी में बाँध हादसे के दौरान मोदी ने बनाया था राहत प्लान

यह घटना 11 अगस्त, 1979 की रात की है। गुजरात के मोरबी में लगातार तीन दिन मूसलाधार बारिश होने से मच्छु नदी पर बना बाँध ओवरफ्लो होकर टूट गया, जिससे भारी तबाही हुई। इस हादसे में आधिकारिक आँकड़े के अनुसार करीब एक हजार लोग असमय मृत्यु के मुँह में समा गए, वहीं हजारों लोग बेघर हो गए। पानी का बहाव इतना तेज था कि कुछ ही घंटों में मोरबी शहर पानी में डूब गया। शवों से कई दिनों तक दुर्गंध आती रही और पूरा सरकारी तंत्र पंगु बना हुआ था। ऐसी परिस्थिति में संघ ने मोरबी में राहत कार्य शुरू करने का बीड़ा उठाया। उस समय नरेंद्र मोदी संगठन के काम से केरल के तिरुवनंतपुरम में थे। मोरबी की खबर सुनते ही वे 13 अगस्त, 1979 को गुजरात लौट आए और राहत कार्य शुरू किया। मोदी ने वहाँ के हालात का जायजा लेने के बाद विस्तार से एक योजना तैयार की। हर टीम को एक खास काम दिया गया, जो आम जनता की अलग-अलग जरूरतों और समस्याओं का निदान करने के लिए तैयार की गई थी। मोदी और उनकी टीम ने मिट्टी को हटाया, लोगों के प्रियजनों का अंतिम संस्कार किया और मरे हुए पशुओं के शवों को उठाया। मोदी के नेतृत्व में बाढ़ आपदा राहत कमेटी का गठन किया गया। इस कमेटी ने बाढ़ पीड़ितों के घरों को बनाने के लिए 14 लाख रुपए इकट्ठा किए। इस कमेटी का काम पीड़ितों को चिकित्सा मदद, अनाज और कपड़े उपलब्ध कराना था। उस बुरे वक्त में मोदी ने लोगों को हिम्मत देने के लिए एक भावुक पत्र लिखा और इसे घर-घर जाकर बाँटा। उस समय गुजरात सरकार की तरफ से राहत कार्य का जिम्मा सँभालने वाले अधिकारियों ने इस अप्रतिम सेवाकार्य के लिए नरेंद्र मोदी की प्रशंसा की थी।

□

देवरस से कई बार मिले राजीव गांधी, सोनिया को रखा बेखबर

राष्ट्रीय स्वयंसेवक संघ की बढ़ती साख को देखते हुए इंदिरा गांधी संघ के साथ संपर्क बनाए रखना चाहती थीं। इमरजेंसी के दौरान ही कराए गए, वर्ष 1977 के लोकसभा चुनाव में वह संघ के विरोध का परिणाम देख चुकी थीं। इसी को ध्यान में रखते हुए इंदिरा गांधी ने वर्ष 1982 में अपने बेटे राजीव गांधी को संघ प्रमुख बालासाहब देवरस के छोटे भाई और संघ के वरिष्ठ अधिकारी भाऊराव देवरस से मिलने के लिए और उनके साथ बातचीत शुरू करने के लिए भेजा था। वर्ष 1982 से 1984 के बीच राजीव गांधी और भाऊराव देवरस के बीच चार बार भेंट हुई थी। पहली और दूसरी बैठक प्रमुख उद्योगपति और मोहन मीकिन ग्रुप के चेयरमैन रहे कपिल मोहन के पूसा रोड आवास पर हुई। तीसरी बैठक कपिल मोहन के भतीजे अनिल बाली के घर पर फ्रेंड्स कॉलोनी में हुई। चौथी मुलाकात 10 जनपथ में वर्ष 1991 में तब हुई थी, जब राजीव गांधी सत्ता से बाहर थे। माखनलाल फोतेदार ने एक बातचीत में खुलासा किया था कि इंदिरा गांधी ने राजीव को संघ के साथ चल रही बातचीत के बारे में घर पर बात करने से मना किया था, क्योंकि वह जानती थीं कि सोनिया गांधी संघ को बिल्कुल पसंद नहीं करती हैं।

□

श्रीगुरुजी के अंतिम संस्कार में गए तो सुप्रीम कोर्ट का जज नहीं बनाया

वर्ष 1982 में सुप्रीम कोर्ट के मुख्य न्यायाधीश वाई.वी. चंद्रचूड़ ने बॉम्बे हाईकोर्ट के मुख्य न्यायाधीश रहे जस्टिस एम.एन. चंदूरकर को सुप्रीम कोर्ट का न्यायाधीश बनाने की संस्तुति की। जस्टिस चंदूरकर अपनी विद्वत्ता और न्यायिक दूरदर्शिता के लिए जाने जाते थे और सी.जे.आई. चंद्रचूड़ उन्हें सर्वोच्च न्यायालय के लिए एक उपयुक्त उम्मीदवार मानते थे, लेकिन तत्कालीन प्रधानमंत्री इंदिरा गांधी ने उनके नाम को तुरंत रिजेक्ट कर दिया। इसकी वजह यह थी कि चंदूरकर ने संघ प्रमुख श्रीगुरुजी के अंतिम संस्कार में हिस्सा लिया था और उन्हें श्रद्धांजलि अर्पित की थी। इतना ही नहीं, अंतिम संस्कार के बाद एक सभा में उन्होंने श्रीगुरुजी के बारे में सकारात्मक बातें भी कही थीं। वाई.वी. चंद्रचूड़ ने जस्टिस चंदूरकर को सुप्रीम कोर्ट का जज नियुक्त करने के लिए दो बार संस्तुति की थी, लेकिन दोनों ही बार कांग्रेस सरकार ने इसे खारिज कर दिया। बरसों बाद इसका खुलासा जस्टिस वाई.वी. चंद्रचूड़ के पोते और पूर्व मुख्य न्यायाधीश डी.वाई. चंद्रचूड़ के बेटे अभिनव चंद्रचूड़ ने किया। उन्होंने अपनी पुस्तक 'सुप्रीम विस्पर्स : सुप्रीम कोर्ट जजेज' में इसकी जानकारी दी है। उन्होंने यह भी बताया कि इंदिरा गांधी ने स्वयं चंद्रचूड़ से इसका खुलासा किया था कि उनको रिजेक्ट करने का कारण यह था कि—"वे हमारी (कांग्रेस सरकार) मदद नहीं कर पाएँगे।"

□

असम दंगे में स्वयंसेवकों ने लगाया पीड़ितों को मरहम

असम में 18 फरवरी, 1983 को फैले दंगे के दौरान संघ के स्वयंसेवकों ने जान की बाजी लगाकर पीड़ितों तक मदद पहुँचाई। ऐसे हालात में जब चारों तरफ अफरा-तफरी मची थी और लोग जान बचाने के लिए सुरक्षित स्थानों की तलाश में थे, तब स्वयंसेवक ही थे, जो पीड़ितों को मरहम लगाने के लिए दंगाग्रस्त इलाकों में पहुँच गए थे। स्वयंसेवक बिना अपनी जान की परवाह किए दंगा पीड़ितों तक मदद पहुँचाने में लगे थे। पीड़ितों के लिए अधिक-से-अधिक सामग्री जुटाई जा सके, इसके लिए 'संघर्ष पीड़ित सहायता समिति' का गठन किया गया। समिति ने दैनिक उपयोग की वस्तुएँ एकत्र कर पीड़ितों के बीच बाँटीं। करीब पाँच हजार परिवारों को बरतन, कंबल, पुस्तकें और भवन निर्माण से संबंधित सामग्री दी गई। इसके अलावा समिति ने करीब 22 लाख रुपए एकत्र किए, जो पीड़ितों को पुनर्वास एवं अन्य मदद के लिए दिए गए। इस दंगे की मूल वजह यह थी कि असम की सीमा बांग्लादेश से लगती है और वहाँ से बड़े पैमाने पर अवैध घुसपैठ हो रही थी। घुसपैठियों ने वोट का अधिकार भी पा लिया था। इसके विरोध में आंदोलन किया जा रहा था। एक तरफ ऑल असम स्टूडेंट यूनियन (आसु) और उसके सहयोगी इस आंदोलन का नेतृत्व कर रहे थे, वहीं दूसरी तरफ इस विरोध की परवाह किए बिना इंदिरा गांधी की सरकार ने फरवरी 1983 में असम में विधानसभा चुनाव का ऐलान कर दिया। आसु की तरफ से चुनाव के बहिष्कार की अपील की गई, लेकिन इसके बावजूद घुसपैठियों ने चुनाव में वोट डाले। इससे उपजे आक्रोश से असम में भीषण दंगा फैल गया। उसके बाद जो मारकाट मची, उसमें करीब आठ हजार लोग मारे गए और कई गाँव जला दिए गए। हजारों लोग बेसहारा और बेघर हो गए।

□

सिख विरोधी दंगों के दौरान सैकड़ों सिखों को नरसंहार से बचाया

संघ ने वर्ष 1984 के सिख विरोधी दंगों के दौरान सिखों की रक्षा करने में महत्त्वपूर्ण भूमिका निभाई थी। स्वयंसेवकों ने सिख परिवारों को न केवल सुरक्षा प्रदान की, बल्कि उनके लिए आश्रय स्थल की भी व्यवस्था की। कई जगहों पर संघ ने शिविर और सुरक्षा व्यवस्था स्थापित की, जिससे सिखों को नरसंहार से बचाया जा सका। प्रसिद्ध लेखक खुशवंत सिंह ने सिखों की मदद करने और उनकी रक्षा करने का श्रेय संघ के स्वयंसेवकों को दिया है। पुस्तक 'ए हिस्ट्री ऑफ द सिख' के लेखक खुशवंत सिंह ने लिखा है, "संघ ने दिल्ली और अन्य स्थानों पर इंदिरा गांधी की हत्या से पहले और बाद में हिंदू-सिख एकता बनाए रखने में महत्त्वपूर्ण भूमिका निभाई थी। वहीं कांग्रेस के नेताओं ने भीड़ को उकसाया, जिसका परिणाम यह हुआ और 3000 से अधिक निर्दोष लोगों की हत्या कर दी गई। सिखों के सैकड़ों धार्मिक स्थलों को नष्ट कर दिया गया तथा सिखों की अनगिनत दुकानें, घरों और संपत्ति नष्ट कर दी गई। उन कठिन दिनों के दौरान साहस दिखाने और असहाय सिखों की रक्षा करने के लिए संघ और भाजपा को उचित श्रेय देना चाहिए।" लेखक खुशवंत सिंह भारतीय जनता पार्टी और उसके नेता अटल बिहारी वाजपेयी के उस समय उठाए गए सराहनीय कदम को याद करते हुए कहते हैं, "गरीब टैक्सी ड्राइवरों की मदद के लिए अटल बिहारी वाजपेयी ने कुछ स्थानों पर हस्तक्षेप कर जो मदद की, वह सराहनीय थी।" वर्ष 1984 में सिख विरोधी दंगों के दौरान संघ के स्वयंसेवकों ने सिखों को हर स्तर पर सुरक्षा प्रदान की थी।

□

भोपाल गैस त्रासदी में जान की बाजी लगाकर पीड़ितों तक मदद पहुँचाई

मध्य प्रदेश की राजधानी भोपाल में 02 दिसंबर, 1984 की रात 8:30 बजे से जहरीली गैस का रिसाव होने से कोहराम मच गया। यूनियन कार्बाइड की फैक्ट्री से मिथाइल आइसोसाइनेट गैस लीक होने लगी थी और इससे तीन हजार से अधिक लोगों की मृत्यु हो गई। दुनिया की सबसे बड़ी औद्योगिक आपदाओं में से एक भोपाल गैस त्रासदी में लगभग ढाई लाख लोगों की आँखों की रोशनी और अन्य अंगों को क्षति पहुँची। भोपाल का हमीदिया अस्पताल गैस पीड़ितों से भर गया। रोगी खुले में जहाँ-तहाँ फर्श पर लेटे हुए थे। न पीने का पानी था, न सफाई की व्यवस्था। ऐसे मुश्किल वक्त में संघ के स्वयंसेवक देवदूत बनकर आए और नगर निगम की मदद से पानी और सफाई की व्यवस्था की। बेकार पड़े शौचालयों की मरम्मत कर उन्हें उपयोग लायक बनाया। पूरा शहर जब गैस रिसाव की चपेट में था और चारों तरफ अफरा-तफरी मची थी, तब जान की बाजी लगाकर स्वयंसेवक बिछड़े लोगों को अपने परिजनों से मिलाने में जुटे थे। परिवार की मदद से शवों की पहचान कर उनके दाह-संस्कार का प्रबंध कर रहे थे। अस्पताल जब मरीजों से भर गए तो पीड़ित लोगों के लिए चिकित्सा शिविर लगाए गए। काशी और दरभंगा से डॉक्टरों की टीम तुरंत बुलाई गई। मध्य प्रदेश के तत्कालीन राज्यपाल के.एम. चांडी ने जब शिविरों का निरीक्षण किया तो स्वयंसेवकों की दक्षता देखकर जमकर उनकी सराहना की। स्वयंसेवकों ने प्रभावित इलाकों में घर-घर ब्रेड, दूध और भोजन के पैकेट बाँटे। दिल्ली से विश्व हिंदू परिषद् और दीनदयाल शोध संस्थान ने आँखों की दवाई के साथ ही अन्य दवाइयाँ और मेडिकल वैन भेजीं। गैस पीड़ितों को मुआवजा दिलवाने के लिए स्वयंसेवकों ने प्रभावित क्षेत्रों का सर्वेक्षण कार्य भी किया।

□

संघ की पहल से दूरदर्शन पर प्रसारित हुई 'रामायण'

दूरदर्शन पर 'रामायण' का प्रसारण नहीं हो पा रहा था। इसके प्रसारण के लिए रामानंद सागर करीब दो साल से दूरदर्शन और सूचना प्रसारण मंत्रालय के चक्कर लगा रहे थे। यों 'रामायण' के दूरदर्शन पर प्रसारण की अनुमति तो रामानंद सागर को वर्ष 1985 में ही मिल गई थी, लेकिन इसके प्रसारण को लेकर दूरदर्शन अधिकारियों से लेकर मंत्रालय स्तर तक के अधिकारी अड़चनें डाल रहे थे। इसके बाद राष्ट्रीय स्वयंसेवक संघ ने 'रामायण' के दूरदर्शन पर प्रसारण को लेकर अपनी पहल शुरू की। संघ ने तत्कालीन प्रधानमंत्री राजीव गांधी तक यह बात पहुँचाई कि रामायण के प्रसारण की अनुमति दी जाए। उस समय कांग्रेस नेता एच.के.एल. भगत ने राजीव गांधी को सावधान किया कि प्रसारण की अनुमति देने से भानुमति का पिटारा खुल जाएगा और भाजपा, संघ तथा विश्व हिंदू परिषद् को रामजन्मभूमि आंदोलन चलाने के लिए अनुकूल वातावरण मिल जाएगा। जब भाऊराव देवरस को इन अड़चनों के बारे में जानकारी मिली तो उन्होंने राजीव गांधी को पत्र लिखा, "चिरंजीवी राजीव, रामायण अगर भारत में नहीं देखी जाएगी तो क्या न्यूयॉर्क में देखी जाएगी।" इसके बाद प्रसारण की अनुमति मिल गई और वर्ष 1987 में इसका टेलीकास्ट शुरू हुआ। रामानंद सागर के बेटे प्रेम सागर ने अपनी पुस्तक 'एन एपिक लाइफ : रामानंद सागर फ्रॉम बरसात टू रामायण' में 'रामायण' के प्रसारण में आई अड़चनों के बारे में विस्तार से लिखा है।

□

गुजरात के सूखा पीड़ितों की मदद में जुटे हजारों स्वयंसेवक

गुजरात में वर्ष 1987–88 में भयंकर सूखा पड़ा था। कई इलाकों में बारिश की एक बूँद भी नहीं गिरने से फसलें बरबाद हो गईं और गरीब तबके के लोग दाने-दाने को मोहताज हो गए। ऐसे में संघ के स्वयंसेवकों ने जरूरतमंदों के लिए राहत शिविर लगाए। सूखा प्रभावित लोगों को भोजन, पानी और अन्य जरूरी सामान उपलब्ध कराए। सूखा पीड़ितों के लिए छाछ सबसे सस्ता और पौष्टिक पेय पदार्थ था। इसे देखते हुए स्वयंसेवकों ने 405 छाछ वितरण केंद्र खोले। पाँच हजार से भी अधिक परिवारों को कई महीने तक निःशुल्क अनाज दिया गया। भुखमरी की चपेट में आए लोगों को डॉक्टरों से चेकअप करवाया गया, जिससे किसी भी प्रकार की बीमारी होने पर समय से इलाज शुरू किया जा सके। गेहूँ के आटे, गुड़ और घी से बनने वाली गुजरात की प्रसिद्ध सुखड़ी रोटी अभियान शुरू किया गया, जिससे सूखा प्रभावितों को पौष्टिक खाना मिल सके। वर्ष 1987 में करीब 16,800 स्वयंसेवकों ने दो लाख से भी अधिक परिवारों के घर-घर जाकर 262 टन सुखड़ियाँ एकत्र कीं। इन सुखड़ियों को छह जिलों के लगभग 14,500 परिवारों में समय-समय पर बाँटा गया। इससे 64,800 लोगों को पौष्टिक भोजन मिल सका। इसी तरह 1988 में 100 टन सुखड़ियाँ एकत्र कर परिवारों में बाँटी गईं। स्वयंसेवकों ने अकाल पीड़ितों की मदद के लिए 'दुष्काल पीड़ित सहायता समिति' का भी गठन किया और इसके माध्यम से लोगों तक सहायता पहुँचाई। संघ ने लोगों के साथ ही पशुधन की भी चिंता की। उन्होंने डेढ़ लाख पशुओं को रखने के लिए 123 शिविर खोले। चारे के उत्पादन और सस्ता चारा खरीदने का काम भी किया। महाराष्ट्र के स्वयंसेवकों ने भी चारा पहुँचाने से लेकर हर स्तर पर सहयोग किया।

□

केरल रेल दुर्घटना में स्वयंसेवकों ने पेश की निस्स्वार्थ सेवा की मिसाल

बेंगलुरु से तिरुवनंतपुरम को जाने वाली आइसलैंड एक्सप्रेस 8 जुलाई, 1988 को बड़े हादसे का शिकार हो गई। केरल के अष्टमुडी झील के ऊपर पेरुमना पुल पर ट्रेन पटरी से उतर गई और कई डिब्बे झील में गिर गए। मानसून के कारण झील में उस समय काफी पानी था, जिससे डिब्बे पानी में समा गए। इस हादसे में 105 लोग मारे गए और 200 लोग घायल हो गए थे। स्थानीय मछुआरों के साथ संघ के स्वयंसेवक घटना की जानकारी मिलते ही दुर्घटनास्थल पर पहुँच गए और डूबते लोगों की प्राण रक्षा के भरसक प्रयास किए। तिरुवनंतपुरम की 'सेवा भारती' और क्विलोन शाखा से संबद्ध कुछ प्रमुख संघ कार्यकर्ता सबसे पहले घटनास्थल पर राहत और बचाव कार्य के लिए पहुँच गए, बाद में और भी स्वयंसेवक पहुँचे। राहत और बचाव कार्य में कई दिन लग गए। पानी में डूबी बोगियों में शव फँसे हुए थे और सड़ने लगे थे। दुर्गंध इतनी ज्यादा थी कि पुलिस और राहत दल बड़ी मुश्किल से काम कर पा रहे थे। प्रमुख मलयायम दैनिक 'मातृभूमि' ने दिनांक 12 जुलाई, 1988 को लिखा—'जहाँ अन्य सभी हिचक रहे थे और सबने अपनी नाक पकड़ ली थी, वहीं संघ के स्वयंसेवकों ने जल में डूबे हुए सड़े शवों को निकालने का बीड़ा उठाया। शवों को संघ के सेवा प्रकल्प 'सेवा भारती' की एंबुलेंस से ढोया गया। अस्पतालों में भी स्वयंसेवक पीड़ितों के लिए रक्तदान करने को तत्पर थे। दुर्घटनास्थल के निकट पेरुमना कयाल स्थित जल क्षेत्र स्वयंसेवकों का कर्म क्षेत्र बन गया था। दुर्घटना के दिन ही स्वयंसेवकों ने डिब्बों में फँसे अनेक यात्रियों का उद्धार किया था। इस कार्य में कुछ स्वयंसेवक भी घायल हो गए।"

□

संघ ने अनुच्छेद 370 को लेकर 50 से अधिक बार पारित किए प्रस्ताव

राष्ट्रीय स्वयंसेवक संघ वर्ष 1953 से कश्मीर में अनुच्छेद 370 का मुद्दा उठाता रहा है। संघ ने वर्ष 1953 से लेकर 2010 तक अपनी विभिन्न बैठकों में 50 से अधिक बार इस मुद्दे पर प्रस्ताव पारित किए। जिन बैठकों में ये प्रस्ताव पारित किए गए, उनमें से कुछ उल्लेखनीय हैं—अखिल भारतीय प्रतिनिधि सभा (1953), अखिल भारतीय प्रतिनिधि सभा (1965), अखिल भारतीय प्रतिनिधि सभा (1986), अखिल भारतीय प्रतिनिधि सभा (1990), अखिल भारतीय कार्यकारी मंडल (1990), अखिल भारतीय कार्यकारी मंडल (1991), अखिल भारतीय कार्यकारी मंडल (1993), अखिल भारतीय कार्यकारी मंडल (1995), अखिल भारतीय कार्यकारी मंडल (1996), अखिल भारतीय प्रतिनिधि सभा (1997), अखिल भारतीय कार्यकारी मंडल (2000), अखिल भारतीय प्रतिनिधि सभा (2001), अखिल भारतीय कार्यकारी मंडल (2002), अखिल भारतीय प्रतिनिधि सभा (2004), अखिल भारतीय प्रतिनिधि सभा (2010) और अखिल भारतीय कार्यकारी मंडल (2010)। इन्हीं प्रस्तावों का परिणाम रहा कि समूचे देश में अनुच्छेद 370 के खिलाफ माहौल बना। इसके बाद जब नरेंद्र मोदी की सरकार सत्ता में आई तो उसने 5 अगस्त, 2019 को न केवल अनुच्छेद 370 के प्रावधानों को खत्म किया, बल्कि संसद में एक कानून लाकर जम्मू-कश्मीर और लद्दाख को दो केंद्र शासित प्रदेशों में परिवर्तित कर दिया। इस कदम के साथ ही देश में डॉ. श्यामा प्रसाद मुकर्जी के 'एक देश, एक विधान' का सपना भी साकार हुआ।

□

□

संघ की सेवा भावना के कायल हुए पूर्व पी.एम. चंद्रशेखर

पूर्व प्रधानमंत्री चंद्रशेखर ने कहा था कि देश के लिए कभी कुछ करना पड़े तो राष्ट्रीय स्वयंसेवक संघ पीछे नहीं हटेगा। यह बात उन्होंने वरिष्ठ पत्रकार रामबहादुर राय के साथ एक इंटरव्यू में कही थी। रामबहादुर राय ने एक साक्षात्कार के दौरान चंद्रशेखर से पूछा था कि आपने एक बार कहा था कि राष्ट्रीय स्वयंसेवक संघ से देश उम्मीद कर सकता है। इस पर आपका क्या खयाल है? इस पर चंद्रशेखर ने कहा था, "देश के लिए कभी कुछ करना पड़े तो वे पीछे नहीं हटेंगे। उनमें एक तबका ऐसा भी है, जिनके लिए राजनीति में एम.पी., एम.एल.ए. होना कोई मायने नहीं रखता। जैसे स्वाधीनता की लड़ाई में एक वर्ग ऐसा भी था, जो जिंदगी भर खादी ही बेचता रहा या गौ सेवा में या हरिजन उद्धार में ही लगा रहा। उसी तरह संघ में एक तबका ऐसा है, जो इन सवालों पर हमेशा आवाज बुलंद करता रहेगा। हमारे समाज में जहाँ भी शक्ति है, उसे हम अस्वीकार नहीं कर सकते।" कुछ मुद्दों पर असहमति के बावजूद संघ के स्वदेशी आंदोलन की सराहना करते हुए, उन्होंने आगे कहा, "स्वदेशी भावना को जाग्रत् करने के लिए एक-एक आदमी तक पहुँचने की बात आप नजरअंदाज नहीं कर सकते। और अगर आप इसे नजरअंदाज करते हैं तो सही मायने में देश की शक्ति का उपयोग नहीं कर सकते। जनतंत्र का एक ही आधार है और किसी भी राष्ट्रीय आंदोलन के लिए जरूरी है कि जिससे जितनी शक्ति मिल सके, उतनी ली जाए। हमको मंजिल तक पहुँचना है तो यह जरूरी नहीं है कि हर आदमी मंजिल तक पहुँच जाएगा, लेकिन जो जितने कदम चल सकता है, उसे साथ लेकर चला जाए। संघ की जो क्षमता है, हमें उसका उपयोग करना चाहिए।"

□

स्वयंसेवकों ने आतंकवादियों के हौसले को किया परास्त

पंजाब के मोगा में 25 जून, 1989 को नेहरू पार्क में राष्ट्रीय स्वयंसेवक संघ की शाखा लगी थी। इस नेहरू पार्क को अब शहीदी पार्क के नाम से जाना जाता है। संघ के स्वयंसेवक शाखा के लिए सुबह 6 बजे जुट गए थे। इस दिन शहर की सभी शाखाओं को सामूहिक रूप से लगाया गया था। सुबह 6 बजकर 25 मिनट पर शाखा में संबोधन का कार्यक्रम शुरू हुआ, लेकिन तभी वहाँ खालिस्तानी आतंकवादी आ धमके और कार्यकर्ताओं से भगवा ध्वज उतारने को कहा। स्वयंसेवकों ने भगवा ध्वज उतारने से मना कर दिया। आतंकवादियों के फरमान पर अमल नहीं हुआ तो उन्होंने फायरिंग शुरू कर दी। अंधाधुंध फायरिंग में 25 स्वयंसेवकों की जान चली गई और उसके बाद बम विस्फोट कर दिया गया, जिसमें कुछ पुलिसकर्मियों की मृत्यु हो गई और कई लोग घायल हो गए। पार्क में चारों तरफ लहूलुहान लोग पड़े थे। बाद में घायलों को अस्पताल ले जाया गया। दरअसल वर्ष 1984 के दंगों को देखते हुए हिंदू-सिख एकता में अलगाव पैदा करने के लिए यह हमला किया गया था, लेकिन स्वयंसेवकों ने उनके मंसूबों पर पानी फेर दिया। आतंकवादी हमले के अगले ही दिन उसी स्थान पर स्वयंसेवकों ने शाखा लगाकर एकता की मिसाल कायम की। शाखा में स्वयंसेवकों ने गीत गाया, "कौन कहंदा हिंदू-सिख वक्ख ने, ए भारत माँ दी सज्जी-खब्बी अक्ख ने" अर्थात् कौन कहता है कि हिंदू-सिख अलग-अलग हैं, ये तो भारत माता की बाईं और दाईं आँख के समान हैं। संघ के इस देशभक्ति गीत ने आतंकियों की योजना को विफल कर दिया।

□

उत्तरकाशी भूकंप में दुर्गम इलाकों में भी राहत सामग्री पहुँचाई

उत्तराखंड के उत्तरकाशी में 20 अक्तूबर, 1991 को आए प्रलयंकारी भूकंप में 700 से ज्यादा लोगों की मृत्यु हो गई और 20 हजार से ज्यादा घर तबाह हो गए। इससे लाखों लोग बेघर हो गए और कड़ाके की ठंड ने उनकी मुसीबत और बढ़ा दी। भूकंप आते ही संघ के स्वयंसेवक सक्रिय हो गए और आपदा पीड़ितों के लिए भोजन, कपड़े और दवाइयाँ एकत्र कर प्रभावित क्षेत्रों में पहुँच गए। उन्होंने बिना कोई समय गँवाए 'उत्तराखंड भूकंप पीड़ित सहायता समिति' का गठन किया और इसके माध्यम से सहायता सामग्री जुटाने और फिर उसे प्रभावित लोगों में बाँटने के काम में जुट गए। राहत सामग्री बाँटने के लिए 20 सहायता केंद्र खोले गए। भूकंप पीड़ितों में खाद्य सामग्री वितरित करने के अलावा करीब तीन सप्ताह तक 60 हजार लोगों के लिए पका हुआ भोजन उपलब्ध कराया। राहत कार्य में संघ से जुड़े संगठन जैसे सेवा भारती, विश्व हिंदू परिषद् एवं अन्यों ने भी अपने स्तर पर धन, राहत सामग्री और अन्य जरूरी सामान जुटाए। संघ के प्रयासों से बड़ी राशि के तिरपाल, तंबू, ऊनी कपड़े, कंबल और अन्य सहायता सामग्री करीब 60 ट्रकों में भरकर आपदा प्रभावित क्षेत्रों में भेजी गई। दो चिकित्सा वाहनों में 10 से ज्यादा डॉक्टरों की टीम लगातार आपदा पीड़ितों की सेवा में जुटी रही। यह स्वयंसेवकों के उत्साह का ही कमाल था कि जहाँ प्रशासन भी नहीं पहुँच पाया, उन दुर्गम इलाकों में भी जंगलों और पहाड़ों को पार कर उन्होंने राहत सामग्री पहुँचाई। गरीबों को घर की मरम्मत और पुनर्वास के लिए 1.5 करोड़ रुपए दिए गए और करीब 10 जिलों में 400 घरों का पुनर्निर्माण भी किया गया। इसके अलावा लोगों को रोजगार से जोड़ने के लिए प्रशिक्षण केंद्र खोला गया। इसमें टाइपिंग, सिलाई, कढ़ाई, थैले बनाने, सेब और टमाटर की चटनी के उत्पादन के गुर सिखाए गए।

□

लातूर भूकंप में राहत से लेकर पुनर्वास तक में जुटे स्वयंसेवक

महाराष्ट्र के लातूर और उस्मानाबाद जिलों के कई इलाकों में वर्ष 1993 में भीषण भूकंप आया। विनाशकारी भूकंप की चपेट में आने से 15 हजार से अधिक लोगों की मृत्यु हो गई और लगभग 113 गाँव पूरी तरह से तबाह हो गए। इससे करीब 38 हजार परिवार प्रभावित हुए और लगभग आठ हजार करोड़ रुपए की आर्थिक हानि हुई। इस विपदा के समय भी संघ के स्वयंसेवक सेवा के लिए सबसे पहले पहुँचने वालों में रहे। संघ से जुड़ी महाराष्ट्र की जन कल्याण समिति पीड़ितों को मदद पहुँचाने में सबसे आगे रही। संघ के करीब पाँच हजार कार्यकर्ता कई दिनों तक दिन-रात सेवा के काम में जुटे रहे। ध्वस्त मकानों के नीचे दबे करीब सात हजार लोगों को मलबा हटाकर सुरक्षित निकाला गया। स्वयंसेवकों की मदद से 15 दिनों में करीब आठ हजार घायलों का अस्पताल में उपचार किया गया। लातूर के विवेकानंद अस्पताल में 45 बड़े ऑपरेशन किए गए। विभिन्न गाँवों के पाँच हजार लोगों को करीब 12 दिन तक भोजन कराया गया। राहत एवं बचाव कार्य के साथ स्वयंसेवक पीड़ितों के पुनर्वास में जुट गए। बेघर हो चुके लोगों के लिए अस्थायी आवास का निर्माण किया गया। लगभग 10 हजार परिवारों में बरतन, खाद्यान्न, वस्त्र और दवाइयाँ बाँटी गईं। बढ़ई, धोबी, दर्जी और जूता बनाने वालों को उनके काम के उपकरण दिए गए। भूकंप पीड़ित क्षेत्रों में छात्रों के लिए टीन शेड में अस्थायी विद्यालय शुरू किए गए। ध्वस्त हो चुकी सड़कों का निर्माण किया गया। संघ की प्रेरणा से देश भर से सहायता के लिए 5.12 करोड़ रुपए जुटाए गए। भूकंप पीड़ितों की सहायता के लिए ब्रिटेन के सेवा इंटरनेशनल और हिंदू स्वयंसेवक संघ ने 1.75 करोड़ रुपए भेजे।

□

□

सूरत में प्लेग फैलने से रोकने में महत्त्वपूर्ण भूमिका निभाई

डायमंड सिटी के नाम से प्रसिद्ध गुजरात के सूरत में सितंबर 1994 में प्लेग की महामारी फैलने से वहाँ भगदड़ मच गई। सूरत के वेड रोड आवासीय इलाके में 10 लोगों की मृत्यु हो गई थी। इससे घबराकर और महामारी फैलने की बात सुनकर सूरत से लगभग 25 फीसदी लोग शहर छोड़कर चले गए। शहर छोड़ने वालों में कई डॉक्टर भी शामिल थे। दूसरे राज्यों से आए कामगार अपने गाँवों को लौट गए। इस भगदड़ के समय जो वहाँ डटे रहे, वे थे राष्ट्रीय स्वयंसेवक संघ के स्वयंसेवक। संघ ने शहरवासियों का मनोबल बढ़ाने के लिए कई बसें भरकर अपने कार्यकर्ताओं को वहाँ भेजा। संघ से संबद्ध डॉक्टरों के संगठन नेशनल मेडिकोज ऑर्गेनाइजेशन (एन.एम.ओ.) के कार्यकर्ताओं ने लोगों को बीमारी के प्रति जागरूक किया। एन.एम.ओ. के डॉक्टरों ने लोगों की चिकित्सा-परिचर्या की। एन.एम.ओ. के अलावा भारतीय किसान संघ और विश्व हिंदू परिषद् के कार्यकर्ता भी शहर में पहुँच चुके थे और अपने शिविर लगाकर लोगों को जागरूक करने का काम कर रहे थे। उन्होंने शहर को स्वच्छ रखने के लिए अभियान चलाया। भारतीय जनता पार्टी के सदस्य भी प्लेग को फैलने से रोकने के लिए शहर को स्वच्छ रखने के अभियान में सबसे आगे खड़े दिखे। एक तरफ जहाँ लोग डरकर शहर छोड़ रहे थे, वहीं संघ के कार्यकर्ता लोगों को साफ-सफाई रखकर प्लेग का मुकाबला करने की नसीहत दे रहे थे। उन्होंने घर-घर जाकर लोगों को स्वच्छता के महत्त्व से अवगत कराया और प्लेग को फैलने से रोकने में महत्त्वपूर्ण भूमिका निभाई।

□

बच्चों को आग से बचाते हुए स्वयंसेवक ने दे दी जान

हरियाणा के सिरसा जिले के मंडी डबवाली में 23 दिसंबर, 1995 को डी.ए.वी. पब्लिक स्कूल के वार्षिक उत्सव के दौरान भीषण आग गई। पंडाल में आग लगते ही चारों तरफ चीख-पुकार मच गई। देखते-ही-देखते पंडाल आग के गोले में बदल गया। आग इतनी भयानक थी कि चंद मिनटों के भीतर 442 लोगों की मृत्यु हो गई, जिनमें आधे से अधिक बच्चे थे। इस हादसे में 150 से अधिक लोग गंभीर रूप से झुलस गए। कार्यक्रम में पत्रकार व राष्ट्रीय स्वयंसेवक संघ के तत्कालीन नगर कार्यवाह अशोक वडेरा भी उपस्थित थे। आग लगने के बाद मची भगदड़ और चीख-पुकार के बीच वे मंच पर पहुँच गए और माइक पकड़कर घोषणा कर भीड़ को नियंत्रित करने का प्रयास किया। इसके बाद उन्होंने धधकती आग में जाकर करीब 15 बच्चों के प्राण बचाए। इस प्रयास में उन्हें अहसास ही नहीं हुआ वे खुद आग की चपेट में आ चुके हैं। अंततः उनकी मृत्यु हो गई। उनका शरीर इतना झुलस गया था कि उनके शव को घटना के तीसरे दिन पहचाना जा सका। अशोक वडेरा की स्मृति को सँजोने के लिए वहाँ के लोगों ने मंडी डबवाली में एक सरस्वती विद्या मंदिर की स्थापना की। संघ के तत्कालीन सरकार्यवाह हो.वे. शेषाद्रि ने इस विद्यालय की नींव रखी थी और इसका उद्घाटन विश्व हिंदू परिषद् के तत्कालीन अध्यक्ष अशोक सिंहल ने किया था। उधर इस अग्नि त्रासदी की जानकारी मिलते ही संघ के अन्य स्वयंसेवक घटनास्थल पर पहुँच गए और राहत एवं बचाव कार्य में जुट गए। सबसे पहले उन्होंने बस अड्डे के पास मुख्य मार्ग पर सूचना केंद्र स्थापित किया। सर्वेक्षण टोलियाँ बनाई गईं, जिन्होंने प्रत्येक गली-मोहल्ले जाकर पीड़ितों की सूची बनाई और बाद में यह रिपोर्ट प्रशासन को सौंपी।

□

स्वयंसेवकों ने जान जोखिम में डालकर मलबे से लोगों को निकाला

यह घटना 6 नवंबर, 1996 की है, जब आंध्र प्रदेश के कुछ इलाकों को विनाशकारी चक्रवात ने अपनी चपेट में ले लिया। गोदावरी जिले के तटवर्ती क्षेत्रों में आए इस भयानक चक्रवात ने 150 गाँवों में कहर बरपा दिया और करीब आठ हजार लोग मारे गए। आपदा को देखते हुए राष्ट्रीय स्वयंसेवक संघ के कार्यकर्ता अपनी जान की परवाह किए बिना राहत कार्य में जुट गए। एक घर के मलबे में जब लोगों के दबे होने का अहसास हुआ तो वे जान को जोखिम में डालकर एक ही परिवार के छह व्यक्तियों को बचाने में सफल रहे। इस तरह के और भी अनेक साहस भरे कार्यों को स्वयंसेवकों ने अंजाम दिया। अगले दिन 7 नवंबर को उन्होंने आश्रय स्थल के लिए शिविरों की स्थापना की और अन्न वितरण केंद्र खोले, जिससे बेघर हुए लोग शिविरों में रह सकें। इन शिविरों में करीब पाँच हजार लोगों ने शरण ली और उनके लिए भोजन की भी व्यवस्था की गई। सहायता कार्य के साथ ही संघ के आह्वान पर देश भर से और विदेशों से भी सहायता राशि और राहत सामग्री पहुँची। सहायता कार्य चलाने की जिम्मेदारी 'जन सक्षम समिति' के जिम्मे था। उसने सर्वेक्षण कर सबसे अधिक प्रभावित 70 गाँवों का चयन किया और वहाँ 10 हजार से भी अधिक परिवारों को वित्तीय सहायता, बरतन, साड़ी और धोती उपलब्ध कराईं। पीड़ितों का पुनर्वास भी किया गया। तीन गाँवों में 300 घरों का निर्माण किया गया, जिस पर 1.75 करोड़ रुपए खर्च हुए। पीड़ित परिवार फिर से रोजी-रोजगार से जुड़ सकें, इसके लिए नारियल का पौधा, धान के बीज, मछली पकड़ने के जाल आदि उन्हें दिए गए। □

स्वयंसेवकों को मसजिद में सम्मानित किया गया

हरियाणा का चरखी दादरी जिला 12 नवंबर, 1996 की शाम को एक भीषण हादसे से दहल उठा। इस हादसे में सऊदी अरेबिया एयरलाइंस और कजाकिस्तान एयरलाइंस के विमान आसमान में ही आपस में टकरा गए थे। इस भयानक दुर्घटना की वजह से चरखी दादरी के आसपास चार-पाँच किलोमीटर तक खेतों में जली-अधजली हालत में 349 शव बिखरे पड़े थे। दुर्घटना की जानकारी मिलते ही भिवानी के तत्कालीन जिला संघचालक जीतराम अन्य स्वयंसेवकों के साथ सरकारी अमले से पहले पहुँच गए। बिना समय गँवाए एक घंटे के भीतर उन लोगों ने पेट्रोमैक्स, जनरेटर, पानी सहित अन्य आवश्यक सामग्रियों का इंतजाम कर लिया। स्वयंसेवकों ने बुरी तरह जले हुए शवों को ट्रैक्टर में उठाया। शवों को सड़ने से बचाने के लिए रात को 11 बजे बर्फ के कारखाने चालू करवाए गए। भिवानी, झज्जर एवं रेवाड़ी से बर्फ की सिल्लियाँ मँगवाई गईं। मृतकों में ज्यादातर मुसलिम या ईसाई थे, ऐसे में दफनाने के लिए ताबूत की व्यवस्था की गई। जीतराम के नेतृत्व में स्वयंसेवकों ने 'विमान दुर्घटना पीड़ित सहायता समिति' का गठन किया। इसमें विश्व हिंदू परिषद्, आर्य समाज, विद्यार्थी परिषद् एवं गुरुद्वारा समिति सहित अनेक सामाजिक संस्थाओं के लोगों को शामिल कर युद्ध स्तर पर काम शुरू कर दिया गया। जिन यात्रियों के परिजन नहीं पहुँच सके, उनको दफनाने का कार्य भी स्वयंसेवकों ने ही किया। अंतिम संस्कार में स्थानीय मौलवी व दिल्ली से आए इसलामिया प्रतिनिधिमंडल की मदद ली गई। तीन दिनों तक दिन-रात स्वयंसेवक इस काम में जुटे रहे। उनके सेवा भाव को देखकर चरखी दादरी के मुसलिम समाज ने स्थानीय मसजिद में स्वयंसेवकों को सम्मानित किया।

□

चांपा रेल दुर्घटना में भरोसे का प्रतीक बने स्वयंसेवक

छत्तीसगढ़ के जांजगीर-चांपा में जब भीषण रेल हादसा हुआ, तब उस समय संघ से संबद्ध विद्या भारती की मध्य प्रदेश इकाई द्वारा संचालित सरस्वती शिशु मंदिर के शिक्षकों का सम्मेलन चल रहा था। रेल हादसे की जानकारी मिलते ही सम्मेलन को तत्काल स्थगित कर दिया गया और सभी कार्यकर्ता राहत एवं बचाव कार्य के लिए दुर्घटनास्थल की ओर रवाना हो गए। जांजगीर-चांपा में 14 सितंबर, 1997 को हसदेव पुल पर अहमदाबाद-हावड़ा एक्सप्रेस दुर्घटनाग्रस्त हो गई। इसमें करीब 100 लोगों की मृत्यु हो गई और 300 से अधिक घायल हो गए। हादसे में ट्रेन के पाँच डिब्बे पलट गए और हसदेव नदी में गिर गए। दुर्घटना की जानकारी मिलते ही संघ की निकटवर्ती शाखाओं के स्वयंसेवक पीड़ितों की मदद के लिए पहुँच गए। सबसे पहले वे घायल यात्रियों को डिब्बे से सुरक्षित निकालने में जुट गए। घायलों में जिन्हें मामूली चोटें आई थीं, उनके लिए स्थानीय सरस्वती शिशु मंदिर में प्राथमिक चिकित्सा केंद्र बनाया गया था। जिन्हें ज्यादा गंभीर चोटें आई थीं, उन्हें बिलासपुर के रेलवे अस्पताल भेजा गया। स्वयंसेवकों ने घायलों के लिए ब्रेड, दूध, चाय और दवाइयों का प्रबंध किया। जो यात्री सकुशल थे, उनके ठहरने की व्यवस्था स्थानीय शिशु मंदिर में की गई। स्वयंसेवकों ने मृतकों और घायलों के बारे में परिजनों तक जानकारी पहुँचाई, जिससे रोते-बिलखते सगे-संबंधियों को राहत मिली। करीब 80 स्वयंसेवकों ने दिन-रात बिलासपुर जिला अस्पताल और रेलवे अस्पताल में पीड़ितों की सेवा की। 25 से अधिक स्वयंसेवकों ने रक्तदान कर कई लोगों की जान बचाई।

□

कांग्रेसी मंत्री का जब संघ से हुआ साक्षात्कार

आंध्र प्रदेश के विशाखापट्टनम में 21 सितंबर, 1997 को हिंदुस्तान पेट्रोलियम कॉरपोरेशन लिमिटेड (एच.पी.सी.एल.) की तेल रिफाइनरी में आग लगने से 56 व्यक्तियों की मृत्यु हो गई। आग इतनी भीषण थी कि ध्वस्त ढाँचे के मलबे से शवों को निकालने के लिए कोई आगे नहीं आ रहा था। रिफाइनरी में आग लगने से हुए विस्फोट ने पूरे शहर को हिलाकर रख दिया, लेकिन राष्ट्रीय स्वयंसेवक संघ के 200 स्वयंसेवक सहायता के लिए फौलादी जज्बा लिये प्लांट के मुख्य द्वार पर पहुँच गए। वे अंदर जाना चाहते थे, लेकिन केंद्रीय औद्योगिक सुरक्षा बल (सी.आई.एस.एफ.) के जवानों ने उन्हें अंदर जाने की अनुमति नहीं दी। हालात बिगड़ते देख स्वयंसेवक चार दलों में बँट गए और इनमें से एक दल सी.आई.एस.एफ. जवानों की नजरों से बचकर परिसर के अंदर प्रवेश कर गया। दूसरा दल मुख्य द्वार पर, तीसरा दल एंबुलेंस के साथ और चौथा दल किंग जॉर्ज अस्पताल में था। शवों को निकालने के लिए नगर निगम के श्रमिक बुलाए गए, लेकिन दुर्घटनास्थल का दृश्य देखने के बाद उन्होंने हाथ खड़े कर दिए। आखिरकार स्वयंसेवकों ने शवों को निकालने का काम शुरू किया। पास के नर्सिंग होम से लाए स्ट्रेचर पर रखकर शवों को एंबुलेंस तक लाया गया और फिर अस्पताल पहुँचाया गया। राज्य सरकार के तत्कालीन कांग्रेसी मंत्री के. विद्याधर राव जब सहायता कार्य का निरीक्षण करने आए तो स्वयंसेवकों की सेवा-भावना देखकर भाव-विभोर हो गए। कार से नीचे उतरकर उनके पास आए और कहा, "अब मैं समझ पाया हूँ कि राष्ट्रीय स्वयंसेवक संघ वास्तव में क्या है। मेरे लिए यह एक नए सत्य का साक्षात्कार है।" उन्होंने हाथ जोड़कर प्रत्येक स्वयंसेवक का अभिनंदन किया।

□

कारगिल युद्ध में 'जय कारगिल-जय भारत कोष' का गठन

वर्ष 1999 में पाकिस्तानी सैनिकों और घुसपैठियों ने जम्मू-कश्मीर के कारगिल सेक्टर में गुपचुप तरीके से कब्जा कर लिया। जैसे ही इसकी जानकारी तत्कालीन प्रधानमंत्री अटल बिहारी वाजपेयी को हुई, उन्होंने तत्काल इसके खिलाफ काररवाई का फैसला किया। 3 मई, 1999 को भारतीय सेना ने पाकिस्तानी सैनिकों और आतंकवादियों को बाहर निकालने के लिए 'ऑपरेशन विजय' शुरू किया। इस कठिन समय में संघ के स्वयंसेवकों ने सरकार और सेना का साथ देते हुए तुरंत सहयोग करने और सहायता पहुँचाने का निर्णय लिया। इस युद्ध के दौरान कई सैनिक और नागरिक पाकिस्तान की ओर से हो रही गोलीबारी में घायल हो गए। संघ के स्वयंसेवकों ने निस्स्वार्थ भाव से उनकी सेवा की और उपचार में मदद दी। घायलों को अस्पताल पहुँचाने में स्वयंसेवकों ने तत्परता से सेना का सहयोग किया। भारतीय वीरों के सम्मान में संघ ने 'जय कारगिल-जय भारत कोष' का गठन किया। स्वयंसेवकों की देशभक्ति व लगन से प्रसन्न होकर मेजर विक्रम जोशी सहित कई सैन्य अधिकारियों ने कहा—"हम सैनिकों को वेतन मिलता है, मृत्यु के बाद परिवार के पालन-पोषण की सुविधाएँ हैं, इसलिए देश की रक्षा करते हैं। परंतु देश में एक ऐसी भी संस्था है (संघ की ओर संकेत करते हुए) जिनके लोगों को कोई सुविधा नहीं, वेतन नहीं, केवल शुद्ध देशभक्ति की भावना से वे जूझते हैं, मरते हैं।" उल्लेखनीय है कि कारगिल युद्ध 2 महीने और 23 दिन तक चला और आखिरकार 26 जुलाई, 1999 को भारत की ऐतिहासिक विजय के साथ समाप्त हुआ।

□

संघ के प्रयासों से अमानवीय कुप्रथा का हुआ अंत

मध्य प्रदेश के भिंड जिले में स्वाधीनता के इतने वर्षों बाद भी एक अमानवीय कुप्रथा गुर्जर और यादव समाज में बदस्तूर जारी थी। यहाँ जन्म लेते ही लड़कियों को मार दिया जाता था। भिंड जिले की मेहगाँव और गोहद तहसील के अधिकांश गुर्जर समाज और यादव (घोसी) समाज वाले गाँवों में यह कुप्रथा थी। राष्ट्रीय स्वयंसेवक संघ को जब इस कुप्रथा की जानकारी हुई तो बुजुर्गों से बात कर कारण तलाशा गया। बुजुर्गों का कहना था कि मुगल शासनकाल में जवान बच्चियों का अपहरण और बलात्कार आम बात थी। आए दिन होने वाली इन घटनाओं से परेशान आकर समाज ने तय किया कि बच्चियों को जवान ही नहीं होने देंगे और जन्म होते ही मार देंगे। कहते हैं कि किसी भी सामाजिक बुराई को समाप्त करने के लिए शिक्षा सबसे बड़ा हथियार होती है। संघ ने इसी मार्ग पर चलते हुए वर्ष 2000 में गितोर गाँव में विद्या भारती द्वारा सरस्वती शिशु मंदिर की शुरुआत की। संघ ने इस कुप्रथा को खत्म करने के लिए सरस्वती शिशु मंदिर के जरिए लोगों में जागरूकता लानी शुरू की। विद्यालय के द्वारा वार्षिकोत्सव, मातृ सम्मेलन और अभिभावक सम्मेलन जैसे कई अन्य कार्यक्रम किए जाने लगे और उनके जरिए चेतना जगाने का काम किया गया। समाज के लोग जाग्रत् होने लगे और धीरे-धीरे यह कुप्रथा समाप्त होने लगी। इस इलाके के गुर्जर और यादव समाज में अब लड़कियों की संख्या लगातार बढ़ रही है। अब गितोर जैसे गाँवों में गलियों एवं सड़कों पर बच्चियाँ खेलती दिख जाती हैं। □

पटना विमान हादसे के बाद जुट पड़े स्वयंसेवक

एलायंस एयर के एक विमान ने 17 जुलाई, 2000 को कोलकाता से नई दिल्ली के लिए उड़ान भरी। इसे बिहार की राजधानी पटना होते हुए जाना था। पटना एयरपोर्ट पर लैंडिंग के पहले विमान गर्दनीबाग इलाके में दुर्घटनाग्रस्त हो गया। दुर्घटना की जानकारी मिलते ही संघ के 150 स्वयंसेवक तुरंत घटनास्थल पर पहुँच गए और राहत एवं बचाव कार्य में जुट गए। इन स्वयंसेवकों का नेतृत्व पटना महानगर प्रचारक नरेन और बाल्मीकि नगर कार्यवाह संजीव कर रहे थे। आग और धुएँ ने बचाव कार्य को मुश्किल बना दिया था। इन मुश्किलों के बीच स्वयंसेवक मलबे से शवों को निकालने में जुट गए। वे प्रशासन को हर स्तर पर मदद कर रहे थे। कुछ स्वयंसेवक आसपास जुटी भीड़ के नियंत्रण में जुटे थे तो कुछ स्वयंसेवकों ने ट्रैफिक के सुचारू संचालन में पुलिस की मदद की। स्वयंसेवकों ने मलबे से शवों को निकालने के बाद उन्हें एंबुलेंस के जरिए अस्पताल पहुँचाया। कुछ स्वयंसेवक पहले ही वहाँ पहुँचकर अस्पताल प्रशासन के साथ शवों को रखने की समुचित व्यवस्था में जुटे थे। स्वयंसेवकों ने दुर्घटना में मृत व्यक्तियों की आत्मा की शांति के लिए प्रार्थना भी की। उल्लेखनीय है कि इस दुर्घटना में विमान में सवार 55 यात्रियों व चालक दल के 6 सदस्यों समेत गर्दनीबाग स्थित सरकारी आवास में रहने वाले 5 लोगों की जान चली गई थी।

□

हिमाचल बाढ़ में स्वयंसेवकों ने निभाई बड़ी भूमिका

हिमाचल प्रदेश के चार जिलों शिमला, किन्नौर, मंडी और कुल्लू में 31 जुलाई, 2000 की रात भीषण बाढ़ आ गई। ग्लेशियरों के पिघलने से सतलुज नदी का जलस्तर बढ़ गया था, जिससे नदी के किनारे वाले इलाकों में भारी तबाही मची। इस त्रासदी में 133 लोगों की जानें गईं, 1673 पशु बह गए और 5383 घर बाढ़ की चपेट में आकर ध्वस्त हो गए। बाढ़ से खेतों में फसलें बरबाद हो गईं और कई किलोमीटर सड़कें ध्वस्त हो गईं। ऐसी विनाशलीला के समय संघ के स्वयंसेवक उनके लिए उम्मीद की किरण बनकर आए। कार्यकर्ता सैकड़ों की संख्या में कंबल, तिरपाल, पतीले, कटोरियाँ, गिलास, प्रेशर कुकर और दवाइयाँ लेकर पहुँचे। भोजन सामग्री से भरे तीन ट्रक पहुँचे, जिनमें चावल, दाल, नमक, मसाले आदि शामिल थे। सेवाकार्यों में सेवा भारती, भारतीय किसान संघ, विश्व हिंदू परिषद् और राष्ट्र सेविका समिति ने बढ़-चढ़कर सहयोग किया। शिमला स्थित डॉ. हेडगेवार स्मारक समिति ने खाद्य सामग्री से भरे दो ट्रक भेजे, जिनमें आटा, दाल, चीनी, नमक, तेल, कंबल, प्रेशर कुकर आदि थे। स्वयंसेवकों ने इन सामग्रियों को प्रत्येक परिवारों में वितरित किया। इसके साथ ही प्रत्येक परिवार को दो-दो तिरपाल भी दिए गए। स्वयंसेवकों ने लोगों को मकान बनाने में भी सहयोग किया।

□

प्रधानमंत्री बनने के बाद जब वाजपेयी संघ मुख्यालय पहुँचे

27 अगस्त, 2000 को अटल बिहारी वाजपेयी नागपुर में राष्ट्रीय स्वयंसेवक संघ के मुख्यालय पहुँचे थे। यह पहला अवसर था जब कोई व्यक्ति प्रधानमंत्री पद पर रहते हुए संघ मुख्यालय पहुँचा। वाजपेयी वहाँ डॉ. हेडगेवार स्मृति मंदिर गए और संघ के संस्थापकों को श्रद्धांजलि अर्पित की। भारत रत्न अटल बिहारी वाजपेयी इसके बाद वर्ष 2004 और फिर 2007 में भी संघ मुख्यालय पहुँचे। वाजपेयी संघ के प्रचारक नारायणराव तरटे के प्रति काफी सम्मान का भाव रखते थे। वे 2004 में उनके स्वास्थ्य की जानकारी लेने के लिए संघ मुख्यालय गए थे। इसके बाद वे 2007 में दूसरे संघ प्रमुख श्रीगुरुजी के शताब्दी वर्ष के समापन समारोह में गए थे। उस दौरान उन्होंने तत्कालीन संघ प्रमुख कुप्.सी. सुदर्शन के साथ मंच साझा किया और अपने भाषण के बाद एक कविता सुनाई। वाजपेयी ने एक बार कहा था, "राष्ट्रीय स्वयंसेवक संघ से मेरे लंबे जुड़ाव का सीधा सा कारण यह है कि मुझे संघ पसंद है। मुझे इसकी विचारधारा पसंद है और सबसे ऊपर मैं लोगों के प्रति संघ के दृष्टिकोण को पसंद करता हूँ, एक-दूसरे के प्रति जो सम्मान संघ में मिलता है, वह अन्यत्र दुर्लभ है। संघ हमारा परिवार है।" वाजपेयी वर्ष 1939 में संघ से जुड़े और 1947 में उन्होंने संघ के पूर्णकालिक प्रचारक के रूप में काम करना शुरू किया। जब वे दसवीं कक्षा में थे, तब उन्होंने 'हिंदू तन-मन, हिंदू जीवन' कविता लिखी थी। वे 'राष्ट्रधर्म' और 'पाञ्चजन्य' के संस्थापक संपादकों में रहे।

□

इक्कीसवीं सदी और संघ

गुजरात के भुज में आए भूकंप के दौरान विश्व हिंदू परिषद् के सेवाकार्य।

गुजरात के भुज में आए भूकंप के दौरान संघ के सेवाकार्य।

तत्कालीन सरसंघचालक सुदर्शनजी।

वर्ष 2011 में सरसंघचालक मोहन भागवत और भारत रत्न लता मंगेशकर की मुलाकात की तसवीर।

बिहार के छपरा जिले में ट्रेन दुर्घटना के समय सेवाकार्य में जुटे स्वयंसेवक।

जम्मू-कश्मीर में 2014 में आए बाढ़ के दौरान सेवाकार्य में जुटे स्वयंसेवक।

वर्ष 2020 में कोरोनाकाल में सेवा में जुटे स्वयंसेवक।

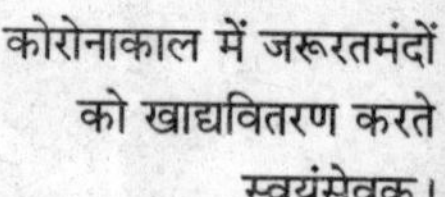

कोरोनाकाल में जरूरतमंदों को खाद्यवितरण करते स्वयंसेवक।

कोरोनाकाल में घर-घर जाकर स्वास्थ्य जाँच करते स्वयंसेवक।

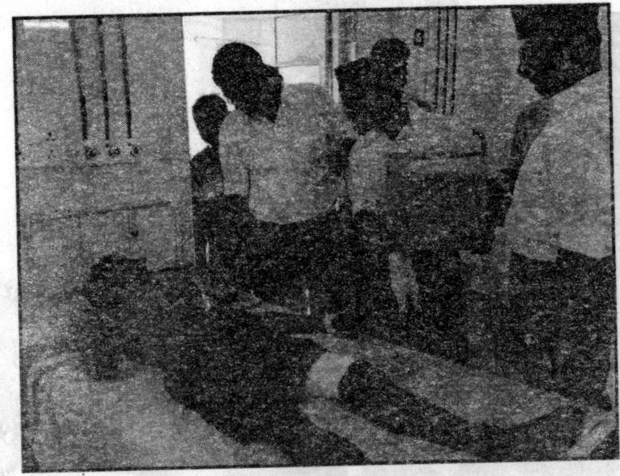

वर्ष 2023 में ओडिशा के बालासोर में रेल दुर्घटना पीड़ितों को सहायता पहुँचाते स्वयंसेवक।

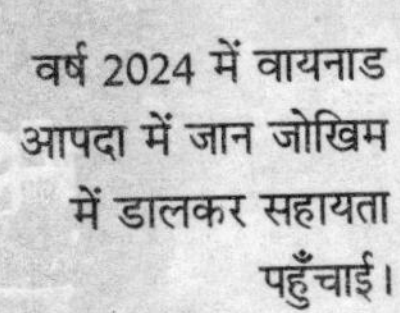

वर्ष 2024 में वायनाड आपदा में जान जोखिम में डालकर सहायता पहुँचाई।

उत्तराखंड में 2025 में बादल फटने से हुई तबाही के दौरान जरूरतमंदों को राहत सामग्री पहुँचाते स्वयंसेवक।

प्रधानमंत्री नरेंद्र मोदी नागपुर में डॉ. हेडगेवार को श्रद्धांजलि अर्पित करते हुए।

नागपुर में डॉ. हेडगेवार स्मारक में पी.एम. मोदी, मोहन भागवत और अन्य।

संघ पर डाक टिकट और स्मारक सिक्का जारी करते प्रधानमंत्री नरेंद्र मोदी। साथ में सरकार्यवाह दत्तात्रेय होसबाले एवं अन्य।

भुज भूकंप राहत कार्य में नरेंद्र मोदी की अहम भूमिका

गुजरात के कच्छ जिले के भुज में 26 जनवरी, 2001 को भीषण भूकंप आया, जिससे पूरा इलाका दहल उठा। देश में जब ज्यादातर लोग टी.वी. पर गणतंत्र दिवस की झाँकियाँ देख रहे थे, गुजरात के 21 जिले भूकंप से हिल गए थे। भुज में हजारों लोगों की जान चली गई और पूरा इलाका एक तरह से श्मशान में बदल गया। ऐसे मुश्किल समय में भी संघ के स्वयंसेवक जोश और उत्साह दिखाते हुए सहायता के लिए सबसे पहले पहुँचे। उस समय नरेंद्र मोदी भी एक स्वयंसेवक के रूप में भुज पहुँचे और राहत कार्य में उनकी अहम भूमिका रही। नरेंद्र मोदी ने भूकंप पीड़ितों की राहत, पुनर्वास और पुनर्निर्माण में मदद की थी। इस आपदा के समय विद्यार्थी परिषद् के कार्यकर्ता भी लोगों की सहायता में जुट गए। बेघर हुए लोगों के लिए शिविर की व्यवस्था की गई। उनके लिए चाय और नाश्ते आदि का प्रबंध किया गया। 10वीं और 12वीं की परीक्षा देने वाले विद्यार्थियों के रहने, भोजन और पढ़ाई करने के लिए नोटबुक और पेन की समुचित व्यवस्था की गई। कई कार्यकर्ता अपने कर्तव्य पथ पर डटकर शवों के अंतिम संस्कार की व्यवस्था में जुटे। भूकंप के कुछ महीने बाद जब नरेंद्र मोदी राज्य के मुख्यमंत्री बने तो स्वयंसेवक के रूप में उनका अनुभव काम आया और फिर भुज का कायाकल्प ही हो गया। यही नहीं, प्रधानमंत्री बनने के बाद नरेंद्र मोदी ने 28 अगस्त, 2022 को भूकंप पीड़ितों की स्मृति में भुज में 'स्मृति वन स्मारक' का उद्घाटन किया। गुजरात के मुख्यमंत्री के रूप में उन्होंने इसे बनाने का फैसला किया था। उन्होंने भूकंप से जान गँवाने वाले प्रत्येक व्यक्ति की स्मृति में इस स्मारक परिसर में एक पेड़ लगाने का सुझाव दिया था और इस तरह वहाँ 13,805 पेड़ भी लगाए गए।

□

पेड़ के नीचे शुरू हुए एकल विद्यालय ने गाँववालों का दिल जीता

संघ से जुड़ी संस्था विद्या भारती गरीबों को शिक्षित करने में किस प्रकार का योगदान दे रही है, इसे पश्चिम बंगाल के उदाहरण से समझा जा सकता है। पश्चिम बंगाल के मालदा जिले के अनुसूचित जनजातीय बहुल ब्लॉक हबीबपुर में वर्ष 2002 में 85 एकल विद्यालय शुरू किए। इससे वहाँ साक्षरता के प्रतिशत में काफी वृद्धि हुई। इसी ब्लॉक में एक गाँव है भालुककोना। वहाँ वर्ष 2002 में एक एकल विद्यालय खोला गया। एक स्वयंसेवक ने यहाँ आचार्य के रूप में पढ़ाना शुरू किया। उस समय विद्यालय के पास कोई साधन नहीं था। एक पेड़ के नीचे विद्यालय चलता था, जिसमें 40 विद्यार्थी पढ़ते थे। दो वर्ष में ही वहाँ के छात्र–छात्राओं के संस्कार देखकर गाँववाले इतने प्रभावित हुए कि उन्होंने 'ग्राम समिति' के सहयोग से विद्यालय के लिए मिट्टी का एक भवन बना दिया। भवन में 200 विद्यार्थियों के बैठने और पढ़ने की सुविधा हो गई। स्वयंसेवक शिक्षक की मेहनत और लगन से पढ़ाई के अच्छे परिणाम आते रहे, छात्रों की संख्या बढ़ती गई और विद्यालय में शिक्षक भी बढ़ते गए। उच्च कक्षाओं में प्रवेश के लिए जो परीक्षा ली जाती थी, उनमें विद्यालय के छात्रों का प्रदर्शन अच्छा रहता था। इससे भालुककोना के विद्यालय की चर्चा दूसरे गाँवों में भी होने लगी। विद्यालय का विस्तार होता गया और यहाँ 500 विद्यार्थी पढ़ने लगे। 500 बच्चों को पढ़ाने के लिए 14 शिक्षक रखे गए। शुरू में कम्युनिस्टों ने इन एकल विद्यालयों का कड़ा विरोध किया, इनके खिलाफ गलत प्रचार किया गया और यहाँ तक कि धमकियाँ भी दी गईं, लेकिन संघ अपने काम में जुटा रहा। निरंतर प्रयास से प्रदेश में एकल विद्यालयों की संख्या दो हजार से अधिक हो गई। इन विद्यालयों के माध्यम से जनजातीय एवं नक्सल प्रभावित इलाकों में शिक्षा क्रांति की अलख जगाई जा रही है।

☐

चेन्नई सुनामी में विद्यार्थी परिषद् ने पेश किया अनुपम उदाहरण

चेन्नई के समुद्र तटों पर 26 दिसंबर, 2004 को सुनामी ने तबाही मचाकर हजारों लोगों की हँसती-खेलती जिंदगी तबाह कर दी। लहरें इतनी रफ्तार से आईं कि तमिलनाडु के पूरे तटीय क्षेत्र में इसका असर महसूस किया गया। हजारों घर, वाहन, पेड़ तहस-नहस हो गए। इस आपदा में हजारों लोगों को अपनी जान गँवानी पड़ी। ऐसे विकट समय में सुनामी पीड़ितों तक सहायता पहुँचाने में राष्ट्रीय स्वयंसेवक संघ के कार्यकर्ता तत्काल जुट गए। स्वयंसेवकों ने सबसे पहले घायलों को अस्पताल पहुँचाने, शवों को उठाने और लापता लोगों की खोज में स्थानीय लोगों की मदद की। चेन्नई, नागपट्टिनम, कडलूर, पांडिचेरी जैसे तटीय इलाकों में राहत कैंप स्थापित किए। इस मदद कार्य में अखिल भारतीय विद्यार्थी परिषद् के कार्यकर्ता सबसे आगे थे। आपदा के आते ही चेन्नई और आसपास के विद्यार्थी परिषद् के कार्यकर्ता सहायता कार्य में जुट गए। उन्होंने तत्काल भोजन के हजारों पैकेट, पानी और कपड़े जुटाए और इन्हें सुनामी प्रभावितों में वितरित किया। नागपट्टिनम में भारी तबाही हुई थी। इसे देखते हुए चार जिलों के करीब 200 कार्यकर्ता नागपट्टिनम पहुँच गए। वहाँ पहले से काम कर रही संघ की संस्था सेवा भारती को राहत सामग्री बाँटने में सहयोग किया। सुनामी प्रभावित इलाकों में लॉरी में भरकर ब्रेड, बिस्कुट एवं अन्य खाद्य सामग्री के साथ दवाइयाँ पहुँचाई गईं। अपने त्वरित राहत कार्य से विद्यार्थी परिषद् के कार्यकर्ताओं ने सुनामी पीड़ितों पर अमिट छाप छोड़ी और देश के सामने अनुपम उदाहरण पेश किया। सुनामी के कारण समुद्र की 20-30 फीट ऊँची लहरों में न जाने कितने लोग बहकर अपनों से सदा के लिए दूर चले गए। इस हादसे में करीब 10 हजार लोगों की मृत्यु हो गई और सैकड़ों लापता हो गए।

□

लोगों की सेवा में जीवन समर्पित किया किशोर स्वयंसेवक ने

1 अगस्त, 2005 को मध्य प्रदेश के इंदौर में भारी बारिश के कारण मारुति नगर बस्ती में पानी भर गया। घरों से बरतन, कपड़े और अन्य सामानों के साथ ही छोटे-छोटे बच्चे भी पानी में बहने लगे। इसी बस्ती में रहने वाले 17 साल के किशोर मनोज चौहान ने अपने दो दोस्तों, बबन पांडे और सुरेश बाथा के साथ मिलकर लोगों की जान बचाने का काम शुरू कर दिया। वे खाली टीन और ट्यूब की मदद से लोगों को सुरक्षित स्थानों तक पहुँचा रहे थे। मनोज खुद बच्चों को गोद में लेकर सुरक्षित जगहों पर पहुँचा रहा था। लगातार पानी में रहने से मनोज की तबियत बिगड़ने लगी। उसके फेफड़ों में पानी चला गया और शरीर कमजोर हो गया। यह सब देखकर संघ के नगर संपर्क प्रमुख डॉ. आनंद प्रकाश मिश्रा ने उसे आराम करने की सलाह दी, लेकिन मनोज नहीं रुका। उसे शाखा में गाया जाने वाला गीत याद आ रहा था—'सेवा है यज्ञ कुंड, समिधा सम हम जलें।' मनोज सुबह 4 बजे से रात 12 बजे तक लगातार पीड़ितों की मदद करता रहा। उसने 18 लोगों की जान बचाई। अगले दिन वह बस्ती में जरूरतमंदों की सूची बनाकर उन्हें राशन और जरूरी सामान दिलाने में जुट गया। लेकिन इस सेवा भाव में वह बीमार हो गया और निमोनिया के कारण 7 अगस्त, 2005 को अस्पताल में उसकी मृत्यु हो गई। गणतंत्र दिवस पर उसे मरणोपरांत अद्वितीय वीरता पुरस्कार से सम्मानित किया गया। मनोज की कहानी आज भी युवाओं को निस्स्वार्थ सेवा और साहस का संदेश देती है।

□

लद्दाख की आपदा में देवदूत बने स्वयंसेवक

6 अगस्त, 2010 की रात लेह–लद्दाख में सबकुछ शांत था। लोग अपने घरों में चैन की नींद सो रहे थे, लेकिन आधी रात को कुदरत का कहर टूटा—बादल फटा और पूरे इलाके में भयंकर बाढ़ आ गई। पानी के साथ बड़े–बड़े पत्थर बहते चले आए। खेत, सड़कें और घर सब बरबाद हो गए। इस भयावह आपदा में ढाई सौ से ज्यादा लोगों की जान चली गई और करीब 9 हजार लोग सीधे तौर पर प्रभावित हुए। उसी समय पास ही के चोगलामसर में राष्ट्रीय स्वयंसेवक संघ का एक शिक्षण वर्ग चल रहा था। जैसे ही वहाँ मौजूद स्वयंसेवकों को खबर मिली, वे मदद के लिए तुरंत निकल पड़े। जम्मू–कश्मीर सेवा भारती भी सक्रिय हुई। सेवा भारती के क्षेत्र संगठन मंत्री जयदेव सिंह के अनुसार, शिक्षा वर्ग को वहीं समाप्त कर सभी स्वयंसेवक राहत कार्य में जुट गए। जान जोखिम में डालकर 27 लोगों की जान बचाई और जरूरतमंदों को तुरंत खाना, पानी, दवाइयाँ, बिस्तर और मच्छरदानियाँ उपलब्ध कराईं। केवल आपदा राहत ही नहीं, सेवा भारती ने पुनर्वास और रोजगार पर भी ध्यान दिया। नाइयों को कटिंग कुरसियाँ, दर्जियों को सिलाई मशीनें, ढाबा चलाने वालों को बरतन और बढ़ई को औजार दिए गए। लद्दाख में महिलाएँ रैनटैक मशीनों से आटा व सत्तू पीसती थीं, लेकिन बाढ़ में 250 मशीनें बह गईं। सेवा भारती ने 90 नई मशीनें वितरित कीं। चोगलामसर में 240 घर पूरी तरह बह गए थे। सेवा भारती ने 100 नए घर बनवाकर लोगों को बसाने में मदद की। इसके साथ ही सरकारी स्कूलों को पुस्तकें, यूनिफॉर्म और पानी की टंकी भी दी गईं। जहाँ सरकार की मदद पहुँचने में समय लगा, वहीं स्वयंसेवक बिना किसी स्वार्थ के देवदूत की तरह सामने आए।

□ □

स्वयंसेवक सरपंच ने गाँव की तसवीर ही बदल दी

मध्य प्रदेश के बुरहानपुर जिले का हरदा गाँव स्वाधीनता के छह दशक बाद भी विकास की बाट जोह रहा था। विकास के नाम पर यहाँ कुछ खास नहीं हुआ था। जनजातीय बहुल हरदा गाँव के लोग इस बात से निराश थे कि उनका गाँव तमाम समस्याएँ झेल रहा है और सुविधाओं से वंचित है। काफी विचार के बाद ग्रामीणों ने सोचा कि क्यों न इस बार गाँव का नेतृत्व संघ के किसी स्वयंसेवक को दी जाए। इसके बाद गाँव के बुजुर्गों की बैठक हुई और वर्ष 2010-11 में गाँववालों ने स्वयंसेवक सुभाष सिंह को सरपंच चुन लिया। सरपंच बनते ही सुभाष ने संघ की जिला टोली से मार्गदर्शन लेकर कई मुद्दों पर कार्य शुरू कर दिया। सफाई-स्वच्छता के साथ पर्यावरण संरक्षण और वृक्षों को काटने पर रोक लगाई गई। ऊर्जा बचत के लिए सी.एफ.एल. बल्ब के उपयोग से लेकर पॉलिथिन मुक्त ग्राम बनाने का संकल्प लिया गया। जन्मदिन और मृत्यु होने पर फलदार वृक्ष लगाने, जल संरक्षण, महापुरुषों पर समय-समय पर संगोष्ठी, छात्रों एवं किसानों को सम्मानित कर प्रोत्साहित किया गया और नशामुक्ति के लिए अभियान चलाकर गाँव को पूर्ण नशामुक्त किया। इन उपायों से कुछ ही वर्षों में गाँव का दृश्य ही बदल गया। मध्य प्रदेश सरकार ने इसे नशामुक्त ग्राम घोषित किया।

□

गौ-वंश संरक्षण के लिए राष्ट्रपति को सौंपे करीब 10 करोड़ हस्ताक्षर

राष्ट्रीय स्वयंसेवक संघ शुरुआत से ही गौ-वंश संरक्षण के लिए काम करता आया है। संघ ने वर्ष 1952 में गौ-हत्या बंदी की माँग के समर्थन में राष्ट्रपति को करीब दो करोड़ हस्ताक्षर सौंपे थे। सबसे महत्त्वपूर्ण बात यह है कि गौरक्षा अभियान के अंतर्गत चार सप्ताह के भीतर संघ के स्वयंसेवकों ने 94,459 गाँवों और कस्बों से 1,79,89,332 लोगों से हस्ताक्षर जुटा लिये थे। इसके बाद संघ के सरसंघचालक श्रीगुरुजी ने 8 दिसंबर, 1952 को उन हस्ताक्षरों को तत्कालीन राष्ट्रपति डॉ. राजेंद्र प्रसाद को सौंपा था। इसी कड़ी में 7 नवंबर, 1966 का वह समय भी आया जब साधु-संतों ने आंदोलन तेज करते हुए संसद का घेराव किया, परंतु इंदिरा गांधी की सरकार ने इस आंदोलन को बुरी तरह से कुचल दिया। गौरक्षा के लिए सतत प्रयत्नशील संघ ने एक बार फिर विभिन्न संगठनों के साथ मिलकर 'विश्व मंगल गौ ग्राम यात्रा' की शुरुआत 30 सितंबर, 2009 को कुरुक्षेत्र से की। इस अभियान का समापन 17 जनवरी, 2010 को नागपुर में हुआ। यात्रा के दौरान गौ-हत्या पर प्रतिबंध लगाने की माँग वाली याचिका पर आठ करोड़ पैंतीस लाख लोगों ने हस्ताक्षर किए। इसके बाद 18 फरवरी, 2011 को आठ करोड़ पैंतीस लाख लोगों के हस्ताक्षर युक्त ज्ञापन तत्कालीन राष्ट्रपति प्रतिभा पाटिल को सौंपा गया था। यह यात्रा 108 दिन चली और देश के 4 लाख 11 हजार, 737 गाँवों तक पहुँची। इस विश्व मंगल गौ ग्राम यात्रा का उद्‍देश्य गौ-वंश संरक्षण के लिए एक केंद्रीय कानून की माँग करना था। इस यात्रा में स्वयंसेवकों की भूमिका केवल हस्ताक्षर जुटाने तक सीमित नहीं थी। उन्होंने लोगों को गौ-संरक्षण के महत्त्व के बारे में जागरूक किया, यात्रा के लिए समर्थन जुटाया और विभिन्न कार्यक्रमों का आयोजन किया।

□

'अहसास यात्रा' ने कश्मीरी छात्रों के दृष्टिकोण बदल दिए

कश्मीर में सेवा भारती द्वारा संचालित कंप्यूटर केंद्र का नाम मदीना है। यहाँ शिक्षा पाने वाले अधिकांश कॉलेज के छात्रों ने बचपन से कश्मीर की आजादी, भारत की गुलामी से छुटकारा, कश्मीर में चलेगा निजाम-ए-मुस्तफा जैसे नारे सुन रखे थे। प्रांत के सेवा प्रमुख को विद्यार्थियों से चर्चा में यह जानकारी हुई कि ये छात्र कभी कश्मीर से बाहर नहीं गए और इनको भारत के विषय में जानकारी नहीं के बराबर है। इसे देखते हुए इन छात्रों को कश्मीर के बाहर कुछ स्थानों का दर्शन कराने की योजना बनाई गई। संघ के सेवा प्रमुख ने इस बारे में वहाँ अर्धसैनिक बल सी.आर.पी.एफ. की 117 बटालियन से संपर्क कर इस योजना के विषय में बात की तो उन्होंने इसमें सहयोग करने के लिए सहमति दे दी। सी.आर.पी.एफ. के एक वरिष्ठ अधिकारी ने यात्रा में महत्त्वपूर्ण भूमिका निभाई। इसे 'अहसास यात्रा' का नाम दिया गया। वर्ष 18 से 22 की आयु के 48 छात्र इस पहली यात्रा में सम्मिलित हुए। मई 2010 में प्रारंभ हुई ग्यारह दिवसीय यात्रा में ये छात्र जम्मू के तत्कालीन पुलिस महानिदेशक से मिले। अमृतसर में वाघा सीमा, दरबार साहेब, जलियाँवाला बाग, चंडीगढ़, दिल्ली, मथुरा, जयपुर, अजमेर तथा गुरुग्राम होते हुए वे कश्मीर वापस आए। इस दौरान वे दिल्ली में तत्कालीन केंद्रीय गृहमंत्री से मिले। सभी स्थानों पर उनके ठहरने व भोजन की व्यवस्था सेवा भारती और विद्या भारती के कार्यकर्ताओं द्वारा की गई थी। यात्रा में जगह-जगह हुए स्वागत से विद्यार्थी भाव-विभोर थे। उन्हें अहसास हुआ कि अपने देश के विषय में उन्हें गलत जानकारी दी गई थी। यात्रा से भारत के प्रति उनका भाव और दृष्टिकोण बदल गया।

□

केदारनाथ आपदा में स्वयंसेवकों ने कायम की मिसाल

उत्तराखंड में 16 जून, 2013 को बादल फटने से आई विनाशकारी बाढ़ ने कई शहरों और गाँवों को तबाह कर दिया। केदारनाथ से दो किलोमीटर दूर चौराबाड़ी झील में बादल फटने से बहकर आए भारी मलबे और विशाल बोल्डर के कारण सैकड़ों लोगों को जान गँवानी पड़ी और हजारों घर तबाह हो गए। इस विनाशकारी जल-प्रलय के समय जब पूरा प्रशासन असहाय महसूस कर रहा था, उस समय भी संघ के स्वयंसेवक अपनी जान की परवाह किए बिना प्रभावित क्षेत्रों में राहत एवं बचाव कार्य के लिए पहुँच गए। बाढ़ से तबाह हुए श्रद्धालु एवं ग्रामीण, जो आश्रयहीन हो गए थे, उन्हें स्वयंसेवकों ने सुरक्षित स्थानों और अस्थायी शिविरों में स्थानांतरित किया। उनके लिए भोजन-पानी की व्यवस्था की। संघ ने पीड़ितों को सहायता पहुँचाने के लिए 'उत्तराखंड दैवीय आपदा पीड़ित सहायता समिति' का गठन किया। 16 जून से 1 जुलाई के बीच केवल देहरादून से 20 ट्रक राहत सामग्री आपदा प्रभावित क्षेत्रों में भेजे गए, जिनमें दालें, चावल, चीनी, चाय, मसाले, कपड़े, कंबल, दूध पाउडर, पानी की बोतलें, दवाइयाँ, बिस्कुट और पैक्ड फूड शामिल थे। स्वयंसेवकों ने हालत की भयावहता को देखते हुए विभिन्न स्थानों पर कुल 15 केंद्र बनाए। हर शिविर को अलग-अलग काम दिए गए, जैसे भोजन वितरण, चिकित्सा सेवा, बचाव सहायता, सुरक्षित स्थानों पर परिवहन, यात्रियों के रिश्तेदारों के लिए हेल्पलाइन केंद्र आदि। लगभग 5,000 स्वयंसेवक बाढ़ प्रभावित क्षेत्रों में दिन-रात लोगों की सेवा में जुटे रहे। इस आपदा में करीब छह हजार तीर्थयात्रियों एवं स्थानीय निवासियों की मृत्यु हो गई। कई तो पानी में बह गए और उनका पता ही नहीं चला।

□

नोबेल पुरस्कार विजेता दलाई लामा पहुँचे संघ मुख्यालय

शांति के लिए नोबेल पुरस्कार विजेता और तिब्बती धर्मगुरु दलाई लामा को दुनिया भर में शांति, करुणा और सहिष्णुता का प्रतीक माना जाता है, लेकिन बहुत कम लोग जानते हैं कि वे राष्ट्रीय स्वयंसेवक संघ के सामाजिक कार्यों की कई बार सराहना कर चुके हैं। इतना ही नहीं, वे 10 जनवरी, 2014 को नागपुर स्थित संघ मुख्यालय भी गए थे और सरसंघचालक डॉ. मोहन भागवत से भेंट की थी। उन्होंने वहाँ संघ के संस्थापक डॉ. केशवराव बलिराम हेडगेवार की समाधि और दूसरे सरसंघचालक श्रीगुरुजी की स्मृति स्थल पर पहुँचकर श्रद्धांजलि अर्पित की और मौन भाव से नमन किया। उन्होंने संघ के अनुशासन, सेवा भावना और समाज के जमीनी स्तर पर काम करने के तौर-तरीकों की प्रशंसा की। उनका कहना था, "संघ जैसे संगठन भारतीय परंपरा और सामाजिक एकता को जीवित रखने में अहम भूमिका निभा रहे हैं।" दलाई लामा ने कहा कि तिब्बत के संघर्ष में राष्ट्रीय स्वयंसेवक संघ का साथ हमेशा मजबूत और प्रेरणादायी रहा है। उन्होंने विशेष रूप से इस बात को रेखांकित किया कि संघ ने तिब्बत और वहाँ की जनता से निरंतर संपर्क बनाए रखा और कठिन समय में हमारा संबल बना रहा। उन्होंने आगे कहा कि राष्ट्रीय स्वयंसेवक संघ जैसे देशभक्त संगठन ने न केवल तिब्बती समुदाय के लिए सहारा प्रदान किया, बल्कि भारत जैसे विशाल और विविधतापूर्ण देश में अनुशासन, समर्पण और सेवा भावना का भाव भी जगाया है। दलाई लामा ने भारत के नैतिक और भौतिक मूल्यों की प्रशंसा करते हुए कहा कि ये मूल्य संपूर्ण विश्व के लिए अनुकरणीय हैं, और संघ द्वारा इन मूल्यों को जीवित रखना एक महत्त्वपूर्ण योगदान है।

□

राजधानी एक्सप्रेस दुर्घटना में बोगियों में फँसे यात्रियों को बाहर निकाला

दिल्ली से असम के डिब्रूगढ़ जा रही दिल्ली-डिब्रूगढ़ राजधानी एक्सप्रेस 25 जून, 2014 को छपरा जिले के पास दुर्घटना का शिकार हो गई। ट्रेन की 11 बोगियाँ पटरी से उतर गईं। इस दुर्घटना में पाँच लोगों की मृत्यु हो गई और करीब 60 लोग घायल हो गए। यह दुर्घटना 24-25 जून की मध्य रात्रि को हुई थी, इसलिए पुलिस प्रशासन को भी घटनास्थल पर पहुँचने में समय लगा। दुर्घटना की जानकारी मिलते ही आसपास रहने वाले संघ के स्वयंसेवक रात में ही घटनास्थल पर पहुँच गए और प्रशासन की प्रतीक्षा किए बिना बोगियों में फँसे यात्रियों को बाहर निकालने का काम शुरू कर दिया। जानकारी मिलने पर आसपास के जिलों के स्वयंसेवक भी घटनास्थल पर पहुँच गए। स्वयंसेवकों ने सबसे पहले घायलों को अस्पताल भेजने की व्यवस्था की। एंबुलेंस मँगवाए और घायल यात्रियों को अस्पताल में भरती करवाया। स्वयंसेवकों की एक टीम ने घायल यात्रियों और राहत कार्य में मदद करने वालों के लिए भोजन की व्यवस्था की। स्वयंसेवकों ने घायल लोगों का सामान सुरक्षित स्थानों पर पहुँचाया। उन्होंने भटके परिजनों को एक-दूसरे से मिलाने में भी अहम भूमिका निभाई। स्वयंसेवकों ने गंभीर रूप से घायल यात्रियों को पटना मेडिकल कॉलेज अस्पताल पहुँचाने में सहायता की। इतना ही नहीं, पटना के स्वयंसेवकों से इन घायल यात्रियों को अस्पताल में हरसंभव सहायता पहुँचाने के लिए भी कहा गया। स्वयंसेवकों की सेवा भावना से रेल यात्रियों के साथ ही स्थानीय नागरिक भी काफी प्रभावित हुए। तत्कालीन रेल मंत्री सदानंद गौड़ा ने स्वयंसेवकों के सेवाकार्यों की काफी सराहना की।

□

कश्मीर बाढ़ में पत्थर खाकर भी मदद पहुँचाते रहे स्वयंसेवक

वर्ष 2014 में सितंबर का महीना जम्मू-कश्मीर के लोगों के लिए विपदा लेकर आया। इलाके में 02 सितंबर, 2014 को शुरू हुई मूसलाधार बारिश ने बाढ़ का रूप ले लिया। हालात इतने बदतर हो गए कि 8 सितंबर, 2014 तक जम्मू-कश्मीर के 450 गाँव जलमग्न हो चुके थे। बाढ़ की विभीषिका में 200 से ज्यादा लोगों ने अपनी जान गँवा दी। हालत इतनी खराब थी कि सेना को भी राहत और बचाव के काम में काफी मुश्किलों का सामना करना पड़ रहा था। ऐसे विपरीत हालात में सेना का साथ देने आगे आए संघ के स्वयंसेवक। सेना की मदद से स्वयंसेवकों ने करीब दो लाख से ज्यादा लोगों को सुरक्षित स्थानों पर पहुँचाया। उनके बीच खाने के पैकेट वितरित किए, उनके लिए कपड़ों का इंतजाम किया गया। सैकड़ों पुलों, सड़कों, सरकारी इमारतों की अस्थायी मरम्मत कर उन्हें बहाल किया गया। संघ के स्वयंसेवकों ने कश्मीर के लोगों तक मदद पहुँचाने में अपनी जान की बाजी भी लगा दी, वहीं घाटी के कुछ नफरती लोगों ने उनके ऊपर पत्थर तक फेंके। इसके बाद भी स्वयंसेवक मानव सेवा के अपने धर्म का पालन करते रहे और कश्मीरियों के पुनर्वास में भी बढ़-चढ़कर मदद की। संघ को यह पता था कि जम्मू-कश्मीर में आबादी मुसलिम बहुल है, इसके बाद भी वे बिना किसी भेदभाव के बचाव कार्य में जुटे रहे। संघ के इस सेवाकार्य की खूब सराहना हुई।

□

सरपंच की दृढ़ता से राज्य सरकार को झुकना पड़ा

यह कहानी वर्ष 2015 की है, जब स्वयंसेवकों के अहिंसक आंदोलन के आगे राज्य सरकार को झुकना पड़ा। आंध्र प्रदेश के श्रीकाकुलम जिले में कोट्टूरु गाँव से तीन किलोमीटर की दूरी पर कन्नेधरा की चोटियों में देवी पोलम्मा का निवास माना जाता है। यहाँ दुर्लभ प्रकार की 56 जड़ी-बूटियाँ पाई जाती हैं। वनवासियों ने यहाँ भगवान् राम का मंदिर भी बनाया है और रामनवमी के उत्सव पर यहाँ हजारों श्रद्धालु जुटते हैं। जब लोगों को पता चला कि इन पर्वतों में ग्रेनाइट का भंडार है तो भूमाफिया, राजनेताओं और व्यापारियों की दृष्टि इस पर्वत पर पड़ी। एक राजनेता के पुत्र ने राज्य सरकार से खनिजों को निकालने की अनुमति भी प्राप्त कर ली। वनवासियों ने इसका विरोध किया। उन्होंने वनवासी कल्याण आश्रम के कार्यकर्ताओं और स्वयंसेवकों से संपर्क किया। गाँव के सरपंच मुखलिंगम के नेतृत्व में धरना-प्रदर्शन दिया गया और सरकारी कार्यालयों का घेराव किया गया। आसपास के 200 गाँवों के करीब तीन हजार वनवासियों ने इस आंदोलन में हिस्सा लिया। सरपंच पर आंदोलन को समाप्त करने का दबाव बनाया गया और प्रलोभन भी दिए गए। सरपंच ने झुकने से साफ मना कर दिया और कहा कि वह संघ के स्वयंसेवक हैं और कोई भी शक्ति उन्हें भयभीत नहीं कर सकती। सरपंच के अडिग रहने और व्यापक आंदोलन को देखते हुए अंततः सरकार को झुकना पड़ा और वर्ष 2015 में खदान की अनुमति निरस्त करनी पड़ी। इस आंदोलन की खास बात यह रही कि स्वयंसेवकों के कुशल नेतृत्व से यह अनुशासित और अहिंसक रहा।

□

नेपाल भूकंप में सेवा और समर्पण का अनुपम उदाहरण

नेपाल में 25 अप्रैल, 2015 को 7.8 तीव्रता का भूकंप आया, जिसने काठमांडू, पोखरा और आसपास के इलाकों में भारी तबाही मचाई। इसमें 9,000 से अधिक लोगों की जान चली गई, लाखों लोग बेघर हो गए और हजारों इमारतें मलबे में बदल गईं। यह नेपाल के इतिहास की सबसे विनाशकारी प्राकृतिक आपदाओं में से एक थी। इसी भयावह स्थिति में राष्ट्रीय स्वयंसेवक संघ के स्वयंसेवकों ने बिना प्रचार और शोरगुल के जमीन पर उतरकर अद्वितीय सेवाकार्य किया। भूकंप के तुरंत बाद संघ और उसके सहयोगी संगठन 'सेवा भारती' और 'सेवा इंटरनेशनल' ने राहत टीमें नेपाल भेजीं। नेपाल में संघ ने अपने सहयोगी संगठन 'हिंदू स्वयंसेवक संघ' के माध्यम से सेवाकार्यों को गति दी। संघ ने नेपाल में 'सेवा केंद्र' बनाए, जहाँ लोगों को अस्थायी आश्रय, चिकित्सा जाँच और परामर्श प्रदान किया गया। पीड़ित लोगों के लिए भोजन, दवा, कंबल, टेंट, प्राथमिक चिकित्सा और बच्चों के लिए दूध जैसी जरूरी चीजों की आपूर्ति की गई। स्वयंसेवकों ने दुर्गम क्षेत्रों तक पैदल जाकर घायलों की सहायता की और मलबे में दबे लोगों को बाहर निकाला। काठमांडू, भक्तपुर, सिंधुपालचौक जैसे क्षेत्रों में स्वयंसेवकों ने मृतकों के अंतिम संस्कार में मदद की। गायों और अन्य पशुओं की देखभाल से लेकर मलबा हटाने के काम में भी प्रशासन की सहायता की। इसके साथ ही भारत और विदेशों में संघ से जुड़े संगठनों जैसे सेवा इंटरनेशनल ने कोष एकत्र कर राहत सामग्री नेपाल पहुँचाई। संघ ने यह कार्य निरपेक्ष भाव से, बिना किसी धार्मिक या जातीय भेदभाव के किया।

□

संघ कार्यालय में प्रदेश कांग्रेस अध्यक्ष ने फहराया तिरंगा

22 फरवरी, 2016 को इंदौर में एक अप्रत्याशित घटना घटी, जब मध्य प्रदेश कांग्रेस अध्यक्ष अरुण यादव राष्ट्रीय स्वयंसेवक संघ के स्थानीय कार्यालय पहुँचे—तिरंगा फहराने के उद्देश्य से, लेकिन जो हुआ, उसने कांग्रेस खेमे को चौंका दिया। दरअसल कांग्रेस लगातार इस बात का दुष्प्रचार करती रही है कि संघ कार्यालय में तिरंगा नहीं फहराया जाता। कांग्रेसी दुष्प्रचार की शिकार कभी-कभी आम जनता ही नहीं, बल्कि कांग्रेस के बड़े नेता भी हो जाते हैं। इसी बात को हथियार बनाकर मध्य प्रदेश कांग्रेस के अध्यक्ष अरुण यादव ने ऐलान किया कि वे इंदौर में संघ के कार्यालय में जाकर तिरंगा फहराएँगे। उनका उद्देश्य सिर्फ राज्य की भाजपा सरकार को ही नहीं, बल्कि केंद्र की मोदी सरकार को भी बदनाम करना था। अरुण यादव 800 कार्यकर्ताओं के साथ संघ कार्यालय की ओर चल पड़े। संघ के पदाधिकारियों से बातचीत के बाद स्थानीय प्रशासन ने मध्य प्रदेश कांग्रेस अध्यक्ष अरुण यादव को मिलाकर 20 कांग्रेसी कार्यकर्ताओं को वहाँ जाने की इजाजत दे दी। यादव जब संघ कार्यालय पहुँचे तो वहाँ उनके स्वागत की पूरी तैयारी पहले से हो रखी थी। न केवल कार्यालय का मुख्य द्वार सजा हुआ था, बल्कि संघ कार्यकर्ताओं ने उन्हें पारंपरिक ढंग से तिलक लगाकर और लाल कालीन बिछाकर स्वागत किया। यह दृश्य कांग्रेस नेताओं के लिए अप्रत्याशित था। अरुण यादव ने संघ कार्यालय की छत पर भगवा ध्वज के पास तिरंगा फहराया। इस दौरान उपस्थित संघ के पदाधिकारियों और स्वयंसेवकों ने तिरंगे के प्रति सम्मान प्रकट करते हुए राष्ट्रगान में भाग लिया। □

पूर्व राष्ट्रपति प्रणब मुखर्जी ने किया संघ मुख्यालय का दौरा

पूर्व राष्ट्रपति भारत रत्न प्रणब मुखर्जी ने 7 जून, 2018 को नागपुर में राष्ट्रीय स्वयंसेवक संघ के मुख्यालय का दौरा किया था। मुख्यालय में मुखर्जी ने संघ के सरसंघचालक मोहन भागवत से भेंट की और स्वयंसेवकों को संबोधित किया। उन्होंने संघ के संस्थापक डॉ. केशवराव बलिराम हेडगेवार को श्रद्धांजलि अर्पित की। 'तृतीय वर्ष संघ शिक्षा वर्ग' के समापन समारोह में पूर्व राष्ट्रपति प्रणब मुखर्जी मुख्य अतिथि के तौर पर सम्मिलित हुए। इस दौरान उन्होंने स्वयंसेवकों को भी संबोधित किया। उन्होंने अपने संबोधन में राष्ट्र, राष्ट्रवाद और बहुलवाद के महत्त्व पर जोर दिया। संघ मुख्यालय का दौरा करके प्रणब मुखर्जी ने एक ऐसा संदेश दिया, जिसने राजनीतिक और सामाजिक विमर्श को फिर से चर्चा में ला दिया। यह दौरा कई मायनों में ऐतिहासिक और अप्रत्याशित था, क्योंकि मुखर्जी कांग्रेस के न सिर्फ एक वरिष्ठ नेता थे, बल्कि वे इंदिरा गांधी, नरसिम्हा राव और मनमोहन सिंह के कार्यकाल में भी वरिष्ठ मंत्री के तौर पर काम कर चुके थे। कांग्रेस की सरकार के दौरान ही वे राष्ट्रपति बने। भारत रत्न प्रणब मुखर्जी के इस दौरे से पहले और बाद में राजनीतिक गलियारों में खूब बहस हुई। कांग्रेस के कई नेताओं ने इस पर आपत्ति जताई, जबकि कुछ ने इसे एक सराहनीय कदम बताया, जो विभिन्न विचारधाराओं के बीच संवाद को बढ़ावा देता है। कांग्रेस ने जहाँ इस पर सवाल उठाए, वहीं मुखर्जी ने इसे विचारों का पुल बनाने का अवसर बताया।

□

इमरान खान ने संयुक्त राष्ट्र में 11 बार की संघ की चर्चा

संयुक्त राष्ट्र संघ में पाकिस्तान के पूर्व प्रधानमंत्री इमरान खान ने राष्ट्रीय स्वयंसेवक संघ का 11 बार नाम लिया था। यह दरशाता है कि पाकिस्तान की नजर में संघ कितना महत्त्वपूर्ण और प्रभावशाली है। पाकिस्तान के प्रधानमंत्री इमरान खान जब 27 सितंबर, 2019 को संयुक्त राष्ट्र महासभा के मंच पर खड़े हुए तो उनके 50 मिनट के भाषण में एक संगठन का नाम 11 बार गूँजा, वह था—राष्ट्रीय स्वयंसेवक संघ। यह कोई साधारण बात नहीं थी। यह उस संगठन की महत्ता, प्रभाव और वैश्विक पहचान का प्रमाण था, जिसे वैश्विक स्तर पर भी महसूस किया जा सकता है। इमरान खान ने अपने भाषण में भारत के आंतरिक मामलों—अनुच्छेद 370 की समाप्ति, जम्मू-कश्मीर की स्थिति और भारत की राजनीति पर बात करते हुए, बार-बार संघ का नाम लिया। संयुक्त राष्ट्र में संघ का बार-बार उल्लेख करना बताता है कि इमरान खान भारत की मोदी सरकार से कितना भयभीत थे। यही वजह है कि भारत सरकार की रणनीति और कूटनीति को संघ का नाम लेकर अपने भय को प्रकट किया। पूरा विश्व जानता है कि पाकिस्तान की सरकार और उसकी सेना हमेशा से भारत में अस्थिरता फैलाने के लिए कट्टरपंथी संगठनों का सहारा लेती रही है। उन्हें भारत की वह शक्ति चुभती है, जो देश को एकजुट, संवेदनशील और राष्ट्रभक्त बनाए रखती है—और संघ यही काम करता है। इमरान खान का भाषण बताता है कि पाकिस्तान के शासकों को डर है कि संघ की वैचारिक शक्ति भारत को अजेय बना रही है। संघ की शक्ति बंदूक में नहीं, विचार में है—और यही बात इमरान खान को सबसे अधिक परेशान कर रही थी।

□

कोरोना पीड़ितों की मदद में जी-जान से जुटे कई संगठन

वर्ष 2020 में जब कोरोना संक्रमण फैला तो पूरे देश में संघ के स्वयंसेवक जरूरतमंदों की मदद के लिए सबसे आगे खड़े दिखाई दिए। संक्रमण के उस दौर में जब कोई व्यक्ति अपने घर से बाहर निकलने के लिए तैयार नहीं था, उस समय स्वयंसेवक जरूरतमंद पीड़ितों के पास ऑक्सीजन से लेकर दवा और भोजन तक पहुँचाने का काम कर रहे थे। स्वयंसेवकों की एक टीम खून और प्लाज्मा की व्यवस्था में जुटी थी तो दूसरी टीम अस्पतालों में खाली बेड का हिसाब-किताब रख रही थी, जिससे कोरोना संक्रमितों को तुरंत बेड मिल सके। संघ ने देश भर में अलग-अलग जिलों में 240 स्थानों पर कोविड अस्पतालों में प्रशासन के साथ मिलकर पीड़ितों तक मेडिकल काउंसलिंग से लेकर एंबुलेंस सेवा की मदद पहुँचाई। संघ ने अपनी ओर से 43 प्रमुख शहरों में कोविड सेवा केंद्र खोले और 2442 वैक्सीनेशन केंद्र चलाए। देश भर में संघ के अभियान के अंतर्गत लगभग 3000 से अधिक लोगों ने प्लाज्मा दान किया। संघ ने प्रशासन और राधास्वामी सत्संग के सहयोग से 2000 बेड्सवाला कोविड केयर सेंटर तैयार किया। 1500 से अधिक स्थानों पर लंगर चलाए गए। सेवा भारती ने दिल्ली के एक बड़े हॉस्पिटल के बाहर प्राणवायु सेवा शुरू की। यहाँ जिन मरीजों को हॉस्पिटल में बेड मिलने में देरी होती, उन्हें ऑक्सीजन उपलब्ध कराई जाती थी। संघ ने शहरों-कस्बों और गाँवों में वैक्सीनेशन को लेकर लोगों में जागरूकता लाने के लिए अभियान चलाया। इतना ही नहीं, इस आपदाकाल में जिन मरीजों की जान चली गई, उनके अंतिम संस्कार की व्यवस्था भी की और इसके लिए व्हाट्सएप ग्रुप बनाया गया था।

□

कोरोना और चक्रवात की दोहरी मार के समय मदद का हाथ बढ़ाया

कोरोनाकाल में महाराष्ट्र के कुछ जिलों के लोगों को दोहरी मार झेलनी पड़ी। एक तरफ कोरोना और दूसरी तरफ 31 मई, 2020 को निसर्ग चक्रवात ने राज्य के रत्नागिरी, रायगढ़ आदि जिलों में कई घर तबाह कर दिए। 110 किलोमीटर की रफ्तार से आई आँधी में बिजली के अनेक खंभे गिर गए तो जहाँ-तहाँ बिजली के तार टूटकर बिखर गए। उस समय देश के कुल कोरोना संक्रमितों में से 35 प्रतिशत महाराष्ट्र में थे। इस दोहरी आपदा के समय राष्ट्रीय स्वयंसेवक संघ, जनकल्याण समिति, विद्यार्थी परिषद् और राष्ट्र सेविका समिति के कार्यकर्ता लोगों की मदद के लिए आगे आए। संघ के 150 स्वयंसेवक, रत्नागिरी और रायगढ़ जिलों में लोगों को मदद पहुँचाने से लेकर तूफान प्रभावित इलाकों में अन्य राहत कामों में जुटे थे। पहले तीन दिन स्वयंसेवकों ने पूरे क्षेत्र के रास्ते को साफ किया, जिससे यातायात शुरू हो सके। स्वयंसेवकों ने प्रभावित गाँवों में शिविर लगाकर लोगों के लिए भोजन-पानी की व्यवस्था की। स्वयंसेवकों की एक टीम ने तूफान के दौरान हुए नुकसान का सर्वेक्षण किया और इस आधार पर पीड़ित परिवारों को घर हेतु छत की चादरें, खप्पर, पशुओं के लिए चारा, पीने का पानी, नारियल के पौधों आदि का वितरण किया। स्वयंसेवकों की कुछ टीमें पहले से ही कोरोना संक्रमितों को हर तरह की मदद पहुँचाने में जुटी थीं। सरकारी तंत्र पर जब कोरोना और तूफान, दोनों का दोहरा भार पड़ रहा था, तब संघ ने सक्रिय होकर अपना दायित्व निभाया। □

कोरोनाकाल में एक वृद्ध स्वयंसेवक ने प्रस्तुत किया उदाहरण

कोरोना की दूसरी लहर के दौरान इतनी ज्यादा संख्या में लोग बीमार होने लगे कि देश के कई शहरों में ऑक्सीजन और बेड की कमी होने लगी। इसी दौरान महाराष्ट्र के नागपुर में संघ के एक वृद्ध स्वयंसेवक 85 वर्षीय नारायण राव दाभाडकर भी कोरोना से संक्रमित हो गए। उनका ऑक्सीजन लेवल घटकर 60 पहुँच गया। इसको देखते हुए उनके दामाद और बेटी ने उन्हें अप्रैल 2021 में नागपुर के इंदिरा गांधी शासकीय अस्पताल में एडमिट कराया। अस्पताल में कोरोना संक्रमितों की संख्या इतनी अधिक थी कि बड़ी मुश्किल से नारायण राव को बेड मिला। उसी दौरान एक महिला अपने 40 वर्षीय पति को अस्पताल लाई। महिला रो रही थी और बेड लेने के लिए डॉक्टरों से मिन्नतें कर रही थी। महिला को बिलखता देख नारायण राव का मन द्रवित हो उठा और उन्होंने अपना बेड देने की पेशकश कर दी। इस पर अस्पताल प्रशासन ने कहा कि उसके लिए सभी मरीज बराबर हैं और अगर वे सही से उपचार नहीं लेंगे तो उनके जीवन को खतरा हो सकता है। इस पर नारायण राव ने कहा, "मैं 85 वर्ष का हो चुका हूँ, मैंने अपनी जिंदगी देख ली है, लेकिन अगर उस स्त्री का पति मर गया तो बच्चे अनाथ हो जाएँगे, इसलिए मेरा कर्तव्य है कि मैं उस व्यक्ति के प्राण बचाऊँ।" नारायण राव के काफी जिद करने पर अस्पताल प्रशासन ने उनसे सहमति-पत्र लिखवाया कि वह दूसरे मरीज के लिए स्वेच्छा से अपना बेड खाली कर रहे हैं। अस्तपाल का बेड छोड़ने के बाद नारायण राव घर चले गए। घर पर उनकी देखभाल की जा रही थी, लेकिन तीन दिन बाद ही उनका निधन हो गया। इस तरह मानवता के लिए जीवन समर्पित करने वाले स्वयंसेवक नारायण राव ने एक अनुपम उदाहरण प्रस्तुत किया।

□

कोरोनाकाल में बहादुर बेटियों ने किया शवों का अंतिम संस्कार

अप्रैल 2021 में कोविड की दूसरी लहर से हर तरफ हाहाकार मचा हुआ था। संक्रमण के डर से कोई भी व्यक्ति घर से निकलने को तैयार नहीं था। लोग डरे-सहमे अपने घरों में कैद थे। ऐसे में सबसे बड़ी चुनौती कोरोना पॉजिटिव शवों के अंतिम संस्कार की थी। गुजरात के भुज के सरकारी अस्पताल में कोरोना पॉजिटिव शवों की संख्या बढ़ती जा रही थी। अस्पताल में अंतिम विदाई की राह देख रहे शवों के अंतिम संस्कार के लिए कोई भी आगे नहीं आ रहा था। ऐसे में 15 अप्रैल, 2021 की शाम को भुज तहसील के विकास अधिकारी ने संघ के स्वयंसेवक रामजी वेलानी को फोन कर इस संबंध में मदद माँगी। इसके बाद संघ कार्यकर्ताओं ने मिलकर इस कार्य के लिए पुरुष स्वयंसेवकों की एक टीम बनाई। पुरुषों की टीम बनने के बाद राष्ट्र सेविका समिति की करीब 10 महिलाएँ भी इस काम में हाथ बँटाने आगे आईं। सौराष्ट्र प्रांत की राष्ट्र सेविका समिति की प्रांत प्रचार प्रमुख हिना दीदी ने कहा, "हम 3-3 की टोली में काम कर रहे थे। नियमित श्मशान घाट की सफाई से लेकर, भीषण गरमी में पी.पी.ई. किट पहनकर अंतिम संस्कार करने में हमें थोड़ी भी कठिनाई महसूस नहीं हुई। गाँव के लोगों ने भी पूरा सहयोग किया, जिनके घरों में लकड़ी थी, उन्होंने लकड़ी दी, कहीं से घी आया तो कहीं से कपूर।" लगभग 45 दिन चले इस अभियान में 450 से अधिक शवों की अंतिम क्रिया संपन्न कराई गई और सम्मानजनक विदाई दी गई। इस नेक काम के लिए साहस दिखाकर स्वयंसेवकों ने 'संघे शक्ति युगे-युगे' को चरितार्थ किया।

□

□

केरल में इको फ्रेंडली चिताग्नि प्रोजेक्ट 13 जिलों में

केरल में छोटी-छोटी बस्तियों में रहने वाले लोगों के सामने एक बहुत बड़ी समस्या यह थी कि उन्हें अपने परिजनों के अंतिम संस्कार के लिए श्मशान में जगह नहीं मिलती थी। वे या तो घर से 10 किलोमीटर दूर जाकर सुनसान जगह पर शवों का अंतिम संस्कार करते थे या फिर अपनी छोटी जमीन में ही घर के पिछवाड़े अपने प्रियजनों को अंतिम विदाई देते थे। कोरोनाकाल में यह समस्या और विकट हो गई। 6 मार्च, 2021 को केरल के छोटे से गाँव अंडोरकोनम में एक वृद्ध व्यक्ति की कोरोना संक्रमण से मृत्यु हो गई। परिजनों की लाख कोशिशों के बाद भी उन्हें श्मशान घाट में अंतिम संस्कार के लिए जगह नहीं मिली। उसके बाद परिजनों ने सेवा भारती से मदद माँगी। कुछ ही घंटे में एक मोबाइल वैन यूनिट पहुँच गई और एल.पी.जी. सिलेंडर का उपयोग कर कार्यकर्ताओं की मदद से अंतिम संस्कार संपन्न किया गया। सेवा भारती को इस समस्या का अहसास पहले ही हो गया था। इसे देखते हुए केरल की सेवा भारती ने वर्ष 2019 में सेवा इंटरनेशनल की मदद से चिताग्नि प्रोजेक्ट की शुरुआत की। इस अनूठे मोबाइल अंतिम संस्कार यूनिट को जरूरतमंद परिवारों तक पहुँचाने का कार्य सेवा भारती अब केरल के 13 जिलों में कर रही है। इससे मात्र 2000 से 2500 रुपए में विधिवत रूप से अंतिम संस्कार संपन्न हो जाता है। खास बात यह है कि चिताग्नि एक इको-फ्रेंडली प्रोजेक्ट है, जिसमें अंतिम संस्कार के लिए लकड़ियों की जरूरत नहीं पड़ती। इस योजना को दक्षिण भारत के 100 जिलों तक पहुँचाने की तैयारी है।

□

कोरोना संक्रमितों के लिए संघ ने चलाया भोजन बैंक

भारत में कोविड-19 का पहला मामला 30 जनवरी, 2020 को सामने आया था। कोरोना महामारी के दौरान जब मामले बढ़ने लगे तो 24 मार्च, 2020 से करीब 68 दिनों तक पूर्ण लॉकडाउन रहा। इस दौरान होटल तथा खाने के स्टॉल आदि सबकुछ बंद थे। लोगों के सामने भोजन की विकट समस्या उत्पन्न हो गई। ऐसे में राष्ट्रीय स्वयंसेवक संघ से जुड़े संगठनों की ओर से देश भर में हजारों स्थानों पर लंगर चलाए गए। भारत में कोरोना का पहला मामला सामने आने के बाद एक साल के भीतर यानी 28 जनवरी, 2021 तक कोरोना संक्रमितों की संख्या 1.07 करोड़ के पार पहुँच गई थी। देश में कई घर ऐसे थे, जहाँ सभी सदस्य कोरोना से संक्रमित थे। इन्हें खाना मिलने में बड़ी दिक्कत होती थी। ऐसे में संघ ने उनकी इस समस्या का निदान निकाला और भोजन बैंक बनाया। भोजन बैंक के अंतर्गत देश भर के कई शहरों में 'केशव रसोई' की शुरुआत की गई। इस रसोई से कोरोना से ग्रस्त व्यक्ति, उनके परिजन, ऐसे परिवार जिनके घर में सभी लोग कोरोना पॉजिटिव थे एवं भोजन की कोई उचित व्यवस्था नहीं थी, उन लोगों तक भोजन पहुँचाया गया। यह प्रयास रहा कि कोई भूखा न सोए। संघ की ओर से विभिन्न राज्यों में हेल्पलाइन नंबर जारी किए गए। लोग हेल्पलाइन पर संपर्क करते और उन घरों तक खाना पहुँचाया जाता। भोजन बैंक से कई महीनों तक कोरोना संक्रमितों की सेवा की गई। कार्यकर्ता शहर में रहने वाले मानसिक रूप से विक्षिप्त एवं बेघर लोगों को भी भोजन का पैकेट उपलब्ध कराते थे। इतना ही नहीं, संघ ने नगर क्षेत्र में विचरण करने वाले पशु-पक्षियों की भी चिंता की और उनके लिए जगह-जगह दाना व पानी की व्यवस्था की गई। इस कार्य में संघ के विविध संगठनों एवं समाज का सहयोग मिला।

□

कोरोनाकाल में दवा बैंक से गरीबों तक पहुँचाई दवाइयाँ

कोरोनाकाल में लोगों की जरूरतों को समझते हुए राष्ट्रीय स्वयंसेवक संघ ने दवा बैंक की शुरुआत की। इसका उद्देश्य गरीब मरीजों तक दवा उपलब्ध कराना था। दवा और मेडिकल सहायता के लिए देश भर में 1,45,159 केंद्र खोले गए, जिनके माध्यम से होम्योपैथिक दवाइयाँ भी वितरित की गईं और आइसोलेशन सेंटर बनाने में मदद की गई। कोरोना की दूसरी लहर में जब स्थितियाँ अधिक गंभीर हो गई थीं, तब संघ ने पुलिस प्रशासन और स्थानीय स्वयंसेवी संगठनों के साथ तालमेल करके 59,91,570 जरूरतमंदों को आयुर्वेदिक काढ़ा वितरित किया। कोरोना संक्रमण बढ़ने के साथ देश में दवाइयों की भी किल्लत हो गई। ऐसे में संघ ने कोरोना संक्रमितों से अपील की कि जिन लोगों के पास दवा बच गई हो तो वे उसे कूड़े में न फेंकें, संघ को दे दें और संघ के कार्यकर्ता उसे जरूरतमंदों तक पहुँचा देंगे। दवा बैंक के लिए संघ ने फोन नंबर भी जारी किए थे, जिस पर दवा लेने और देने वाले संपर्क कर सकते थे। संघ ने देश के प्रमुख शहरों में कोविड सेवा केंद्र खोले, जिससे कोरोना संक्रमितों को समय पर मदद मिल सके। कोरोना से बचाव के लिए जब टीका लगाया जा रहा था, तब संघ ने देश भर में वैक्सीनेशन केंद्र खोले, जिससे दूरदराज के इलाकों में भी लोगों का वैक्सीनेशन हो सके। संघ ने शहरों, कस्बों और गाँवों में वैक्सीनेशन को लेकर लोगों में जागरूकता जगाने के लिए बड़े पैमाने पर अभियान भी चलाया। □

कोरोनाकाल में संघ की मदद से लाखों घरों में जले चूल्हे

मार्च 2020 में देश में कोरोना फैलने और लॉकडाउन लागू होने के बाद लोगों के सामने अनेक तरह के संकट आए। देश में जब सभी प्रमुख बाजार और दुकानें बंद थीं, तब दूरदराज के लोगों और गरीबों के सामने सबसे बड़ी समस्या यह थी कि घर का चूल्हा कैसे जले? ऐसे कठिन समय में स्वयंसेवक उनके लिए आशा की किरण बनकर आए। संघ ने इस समस्या को समझते हुए देश भर में अपने पाँच लाख से अधिक स्वयंसेवकों को लोगों की सेवा के लिए उतार दिया। स्वयंसेवकों ने सेवा की मिसाल प्रस्तुत करते हुए लॉकडाउन के दौरान पाँच करोड़ से अधिक भोजन के पैकेट बाँटे और 73.81 लाख से अधिक परिवारों में सूखा राशन वितरित किया। स्वयंसेवकों ने अपनी जान की परवाह किए बिना घर-घर जाकर ये कार्य किया और लाखों घरों में चूल्हा बुझने नहीं दिया। संघ ने कोरोनाकाल में 92,656 सेवा स्थान बनाए; 5,07,656 कार्यकर्ता दिन-रात सेवारत रहे; 73,81,802 परिवारों में राशन किट बाँटी गई; 4,66,34,730 तैयार भोजन के पैकेट बाँटे गए; 89,23,131 मास्क बाँटे गए; 10,91,661 स्टे होम बनाए और दूसरे प्रांतों से आए 19,42,179 लोगों को हर प्रकार की सहायता पहुँचाई। सेवा भारती ने कोरोनाकाल में चलाए गए सेवा अभियानों को लेकर लघु वृत्तचित्र '100 दिन सेवा के' में पूरे देश में सेवाकार्यों की जानकारी दी है।

□ □

10 किलोमीटर पैदल चलकर कंधे पर सहायता सामग्री पहुँचाई

लॉकडाउन के समय असम के कछार जिले के दुर्गम इलाकों में सहायता सामग्री पहुँचाना आसान नहीं था। इस जिले में मुख्यतया रियांग समुदाय बसता है, जो कि जनजातीय समूह है। कछार जिले के मुख्यालय सिल्चर से करीब 70 किलोमीटर दूर कालाखाल, बालीखाल और ढोलाखाल गाँवों में इनकी बस्ती है। दुर्गम इलाका होने के कारण इन गाँवों तक पहुँचने के लिए करीब 10 किलोमीटर का रास्ता पैदल तय करना पड़ता है। कोरोना के कारण जब लॉकडाउन लगा, तब कछार जिले के स्वयंसेवकों ने ये सर्वेक्षण करना शुरू कर दिया था कि जिले में कहाँ-कहाँ सहायता की जरूरत है। उसी दौरान उन्हें इन गाँवों की जानकारी हुई। उन्हें पता चला रियांग समुदाय के पास खाने-पीने का सामान नहीं है। यह जानकारी मिलते ही 'केशव स्मारक संस्कृति सुरभि' के स्वयंसेवकों ने गाँव में खाद्य सामग्री पहुँचाने की ठानी। स्थानीय कार्यकर्ताओं की मदद से उन्होंने कंधे पर खाद्य सामग्री उठाई और 10 किलोमीटर पैदल चलकर गाँवों तक पहुँचे। 12 अप्रैल और 27 अप्रैल, 2020 को उन्होंने गाँववालों के बीच खाद्य सामग्री के साथ ही अन्य आवश्यक सामग्री का वितरण किया। इसके बाद भी स्वयंसेवक लगातार गाँववालों के संपर्क में रहे और सहायता सामग्री पहुँचाई। इन गाँवों के मुखिया ब्रिखोराम रियांग, नंदलाल रियांग और रोशिदा रियांग ने कहा, "संघ को छोड़कर किसी और संस्थान ने इन दुर्गम गाँवों में आने की चिंता नहीं की।" 'केशव स्मारक संस्कृति सुरभि' रियांग समुदाय के लोगों का जीवन स्तर सुधारने के प्रयास में भी जुटी है।

□

लॉकडाउन में संघ की हेल्पलाइन बनी लाइफलाइन

कोरोनाकाल में देश में 25 मार्च, 2020 से 31 मई, 2020 तक लॉकडाउन के दौरान जिस चीज की सबसे ज्यादा जरूरत थी, वह थी जरूरतमंदों तक सहायता सामग्री पहुँचे, कोरोना को लेकर उनके मन में बसा डर दूर हो और मेडिकल संबंधी जरूरतें पूरी हों। इसे समझते हुए संघ ने हेल्पलाइन सेवा शुरू की। संघ की शाखाएँ देश भर में हैं, वहीं 'सेवा भारती' की शाखाएँ भी देश के कोने-कोने में हैं। संघ से जुड़ी अन्य संस्थाओं की मदद से देश के सभी शहरों में मार्च के अंतिम सप्ताह में हेल्पलाइन की सेवाएँ शुरू की गईं। केरल में संघ के माध्यम से टेलीफोन काउंसिलिंग की व्यवस्था की गई। 14 काउंसलर लगातार तीन महीने तक प्रतिदिन लोगों की समस्याओं को दूर कर रहे थे। गोरखपुर में चिकित्सा संबंधी परामर्श के लिए हेल्पलाइन नंबर 9389045050 जारी किया गया था। भोपाल में 'सेवा भारती दूरभाष मित्र अभियान' शुरू किया गया और कुछ ही दिनों में हजारों लोगों से संपर्क किया गया। इनमें कोरोना संक्रमित मरीज और बुजुर्ग शामिल थे। दिल्ली में हेल्पलाइन नंबर 8100066066 जारी किया गया था और पहले ही दिन दो हजार से अधिक कॉल आईं। इस सेंटर में शुरू में कॉल सुनने के लिए सात लोग थे, बाद में कॉल बढ़ने पर कार्यकर्ताओं की संख्या बढ़ाई गई। राँची में 'हेलो डॉक्टर' नाम से हेल्पलाइन शुरू की गई। तेलंगाना के हैदराबाद में 'सेवा भारती कोविड हेल्पलाइन कॉल सेंटर' में 50 महिलाओं की टीम ने लगातार काम किया। हेल्पलाइन सेवा के माध्यम से सर्दी, जुकाम, बुखार पर डॉक्टरों से बात कर उचित परामर्श देने से लेकर गर्भवती महिलाओं को भी हरसंभव सहायता पहुँचाई गई। कोरोना संक्रमित मरीजों को घर पर ही कोरोना किट भेजी गई, जिससे संक्रमण और नहीं फैले।

□

स्वयंसेवकों के प्रति अनोखे तरीके से व्यक्त की कृतज्ञता

कोरोनाकाल के लॉकडाउन में संघ के सेवाकार्य के प्रति आम नागरिकों में किस कदर सम्मान का भाव था, यह अनेक रूपों में सामने आया है। इस तरह का एक अनुपम उदाहरण सुभाषचंद्र पांडे का है। गोरखपुर जिले के पिपराइच गाँव के रहने वाले सुभाषचंद्र पांडे मुंबई में ऑटो रिक्शा चलाते थे। लॉकडाउन में जब सबकुछ ठप हो गया तो वे अपने परिवार के साथ ऑटो से अपने गाँव के लिए निकले। मुंबई से उनके घर तक की कुल दूरी 1,682 किलोमीटर थी। गाँव लौटते समय वे इंदौर में परिवार को भोजन कराने के लिए रुके, लेकिन लॉकडाउन में सबकुछ बंद होने से कुछ भी नहीं मिल रहा था। ऐसे में संघ के स्वयंसेवकों ने उनकी परेशानी को भाँपते हुए उनके लिए भोजन-पानी, दवाई और अन्य आवश्यक वस्तुओं के साथ ही विश्राम की व्यवस्था की। इंदौर में कुछ समय आराम करने के बाद वे परिवार सहित गाँव लौट गए, लेकिन स्वयंसेवकों की सेवा भावना और इंदौर का एहसान उनके मन में बस गया। बाद में अनलॉक की प्रक्रिया शुरू होने के बाद सुभाषचंद्र अपने परिवार के साथ उसी ऑटो से वापस मुंबई के लिए निकल पड़े। रास्ते में इंदौर बाईपास पर यह परिवार रुका। सुभाषचंद्र और उनकी पत्नी उपमा पांडे एक साथ सड़क के किनारे बैठे। घर से साथ में लाया भोजन निकाला और उस भोजन का पहला कौर इंदौर को अर्पित किया। फिर कृतज्ञ भाव से उन्होंने भोजन किया। उपमा पांडे ने भावुक होकर कहा, "जिस इंदौर ने उस संकट काल में हमारे भूखे-प्यासे बच्चों को खाना खिलाया, पानी पिलाया और दवाई दी, भगवान् करे, उस इंदौर के लोग कभी भूखे न रहें।"

□

स्वयंसेवकों ने महिलाओं का जीवन बचा लिया

पश्चिम बंगाल के मुर्शिदाबाद और मेदिनीपुर जिले की कुछ महिलाएँ पड़ोसी राज्य ओडिशा में मजदूरी के लिए जाती थीं। इन जिलों की सात महिलाओं की टोली जब वहाँ काम कर रही थी, उसी समय लॉकडाउन लग गया। लॉकडाउन लग जाने से काम बंद हो गया। काम बंद होने से खाने-पीने और रहने की समस्या उत्पन्न हो गई। जैसे-तैसे उन्होंने कुछ दिन काटे। जब श्रमिकों के गाँव लौटने के समाचार आने लगे तो ये महिलाएँ भी गाँव के लिए निकल पड़ीं। तीन दिन लगातार चलने के बाद वे ओडिशा-पश्चिम बंगाल के बॉर्डर जमशोला पहुँचीं। वहाँ बंगाल सरकार की तरफ से श्रमिकों के लिए कोई व्यवस्था नहीं थी। जमशोला गाँव का कुछ हिस्सा बंगाल में तो कुछ हिस्सा ओडिशा में पड़ता है। वहाँ से बंगाल जाने के लिए दिन भर में केवल दो बसें चलती थीं, लेकिन वे पहले ही खचाखच भर जाती थीं। बंगाल में आगे कैसे जाएँ? अपने गाँव तक किस तरह पहुँचें, गाँव जाकर क्या काम करेंगी, काम नहीं करेंगी तो खाएँगी क्या? यह समस्या उनके सामने मुँह बाए खड़ी थी। तीन दिन लगातार चलने से वे काफी कमजोर हो गई थीं और इस मानसिक ऊहापोह के बीच सातों महिलाओं ने सुवणरिखा नदी में छलाँग लगाकर जीवनलीला समाप्त करने का निश्चय किया। जमशोला में संघ के कुछ स्वयंसेवक श्रमिकों की सेवा में लगे थे। उन्होंने जब इन हताश महिलाओं को देखा तो बातचीत की। उनकी पीड़ा जानकर उन्होंने महिलाओं को ढाँढ़स बँधाया कि सबकुछ ठीक हो जाएगा। स्वयंसेवकों ने उनके खाने-पीने से लेकर अन्य सारी व्यवस्था की। उनके अपने गाँव लौटने की व्यवस्था भी की। इस तरह स्वयंसेवकों की जागरूकता से सात महिलाओं का जीवन बच गया।

□

स्वयंसेवक के रक्तदान से परिवारों में गूँजी किलकारियाँ

लॉकडाउन के दौरान 29 मार्च, 2020 को मध्य प्रदेश के मालवा क्षेत्र में संघ के स्वयंसेवक मौसम वाडिया को सुबह चार बजे जानकारी मिली कि एक गर्भवती महिला को रक्त की जरूरत है। वे तत्काल बिस्तर से उठे और सीधा अस्पताल पहुँचकर रक्तदान किया। गर्भवती महिला प्रसव पीड़ा से कराह रही थी, लेकिन जाँच में पता चला कि महिला के शरीर में प्लेटलेट्स की संख्या बहुत कम है। ऐसी हालत में प्रसव कराने पर जच्चा और बच्चा दोनों की जान को खतरा था। अस्पताल में भरती महिला के परिजनों ने तब मदद की गुहार लगाई। लेकिन लॉकडाउन के चलते न तो उन्हें ब्लड बैंक से खून मिल पा रहा था और न कोई बाहरी डोनर अस्पताल आने को तैयार था। इसी बीच महिला के परिजनों को संघ के स्वयंसेवक मौसम वाडिया के बारे में जानकारी मिली तो उन्होंने उनसे संपर्क साधा और सहायता माँगी। वाडिया के रक्तदान करने के बाद ब्लड को फिल्टर कर डॉक्टरों ने महिला को प्लाज्मा प्लेटलेट्स चढ़ाए। प्लेटलेट्स की संख्या में वृद्धि होते ही चंद घंटे में प्रसूता ने स्वस्थ बालक को जन्म दिया। इस तरह स्वयंसेवक ने रक्तदान कर माँ और शिशु को नया जीवन दिया। इसी तरह इंदौर में लॉकडाउन के दौरान एक गर्भवती महिला को प्रसव पीड़ा हुई। जाँच में प्लेटलेट्स कम होने की जानकारी मिली। तब इंदौर के स्वयंसेवक अजय मस्तूद ने 1 अप्रैल, 2020 को रक्तदान किया और फिर महिला को प्लाज्मा प्लेटलेट्स चढ़ाने के बाद प्रसव कराया गया। एक स्वयंसेवक के रक्तदान से माँ और नवजात की जान बच गई। मौसम वाडिया और अजय जैसे अनेक स्वयंसेवकों के तत्काल रक्तदान से जहाँ लोगों की जान बची, वहीं परिवारों में किलकारियाँ भी गूँज उठीं।

□

स्वयंसेवकों की सेवा ने इशरत का दिल जीता

देश भर में 25 मार्च, 2020 से लॉकडाउन लागू होने के बाद फैक्ट्री और कंपनियाँ भी बंद हो गईं। ऐसे में प्रवासी श्रमिकों ने अपने गाँव जाना शुरू कर दिया। कोई पैदल जा रहा था तो कोई साइकिल से, कहीं किसी को जो भी वाहन मिला, उसी में सवार होकर अपने गाँव की तरफ चल दिया। गुजरात और महाराष्ट्र के प्रवासी श्रमिक जलगाँव होते हुए अपने गाँव लौट रहे थे। वहाँ लोगों को किसी तरह की परेशानी नहीं हो, इसको ध्यान में रखते हुए स्वयंसेवकों ने भोजन से लेकर सभी आवश्यक व्यवस्थाएँ की थीं। इन्हीं में एक प्रवासी श्रमिक थे नूर मोहम्मद। नूर सूरत में कपड़ों की फेरी लगाकर जीवनयापन करते थे। वे और उनकी पत्नी इशरत सूरत से पैदल उत्तर प्रदेश के मेरठ में अपने गाँव के लिए चल दिए। जब वे जलगाँव शहर से गुजर रहे थे तो अचानक उनकी पत्नी को प्रसव पीड़ा हुई। लॉकडाउन के कारण नूर मोहम्मद को कोई मदद नहीं मिल पा रही थी। इसी बीच किसी ने उन्हें संघ के स्वयंसेवक रवि कासार का मोबाइल नंबर दिया। नूर ने उनसे बात कर मदद माँगी। रवि तुरंत नूर के पास पहुँचे और साथ में एंबुलेंस भी ले आए। एंबुलेंस से जैसे ही नूर की पत्नी इशरत को अस्पताल ले जाने लगे कि तभी प्रसव पीड़ा और तेज हो गई। रवि ने साथियों की मदद से वहीं इशरत की प्रसूति करवाई और उसके बाद तुरंत अस्पताल पहुँचाया। इसके साथ ही रवि ने उनके लिए भोजन और अन्य सहायता सामग्री उपलब्ध करवाई। स्वयंसेवक की सेवा भावना से भाव-विभोर इशरत ने कहा, "आप तो हमारे लिए खुदा हो।"

□

□

पिता के अंतिम संस्कार के लिए युवक को चेन्नई से बिहार पहुँचाया

कोरोना के समय लॉकडाउन में सेवा भारती की एक टीम ने कोरोना टास्क फोर्स का गठन किया था। इसके अंतर्गत एक हेल्पलाइन भी जारी की गई थी। कोई भी जरूरतमंद देश में कहीं से भी इस पर संपर्क कर सकता था। मई 2020 में इस हेल्पलाइन पर चेन्नई में रहने वाले चंदन का फोन आया। चंदन बिहार के गया जिले में कल्हण गाँव का रहने वाला था। वह चेन्नई में एक प्राइवेट कंपनी में नौकरी करता था, लेकिन लॉकडाउन के कारण कंपनी बंद हो गई। वह अपनी कमाई में से हर महीने अपनी छोटी बहन की शादी और बीमार पिताजी की देखभाल के लिए पैसे भेजता था। वह खुद पर बहुत कम खर्च करता था। कंपनी बंद होने के बाद उसके चेन्नई में रहने, खाने-पीने की समस्या उत्पन्न हो गई। इसी बीच उसके पिता के निधन की खबर आई। उसके पास घर लौटने तक के लिए भी पैसे नहीं थे। हेल्पलाइन पर संपर्क करने के बाद कोरोना टास्क फोर्स के कार्यकर्ता सक्रिय हो गए। उन्होंने उसे चेन्नई से पटना जाने वाली श्रमिक स्पेशल ट्रेन में बिठाया और टिकट के साथ ही रास्ते के खर्च के लिए पैसे भी दिए। कोरोना टास्क फोर्स के कार्यकर्ता चंदन के पटना पहुँचने तक उसके संपर्क में थे। पटना पहुँचने पर पटना के स्वयंसेवक स्वयं चंदन को गाँव छोड़कर आए। पिता के अंतिम संस्कार के बाद चंदन ने हेल्पलाइन को एक भावुक पत्र लिखा और आभार व्यक्त किया। इस तरह की कई मानवीय कहानियाँ हैं, जिसे संघ से जुड़े कोरोना टास्क फोर्स ने अंजाम तक पहुँचाया।

□

ओडिशा रेल हादसे में प्रशासन से पहले पहुँचे स्वयंसेवक

ओडिशा के बालासोर में 02 जून, 2023 को हुई भीषण रेल दुर्घटना के बाद संघ के स्वयंसेवक प्रशासन से भी पहले घटनास्थल पर पहुँचे। दुर्घटनास्थल के पास के गाँव में ही संघ की शाखा होने के कारण स्वयंसेवक शाम को दुर्घटना होते ही तत्काल वहाँ पहुँच गए। वहीं व्हाट्सएप पर सूचना दे दी गई, जिससे रात होते-होते करीब 300 स्वयंसेवक बालेश्वर और भद्रक जिलों से घटनास्थल पर पहुँच गए। वहाँ स्वयंसेवकों को सामने जो भी काम दिखा, उसी में जुट गए। इस भीषण दुर्घटना में सबसे पहले घायलों को राहत पहुँचाने की आवश्यकता थी। जिन्होंने अभी-अभी मृत्यु को करीब से देखा, स्वयंसेवकों ने उन्हें सहारा देने का काम किया। ट्रेन की बोगियों में फँसे यात्रियों को निकालना कम चुनौतीपूर्ण नहीं था। ऐसे में एन.डी.आर.एफ. और प्रशासन को मदद करने में स्वयंसेवकों ने कोई कोर-कसर बाकी नहीं छोड़ी। न केवल यात्रियों को बोगियों से बाहर निकाला, बल्कि उन्हें चिकित्सा के लिए अस्पताल भी पहुँचाया। घायलों को तुरंत इलाज मिले, इसके लिए स्वयंसेवकों ने ऑटो और अपनी मोटरसाइकिल का सहारा लिया। घायल यात्रियों के लिए भोजन, पानी और बिस्तर आदि का प्रबंध किया। खून की जरूरत पड़ी तो सैकड़ों यूनिट रक्तदान किया। शवों को प्लास्टिक में बाँधने के बाद सम्मानजनक ढंग से परिजनों को सौंपा। लापता लोगों की खोज की और उन्हें परिजनों से मिलाया। अखिल भारतीय विद्यार्थी परिषद्, हिंदू जागरण मंच, बजरंग दल, सेवा भारती के स्वयंसेवकों की एक यूनिट बालेश्वर जिला अस्पताल, भद्रक जिला मुख्यालय अस्पताल, सोरो अस्पताल, कटक स्थित एस.सी. बी. मेडिकल कॉलेज व अन्य अस्पतालों में भी डटी रही। इस हादसे में कम-से-कम 233 लोग मारे गए तो वहीं 900 से अधिक घायल हुए।

□

बिहार रेल दुर्घटना में यात्रियों की सेवा में रात भर जुटे रहे

बिहार में 11 अक्तूबर, 2023 को दानापुर-बक्सर रेलखंड पर रघुनाथपुर रेलवे स्टेशन के पास रात करीब 10 बजे नॉर्थ-ईस्ट एक्सप्रेस दुर्घटनाग्रस्त हो गई। ट्रेन के 23 डिब्बे पटरी से उतर गए, जिससे चार यात्रियों की मृत्यु हो गई और 70 से अधिक घायल हो गए। बोगियों के पटरी से उतरते ही लोगों में चीख-पुकार मच गई। आसपास के स्थानीय लोग दुर्घटनास्थल पर पहुँच गए। घटना की जानकारी मिलते ही रघुनाथपुर के स्वयंसेवक दुर्घटनास्थल की ओर मदद के लिए दौड़ पड़े। करीब एक घंटे के भीतर आसपास के जिले के स्वयंसेवक भी दुर्घटनास्थल पर पहुँच गए। स्वयंसेवकों ने सबसे पहले बदहवास घायल यात्रियों को बोगियों से निकाला और उन्हें सुरक्षित एंबुलेंस तक पहुँचाया। वहाँ से उन्हें अस्पताल पहुँचाया गया। स्वयंसेवकों की एक टीम अस्पताल पहुँच गई थी, जिससे घटनास्थल से लाए जाने वाले घायलों को तुरंत उपचार मिल सके। बक्सर और आरा के अस्पतालों में भी घायलों के तुरंत इलाज की व्यवस्था की गई। स्वयंसेवकों ने यात्रियों का सामान ट्रेन से निकालकर सुरक्षित रखवाया। यात्रियों के लिए भोजन और पानी की व्यवस्था की। स्वयंसेवक रात भर यात्रियों को हर तरह की सहायता पहुँचाने में जुटे रहे। इन सभी कार्यों में स्वयंसेवक प्रशासन को हर कदम पर सहयोग कर रहे थे। इतना ही नहीं, यात्रियों को सुरक्षित निकालने के बाद ट्रैक पर पड़े मलबे को हटाने में भी प्रशासन की मदद की, जिससे रेल सेवा दोबारा सुचारू रूप से संचालित हो सकी।

□

बजरंग दल ने 86 लाख गौ-वंश की जान बचाई

विश्व हिंदू परिषद् की युवा इकाई बजरंग दल ने वर्ष 1996 से गौ-वंश की रक्षा के लिए अभियान शुरू किया। वर्ष 1996 से 2023 तक यानी करीब 27 वर्षों में बजरंग दल ने 86 लाख गौ-वंश की रक्षा की। इन वर्षों के दौरान बजरंग दल ने गायों की तस्करी रोकने और वध के लिए ले जाई जा रही गायों को बचाने के लिए देश भर में अभियान चलाया। अभियान के अंतर्गत गौ-वंश की रक्षा कर उन्हें गौशालाओं में पहुँचाया गया। इस निमित्त कई गौशालाओं की स्थापना भी की गई। गौरतलब है कि प्रयागराज के नैनी में 21 मई से 28 मई, 2023 के बीच शौर्य प्रशिक्षण वर्ग का आयोजन किया गया। इस कार्यक्रम के समापन के अवसर पर बजरंग दल के राष्ट्रीय संयोजक नीरज दौनेरिया ने बताया, "वर्ष 1996 में बजरंग दल के 25,000 कार्यकर्ताओं ने प्रयागराज में संगम के तट पर संकल्प लिया था कि 'गाय नहीं कटने देंगे, देश नहीं बँटने देंगे'।" उन्होंने कहा, "जो गौ-वंश कटने जा रहे थे, ऐसे 86 लाख गौ-वंशों की बजरंग दल के कार्यकर्ताओं ने रक्षा की है और इसी का परिणाम है कि आज विश्व हिंदू परिषद् 550 गौशालाएँ चला रही है।" उल्लेखनीय है कि वर्ष 1984 में बजरंग दल का गठन हुआ और 1993 में पूरे देश में इसका संगठनात्मक तंत्र खड़ा किया गया। आज बजरंग दल में 52,000 संयोजक, 3.50 लाख कार्यकर्ता और करीब एक करोड़ सक्रिय सदस्य हैं। □

□

संघ पर लगी पाबंदी पर हाईकोर्ट की सख्त टिप्पणी

राष्ट्रीय स्वयंसेवक संघ की लोकप्रियता से कांग्रेस किस प्रकार खौफ खाती थी, इसका एक उदाहरण इंदिरा गांधी की सरकार द्वारा लगाई गई एक पाबंदी है। वर्ष 1966 में तत्कालीन इंदिरा गांधी की सरकार ने एक सरकारी आदेश जारी किया कि कोई भी केंद्रीय कर्मचारी संघ की गतिविधियों में भाग नहीं ले सकता। इसके बाद वर्ष 1975 और 1980 में भी इस आशय के दो और आदेश जारी किए गए, जिससे यह निषेध प्रभावी बना रहा। यह पाबंदी पाँच दशक से भी अधिक समय तक लगी रही। केंद्र में नरेंद्र मोदी सरकार आने के बाद 9 जुलाई, 2024 को सरकारी आदेश द्वारा इस प्रतिबंध को हटाया गया। हालाँकि इस बीच केंद्र सरकार के एक सेवानिवृत्त अधिकारी पुरुषोत्तम गुप्ता ने मध्य प्रदेश उच्च न्यायालय (इंदौर पीठ) में याचिका दाखिल की थी। उन्होंने तर्क दिया कि संघ पर प्रतिबंध के कारण उन्हें अपने संवैधानिक अधिकारों से वंचित किया गया, जबकि संघ कोई प्रतिबंधित संगठन नहीं है। इस याचिका पर सुनवाई करते हुए अदालत ने महत्त्वपूर्ण टिप्पणी की। 25 जुलाई, 2024 को आदेश देते हुए उच्च न्यायालय ने कहा कि सरकार को इस गलती को सुधारने में पाँच दशक लग गए, जो बेहद खेदजनक है। अदालत ने कहा कि संघ आज अंतरराष्ट्रीय स्तर पर ख्याति प्राप्त संगठन है और उस पर प्रतिबंध तथ्यों, ठोस आधार और रिपोर्ट के अभाव में लिया गया राजनीतिक निर्णय प्रतीत होता है। इसके साथ ही कोर्ट ने केंद्र सरकार को निर्देश दिया कि वह प्रतिबंध हटाने वाले 9 जुलाई, 2024 के उस आदेश को सभी सरकारी विभागों व संस्थाओं तक औपचारिक रूप से प्रेषित करे और अपनी वेबसाइट पर प्रमुखता से प्रकाशित भी करे।

□

सुप्रीम कोर्ट ने कहा : संघ के सदस्य अपराधी नहीं हैं

राष्ट्रीय स्वयंसेवक संघ 02 अक्तूबर, 2022 को यानी गांधी जयंती और विजयादशमी के दिन तमिलनाडु में रैली आयोजित करना चाहता था। लेकिन राज्य में स्टालिन की सरकार ने पथ-संचलन की अनुमति देने से इनकार कर दिया। राज्य सरकार ने यह कहकर रैली पर पाबंदी लगा दी कि राज्य में पॉपुलर फ्रंट ऑफ इंडिया यानी पी.एफ.आई. जैसे प्रतिबंधित संगठनों की गतिविधियों को देखते हुए सुरक्षा खतरों को नजरअंदाज नहीं किया जा सकता। इसके बाद संघ मद्रास हाईकोर्ट पहुँचा, जहाँ उसे पथ-संचलन की अनुमति मिली। कोर्ट ने कहा कि शांतिपूर्ण रैली में हिस्सा लेना संवैधानिक अधिकार है और राज्य को 'उचित सुरक्षा सुविधा' प्रदान करनी चाहिए। इसके उपरांत फरवरी 2023 में तमिलनाडु सरकार ने सुप्रीम कोर्ट का दरवाजा खटखटाया, लेकिन 11 अप्रैल, 2023 को सर्वोच्च न्यायालय ने हाईकोर्ट के आदेश को बरकरार रखते हुए राज्य सरकार की अपील को खारिज कर दिया। न्यायालय ने स्पष्ट किया कि अगर संघ के सदस्यों पर हमला होने की संभावना है तो राज्य की जिम्मेदारी है कि वह उन्हें सुरक्षा प्रदान करे, न कि अधिकारों पर प्रतिबंध लगाए। इसके बाद एक बार फिर सुप्रीम कोर्ट ने 6 नवंबर, 2023 को रैली आयोजित करने के लिए राज्य सरकार को अनुमति देने और मार्ग निर्धारित करने का निर्देश दिया; साथ ही सार्वजनिक व्यवस्था बनाए रखने की जिम्मेदारी भी सौंपी। फैसले के दौरान सर्वोच्च अदालत ने एक महत्त्वपूर्ण बात कही। सुप्रीम कोर्ट ने यह स्पष्ट किया कि संघ के सदस्य कोई अपराधी नहीं हैं, बल्कि राज्य सरकार द्वारा प्रस्तुत आँकड़ों से यह पता चलता है कि अधिकांश मामलों में वे स्वयं हमलों के शिकार या पीड़ित पक्ष रहे हैं। □

वायनाड आपदा में जान जोखिम में डालकर सहायता पहुँचाई

29 जुलाई, 2024 को केरल के वायनाड में भारी बारिश के बाद कई जगहों पर भूस्खलन हुआ। पहाड़ से बहकर आए सैलाब ने पूरे इलाके में हाहाकार मचा दिया। करीब 22 हजार की आबादी वाले चार गाँव तो सिर्फ 4 घंटे में तबाह हो गए। कई घर पानी में बह गए, कई क्षतिग्रस्त हो गए और सैकड़ों लोग मलबे में दब गए। मौसम अत्यधिक खराब होने के कारण किसी के लिए भी वहाँ तक पहुँचना आसान नहीं था। खास बात ये है कि इस संसदीय सीट से जुड़े सांसद राहुल गांधी और प्रियंका गांधी वाड्रा को भी यहाँ पहुँचने में चार दिन लग गए। लेकिन संघ के स्वयंसेवक अपनी जान की परवाह न करते हुए राहत और बचाव कार्य के लिए वहाँ तत्काल पहुँच गए। स्वयंसेवकों ने बिना किसी देरी के मानव सेवा में दिन-रात एक कर दिया। राहत और बचाव कार्य में समन्वय के लिए स्वयंसेवकों ने मेप्पाडी में एक सहायता डेस्क स्थापित किया। संघ के स्वयंसेवक और सेवा भारती के कार्यकर्ताओं ने सबसे पहले घायलों को अस्पताल पहुँचाया। उन्होंने लोगों को मलबे से निकाला, बाढ़ में बेघर हुए लोगों के रहने के लिए शिविर की व्यवस्था की और उनके लिए खाने-पीने के साथ ही दवाइयों का प्रबंध किया। इतना ही नहीं, उन्होंने मृतकों के अंतिम संस्कार की भी व्यवस्था की। यहाँ शवों को ढूँढ़ने का काम कई दिनों तक चलता रहा और इस काम में स्वयंसेवकों ने सेना और आपदा बल को हर स्तर पर सहयोग किया। राहत कार्य में वायनाड के स्वयंसेवकों के साथ ही पड़ोसी जिले नीलगिरि के स्वयंसेवकों ने भी हाथ बँटाया। उल्लेखनीय है कि वायनाड आपदा में करीब 400 लोगों की मृत्यु हो गई।

□

कच्छ के घुमंतू वाढ़ा समाज में 'अपना घर' मिलने की खुशी

गुजरात के कच्छ जिले के बन्नी इलाके में वाढ़ा समुदाय घुमंतू प्रवृत्ति से जीवनयापन करते आ रहे थे। वे मूलभूत सुविधाओं से भी वंचित थे। उनका अपना घर नहीं था। वे जंगलों में इधर-उधर भटकते हुए अपना जीवन गुजर-बसर करते थे। इस तरह वाढ़ा समुदाय के लोग काफी कष्टमय जीवन जीने के लिए विवश थे। न रहने के लिए घर और न ही पीने के लिए पानी जैसी मूलभूत सुविधा थी। ऐसे में उनकी सुध राष्ट्रीय स्वयंसेवक संघ ने ली। संघ से जुड़ी 'सेवा साधना, कच्छ' ने उनका जीवन स्तर बेहतर करने का बीड़ा उठाया और दानदाताओं से संपर्क किया। सेवा साधना ने समाज के सुधी जनों से दान में मिली धनराशि की मदद से चार गाँवों में 65 मकानों का निर्माण कराया, जिससे धूप और बारिश से उन्हें सुरक्षा मिले। इसके साथ ही उन्हें साक्षर कर सबल बनाने और मुख्यधारा से जोड़ने पर बल दिया गया। गाँव में मकानों के साथ ही मंदिर का भी निर्माण किया गया, जिससे वे अपनी संस्कृति से जुड़े रहें। संघ के प्रयासों और दानदाताओं की मदद से 8 दिसंबर, 2024 को वाढ़ा समाज का पहला सामूहिक विवाह संपन्न हुआ। इस समारोह का हिस्सा बनकर वाढ़ा समाज के लोगों की खुशी का ठिकाना नहीं रहा। संघ की अखिल भारतीय प्रतिनिधि सभा के वार्षिक प्रतिवेदन 2024-25 में भी वाढ़ा समाज में आई प्रगति की चर्चा की गई है।

□

महाकुंभ-2025 में
16 हजार स्वयंसेवकों ने सँभाला ट्रैफिक

उत्तर प्रदेश के प्रयागराज में 13 जनवरी से 26 फरवरी, 2025 तक आयोजित किया गया महाकुंभ मेला ऐतिहासिक रहा। पिछले सभी रिकॉर्ड को ध्वस्त करते हुए यह मानव इतिहास का अब तक का सबसे बड़ा जमावड़ा सिद्ध हुआ। प्रयागराज महाकुंभ के दौरान 66 करोड़ से अधिक श्रद्धालुओं ने संगम में डुबकी लगाई। यह आँकड़ा दुनिया के कई देशों की जनसंख्या से भी अधिक है। देश में इतना बड़ा आयोजन हो तो स्वाभाविक है कि राष्ट्रीय स्वयंसेवक संघ की भूमिका भी महत्त्वपूर्ण हो जाती है। संघ हर स्तर पर मदद करने के लिए आगे आया। इतनी बड़ी संख्या में लोगों के प्रयागराज पहुँचने के कारण ट्रैफिक व्यवस्था सुचारू रखना सबसे चुनौतीपूर्ण काम था, जिससे बिना किसी व्यवधान के महाकुंभ सफलतापूर्वक संपन्न हो सके। इसे ध्यान में रखते हुए संघ के 16 हजार कार्यकर्ता ट्रैफिक व्यवस्था सुचारू बनाए रखने के काम में जुट गए। ये स्वयंसेवक मेला क्षेत्र के विभिन्न चौराहों पर तैनात थे और आने वाले श्रद्धालुओं को रास्ता बता रहे थे और पुलिस को ट्रैफिक संचालन में मदद दे रहे थे। इसके लिए बाकायदा स्वयंसेवकों को प्रशिक्षण दिया गया था और यह तय किया गया था कि श्रद्धालुओं को हरसंभव मदद पहुँचाने के लिए वे पुलिस के साथ मिलकर काम करेंगे। इसके अलावा स्वयंसेवकों ने मेला क्षेत्र की साफ-सफाई और स्वास्थ्य सेवा के साथ ही अन्य सेवाओं में भी योगदान दिया।

□

महाकुंभ में संघ की पहल से 140 करोड़ की बचत

प्रयागराज महाकुंभ-2025 में पर्यावरण और स्वच्छता को बनाए रखने के लिए अनेक उपाय किए गए। सरकार के प्रयासों के बीच महाकुंभ के आयोजन को भव्य और पर्यावरण अनुकूल बनाने के लिए संघ ने 'हरित कुंभ' के नाम से एक अनोखी पहल की। इसके लिए संघ के कार्यकर्ताओं ने दिसंबर के अंतिम सप्ताह से ही स्टील की थालियों और जूट एवं कपड़ों के थैलों का मुफ्त वितरण शुरू कर दिया। इन्हें संघ की विभिन्न संस्थाओं ने देश भर से जुटाया था। दरअसल, अखाड़ों के कुंभ प्रवेश के समय से ही साधु-संतों के शिविर लग गए और उनके यहाँ अन्न क्षेत्र प्रारंभ हो गए। कार्यकर्ता पहले शिविरों में जाकर थाली की उपयोगिता और संख्या का अनुमान लगाते थे और उसी के अनुरूप भंडारे को थालियाँ दी जाती थीं। महाकुंभ क्षेत्र में 15 लाख थालियाँ और 15 लाख थैले बाँटने का लक्ष्य रखा गया था, लेकिन श्रद्धालुओं की बढ़ती संख्या को देखते हुए इससे कहीं ज्यादा थैलों और थालियों का वितरण किया गया। भंडारों में बड़े पैमाने पर डिस्पोजल बरतनों, पत्तलों और प्लास्टिक के बैग के उपयोग की संभावना थी, जिससे बड़े पैमाने पर कचरा तैयार होता। इसे रोकने के लिए ही थालियों और थैले बाँटने का अभियान शुरू किया गया। थाली मिलने के बाद कई अखाड़ों और संतों ने प्लास्टिक की लाखों थालियों और पत्तलों का ऑर्डर कैंसिल कर दिया। इससे जहाँ लगभग 140 करोड़ रुपए की बचत हुई, वहीं तकरीबन 29,000 टन कचरे के उत्पादन से राहत मिली। थालियों और थैले वितरण के लिए सेक्टर को क्लस्टर बनाकर भंडार स्थापित किए गए। थाली और थैला वितरण में विश्व हिंदू परिषद्, माधव आश्रम और विद्या भारती जैसी संस्थाओं ने महत्त्वपूर्ण भूमिका निभाई।

□

वंचित वर्गों के 8 हजार विद्यार्थियों को कराया 'कुंभ दर्शन'

राष्ट्रीय स्वयंसेवक संघ ने महाकुंभ-2025 के दौरान वंचित वर्गों को भारतीय संस्कृति और परंपराओं से जोड़ने के लिए एक अनोखी पहल की। संघ की संस्था विद्या भारती ने दलित, जनजातीय और वंचित वर्गों से जुड़े 8 हजार विद्यार्थियों को 'कुंभ दर्शन' की योजना बनाई। यह पहल 16 जनवरी से प्रारंभ हुई, जिसके अंतर्गत 10 वर्ष से अधिक आयु के छात्रों को उनके माता-पिता के साथ महाकुंभ मेले का दौरा कराया गया। विद्या भारती के अनुसार इस यात्रा का उद्‌देश्य दलित और जनजातीय छात्रों को हिंदू परंपराओं, भारतीय संस्कृति और महाकुंभ के आध्यात्मिक महत्त्व से परिचित कराना था। इसका एक उद्‌देश्य यह भी था कि वे अपनी जड़ों से जुड़ें, ताकि धर्मांतरण के प्रयासों से प्रभावित न हों। कुंभ यात्रा के दौरान छात्रों और उनके माता-पिता के ठहरने के लिए मेला क्षेत्र के सेक्टर 9 में एक विशेष शिविर स्थापित किया गया था। अवध क्षेत्र के सेवा भारती विद्यालयों के प्रशिक्षक रामजी सिंह के अनुसार इस दौरान छात्रों को संतों के आश्रम और अखाड़ों को निकट से देखने का अवसर मिला। उन्होंने संगम घाट के दर्शन किए और उन्हें इसके पौराणिक महत्त्व से अवगत कराया गया। इस यात्रा से छात्र भारतीय परंपरा और महाकुंभ के आध्यात्मिक पहलुओं से अवगत हुए। इस प्रयास ने उन्हें अपनी जड़ों से जोड़ने में महत्त्वपूर्ण भूमिका निभाई।

□

54 हजार बिछड़े लोगों को परिजनों से मिलाने में सहायता

महाकुंभ-2025 के विशाल समागम में करोड़ों श्रद्धालु पवित्र स्नान के लिए उमड़े। इसका अनुमान पहले से लगाया गया था और इसी के मद्देनजर संघ ने अपने स्वयंसेवकों को अलग-अलग दायित्व सौंपकर प्रशासन की मदद करने का निश्चय किया था। महाकुंभ मेले के दौरान 45 दिनों तक उमड़े श्रद्धालुओं के जनसैलाब में 54 हजार से अधिक लोग बिछड़ गए, लेकिन सभी बिछड़े लोगों को उनके परिजनों से मिला दिया गया। प्रशासन ने इस समस्या से निपटने के लिए 10 डिजिटल खोया-पाया केंद्र स्थापित किए थे, लेकिन बिछड़े लोगों को परिजनों से मिलाने में स्वयंसेवकों की भूमिका सबसे अहम रही। इसकी वजह यह थी कि वे मेला परिसर और संगम तट पर तो मौजूद थे ही, इसके साथ ही उनकी उपस्थिति रेलवे और बस स्टेशनों से लेकर शहर के मुख्य चौक-चौराहे तक थी। संघ ने खोए हुए श्रद्धालुओं को मिलवाने के लिए एक 'व्हाट्सऐप ग्रुप' बनाया था, जिसमें देश भर के स्वयंसेवक जुड़े हुए थे। इसकी वजह से बिछड़े लोगों को परिजनों से मिलाने में काफी मदद मिली। स्वयंसेवक महाकुंभ में हर जगह उपस्थित थे। एक तरफ वे गंगा-दूत बनकर संगम तट की सफाई का ध्यान रख रहे थे, वहीं संघ की संस्था सेवा भारती ने विशाल भंडारे का आयोजन किया था, जिसमें प्रतिदिन हजारों श्रद्धालुओं को भोजन कराया गया। यहाँ तक कि प्रशासन भी संघ की मदद ले रहा था।

□

अहमदाबाद-लंदन विमान हादसे के समय हर मोरचे पर डटे स्वयंसेवक

12 जून, 2025 को अहमदाबाद से लंदन जा रही एयर इंडिया की फ्लाइट ए.आई.-171, बोइंग 787-8 ड्रीमलाइनर, उड़ान भरने के कुछ ही क्षणों बाद दुर्घटनाग्रस्त हो गई। इस हादसे में विमान में सवार 241 लोगों सहित बीजे मेडिकल कॉलेज के छात्रावास में भी कई लोगों की मृत्यु हो गई, जिससे कुल मृतकों की संख्या 265 से अधिक हो गई। हादसा बहुत भयावह था; पूरा देश शोक में डूब गया था। देश भर में जहाँ इसे लेकर चर्चा चल रही थी, वहीं संघ के स्वयंसेवक संकट के समय घटनास्थल पर पहुँचकर राहत और बचाव कार्य में जुट गए। घटनास्थल पर भीड़ बढ़ती देखकर उन्होंने भीड़-नियंत्रण का मोरचा भी सँभाल लिया। स्वयंसेवकों ने पुलिस और प्रशासन के साथ मिलकर ग्रीन कॉरिडोर बनाया, जिससे घायलों को जल्द-से-जल्द सिविल अस्पताल पहुँचाया गया। अस्पताल में मौजूद स्वयंसेवकों ने परिजनों को ढाँढ़स बँधाया और पीड़ितों को तत्काल चिकित्सा सहायता दिलाने में मदद की। रक्त की जरूरत पड़ी तो रक्तदान के लिए वे सबसे आगे आए। दुर्घटनास्थल एवं अस्पताल में मौजूद परिजनों, राहत कार्य करने वालों और जरूरतमंदों के लिए भोजन और पानी की व्यवस्था की। दुर्घटनास्थल और अस्पताल के बाहर भीड़-नियंत्रण में स्वयंसेवकों ने महत्त्वपूर्ण भूमिका निभाई। शहर की ट्रैफिक व्यवस्था को सुचारू रखने में उन्होंने पुलिस की हरसंभव मदद की। अस्पताल के बाहर राहत केंद्रों पर स्वयंसेवक लगातार अपनी सेवा देते रहे। विभिन्न शहरों से आने वाले परिजनों को जानकारी देने और भोजन-पानी देने से लेकर हर प्रकार की सहायता की। जहाँ भी मानव सेवा की जरूरत पड़ी, संघ के कार्यकर्ता तत्परता से अपनी सेवा देने में जुटे रहे।

□

संघ भारत की अमर संस्कृति का वटवृक्ष : पी.एम. मोदी

नरेंद्र मोदी ने प्रधानमंत्री के रूप में 30 मार्च, 2025 को संघ मुख्यालय का दौरा किया। पी.एम. मोदी ऐसे समय में संघ मुख्यालय पहुँचे, जब संघ ने अपनी स्थापना के 100 वर्ष पूरे किए। मोदी ने डॉ. हेडगेवार स्मारक स्थित स्मृति भवन में संघ के पदाधिकारियों से मुलाकात की। उन्होंने डॉ. हेडगेवार स्मृति मंदिर जाकर संघ के संस्थापकों को श्रद्धांजलि दी। स्मृति मंदिर में संदेश पुस्तिका पर उन्होंने लिखा—यह स्मारक भारतीय संस्कृति, राष्ट्रवाद और संगठन के मूल्यों को समर्पित है। प्रधानमंत्री ने अपने संदेश में लिखा, "संघ के दो मजबूत स्तंभों का स्मारक उन लाखों स्वयंसेवकों के लिए प्रेरणा है, जिन्होंने राष्ट्र की सेवा के लिए स्वयं को समर्पित कर दिया है। मैं 'स्मृति मंदिर' में आकर अभिभूत हूँ। यह स्थल परम पूज्य डॉ. हेडगेवार और पूज्य श्रीगुरुजी की स्मृतियों को सँजोए हुए है।" प्रधानमंत्री मोदी ने 'माधव नेत्रालय प्रीमियम सेंटर' की आधारशिला रखी। यह सेंटर माधव नेत्रालय नेत्र संस्थान और अनुसंधान केंद्र का नया विस्तार भवन है, जिसका नाम पूर्व संघ प्रमुख माधवराव गोलवलकर 'श्रीगुरुजी' के नाम पर रखा गया है। संघ को वटवृक्ष की संज्ञा देते हुए पी.एम. मोदी ने कहा, "संघ भारत की अमर संस्कृति और आधुनिकीकरण का वटवृक्ष है, जिसके आदर्श और सिद्धांत राष्ट्रीय चेतना की रक्षा करना है। संघ के स्वयंसेवक देश के विभिन्न क्षेत्रों एवं हिस्सों में निस्स्वार्थ भाव से काम कर रहे हैं।" मोदी ने कहा कि सेवा की भावना संघ के स्वयंसेवकों की पीढ़ियों को अथक परिश्रम के लिए प्रेरित करती है और यह समर्पण स्वयंसेवकों को निरंतर सक्रिय रखता है तथा उन्हें कभी थकने या रुकने नहीं देता। इससे पहले मोदी दो बार वर्ष 2012 और 2013 में संघ मुख्यालय पहुँचे थे, जब वे गुजरात के मुख्यमंत्री थे।

□

धराली आपदा में स्वयंसेवक बने उम्मीद की किरण

5 अगस्त, 2025 को उत्तराखंड के उत्तरकाशी जनपद के धराली क्षेत्र में आई भीषण प्राकृतिक आपदा ने भारी तबाही मचाई। सैकड़ों परिवार बेघर हो गए और उनके सामने खाद्य सामग्री से लेकर रहने तक का संकट उत्पन्न हो गया। इस चुनौतीपूर्ण संकट के समय संघ के स्वयंसेवक सेवा के मोरचे पर तत्काल जुट गए। संकटग्रस्त परिवारों की सहायता के लिए राष्ट्रीय स्वयंसेवक संघ ने त्वरित कदम उठाए और 'उत्तरांचल दैवीय आपदा पीड़ित सहायता समिति' का गठन किया। धराली गाँव के कुल 280 परिवारों में से 80 परिवार ऐसे थे, जो इस आपदा से सर्वाधिक प्रभावित हुए। इनके पास न तो भोजन पकाने और न ही जीवनयापन की अन्य आवश्यक सामग्री थी। इस विकट स्थिति को देखते हुए स्वयंसेवकों ने जरूरतमंदों को भोजन सामग्री के साथ ही आवश्यक वस्तुओं के पैकेट वितरित किए। आपदा से बेघर हुए लोगों के लिए हर दिन एक नई चुनौती बनकर सामने आ रहा था। इसे देखते हुए संघ ने ऋषिकेश से राहत सामग्री से भरे ट्रक को धराली के लिए रवाना किया। इस ट्रक में आवश्यक खाद्य सामग्री, दैनिक उपयोग की वस्तुएँ और गैस सिलेंडर जैसी जीवनदायिनी सामग्री शामिल थीं। ऋषिकेश के महापौर शंभु पासवान ने इस पहल की सराहना करते हुए कहा, "यह अत्यंत सराहनीय पहल है। ऐसे समय में जब धराली के लोग गहरे संकट में हैं, संघ की यह मदद उन्हें बड़ी राहत देगी।" आपदा की इस घड़ी में राष्ट्रीय स्वयंसेवक संघ धराली के पीड़ित परिवारों के लिए न केवल भौतिक सहायता, बल्कि एक नई उम्मीद और जीने की हिम्मत लेकर आया। □

संघ के शताब्दी वर्ष पर लाल किले से गुणगान

15 अगस्त, 2025 को 79वें स्वतंत्रता दिवस पर प्रधानमंत्री नरेंद्र मोदी ने लाल किले से राष्ट्र को संबोधित करते हुए राष्ट्रीय स्वयंसेवक संघ की सराहना की। यह पहला अवसर था, जब किसी प्रधानमंत्री ने लाल किले से भाषण में संघ का उल्लेख किया। प्रधानमंत्री मोदी ने अपने संबोधन में कहा, "आज मैं बहुत गर्व के साथ एक बात का जिक्र करना चाहता हूँ। आज से 100 साल पहले एक संगठन का जन्म हुआ—राष्ट्रीय स्वयंसेवक संघ। 100 साल की राष्ट्र की सेवा, एक बहुत ही गौरवपूर्ण स्वर्णिम पृष्ठ है। व्यक्ति निर्माण से राष्ट्र निर्माण के संकल्प को लेकर 100 साल तक माँ भारती के कल्याण का लक्ष्य लेकर स्वयंसेवकों ने अपना जीवन समर्पित किया है। सेवा, समर्पण, संगठन और अप्रतिम अनुशासन, यह जिसकी पहचान रही है। राष्ट्रीय स्वयंसेवक संघ एक प्रकार से दुनिया का सबसे बड़ा एन.जी.ओ. है। 100 साल का उसका समर्पण का इतिहास है। मैं आज यहाँ लाल किले की प्राचीर से 100 साल की इस राष्ट्र सेवा की यात्रा में योगदान करने वाले सभी स्वयंसेवकों को आदरपूर्वक स्मरण करता हूँ। राष्ट्रीय स्वयंसेवक संघ की इस 100 साल की भव्य समर्पित यात्रा पर देश गर्व करता है और यह हमें प्रेरणा देती रहेगी।" उल्लेखनीय है कि प्रधानमंत्री मोदी ने 30 मार्च, 2025 को राष्ट्रीय स्वयंसेवक संघ के मुख्यालय का दौरा किया था और वहाँ भी संघ के कार्यों की प्रशंसा की थी। वहीं, मार्च 2025 में अमरीकी पॉडकास्टर लेक्स फ्रिडमैन के साथ हुए साक्षात्कार में प्रधानमंत्री मोदी ने संघ के उनके जीवन पर प्रभाव की चर्चा की थी। उन्होंने संघ के सेवाकार्यों को महत्त्वपूर्ण बताया था।

□

शतवर्षीय यात्रा पर विशेष डाक टिकट और सिक्का

संघ की 100वीं वर्षगाँठ पर भारत सरकार ने एक विशेष कार्यक्रम का आयोजन किया। नई दिल्ली के आंबेडकर इंटरनेशनल सेंटर में 1 अक्तूबर, 2025 को आयोजित इस कार्यक्रम में प्रधानमंत्री नरेंद्र मोदी और राष्ट्रीय स्वयंसेवक संघ के सरकार्यवाह दत्तात्रेय होसबाले के अतिरिक्त कई गणमान्य लोग उपस्थित थे। इस कार्यक्रम के माध्यम से केंद्र सरकार ने संघ के योगदान को सार्वजनिक रूप से न केवल सराहा, बल्कि पहली बार विशेष डाक टिकट और स्मारक सिक्का भी जारी किया। इस विशेष स्मारक डाक टिकट में सरकार ने वर्ष 1963 में गणतंत्र दिवस परेड के दौरान संघ के स्वयंसेवकों के मार्च के यादगार पल को उकेरा है। 100 रुपए के स्मारक सिक्के के एक ओर राष्ट्रीय प्रतीक चिह्न तो दूसरी तरफ सिंह के साथ वरद मुद्रा में भारत माता की भव्य छवि अंकित है, जिन्हें स्वयंसेवकों द्वारा नमन किया जा रहा है। इस अवसर पर प्रधानमंत्री मोदी ने कहा, “स्वतंत्र भारत के इतिहास में संभवत: यह पहली बार है, जब भारत माता की छवि भारतीय मुद्रा पर दिखाई दी है। सिक्के पर संघ का मार्गदर्शक आदर्श वाक्य—‘राष्ट्राय स्वाहा, इदं राष्ट्राय, इदं न मम’ भी अंकित है।”

□

संगठन

संघ उत्सव के दौरान बाल स्वयंसेवक।

संघ उत्सव के दौरान स्वयंसेवक।

स्वयंसेवकों का पथ संचलन।

शाखा के दौरान भारत माता की वंदना।

शाखा में शामिल स्वयंसेवक।

राष्ट्र रक्षा के यज्ञ में आहुति के लिए संघ का गठन

मुट्ठी भर अंग्रेजों का करीब सात हजार किलोमीटर दूर से आकर भारत जैसे विशाल देश पर राज करना, कांग्रेस पार्टी का मुसलिम तुष्टीकरण, देशवासियों में राष्ट्रप्रेम की भावना का अभाव और हिंदुओं का संगठित नहीं होना एवं जातियों में बँटा होना, ये कुछ ऐसे सवाल थे, जो डॉ. हेडगेवार के मन-मस्तिष्क को बार-बार कुरेद रहे थे। राष्ट्रीय स्वयंसेवक संघ की स्थापना के पीछे ये कुछ ऐसे आधार बिंदु थे, जिनसे वह हिंदुस्तान के राष्ट्रीय फलक को तैयार करना चाहते थे। सांस्कृतिक स्वाभिमान के माध्यम से वह भारत की सर्वांग स्वतंत्रता का रास्ता तय करना चाहते थे। डॉ. हेडगेवार का मानना था, "राष्ट्र रक्षा के समान कोई पुण्य नहीं, राष्ट्र रक्षा के समान कोई व्रत नहीं, राष्ट्र रक्षा के समान कोई यज्ञ नहीं। अतः राष्ट्र रक्षा सर्वोपरि होनी चाहिए।" इन्हीं सूत्रों को आत्मसात् करते हुए उन्होंने 1925 में विजयादशमी के दिन राष्ट्रीय स्वयंसेवक संघ का गठन किया। स्वतंत्रता आंदोलन के लिए संघ के जरिए वे देशवासियों विशेषकर नवयुवकों को एकजुट करना चाहते थे। उनका यह भी मानना था, "अनुशासन अपने संगठन की नींव है, इसी पर हमें विशाल इमारत को खड़ा करना है। किसी भी भूल से यदि नींव जरा सी भी कच्ची रह गई तो इमारत का उस ओर का भाग ढल जाएगा। इमारत में दरार पड़ जाएगी और आखिर में वह संपूर्ण इमारत ढह जाएगी। जीवन में निस्स्वार्थ भावना आए बिना खरे अनुशासन का निर्माण नहीं होता।" वे भारत के मूल्यों, संस्कृति और परंपराओं के आधार पर समाज और राष्ट्र को संगठित करना चाहते थे। उन्हें व्यक्ति पूजा से घृणा थी और इसलिए उन्होंने वर्ष 1923 में कांग्रेस पार्टी छोड़ दी। उनका मानना था व्यक्ति आज है, कल नहीं होगा। यही वजह है कि उन्होंने संघ में व्यक्ति को महत्त्व न देकर, विचार को महत्त्व दिया।

□

पहले गुरु-दक्षिणा कार्यक्रम में एकत्र हुए 84.50 रुपए

राष्ट्रीय स्वयंसेवक संघ सबसे कम खर्च में चलने वाला समाजसेवी संगठन है। एक समय ये कहावत थी कि संघ की शाखा चलाने के लिए क्या चाहिए? एक डंडा और एक झंडा। इसके अलावा वरदी आदि की जो जरूरत होती है, उसकी व्यवस्था स्वयंसेवक खुद ही करते हैं। संघ के संस्थापक डॉ. हेडगेवार ने सभी कार्यकर्ताओं को शाखा चलाने और देश सेवा से लेकर अन्य सभी काम करने के दौरान सादगी से चलने पर जोर दिया था। वर्ष 1925 में संघ की स्थापना के बाद कार्यक्रमों एवं समारोहों के लिए धन की आवश्यकता अनुभव हुई तो 1928 में संघ ने अपनी गतिविधियों के लिए गुरु-दक्षिणा कार्यक्रम की शुरुआत की। वर्ष 1928 में पहली गुरु-दक्षिणा कार्यक्रम में 84.50 रुपए एकत्र हुए थे। उसके बाद यह संघ का वार्षिक कार्यक्रम बन गया। गुरु-दक्षिणा कार्यक्रम में सम्मिलित होने वाले संघ के लिए गुप्त दान करते हैं। हिंदू कैंलेडर के हिसाब से गुरु पूर्णिमा से रक्षाबंधन तक यानी एक महीने गुरु-दक्षिणा का कार्यक्रम चलता है। इस दौरान स्वयंसेवक संघ में गुरु माने जाने वाले भगवा ध्वज के सामने अपनी इच्छा से दक्षिणा की राशि समर्पित करते हैं। इसे गुप्त रखा जाता है यानी दक्षिणा की राशि और देने वाले का नाम सार्वजनिक नहीं किया जाता, लेकिन हर एक पैसे का पूरा हिसाब रखा जाता है। किसी भी संगठन के भ्रष्ट होने और खत्म होने का सबसे बड़ा कारण आर्थिक तौर पर दूसरों या सरकारों पर निर्भर होना होता है। डॉ. हेडगेवार ने इसे पहले ही भाँप लिया था; इसीलिए उन्होंने संघ को आत्मनिर्भर बनाया और इसके लिए गुरु-दक्षिणा की परंपरा प्रारंभ की।

□

इस तरह हुआ 'राष्ट्रीय स्वयंसेवक संघ' का नामकरण

राष्ट्रीय स्वयंसेवक संघ की स्थापना वर्ष 1925 में 'विजयादशमी' के दिन हुई, लेकिन संगठन का नाम करीब छह माह बाद तय किया गया। 17 अप्रैल, 1926 को डॉ. हेडगेवार ने एक बैठक बुलाई, जिसमें संगठन का नाम तय करने के लिए विस्तृत चर्चा हुई। कई दौर की बैठक के बाद तीन नामों को अंतिम रूप दिया गया—राष्ट्रीय स्वयंसेवक संघ, जरीपताका मंडल और भद्रातोद्धारक मंडल। इन तीन नामों पर अधिक विचार-विमर्श हुआ और अंतत: 'राष्ट्रीय स्वयंसेवक संघ' नाम चुना गया। प्राध्यापक पांडुरंग कृष्णराव सावलापुरकर ने बैठक का वृत्तांत बताते हुए कहा कि बैठक में 26 स्वयंसेवक उपस्थित थे। उनमें से बहुत सारे स्वयंसेवकों की आयु तो बीस वर्ष से भी कम होगी, लेकिन डॉ. हेडगेवार ने सभी को खुली चर्चा करने का अवसर दिया। सावलापुरकर ने भी आधा घंटा भाषण दिया। बाद में सबकी सहमति से 'राष्ट्रीय स्वयंसेवक संघ' नाम स्वीकृत किया गया।

□

इस तरह तय हुई संघ की प्रार्थना 'नमस्ते सदा वत्सले मातृभूमे'

राष्ट्रीय स्वयंसेवक संघ की शाखाओं में नियमित रूप से गाई जाने वाली प्रार्थना संघ की स्थापना के 14 साल बाद तय की गई। यह प्रार्थना 'नमस्ते सदा वत्सले मातृभूमे' अब इसके कामकाज का अनिवार्य अंग ही नहीं, पहचान भी बन चुकी है। पूरी प्रार्थना संस्कृत में है। संघ की प्रार्थना की रचना व प्रारूप सबसे पहले फरवरी 1939 में नागपुर के पास सिंदी में हुई बैठक में तैयार किया गया। संघ की प्रार्थना संघ संस्थापक डॉ. केशवराव बलिराम हेडगेवार, माधव सदाशिव गोलवलकर तथा अन्य वरिष्ठ कार्यकर्ताओं के मार्गदर्शन में संस्कृत के प्राध्यापक नरहरि नारायण भिड़े ने लिखी थी। संघ प्रार्थना में ही संघ के कार्यकर्ताओं का उद्‍देश्य, लक्ष्य, स्वप्न, देश के प्रति कर्तव्य का वर्णन है। शुरुआत में प्रार्थना मराठी और हिंदी में रखने पर भी विचार हुआ। फिर अंत में प्रार्थना को केवल संस्कृत भाषा में रखने का निर्णय हुआ, ताकि सारे देश में एक स्वरूप एवं एक भाषा में प्रार्थना हो।

□

स्वयंसेवकों ने प्रस्तुत की अनुशासन की मिसाल

वर्ष 1937 में नागपुर में संघ के स्वयंसेवकों का एक शिविर लगाया गया। इसमें दो हजार से अधिक स्वयंसेवकों ने भाग लिया था। एक तो उस समय सुविधाओं का अभाव था और ऊपर से इतनी भारी संख्या में स्वयंसेवकों की व्यवस्था करना टेढ़ी खीर था। परंतु देश और समाज के प्रति संघ की सेवा से प्रेरित लोगों के सहयोग से इसमें कोई दिक्कत नहीं आई। स्वयंसेवकों के ठहरने एवं भोजन का प्रबंध शहर के शुभचिंतकों की मदद से हो गया, लेकिन एक साथ इतने लोगों के स्नान आदि की व्यवस्था करना भी कम चुनौतीपूर्ण नहीं था। शहर के पास ही दिलावर खान का संतरे का बगीचा था और उसी से सटा टैंक था। दिलावर खान ने टैंक में स्वयंसेवकों को स्नान करने की अनुमति तो दे दी, लेकिन उसे अंदर-अंदर संतरे के चोरी होने का भय सताता रहा। शिविर जब संपन्न हुआ तो उसने अपने संतरे के बगीचे का निरीक्षण किया और पाया कि एक भी संतरा चोरी नहीं हुआ था। वह यह देखकर चकित रह गया। स्वयंसेवकों के अनुशासन से प्रभावित होकर उसने कार्यकर्ताओं के लिए संतरे की कई टोकरियाँ डॉ. हेडगेवार को भेंट कीं। जाहिर है डॉ. हेडगेवार ने संघ में अनुशासन का जो बीज बोया, आज वह वटवृक्ष बनकर संगठन के उद्देश्यों को प्राप्त करने में बहुत बड़ी भूमिका निभा रहा है।

□

डॉ. हेडगेवार की आखिरी चिट से चुने गए संघ के दूसरे प्रमुख

किसी को अंदाजा नहीं था कि डॉ. हेडगेवार अपने बाद संघ की कमान 34 वर्षीय माधवराव सदाशिवराव गोलवलकर 'श्रीगुरुजी' को सौंपकर जाएँगे। 21 जून, 1940 को डॉ. हेडगेवार का 51 वर्ष की आयु में निधन हो गया। उस समय श्रीगुरुजी से अधिक वरिष्ठ स्वयंसेवक संघ में मौजूद थे। अपनी मृत्यु से एक दिन पहले डॉ. हेडगेवार ने श्रीगुरुजी को एक चिट पकड़ाई थी। डॉ. हेडगेवार की मृत्यु के बाद 13 दिन तक शोक रहा। 3 जुलाई, 1940 को संघ के सारे बड़े अधिकारी नागपुर में जुटे। बैठक में डॉ. हेडगेवार की वह चिट पढ़ी गई। चिट में लिखा था—"इससे पहले कि तुम मेरे शरीर को डॉक्टरों के हवाले करो, मैं तुमसे कहना चाहता हूँ कि अब से संगठन को चलाने की पूरी जिम्मेदारी तुम्हारी होगी।" पुस्तक 'द ब्रदरहुड इन सैफरन' के अनुसार, इस बैठक से पहले कयास लग रहे थे कि अप्पाजी जोशी को डॉ. हेडगेवार अपना उत्तराधिकारी चुनेंगे। जब श्रीगुरुजी का नाम आया तो संघ के सभी लोग हैरान रह गए। डॉ. हेडगेवार ने श्रीगुरुजी के समर्पण और भविष्य के संघ को गढ़ने एवं तेजी से इसके विस्तार के लिए गोलवलकर को चुना था। संघ के कार्यकर्ताओं का डॉ. हेडगेवार के प्रति अगाध श्रद्धा भाव ही था कि उन्होंने उनके निर्णय को सहर्ष स्वीकार किया।

□

विदेश में संघ की पहली शाखा केन्या के मोंबासा में लगी

राष्ट्रीय स्वयंसेवक संघ की देश से बाहर पहली शाखा पानी के जहाज पर लगी थी, वहीं विदेशी धरती पर पहली शाखा केन्या के मोंबासा में लगी थी। भारत की स्वाधीनता से कुछ ही महीने पहले वर्ष 1946 के अंत में भारतीयों को लेकर अफ्रीका जा रहे एक जहाज पर पंजाब के एक स्वयंसेवक की इच्छा अपने संगठन की प्रार्थना गाने की हुई। उन्होंने संघ की प्रार्थना 'नमस्ते सदा वत्सले मातृभूमे' गाना शुरू किया तो देखा कि कुछ और लोग भी उनके साथ गा रहे हैं। संघ के उस कार्यकर्ता का नाम जगदीश चंद्र शारदा था। यहीं उनकी भेंट संघ के दूसरे स्वयंसेवक मानेक भाई रुगानी से हुई। वे दोनों केन्या जा रहे थे। इसके बाद दोनों ने जहाज पर ही शाखा लगाने का निर्णय किया। उन्होंने उसी जहाज पर शाखा लगाई। जहाज पर लगी उस शाखा को संघ की भारत के बाहर लगी पहली शाखा माना गया। इसके बाद केन्या के शहर मोंबासा पहुँचकर उन्होंने 'भारत स्वयंसेवक संघ' का गठन किया और शाखा लगाई। बाद में इसे 'हिंदू स्वयंसेवक संघ' नाम दिया गया। इस तरह विदेश में संघ की पहली शाखा केन्या के मोंबासा में लगी। विदेशी धरती पर संघ की इसी पहली शाखा के सदस्यों ने तंजानिया, युगांडा, मॉरीशस और अफ्रीका के अन्य हिस्सों में संगठन का प्रचार-प्रसार किया। उल्लेखनीय है कि राष्ट्रीय स्वयंसेवक संघ विदेशों में हिंदू स्वयंसेवक संघ के नाम से कार्य करता है, जो 40 देशों में पंजीकृत है। अरब के कुछ देशों में संघ की शाखा बंद कमरे के भीतर लगाई जाती है। फिनलैंड एवं कुछ अन्य देशों में ऑनलाइन शाखा लगाई जाती है।

□

संघ की 83 हजार शाखाओं से जुड़े हैं एक करोड़ स्वयंसेवक

देश में राष्ट्रीय स्वयंसेवक संघ की 83,129 शाखाएँ हैं। संघ की संगठनात्मक संरचना में पूरे भारत में 46 प्रांत, 922 जिले, 6,597 खंड और 27,720 मंडल में 83,129 दैनिक शाखाएँ हैं। संघ स्थान की बात करें तो ये 52 हजार के करीब हैं। संघ के मिलन कार्यक्रमों की संख्या 32,147 है। इसी तरह संघ की मंडली की संख्या 12,091 है। ये आँकड़े 13 मार्च, 2025 तक के हैं। 21 मार्च से 23 मार्च, 2025 को कर्नाटक की राजधानी बेंगलुरु में हुई संघ की अखिल भारतीय प्रतिनिधि सभा की बैठक में सह सरकार्यवाह सी.आर. मुकुंद ने यह जानकारी दी। संघ की ओर से बताया गया कि वर्तमान में देश भर में 73,646 स्थानों पर संघ की गतिविधियाँ चल रही हैं। इनमें से 51,710 स्थान पर दैनिक गतिविधियाँ और 21,936 स्थान पर साप्ताहिक गतिविधियाँ चल रही हैं। मुकुंद ने बताया कि कुल 58,981 ग्रामीण मंडलों में से 30,770 स्थानों पर शाखाएँ लग रही हैं। संघ संगठन क्षमता की जानकारी देते हुए उन्होंने बताया कि देश भर में एक करोड़ से अधिक स्वयंसेवक हैं और इनमें से करीब 6 लाख प्रतिदिन शाखा जाते हैं। इसके अतिरिक्त भी कई स्वयंसेवक विविध क्षेत्रों में संघ प्रेरित संगठनों में कार्यरत हैं। उल्लेखनीय है कि साल 2012 से मार्च 2025 तक 12,73,453 से अधिक लोग संघ से जुड़े हैं।

□

इन वजहों से तीन बार लगा था संघ पर बैन, फिर ऐसे हटा

संघ के 100 साल के इतिहास में उस पर तीन बार 1948, 1975 और 1992 में प्रतिबंध लगाया गया। इन तीनों ही अवसरों पर जाँच के बाद यह पता चला कि संगठन के विरूद्ध लगाए गए आरोप निराधार थे और कोई सबूत नहीं मिला। इसके बाद प्रतिबंध हटाना पड़ा। संघ पर पहला प्रतिबंध महात्मा गांधी की हत्या के बाद 4 फरवरी, 1948 को लगाया गया और संघ प्रमुख श्रीगुरुजी सहित सैकड़ों स्वयंसेवकों को गिरफ्तार किया गया। हालाँकि जाँच के बाद गांधी हत्या मामले में संघ की संलिप्तता का कोई प्रमाण नहीं मिला। 18 महीने तक चली विस्तृत जाँच में कोई आरोप सिद्ध नहीं हुआ, जिसके बाद सरकार ने 11 जुलाई, 1949 को संघ से प्रतिबंध हटा लिया। दूसरा प्रतिबंध आपातकाल के दौरान लगाया गया। 25 जून, 1975 को तत्कालीन प्रधानमंत्री इंदिरा गांधी ने देश में आपातकाल की घोषणा की। उस दौरान संघ ने खुलकर आपातकाल का विरोध किया था। इसे देखते हुए संघ पर प्रतिबंध लगा दिया गया। इस दौरान हजारों संघ कार्यकर्ताओं को गिरफ्तार किया गया। जनता पार्टी सरकार ने 22 मार्च, 1977 को संघ सहित सभी प्रतिबंधित संगठनों से प्रतिबंध हटा दिया। तीसरा प्रतिबंध 6 दिसंबर, 1992 को अयोध्या में विवादित ढाँचे के विध्वंस के बाद लगाया गया। सरकार ने संघ पर विध्वंस की साजिश रचने और सांप्रदायिक तनाव भड़काने का आरोप लगाते हुए 10 दिसंबर, 1992 को उस पर प्रतिबंध लगा दिया। इस मामले की सुनवाई कर रहे विशेष न्यायाधीकरण ने पाया कि सरकार के पास संघ पर प्रतिबंध लगाने के लिए पर्याप्त प्रमाण नहीं थे कि वह विध्वंस या सांप्रदायिक हिंसा में शामिल था। इसके बाद 4 जून, 1993 को प्रतिबंध हटा लिया गया।

□

संघ ने देश को दिया राजनीतिक विकल्प

देश की स्वाधीनता के दौरान महात्मा गांधी ने यह इच्छा जताई थी कि कांग्रेस को अब समाप्त कर देना चाहिए। कांग्रेस समाप्त तो नहीं हुई, मगर धीरे-धीरे कांग्रेस का आभामंडल क्षीण होता चला गया। जाहिर है देश में नेहरू के एकतरफा फैसले और तुष्टीकरण की नीतियों के खिलाफ एक वैकल्पिक राजनीतिक दल की आवश्यकता महसूस की जा रही थी। इस बात को तब और बल मिला, जब नेहरू मंत्रिमंडल में उद्योग मंत्री रहे डॉ. श्यामा प्रसाद मुकर्जी ने अपने पद से त्याग-पत्र दे दिया। उन्होंने नेहरू-लियाकत समझौते को मुसलिम तुष्टीकरण की संज्ञा देते हुए 19 अप्रैल, 1950 को मंत्रिमंडल से इस्तीफा दे दिया। डॉ. मुकर्जी ने नेहरू की नीतियों के विरोध में और कांग्रेस के विकल्प के रूप में एक नई राजनीतिक पार्टी खड़ा करने का बीड़ा उठाया। सरकार से हटने के बाद डॉ. मुकर्जी ने संघ प्रमुख श्रीगुरुजी से नागपुर में भेंट की और अपनी बात रखी। श्रीगुरुजी ने उनका समर्थन किया, लेकिन एक शर्त रखी कि संघ सीधे राजनीति में नहीं आएगा, लेकिन जनसंघ को प्रचारक कार्यकर्ता देगा। श्रीगुरुजी ने डॉ. मुकर्जी के नेतृत्व में संघ प्रचारक दीनदयाल उपाध्याय, अटल बिहारी वाजपेयी, नानाजी देशमुख और बलराज मधोक को नई राजनीतिक पार्टी खड़ा करने की जिम्मेदारी सौंपी। बाद में ये नेता नए दल जनसंघ के स्तंभ बने। संघ के सहयोग से 21 अक्तूबर, 1951 को दिल्ली के राघोमल कन्या विद्यालय में भारतीय जनसंघ की नींव रखी गई, जिसका चुनाव चिह्न दीपक था। 1977 में जनसंघ का विलय जनता पार्टी में किया गया, लेकिन 1980 में यह पुनः भारतीय जनता पार्टी (BJP) के रूप में अस्तित्व में आया। आज दुनिया की सबसे बड़ी पार्टी बन चुकी भारतीय जनता पार्टी के वरिष्ठ नेताओं में संघ के स्वयंसेवकों की लंबी-चौड़ी सूची है।

□

संघ ने दिए राष्ट्रपति, उपराष्ट्रपति और मोदी सहित दो प्रधानमंत्री

संघ के इतिहास में 2014 कई मायनों में स्वर्णिम साल के रूप में गिना जाएगा। इस साल उसके एक प्रचारक नरेंद्र मोदी को देश ने पूर्ण बहुमत के साथ प्रधानमंत्री के रूप में चुना। नरेंद्र मोदी 8 साल की उम्र में बाल स्वयंसेवक के रूप में संघ की वडनगर शाखा से जुड़े। नरेंद्र मोदी करीब 20 वर्ष की आयु में 1970 में राष्ट्रीय स्वयंसेवक संघ से कार्यकर्ता के रूप में जुड़ गए। उनका लक्ष्य बेहद स्पष्ट और निर्धारित था। उन्होंने देश सेवा का प्रण लिया और संघ के कार्यकर्ता बन गए। वर्ष 1972 में वह पूर्णकालिक प्रचारक बने। आपातकाल के दौरान पी.एम. मोदी ने परदे के पीछे रहकर महत्त्वपूर्ण भूमिकाएँ निभाईं। नरेंद्र मोदी अनवरत संघ के काम में जुटे रहे और उनके संगठनात्मक कौशल की सराहना होती रही। फिर एक दिन उन्हें दिल्ली बुलाया गया। वर्ष 1987 में वह भाजपा में सम्मिलित हुए। बाद में उन्हें पार्टी में बड़ी जिम्मेदारियाँ मिलती गईं। वर्ष 1988-89 के दौरान मोदी को गुजरात भाजपा में महासचिव की जिम्मेदारी सौंपी गई। वर्ष 1995 में उन्हें भाजपा का राष्ट्रीय सचिव बनाया गया। इसके बाद वह पाँच राज्यों के प्रभारी बनाए गए। मोदी वर्ष 2001 में गुजरात के मुख्यमंत्री बने और 2014 में देश के प्रधानमंत्री बने। इससे पहले संघ परिवार से अटल बिहारी वाजपेयी प्रधानमंत्री बने थे। वाजपेयी भी संघ के प्रचारक रहे। यही नहीं, पूर्व राष्ट्रपति राम नाथ कोविंद, पूर्व उपराष्ट्रपति वेंकैया नायडू भी संघ के स्वयंसेवक रह चुके हैं।

□

सामाजिक समरसता के लिए 9 हजार गाँवों का सर्वेक्षण

राष्ट्रीय स्वयंसेवक संघ ने 2025 में अपनी स्थापना के शताब्दी वर्ष में एक बड़ा कार्य अपने हाथों में लिया। संघ ने सत्य का प्रचार करके और उसे जमीनी स्तर पर लागू करके देश में अस्पृश्यता और जातिगत भेदभाव को मिटाने के लिए महत्त्वपूर्ण प्रयास किए हैं। समाज में समरसता लाने और लोगों के सामने आने वाली विभिन्न समस्याओं की पहचान करने एवं उनका समाधान करने के लिए संघ के द्वारा एक व्यापक सामाजिक सर्वेक्षण को परिणति तक पहुँचाया गया। करीब 9 हजार गाँवों का विस्तारपूर्वक सर्वेक्षण किया गया, जिसमें कई महत्त्वपूर्ण जानकारी सामने आई। इसके बाद संघ के स्वयंसेवकों ने गाँवों की समस्याओं के समाधान के लिए उपाय भी शुरू कर दिए। इसके अलावा स्वयंसेवक विभिन्न बस्तियों, गाँवों और अन्य हिस्सों में क्षेत्र विशेष के मुद्दों पर भी ध्यान केंद्रित कर रहे हैं, जैसे कि सीवेज, सड़क संपर्क, स्वच्छता, अंतरजातीय संघर्ष जैसी समस्याओं से लेकर स्वास्थ्य, शिक्षा और विकास आदि। संघ की सोच यह रही कि इन मुद्दों को सामूहिक प्रयासों से हल किया जाए।

□

गणवेश में तीन लाख से अधिक स्वयंसेवकों के एकत्र होने का रिकॉर्ड

क्रांतिवीरों की धरती मेरठ पर राष्ट्रीय स्वयंसेवक संघ ने 25 फरवरी, 2018 को एक अनोखा रिकॉर्ड बनाया। समागम राष्ट्रोदय कार्यक्रम में तीन लाख से अधिक स्वयंसेवकों ने पूर्ण गणवेश में हिस्सा लेकर विश्व रिकॉर्ड बनाया। यह संघ का एक स्थान पर अब तक का सबसे बड़ा कार्यक्रम था, जिसमें एकता का संदेश दिया गया। इस कार्यक्रम में भाग लेने के लिए हर वर्ग और समुदाय से लोगों ने पंजीकरण कराया। करीब सवा तीन लाख पंजीकरण में सवा दो लाख स्वयंसेवक चालीस साल से कम आयु के थे। अलग-अलग श्रेणी में 94,498 स्टूडेंट, 70,580 व्यापारी, 53,368 नौकरीपेशा, 46,572 किसान, 33,348 वकील, 12,534 शिक्षक, 4,205 डॉक्टर और 25,181 अन्य लोगों ने बतौर स्वयंसेवक समागम में सम्मिलित होने के लिए पंजीकरण कराया। लोगों के लिए भोजन की व्यवस्था भी तीन लाख परिवारों की तरफ से की गई थी। समागम में सम्मिलित होने वाले लोगों के लिए भोजन के 6 लाख से अधिक पैकेट तैयार किए गए थे। समागम के जरिए तीन लाख परिवारों को साथ जोड़कर जातिगत भेदभाव मिटाने का एक खास संदेश दिया गया। इससे पहले केरल के कोल्लम में वर्ष 2010 में 92 हजार स्वयंसेवक एक जगह जुटे थे।

□

दुनिया की सबसे ऊँची चोटी पर संघ की शाखा

राष्ट्रीय स्वयंसेवक संघ के स्वयंसेवक और पर्वतारोही विपिन चौधरी ने 22 मई, 2019 को माउंट एवरेस्ट को फतह किया। संघ के अनुशासित सिपाही चौधरी ने माउंट एवरेस्ट की चोटी पर पहुँचकर सबसे पहले देश के प्रति सम्मान प्रकट करते हुए राष्ट्रीय तिरंगा झंडा लहराया। इसके बाद उन्होंने संघ का भगवा ध्वज फहराया। चौधरी यहीं नहीं रुके, उन्होंने वहाँ शाखा भी लगाई। एक तो माउंट एवरेस्ट की चोटी पर चढ़ना ही अपने आप में मुश्किल भरा काम है और उस पर वहाँ विपरीत मौसम में तेज हवाओं के बीच दो-दो झंडे फहराना और शाखा लगाना कम साहस की बात नहीं है। चौधरी ने कहा, "जब मैं माउंट एवरेस्ट पर पहुँचा तो मैंने सबसे पहले राष्ट्रीय तिरंगा लहराया, और फिर मैंने भगवा ध्वज फहराया और वहाँ संघ की शाखा लगाई। यह एक सपना सच होने जैसा था।" चौधरी ने कहा, "इन चोटियों पर चढ़ना जितना मुश्किल है, उतना ही उतरना भी। वहाँ की परिस्थितियाँ बहुत ही मुश्किल भरी हैं। इसके बाद आप वहाँ बस कुछ मिनट ही रुक पाते हैं। इन चोटियों पर चढ़ने के लिए बहुत अधिक शारीरिक श्रम की आवश्यकता होती है।" चौधरी उत्तर प्रदेश के मुरादनगर में संघ से जुड़े रहे हैं।

□

ब्रिटिश मीडिया ने बताया 'दुनिया का सबसे शक्तिशाली स्वयंसेवक समूह'

दुनिया भर के मीडिया संस्थान जहाँ राष्ट्रीय स्वयंसेवक संघ को अकसर भारतीय राजनीति से जोड़कर देखते हैं, वहीं ब्रिटेन के प्रतिष्ठित-पत्र 'द इकोनॉमिस्ट' ने दिसंबर 2024 में संघ की कार्यप्रणाली और सामाजिक प्रभाव पर एक विस्तृत लेख प्रकाशित किया, जिसका शीर्षक था—'Inside the RSS, the world's most powerful volunteer group.' इस लेख में संघ को 'दुनिया का सबसे शक्तिशाली स्वयंसेवक संगठन' कहा गया। यह उपाधि सिर्फ प्रशंसा नहीं, बल्कि संघ के अनुशासन, संगठनात्मक क्षमता और राष्ट्र निर्माण में सहभागिता की वैश्विक स्तर पर मान्यता है। रिपोर्ट में नागपुर स्थित मुख्यालय और शाखा गतिविधियों का निरीक्षण करते हुए इसे 'सैन्य परेड और स्कूल स्पोर्ट्स डे का मिला-जुला रूप' जैसा बताया गया, जहाँ अनुशासन, ऊर्जा और सामाजिक समर्पण की झलक स्पष्ट थी। लेख में यह भी कहा गया कि संघ युवाओं को उद्देश्य और आत्मगौरव प्रदान करता है, और यही वजह है कि यह संगठन लगातार युवाओं को जोड़ने में सफल रहा है। 'द इकोनॉमिस्ट' ने संघ को हिंदू राष्ट्रवाद के 'पैदल सैनिक' की संज्ञा दी, लेकिन साथ ही यह स्वीकार किया कि वह एक सामाजिक संरचना के रूप में स्थानीय और राष्ट्रीय स्तर पर सेवाकार्यों में अग्रणी भूमिका निभाता है। इस लेख के साथ 'द इकोनॉमिस्ट' ने एक पॉडकास्ट भी जारी किया, जिसका शीर्षक था—'The most powerful volunteer group you've never heard of.'

□

समाजसेवा करते बलिदान हुए सैकड़ों स्वयंसेवक

राष्ट्रीय स्वयंसेवक संघ शुरू से ही भारतीय संस्कृति और समाजसेवा को लेकर अग्रणी भूमिका निभाता रहा है। लेकिन कई राज्यों में उसे इसकी भारी कीमत चुकानी पड़ी है। सिर्फ केरल, त्रिपुरा और पश्चिम बंगाल में ही सैकड़ों स्वयंसेवकों को अपनी जान गँवानी पड़ी है। केरल की बात करें तो यहाँ संघ की चार हजार से अधिक शाखाएँ हैं और 2.5 लाख से अधिक स्वयंसेवक हैं। राज्य में पिछले 85 साल में 250 से ज्यादा स्वयंसेवकों ने जान गँवाई है। अकेले कन्नूर में 80 से ज्यादा स्वयंसेवकों की हत्या हुई है। इसी तरह का हाल त्रिपुरा का रहा है। राज्य के धलाई जिले के धूमचेरा में संघ द्वारा जनजातीय छात्रों के लिए वनवासी कल्याण आश्रम चलाया जाता है। इसी आश्रम से 6 अगस्त, 1999 को संघ के चार वरिष्ठ प्रचारकों श्यामल कांति सेनगुप्ता, दिनेंद्रनाथ डे, सुधामय दत्ता और शुभंकर चक्रवर्ती को अगवा करके बांग्लादेश ले जाया गया, जहाँ उनकी हत्या कर दी गई। पश्चिम बंगाल में भी कई स्वयंसेवकों की जान की हानि हुई। दक्षिण 24 परगना के सोनाखली में 10 फरवरी, 2001 को चार स्वयंसेवकों—अभिजीत सरदार, पतित्पवन नस्कर, सुजीत नस्कर और अनादी नस्कर को निर्मम ढंग से गोली मार दी गई। मुर्शिदाबाद में 8 अक्तूबर, 2019 को स्वयंसेवक बंधु प्रकाश पाल, उनकी गर्भवती पत्नी और आठ वर्षीय पुत्र की निर्दयतापूर्वक हत्या कर दी गई। इस तरह की अनेक घटनाएँ बर्द्धमान, हावड़ा और अन्य जिलों में हुई हैं। इतना सब कुछ होने के बाद भी स्वयंसेवकों ने हार नहीं मानी और इन राज्यों में अपनी सेवा लगातार जारी रखी है।

□

मूँगफली बेचकर किशोर स्वयंसेवक ने की गुरु-दक्षिणा

संघ में देश के लिए समर्पित होने की प्रतिज्ञा की भावना की पुष्टि के लिए गुरु-दक्षिणा कार्यक्रम होता है। इसी से जुड़ी एक अनोखी कहानी है नौवीं में पढ़ने वाले स्वयंसेवक श्यामू पवार की। उसके पिता मजदूरी करते थे। घर की माली हालत खस्ताहाल थी। रोज की कमाई से किसी तरह घर चलता था। उसने निश्चय किया कि इस बार गुरु-दक्षिणा में 21 रुपए समर्पित करेगा। उसने अपनी माँ से मूँगफली बनवाकर तीन महीने तक सिनेमा टॉकीज के इंटरवल में मूँगफली बेचकर 21 रुपए जमा किए और गुरु-दक्षिणा में सहर्ष समर्पित किया। '100 वर्ष की संघ यात्रा—नए क्षितिज' कार्यक्रम में सरसंघचालक मोहन भागवत ने अपने व्याख्यान में कई किस्से उदाहरण के रूप में बताए। एक अन्य उदाहरण में उन्होंने एक और कहानी बताई। एक युवा कार्यकर्ता अनुसूचित जाति से था, जिसे संघ के बारे में गलत जानकारी देकर कुछ लोग भड़काना चाहते थे। वे यह कहकर भड़काते थे कि तुमसे केवल झाड़ू लगवाएँगे। एक दिन वह गरमी की भरी दोपहर में संघ प्रचारक यशवंतराव केलकर के घर पहुँच गया। उन्होंने कहा, "अरे दोपहर में इतनी गरमी में कैसे आए। आओ-आओ बैठो। क्या बात है?" श्यामू ने कहा, "मुझे बहुत प्यास लगी है।" केलकरजी ने कहा, "अंदर जाओ, किचन में पानी है, तुम पी लो। आते समय एक गिलास मेरे लिए भी ले आना।" उसने पानी पिया और केलकरजी के लिए भी ले आया। इस सहज व्यवहार ने कार्यकर्ता के मन से सारे पूर्वाग्रह और शक दूर कर दिए। जब केलकरजी ने पूछा कि वह क्यों आया था तो कार्यकर्ता ने जवाब दिया, "अब मेरा काम हो गया।"

□

संघ प्रचारक का समर्पण और समाज का अटूट बंधन

डॉ. हेडगेवार ने संघ के विस्तार के लिए नागपुर से एक प्रचारक को बिहार के भागलपुर भेजा। जैसे-तैसे उनको टिकट का पैसा दिया। उस समय 3 रुपए 12 आना भागलपुर तक का टिकट था। भागलपुर पहुँचने के बाद प्रचारक के पास केवल सवा रुपए बचे थे। शहर में न कोई परिचित था, न रहने की जगह। ऐसे में वे रात में स्टेशन पर खड़ी पैसेंजर ट्रेन में सोते और स्टेशन पर ही अपना नित्यकर्म करते थे। उनके प्रयासों से वहाँ शाखा प्रारंभ हुई। एक दिन एक बाल स्वयंसेवक के घर पर्व का अवसर था। जब उस परिवार को प्रचारक के इस समर्पण भाव का पता चला तो उन्होंने भोजन पर आमंत्रित किया। बाल स्वयंसेवक की माताजी ने भावविभोर होकर कहा, "अगर कभी भोजन की व्यवस्था न हो, तो निःसंकोच हमारे घर आ जाइए।" '100 वर्ष की संघ यात्रा-नए क्षितिज' कार्यक्रम में सरसंघचालक मोहन भागवत ने यह किस्सा सुनाते हुए बताया कि किस प्रकार स्वयंसेवकों ने समर्पित भाव से काम करते हुए संघ के मिशन को आगे बढ़ाया है। वो आगे कहते हैं कि बाद में जब वे क्षेत्र प्रचारक बनकर भागलपुर गए तो उन्होंने देखा कि वह बाल स्वयंसेवक अब विभाग संघचालक बन चुका था। मोहन भागवत ने कहा, "एक बड़े प्रसिद्ध चिकित्सक के यहाँ हमारा भोजन था। वहाँ वे विभाग संघचालकजी भी थे। हमने भोजन के लिए बोला तो वे बोले मेरा भोजन घर में बना है।" उन्होंने कहा, "तो फिर जाइए, समय हो गया।" विभाग संचालक ने कहा, "नहीं, आपका भोजन पूरा होने के बाद मुझे सूचित करना पड़ेगा तब घर में बहुएँ भोजन करेंगी।" बाल स्वयंसेवक की माताजी का निमंत्रण और बहुओं का प्रतीक्षा करना यह दरशाता है कि संघ के प्रति सम्मान का भाव केवल एक व्यक्ति तक सीमित नहीं रहा, बल्कि पीढ़ियों तक पूरे परिवार के आचरण में समाहित हो गया। □

जब एक प्रधानमंत्री बन गए स्वयंसेवक

एक स्वयंसेवक के जीवन में संघ का क्या महत्त्व है, इसे प्रधानमंत्री नरेंद्र मोदी के 11 सितंबर, 2025 के ब्लॉग से समझा जा सकता है। इसमें उन्होंने एक स्वयंसेवक की भाँति संघ प्रमुख मोहन भागवत को लेकर एक आलेख लिखा। पहली बार किसी प्रधानमंत्री ने सार्वजनिक रूप से संघ प्रमुख के लिए इस प्रकार का लेख लिखा है। यह इसलिए भी विशेष था, क्योंकि सरसंघचालक मोहन भागवत का यह 75वाँ जन्मदिवस था। प्रधानमंत्री मोदी लिखते हैं, "यह भारत और विश्व भर के लाखों स्वयंसेवकों के लिए एक ऐतिहासिक अवसर है। हम स्वयंसेवकों का सौभाग्य है कि हमारे पास मोहन भागवतजी जैसे दूरदर्शी और परिश्रमी सरसंघचालक हैं, जो ऐसे समय में संगठन का नेतृत्व कर रहे हैं।" इस ब्लॉग में प्रधानमंत्री मोदी बताते हैं कि किस प्रकार मोहन भागवत ने आपातकाल से लेकर कोरोनाकाल तक समाज के बीच रहकर निरंतर कार्य किया है। वे लिखते हैं, "एक युवा स्वयंसेवक से लेकर सरसंघचालक तक की उनकी जीवन यात्रा उनकी निष्ठा और वैचारिक दृढ़ता को दरशाती है। विचार के प्रति पूर्ण समर्पण और व्यवस्थाओं में समयानुकूल परिवर्तन करते हुए उनके नेतृत्व में संघकार्य का निरंतर विस्तार हो रहा है।" इस लेख में प्रधानमंत्री मोदी यह भी बताते हैं किस प्रकार मोहन भागवत का कार्यकाल संघ में सर्वाधिक परिवर्तन का कालखंड रहा है। चाहे वह गणवेश परिवर्तन हो, संघ शिक्षा वर्गों में बदलाव हो आदि।

□

दुनिया की सबसे बड़ी अनौपचारिक संस्था

राष्ट्रीय स्वयंसेवक संघ दुनिया का सबसे बड़ा स्वयंसेवी संगठन है। संघ दुनिया का इकलौता ऐसा संगठन है, जो इतना व्यापक और प्रभावशाली होने के बाद भी कहीं पंजीकृत नहीं है। वर्ष 1925 में 5 लोगों से शुरू हुई पहली शाखा आज देश के कोने-कोने तक पहुँच चुकी है, लेकिन कहीं कोई दस्तावेज नहीं है। संघ से कितने लोग जुड़े हुए हैं, इसकी कोई आधिकारिक संख्या उपलब्ध नहीं है। एक अनुमान के मुताबिक देश में संघ से करीब एक करोड़ स्वयंसेवक जुड़े हैं। संघ के अनगिनत आनुषंगिक संगठन हैं, वो भी एक से बढ़कर एक, कोई दुनिया का सबसे बड़ा राजनीतिक दल, कोई दुनिया का सबसे बड़ा मजदूर संगठन और कोई विद्यार्थियों का सबसे बड़ा संगठन। ये जितने आँकड़े बताए गए हैं, उससे अधिक आँकड़े तो कभी दर्ज ही नहीं हो पाए, क्योंकि किसी ने रिकॉर्ड ही नहीं रखा। संघ अपने स्वयंसेवकों का कोई औपचारिक रिकॉर्ड या सदस्यता सूची नहीं रखता। कोई भी व्यक्ति जो संघ की शाखाओं में जाना शुरू कर देता है, उसे स्वयंसेवक माना जाता है। चूँकि कोई औपचारिक सदस्यता नहीं होती, इसलिए इससे अलग होने के लिए भी कोई त्याग-पत्र देने की आवश्यकता नहीं होती। व्यक्ति अपनी इच्छा से शाखाओं में आना बंद कर सकता है। संघ के काम के लिए संगठन के बाहर से कोई पैसा नहीं लिया जाता, भले ही वह स्वेच्छा से दिया गया हो। संघ अपना समस्त व्यय उस गुरु-दक्षिणा से पूरा करता है, जो साल में एक बार संघ के स्वयंसेवक भगवा ध्वज को गुरु मानकर समर्पित करते हैं। रजिस्टर्ड नहीं होने के कारण संघ इन्कम टैक्स या आयकर रिटर्न फाइल नहीं करता, लेकिन अपनी विश्वसनीयता बनाए रखने के लिए संघ एक-एक पाई का हिसाब रखता है और हर साल ऑडिट करता है।

□

जननी
जन्मभूमिश्च
स्वर्गादपि
गरीयसी

संघ की प्रार्थना का हिंदी में अनुवाद

नमस्ते सदा वत्सले मातृभूमे, त्वया हिन्दुभूमे सुखं वर्धितोऽहम्।
हे प्यार करने वाली मातृभूमि! मैं तुझे सदा (सदैव) नमस्कार करता हूँ।
तूने मेरा सुख से पालन-पोषण किया है।

महामङ्गले पुण्यभूमे त्वदर्थे, पतत्वेष कायो नमस्ते नमस्ते।। १।।
हे महामंगलमयी पुण्यभूमि! तेरे ही कार्य में मेरा यह शरीर अर्पण हो।
मैं तुझे बारंबार नमस्कार करता हूँ।

प्रभो शक्ति मन्हिन्दुराष्ट्राङ्गभूता, इमे सादरं त्वाम नमामो वयम् त्वदीयाय
कार्याय बध्दा कटीयं, शुभामाशिषम देहि तत्पूर्तये।
हे सर्वशक्तिशाली परमेश्वर! हम हिंदू राष्ट्र के सुपुत्र तुझे आदर सहित
प्रणाम करते हैं। तेरे ही कार्य के लिए हमने अपनी कमर कसी है।
उसकी पूर्ति के लिए हमें अपना शुभाशीर्वाद दें।

अजय्यां च विश्वस्य देहीश शक्तिम, सुशीलं जगद्येन नम्रं भवेत्,
श्रुतं चैव यत्कण्टकाकीर्ण मार्गं, स्वयं स्वीकृतं नः सुगं कारयेत्।। २।।
हे प्रभु! हमें ऐसी शक्ति दे, जिसे विश्व में कभी कोई चुनौती न दे सके,
ऐसा शुद्ध चारित्र्य दे, जिसके समक्ष संपूर्ण विश्व नतमस्तक हो जाए। ऐसा ज्ञान दे कि
स्वयं के द्वारा स्वीकृत किया गया यह कंटकाकीर्ण मार्ग सुगम हो जाए।

समुत्कर्षनिःश्रेयसस्यैकमुग्रं, परं साधनं नाम वीरव्रतम्
तदन्तः स्फुरत्वक्षया ध्येयनिष्ठा, हृदन्तः प्रजागर्तु तीव्राऽनिशम्।
उग्र वीरव्रती की भावना हम में उत्स्फूर्त होती रहे, जो उच्चतम आध्यात्मिक
सुख एवं महानतम ऐहिक समृद्धि प्राप्त करने का एकमेव श्रेष्ठतम साधन है।
तीव्र एवं अखंड ध्येयनिष्ठा हमारे अंतःकरणों में सदैव जागती रहे।

विजेत्री च नः संहता कार्यशक्तिर्, विधायास्य धर्मस्य संरक्षणम्।
परं वैभवं नेतुमेतत् स्वराष्ट्रं, समर्था भवत्वाशिषा ते भृशम्।। ३।।
हे माँ! तेरी कृपा से हमारी यह विजयशालिनी संघटित कार्यशक्ति हमारे धर्म का संरक्षण
कर इस राष्ट्र को वैभव के उच्चतम शिखर पर पहुँचाने में समर्थ हो।

।। भारत माता की जय।।

डॉक्टर केशवराव बलिराम हेडगेवार

उपाख्य—डॉक्टरजी

कार्यकाल—27 सितंबर, 1925-21 जून, 1940

डॉ. केशवराव बलिराम हेडगेवार का जन्म 1 अप्रैल, 1889 को नागपुर में हुआ था। उनका परिवार मूलरूप से तेलंगाना के कंदकुर्ती गाँव का रहने वाला था, लेकिन निजाम शासन के अत्याचारों से तंग आकर उनके पूर्वज नागपुर आ बसे। घर में आर्थिक तंगी थी और केशव महज 13 वर्ष के थे, जब प्लेग के कारण उनके माता-पिता का निधन हो गया। इसके बावजूद उन्होंने कलकत्ता से डॉक्टरी की पढ़ाई पूरी की। उन्होंने संघ की स्थापना देश की स्वाधीनता, भारतीय संस्कृति के पुनरोत्थान तथा इसे परम वैभव पर पहुँचाने के उद्‌देश्य से की। उन्होंने व्यक्ति निर्माण और राष्ट्र जागरण के लिए शाखा जैसी अभिनव प्रणाली विकसित की। उनकी सोच ने करोड़ों राष्ट्रभक्तों को नई दिशा दी। 21 जून, 1940 को उनका निधन हुआ, लेकिन उनके विचार आज भी जनमानस को प्रेरित करते हैं।

माधवराव सदाशिवराव गोलवलकर

उपाख्य—श्रीगुरुजी

कार्यकाल—22 जून, 1940–5 जून, 1973

श्रीगुरुजी का जन्म 19 फरवरी, 1906 को नागपुर के पास रामटेक में हुआ। वर्ष 1927 में उन्होंने बी.एच.यू. से एम.एससी., एल.एल.बी. की डिग्री हासिल की। डॉ. हेडगेवार ने अपने गिरते स्वास्थ्य को देखते हुए 13 अगस्त, 1939 को रक्षाबंधन के अवसर पर श्रीगुरुजी को 'सरकार्यवाह' का दायित्व दिया था। संघ-संस्थापक डॉ. केशवराव बलिराम हेडगेवार के निधन के बाद वर्ष 1940 में वे संघ के दूसरे सरसंघचालक बने। वर्ष 1940 से 1973 तक यानी 33 सालों तक उन्होंने संघ के स्वरूप को विस्तार देने के लिए काम किया। 5 जून, 1973 को उनका देहांत हो गया।

मधुकर दत्तात्रेय देवरस

उपाख्य—बालासाहब देवरस

कार्यकाल—6 जून, 1973-10 मार्च, 1994

बालासाहब देवरस का जन्म 11 दिसंबर, 1915 को नागपुर में हुआ। वर्ष 1937 में बी.ए., एल.एल.बी. की पढ़ाई पूरी करने के बाद बालासाहब देवरस नागपुर के नगर कार्यवाह बने। आपातकाल में 30 जून को देवरस को गिरफ्तार करके पुणे की यरवदा जेल भेज दिया गया। वे करीब 20 महीने तक जेल में रहे। उनके छोटे भाई भाऊराव देवरस भी आजीवन संघ के प्रचारक रहे और उन्होंने संघ के विस्तार में महत्त्वपूर्ण भूमिका निभाई। लंबे समय से अस्वस्थ रहने के कारण उन्होंने 11 मार्च, 1994 को प्रो. राजेंद्र सिंह को संघ का सरसंघचालक नियुक्त कर दिया। 17 जून, 1996 को उनका निधन हो गया।

प्रोफेसर राजेंद्र सिंह

उपाख्य—रज्जू भैया

कार्यकाल—11 मार्च, 1994-9 मार्च, 2000

प्रोफेसर राजेंद्र सिंह का जन्म 29 जनवरी, 1922 को उत्तर प्रदेश के बुलंदशहर जिले में हुआ। उन्हें पढ़ने के लिए प्रयागराज भेजा गया। उन्होंने प्रथम श्रेणी में एम.एससी. की परीक्षा उत्तीर्ण की और फिर वहीं भौतिक विज्ञान के प्राध्यापक हो गए। नोबेल पुरस्कार विजेता प्रसिद्ध वैज्ञानिक सी.वी. रमन ने रज्जू भैया की परीक्षा ली थी और उनसे अत्यधिक प्रभावित होकर उनको शत-प्रतिशत अंक दिए थे। प्रयागराज में उनका संपर्क संघ से हुआ और वे नियमित शाखा जाने लगे। वर्ष 1966 में उन्होंने विश्वविद्यालय की नौकरी से त्याग-पत्र दे दिया और पूरा समय संघ को ही देने लगे। बीमारी के कारण उन्होंने 10 मार्च, 2000 को सुदर्शनजी को सरसंघचालक का दायित्व दे दिया। 14 जुलाई, 2003 को पुणे में उनका निधन हो गया।

कुप्पहल्ली सीतारमैया सुदर्शन

उपाख्य—सुदर्शनजी

कार्यकाल—10 मार्च, 2000-20 मार्च, 2009

कुप्.सी. सुदर्शन का जन्म 18 जून, 1931 को छत्तीसगढ़ की राजधानी रायपुर में हुआ। वे मूलत: तमिलनाडु और कर्नाटक की सीमा पर बसे कुप्पहल्ली (मैसूर) ग्राम के निवासी थे। वर्ष 1954 में सागर विश्वविद्यालय से बी.ई. की उपाधि प्राप्त कर वे 23 वर्ष की उम्र में संघ के पूर्णकालिक प्रचारक बने। वर्ष 1979 में उन्हें अखिल भारतीय बौद्धिक प्रमुख और 1990 में सह-सरकार्यवाह का दायित्व सौंपा गया। 15 सितंबर, 2012 को रायपुर में उन्होंने अंतिम साँस ली। वे जब संघ प्रमुख थे, उसी दौरान 'राष्ट्रीय मुसलिम मंच' की स्थापना हुई।

डॉ. मोहन मधुकरराव भागवत

उपाख्य—भागवतजी

कार्यकाल—21 मार्च, 2009–वर्तमान

सरसंघचालक मोहन भागवत का जन्म 11 सितंबर, 1950 में महाराष्ट्र के शहर चंद्रपुर में हुआ। भागवत ने चंद्रपुर से बी.एससी. की पढ़ाई की। इसके बाद उन्होंने पंजाबराव देशमुख कृषि विद्यापीठ अकोला से पशुचिकित्सा और पशुपालन में स्नातक की डिग्री हासिल की। इनका पूरा परिवार राष्ट्रीय स्वयंसेवक संघ से जुड़ा हुआ था। मोहन भागवत के पिता मधुकरराव भागवत चंद्रपुर क्षेत्र के अध्यक्ष और गुजरात के प्रांत प्रचारक थे। उनकी माँ मालती भागवत राष्ट्र सेविका समिति की सदस्य रहीं। यही नहीं, मोहन भागवत के बाबा नानासाहेब भी संघ से जुड़े रहे और उन्होंने डॉ. हेगडेवार के साथ मिलकर लंबे समय तक काम किया। मोहन भागवत लंबे समय से संघ से जुड़े हैं। छात्र जीवन में वे शाखा में हिस्सा लिया करते थे। आपातकाल के समय वर्ष 1975 में वे पूर्ण रूप से संघ में सक्रिय हो गए।

राष्ट्रीय स्वयंसेवक संघ के सरसंघचालक

1. डॉक्टर केशवराव बलिराम हेडगेवार 1925–1940
2. माधवराव सदाशिवराव गोलवलकर 1940–1973
3. मधुकर दत्तात्रेय देवरस 1973–1994
4. प्रोफेसर राजेंद्र सिंह 1994–2000
5. कुप्पहल्ली सीतारमैया सुदर्शन 2000–2009
6. डॉ. मोहन मधुकरराव भागवत 2009–वर्तमान

राष्ट्रीय स्वयंसेवक संघ के सरकार्यवाह

1. गोपाल मुकुंद हुद्दार (बालाजी) 1929–1931
2. डी.आर. लिमये 1931–1934
3. एच.वी. कुलकर्णी 1934–1937
4. जी.एस. पाध्ये 1937–1939
5. मा.स. गोलवलकर (श्रीगुरुजी) 1939–1940
6. मल्हार नारायण काले (भैयासाहेब) 1940–1945
7. प्रभाकर बलवंत दाणी (भैयाजी दाणी) 1945–1956, 1962–1965
8. एकनाथ रानाडे 1956–1962
9. मधुकर दत्तात्रेय देवरस (बालासाहबजी) 1965–1973
10. माधव कोंडोपंत मुले 1973–1977
11. प्रोफेसर राजेंद्र सिंह (रज्जू भैया) 1977–1987
12. हो.वे. शेषाद्रि 1987–2000
13. डॉ. मोहन मधुकरराव भागवत 2000–2009
14. सुरेश जोशी (भैयाजी जोशी) 2009–2021
15. दत्तात्रेय होसबाले 2021–वर्तमान

गोपाल मुकुंद हुद्दार

उपाख्य—बालाजी हुद्दार

कार्यकाल—1929-1931

गोपाल मुकुंद हुद्दार (बालाजी हुद्दार) का जन्म 1902 में मध्य प्रदेश के मंडला में हुआ। हुद्दार ने अपना राजनीतिक जीवन हिंदू महासभा से आरंभ किया। 1925 में संघ की स्थापना के समय डॉ. हेडगेवार ने जिन लोगों को चुना, उनमें बालाजी हुद्दार भी थे। वे 1929 में संघ के सरकार्यवाह (महासचिव) बनाए गए। 1931 में 'बालाघाट षड्यंत्र केस' में उन्हें हथियार इकट्ठा करने के आरोप में गिरफ्तार कर लिया गया और फिर 1935 में जेल से रिहा किया गया। इसके बाद उनका झुकाव सशस्त्र आंदोलन की तरफ हो गया।

डी.आर. लिमये

कार्यकाल—1931-1934

संघ का शुरुआती काल (1925-1935) निर्माण और संगठन के विस्तार का दौर था। इसी कालखंड में डी.आर. लिमये को 1931 में सरकार्यवाह के रूप में नियुक्त किया गया, ताकि संगठन के संचालन में डॉ. हेडगेवार का सहयोग कर सकें। उस समय संगठन का विस्तार सांस्कृतिक राष्ट्रवाद, अनुशासन और शाखा कार्य के माध्यम से किया जा रहा था, जिसमें उन्होंने महत्त्वपूर्ण भूमिका निभाई। लिमये ने शाखाओं के नियमित संचालन, प्रशिक्षण वर्गों और स्वयंसेवकों की आंतरिक व्यवस्था को सुदृढ़ करने का काम किया। उन्होंने संघ के प्रारंभिक ढाँचे का संगठनात्मक रूप में विस्तार भी किया। लिमये ने स्थानीय और क्षेत्रीय स्तर पर संघ के विचारों को मजबूती प्रदान की।

एच.वी. कुलकर्णी

कार्यकाल—1934-1937

डॉ. हेडगेवार के निकट सहयोगी रहे हनुमंतराव विनायक कुलकर्णी संघ के शुरुआती प्रचारकों में से एक थे। एच.वी. कुलकर्णी ने संघ के तीसरे सरकार्यवाह का दायित्व 1934 में सँभाला। वे अत्यंत अनुशासित, कार्यकुशल एवं संगठनकर्ता माने जाते थे। उन्होंने शाखाओं में खेल, व्यायाम और बौद्धिक सत्रों की संरचना को बेहतर बनाया। इसके साथ ही कार्यकर्ताओं को प्रचारक के रूप में बाहर भेजने की परंपरा को बढ़ावा दिया, जिससे संघ महाराष्ट्र के बाहर फैलना शुरू हुआ। कुलकर्णी के तीन साल के कार्यकाल में संगठनात्मक विस्तार को काफी मजबूती मिली।

जी.एस. पाध्ये

कार्यकाल—1937–1939

गणेश सदाशिव पाध्ये संघ के चौथे सरकार्यवाह बने। महाराष्ट्र में जनमे पाध्ये डॉ. हेडगेवार के विश्वसनीय सहयोगी और प्रारंभिक स्वयंसेवकों में से एक थे। वे अपने शांत और सादगीपूर्ण स्वभाव के लिए जाने जाते थे। उन्होंने 1937 में सरकार्यवाह का दायित्व सँभाला। इस समय संघ महाराष्ट्र की सीमाओं से निकलकर मध्य प्रांत और अन्य हिंदी भाषी क्षेत्रों में प्रवेश कर रहा था। उनके कार्यकाल में नियमित शाखाओं की परंपरा और अधिक मजबूत हुई। जी.एस. पाध्ये के कार्यकाल के समय ही संघ शिक्षा वर्गों, यानी ट्रेनिंग कैंप्स का प्रारंभिक रूप और व्यवस्थित हुआ। उन्होंने जहाँ प्रचारक परंपरा को और गति दी, वहीं नए स्वयंसेवकों को नेतृत्व और संगठनात्मक प्रशिक्षण देने के काम को और आगे बढ़ाया।

मल्हार नारायण काले

उपाख्य—भैयासाहेब काले

कार्यकाल—1940-1945

भैयासाहेब काले छात्र जीवन से ही राष्ट्रवादी विचारों से प्रभावित थे। इसी दौरान वे डॉ. हेडगेवार के संपर्क में आए और उनसे प्रेरित होकर 1925 में संघ के संस्थापक सदस्यों में शामिल हो गए। भैयासाहेब काले ने अपना जीवन संघ के कार्यों को समर्पित कर दिया और वे एक पूर्णकालिक प्रचारक बन गए। उन्होंने संघ के विस्तार के लिए देश के विभिन्न हिस्सों में काम किया, खासकर महाराष्ट्र और मध्य भारत में।

प्रभाकर बलवंत दाणी

उपाख्य—भैयाजी दाणी

प्रथम कार्यकाल—1945-1956

द्वितीय कार्यकाल—1962-1965

प्रभाकर बलवंत दाणी का जन्म 9 अक्तूबर, 1907 को नागपुर में हुआ। शिक्षा ग्रहण करने के दौरान वे डॉ. हेडगेवार के संपर्क में आए। 1925 में संघ की स्थापना की निर्णायक बैठक में उपस्थित रहे। नागपुर प्रांत के बाहर पहली शाखा भैयाजी ने काशी हिंदू विश्वविद्यालय में प्रारंभ की। उनके ही प्रयास से श्रीगुरुजी संघ में आए। 1942 में गृहस्थ प्रचारक बनकर मध्य भारत प्रांत में गए और मध्य भारत के प्रांत प्रचारक बने। 1945 में उन्हें सरकार्यवाह का दायित्व मिला। 1956 तक उन्होंने इस दायित्व का निर्वहन किया। भैयाजी दाणी की कार्यकुशलता को देखते हुए 1962 में उन्हें पुनः सरकार्यवाह चुना गया। 1965 तक उन्होंने इस दायित्व का निर्वहन किया। 2 मई, 1965 को उनका निधन हो गया।

एकनाथ रानाडे

उपाख्य—एकनाथजी

कार्यकाल—1956-1962

अमरावती में 19 नवंबर, 1914 को जनमे एकनाथ रानाडे डॉ. हेडगेवार के संपर्क में आकर बाल्यकाल में संघ के स्वयंसेवक बने। 1936 में संघ के प्रचारक बनने के बाद 1938 तक उन्होंने नागपुर में संघकार्य का विस्तार किया। 1938 से 1947 तक महाकौशल के प्रांत प्रचारक रहे। संघ के लिखित संविधान का मसौदा तैयार करने में उनकी प्रमुख भूमिका रही। वे 1953 से 1956 तक अखिल भारतीय प्रचारक प्रमुख रहे। 1956 से 1962 तक उन्होंने सरकार्यवाह का दायित्व निभाया। कन्याकुमारी में विवेकानंद रॉक मेमोरियल की योजना और निर्माण का श्रेय रानाडे को ही जाता है। उन्होंने 'Rousing Call to Hindu Nation' समेत कई अन्य पुस्तकों का लेखन भी किया। 22 अगस्त, 1982 को उनका निधन हो गया।

माधव कोंडोपंत मुले

कार्यकाल—1973-1977

माधव मुले का जन्म महाराष्ट्र के रत्नागिरि जिले में 7 नवंबर, 1912 को हुआ। 1923 में डॉ. हेडगेवार के संपर्क में आए। 1931 में आजीवन संघकार्य करने का संकल्प लिया। डॉ. हेडगेवार के साथ महाराष्ट्र के प्रवास में साथ रहे। 21 जुलाई, 1940 को पंजाब के प्रांत प्रचारक नियुक्त हुए। पंजाब में उनके कुशल नेतृत्व का प्रभाव इतना व्यापक रहा कि 1942 में उनके प्रयास एवं प्रेरणा से 58 प्रचारक तैयार हुए। भारत विभाजन के संकटकाल में उन्होंने स्वयंसेवकों का मार्गदर्शन किया। साथ ही विदेशों में संघकार्य का विस्तार करने के लिए स्वयंसेवकों को प्रेरणा दी। 30 सितंबर, 1978 को उनका निधन हो गया।

होंगसंद्र वेंकटरमैया शेषाद्रि

कार्यकाल—1987–2000

होंगसंद्र वेंकटरमैया शेषाद्रि का जन्म 26 मई, 1926 को कर्नाटक के बेंगलौर में हुआ। वे 1934 में विद्यार्थी जीवन में ही स्वयंसेवक बन गए। 1946 में अध्ययन पूरा करने के बाद पूर्णकालिक प्रचारक बने। वर्ष 1986 तक दक्षिण भारत में संघकार्य को विस्तार देने में जुटे रहे। दक्षिण भारत में शाखाओं और संघ की वैचारिक पकड़ मजबूत करने में शेषाद्रि की महत्त्वपूर्ण भूमिका रही। संघ तथा अन्य हिंदू साहित्य के प्रकाशन के लिए बेंगलौर में 'राष्ट्रोत्थान परिषद्' की स्थापना की। 1987 में उन्हें सरकार्यवाह का दायित्व मिला। उन्होंने अनेक पुस्तकें लिखीं, जिनमें प्रमुख हैं—'The Tragic Story of Partition' और 'RSS A Vision in Action'. उनके लेखन ने संघ की वैचारिक स्पष्टता को और मजबूती दी। 14 अगस्त, 2005 को उनका निधन हो गया।

सुरेश जोशी

उपाख्य—भैयाजी जोशी

कार्यकाल—2009–2021

भैयाजी जोशी का जन्म 1947 में इंदौर में हुआ। भैयाजी बाल्यकाल से ही संघ से जुड़ गए। वे 1975 में प्रचारक बने। महाराष्ट्र प्रांत में विभिन्न स्तरों पर कार्य करते हुए उन्होंने संगठनात्मक दक्षता दिखाई। बाद में उन्हें अखिल भारतीय सह-कार्यवाह की जिम्मेदारी मिली। मार्च 2009 की प्रतिनिधि सभा में उन्हें पहली बार सरकार्यवाह चुना गया। इसके बाद 2012 तथा 2015 में उन्हें फिर से इस दायित्व के लिए चुना गया। उत्तर प्रदेश से लेकर पूर्वोत्तर भारत में संघकार्य के विस्तार में भैयाजी की महत्त्वपूर्ण भूमिका रही है। वर्तमान में वे संघ की अखिल भारतीय कार्यकारिणी सदस्य के रूप में अपने दायित्व का निर्वहन कर रहे हैं।

दत्तात्रेय होसबाले

उपाख्य—दत्ताजी

कार्यकाल—2021 से वर्तमान

दत्तात्रेय होसबाले का जन्म 1 दिसंबर, 1954 को कर्नाटक के शिमोगा जिले में हुआ। 1968 में मात्र 13 वर्ष की आयु में वे संघ के स्वयंसेवक बने। 1972 में वे अखिल भारतीय विद्यार्थी परिषद् से जुड़े। वर्ष 1978 में स्नातकोत्तर की डिग्री हासिल करने के बाद पूर्णकालिक प्रचारक बने। विद्यार्थी परिषद् में विभिन्न दायित्वों का निर्वहन करने के पश्चात् 1992 से 2003 यानी 11 वर्षों तक अखिल भारतीय संगठन मंत्री रहे। 2003 में संघ के अखिल भारतीय सह-बौद्धिक प्रमुख बनाए गए। 2009 से 2021 तक वे सह-सरकार्यवाह रहे। मार्च 2021 में उन्होंने सरकार्यवाह का दायित्व सँभाला। उनकी कार्यकुशलता और प्रतिबद्धता को देखते हुए मार्च 2024 में पुनः उन्हें सर्वसम्मति से सरकार्यवाह चुना गया। आपातकाल (1975-77) के दौरान उन्होंने 16 महीने जेल की सजा काटी।

□

संघ की 100 महान् विभूतियाँ

1. मधुकरराव भागवत
2. राजाभाऊ पातुरकर
3. हरिकृष्ण जोशी (अप्पाजी जोशी)
4. मुरलीधर दत्तात्रेय देवरस (भाऊराव देवरस)
5. वसंतराव ओक
6. यादव कृष्ण जोशी (यादवराव जोशी)
7. लेखराज शर्मा
8. नरहरपंत बालाजी पारखी
9. गोविंद सीताराम परमार्थ (दादाराव परमार्थ)
10. उमाकांत केशव (बाबासाहेब आपटे)
11. गोपालराव येकुंटवार
12. मोरुभाऊ मुंजे
13. विठलराव रामचंद्रराव पत्तकी
14. नारायणराव तरटे
15. बाबूराव पालधीकर
16. चंडिकादास अमृतराव देशमुख (नानाजी देशमुख)
17. रामभाऊ मालोदे
18. बलवंत नारायण (बालासाहेब इंदुरकर)
19. त्र्यंबकराव जुमड़े
20. मुरलीधर कृष्णराव (बाबूराव) चौथाईवाले
21. भैयाजी शहादाणी
22. बापूराव भिशीकर
23. शिवराम शंकर (दादासाहब) आप्टे
24. लक्ष्मण माधव (बाबूराव) देशपांडे

25. मोरूभाऊ केतकर
26. ठाकुर राम सिंह
27. गोविंद कृष्ण (भाऊसाहब) भुस्कुटे
28. केशवराव गोरे
29. यादवराव कालकर
30. बच्छराज व्यास
31. पं. दीनदयाल उपाध्याय
32. प्रभाकर गजानन (भैयाजी) सहस्त्रबुद्धे
33. लक्ष्मणराव इनामदार (वकील साहब)
34. शिवराम पंत जोगलेकर
35. माधवराव देशमुख
36. अनंतराव गोखले
37. डॉ. वासुदेव केशव (आबाजी) थत्ते
38. लक्ष्मण श्रीकृष्ण भिड़े
39. भास्करराव कलंबी
40. मोरेश्वर नीलकंठ (मोरोपंत) पिंगले
41. आचार्य गिरिराज किशोर
42. बापूराव लेले
43. चमनलाल
44. नरहरि पांडुरंग (राजाभाऊ) सावरगाँवकर
45. ब्रह्मदेव
46. जगन्नाथराव जोशी
47. दत्तोपंत ठेंगड़ी
48. दत्तात्रेय भीकाजी (बाबूराव) पालधीकर
49. सुंदर सिंह भंडारी
50. कृष्णचंद्र गांधी
51. दत्तात्रेय गंगाधर (भैयाजी) कस्तूरे
52. नारायण बलवंत (राजाभाऊ) महाकाल
53. जयगोपाल

54. सोहन सिंह
55. ठाकुर संकटा प्रसाद सिंह
56. दत्तात्रेय बालकृष्ण (नाना) भागवत
57. के. सूर्यनारायण राव 'सुरुजी'
58. केशवराव दत्तात्रेय दीक्षित
59. विश्वनाथ
60. रामनरेश सिंह
61. ओमप्रकाश गर्ग
62. रामप्रकाश धीर
63. लक्ष्मण सिंह शेखावत
64. ओमप्रकाश
65. कौशल किशोर
66. लज्जाराम तोमर
67. सरदार चिरंजीव सिंह
68. रंगा हरि
69. ना. कृष्णप्पा
70. अजीत कुमार
71. मोहन जोशी
72. श्रीपति शास्त्री
73. श्रीकांत जोशी
74. सुब्बूराव श्रीनिवास
75. मुकुंदराव आत्माराम पणशीकर
76. मदनदास देवी
77. बालकृष्ण उत्तमराव नाईक
78. रामचंद्र नरहरी (बबनराव) सहस्त्रभोजनी
79. महावीर
80. पांडुरंग पंत क्षीरसागर
81. बापूराव मोघे
82. सुरेश रामचंद्र केतकर

83. मधुभाई कुलकर्णी
84. वीरेंद्र भटनागर
85. बालकृष्ण
86. धनप्रकाश त्यागी
87. बाबा योगेंद्र
88. जगदीश चंद्र त्रिपाठी
89. कृष्णराव सप्रे
90. ओंकार भावे
91. पंढरीराव कृदत्त
92. दत्ताजी डिंडोलकर
93. गोविंदराव कात्रे
94. अवधबिहारी
95. कृष्णराव मोहरिर
96. माधवराव बनहट्टी
97. पंडित रामनारायण शास्त्री
98. मिश्रीलाल तिवारी
99. मधुसूदन देव
100. उत्तमचंद इसराणी

1. मधुकरराव भागवत

जन्म : 1920, **निधन :** 10 अगस्त, 2001

1933 में संघ शिक्षा वर्ग का तृतीय वर्ष शिक्षण पूर्ण किया। 1940 में प्रचारक बने। 1941 में कटनी में महाकौशल प्रांत के प्रचारक रहे। 1942 से 1948 तक गुजरात के प्रांत प्रचारक रहे। इस कालखंड में 115 शाखाएँ प्रारंभ हुईं तथा गुजरात प्रांत से 45 प्रचारकों ने दायित्व सँभाला। 1943 में पिताजी के वचन की पूर्ति के लिए गृहस्थ जीवन में आए। 1943 में गुजरात में पुनः लौटकर 1951 तक गृहस्थ प्रचारक के रूप में कार्य किया।

2. राजाभाऊ पातुरकर

जन्म : जून 1915, **निधन :** 2 जनवरी, 1988

10वीं की पढ़ाई के बाद डॉ. हेडगेवार ने 1937 में उन्हें प्रचारक के रूप में संघकार्य विस्तार और आगे की पढ़ाई के लिए पंजाब प्रांत में लाहौर भेजा। 1949 में नागपुर वापस बुलाया गया और विदर्भ के प्रांत प्रचारक का दायित्व मिला। 1952 से 1957 तक संघकार्य विस्तार के लिए मध्य भारत भेजे गए। पूरे भारत में 'सिखों का इतिहास एवं डॉ. हेडगेवार की चित्रमय प्रदर्शनी' का आयोजन किया।

3. हरिकृष्ण जोशी (अप्पाजी जोशी)

जन्म : 30 मार्च, 1897, **निधन :** 21 दिसंबर, 1979

1911 में राष्ट्रीय स्वयंसेवक मंडल की स्थापना की। 1914 से 1918 तक डॉ. हेडगेवार के साथ आंदोलन में भाग लिया। 1917 में कुछ चुने हुए युवकों को प्रशिक्षण दिया गया, उसमें अप्पाजी भी शामिल थे। इसी शिविर में डॉक्टर हेडगेवार से उनकी निकटता हुई और आखिर तक उनके साथ कार्य किया। 1946 में कुछ समय के लिए सरकार्यवाह नियुक्त हुए। 1961 से अंतिम साँस तक विदर्भ प्रांत के संघचालक के रूप में काम किया।

4. मुरलीधर दत्तात्रेय देवरस (भाऊराव देवरस)

जन्म : 5 नवंबर, 1916, **निधन :** 13 मई, 1992

1926 के प्रारंभ के दिनों में डॉ. हेडगेवार के संपर्क में आए। विद्यार्थी जीवन पूर्ण होने के बाद संघकार्य और आगे की पढ़ाई हेतु लखनऊ भेजे गए। 1939 में पूर्णकालिक के रूप में संघकार्यों में समर्पित हो गए। बाद में उत्तर प्रदेश के प्रांत प्रचारक बने और वहाँ संघकार्यों के विस्तार में अहम भूमिका निभाई। बिहार एवं दिल्ली में भी संघ को मजबूती प्रदान की। वे सह-सरकार्यवाह भी बने और अनेक संगठनों की स्थापना और विकास को प्रेरणा दी। 'विद्या भारती' और 'राष्ट्रीय सिख संगत' की स्थापना, विस्तार एवं विकास के मार्गदर्शक रहे।

5. वसंतराव ओक

जन्म : 13 मई, 1914, **निधन :** 9 अगस्त, 2000

डॉ. हेडगेवार के प्रथम पंक्ति के कार्यकर्ताओं में उनकी गणना होती है। 1936 में दिल्ली में संघकार्य का औपचारिक प्रारंभ किया और पहली शाखा हिंदू भवन में लगाई। 1937 में हरियाणा प्रांत में भी शाखा प्रारंभ की। उनके अथक प्रयासों से दिल्ली में संघकार्य का प्रभाव निरंतर बढ़ता गया। 1942 के भारत छोड़ो आंदोलन के दौरान स्वयंसेवकों का संचालन किया। गोवा मुक्ति संग्राम में संघ की योजना के अंतर्गत सक्रिय भागीदारी की और गोलीबारी में घायल भी हुए। 1999 में भारत सरकार ने 'गोमांतक संग्राम सैनिक' के रूप में मान्यता प्रदान की।

6. यादव कृष्ण जोशी (यादवराव जोशी)

जन्म : 3 सितंबर, 1914, **निधन :** 20 अगस्त, 1992

1926 में डॉ. हेडगेवार के संपर्क में आए। उनकी प्रेरणा से अपना जीवन संघकार्य के लिए समर्पित करने का संकल्प लिया। 1940 में उत्तर प्रदेश के झाँसी में प्रचारक नियुक्त किए गए। 1941 में कर्नाटक के प्रांत प्रचारक बने। इसके साथ ही दक्षिण क्षेत्र प्रचारक, अखिल भारतीय बौद्धिक प्रमुख और अखिल भारतीय प्रचारक प्रमुख के दायित्वों का भी निर्वहन किया। 51 वर्ष तक संपूर्ण दक्षिण भारत में संघकार्य का विस्तार तथा विकास किया। 1940 के संघ शिक्षा वर्ग में प्रार्थना को सर्वप्रथम स्वर देकर गायन किया। 1977 से 1984 तक सह-सरकार्यवाह रहे। संघ विचारों के प्रचार-प्रसार के लिए 'राष्ट्रोत्थान परिषद्' की स्थापना की।

7. लेखराज शर्मा

1940 में पंजाब के मुल्तान भेजे गए। 4 मार्च, 1947 को मुल्तान में मुसलमानों ने संघ के एक शिविर पर हमला कर दिया। विभाग प्रचारक के नाते लेखराजजी ने प्रतिकार किया। इस दौरान वे गंभीर रूप से घायल हो गए। 1949 में वे राजस्थान के पहले प्रांत प्रचारक बने। 1959 तक इस दायित्व को संभाला।

8. नरहरपंत बालाजी पारखी

बिहार का प्रचारक बनाकर भेजा गया। 1942 से आंध्र प्रदेश के प्रांत प्रचारक रहे।

9. गोविंद सीताराम परमार्थ (दादाराव परमार्थ)

जन्म : 1904, **निधन :** 27 जून, 1963

डॉ. हेडगेवार के साथ जंगल सत्याग्रह में भाग लिया। उनसे प्रभावित होकर आजीवन संघकार्य करने का संकल्प लिया। प्रारंभ में नागपुर परिसर में संघकार्य का विस्तार करने में लगे। बाद में 8 से 10 वर्षों तक दिल्ली, उत्तर प्रदेश, गुजरात, महाराष्ट्र में संघकार्य का बीजारोपण किया। 1935 में महाराष्ट्र के पुणे भेजे गए। 1936 में दिल्ली में पहली शाखा प्रारंभ करने में महत्त्वपूर्ण योगदान दिया। 1936-37 में काशी हिंदू विश्वविद्यालय में शाखा को नियमित करने का प्रयास किया।

10. उमाकांत केशव (बाबासाहेब आपटे)

जन्म : 28 अगस्त, 1903, **निधन :** 26 जुलाई, 1972

वर्ष 1926 में डॉ. हेडगेवार द्वारा प्रतिज्ञा लेकर संघ के स्वयंसेवक बने। 1927 में संघ के पहले संघ शिक्षा वर्ग के बौद्धिक प्रमुख का दायित्व सँभाला। 1932 में नौकरी से त्यागपत्र देकर संघ के पूर्णकालिक कार्यकर्ता बने। 1934 में प्रचारक योजना प्रारंभ होते ही विदर्भ के यवतमाल में प्रचारक का दायित्व मिला। इसके बाद 1935 में पंजाब प्रांत के लाहौर में प्रचारक की जिम्मेदारी सँभाली।

11. गोपालराव येकुंटवार

संघकार्य के लिए 1935 में एक वर्ष के लिए सांगली में नियुक्त किए गए और उसके बाद बंबई में दायित्व मिला। डॉ. हेडगेवार ने संघकार्य के विस्तार के लिए 1938 में विशाखापट्टनम भेजा, जहाँ उन्होंने संगठन को मजबूत आधार दिया।

12. मोरुभाऊ मुंजे

जन्म : 18 नवंबर, 1916, **निधन :** 8 दिसंबर, 2007

मोरुभाऊ मुंजे 1938 में रावलपिंडी विभाग के प्रचारक बने। अपने दायित्व का निर्वाह करते हुए उन्होंने झेलम, गुजराँवाला, पेशावर आदि स्थानों पर शाखाएँ प्रारंभ कीं। उन्हें सुदृढ़ किया तथा स्थानीय युवकों को प्रेरित कर उन्हें संघ की विचारधारा से जोड़कर समर्पित स्वयंसेवक एवं प्रचारक बनने के लिए प्रशिक्षित किया। इस प्रकार पूरे विभाग में संघ के संगठन को एक सुदृढ़ आकार दिया।

13. विठलराव रामचंद्रराव पत्तकी

जन्म : 18 जनवरी, 1911, **निधन** : 13 अप्रैल, 1970

नागपुर की एक प्रसिद्ध व्यायामशाला के मल्ल (पहलवान) थे और डॉ. हेडगेवार के स्नेह से संघ के स्वयंसेवक बने। 1939 में कलकत्ता में प्रचारक नियुक्त हुए। 22 मार्च, 1939 को वहाँ पहली शाखा प्रारंभ की और संघकार्य की नींव रखी। 1940 से 1945 तक बंगाल के प्रांत प्रचारक रहे और इस अवधि में शाखाओं की संख्या व स्वयंसेवकों की सक्रियता में उल्लेखनीय वृद्धि हुई।

14. नारायणराव तरटे

जन्म : 13 मार्च, 1913, **निधन** : 1 अगस्त, 2005

1932 में संघ शिक्षा वर्ग में नागपुर आए। डॉ. हेडगेवार की प्रेरणा से प्रचारक बनने का संकल्प लिया। 1938 में मध्य भारत प्रांत के ग्वालियर भेजे गए, जहाँ संघ की शाखा प्रारंभ की। नारायणराव पहले ऐसे प्रचारक बने, जो नागपुर से नहीं थे और उन्हें संघकार्य के लिए बाहर भेजा गया। वे विदर्भ से ग्वालियर गए थे। 1944 से 1947 तक उत्तर प्रदेश के पीलीभीत जिला प्रचारक रहते हुए संघकार्य का विस्तार किया। 1947 के अंत में लखनऊ भेजा गया। 'हिंदुस्थान समाचार' संस्था के कार्य के लिए विभिन्न शहरों में रहकर 18 वर्ष काम किया। 1966 से लगातार 19 वर्षों तक विश्व हिंदू परिषद् की मासिक पत्रिका 'हिंदू विश्व' का संपादन किया।

15. बाबूराव पालधीकर

जन्म : 21 जनवरी, 1921, **निधन :** 12 अक्तूबर, 2003

बाबूराव ने 1940 में तृतीय वर्ष का प्रशिक्षण पूरा किया। उसी वर्ष वे प्रचारक बने और पंजाब के फिरोजपुर में दायित्व दिया गया। 1944 में विभाग प्रचारक तथा 1947 में सह-प्रांत प्रचारक बने। 1949 में ओडिशा का प्रांत प्रचारक बनाकर भेजा गया। ओडिशा में तब केवल चार शाखाएँ थीं, जो बाद में बढ़कर 200 हो गईं। 1980 में उन्हें पूर्वी क्षेत्र के क्षेत्र प्रचारक का दायित्व मिला। वृद्धावस्था के कारण 1992 में उन्हें दायित्व से विश्राम दे दिया गया।

16. चंडिकादास अमृतराव देशमुख (नानाजी देशमुख)

जन्म : 11 अक्तूबर, 1916, **निधन :** 27 फरवरी, 2010

भारत रत्न नानाजी देशमुख ने शिक्षा पूरी करने के बाद 1939 में गोरखपुर में प्रचारक का दायित्व सँभाला। उन्होंने उत्तर प्रदेश सह-प्रांत प्रचारक के दायित्व का भी निर्वहन किया। 1950 में गोरखपुर में पहले शिशु मंदिर की स्थापना में उनकी महत्त्वपूर्ण भूमिका रही। उन्होंने 'पाञ्चजन्य', 'राष्ट्रधर्म', 'स्वदेश' आदि पत्रिकाओं में संपादकीय व संगठनात्मक सेवा दी। भारतीय जनसंघ के काम के साथ ही वे जनता पार्टी की स्थापना के प्रमुख शिल्पकार रहे। 1972 में दीनदयाल शोध संस्थान की स्थापना की, जबकि चित्रकूट में ग्रामोदय विश्वविद्यालय का शुभारंभ किया। 1999 में राज्यसभा सदस्य नियुक्त किए गए। 2019 में उन्हें मरणोपरांत 'भारत रत्न' से सम्मानित किया गया।

17. रामभाऊ मालोदे

1931 में डॉ. हेडगेवार के संपर्क में आए। वे मूलतः वाशिम के स्वयंसेवक थे। 1935 में शिक्षण पूर्ण करने के पश्चात् मद्रास में प्रचारक का दायित्व सौंपा गया। मद्रास के आर्य-द्रविड़ संघर्ष की कठिन पृष्ठभूमि में अपने अथक परिश्रम एवं कुशल नेतृत्व से संघकार्य का विस्तार किया। वे अपनी भाषा, वेशभूषा और आहार-विहार से पूर्णतः मद्रासी बन गए थे।

18. बलवंत नारायण (बालासाहेब इंदुरकर)

निधन : 22 अक्तूबर, 2001

संघ के प्रारंभिक काल के प्रमुख प्रचारकों में से एक। डॉ. हेडगेवार से संपर्क के बाद संघकार्य से जुड़े और उनकी प्रेरणा से प्रचारक बने। 20 वर्ष की आयु में पंजाब प्रांत के लाहौर में नियुक्त हुए। प्रथम संघ प्रतिबंध के समय उन्हें हिमाचल प्रदेश की जेल में रखा गया। जेल से लौटने के बाद भी उन्होंने संघकार्य में सक्रिय भूमिका निभाई।

19. त्र्यंबकराव जुमड़े

जन्म : 1915, **निधन :** 3 अप्रैल, 1997

1934 में संघ के तृतीय वर्ष का प्रशिक्षण लिया। 1939 में अमरावती और फिर 1942 में खंडवा जिले में संघकार्य के विस्तार हेतु भेजा गया। वे पैदल, साइकिल या बैलगाड़ी से प्रवास करते थे। उनके प्रयत्नों से वहाँ शाखाओं की संख्या में अच्छी वृद्धि हुई। 1963 तक

महाकौशल प्रांत में विभिन्न दायित्वों पर कार्य किया। 1967 में उन्हें भारतीय मजदूर संघ के मध्य प्रदेश प्रांत का संगठन मंत्री बनाया गया और इस भूमिका में उन्होंने श्रमिकों को संगठित कर संघ के विचारों का व्यापक प्रचार किया।

२०. मुरलीधर कृष्णराव (बाबूराव) चौथाईवाले

जन्म : 27 जुलाई, 1922, **निधन** : 4 फरवरी, 1996

दो वर्ष छिंदवाड़ा में प्रचारक के रूप में कार्य किया। इसके बाद नागपुर से बी.ए., बी.एड. तथा एम.ए. की उपाधियाँ अर्जित कीं। 1954 से सरसंघचालक श्रीगुरुजी का पत्र-व्यवहार सँभालने लगे। लगभग 11 हजार पत्रों की प्रतिलिपियों से 'पत्ररूप श्रीगुरुजी' ग्रंथ का संकलन किया। तृतीय सरसंघचालक बालासाहब देवरस के देहांत के बाद 'मेरे देखे हुए श्री बालासाहब देवरस' नामक पुस्तक का लेखन किया, जो उनके संस्मरणों और अनुभवों पर आधारित महत्त्वपूर्ण कृति है।

२१. भैयाजी शहादाणी

निधन : 26 मार्च, 1971

संघ स्थापना के बाद इतवारी शाखा से जुड़कर स्वयंसेवक बने। नागपुर से बी.ए. तक की शिक्षा पूर्ण करने के बाद सन् 1938 में प्रचारक नियुक्त हुए। कुछ वर्ष बिहार में प्रचारक रहने के पश्चात् लंबे समय तक नागपुर और भंडारा विभाग प्रचारक के रूप में कार्य किया। श्रीगुरुजी का पत्र-व्यवहार दीर्घ अवधि तक सुव्यवस्थित रूप से सँभालते रहे।

२२. बापूराव भिशीकर

सन् 1935 में धमतरी में विस्तारक का दायित्व सँभालते हुए पहली शाखा स्थापित की। सन् 1938 में संघकार्य के विस्तार हेतु कराची भेजा गया, जहाँ सिंध प्रांत में संघकार्य का औपचारिक शुभारंभ किया। उनके अथक प्रयासों से ही डॉ. हेडगेवार की संघकार्य विस्तार की कल्पना साकार हुई, जिसके अंतर्गत 3 प्रतिशत शहरी तथा 1 प्रतिशत ग्रामीण क्षेत्र में स्वयंसेवकों की उपस्थिति सुनिश्चित करने वाला सिंध पहला प्रांत बना।

२३. शिवराम शंकर (दादासाहब) आप्टे

जन्म : 2 फरवरी, 1905, **निधन** : 10 अक्तूबर, 1985

गुजरात के वडोदरा में जन्म। शिवराम शंकर आप्टे 1939 में स्वयंसेवक बने और 1944 में प्रचारक के रूप में कार्यभार ग्रहण किया। संघकार्य विस्तार के लिए तमिलनाडु भेजे गए, जहाँ उन्होंने संगठन को नई दिशा प्रदान की। संघ तथा विश्व हिंदू परिषद् का संविधान निर्माण करने में उनकी भूमिका महत्त्वपूर्ण रही। 10 अप्रैल, 1948 को भारत की प्रथम बहुभाषी समाचार एजेंसी 'हिंदुस्थान समाचार' की स्थापना का श्रेय भी उन्हें ही जाता है। इसी क्रम में, देवनागरी लिपि में 'टेलीप्रिंटर' का आविष्कार कर उन्होंने संचार जगत् में ऐतिहासिक योगदान दिया। सन् 1964 में उन्हें विश्व हिंदू परिषद् का संस्थापक महासचिव नियुक्त किया गया।

24. लक्ष्मण माधव (बाबूराव) देशपांडे

जन्म : 11 दिसंबर, 1913, **निधन :** 14 मई, 2009

महाराष्ट्र के अमरावती में जन्म। सन् 1941 में प्रचारक जीवन आरंभ किया। 1945 में बिहार भेजे गए, जहाँ श्रीगुरुजी के प्रवास के दौरान उन्होंने अपनी रेखांकन कला से विशेष पहचान बनाई। अपने जीवन के अंतिम चरण में भी उनकी जीवंतता अद्भुत थी। श्रीराम जन्मभूमि आंदोलन की प्रथम कारसेवा में वे अपने गाँव मंगरुल से अयोध्या तक पैदल पहुँचकर सहभागी बने। उनका संपूर्ण जीवन समर्पण, अनुशासन और निष्ठा का प्रेरक आदर्श प्रस्तुत करता है।

25. मोरूभाऊ केतकर

जन्म : 14 सितंबर, 1914, **निधन :** 9 जून, 1993

महाराष्ट्र के नागपुर में जन्म। सन् 1943 में नौकरी छोड़कर प्रचारक जीवन अपनाया। बालासाहब देशपांडे द्वारा स्थापित वनवासी कल्याण आश्रम के कार्यों से वे प्रारंभ से ही जुड़े रहे। 10 नवंबर, 1952 को उन्होंने आश्रम के विस्तार हेतु जशपुर के महाराजा विजय भूषण सिंह से महत्त्वपूर्ण सहयोग प्राप्त किया। वनवासी बच्चों की शिक्षा के लिए छात्रावास स्थापित किए, जिनमें से पहला जशपुर में और दूसरा जशपुर से लगभग 150 किलोमीटर दूर बगीचा में प्रारंभ किया गया। वनवासी समाज के उत्थान एवं शिक्षा के क्षेत्र में उनका योगदान अनुकरणीय और प्रेरणादायक माना जाता है।

२६. ठाकुर राम सिंह

जन्म : 16 फरवरी, 1915, **निधन :** 6 दिसंबर, 2010

हिमाचल प्रदेश के हमीरपुर में जन्म। पढ़ाई के दौरान ही स्वयंसेवक बने। सन् 1942 में अध्यापक की नौकरी छोड़कर प्रचारक बने और अपने साथ 10 युवाओं को भी प्रचारक बनाकर संघकार्य को नई दिशा दी। सन् 1949 में पूर्वोत्तर भेजे गए, जहाँ 1962 के चीन युद्ध के समय असम में शांति बनाए रखने में महत्त्वपूर्ण भूमिका निभाई। वे क्रमश: 1971 में पंजाब के सह-प्रांत प्रचारक, 1974 में प्रांत प्रचारक और 1978 में क्षेत्र प्रचारक बने। सन् 1984 में उन्हें 'अखिल भारतीय इतिहास संकलन योजना समिति' में महत्त्वपूर्ण दायित्व सौंपा गया। इसके पश्चात् 2006 में उन्होंने हमीरपुर जिले के नेरी में 'ठाकुर जगदेवचंद्र स्मृति इतिहास शोध संस्थान' की स्थापना की और जीवनपर्यंत इतिहास के पुनर्लेखन तथा सांस्कृतिक पुनर्जागरण के कार्य में सक्रिय रहे।

२७. गोविंद कृष्ण (भाऊसाहब) भुस्कुटे

जन्म : 14 जून, 1915, **निधन :** 1 जनवरी, 1991

मध्य प्रदेश के बुरहानपुर में जन्म। सन् 1932 से नियमित रूप से शाखा में जाने लगे। सन् 1941 में उनका विवाह हुआ और वे संघ के प्रथम गृहस्थ प्रचारक के रूप में प्रतिष्ठित हुए। संघ में उन्होंने विभिन्न दायित्व निभाते हुए अंतत: क्षेत्र प्रचारक तक की भूमिका निभाई। 'भारतीय किसान संघ' की स्थापना में भी उन्होंने मार्गदर्शक की भूमिका का निर्वहन किया और संगठन को सशक्त आधार प्रदान किया।

२८. केशवराव गोरे

जन्म : 1 सितंबर, 1915, **निधन :** 28 अक्तूबर, 2001

महाराष्ट्र के गोंदिया में जन्म। 1938 में मध्य प्रदेश आकर किराने की दुकान खोली। सन् 1939-40 में श्रीगुरुजी के प्रवास के दौरान बड़े भाई यशवंतराव गोरे के आग्रह पर प्रचारक बन गए। वे जन्मजात वास्तुकार थे। जबलपुर में प्रांतीय कार्यालय 'केशव-कुंज' का निर्माण कराया और इंदौर कार्यालय के निर्माण में महत्त्वपूर्ण भूमिका निभाई। इसके बाद उन्हें नागपुर केंद्रीय कार्यालय प्रमुख तथा अखिल भारतीय व्यवस्था प्रमुख का दायित्व सौंपा गया।

२९. यादवराव कालकर

जन्म : 10 मई, 1916, **निधन :** 7 फरवरी, 1985

महाराष्ट्र के देउलघाट में जन्म। सन् 1942 में होशंगाबाद में सरकारी नौकरी छोड़कर प्रचारक बने। बाद में महाकौशल के प्रांत प्रचारक नियुक्त किए गए। अत्यंत परिश्रमी कालकरजी कई बार शाखाएँ लगाने के लिए 35-45 किलोमीटर तक पैदल यात्रा करते थे। सन् 1948 में प्रतिबंध के दौरान वे जेल में रहे और सन् 1975 के आपातकाल में बंदी तथा सत्याग्रही कार्यकर्ताओं के परिवारों की जिम्मेदारी सफलतापूर्वक निभाई।

30. बच्छराज व्यास

जन्म : 24 सितंबर, 1916, **निधन :** 15 मार्च, 1972

राजस्थान के डीडवाना में जन्म। कॉलेज की पढ़ाई के दौरान ही बालासाहब देवरस के संपर्क में आए और स्वयंसेवक बने। छात्र जीवन में विवाह के बावजूद, श्रीगुरुजी की इच्छा पर सन् 1944 से 1947 तक राजस्थान में प्रचारक के रूप में कार्य किया। सन् 1948 में संघ पर प्रतिबंध के समय उन्होंने नागपुर केंद्र सँभालते हुए पूरे देश में सत्याग्रह को गति दी। 1958 से 1962 तक महाराष्ट्र विधान परिषद् के सदस्य रहे। सन् 1965 में श्रीगुरुजी और बालासाहब देवरस के आदेश पर भारतीय जनसंघ के राष्ट्रीय अध्यक्ष बने। संघ जीवन के आदर्श उन्होंने राजनीतिक क्षेत्र में भी बनाए रखे।

31. पं. दीनदयाल उपाध्याय

जन्म : 25 सितंबर, 1916, **निधन :** 11 फरवरी, 1968

'एकात्म मानव दर्शन' के प्रणेता पं. दीनदयाल उपाध्याय का जन्म राजस्थान के धानक्या गाँव में हुआ। कॉलेज की पढ़ाई के दौरान वे प्रांत प्रचारक भाऊराव देवरस के संपर्क में आए और स्वयंसेवक बने। लखनऊ में राष्ट्रधर्म प्रकाशन की स्थापना के साथ ही उन्होंने 'एकात्म मानव दर्शन' नामक सामाजिक-आर्थिक चिंतन प्रस्तुत किया। सन् 1967 में केरल में आयोजित अधिवेशन में सर्वसम्मति से भारतीय जनसंघ के अध्यक्ष बनाए गए। 11 फरवरी, 1968 को दीनदयालजी की लखनऊ से पटना रेल-यात्रा के दौरान मुगलसराय स्टेशन पर रहस्यमय ढंग से हत्या कर दी गई।

32. प्रभाकर गजानन (भैयाजी) सहस्त्रबुद्धे

जन्म : 18 सितंबर, 1917, **निधन :** 14 मई, 2007

मध्य प्रदेश के खंडवा में जन्म। सन् 1935 में स्वयंसेवक और 1942 में प्रचारक बनकर संघकार्य हेतु प्रवृत्त हुए। सन् 1948 में संघ पर प्रतिबंध के समय वे उत्तर प्रदेश के सह-प्रांत प्रचारक रहे और प्रतिबंध हटने के बाद 1950 में मध्य भारत के प्रांत प्रचारक बनाए गए। सन् 1975 के आपातकाल में नागपुर जेल में रहे। उन्होंने 125 पुस्तकों की रचना की, जिनमें 'जीवन मूल्य' अत्यंत लोकप्रिय रही। उन्होंने प्रख्यात इतिहासकार हरिभाऊ वाकणकर के साथ वैदिक सरस्वती नदी पर शोध कार्य भी किया।

33. लक्ष्मणराव इनामदार (वकील साहब)

जन्म : 21 सितंबर, 1917, **निधन :** 15 जुलाई, 1985

गुजरात में संघकार्य के शिल्पी कहे जाने वाले लक्ष्मणराव इनामदार का जन्म महाराष्ट्र के सतारा में हुआ। वे एल.एल.बी. की शिक्षा पूर्ण नहीं कर पाए, लेकिन आजीवन 'वकील साहब' के नाम से प्रसिद्ध रहे। सन् 1941 में प्रचारक बने और गुजरात के नवसारी भेजे गए। सन् 1952 में गुजरात प्रांत प्रचारक तथा 1973 में क्षेत्र प्रचारक बनाए गए। बाद में उन्हें अखिल भारतीय व्यवस्था प्रमुख का दायित्व सौंपा गया। देश के विभाजन, 1948 और 1975 के संघ प्रतिबंध, सोमनाथ मंदिर निर्माण, गोहत्या बंदी सत्याग्रह, चीन और पाकिस्तान के आक्रमण, विवेकानंद जन्मशती, मीनाक्षीपुरम धर्मांतरण प्रकरण तथा गुजरात में बार-बार आने वाले अकाल, बाढ़ और भूकंप जैसी अनेक चुनौतियों का उन्होंने धैर्य और साहस से सामना किया और संगठन को मजबूती प्रदान की।

34. शिवराम पंत जोगलेकर

जन्म : 1917, **निधन :** 29 जून, 1999

कर्नाटक के बागलकोट में जन्म। सन् 1932 में डॉ. हेडगेवार के दर्शन के साथ संघ में प्रवेश हुआ। 1936 में उन्हें पुणे नगर कार्यवाह की जिम्मेदारी दी गई। सन् 1942 में स्वर्ण पदक के साथ एम.एससी. पूरी करने के बाद प्रचारक बनने का निर्णय लिया। सन् 1943 में मद्रास भेजे गए, जहाँ सेवा के माध्यम से हिंदुत्व जागरण और शाखा प्रसार के अभिनव प्रयोग किए। वे शिक्षित लोगों को 'संपादक के नाम पत्र' लिखने के लिए प्रेरित करते थे, और इसी पहल से 'विजिल' नामक संस्था की स्थापना हुई। 60 वर्ष तक उन्होंने तमिलनाडु में संघ के विविध दायित्व निभाए।

35. माधवराव देशमुख

जन्म : 2 जनवरी, 1918, **निधन :** 14 मई, 1982

उत्तर प्रदेश के काशी में जन्म। सन् 1937 में स्वयंसेवक जीवन आरंभ किया और इसके बाद प्रचारक की जिम्मेदारी सँभाली। सन् 1956 में गृहस्थ जीवन में प्रवेश किया; 1964 में विश्व हिंदू परिषद् की स्थापना के साथ ही उन्हें इसके संगठन का काम सौंपा गया। सन् 1975 में संघ पर प्रतिबंध लगने पर वे डेढ़ साल तक वाराणसी, नैनी सहित कई जेलों में रहे।

36. अनंतराव गोखले

जन्म : 23 सितंबर, 1918, **निधन :** 25 मई, 2014

मध्य प्रदेश के खंडवा में जन्म। संघ से जुड़ाव विद्यार्थी जीवन में ही हो गया। सन् 1940 में श्रीगुरुजी के आह्वान पर प्रचारक बने। सन् 1948 में संघ पर प्रतिबंध के समय उन्होंने अखिल भारतीय विद्यार्थी परिषद् (ए.बी.वी.पी.) की ओर से 150 स्वयंसेवकों को गाँव-गाँव जागरूकता फैलाने के लिए भेजा। बाद में लखनऊ में 'लोकहित प्रकाशन' का कार्य किया और 150 नई तथा प्रामाणिक पुस्तकों का प्रकाशन सुनिश्चित किया। सन् 1991 में उन्होंने अपने हिस्से की संपत्ति संघ को दान कर दी, जिस पर संघ कार्यालय का निर्माण हुआ और जिसे 'शिवनेरी' नाम दिया गया।

37. डॉ. वासुदेव केशव (आबाजी) थत्ते

जन्म : 24 नवंबर,1918, **निधन :** 27 नवंबर, 1995

एम.बी.बी.एस. की पढ़ाई पूरी करने के बाद प्रचारक बनने का संकल्प लिया। इससे पहले वे बड़े भाई अप्पाजी की प्रेरणा से शाखा से जुड़ चुके थे। सन् 1944-45 में बालासाहब देवरस ने उन्हें नागपुर बुलाया। चिकित्सा अनुभव प्राप्त करने के बाद उन्हें बंगाल के शिवपुर भेजा गया। सन् 1950 में प्रतिबंध हटने के बाद उन्हें श्रीगुरुजी के साथ कार्य करने को कहा गया। कालांतर में वे अखिल भारतीय प्रचारक प्रमुख बनाए गए। उन्होंने ग्राहक पंचायत, सहकार भारती, राष्ट्र सेविका समिति तथा अन्य महिला संगठनों के समन्वय का दायित्व कुशलतापूर्वक सँभाला।

38. लक्ष्मण श्रीकृष्ण भिड़े

जन्म : 1918, **निधन :** 7 जनवरी, 2001

महाराष्ट्र के अकोला में जन्म। कई स्थानों पर संघ का दायित्व सँभाला। सन् 1941 में प्रचारक बने और 1942 में लखनऊ भेजे गए। सन् 1957 में उन्हें केन्या भेजा गया और 1961 में वे उत्तर प्रदेश लौटे। सन् 1973 में उन्हें विश्व विभाग का कार्य सौंपा गया। 1978 में 'फ्रेंड्स ऑफ इंडिया सोसाइटी इंटरनेशनल' की स्थापना में उनका प्रमुख योगदान रहा और 1990 में 'ओवरसीज फ्रेंड्स ऑफ बीजेपी' की स्थापना की। सन् 1992 में उन्हें दीनदयाल शोध संस्थान का अध्यक्ष बनाया गया। संघ से उनके गहरे लगाव का परिचय दिसंबर 2000 में विश्व संघ शिविर में मिला, जब स्वास्थ्य खराब होने के बावजूद वे वहाँ पहुँचे और बिना बोले सभी से मिलकर संतोष और प्रसन्नता व्यक्त की।

39. भास्करराव कलंबी

जन्म : 5 अक्तूबर, 1919, **निधन :** 12 जनवरी, 2002

म्याँमार के रंगून में जन्म। सन् 1935 में बंबई में स्वयंसेवक बने। सन् 1945 में कोच्चि में प्रचारक के रूप में भेजे गए। सन् 1964 में केरल के प्रथम प्रांत प्रचारक बने, जहाँ उन्होंने निर्धन मछुआरों के बीच रात्रि शाखाओं का अभिनव प्रयोग किया। सन् 1981 में संघ शिक्षा वर्ग में उन्हें भीषण हृदयाघात हुआ और 1983 में बाईपास सर्जरी हुई। इसके बावजूद वे संघ सेवा में लगातार जुटे रहे। सन् 1984 में उन्होंने 'वनवासी कल्याण आश्रम' के अखिल भारतीय संगठन मंत्री का दायित्व सँभाला और जनजातियों के गौरवशाली इतिहास एवं परंपराओं को सबके सामने लाने का कार्य किया।

40. मोरेश्वर नीलकंठ (मोरोपंत) पिंगले

जन्म : 30 अक्तूबर,1919, **निधन :** 21 सितंबर, 2003

सन् 1930 में स्वयंसेवक बने और 1941 में प्रचारक। उन्होंने सह-विभाग प्रचारक, प्रांत प्रचारक, अखिल भारतीय शारीरिक प्रमुख, बौद्धिक प्रमुख, प्रचारक प्रमुख तथा सह-सरकार्यवाह जैसे महत्त्वपूर्ण दायित्वों का निर्वहन किया। छत्रपति शिवाजी की 300वीं पुण्यतिथि पर रायगढ़ में आयोजित भव्य कार्यक्रम, डॉ. हेडगेवार के समाधि निर्माण और बाबासाहेब आप्टे स्मारक समिति के कार्यक्रम उन्होंने सफलतापूर्वक संपन्न कराए। सन् 1981 में मीनाक्षीपुरम कांड के बाद 'संस्कृति रक्षा निधि' का संग्रह और 'एकात्मता रथ यात्रा' का आयोजन भी उनके नेतृत्व में अत्यंत सफल रहा। वे विश्व हिंदू परिषद् के प्रमुख मार्गदर्शकों में से एक रहे और जीवनपर्यंत संगठनात्मक कार्यों में सक्रिय रहे।

41. आचार्य गिरिराज किशोर

जन्म : 4 फरवरी, 1920, **निधन :** 13 जुलाई, 2014

उत्तर प्रदेश के एटा में जन्म। आगरा में स्वयंसेवक बने और 1948 के प्रतिबंध के समय मैनपुरी, आगरा, बरेली और बनारस की जेलों में लगातार 13 महीने तक बंदी रहे। छोटे भाई की असमय मृत्यु के कारण घर की जिम्मेदारी निभाने हेतु मध्य प्रदेश के भिंड जिले में प्राचार्य बने। वे अखिल भारतीय विद्यार्थी परिषद् (अ.भा.वि.प.) के राष्ट्रीय उपाध्यक्ष और संगठन मंत्री रहे। बाद में नौकरी छोड़कर भारतीय जनसंघ के राजस्थान प्रांत के संगठन मंत्री बनाए गए। सन् 1983 में उन्हें विश्व हिंदू परिषद् का कार्य सौंपा गया और जीवनपर्यंत हिंदू समाज को संगठित करने के कार्य में सक्रिय रहे।

42. बापूराव लेले

जन्म : 29 फरवरी, 1920, **निधन :** 11 अगस्त, 2002

महाराष्ट्र के जलगाँव में जन्म। बाल्यकाल में ही संघ से जुड़ गए। सन् 1940 में प्रचारक बने और दादासाहेब आप्टे के साथ 'हिंदुस्थान समाचार' संस्था में कार्य किया। पाँच वर्ष तक भारतीय प्रेस परिषद् के सदस्य रहे। सन् 1962 में राष्ट्रपति डॉ. एस. राधाकृष्णन के साथ ब्रिटेन और 1966 में प्रधानमंत्री लालबहादुर शास्त्री के साथ ताशकंद गए। अपने षष्ठीपूर्ति कार्यक्रम में प्राप्त 61,000 रुपए उन्होंने 'तरुण भारत' को दान कर दिए और पत्रकारिता व राष्ट्रसेवा के प्रति अपनी गहरी प्रतिबद्धता का परिचय दिया।

43. चमनलाल

जन्म : 25 मार्च, 1920, **निधन :** 10 फरवरी, 2003

संघ के चलते-फिरते 'विश्वकोश' कहे जाने वाले चमनलालजी का जन्म सियालकोट (वर्तमान पाकिस्तान) में हुआ। सन् 1932 में स्वयंसेवक बने और 1942 में प्रचारक। सन् 1946 में लाहौर में विभाजन की विभीषिका के प्रत्यक्षदर्शी के रूप में उन्होंने हर दिन की घटनाओं को डायरी में लिपिबद्ध किया। सन् 1950 में दिल्ली आए और झंडेवाला कार्यालय की व्यवस्था सँभाली। विदेश से आने वाले कार्यकर्ताओं के नाम, पते और फोन नंबर सुरक्षित रखते हुए वे भारत में रहते हुए भी दुनिया भर के स्वयंसेवकों के लिए एक महत्त्वपूर्ण सेतु बन गए। उन्हें मॉरीशस के राष्ट्रपति सर अनिरुद्ध जगन्नाथ ने अपने पुत्र के विवाह में राजकीय अतिथि के रूप में पोर्ट लुई आमंत्रित किया, जो उनके अंतरराष्ट्रीय सम्मान और प्रतिष्ठा का प्रमाण है।

44. नरहरि पांडुरंग (राजाभाऊ) सावरगाँवकर

जन्म : 21 मई, 1920, **निधन :** 10 अप्रैल, 2000

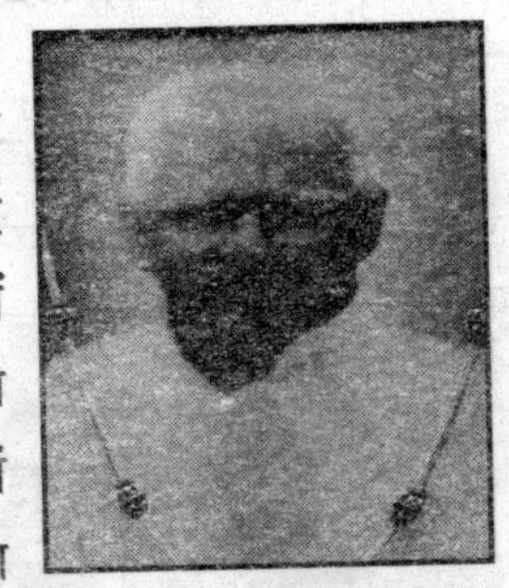

महाराष्ट्र के यवतमाल में जन्म। मात्र 11 वर्ष की आयु में स्वयंसेवक बने और संघ के तीनों वर्गों का प्रशिक्षण पूर्ण किया। सन् 1944 में प्रचारक बने और उन्हें बिहार भेजा गया। वे प्रतिवर्ष संघ शिक्षा वर्ग में शिक्षक बनकर जाते थे। उन्हें दीनदयाल उपाध्याय, अटल बिहारी वाजपेयी, रज्जू भैय्या जैसे वरिष्ठ कार्यकर्ताओं को प्रशिक्षण देने का सौभाग्य प्राप्त हुआ। इसके अलावा उन्होंने बिहार प्रांत के वनवासी कल्याण आश्रम के मार्गदर्शक के रूप में भी महत्त्वपूर्ण योगदान दिया।

45. ब्रह्मदेव

जन्म : 15 जून, 1920, **निधन :** 24 फरवरी, 2002

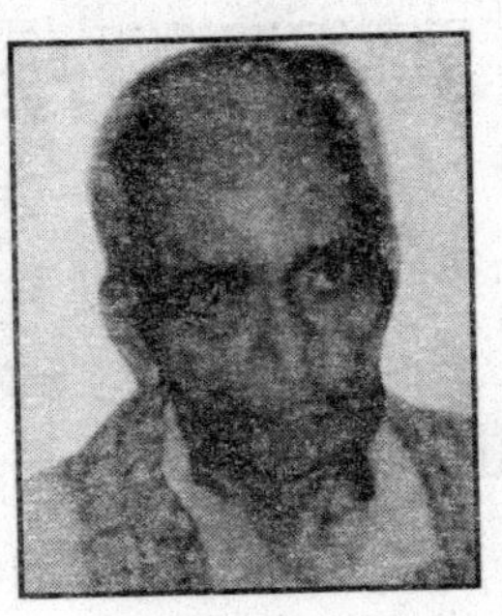

दिल्ली के नजफगढ़ में जन्म। सन् 1937 में स्वयंसेवक बने। मेरठ के सैन्य लेखा कार्यालय में नौकरी की, लेकिन भारतीयों के अपमान पर नौकरी त्याग दी। सन् 1943 में उन्हें प्रचारक के रूप में पंजाब भेजा गया। सन् 1959 में उन्हें राजस्थान प्रांत प्रचारक का दायित्व मिला। सन् 1977 में आपातकाल के बाद उन्हें उत्तरी क्षेत्र का क्षेत्र प्रचारक बनाया गया। सन् 1989 में वे विश्व हिंदू परिषद् के केंद्रीय मंत्री बनाए गए।

46. जगन्नाथराव जोशी

जन्म : 23 जून, 1920, **निधन :** 15 जुलाई, 1991

कर्नाटक के नरगुंड गाँव में जन्म। बी.एड. करने के बाद उन्हें सरकारी नौकरी मिली, लेकिन देश के प्रति समर्पण भाव इतना गहरा था कि उन्होंने नौकरी छोड़कर संघ का प्रचारक बनने का निर्णय लिया। वे गोवा मुक्ति आंदोलन के पहले जत्थे के नेता रहे और करीब पौने दो साल तक लिस्बन जेल में रहे। सन् 1966 में कच्छ समझौतों के विरोध में आंदोलन कर अपनी अमोघ वाणी से जागृति फैलाई। सन् 1967 में वे सांसद बने। जनता पार्टी के शासनकाल में राज्यपाल का पद अस्वीकार कर संगठन को सबल बनाने का कार्य किया। कर्नाटक में संगठन को ग्राम स्तर तक पहुँचाने के लिए उन्हें 'कर्नाटक केसरी' कहा गया।

47. दत्तोपंत ठेंगड़ी

जन्म : 10 अक्तूबर, 1920, **निधन :** 14 अक्तूबर, 2004

महाराष्ट्र के आर्वी में जन्म। सन् 1935 में स्वतंत्रता आंदोलन की 'वानरसेना' के आर्वी तालुका अध्यक्ष थे। सन् 1941 में संघ के प्रचारक बने और केरल भेजे गए, जहाँ उन्होंने राष्ट्रभाषा प्रचार समिति का कार्य भी सँभाला। केरल के बाद उन्हें बंगाल और फिर असम भेजा गया। संघ की योजना से मजदूर क्षेत्र में कार्य करने के लिए इंडियन नेशनल ट्रेड यूनियन कांग्रेस (इंटक) और शेतकारी कामगार फेडरेशन जैसे संगठनों में जाकर अनुभव प्राप्त किया और 'भारतीय मजदूर संघ' की स्थापना की। 'स्वदेशी जागरण मंच' में भी उनकी सक्रिय भूमिका रही। एक लेखक के रूप में उनकी हिंदी में 28, अंग्रेजी में 12 और मराठी में 3 पुस्तकें प्रकाशित हैं, जिनसे संगठन और राष्ट्रीय चिंतन को एक नई दिशा मिली।

48. दत्तात्रेय भीकाजी (बाबूराव) पालधीकर

जन्म : 21 जनवरी, 1921, **निधन :** 12 अक्तूबर, 2023

महाराष्ट्र के वर्धा में जन्म। दत्तोपंत ठेंगड़ी ने स्वयंसेवक बनाया। बी.ए. करने के बाद सन् 1940 में प्रचारक बने और फिरोजपुर (पंजाब) भेजे गए। वे मराठी, संस्कृत, अंग्रेजी, हिंदी, उर्दू और पंजाबी भाषाओं के जानकार थे। विभाजन के समय हिंदुओं की रक्षा में उनकी भूमिका अत्यंत महत्त्वपूर्ण रही। सन् 1948 में संघ पर प्रतिबंध के बाद उन्हें उड़ीसा का प्रांत प्रचारक बनाया गया, सन् 1980 में उन्हें पूर्वी क्षेत्र का क्षेत्र प्रचारक नियुक्त किया गया।

49. सुंदर सिंह भंडारी

जन्म : 12 अप्रैल, 1921, **निधन :** 22 जून, 2005

राजस्थान के उदयपुर में जन्म। सन् 1937 में पं. दीनदयाल उपाध्याय के साथ संघ में प्रवेश किया। सन् 1946 में प्रचारक बने और जोधपुर भेजे गए। सन् 1951 में उन्हें श्रीगुरुजी द्वारा दीनदयालजी और नानाजी देशमुख के साथ जनसंघ में भेजा गया। सन् 1954 में वे जनसंघ के केंद्रीय मंत्री और 1967 में महामंत्री बने। 1968 में दीनदयालजी की हत्या के बाद उन्हें राष्ट्रीय संगठन मंत्री बनाया गया। सन् 1980 में भारतीय जनता पार्टी का संविधान उनकी देख-रेख में तैयार हुआ। वे भारतीय जनता पार्टी के राष्ट्रीय अध्यक्ष तथा तीन बार राज्यसभा सदस्य रहने के साथ-साथ बिहार एवं गुजरात के राज्यपाल भी रहे।

50. कृष्णचंद्र गांधी

जन्म : 11 अक्तूबर, 1921, **निधन :** 24 नवंबर, 2002

उत्तर प्रदेश के मेरठ में जन्म। सन् 1943 में स्वयंसेवक बने। 1944 में बी.ए. करने के बाद वे प्रचारक बन गए। 1945 में मथुरा जिला प्रचारक बने। मथुरा में प्रचारक रहते हुए उन्होंने केशवदुर्ग कार्यालय का निर्माण करवाया। श्रम और श्रमिकों के प्रति प्रेम, आदर और करुणा के कारण वे आजीवन रिक्शा पर नहीं बैठे। सन् 1952 में नानाजी देशमुख के साथ विभाग प्रचारक के रूप में गोरखपुर में देश का पहला सरस्वती शिशु मंदिर प्रारंभ किया। उत्तर प्रदेश के बाद उन्हें पूर्वोत्तर भारत भेजा गया। वहाँ उन्होंने वनवासी शिक्षा का स्वरूप तैयार किया।

51. दत्तात्रेय गंगाधर (भैयाजी) कस्तूरे

जन्म : 12 दिसंबर, 1921, **निधन :** 2 जनवरी, 2006

मध्य प्रदेश में महाकाल की नगरी उज्जैन में जन्म। सन् 1936 में स्वयंसेवक बने और भारत छोड़ो आंदोलन की समाप्ति के बाद प्रचारक का जीवन अपनाया। प्रचारक रहते हुए उन्होंने बाबा ओंकारनाथजी से दीक्षा ली और नर्मदा तट पर 24 लाख जाप करते हुए 'गायत्री पुरश्चरण' की अखंड साधना पूरी की। सन् 1975 में आपातकाल से पूर्व उन्हें विश्व हिंदू परिषद् का दायित्व सौंपा गया। उन्होंने विहिप द्वारा प्रकाशित 'हिंदू चेतना' की जिम्मेदारी भी कुशलतापूर्वक सँभाली और इसे हिंदू समाज में जागरण का प्रभावी माध्यम बनाया।

52. नारायण बलवंत (राजाभाऊ) महाकाल

जन्म : 26 जनवरी, 1923, **निधन :** 15 अगस्त, 1955

मध्य प्रदेश के उज्जैन में प्रचारक रहे दिगंबर राव तिजोर के संपर्क में आकर राजाभाऊ स्वयंसेवक बने। 1942 में प्रचारक बनने का संकल्प लिया। 1948 में प्रतिबंध के समय होटल खोलकर धन और बैठक दोनों की व्यवस्था की। 1955 में गोवा मुक्ति आंदोलन में उज्जैन जत्थे का नेतृत्व किया। पुर्तगाली सैनिक की गोली सिर पर लगने पर भी उन्होंने तिरंगा नहीं छोड़ा। गोवा की स्वतंत्रता के अमर सेनानी नारायण बलवंत की अस्थियों को उनकी जन्मभूमि उज्जैन में माँ क्षिप्रा के पवित्र जल में विसर्जित किया गया।

53. जयगोपाल

जन्म : 10 जुलाई, 1923, **निधन :** 2 अगस्त, 2005

पश्चिमोत्तर सीमा प्रांत डेरा इस्माइल खाँ (अब पाकिस्तान में) में जन्म। छात्र जीवन में ही स्वयंसेवक बने। अभियंता की पढ़ाई करने लखनऊ आए, जहाँ उनकी भेंट भाऊराव देवरस से हुई। 1942 में प्रचारक बने और तीन वर्ष तक काठमांडू (नेपाल) में संघकार्य किया। उन्हें लखनऊ में विद्या भारती, उत्तर प्रदेश का संरक्षक बनाया गया। 1973 में पूर्वी उत्तर प्रदेश के प्रांत प्रचारक और 1989 में उत्तरी क्षेत्र के क्षेत्र प्रचारक बने। उन्होंने लद्दाख जैसे क्षेत्र में भी संघकार्य का बीजारोपण किया।

54. सोहन सिंह

जन्म : 18 अक्तूबर, 1923, **निधन :** 4 जुलाई, 2015

उत्तर प्रदेश के बुलंदशहर में जन्म। बाल्यावस्था में ही हिंदू महासभा भवन शाखा में स्वयंसेवक बने। 1943 में प्रचारक बनकर करनाल गए और हरियाणा में संभाग प्रचारक भी रहे। दिल्ली में संभाग प्रचारक रहते हुए 1969 में पीरागढ़ी शिविर की व्यवस्थाओं को देखकर श्रीगुरुजी ने कहा—'न भूतो न भविष्यति।' वे जयपुर के विभाग प्रचारक, राजस्थान के प्रांत प्रचारक तथा दिल्ली और राजस्थान के क्षेत्र प्रचारक भी रहे। सन् 1994 में अखिल भारतीय धर्म जागरण प्रमुख और उसके बाद उत्तर क्षेत्र के प्रचारक प्रमुख बनाए गए।

55. ठाकुर संकटा प्रसाद सिंह

जन्म : 23 नवंबर, 1923, **निधन :** 20 अक्तूबर, 2017

उत्तर प्रदेश के गाजीपुर में जन्म। सन् 1942 के भारत छोड़ो आंदोलन के दौरान संघ से जुड़े। सन् 1944 में उन्हें प्रचारक बनाकर भदोही की मिर्जापुर तहसील भेजा गया, जहाँ उन्होंने तहसील, जिला और विभाग प्रचारक के रूप में कार्य किया। बाद में वे अखिल भारतीय किसान संघ में गए, जहाँ उन्होंने उत्तर प्रदेश के संगठन मंत्री, राष्ट्रीय संगठन मंत्री और राष्ट्रीय अध्यक्ष के रूप में दायित्व निभाया। वे संघ शिक्षा वर्ग, उत्तर प्रदेश के पहले मुख्य शिक्षक भी बने।

56. दत्तात्रेय बालकृष्ण (नाना) भागवत

जन्म : 4 दिसंबर, 1923, **निधन** : 29 दिसंबर, 2006

राम मंदिर आंदोलन में शिलापूजन कार्य की व्यवस्था सँभालने वाले दत्तात्रेय बालकृष्ण भागवत का जन्म महाराष्ट्र के वर्धा में हुआ। वे छात्र जीवन में ही स्वयंसेवक बने और सन् 1944 में प्रचारक बने। पहले कर्नाटक और फिर 1946 में बिहार भेजे गए। आपातकाल के बाद वे विश्व हिंदू परिषद्, बिहार प्रांत के संगठन मंत्री बने। सन् 1980 में बिहार और उत्तर प्रदेश के सह-क्षेत्रीय संगठन मंत्री और 1985-86 में विश्व हिंदू परिषद् के केंद्रीय मंत्री रहे। वे पंजाब में आतंकवाद के दौरान 'सद्भावना यात्रा' तथा नेपाल के पशुपतिनाथ से चली पहली 'एकात्मता यात्रा' के संयोजक भी रहे।

57. के. सूर्यनारायण राव 'सुरुजी'

जन्म : 20 अगस्त, 1924, **निधन** : 18 नवंबर, 2016

कर्नाटक के बेंगलुरु में जन्म। सन् 1942 में छात्र जीवन में स्वयंसेवक बने। बी.एससी. (गणित) करने के बाद सन् 1946 में प्रचारक बने और कर्नाटक में विभाग प्रचारक का दायित्व मिला। सन् 1972 से 1984 तक तमिलनाडु के प्रांत प्रचारक रहे और बाद में तमिलनाडु एवं केरल के क्षेत्र प्रचारक बने। इसके बाद उन्हें अखिल भारतीय सेवा प्रमुख बनाया गया। उन्होंने विश्व हिंदू परिषद्, वनवासी कल्याण आश्रम, आरोग्य भारती, सेवा भारती जैसी संस्थाओं से जुड़कर कार्य किया। सन् 1969 में उडुपी (कर्नाटक) में संत सम्मेलन की जिम्मेदारी सँभाली, जिसमें धर्माचार्यों ने हिंदू समाज में छुआछूत समाप्ति का ऐतिहासिक प्रस्ताव स्वीकार किया।

58. केशवराव दत्तात्रेय दीक्षित

जन्म : 1 अगस्त,1925, **निधन :** 20 सितंबर, 2022

महाराष्ट्र के वर्धा में जन्म। बाल्यकाल में ही स्वयंसेवक बन गए। सन् 1939 से लेकर 1941 तक लगातार प्रथम, द्वितीय और तृतीय वर्ष का प्रशिक्षण पूरा किया। सन् 1950 में प्रचारक बने और पश्चिम बंगाल भेजे गए, जहाँ उन्होंने 72 वर्षों तक राष्ट्र-निर्माण का कार्य किया। उन्होंने कोलकाता महानगर प्रचारक, प्रांत संपर्क प्रमुख, प्रांत प्रचारक, क्षेत्र बौद्धिक प्रमुख और क्षेत्र प्रचारक जैसे दायित्व निभाए। बंगाल के कार्यकर्ता कहते थे कि 'बंगमाता ने केशवजी को अपनी संतान के रूप में गोद लिया था।'

59. विश्वनाथ

जन्म : 1925, **निधन :** 24 मई, 2007

पंजाब के श्रीगोइंदवाल साहिब में जन्म। छात्र जीवन में ही संघ के संपर्क में आए। सन् 1945 में प्रचारक बने। विभाजन के समय हिंदू रक्षा के लिए युवकों की टोली बनाई। सन् 1978 में पंजाब के प्रांत प्रचारक बनाए गए और स्थिति सँभालने में महत्त्वपूर्ण योगदान दिया। सन् 1990 में उन्हें उत्तर क्षेत्र का क्षेत्र प्रचारक बनाया गया। सन् 2001 से 2006 तक धर्मजागरण विभाग के प्रमुख रहे। जीवन के अंतिम दिनों में अमृतसर कार्यालय में रहकर नियमित शाखा जाते रहे।

60. रामनरेश सिंह

जन्म : 1925, **निधन :** 2 मई, 1985

उत्तर प्रदेश के मिर्जापुर में जन्म। हाई स्कूल की शिक्षा पूरी होते ही लिपिक की नौकरी लग गई, लेकिन संघ से जुड़ाव पहले से ही था। सन् 1946 में स्थायी सरकारी नौकरी छोड़कर प्रचारक बन गए। सन् 1950 में पुरुषोत्तम चिकित्सालय, 1952 में माधव विद्या मंदिर और 1953 में पंडा समाज की स्थापना की। भारतीय मजदूर संघ की स्थापना के बाद इससे जुड़े और आगे चलकर इसके राष्ट्रीय महामंत्री बने। मजदूरों के हित में कई लेखों का प्रकाशन किया और राज्य तथा राष्ट्र स्तर पर अनेक संस्थाओं का निर्माण कर मजदूर संघ को आगे बढ़ाया।

61. ओमप्रकाश गर्ग

जन्म : 21 जून, 1926, **निधन :** 6 नवंबर, 2021

उत्तर प्रदेश के गाजियाबाद में जन्म। बाल्यकाल में ही स्वयंसेवक बने। बी.एससी. करने के बाद 1946 में प्रचारक जीवन स्वीकार किया। 1964 में भारतीय जनसंघ का संगठन मंत्री बनाया गया। 1974 में पटना के विभाग प्रचारक, 1981 में बिहार के सह-प्रांत प्रचारक और 1985 में उत्तर बिहार प्रांत प्रचारक रहे। 1991 में उन्हें नेपाल राष्ट्र के प्रचारक का दायित्व सौंपा गया। 2007 में वे विश्व हिंदू परिषद् के केंद्रीय मंत्री तथा नेपाल के प्रभारी बनाए गए।

62. रामप्रकाश धीर

जन्म : 16 नवंबर, 1926, **निधन** : 20 जून, 2014

म्याँमार के मोनीवा में जन्म। पंजाब विश्वविद्यालय से बी.ए. किया। 1947 में प्रचारक बने और सबसे पहले म्याँमार भेजे गए। बाद में कुछ समय तक पंजाब में प्रचारक रहे। 1950 में डॉ. मंगल सेन के सहयोग से उन्होंने म्याँमार में 'भारतीय स्वयंसेवक संघ' की स्थापना की, जो आगे चलकर 'सनातन धर्म स्वयंसेवक संघ' के नाम से प्रसिद्ध हुआ। उन्हें 1956 में पुनः म्याँमार का दायित्व मिला। वृद्धावस्था में वे यांगून के निकट स्थित 'मंगल आश्रम छात्रावास' में रहे और यहीं म्याँमार में संघकार्य के इतिहास का लेखन किया।

63. लक्ष्मण सिंह शेखावत

जन्म : 1926, **निधन** : 29 दिसंबर, 2000

राजस्थान के झुंझुनूं में जन्म। सन् 1944 में स्वयंसेवक बने और 1947 में प्रचारक निकले। 1987 से 1992 तक राजस्थान के सह-प्रांत प्रचारक रहे। 1992 से उन्होंने जोधपुर प्रांत प्रचारक का दायित्व सँभाला। उनके प्रयासों से मेवाड़ के महाराणा भगवतसिंह और गढ़ी के राव इंद्रजीत सिंह जैसे प्रभावशाली व्यक्तित्व विश्व हिंदू परिषद् में सक्रिय हुए। आगे चलकर भारतीय किसान संघ के अखिल भारतीय मंत्री भी बनाए गए और किसानों के संगठन एवं नेतृत्व में महत्त्वपूर्ण योगदान दिया।

64. ओमप्रकाश

जन्म : 30 अगस्त, 1927, **निधन** : 4 अगस्त, 2019

हरियाणा के पलवल में जन्म। सन् 1944 में स्वयंसेवक बने। 1947 में तृतीय वर्ष प्रशिक्षण के बाद उन्होंने अलीगढ़ जनपद के अतरौली से प्रचारक जीवन आरंभ किया। 1948 में प्रतिबंध के दौरान अलीगढ़ जेल में रहे। आपातकाल में रामपुर जिले के शाहबाद में पुलिस ने उन्हें तत्कालीन प्रांत प्रचारक माधवराव देवड़े के साथ गिरफ्तार किया। आपातकाल के बाद 1978 में पश्चिमी उत्तर प्रदेश के प्रांत प्रचारक बने। 1989 में उन्हें सह-क्षेत्र प्रचारक, 1994 में क्षेत्र प्रचारक और 2004 में अखिल भारतीय सह-सेवा प्रमुख का दायित्व सौंपा गया। 2006 में वे केंद्रीय कार्यकारिणी सदस्य एवं अखिल भारतीय गो सेवा प्रमुख बने और इस भूमिका में उन्होंने गो संरक्षण एवं सेवा कार्यों को सशक्त बनाया तथा संगठनात्मक गतिविधियों को नई दिशा प्रदान की।

65. कौशल किशोर

जन्म : 14 सितंबर, 1928, **निधन** : 27 अगस्त, 2003

उत्तर प्रदेश के रायबरेली में जन्म। बाल्यकाल में ही स्वयंसेवक बने। 1946 में इंटरमीडिएट उत्तीर्ण करने के बाद प्रचारक बने। 1971 में उन्हें उत्तर प्रदेश जनसंघ का संगठन मंत्री बनाया गया। 1975 में आपातकाल के दौरान 'मीसा बंदी' रहे। 1980 में राजनीति से संन्यास लेकर पुन: संघकार्य में जुट गए। बाद में उन्हें जम्मू संभाग का सह-प्रांत प्रचारक नियुक्त किया गया। इसके बाद उन्होंने दिल्ली में कार्य किया और फिर अखिल भारतीय सह बौद्धिक प्रमुख बने। संघ के संपर्क विभाग का गठन होने पर इसके पहले अखिल भारतीय संपर्क प्रमुख बने और इस भूमिका में उन्होंने राष्ट्र जीवन के विभिन्न क्षेत्रों के प्रतिष्ठित व्यक्तियों से संवाद स्थापित कर संघ के संपर्क को मजबूत किया।

66. लज्जाराम तोमर

जन्म : 21 जुलाई, 1930, **निधन :** 17 नवंबर, 2004

मध्य प्रदेश के मुरैना में जन्म। सन् 1945 में स्वयंसेवक बने। उन्होंने सरकारी नौकरी छोड़कर 'सरस्वती शिशु मंदिर' योजना में योगदान देना शुरू किया। आपातकाल के दौरान उनके एकमात्र पुत्र का देहांत हो गया। इस गहन आघात से वे संन्यास की ओर प्रवृत्त हुए, किंतु भाऊरावजी की प्रेरणा से उन्होंने शेष जीवन शिक्षा कार्य के लिए समर्पित कर दिया। 1979 में विद्या भारती के गठन पर उन्हें राष्ट्रीय संगठन मंत्री बनाया गया। भारतीय चिंतन दृष्टि पर आधारित अनेक पुस्तकों का लेखन और प्रकाशन उनका उल्लेखनीय कार्य रहा। उनकी ही प्रेरणा से कुरुक्षेत्र के गीता विद्यालय परिसर में 'संस्कृति संग्रहालय' की स्थापना हुई।

67. सरदार चिरंजीव सिंह

जन्म : 1 अक्तूबर, 1930, **निधन :** 20 नवंबर, 2023

पंजाब के पटियाला में जन्म। सन् 1944 में स्वयंसेवक बने। 1946 में गीता विद्यालय, कुरुक्षेत्र की स्थापना पर श्रीगुरुजी के भाषण ने उनके जीवन पर गहरी छाप छोड़ी। 1953 में वे प्रचारक बने और पंजाब के विभिन्न जिलों में संघकार्य विस्तार का दायित्व सँभाला। 1984 में उन्हें विश्व हिंदू परिषद् (पंजाब) का संगठन मंत्री नियुक्त किया गया। 1986 में अमृतसर में गुरु नानक देवजी के प्रकाश पर्व पर 'राष्ट्रीय सिख संगत' का गठन हुआ, जिसके वे महासचिव बने। 1990 में शमशेर सिंह गिल के निधन के बाद वे इसके अध्यक्ष बने और 2003 तक इस दायित्व का निर्वहन किया।

६८. रंगा हरि

जन्म : 5 दिसंबर, 1930, **निधन :** 29 अक्तूबर, 2023

केरल के कोच्चि में जन्म। बाल्यकाल में ही स्वयंसेवक बन गए और 1951 में प्रचारक जीवन आरंभ किया। कई भाषाओं में लेखन करने वाले रंगा हरि ने साहित्यिक और वैचारिक योगदान के रूप में मलयालम में 20, हिंदी में 8 और कोंकणी में 1 पुस्तक की रचना की। इसके अतिरिक्त उन्होंने 'श्रीगुरुजी समग्र' का 12 खंडों में संपादन भी किया। संघकार्य में वे 1983 से 1990 तक केरल के प्रांत प्रचारक रहे। 1990 में उन्हें अखिल भारतीय सह-बौद्धिक प्रमुख और 1991 से 2005 तक अखिल भारतीय बौद्धिक प्रमुख का दायित्व सौंपा गया। 2005 तक वे एशिया और ऑस्ट्रेलिया में हिंदू स्वयंसेवक संघ के मार्गदर्शक भी रहे।

६९. ना. कृष्णप्पा

जन्म : 1932, **निधन :** 10 अगस्त, 2015

कर्नाटक के मैसूर में जन्म। कॉलेज में अध्ययन के दौरान ही स्वयंसेवक बने। 1954 में वे प्रचारक बने। 1955 से 1962 तक क्रमशः जिला प्रचारक और उसके बाद विभाग प्रचारक रहे। 1975 में आपातकाल के दौरान उन्होंने मेंगलुरु विभाग में आंदोलन का नेतृत्व किया। 1978 में वे प्रांत बौद्धिक प्रमुख, 1980 में कर्नाटक प्रांत प्रचारक और 1989 में दक्षिण क्षेत्र के क्षेत्र प्रचारक बनाए गए। 2004 से 2014 तक वे अखिल भारतीय कार्यकारिणी सदस्य के रूप में कार्य करते रहे और संगठन को सुदृढ़ बनाने में अपना महत्त्वपूर्ण योगदान दिया।

70. अजीत कुमार

जन्म : 27 अगस्त, 1934, **निधन :** 3 दिसंबर, 1990

कर्नाटक के गुंडीवंडेयवर में जन्म। बाल्यकाल में ही स्वयंसेवक बने। इलेक्ट्रिकल और मैकेनिकल इंजीनियरिंग करने के उपरांत 1957 में प्रचारक निकले। संघ शिक्षा वर्ग के लिए उन्होंने योगासन का पाठ्यक्रम बनाया। आपातकाल के दौरान जेल में रहते हुए भी उन्होंने योग की कक्षाएँ संचालित कीं। उन्होंने 'हिंदू सेवा प्रतिष्ठान संस्था' के माध्यम से सैकड़ों युवाओं को संगठन से जोड़ा। साथ ही उन्होंने संस्कृत संभाषण योजना की शुरुआत की। कार्य के प्रति उनकी लगन और तत्परता के कारण लोग उन्हें 'Saint in a hurry' कहते थे।

71. मोहन जोशी

जन्म : 13 दिसंबर, 1934, **निधन :** 4 दिसंबर, 2017

राजस्थान के कोटा में जन्म। एम.ए. (साहित्य रत्न) की पढ़ाई पूरी की। संघ से जुड़ने के बाद 1957 में प्रचारक बने। 1960 से 1984 तक उनका केंद्र जयपुर रहा। उन्होंने अखिल भारतीय विद्यार्थी परिषद् की त्रैमासिक पत्रिका 'तरुण शक्ति' का संपादन किया। 1977 में उन्हें विहिप राजस्थान का संगठन मंत्री बनाया गया। 1984 में विहिप में परावर्तन विभाग की स्थापना की गई, जिसे अब धर्म जागरण विभाग के नाम से जाना जाता है। इसके अतिरिक्त उन्होंने 'भारत जनसेवा संस्थान' की स्थापना कर हजारों लोगों को पुनः हिंदू धर्म में लौटने के लिए प्रेरित किया।

72. श्रीपति शास्त्री

जन्म : 19 जून, 1935, **निधन :** 27 फरवरी, 2010

कर्नाटक के चित्रदुर्ग में जन्म। एम.ए. के बाद पीएच. डी. की। छात्र जीवन में ही स्वयंसेवक बने। तात्या बापट और दामु अण्णा दाते के साथ मिलकर उन्होंने 'पतित पावन संस्था' की स्थापना कर समाज के वंचित वर्गों को संघ से जोड़ने का कार्य किया। संघ में उन्होंने प्रांत, क्षेत्र और अखिल भारतीय सह-बौद्धिक प्रमुख के साथ-साथ अखिल भारतीय सह-संपर्क प्रमुख के दायित्व निभाए। वे कन्नड़, तमिल, हिंदी, अंग्रेजी और मराठी भाषाओं में निपुण थे। उन्होंने महाराष्ट्र की जनकल्याण समिति को सुव्यवस्थित किया और पुणे विश्वविद्यालय में इतिहास विभागाध्यक्ष के पद पर भी कार्य किया।

73. श्रीकांत जोशी

जन्म : 21 दिसंबर, 1936, **निधन :** 8 जनवरी, 2013

महाराष्ट्र के रत्नागिरी में जन्म। बी.ए. की पढ़ाई के दौरान स्वयंसेवक बन गए। 1960 में प्रचारक बनकर नांदेड़ गए और 1963 में तेजपुर विभाग प्रचारक के रूप में असम भेजे गए। 1967 में उन्होंने विहिप के सम्मेलनों और विवेकानंद शिला स्मारक के लिए निधि संग्रह का संयोजन किया। 1979-1985 तक घुसपैठ विरोधी आंदोलन पर उनकी पुस्तक 'घुसपैठ : एक निःशब्द आक्रमण' बहुचर्चित रही। 1987-1996 तक वे सरसंघचालक बालासाहब देवरस के निजी सचिव रहे। 1996 से 1998 तक अखिल भारतीय सह-प्रचार प्रमुख, फिर 2004 तक अखिल भारतीय प्रचार प्रमुख रहे। उन्होंने 2001 में हिंदुस्थान समाचार संवाद समिति को पुनर्जीवित किया।

74. सुब्बूराव श्रीनिवास

जन्म : 10 अप्रैल, 1940, **निधन :** 18 जनवरी, 2005

1962 में कर्नाटक प्रांत प्रचारक यादवराव जोशी की प्रेरणा से प्रचारक बने। पुणे में चल रही घोष शाखा में रुचि के कारण उन्होंने छह माह तक सघन प्रशिक्षण लिया और इसके बाद कर्नाटक प्रांत के घोष प्रमुख बने। इसके बाद उन्होंने घोष के शब्द, स्वर और लिपि का भारतीयकरण किया। जब घोष विभाग को स्वतंत्र विभाग बनाया गया, तो उन्हें अखिल भारतीय घोष प्रमुख की जिम्मेदारी दी गई। उन्होंने देश के हर प्रांत में घोष वादकों के शिविर लगाए, जिससे कुछ ही वर्षों में हजारों नए वादक और घोष प्रमुख तैयार हुए।

75. मुकुंदराव आत्माराम पणशीकर

जन्म : 27 मई, 1940, **निधन :** 7 मई, 2015

महाराष्ट्र की राजधानी बंबई में जन्म। सन् 1947 में स्वयंसेवक और 1962 में प्रचारक बने। उन्होंने तहसील, जिला, विभाग, बंबई महानगर, महाराष्ट्र सह-प्रांत प्रचारक, प्रांत प्रचारक और पश्चिम क्षेत्र के क्षेत्र प्रचारक के दायित्वों का निर्वहन किया। इसके अतिरिक्त वे अखिल भारतीय धर्मजागरण विभाग प्रमुख भी रहे। उन्होंने धर्मजागरण के पाँच आयाम—परियोजना, शासन, संस्कृति, विधि और विनियमन को व्यवस्थित रूप से संगठित किया। 2006 में उन्होंने शबरी कुंभ (डांग, गुजरात) का सफल आयोजन किया और 2011 में हरिहरनाथ (बिहार) से मुक्तिनाथ (नेपाल) तक की यात्रा के सूत्रधार रहे।

76. मदनदास देवी

जन्म : 9 जुलाई, 1942, **निधन** : 24 जुलाई, 2023

महाराष्ट्र के सोलापुर में जन्म। बाल्यकाल में ही वे स्वयंसेवक बन गए। 1962 में तृतीय वर्ष पूर्ण करने के बाद 1964 में विद्यार्थी परिषद् से जुड़े और 1969 में उन्हें प्रचारक बनाया गया। 1970 से 1992 तक वे विद्यार्थी परिषद् के राष्ट्रीय संगठन मंत्री रहे। ऐसे अनेक कार्यकर्ता गढ़े, जो आज देश में महत्त्वपूर्ण दायित्वों का निर्वहन कर रहे हैं। उन्होंने बी.कॉम., एल.एल.बी. और चार्टर्ड अकाउंटेंट की पढ़ाई की। अनेक वर्षों तक विश्व विभाग के पालक अधिकारी भी रहे। आज यदि 180 देशों में हिंदू संगठन का कार्य दिखाई देता है, तो इसके पीछे उनका अप्रतिम योगदान है। उन्होंने छह वर्षों तक राजनीतिक क्षेत्र में संपर्क का भी दायित्व सँभाला।

77. बालकृष्ण उत्तमराव नाईक

जन्म : 1942, **निधन** : 18 नवंबर, 2020

महाराष्ट्र के संभाजीनगर में जन्म। अमेरिका के स्टैनफोर्ड विश्वविद्यालय से इंजीनियरिंग की। 1966 में भारत लौटकर संघ के प्रचारक बने। 1974 में उन्हें विश्व हिंदू परिषद् (विहिप) में विभाग संगठन मंत्री बनाया गया। 1976 में प्रांत के मंत्री का दायित्व मिला। 1990 में वे पश्चिमांचल संगठन मंत्री बनकर मुंबई आए। 1995 में उन्होंने विहिप के केंद्रीय मंत्री (विश्व समन्वय) के रूप में कार्य सँभाला और फिर संयुक्त महामंत्री एवं उपाध्यक्ष रहे। उन्होंने सिख, बौद्ध, जैन सहित विभिन्न धर्म-संप्रदायों के साधु-संतों के साथ निरंतर संपर्क बनाए रखा। वे विपश्यना के सिद्ध साधक भी थे।

78. रामचंद्र नरहरी (बबनराव) सहस्त्रभोजनी

जन्म : 5 सितंबर, 1944, **निधन** : 30 सितंबर, 2020

महाराष्ट्र के नागपुर में जन्म। 1950 में बाल्यकाल में ही स्वयंसेवक बने। इतिहास में एम.ए. किया। 1970 में बंगाल के मुर्शिदाबाद जिले से प्रचारक जीवन आरंभ किया। बाद में कलकत्ता महानगर प्रचारक बने। 1982 में उन्हें असम प्रांत के त्रिपुरा विभाग का प्रचारक नियुक्त किया गया। इसके अतिरिक्त दक्षिण बिहार के सह-प्रांत प्रचारक तथा विदर्भ प्रांत प्रचारक प्रमुख भी रहे। 1991 में रामजन्मभूमि आंदोलन के समय वे असम क्षेत्र विहिप के सह-संगठन मंत्री बने। इसके बाद उन्हें अखिल भारतीय सह-शारीरिक प्रमुख का दायित्व भी मिला।

79. महावीर

जन्म : 22 नवंबर, 1951, **निधन** : 24 अक्तूबर, 2017

पंजाब के मनसा में जन्म। एम.एससी. तक पढ़ाई की। उनके पिता भी संघ के स्वयंसेवक थे, इस कारण वे बाल्यावस्था से ही संघ से जुड़ गए। 1972 में प्रचारक बने। उन्होंने हिमाचल प्रदेश में जिला, विभाग और सह-प्रांत प्रचारक के दायित्व सँभाले। पंजाब के प्रांत प्रचारक रहते हुए अमृतसर में 119 बस्तियों में से 100 को शाखायुक्त करने में सफलता प्राप्त की। इसके बाद वे उत्तरी क्षेत्र के प्रचारक और अखिल भारतीय सह-बौद्धिक प्रमुख बनाए गए। उन्होंने संघ की केंद्रीय कार्यकारिणी के सदस्य के रूप में भी सेवा दी। महावीर का विश्वास था कि सटीक समय प्रबंधन से सीमित समय में भी अधिक कार्य किया जा सकता है।

80. पांडुरंग पंत क्षीरसागर

जन्म : 10 जून, 1918, **निधन** : 23 मार्च, 1976

महाराष्ट्र के वर्धा में जन्म। बाल्यकाल से ही संघ से जुड़ गए। उन्हें बंगाल भेजा गया, जहाँ 4-5 वर्षों तक उन्होंने सेवा कार्य किया। 1950 में नागपुर कार्यालय का कार्यभार सँभाला और 1955 में अखिल भारतीय व्यवस्था प्रमुख बने। 1962 में 'स्मृति मंदिर' के निर्माण की जिम्मेदारी उन्हें सौंपी गई। आपातकाल के दौरान उनके व्यवस्थित हिसाब-किताब को देखकर सरकारी अधिकारी भी उनकी सराहना करने से खुद को रोक नहीं पाए। एक बार एक अधिकारी ने उनसे कहा—"सार्वजनिक संस्थाओं का हिसाब-किताब कैसा होना चाहिए, यह संघ से सीखना चाहिए।"

81. बापूराव मोघे

महाराष्ट्र के नागपुर में जन्म। प्रयाग विश्वविद्यालय में एम.एससी. के अध्ययन के दौरान संघकार्य भी करते थे। वे अध्यापन कर अपनी और भाऊरावजी की व्यय व्यवस्था करते थे। प्रयाग विश्वविद्यालय में उन्होंने कई विद्यार्थियों के मन में संघ के विचारों का बीजारोपण किया, जिनमें प्रो. राजेंद्र सिंह (रज्जू भैया) और डॉ. मुरली मनोहर जोशी प्रमुख थे। 1942 में लखनऊ के प्रथम संघ शिक्षा वर्ग के मुख्य शिक्षक बने। 1950 में आंध्र प्रदेश के प्रांत प्रचारक नियुक्त हुए। इसके अतिरिक्त उन्होंने अखिल भारतीय व्यवस्था और बौद्धिक प्रमुख के दायित्व को भी सँभाला।

८२. सुरेश रामचंद्र केतकर

जन्म : 28 सितंबर, 1934, **निधन :** 16 जुलाई, 2016

महाराष्ट्र के पुणे में जन्म। बी.एससी. और बी.एड. की पढ़ाई की। 1958 में प्रचारक बने और सोलापुर जिले के सांगली तथा लातूर विभाग में कार्यरत रहे। उन्होंने प्रांत शारीरिक शिक्षण प्रमुख, क्षेत्र प्रचारक, अखिल भारतीय शारीरिक शिक्षण प्रमुख, सह–सरकार्यवाह तथा अखिल भारतीय प्रचारक प्रमुख जैसे महत्त्वपूर्ण दायित्वों का निर्वहन किया। पूरे देश में यात्रा करते हुए मिलने वाले कार्यकर्ताओं की जानकारी स्मरण रखने वाले केतकरजी संघकार्य के जीवंत स्मृतिकोष माने जाते थे। इसके अतिरिक्त उन्होंने भारतीय मजदूर संघ, संस्कार भारती, भारतीय किसान संघ आदि संस्थाओं का भी दायित्व सँभाला और इन संगठनों के माध्यम से समाज जीवन के विविध क्षेत्रों में राष्ट्रभावना का संचार किया।

८३. मधुभाई कुलकर्णी

जन्म : 17 मई, 1938, **निधन :** 18 सितंबर, 2025

1962 में संघ के प्रचारक के रूप में कार्य प्रारंभ किया तथा तालुका, जिला, विभाग, पुणे महानगर, गुजरात प्रांत और पश्चिम क्षेत्र प्रचारक जैसे विभिन्न दायित्व निभाए। बाद में अखिल भारतीय बौद्धिक प्रमुख और 2015 तक कार्यकारी मंडल के सदस्य भी रहे। नए कार्यकर्ताओं और समाज तक संघ के विचारों को पहुँचाने के लिए उन्होंने 'अथातो संघजिज्ञासा' नामक पुस्तक लिखी, जिसका कई भाषाओं में अनुवाद हुआ। अपने अंतिम दिनों तक वे शाखा, यात्राओं, संवाद और कार्यक्रमों में सक्रिय रहे।

84. वीरेंद्र भटनागर

जन्म : 15 जून, 1930, **निधन :** 25 जनवरी, 2015

सन् 1947 में काशी से संघ शिक्षा वर्ग का प्रथम वर्ष करते हुए प्रचारक बनने का निर्णय लिया। 1948 में संघ पर प्रतिबंध के दौरान लखनऊ जेल में रहे। 1962 में उन्हें रायबरेली नगर और गाजियाबाद तहसील प्रचारक बनाया गया। 1962-1986 तक उन्होंने उत्तर प्रदेश में भारतीय मजदूर संघ के विभिन्न दायित्वों का निर्वहन किया। 1986 में उन्हें उत्तर प्रदेश में सेवा कार्यों के विस्तार का काम सौंपा गया, जिसके अंतर्गत उन्होंने 10 वर्ष तक व्यापक प्रवास किया।

85. बालकृष्ण

जन्म : 5 मार्च, 1937, **निधन :** 20 अगस्त, 2024

सन् 1962 में नौकरी छोड़कर संघकार्य का संकल्प लिया और कानपुर के तत्कालीन विभाग प्रचारक अशोक सिंहलजी की प्रेरणा से प्रचारक बने। उन्होंने तहसील प्रचारक से लेकर नगर प्रचारक, जिला प्रचारक, प्रांत शारीरिक प्रमुख, सह-प्रांत प्रचारक, प्रांत प्रचारक (अवध प्रांत), संयुक्त क्षेत्र संपर्क प्रमुख और अखिल भारतीय सह-व्यवस्था प्रमुख जैसे महत्त्वपूर्ण दायित्वों का निर्वहन किया। बालकृष्णजी को 'स्वयंसेवकों को मूर्तिकार की तरह निखारने वाला' प्रचारक माना जाता था। उन्होंने अपने जीवनकाल में हजारों स्वयंसेवकों को देशसेवा के लिए प्रेरित किया।

86. धनप्रकाश त्यागी

जन्म : 10 जनवरी, 1918, **निधन :** 24 जनवरी, 2020

सन् 1943 में दिल्ली में संघ विस्तारक के रूप में कार्य शुरू किया; सहारनपुर नगर और अलीगढ़ नगर प्रचारक के रूप में संघकार्य किया। इसके अतिरिक्त अंबाला, हिसार, गुरुग्राम, शिमला एवं होशियारपुर में जिला प्रचारक भी रहे। 1962-1965 तक जम्मू विभाग प्रचारक और 1965-1971 तक जयपुर विभाग प्रचारक रहे। आपातकाल के दौरान जेल भी गए। 1971-1986 तक भारतीय मजदूर संघ में विभिन्न दायित्वों का निर्वहन किया और 2000-2005 तक सेवा भारती जागरण पत्रक के प्रकाशन का कार्यभार सँभाला।

87. बाबा योगेंद्र

जन्म : 7 जनवरी, 1924, **निधन :** 10 जून, 2022

छात्र जीवन में गोरखपुर में नानाजी देशमुख के संपर्क में आए और स्वयं को संघकार्य के लिए समर्पित करने का निश्चय किया। 1942 में लखनऊ में संघ शिक्षा वर्ग के प्रथम वर्ष का प्रशिक्षण लिया और 1945 में प्रचारक बने। उनका कार्यक्षेत्र बस्ती, महराजगंज, पडरौना, प्रयागराज, बहराइच, बरेली, बदायूँ, हरदोई और सीतापुर तक फैला। उन्होंने 'देश-विभाजन', 'जलती कश्मीर' और 'भारत की विश्व को देन' जैसी अनेक प्रदर्शनियों के माध्यम से सामाजिक जागरूकता फैलाई। 1981 में उन्हें 'संस्कार भारती' का कार्यभार सौंपा गया।

८८. जगदीश चंद्र त्रिपाठी

जन्म : 3 जनवरी, 1936, **निधन :** 12 मार्च, 2015

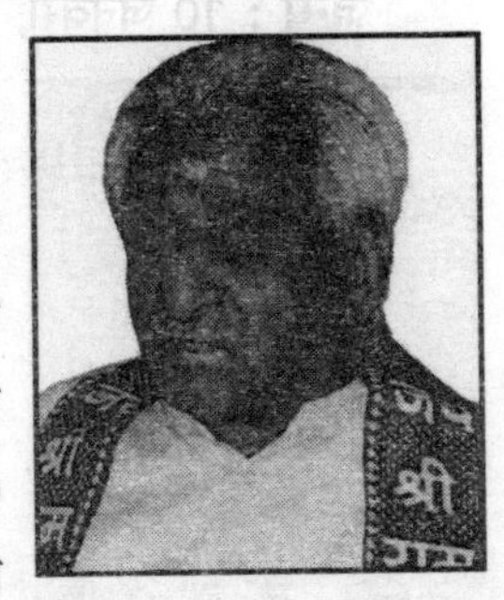

सन् 1956 में संघ के प्रचारक बने। उत्तर प्रदेश के पूरनपुर, शाहजीपुर, एटा, शामली, गाजियाबाद, श्रीनगर गढ़वाल और रामपुर में नगर, तहसील और जिला प्रचारक के रूप में संघकार्य किया। 1967 में असम के तेजपुर भेजे गए और कई वर्षों तक बंगाल में वर्धमान विभाग प्रचारक और कलकत्ता प्रांतीय कार्यालय प्रमुख रहे। 1984-1990 तक संघ के वरिष्ठ प्रचारक भाऊराव देवरस के निजी सहायक रहे। इसके बाद उन्होंने उत्तरांचल उत्थान परिषद्, वनवासी कल्याण आश्रम, लोकभारती लखनऊ और विश्व संवाद केंद्र अल्मोड़ा का कार्यभार सँभाला। सन् 2000 में उन्हें विश्व हिंदू परिषद् में एक दायित्व सौंपा गया, जिसके माध्यम से उन्होंने हरिद्वार और वृंदावन में धर्माचार्यों से संपर्क का कार्य किया। 2004 में विहिप के दिल्ली केंद्रीय कार्यालय में व्यवस्था प्रमुख बने।

८९. कृष्णराव सप्रे

जन्म : 4 सितंबर, 1931, **निधन :** 27 जनवरी, 1999

मध्य प्रदेश के जबलपुर में जन्म। वे ऐसे परिवार से थे, जिनके माता-पिता भी संघ से जुड़े हुए थे। इसी कारण वे और उनके तीनों भाई स्वयंसेवक बने। शिक्षा पूर्ण करने के बाद कृष्णराव प्रचारक बने। उन्हें पहले रायगढ़ और फिर छिंदवाड़ा विभाग का कार्य सौंपा गया। उन्होंने 'भारतीय जनजातीय सांस्कृतिक मंच' की स्थापना कर अनेक गतिविधियाँ प्रारंभ कीं, जिससे जनजातीय क्षेत्रों में धर्मांतरण की प्रवृत्ति पर रोक लगी। आम लोगों और कार्यकर्ताओं को जागरूक करने के लिए उन्होंने कई पुस्तकें भी लिखीं।

90. ओंकार भावे

जन्म : 26 जुलाई, 1924, **निधन :** 23 जुलाई, 2009

उत्तर प्रदेश के आजमगढ़ में जन्म। 14 वर्ष की आयु में स्वयंसेवक बने। 1940, 41 व 42 में नागपुर से संघ शिक्षा वर्ग के प्रथम, द्वितीय और तृतीय वर्ष पूर्ण किए। 1945 में प्रयाग विश्वविद्यालय से बी.ए. करने के बाद प्रचारक जीवन अपनाया; प्रयाग, हरदोई और अलीगढ़ में जिला प्रचारक तथा आगरा और लखनऊ में विभाग प्रचारक के रूप में कार्य किया। लखनऊ में 'राष्ट्रधर्म प्रकाशन' के व्यवस्थापक और 'राष्ट्रधर्म' मासिक के सह-संपादक भी रहे। आगे चलकर पूर्वी उत्तर प्रदेश में शारीरिक व व्यवस्था प्रमुख का दायित्व सँभाला। 1984 में उन्हें उत्तर प्रदेश और मध्य प्रदेश में विश्व हिंदू परिषद् के संगठन का विस्तार कार्य सौंपा गया। 1991 में वे परिषद् के केंद्रीय मंत्री, 1995 में संयुक्त महामंत्री और 2009 में उपाध्यक्ष बने।

91. पंढरीराव कृदत्त

जन्म : 14 मार्च 1922, **निधन :** 20 जनवरी, 2009

1935 में अपनी बाल्यावस्था में शाखा जाने लगे थे। 1938 में नागपुर संघ शिक्षा वर्ग में उन्होंने डॉ. हेडगेवार के दर्शन किए और उनकी प्रेरक वाणी सुनी। 1939 में गृहस्थ जीवन में प्रवेश के बाद भी उनके जीवन की प्राथमिकता संघकार्य ही रही। उन्हें 1952, 1957 और 1967 के चुनावों में जनसंघ ने छत्तीसगढ़ के धमतरी विधानसभा का प्रत्याशी बनाया और वे तीनों बार भारी मतों से विजयी हुए। 1969 में श्रीगुरुजी के संकेत पर उन्होंने राजनीति छोड़कर पुनः संघकार्य में प्रवेश किया। श्रीगुरुजी ने उन्हें रायपुर विभाग कार्यवाह का दायित्व दिया। इसके बाद वे रायपुर विभाग के सहसंघचालक और फिर छत्तीसगढ़ प्रांत के संघचालक भी रहे।

९२. दत्ताजी डिंडोलकर

जन्म : 7 अगस्त, 1923, **निधन :** 14 अक्तूबर, 1990

युवा स्वयंसेवक के रूप में राष्ट्रीय स्वयंसेवक संघ में सक्रियता दिखाई और बाद में पूर्णकालिक प्रचारक बने। काफी समय तक केरल तथा तमिलनाडु में प्रचारक के नाते शाखा विस्तार का कार्य किया। दत्ताजी विद्यार्थी परिषद् के संस्थापक सदस्य थे और लंबे समय तक इसके अध्यक्ष भी रहे। उन्होंने विद्यार्थी परिषद् के संगठन और वैचारिक नींव को मजबूत करने में महत्त्वपूर्ण भूमिका निभाई। 1989 में जब संघ संस्थापक डॉ. हेडगेवार की जन्म शताब्दी मनाई गई, तो उसके क्रियान्वयन के लिए बनी समिति के वे केंद्रीय सहसचिव भी थे।

९३. गोविंदराव कात्रे

जन्म : 23 नवंबर, 1901, **निधन :** 16 मई, 1977

रेल विभाग में नौकरी के दौरान 1943 में संघ से संपर्क हुआ। कात्रेजी कुष्ठ रोग ग्रसित थे, जिसके कारण उनकी पुत्री का विवाह नहीं हो रहा था। सरसंघचालक श्रीगुरुजी के आग्रह पर एक स्वयंसेवक ने 1952 में उनकी पुत्री से विवाह कर लिया। संघ से प्रेरित होकर उन्होंने अपना जीवन कुष्ठ रोग से पीड़ित लोगों की सेवा के लिए समर्पित कर दिया। उन्होंने कुष्ठ रोगियों के लिए काम करने को लेकर श्रीगुरुजी और जुगल किशोर बिड़ला को पत्र लिखा। आखिरकार उस समय बड़ी सफलता मिली, जब 5 मई, 1962 को 'भारतीय कुष्ठ निवारक संघ' का गठन हुआ। छत्तीसगढ़ के चाँपा में आश्रम और चिकित्सालय प्रारंभ हो गया।

94. अवधबिहारी

जन्म : 5 जुलाई, 1926, **निधन :** 12 मई, 2017

संघ से संपर्क 1942 में हुआ, जब वे मात्र 16 वर्ष के थे। 1946 में उन्होंने पढ़ाई को विराम देकर प्रचारक जीवन अपना लिया। उनके जीवन पर सरसंघचालक श्रीगुरुजी का विशेष प्रभाव रहा। 1946 से 1977 तक उन्होंने उत्तर प्रदेश के विभिन्न जिलों में कई दायित्वों का निर्वहन किया। 1982 से 1986 तक राँची उनका केंद्र रहा। 1987 से 1997 तक मध्य प्रदेश का दायित्व सँभाला। 1997 में उन्हें वनवासी कल्याण आश्रम का राष्ट्रीय सह-संगठन मंत्री नियुक्त कर पुनः राँची भेजा गया। 2007 में उन्हें 'अखिल भारतीय कार्यकर्ता प्रमुख' की जिम्मेदारी सौंपी गई।

95. कृष्णराव मोहरिर

जन्म : 1910, **निधन :** 1982

सन् 1938 में संघ के स्वयंसेवक बने। वे जीवनपर्यंत नागपुर स्थित संघ के केंद्रीय कार्यालय के प्रमुख रहे। जैसे-जैसे संघ का कार्य विस्तृत होता गया, नागपुर का कार्यालय केंद्रीय कार्यालय के रूप में विकसित होता गया। डॉ. हेडगेवार ने कार्यालय का संपूर्ण दायित्व कृष्णरावजी को सौंप दिया। इस नाते वे अतिथियों के स्वागत-सत्कार, पत्र-व्यवहार और रेलवे स्टेशन पर आने-जाने जैसे अनेक कार्य सँभालते थे। किसी का स्वागत, अगवानी या विदाई की व्यवस्था करनी हो, किसी बीमार की देखभाल करनी हो या किसी कार्यकर्ता की व्यक्तिगत समस्या में सहयोग देना हो—कृष्णरावजी सदैव तत्पर रहते थे।

96. माधवराव बनहट्टी

जन्म : 19 फरवरी, 1927, **निधन :** 1 अप्रैल, 2000

नागपुर में जन्म। 1945 में बी.एससी. करने के बाद एक वर्ष डाक-तार विभाग में कार्य किया, लेकिन शीघ्र ही प्रचारक जीवन अपना लिया। प्रारंभ में उन्हें बंगाल के बांकुड़ा जिले में भेजा गया। बाद में वे चौबीस परगना विभाग सहित बंगाल के विभिन्न दायित्वों पर कार्यरत रहे। 1977 में उन्हें मॉरीशस भेजा गया, जहाँ 12 वर्षों तक रहकर उन्होंने मॉरीशस और दक्षिण अफ्रीका में संघकार्य को मजबूत आधार दिया। भारत लौटने पर वे विश्व हिंदू परिषद् से जुड़े और पूर्वांचल क्षेत्र के संगठन मंत्री बने। 1997 में दिल्ली में उन्हें परिषद् के संयुक्त मंत्री और बाद में केंद्रीय मंत्री की जिम्मेदारी सौंपी गई। विदेश विभाग और वैश्विक समन्वय के क्षेत्र में उनकी भूमिका अत्यंत महत्त्वपूर्ण रही।

97. पंडित रामनारायण शास्त्री

जन्म : 11 फरवरी, 1913, **निधन :** 28 दिसंबर, 1979

वे देश के अग्रणी आयुर्वेदाचार्य थे। संघ से परिचय 1943 में हुआ, जब वे इंदौर की मल्हारगंज शाखा में जाने लगे। धीरे-धीरे संघ से उनका जुड़ाव इतना गहरा हुआ कि वह उनके जीवन की धड़कन बन गया। अनेक दायित्वों का निर्वहन करने के बाद उन्हें मध्य भारत का प्रांत संघचालक नियुक्त किया गया और यह दायित्व उन्होंने जीवन के अंतिम क्षण तक निभाया। चिकित्सा का सफल व्यवसाय होते हुए भी शास्त्रीजी ने देश और संघ पर आने वाली हर चुनौती को स्वीकार किया। वे इंदौर से प्रकाशित हिंदी समाचार-पत्र 'स्वदेश' की संचालन संस्था 'श्री रेवा प्रकाशन लिमिटेड' के आजीवन अध्यक्ष रहे।

९८. मिश्रीलाल तिवारी

जन्म : 1916, **निधन :** 10 जुलाई, 2001

मध्य प्रदेश के शाजापुर में जन्म। विद्यार्थी जीवन में ही संघ के संपर्क में आए, जिससे उनमें समाज कार्य की गहरी इच्छा जगी। 1946 में उन्होंने सरकारी नौकरी छोड़कर प्रचारक जीवन अपना लिया। संघ में विभिन्न दायित्व निभाने के बाद 1968 में मध्य प्रांत में वनवासी कल्याण आश्रम का कार्य प्रारंभ करने की योजना बनी और इसका दायित्व मिश्रीलालजी को सौंपा गया। उनके प्रयासों से प्रांत में छात्रावासों सहित कई सेवा प्रकल्पों की शुरुआत हुई। 1978 में उन्हें वनवासी कल्याण आश्रम का महामंत्री नियुक्त किया गया। इसके पश्चात् 1987 में वे अखिल भारतीय वनवासी कल्याण आश्रम के उपाध्यक्ष बने और समाजसेवा के क्षेत्र में उल्लेखनीय योगदान दिया।

९९. मधुसूदन देव

जन्म : 8 जून, 1918, **निधन :** 12 दिसंबर 2006

नागपुर में जन्म। उनकी डॉ. हेडगेवार से गहरी मित्रता थी। जब वे धंतोली सायं शाखा के मुख्य शिक्षक बने, तो वह शाखा नागपुर की आदर्श शाखाओं में गिनी जाने लगी। 1942 में उन्होंने नौकरी छोड़कर प्रचारक जीवन अपनाया। श्रीगुरुजी के निर्देश पर उन्हें बिहार भेजा गया और फिर वे वहीं के होकर रह गए। 1957 में वे बिहार के प्रांत प्रचारक बने। आपातकाल के बाद 1977 में उन्हें उत्तर प्रदेश और बिहार का सह-क्षेत्र प्रचारक नियुक्त किया गया। 1980 में वे बिहार के क्षेत्र प्रचारक बने। आगे चलकर उन्हें बिहार, बंगाल और उड़ीसा का दायित्व सौंपा गया। 1995 में देवजी को बिहार में 'विद्या भारती' का संरक्षक बनाया गया।

100. उत्तमचंद इसराणी

जन्म : 10 नवंबर, 1923, **निधन :** 5 दिसंबर, 2007

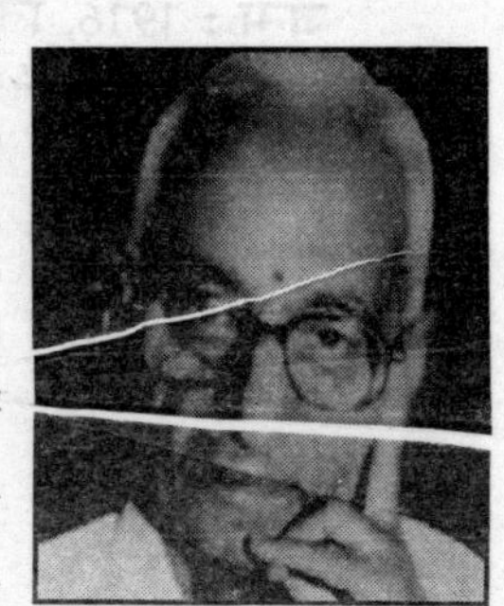

सिंध प्रांत (अब पाकिस्तान) के सक्खर जिले में जन्म। बाल्यकाल में ही संघ के स्वयंसेवक बने। देश विभाजन के समय वे अपने परिवार सहित मध्य प्रदेश के भोपाल आकर बस गए और यहाँ वकालत प्रारंभ की। साथ ही वे संघकार्य में भी सक्रिय रहे। प्रारंभ में उन्हें भोपाल विभाग कार्यवाह का दायित्व मिला, इसके बाद वे प्रांत कार्यवाह और फिर प्रांत संघचालक बने। जब मध्य भारत, महाकौशल और छत्तीसगढ़ प्रांतों को मिलाकर एक क्षेत्र बनाया गया, तो उन्हें क्षेत्र संघचालक की जिम्मेदारी सौंपी गई। इसके अतिरिक्त वे 'अखिल भारतीय अधिवक्ता परिषद्' के राष्ट्रीय अध्यक्ष के रूप में भी सक्रिय रहे और निरंतर कार्य करते रहे।

□

संघ की प्रेरणा से संचालित कुछ प्रमुख संगठन

1. राष्ट्र सेविका समिति—1936
2. अखिल भारतीय विद्यार्थी परिषद्—1948
3. विद्या भारती—1952
4. वनवासी कल्याण आश्रम—1952
5. भारतीय मजदूर संघ—1955
6. भारतीय कुष्ठ निवारक संघ—1962
7. भारत विकास परिषद्—1963
8. विश्व हिंदू परिषद्—1964
9. अखिल भारतीय साहित्य परिषद्—1966
10. भारतीय शिक्षण मंडल—1969
11. दीनदयाल शोध संस्थान—1968
12. अखिल भारतीय ग्राहक पंचायत—1974
13. नेशनल मेडिकोज ऑर्गेनाइजेशन—1977
14. सहकार भारती—1978
15. भारतीय किसान संघ—1979
16. भारतीय जनता पार्टी—1980
17. प्रज्ञा प्रवाह—1980
18. संस्कार भारती—1981
19. संस्कृत भारती—1981
20. हिंदू जागरण मंच—1982
21. सीमा जागरण मंच—1985
22. एकल विद्यालय—1986

23. विज्ञान भारती—1991
24. स्वदेशी जागरण मंच—1991
25. अखिल भारतीय अधिवक्ता परिषद्—1992
26. क्रीड़ा भारती—1992
27. पूर्व सैनिक सेवा परिषद्—1993
28. अखिल भारतीय इतिहास संकलन योजना—1994
29. लघु उद्योग भारती—1994
30. आरोग्य भारती—2002
31. सेवा भारती—2003
32. शिक्षा संस्कृति उत्थान न्यास—2007
33. सक्षम—2008

1. राष्ट्र सेविका समिति

संघ में महिलाओं की भागीदारी बढ़ाने के लिए 'राष्ट्र सेविका समिति' की स्थापना वर्ष 1936 में विजयादशमी के दिन की गई। विजयादशमी के शुभ मुहूर्त पर समिति की प्रथम शाखा वर्धा में प्रारंभ हुई। इसकी संस्थापिका लक्ष्मीबाई केलकर (मौसीजी) थीं। समिति का ध्येय तेजस्वी 'राष्ट्र का निर्माण' और सूत्र वाक्य 'स्त्री राष्ट्र की आधारशक्ति' है। आज राष्ट्र सेविका समिति भारत का सबसे बड़ा महिला संगठन है और देश के हर हिस्से में इसकी शाखाएँ हैं। देश भर में समिति की 3 लाख से अधिक सेविकाएँ हैं और 584 जिलों में समिति की हजारों नियमित शाखाएँ संचालित होती हैं। समिति आज सैकड़ों सेवाकार्य कर रही है; इनमें महिला छात्रावासों का संचालन, निःशुल्क चिकित्सा केंद्रों का संचालन, लघु उद्योग से जुड़े स्वयं सहायता समूहों का गठन आदि शामिल हैं।

2. अखिल भारतीय विद्यार्थी परिषद्

राष्ट्रीय स्वयंसेवक संघ से जुड़े छात्र संगठन 'अखिल भारतीय विद्यार्थी परिषद्' (ए.बी.वी.पी.) की स्थापना वर्ष 1948 में हुई, लेकिन इसका औपचारिक पंजीकरण 9 जुलाई, 1949 को हुआ। स्वाधीनता प्राप्ति के बाद एक मजबूत राष्ट्र के निर्माण, अपनी संस्कृति को बचाए और बनाए रखने के लिए पूरे देश ने एक विकसित और समृद्ध देश का सपना देखा। इसमें विश्वविद्यालयों में पढ़ने वाले विद्यार्थियों की समुचित भागीदारी के लिए अखिल भारतीय विद्यार्थी परिषद् की स्थापना की गई। प्रो. ओम प्रकाश बहल प्रथम राष्ट्रीय अध्यक्ष और केशव देव वर्मा पहले महामंत्री बने। संघ की योजना के अनुसार 1958-59 में यशवंतराव केलकर ने विद्यार्थी परिषद् का दायित्व सँभाला। वर्ष 1967-68 में वे विद्यार्थी परिषद् के अखिल भारतीय अध्यक्ष रहे। उसके बाद मदनदास देवीजी और प्रो. बाल आपटे से संगठन को मजबूती मिली। इसकी सदस्य संख्या करीब 33 लाख से अधिक है।

3. विद्या भारती

भारतीय संस्कृति, संस्कार और राष्ट्रभक्ति पर आधारित शिक्षा को जन-जन तक पहुँचाने के उद्देश्य से शुरू हुआ 'विद्या भारती' का आंदोलन आज देश भर में एक व्यापक शैक्षिक अभियान बन चुका है। इसकी शुरुआत 1 जुलाई, 1952

को गोरखपुर के पक्की बाग में हुई, जब संघ के ज्येष्ठ कार्यकर्ताओं कृष्णचंद्र गांधी, भाऊराव देवरस और नानाजी देशमुख ने देश का पहला सरस्वती शिशु मंदिर स्थापित किया। इसका उद्देश्य भारतीय संस्कृति और मूल्यों पर आधारित शिक्षा देना था। वर्ष 1977 में इस शिक्षा अभियान को संगठित रूप देने के लिए 'विद्या भारती अखिल भारतीय शिक्षा संस्थान' की स्थापना हुई। वर्तमान में विद्या भारती देश भर में 13 हजार से अधिक विद्यालय संचालित कर रही है, जिनमें लगभग 1.5 लाख शिक्षक और 35 लाख विद्यार्थी हैं। इनमें 40 हजार से अधिक मुसलिम छात्र भी हैं। संस्था सीमावर्ती 127 जिलों में दो सौ से अधिक स्कूल चला रही है और राष्ट्र निर्माण में शिक्षा के माध्यम से योगदान दे रही है।

4. वनवासी कल्याण आश्रम

'वनवासी कल्याण आश्रम' की स्थापना छत्तीसगढ़ के जशपुर में 26 दिसंबर, 1952 को रमाकांत केशव देशपांडे ने की, जिन्हें बालासाहब देशपांडे के नाम से भी जाना जाता है। वनवासी कल्याण आश्रम जनजातियों के बीच काम करता है। भारत में 12 करोड़ से अधिक जनजातियों को समाज की मुख्यधारा से जोड़ने और उनके विकास के लिए यह संस्था जुटी हुई है। जनजातीय समाज के विकास के लिए संस्था द्वारा 21 हजार से अधिक सेवा प्रकल्प चलाए जा रहे हैं। लगभग 240 जनजातियों, 247 वनवासी जिलों तथा साढ़े नौ हजार से अधिक गाँवों में वनवासी कल्याण आश्रम का कार्य संचालित है।

5. भारतीय मजदूर संघ

'भारतीय मजदूर संघ' (बी.एम.एस.) की स्थापना 23 जुलाई, 1955 को दत्तोपंत ठेंगड़ी ने की थी। बी.एम.एस. से दर्जनों फेडरेशंस जुड़े हैं, जिनके अंतर्गत संगठित व असंगठित क्षेत्रों की कुल 5 हजार से अधिक यूनियन हैं। इसने श्रमिकों की स्थिति तथा श्रमिकों के अधिकारों की दिशा में गहन अध्ययन कार्य किया है। भारतीय मजदूर संघ द्वारा पुणे में स्थापित शोध केंद्र 'भारतीय श्रमशोध मंडली' में सेवा क्षेत्र जैसे बिजनेस प्रोसेस आउटसोर्सिंग (बी.पी.ओ.) और अन्य नए उभरते कार्यक्षेत्रों का अध्ययन किया जाता है। भारतीय मजदूर संघ के अंतर्गत अन्य शोध केंद्र, यथा—दिल्ली में समदर्शी शोध संस्थान (एस.आर.आई.) तथा एर्नाकुलम में

श्रमिक शोध केंद्र भविष्य की श्रमिक नीतियाँ तैयार करने में अहम भूमिका निभा रहे हैं। ये संस्थाएँ श्रमिकों से संबंधित नीतियों पर मंत्रालयों तथा अन्य सरकारी संगठनों को सुझाव भी देती हैं। श्रम मंत्रालय के अनुसार बी.एम.एस. की सदस्य संख्या साठ लाख से अधिक है।

6. भारतीय कुष्ठ निवारक संघ

'भारतीय कुष्ठ निवारक संघ' की स्थापना 5 अप्रैल, 1962 को हुई। यह संगठन कुष्ठ रोगियों के कल्याण के लिए काम करती है। छत्तीसगढ़ के चांपा में स्थित इसका परिसर 100 एकड़ में फैला है। इस परिसर में ही अस्पताल है, जहाँ कुष्ठ रोगियों के इलाज की पूरी व्यवस्था है। भारतीय कुष्ठ निवारक संघ कुष्ठ रोगियों को रोग मुक्त करने के साथ ही उनको रोजगार भी मुहैया करा रहा है। यहाँ चल रहा छात्रावास गरीब और असहाय बच्चों के लिए किसी वरदान से कम नहीं है।

7. भारत विकास परिषद्

'भारत विकास परिषद्' एक ऐसी संस्था है, जो भारत राष्ट्र के सर्वांगीण विकास के लिए विभिन्न क्षेत्रों में कार्य करती है। इसकी स्थापना 12 जुलाई, 1963 को की गई, लेकिन पंजीकरण 10 जुलाई, 1963 को हुआ। भारतीय संस्कृति और भारतीय जीवन मूल्य परिषद् का मूल मंत्र है। परिषद् देश भर में शिक्षा, संस्कार और सेवा के सैकड़ों केंद्र चला रही है। दिव्यांगों की सहायता के लिए इसने महत्त्वपूर्ण काम किया है। समाज के निचले वर्ग के विकास के लिए भी यह निरंतर काम कर रही है।

8. विश्व हिंदू परिषद्

देश-विदेश तक फैले हिंदू समाज को एकजुट करने और उन्हें भारतीय संस्कृति से जोड़ने के लिए 'विश्व हिंदू परिषद्' की स्थापना 29 अगस्त, 1964 को हुई। विहिप का उद्देश्य हिंदू समाज को संगठित करना, हिंदू धर्म की रक्षा करना और समाज की सेवा करना है। विहिप गौ-रक्षा, धर्मांतरण, आतंकवाद और हिंदू मठ-मंदिर का मुद्दा उठाती रही है। इसने सामाजिक कुरीतियों के उन्मूलन के लिए अथक प्रयास किए हैं। समाज में हिंदू गौरव और एकता की वृद्धि के लिए यह लगातार काम कर रही है। स्वास्थ्य-शिक्षा, आत्म-सशक्तीकरण आदि के

क्षेत्रों में चार हजार से अधिक सेवा परियोजनाओं के माध्यम से परिषद् हिंदू समाज की जड़ों को मजबूत करने में जुटा है।

9. अखिल भारतीय साहित्य परिषद्

'अखिल भारतीय साहित्य परिषद्' की स्थापना 27 अक्तूबर, 1966 को नई दिल्ली में हुई। यह भारतीय भाषाओं का देशव्यापी संगठन है। इस संगठन का उद्देश्य भारतीय भाषाओं के साहित्यकारों, समालोचकों और विचारकों को एक मंच प्रदान करना है। इसका पहला वार्षिक अधिवेशन 1966 में प्रसिद्ध साहित्यकार जैनेंद्र कुमार की अध्यक्षता में संपन्न हुआ था। काव्य गोष्ठियों, कवि सम्मेलनों एवं काव्यपाठ प्रतियोगिताओं, साहित्यकार सम्मेलनों, साहित्यकार सम्मान समारोहों के माध्यम से नवोदित प्रतिभाओं का प्रोत्साहन किया जाता है।

10. भारतीय शिक्षण मंडल

शिक्षा के क्षेत्र में भारतीय जीवन मूल्यों की स्थापना और राष्ट्र विरोधी प्रवृत्तियों की रोकथाम के लिए भारतीय शिक्षण मंडल की स्थापना वर्ष 1969 में की गई। संस्था शिक्षा क्षेत्र में राष्ट्रीय पुनरुत्थान के उद्देश्य से कार्यरत है। इसका उद्देश्य भारत की एकात्म जीवनदृष्टि पर आधारित तथा देश की सांस्कृतिक एवं ऐतिहासिक अनुभूति से उपजी शिक्षा व्यवस्था के लिए वातावरण तैयार करना है। संस्था राष्ट्र के समग्र विकास पर केंद्रित राष्ट्रीय शिक्षा नीति, पाठ्यचर्या, व्यवस्था तथा शिक्षण विधि पर जोर देती है। इसका केंद्रीय कार्यालय नागपुर में है।

11. दीनदयाल शोध संस्थान

'दीनदयाल शोध संस्थान' की स्थापना 8 मार्च, 1968 को नानाजी देशमुख ने की थी। वे दीनदयाल उपाध्याय के 'एकात्म मानववाद' दर्शन से प्रेरित थे और चाहते थे कि गाँवों का विकास गाँववालों की भागीदारी से हो। इसके लिए उन्होंने एक समग्र कार्यक्रम शुरू किया, जिसमें स्वास्थ्य, स्वच्छता, शिक्षा, कृषि, आय सृजन और प्राकृतिक संसाधनों का संरक्षण शामिल था। इसका पहला प्रयोग 1978 में गोंडा (उत्तर प्रदेश) के एक गाँव में किया गया, जिसकी सफलता के बाद यह मॉडल मध्य प्रदेश के चित्रकूट, बिहार और महाराष्ट्र तक पहुँचा। संस्था की सबसे अनोखी पहल

है 'समाज शिल्पी दंपती' योजना, जिसके अंतर्गत एक समर्पित नवविवाहित स्नातक जोड़ा गाँव में रहकर पाँच वर्षों तक सेवा करता है और बदलाव का माध्यम बनता है।

12. अखिल भारतीय ग्राहक पंचायत

'अखिल भारतीय ग्राहक पंचायत' की स्थापना वर्ष 1974 में पुणे में हुई। बिंदु माधव जोशी द्वारा स्थापित यह संगठन उपभोक्ता अधिकारों व जागरूकता के लिए काम करता है। इस संगठन का मूल उद्देश्य ग्राहक को अपने अधिकारों के प्रति जागरूक करना एवं उसे उचित मूल्य पर अच्छी गुणवत्ता, सही नाप, विक्रय उपरांत सेवा एवं अच्छा व्यवहार दिलवाना है। इस संगठन की सबसे बड़ी उपलब्धि उपभोक्ता संरक्षण अधिनियम, 1986 लागू करवाना रही है।

13. नेशनल मेडिकोज ऑर्गेनाइजेशन

राष्ट्रीय स्वयंसेक संघ से जुड़े डॉक्टरों के संगठन 'नेशनल मेडिकोज ऑर्गेनाइजेशन' (एन.एम.ओ.) की स्थापना 5 नवंबर, 1977 को वाराणसी में हुई। इसी साल अखिल भारतीय विद्यार्थी परिषद् (ए.बी.वी.पी.) के 23वें राष्ट्रीय सम्मेलन के अवसर पर आयोजित मेडिकल छात्रों और डॉक्टरों के एक सम्मेलन में विशेष रूप से ग्रामीण क्षेत्रों में गरीबों की सेवा के लिए चिकित्सकों को एक साझा मंच पर लाने का निर्णय लिया गया। संगठन का उद्देश्य राष्ट्रीय चरित्र का विकास करना, राष्ट्र और मानवता के प्रति समर्पण की भावना पैदा करना और चिकित्सा की विभिन्न प्रणालियों के छात्रों के बीच भाईचारा पैदा करना तय किया गया। जब भी देश के किसी भूभाग में प्राकृतिक विपदा आती है, एन.एम.ओ. के कार्यकर्ता निस्स्वार्थ भाव से सेवा देते आए हैं।

14. सहकार भारती

'सहकार भारती' की स्थापना 11 जनवरी, 1978 को संघ के वरिष्ठ प्रचारक लक्ष्मणराव इनामदार (वकील साहब) ने पुणे में की थी। इसका उद्देश्य भारत में स्वदेशी सोच पर आधारित सहकारी आंदोलन को बढ़ावा देना था। सहकारी संस्थाओं को स्वदेशी और राष्ट्रवादी सोच के साथ सशक्त बनाना और किसानों, ग्रामीणों और लघु उद्यमों को आत्मनिर्भर बनाना इसका लक्ष्य है। इसकी स्थापना ऐसे समय में

हुई, जब सहकारिता को केवल सरकारी योजनाओं तक सीमित मान लिया गया था। सहकार भारती ने इसे जनांदोलन बनाने का प्रयास किया, जिससे आम लोग, किसान, कारीगर और छोटे उद्यमी जुड़ सकें। आज यह संस्था सहकारी बैंकों, दुग्धसंघों, कृषिमंडियों, क्रेडिट सोसाइटियों आदि में कार्यरत लाखों लोगों को संगठनात्मक मार्गदर्शन और नीतिगत सलाह देती है। इसका उद्देश्य है—आत्मनिर्भर भारत के निर्माण में सहकारिता की भूमिका को मजबूत करना।

15. भारतीय किसान संघ

'भारतीय किसान संघ' किसानों का एक संघ है, जिसका लक्ष्य भारतीय किसानों का समग्र विकास है। 'किसानों की, किसानों के लिए, किसानों द्वारा' इसका उद्देश्य है। भारतीय किसान संघ की स्थापना राष्ट्रवादी ट्रेड यूनियन नेता दत्तोपंत ठेंगड़ी ने की। दत्तोपंतजी ने संपूर्ण देश की यात्रा की और सभी राज्यों के किसानों की समस्याएँ जानीं। उन्होंने देश भर में से 650 से अधिक किसान प्रतिनिधियों का चयन किया और राजस्थान के कोटा शहर में एक अधिवेशन आयोजित कर 4 मार्च, 1979 को भारतीय किसान संघ की स्थापना की घोषणा की। भारतीय किसान संघ देश के किसानों तथा कृषि मजदूरों की आवाज उठाने वाला और ग्राम विकास की प्रक्रिया में सहयोग देने वाला एक प्रमुख संगठन है। यह भारत के सबसे बड़े किसान संगठन के रूप में जाना जाता है।

16. भारतीय जनता पार्टी

भारत को एक समर्थ राष्ट्र बनाने के लक्ष्य के साथ 'भारतीय जनता पार्टी' (भाजपा) का गठन 6 अप्रैल, 1980 को नई दिल्ली के कोटला मैदान में आयोजित एक कार्यकर्ता अधिवेशन में किया गया। इसके प्रथम अध्यक्ष अटल बिहारी वाजपेयी निर्वाचित हुए। हालाँकि भाजपा का गठन 6 अप्रैल, 1980 को हुआ, लेकिन इसका इतिहास भारतीय जनसंघ से जुड़ा हुआ है। भारतीय जनसंघ की स्थापना 21 अक्तूबर, 1951 को डॉ. श्यामा प्रसाद मुकर्जी की अध्यक्षता में दिल्ली के राघोमल आर्य कन्या उच्च विद्यालय में हुई। 01 मई, 1977 को भारतीय जनसंघ ने करीब 5000 प्रतिनिधियों के एक अधिवेशन में अपना विलय जनता पार्टी में कर दिया। 4 अप्रैल, 1980 को जनता पार्टी की राष्ट्रीय कार्य समिति ने अपने सदस्यों के राष्ट्रीय स्वयंसेवक संघ से

जुड़ने पर प्रतिबंध लगा दिया। भारतीय जनसंघ से संबद्ध सदस्यों ने इसका विरोध किया और जनता पार्टी से अलग होकर 6 अप्रैल, 1980 को 'भारतीय जनता पार्टी' के गठन की घोषणा की।

17. प्रज्ञा प्रवाह

'प्रज्ञा प्रवाह' राष्ट्रीय स्वयंसेवक संघ की एक प्रमुख वैचारिक इकाई है। इसकी स्थापना 1980 के दशक के आरंभ में भारत के बौद्धिक क्षेत्र को राष्ट्रवादी सोच से जोड़ने के उद्देश्य से की गई थी। इसकी शुरुआत कुप्.सी. सुदर्शन, दत्तोपंत ठेंगड़ी और पी. परमेश्वरन जैसे प्रखर विचारकों ने मिलकर की थी। उन्होंने यह अनुभव किया कि भारतीय संस्कृति और परंपराओं पर आधारित विचारधारा को शिक्षा और समाज के विमर्श में सशक्त रूप से प्रस्तुत किया जाना चाहिए। प्रज्ञा प्रवाह का उद्देश्य है भारतीय संस्कृति, शिक्षा और मूल्यों के संरक्षण के साथ-साथ समाज में सकारात्मक बदलाव लाना। यह संगठन शिक्षकों, शोधकर्ताओं और युवाओं को जोड़ते हुए देश के सैकड़ों विश्वविद्यालयों में सक्रिय है और संगोष्ठियों, विमर्शों और शोधकार्यों के जरिए राष्ट्रनिष्ठ सोच को विस्तार देने का कार्य करता है।

18. संस्कार भारती

'संस्कार भारती' की स्थापना कला एवं संस्कृति के क्षेत्र में राष्ट्रीय चेतना लाने के उद्देश्य से जनवरी 1981 में लखनऊ में हुई। कला एवं संस्कृति किसी भी समाज और राष्ट्र की पहचान होती है और इसी भावना को लेकर संस्कार भारती समाज में जागरूकता लाने के लिए काम कर रही है। संस्कार भारती समाज से सांस्कृतिक प्रदूषण को दूर कर भारतीय संस्कृति की रक्षा में जुटी है। संस्था विभिन्न कार्यक्रमों के माध्यम से भारतीय संस्कृति के पोषण में लगी है और वर्तमान पीढ़ी को अपनी संस्कृति से जोड़ रही है।

19. संस्कृत भारती

'संस्कृत भारती' एक ऐसा सामाजिक संगठन है, जो संस्कृत के प्रचार-प्रसार का कार्य कर रहा है और शिक्षण के माध्यम के रूप में संस्कृत को स्थापित करने की दिशा में गंभीरतापूर्वक प्रयत्नशील है। वर्ष 1981 में गठित यह संस्था संस्कृत अध्ययन

के अल्पकालीन पाठ्यक्रम चलाती है। आज संस्कृत भारती के दुनिया के करीब दो दर्जन से अधिक देशों में 4,500 सेंटर हैं। इसने अब तक देश-विदेश में 1 करोड़ से अधिक लोगों को संस्कृत बोलने के लिए प्रशिक्षित किया है और एक लाख संस्कृत शिक्षकों को शिक्षण के लिए प्रशिक्षण दिया है। चीन सहित 40 देशों के ढाई सौ से अधिक विश्वविद्यालयों में संस्कृत शिक्षण और शोध कार्य किए जा रहे हैं। इसकी गतिविधियाँ अमेरिका में भी चलती हैं, जहाँ कैलीफोर्निया में इसका मुख्यालय है। ब्रिटेन के स्कूलों में संस्कृत बहुत प्रिय विषय है। जर्मनी के चौदह शीर्ष विश्वविद्यालयों में संस्कृत पढ़ाई जाती है। स्विट्जरलैंड और इटली में ग्रीष्मकालीन संस्कृत संभाषण स्कूलों में भाग लेने वालों की संख्या काफी बढ़ी है।

20. हिंदू जागरण मंच

'हिंदू जागरण मंच' की स्थापना 1982 में हुई थी। इसका उद्देश्य देश भर में हिंदू समाज को जाग्रत्, संगठित, सक्रिय और सुरक्षित बनाना है। यह मंच आज भारत के लगभग सभी राज्यों में कार्य कर रहा है और कई जगहों पर क्षेत्रीय नामों से भी सक्रिय है। इससे जुड़ा एक प्रमुख संगठन है 'धर्म जागरण समिति', जो उन लोगों को फिर से हिंदू धर्म में लौटाने के लिए कार्य करती है, जिन्होंने किसी भी कारण से अन्य धर्म अपना लिये थे। मंच धार्मिक ही नहीं, सामाजिक और सांस्कृतिक जागरूकता के क्षेत्रों में भी अपनी अहम भूमिका निभा रहा है।

21. सीमा जागरण मंच

'सीमा जागरण मंच' की स्थापना वर्ष 1985 में रामनवमी के दिन राजस्थान के जैसलमेर में हुई थी। भारत सैकड़ों वर्षों से पश्चिम से होने वाले आक्रमण को झेलता रहा है और उत्तर की ओर से भी सीमा को संकुचित करने का कुत्सित प्रयास किया जाता रहा है। इसी मुद्दे को लेकर भारतीय जनमानस के भीतर सीमावर्ती विषयों के संदर्भ में चेतना जगाने और सीमा से जुड़े विषयों के प्रति उन्हें अधिक संवेदनशील बनाने के लिए इस संस्था का गठन किया गया। संस्था सीमाओं की सुरक्षा के लिए नागरिकों की सकारात्मक भूमिका को सुनिश्चित कराने का भी प्रयास करती है। वर्तमान में यह संगठन देश के समस्त 24 सीमावर्ती राज्यों में विभिन्न नामों के साथ कार्यरत है।

22. एकल विद्यालय

'एकल विद्यालय अभियान' की शुरुआत 1986 को झारखंड के गुमला जिले के एक गाँव से हुई थी। इसकी स्थापना के पीछे भाऊराव देवरस की परिकल्पना थी, जबकि आई.आई.टी. कानपुर में परमाणु भौतिकी के प्रोफेसर डॉ. राकेश पोपली और उनकी पत्नी प्राथमिक शिक्षा विशेषज्ञ रमा पोपली ने महत्त्वपूर्ण भूमिका निभाई। इस अभियान का उद्देश्य दूरदराज के ग्रामीण और जनजातीय क्षेत्रों में 'एक शिक्षक-एक विद्यालय' मॉडल के अंतर्गत बच्चों को मातृभाषा में प्राथमिक शिक्षा, संस्कार, स्वास्थ्य जागरूकता और स्वावलंबन से जोड़ना है। यह गाँव के ही युवाओं को प्रशिक्षित कर शिक्षक बनाता है, जिससे शिक्षा के साथ-साथ ग्राम विकास, महिला सशक्तीकरण और सामाजिक समरसता को भी बढ़ावा मिलता है। इस अभियान को व्यापक रूप देने में संघ के वरिष्ठ प्रचारक श्यामजी गुप्त की भूमिका भी महत्त्वपूर्ण रही। एकल विद्यालय आज देश भर में एक लाख से अधिक गाँवों में सक्रिय हैं और करोड़ों बच्चों की शिक्षा का माध्यम बन चुके हैं।

23. विज्ञान भारती

'विज्ञान भारती' की स्थापना 21 अक्तूबर, 1991 को हुई थी। यह एक गैर-सरकारी संगठन है, जो भारत में स्वदेशी विज्ञान को बढ़ावा देने के लिए काम करता है। विज्ञान भारती को 'विभा' के नाम से भी जाना जाता है। विज्ञान भारती 'स्वदेशी विज्ञान' के सिद्धांत को बढ़ावा देने के साथ ही भारतीय विरासत को विज्ञान के साथ जोड़ने के लिए भी काम करती है। एक तरफ यह संस्था भारतीय विज्ञान और प्रौद्योगिकी में आत्मनिर्भरता और नवाचार को प्रोत्साहित करती है, वहीं दूसरी तरफ भारतीय ज्ञान-परंपरा के साथ आधुनिक विज्ञान का समन्वय करती है। भारतीय भाषाओं में वैज्ञानिक साक्षरता को बढ़ावा देने के साथ ही संस्था आयुर्वेद, वास्तुविद्या, खगोल विज्ञान के क्षेत्र में भी काम करती है।

24. स्वदेशी जागरण मंच

वरिष्ठ संघ प्रचारक दत्तोपंत ठेंगड़ी के नेतृत्व में 22 नवंबर, 1991 को महाराष्ट्र के नागपुर में 'स्वदेशी जागरण मंच' की स्थापना हुई। यह वही दौर था, जब भारत उदारीकरण के एक नए युग की ओर कदम बढ़ा रहा था। वर्ष 1996 में मंच ने हिंदी

और अंग्रेजी दोनों भाषाओं में मासिक पत्रिका 'स्वदेशी' शुरू की। स्वदेशी जागरण मंच अपनी गतिविधियों और अन्य माध्यमों से योगदान कर देश की आर्थिक स्थिति को दिशा देने में सहयोग करता रहा है। भारत का हित स्वदेशी दृष्टिकोण में है, इसलिए स्वदेशी जागरण मंच गाँव-गाँव में स्वेदशी की भावना मजबूत कर रहा है, जिससे देश सशक्त बने।

25. अखिल भारतीय अधिवक्ता परिषद्

'अखिल भारतीय अधिवक्ता परिषद्' की स्थापना 7 सितंबर, 1992 को नई दिल्ली में की गई थी। इस अवसर पर संगठन के प्रेरणास्रोत दत्तोपंत ठेंगड़ी ने परिषद् के कार्यकर्ताओं को संबोधित करते हुए एक मजबूत, आत्मनिर्भर और न्यायप्रिय भारत के अपने सपने को साझा किया और उसमें अधिवक्ताओं की भूमिका को महत्त्वपूर्ण बताया। यह परिषद् देश भर के अधिवक्ताओं को एक मंच पर लाने का प्रयास है, जिससे वे न केवल अपने अधिकारों और दायित्वों को समझें, बल्कि न्याय व्यवस्था में नैतिक मूल्यों और राष्ट्रीय दृष्टिकोण को भी स्थापित करें। अपनी स्थापना के समय से ही परिषद् भारतीय संस्कृति और आदर्शों को पुनर्जीवित करने, अधिवक्ताओं में सेवा और आदर्शवाद की भावना जगाने एवं न्यायपालिका की गुणवत्ता व प्रभावशीलता बढ़ाने का कार्य कर रही है।

26. क्रीड़ा भारती

'क्रीड़ा भारती' में युवकों को शारीरिक और मानसिक खेल के प्रशिक्षण दिए जाते हैं। क्रीड़ा भारती की स्थापना वर्ष 1992 में 'स्वस्थ भारत-समर्थ भारत' के ध्येय के साथ पुणे (महाराष्ट्र) में की गई। इसका बोधवाक्य 'क्रीड़ा से निर्माण चरित्र का, चरित्र से निर्माण राष्ट्र का' है। इसका लक्ष्य है देश के अन्य स्थापित खेलों के साथ-साथ स्वदेशी खेलों को भी बढ़ावा मिले, समाज के सभी वर्गों में खेलों के प्रति आकर्षण बढ़े और खेलों के माध्यम से राष्ट्रीय चरित्र की भावना का निर्माण हो। इसके अलावा देश में एक खेल संस्कृति का निर्माण हो और अंतरराष्ट्रीय स्पर्धाओं में देश विश्व के अग्रणी देशों में गिना जाए, क्रीड़ा भारती इस दिशा में अहम भूमिका निभा रही है।

27. पूर्व सैनिक सेवा परिषद्

पूर्व सैनिकों के पुनर्वास में सहायता करने तथा उनकी देशभक्ति और अनुशासन का उपयोग देशहित में करने के लिए 'पूर्व सैनिक सेवा परिषद्' का गठन 4 जून, 1993 को किया गया। पूर्व सैनिकों की देशभक्ति से समाज को जोड़ने के साथ-साथ पूरे भारत में, विशेष रूप से दूरदराज के ग्रामीण इलाकों में रहने वाले पूर्व सैन्यकर्मियों के परिवारों के हित के लिए भी काम किया जाता है।

28. अखिल भारतीय इतिहास संकलन योजना

'अखिल भारतीय इतिहास संकलन योजना' की परिकल्पना 1973 में संघ के प्रचारक मोरोपंत पिंगले ने की थी। वर्ष 1973 में नागपुर में भारतीय इतिहास लेखन, संकलन तथा प्रकाशन आदि के लिए 'बाबासाहेब आपटे स्मारक समिति' की स्थापना हुई। बाद में 1994 में 'अखिल भारतीय इतिहास संकलन योजना' नामक राष्ट्रीय संगठन दिल्ली में पंजीकृत हुआ। इतिहास संकलन योजना इतिहास के क्षेत्र में कार्यरत विद्वज्जनों का एक राष्ट्रव्यापी संगठन है, जो इतिहास, संस्कृति, परंपरा आदि क्षेत्र में प्रामाणिक और तथ्यपरक इतिहास-लेखन तथा प्रकाशन की दिशा में कार्यरत है। देश एवं विदेशों में रह रहे इतिहास एवं पुरातत्व के विद्वान्, विश्वविद्यालयों में कार्यरत प्राध्यापक, अध्यापक, अनुसंधान केंद्रों के संचालक, भूगोल, खगोल आदि अनेक क्षेत्रों के विद्वान् और इतिहास में रुचि रखने वाले विद्वान् इस कार्य से जुड़े हुए हैं।

29. लघु उद्योग भारती

'लघु उद्योग भारती' छोटे (सूक्ष्म) व लघु उद्योगों का राष्ट्रव्यापी संगठन है। इसकी स्थापना वर्ष 1994 में की गई। लगभग सभी राज्यों में इसकी इकाइयाँ कार्यरत है। इसका पंजीकृत कार्यालय नागपुर में व प्रशासनिक कार्यालय दिल्ली में स्थित है। देश में अनेक प्रभावशाली औद्योगिक संगठन हैं, लेकिन वे सामान्यतया बड़े उद्योगों के हित के लिए ही सरकार के नीति निर्धारकों के समक्ष पैरवी करते हैं। इस कारण पूरे देश में फैले हुए लघु उद्योगों की आवश्यकताओं व समस्याओं को सही ढंग से प्रस्तुत करने वाला कोई प्रभावी संगठन नहीं था। लघु उद्योग भारती इस भूमिका को सशक्त रूप से निभा रही है।

30. आरोग्य भारती

'आरोग्य भारती' भारतीय जीवन मूल्य पर आधारित स्वास्थ्य के क्षेत्र में रुचि रखने वाले विभिन्न चिकित्सा पद्धति के चिकित्सक एवं सेवा में जुटे व्यक्तियों का संगठन है। इसकी स्थापना 2 नवंबर, 2002 को कोच्चि में हुई थी। संस्था का विधिवत् पंजीयन 29 जुलाई, 2004 को भोपाल में हुआ। स्वास्थ्य के प्रति लोगों में जागरूकता लाने के लिए इसका गठन किया गया। वर्तमान में देश के सभी राज्यों में इसकी प्रांतीय इकाइयाँ हैं। आरोग्य भारती की राष्ट्रीय कार्यकारिणी में मान्य चिकित्सा पद्धतियों के चिकित्सक, विशेषज्ञ एवं गणमान्य व्यक्ति होते हैं, जो विभिन्न प्रकार के जागरण, सेवाकार्यों का संचालन करने और संगठनात्मक दिशा-निर्देश तैयार करते हैं।

31. सेवा भारती

'सेवा भारती' एक गैर-सरकारी संगठन (एन.जी.ओ.) की तरह कार्य करती है और यह आर्थिक रूप से कमजोर वर्गों में सामाजिक-आर्थिक रूप से हाशिए वाले, जनजातीय और स्वदेशी समुदायों पर विशेष ध्यान केंद्रित करती है। इसका पंजीकरण 8 दिसंबर, 2003 को हुआ। आज देश भर में 1246 संस्थाएँ सेवा भारती से संबद्ध होकर आपस में मिलकर सेवाकार्य कर रही हैं। संस्था देश में पिछड़े एवं अभावग्रस्त लोगों के बीच शिक्षा, स्वास्थ्य, सामाजिक एवं स्वावलंबन के विभिन्न प्रकल्पों के द्वारा स्वैच्छिक संस्थाओं और समर्पित कार्यकर्ताओं के सहयोग से समरस समाज का निर्माण करने में जुटी है।

32. शिक्षा संस्कृति उत्थान न्यास

भारत की प्राचीन और संस्कारित शिक्षा पद्धति की स्थापना के उद्देश्य से 24 मई, 2007 को 'शिक्षा संस्कृति उत्थान न्यास' का गठन किया गया। चरित्र निर्माण के साथ-साथ व्यक्तित्व का समग्र विकास न्यास का ध्येय है। भारत की शिक्षा, भारत की संस्कृति, प्रकृति एवं प्रगति के अनुरूप हो, इस उद्देश्य के साथ न्यास अपने काम को आगे बढ़ा रहा है। चरित्र निर्माण के साथ-साथ मूल्य आधारित शिक्षा, मातृभाषा में शिक्षा, वैदिक गणित, पर्यावरण शिक्षा और शिक्षा की स्वायत्तता पर इसने खूब काम किया है। न्यायपालिका और विधि शिक्षा में भी भारतीय भाषाओं के प्रयोग को बढ़ावा मिले, इसके प्रयास भी किए गए हैं।

33. सक्षम

देश में दिव्यांगों के कल्याण का उद्देश्य लेकर 'सक्षम' की स्थापना 20 जून, 2008 को नागपुर में हुई थी। सक्षम देश भर में दिव्यांग लोगों की सहायता कर रही है, जिसमें उनकी पेंशन, कृत्रिम अंग लगवाना, उपचार करवाना और ऑपरेशन में सहायता करना भी शामिल है। संस्था अपनी ओर से इसका व्यय भी उठाती है। दृष्टि बाधित और कम दृष्टि वाले प्रत्येक व्यक्ति को उज्ज्वल भविष्य के लिए सर्वश्रेष्ठ अवसर मिले, इसके लिए भी कार्य किया जाता है।

□□□

प्रेरणाप्रद संघ साहित्य